lonely planet

Alaska

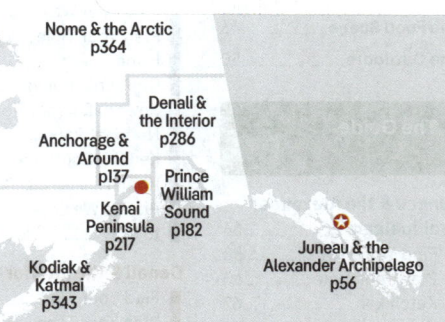

- Nome & the Arctic p364
- Denali & the Interior p286
- Anchorage & Around p137
- Prince William Sound p182
- Kenai Peninsula p217
- Juneau & the Alexander Archipelago p56
- Kodiak & Katmai p343

Regis St Louis, Melody Burdette,
Kevin Raub, Mara Vorhees

CONTENTS

Plan Your Trip

The Journey Begins Here 4
Alaska Map 6
Our Picks 8
Regions & Cities 20
Itineraries 22
When to Go 30
Get Prepared for Alaska 32
Cruising Alaska 34
The Alaska Railroad 38
Alaska's Parks & Wildlife 40
Trip Planner: Bears,
Bears, Bears 44
The Food Scene 46
The Outdoors 50

The Guide

Juneau & the Alexander Archipelago 56
Find Your Way 58
Plan Your Time 60
Ketchikan 62
Wrangell 76
Petersburg 81
Sitka 87
Juneau 96
Glacier Bay
National Park & Preserve. 109
Haines 115
Skagway 122
Places We Love
to Stay 134

Anchorage & Around 137
Find Your Way 138
Plan Your Time 140
Anchorage 142
Palmer 163
Girdwood 172
Places We Love
to Stay 181

Prince William Sound 182
Find Your Way 184
Plan Your Time 186
Valdez 188
Cordova 198
Whittier 208
Places We Love
to Stay 215

Kenai Peninsula 217
Find Your Way 218
Plan Your Time 220
Hope 222
Cooper Landing 232
Seward & Kenai Fjords
National Park 245
Kenai & Soldotna 258
Homer 267
Places We Love
to Stay 284

Denali & the Interior 286
Find Your Way 288
Plan Your Time 290
Talkeetna 292
Denali State Park 300
Denali National Park
& Preserve 303

Totem Bight State Historical Park (p67)

Fairbanks 316
Tok & the Taylor
Highway 330
Wrangell-St Elias
National Park &
Preserve 334
Places We Love
to Stay 340

Kodiak & Katmai 343
Find Your Way 344
Plan Your Time 345
Kodiak 346
Katmai National Park
& Preserve 358
Places We Love
to Stay 363

Nome & the Arctic 364
Find Your Way 366
Plan Your Time 367
Nome 368
Utqiaġvik 379
Dalton Highway 383
Places We Love
to Stay 387

Ice climber, Matanuska Glacier (p160)

Brown bears, Lake Clark National Park & Preserve (p278)

Toolkit

Arriving	390
Getting Around	391
Money	392
Accommodations	393
Family Travel	394
Health & Safe Travel	395
Food, Drink & Nightlife	396
Responsible Travel	398
LGBTIQ+ Travelers	400
Accessible Travel	401
Nuts & Bolts	403

Storybook

A History of Alaska in 15 Places	406
Meet the Alaskans	410
Russian Imperialism & Tlingit Resistance	412
Alaska by Air	414

Acknowledgement of Land

Lonely Planet respectfully acknowledges that Alaska is the traditional homelands of 229 state and federally recognized Tribes and Alaska Native communities. We honor their enduring connection to the lands, waters and ways of life that have sustained Alaska Native peoples since time immemorial. We encourage travelers to learn about these communities, reflect upon their histories, and recognize the strength and vitality of Alaska Native peoples today.

Mountains of Kachemak Bay State Park (p280)

ALASKA
THE JOURNEY BEGINS HERE

Alaska has always drawn adventurers, iconoclasts and fortune seekers, as well as people like me who simply have an abiding love for the world's wild places. Wilderness is deeply woven into Alaska, and not just as an abstract concept. It's in the backyard of the state capital – a place so remote you can't get there by road – where rainforest trails to craggy peaks begin a short walk from downtown. The spirit of the wild touches every part of this great state, from its forested seashores and glaciated fjords in the south to the mountainous national parks and rolling desert-like tundra of the north, but also in surprising places like the sparkling waterways that snake through Alaska's largest settlements. This wildness is increasingly rare in today's world, and of vital importance for the ecosystems and the people who visit them. It's the reason why so many fall under the spell of 'the Great Land', or Alyeska, as the Aleut called it.

Regis St Louis

@regisstlouis

The son of two Coloradans, Regis has spent two decades exploring the world's wild places. He has written numerous guides for Lonely Planet and other publishers.

My favourite experience is taking an early morning water taxi from Homer to **Kachemak Bay State Park** (p280) for a day of hiking followed by a picnic overlooking a glacial lagoon.

WHO GOES WHERE

Our writers and experts choose the places which, for them, define Alaska.

I left the crowds behind when I hopped off the tourist train in Skagway to hike to **Laughton Glacier** (p132). Incredible 360-degree views from the trail, which ended at the face of the glacier itself. I climbed on the scree and snow and got my feet wet in the icy glacial runoff – a reminder that Earth is a wild and wonderful place.

Mara Vorhees
havetwinswilltravel.com

Mara writes about family travel around the world. She is co-author of The Last Stand of the Raven Clan, a narrative nonfiction book about the Tlingit-Russian War.

At the end of the 84-mile Nome–Taylor Rd, deep on the Seward Peninsula, I kicked off my shoes and walked barefoot onto the wood-decked **Kougarok Bridge** (p375). It was a rare hot afternoon in the Arctic, and the sun washed the tundra around me in gold. I hadn't seen anyone for hours, and felt like I'd stumbled into Alaska from another time – raw, endless and untouched. That barefoot pause reminded me why exploring the edges of the map matters most.

Melody Burdette
@melskyburd

Melody is a freelance writer, photographer and nomadic van-lifer based in Alaska.

It's hard to beat Prince William Sound's trifecta of often quirky, always isolated, fishing towns, each with a unique personality but united by their far-flung locales bound by jaw-dropping nature. **Cordova** (p198) is my favourite because I love a place unreachable by road, but Whittier's unique history and Valdez' lively craft breweries and wonderful food trucks run a close second. These are quintessential Alaska harbors hellbent on 'I'd Rather Be Fishing' attitudes, salmon diets and thriving in some of the world's most tragically beautiful places.

Kevin Raub
@RaubontheRoad

Kevin is a travel journalist and craft-beer connoisseur, and the co-author of over 125 Lonely Planet guidebooks on four continents.

Fairbanks
Explore gold-mining history and see migratory birds (p316)

Denali National Park & Preserve
Spot wildlife on ranger-led Discovery Hikes (p303)

Talkeetna
Browse craft shops and take a scenic flight (p292)

Juneau
Learn about Alaska Native heritage (p96)

Cordova
Discover the wonders surrounding this remote town (p198)

Valdez
Be awed by Columbia and Meares glaciers (p188)

Seward
Tour the waters and glaciers of Kenai Fjords (p245)

Petersburg
Hike lush trails in the Tongass National Forest (p81)

Ketchikan
Walk beneath towering totem poles (p62)

THE WILD THINGS

Alaska's wildlife – on land, at sea and in the air – offers once-in-a-lifetime animal encounters. In remote national parks you can see bears gorging on salmon, or digging for clams on a beach. Amid glacier-backed fjords, small tour boats wind past breaching humpback whales and tufted puffins diving for fish, while Steller sea lions look blithely on from rocky shorelines. Scenic flights over mountain valleys offer dramatic views over herds of caribou or moose lumbering along stream beds.

Bear Essentials

Alaska provides habitat for black, brown and polar bears (pictured). Black bears are prevalent in forests, brown bears prefer upland meadows and salmon streams, and polar bears hunt on Arctic pack ice.

Optical Advantage

Binoculars are a must for looking at wildlife, and a spotting scope is even better. If you're lacking, you can purchase gear at shops in larger towns.

Roadside Etiquette

If you spot an animal while driving, don't block traffic. Instead pull completely off the road, and view safely from there.

Brown bears fishing, Brooks Falls (p358)

PLAN YOUR TRIP OUR PICKS

BEST WILDLIFE EXPERIENCES

See the annual migration of sandhill cranes at ❶ **Creamer's Field** (p325) in Fairbanks each August.

Hop on a bus and travel the ❷ **Denali Park Rd** (p307), looking for grizzly (brown) bears in Alaska's most popular national park.

Be amazed by the largest brown bear concentration in the world at ❸ **Brooks Falls** (p358) in Katmai National Park & Preserve.

Take a ❹ **Kenai Fjords National Park** (p248) cruise to look for humpback whales, orcas and Dall's porpoises.

Spot sea otters, seals, puffins and elusive whales on a day boat tour in ❺ **Glacier Bay National Park** (p109).

Kayaking, Resurrection Bay (p249)

OUT ON THE WATER

Alaska has nearly 34,000 miles of shoreline, 12,000 rivers and three million lakes. There are plenty of opportunities to float, paddle or row across pristine wilderness waterways, from the placid mountain lakes of the Kenai Peninsula to the island-backed coves of the Southeast and the roaring rivers of the Interior and the Arctic.

Be Prepared

Alaska's waters are cold, so pack non-cotton layers, waterproof gloves and rubber boots or neoprene booties to stay insulated in variable weather conditions.

Watery Parks

Homer's **Kachemak Bay State Park** (p280) and the calm bays around **Misty Fjords National Monument** (p72) are pristine locations for day or overnight paddling trips.

BEST WATER-BASED EXPERIENCES

Look for bald eagles and sea stars while paddling amid the towering rainforests in Clover Pass or Naha Bay in ❶ **Ketchikan** (p62).

Join a rafting trip, whether easygoing or thrilling with Class IV rapids, on the ❷ **Nenana River** (p311) near Denali National Park.

Get up close to majestic ❸ **Columbia Glacier** (p190) or Meares Glacier with Stan Stephens Glacier & Wildlife Cruises.

Take a water taxi to ❹ **Blackstone Bay** (p213) to kayak among floating ice and the calving ice of Blackstone Glacier.

Kayak through a topaz-blue glacial lagoon off ❺ **Resurrection Bay** (p250), home to quiet coves and rushing waterfalls.

TRACKS & TRAILS

Ask any Alaskan about their favorite outdoor activity, and hiking will frequently top the list. It's no surprise given the incredible wilderness accessible in every part of the state. Mountains, forests and coastlines set the stage for memorable outings on Alaska's 1000-plus trails, which range from short jaunts to epic treks like the 2300-mile Iditarod National Historic Trail.

BEST HIKING EXPERIENCES

Hike to a majestic viewpoint along Denali National Park's Savage Alpine Trail or enjoy an easier but equally scenic route along the ❶ **Savage River Loop** (p306).

Enjoy sweeping views of the Anchorage Bowl, Cook Inlet and Denali on Anchorage's most popular hike, ❷ **Flattop Mountain** (p146).

Take a water taxi to Kachemak Bay State Park and follow the ❸ **Glacier Lake Trail** (p281) through forest to a waterway full of sparkling icebergs.

Experience Tongass National Forest's lush beauty on ❹ **Petersburg's trails** (p85), with moss-covered stumps, soaring spruce trees and views over the water.

Immerse yourself in the landscapes of Kodiak island, starting with a hike near rugged shores at ❺ **Termination Point** (p354).

Go Guided

Alaska's rugged landscape can be intimidating. Hiking with a naturalist guide can provide interesting information about an area and situational experience for those unaccustomed to wilderness adventuring.

Urban Wilderness

Anchorage has more than 300 miles of walking, biking, skiing and hiking trails within easy reach, with most also interconnecting with state or federal lands.

Stay Safe

Exploring on a trail means a higher chance of encountering wildlife, inclement weather or other hazards. Be prepared with bear spray, appropriate clothing and footwear suitable for the terrain.

PLAN YOUR TRIP OUR PICKS

BEHIND THE WHEEL

The open road awaits. As you hop into the driver's seat and hit the highway, you can chart a course through some of the world's most striking landscapes. Soaring snow-covered peaks, glacially carved valleys and rolling tundra set the stage for memorable adventures in the land of the midnight sun. Apart from the panoramic views along the way, you can stop for wilderness walks and refueling in tiny communities, far from the drone of city life.

4WD Required

You'll need to hire a 4WD from a specialty rental (such as Arctic Outfitters in Fairbanks) to drive most unpaved roads and highways.

Wildlife Safety

Be mindful of driving in the early morning or evening when wildlife is most active, as moose and other animals can wander onto the road.

Fill up the Tank

Keep the fuel tank topped up wherever you roam, especially in remote parts of the Interior where service stations are few and far between.

Dalton Highway (p383)

BEST ROAD-TRIP EXPERIENCES

Fly to ❶ **Nome** (p368), then spend three days driving each of its fascinatingly diverse roads out of town, past ghostly ruins, hot springs and grazing musk ox.

Take the long way around ❷ **Prince William Sound** (p182), skirting glaciers, dramatic mountain passes and sparkling waterways where you might spy beluga whales.

Tackle the wild and remote ❸ **Dalton Hwy** (p383), gateway to an unforgettable journey through boreal forests and rolling tundra to the Arctic Ocean.

Get well off the beaten path on the ❹ **Taylor Hwy** (p330) as you motor out to former gold-mining settlements amid jaw-dropping wilderness.

Drive past rushing rivers and pause at scenic viewpoints along the rugged ❺ **McCarthy Rd** (p338), gateway to America's largest national park.

Salmon fishing near Cooper Landing (p232)

CAST A LINE

Home to some of the best fishing on the planet, Alaska is the place to set your sights on teeming salmon streams, deep-water hunting for halibut, or fly-fishing for rainbow trout or grayling. Each summer, anglers flock to the state's picturesque coastlines, forest-lined rivers and mountain streams to fish and hopefully reel in a trophy catch.

Salmon by Any Other Name

Alaska's waters house five species of salmon: chum, sockeye, pink, chinook and coho. Each spawns at different times of year, beginning with chinook in late spring.

Plying the Rivers

For optimum species variety, fly-fishing is best in June or early July, with braided streams and rivers giving anglers a chance to try different fly patterns.

BEST FISHING EXPERIENCES

Time your visit just right to the upper Kenai Peninsula, where you can enjoy world-class salmon fishing on scenic rivers near ❶ **Cooper Landing** (p232).

Head out from ❷ **Homer** (p267) for a day of adventure-filled deep-sea fishing for halibut on the mountain-backed waters of Cook Inlet.

Experience one of Alaska's legendary fishing spots at ❸ **Ship Creek** (p146) in Anchorage, casting your line for trophy salmon.

Fly-fish the sparkling waters of the ❹ **Little Tok River** (p330) near the community of Tok.

Try the family-friendly ❺ **Bering Sea Crab Fishermen's Tour** (p68) in Ketchikan for a look at the dangerous deep-sea crab industry.

LOOK BACK

Alaskans are proud of their home, and they appreciate the ancient roots of a land far removed from the rest of the United States. Its network of museums and historic sites can provide valuable perspective as you travel throughout this richly layered state, with its mix of archeological sites, former Russian enclaves and well-preserved homesteads.

Gateways to History

Browse **Anchorage Museum**'s (pictured; p148) large archive of photos, letters and other records, or the articles, film and books of Juneau's Alaska State Library & Archives.

Fly High

Aviation has played a major role in Alaska's growth. Anchorage's **Lake Hood** (pictured; p157) seaplane base is the busiest in the world, and adjacent is the Aviation Heritage Museum.

Exploring the Past

Wrangell History Unlocked is a highly engaging podcast covering one of Alaska's earliest settlements, with episodes that explore everything from Alaska Native history to true-crime stories.

BEST HISTORY EXPERIENCES

Explore vestiges of the boomtown that fueled the rise of Juneau at the ❶ **Treadwell Mine Historic Trail** (p103) on Douglas Island.

Wander through the log-cabin museums in Fairbanks' ❷ **Pioneer Park** (p321), then return in the evening for a whimsical history-esque production of the Golden Heart Redux.

Stroll the sites of ❸ **Old Valdez** (p195), and see reminders of a powerful 1964 earthquake that destroyed the city.

Learn about the native Tlingit and 18th-century Russian colonizers in ❹ **Sitka** (p87), home to Orthodox landmarks, striking totem poles and a moving national historical park.

Take a guided tour through the deserted streets of ❺ **Kennecott** (p334), a former copper-mining town now preserved within Wrangell-St Elias National Park.

FROM LEFT: LINDA HARMS/SHUTTERSTOCK, DEE BROWNING/SHUTTERSTOCK

ALASKA'S FIRST PEOPLE

Alaska Natives play an integral part in the Great Land's modern-day politics, culture and commerce. While their cultural imprint stretches back more than 10,000 years, present-day traditions and practices are constantly evolving – subsistence living and art and craft traditions remain alive and well, however, following a remarkable renaissance over the past generation. Visitors can learn more through Indigenous-run galleries, important historic sites and open-air museums that showcase the artful ingenuity of Alaska's first peoples.

Tribal Collaboration

The **Alaska Native Heritage Center** (pictured; p154) in Anchorage opened in 1999 as a hub for education and information about the 11 main tribal groups inhabiting Alaska for time immemorial.

Clashes with Europeans

On an island amid towering spruce and hemlock, **Sitka National Historical Park** (pictured; p92) preserves the site of a deadly 1804 skirmish between invading Russian traders and Indigenous Kiks.ádi Tlingit.

Dancing & Drumming

Learn about the Arctic's tribal groups and traditions, such as mask-making, drumming and dancing at the **Iñupiat Heritage Center** (p379) in Utqiagvik.

Totem Bight State Historical Park (p67)

PLAN YOUR TRIP

OUR PICKS

BEST ALASKA NATIVE CULTURAL EXPERIENCES

Gather insight into Iñupiat culture at the ❶ **Katirvik Cultural Center** in Nome's **Richard Foster Building** (p370) and witness the longstanding traditions of the far-northern tribal groups.

Explore the atmospheric galleries of the ❷ **University of Alaska Museum of the North** (p322), which has a brilliant collection of Indigenous artifacts from all of Alaska's distinct regions.

Wander the Arctic Studies exhibition in the ❸ **Anchorage Museum** (p148).

Visit the ❹ **Sealaska Heritage Institute** (p98) in Juneau, where you can enter a full-scale replica of a clan house.

See the world's largest collection of totems at ❺ **Totem Bight State Historical Park** (p67) in Ketchikan.

17

Wrangell-St Elias National Park & Preserve (p334)

ADRENALINE RUSHES

For heart-pounding adventure, Alaska delivers the best of the best. From soaring above North America's highest peak to rafting a raging Class V river, the list of activities is endless, and each region features its own brand of excitement, from mountain biking to kayaking to skating on frozen lakes in the winter.

Push the Pedals

Mountain biking is one of Alaska's fastest-growing sports, with tracks for riders of any ability. Try Prince of Wales Island for gravel, or Anchorage for forested singletrack.

Fly to Remote Wilderness

Hop on a plane in Talkeetna for up-close views of Denali, or fly from Homer across Cook Inlet for a beach landing and bear viewing.

BEST ADRENALINE-FUELED EXPERIENCES

Brave the howling winds and go for a swim in the Arctic Ocean near ❶ **Utqiaġvik** (p379) for a chilling, yet invigorating experience.

Join a guided tour – or go on your own – for an otherworldly walk across the crunchy icy expanse of ❷ **Root Glacier** (p335) in Wrangell-St Elias National Park.

Hold on tight while bouncing over Class V rapids during a thrilling white-water trip along ❸ **Six Mile Creek** (p222) on the Kenai Peninsula.

Take a heli-ski tour in ❹ **Valdez** (p193) for some of the most challenging backcountry ski terrain in the world.

Rent a mountain bike in ❺ **Girdwood** (p172) and hit some of the spectacular routes just outside of town, such as the Lower Iditarod Trail.

SMALL-TOWN LIFE

Alaska's diverse collection of small towns make up the state's heart and soul. Tight-knit art communities, mom-and-pop restaurants and streets leading to dramatic viewpoints and forest-backed shorelines: these quiet corners make fascinating destinations in between outdoor adventures. The locals are a big part of the draw, and are often happy to show off their community to out-of-towners.

BEST SMALL-TOWN EXPERIENCES

Catch a boat from Homer to ❶ **Seldovia** (p277), where you can wander an old-fashioned main street or hike a lovely forest trail blazed by high school students.

Under One Roof

Whittier is a town of roughly 250 residents, nearly all of whom live in a Cold War–era 14-story apartment building (pictured) with its own grocery store and post office.

Tiny Town

Kupreanof (pictured; p86) is one of Alaska's smallest towns. It's home to around 20 residents, and you can only get there by boat from nearby Petersburg.

Fly or sail to remote ❷ **Cordova** (p198), home to varied attractions (a glacier, a science museum) and quirky events (the Iceworm Festival).

Explore the charming downtown of ❸ **Petersburg** (p81), then take a stroll to Sandy Beach Park to look for petroglyphs.

Spend a day in ❹ **Talkeetna** (p292), browsing the craft shops and historic sites, followed by outdoor dining and drinks on the main street.

Discover the many charms of ❺ **Kodiak** (p346) by visiting its intriguing museums then hitting the WWII sites just outside of town.

Market Day

Try to catch at least one farmers market while you're in Alaska *(alaskafarmersmarkets.org)*. Apart from foods and crafts, you'll find a vibrant community spirit.

REGIONS & CITIES

Find the places that tick all your boxes.

Nome & the Arctic

IÑUPIAT TRADITIONS, TUNDRA AND ROAD TRIPS

Head to Nome to experience the extraordinary landscapes and wildlife of the far north. This vast region is also the place for stunning aurora borealis displays, learning about Iñupiat traditions in Utqiaġvik and epic drives along the Dalton Hwy, passing rolling tundra and otherworldly views en route to the Arctic Ocean.

Anchorage & Around

LOCALLY STEEPED URBAN PLAYGROUND AND INCREDIBLE NATURE

Found on the traditional homeland of the Dena'ina Athabascan people, this is the place to play, with lakes, mountains and rivers set amid Alaska's urban hub. Go remote easily with thousands of acres of public land available for recreation. Bike, hike or paddle with locals and dine at some of the state's most famous restaurants.

Kodiak & Katmai

BROWN BEARS AND WILDERNESS

See brown bears fishing for salmon at Katmai National Park & Preserve, one of Alaska's most famous destinations for wildlife encounters. On Kodiak Island, you can learn about Alaska Native heritage, explore WWII sites and head off on some outstanding hikes to lofty mountaintops and rugged shorelines.

Kodiak & Katmai p343

Denali & the Interior

TOWERING PEAKS AND CREATIVE TOWNS

The ancestral home to the Athabascan people, and later gold miners, this is the region for epic road trips. Amid the stunning national parks of Denali and Wrangell-St Elias, there's legendary hiking, wildlife-watching, rafting and scenic flights. Don't miss the varied attractions of Fairbanks or the captivating little settlements of Talkeetna and McCarthy.

Nome & the Arctic p364

Prince William Sound

IMPOSING GLACIERS AND ISOLATED FISHING PORTS

This stunning area features prime salmon and halibut fishing for serious anglers and scenic coves perfect for kayaking. Set your sights on Whittier, a gateway to glacier adventures and wildlife-watching, and the vibrant little city of Valdez, with abundant activities and craft breweries. There's also remote Cordova, surrounded by breathtaking scenery.

Denali & the Interior p286

Anchorage & Around p137

Prince William Sound p182

Kenai Peninsula p217

Juneau & the Alexander Archipelago p56

Kenai Peninsula

ADVENTURES ON LAND AND SEA

Alaska in miniature, with mountains, lakes, glaciers and fjords, the Kenai Peninsula is easily reached from Anchorage, making it a popular destination for fishing, hiking and mountain biking. Charming towns such as arts-minded Homer and historic Seward make great bases for wilderness adventures in Chugach National Forest and Kenai Fjords National Park.

Juneau & the Alexander Archipelago

RAINFORESTS, GLACIERS AND TOTEM POLES

Lush rainforests meet briny ocean waters in Southeast Alaska. Mountains tower over island towns unreachable by road, and wildlife flourishes in the waters and on the traditional lands of Tlingit, Haida and Tsimshian peoples. Watch for humpback whales, sea otters and brown bears, and take time to explore the hilly streets of Alaska's capital city.

Glacier Bay National Park (p109)

ITINERARIES

Exploring the Inside Passage

Allow: 11 days   **Distance:** 675 miles

This Alexander Archipelago makes a fabled introduction to Alaska's natural and cultural treasures. You'll see exquisitely carved totem poles, visit replica clan houses and wander galleries of archeological treasures. Couple this with glacier boat trips, rainforest hikes and wildlife-watching to see why so many fall in love with the southeast.

❶ KETCHIKAN ⏱ 2 DAYS

Explore the downtown's lanes and Ketchikan's wildlife and cultural **museums** (p66), then catch the bus to see the carved masterpieces at **Totem Bight State Historical Park** (p67). On day two, get out on the water, with a fishing tour such as **Bering Sea Crab Fishermen's Tour** (p68) or an active paddling trip amid sea lions and starfish with the likes of **Ketchikan Kayak Company** (p71). ✈ *45min*

❷ WRANGELL ⏱ 1 DAY

Located at the mouth of the Stikine River, Wrangell offers excursions to **Anan Creek Wildlife Observatory** (p78), where you can see bears feasting on salmon. There are also some great trails here, plus ancient rock carvings on **Petroglyph Beach** (p79). ✈ *45min*

✈ *Detour: Catch a daily 30-minute flight (or weekly ferry) to **Petersburg** (p81), a base for glacier boat trips and mountain hikes.* ✈ *1 day*

❸ JUNEAU ⏱ 2 DAYS

Alaska's capital is a great place to explore the past and learn about Alaska Native traditions, particularly in the **Alaska State Museum** (p96) and the **Sealaska Heritage Institute** (p98). Stroll the shops and cafes of downtown and leave time for the wonders outside of town: **Mendenhall Glacier** (p100), the **Perseverance Trail** (p104) and the **Treadwell Mine** (p103). Enjoy a seafood feast and drinks in a **historic bar** (p107). ✈ *45min*

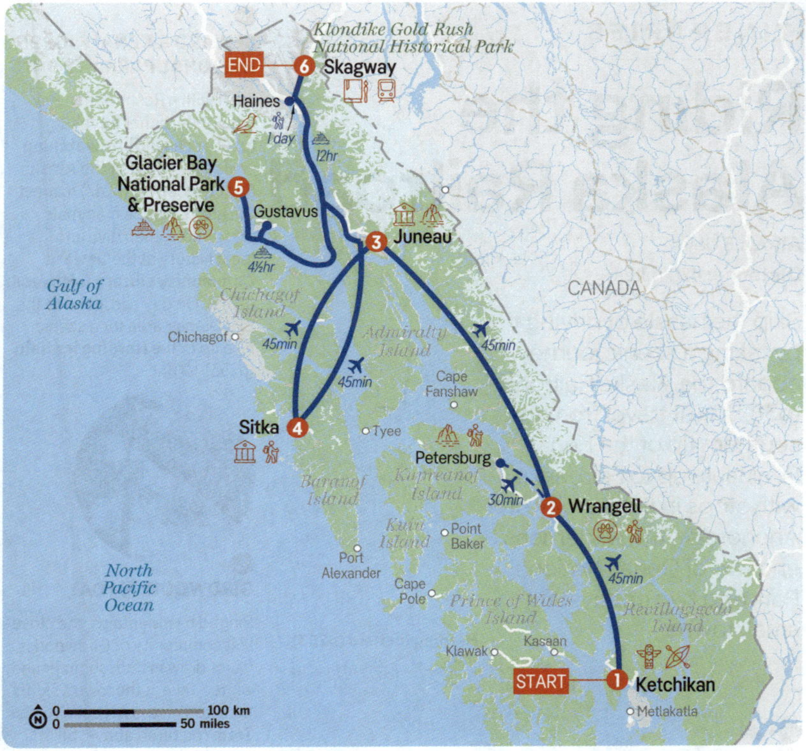

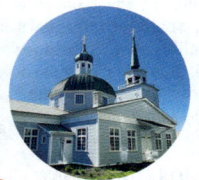

4

SITKA 2 DAYS

The former capital of Russian Alaska has preserved historic buildings, including a cathedral and **bishop's house** (pictured; p90). Be immersed in Indigenous culture at **Sheldon Jackson Museum** (p91) and see totem poles amid **Sitka National Historical Park** (p92). Sitka is a launchpad for adventure, whether hiking, kayaking, mountain biking or island hopping. From Sitka, fly to Juneau then take a boat to Gustavus and Glacier Bay. *45min & 4.5hr*

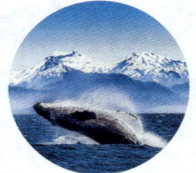

5

GLACIER BAY NATIONAL PARK & PRESERVE 1 DAY

Head out for a full-day **boat trip** (p112) through a cinematic landscape of glaciers, peaks and untrammeled shorelines. Wildlife plays a starring role – you might see sea otters, whales, brown bears and mountain goats. Later, take in exhibits at the visitor center and visit the **Huna Tribal House** (p110). You can also stretch your legs on the **Bartlett River Trail** (p111). *12hr*

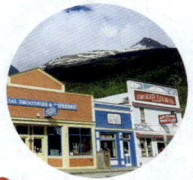

6

SKAGWAY 2 DAYS

Get an early start to beat the cruise-ship crowds on a wander through the photogenic old-time downtown (aka the **Klondike Gold Rush National Historical Park**, p123). Later, ride a vintage **railway** (p130), explore the former boom town of **Dyea** (p132) and hit the trail.

*Detour: Make the one-hour boat ride to **Haines (p115)**, home to a bald-eagle preserve, early-20th-century architecture and a trail up 3600ft Mt Ripinsky. 1 day*

FROM LEFT: VENDI SAPUTRA/SHUTTERSTOCK, BETTY WILEY/GETTY IMAGES, RICHARD CUMMINS/GETTY IMAGES

ITINERARIES

Riding the Alaska Railroad

Allow: 8 days
Distance: 470 miles

Skip the hassle of driving by taking a scenic journey aboard the Alaska Railroad (p38). You'll travel from the southern tip of the Kenai Peninsula up to Fairbanks, with stops in the big city of Anchorage, the wilderness enclave of Denali National Park and two captivating small towns.

Harding Icefield (p253)

① SEWARD & KENAI FJORDS NATIONAL PARK ⏱ 2 DAYS

Start with a Resurrection Bay adventure, either **kayaking** (p250) or a **wildlife-watching cruise** (p248). Visit the **Alaska SeaLife Center** (p247) to meet the area's marine mammals and birdlife, then dive into local history at the **Seward Community Library & Museum** (p245). On day two, head to the Exit Glacier area for a scenic hike up to the **Harding Icefield** (p253). 🚆 3hr

② GIRDWOOD ⏱ 1 DAY

Ringed by mountains, the close-knit community of Girdwood is a major draw in both summer and winter. Take in the town's sights then hop on the **Alyeska Aerial Tram** (pictured above; p175) for a ride to a 2300ft summit. Continue the adventure while walking between lofty peaks on the **Veilbreaker Skybridges** (p175). Or, try gold panning at the **Crow Creek Gold Mine** (p177). 🚆 1hr 20 min

③ ANCHORAGE ⏱ 1 DAY

Start the day with breakfast at **Snow City Cafe** (p143), then head to the **Anchorage Museum** (p148) for a wander through galleries devoted to Alaska's First Peoples. Hit the stores for unique souvenirs (p155). Later, go seaplane spotting while biking around **Lake Hood** (p157). By night, indulge in seafood at **Humpy's Great Alaskan Alehouse** (p143) and craft beer at **Tent City Taphouse** (p149). 🚆 3hr

FROM LEFT: ATTILIO PREGNOLATO/SHUTTERSTOCK, SARAH_XIE7/SHUTTERSTOCK, CZECH THE WORLD/SHUTTERSTOCK

④ TALKEETNA ⏱ 1 DAY

Enjoy espresso and crepes from **Conscious Coffee** (p294), then go for a stroll around town. Stop in the **Talkeetna Historical Society Museum** (p292) to learn about homesteaders, bush pilots, miners and the climbers who've reached the summit of Denali. Later enjoy some adventure, either jet boating on the **Susitna River** (p294) or enjoying a spectacular scenic **flight** (p298) around North America's highest mountain. 🚆 4½hr

⑤ DENALI NATIONAL PARK & PRESERVE ⏱ 2 DAYS

Get the lay of the land in the **Denali Visitor Center** (p305), then visit the park's cuddliest rangers at the **Sled Dog Kennels** (p305). Afterwards, tackle the **Mt Healy Overlook Trail** (pictured below; p306). On day two, go on a ranger-led **Discovery Hike** (p307) or enjoy some less strenuous wildlife-watching on a **naturalist-led bus tour** (p307). 🚆 4hr

⑥ FAIRBANKS ⏱ 1 DAY

Learn about Fairbanks' history through the exhibits of the **Morris Thompson Cultural & Visitors Center** (p316). Stroll through downtown and along the **Chena River** (p320) or go **canoeing** (p321). Next, head to the **University of Alaska Museum of the North** (p322) to explore its outstanding exhibits on Alaska Native culture and the blooming **botanical garden** (p323) nearby. End the day at the riverside **Pump House** (p322).

Sea otter, Prince William Sound (p188)

ITINERARIES

Seaside Adventures in Southcentral

Allow: 9 days   **Distance:** 730 miles

Glaciers, fjords and mountain backdrops feature on this cinematic journey around Prince William Sound, down the Kenai Peninsula and across to Kodiak Island. Apart from the grand scenery, you can enjoy rewarding hikes and boat trips, plus memorable wildlife-watching, with the chance to see brown bears fishing for salmon at the trip's end.

❶ VALDEZ ⏱ 1 DAY

Located at the head of a deep fjord, Valdez is truly a mountains-to-sound city, with soaring peaks, wildlife and access to hundreds of miles of wilderness. Go glacier gazing (pictured; with plenty of wildlife spotting) on a full-day **boat trip** (p188). On day two, see the Alaska Native artifacts at the **Maxine & Jesse Whitney Museum** (p192) and take a coastal hike along the **Shoup Bay Trail** (p191). 🚗 5hr

❷ PALMER ⏱ 1 DAY

See Alaska's wildlife on a tour of **Musk Ox Farm** (pictured; p168), then enjoy more close animal encounters (including feeding opportunities) at **Reindeer Farm** (p168). Stroll into the 1930s by checking out the town's **historic buildings** (p166), followed by snacks and drinks at the **Matanuska Brewing Company** (p165). Or, end the day with a hike along the **Bodenburg Butte Trail** (p167). 🚗 2hr

❸ WHITTIER ⏱ 1 DAY

It's an adventure – driving through North America's longest highway tunnel (pictured) – just reaching Whittier. On arrival, wander through this former military base turned modern-day community checking out Cold War architecture and the **Prince William Sound Museum** (p211). Hike to Portage Glacier on the **Portage Pass Trail** (p210). By night, dine on seafood with a view at the **Inn at Whittier** (p215). 🚗 1¼hr

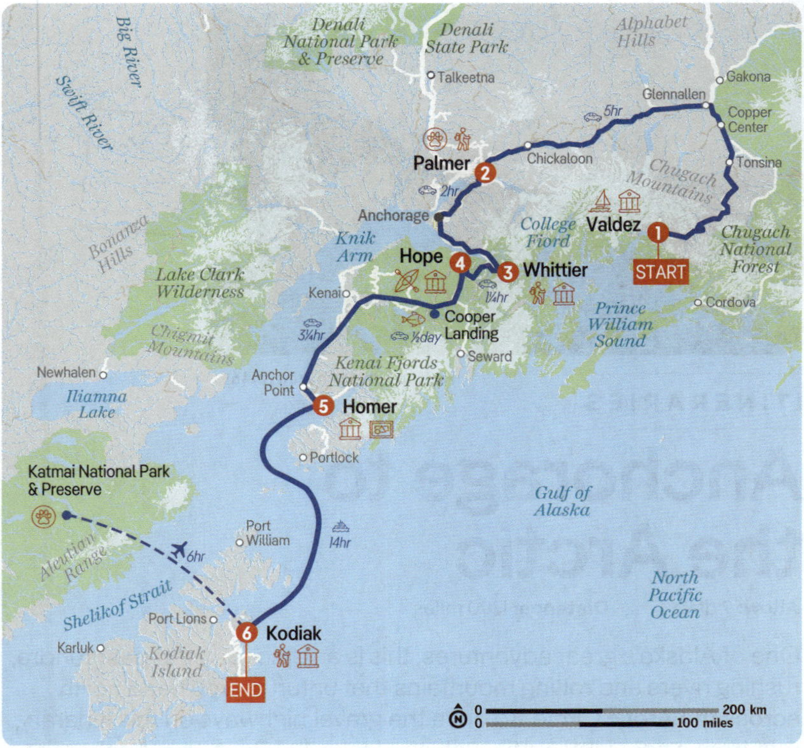

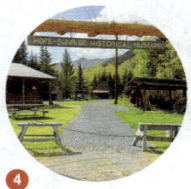

4

HOPE 1 DAY

Head on a thrilling rafting trip over the Class V rapids of **Six Mile Creek** (p224). After, enjoy a peaceful wander through log cabins packed with curios at the **Hope & Sunrise Historical Society Museum** (p224). *3¼hr*

*Detour: Make the one-hour drive to **Cooper Landing** for world-class salmon fishing (p232), followed by a walk through an ancient fishing camp at the **K'Beq' Cultural Heritage Interpretive Site** (p237). Half-day*

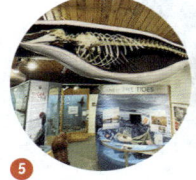

5

HOMER 2 DAYS

Learn about the people who shaped Homer's history at the **Pratt Museum** (pictured; p267), then explore the interactive wildlife exhibits at the **Alaska Islands & Ocean Visitor Center** (p271). Tour a few **galleries** (p272) before heading to the **Spit** (p270) for a stroll. On day two, go fishing for halibut or take a boat to **Kachemak Bay State Park** (p280) for a hike to a glacial lagoon. *14hr*

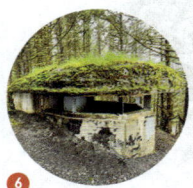

6

KODIAK 2 DAYS

If you've timed your visit right, you can catch an overnight ferry from Homer. Once in Kodiak, visit the **Alutiiq Museum** (p347) and **Kodiak History Museum** (p347), then see the WWII sites (pictured) in **Fort Abercrombie State Historical Park** (p351) and hike the **Termination Point Loop** (p354).

*Detour: Take a half-day flightseeing tour to **Katmai National Park & Preserve** (p358) to watch brown bears in the wild. 6hr*

FROM LEFT: HW22/SHUTTERSTOCK, REGIS ST LOUIS/LONELY PLANET, KARENFOLEYPHOTOGRAPHY/SHUTTERSTOCK

Flattop Mountain Trail (p146)

ITINERARIES

Anchorage to the Arctic

Allow: 9 days **Distance:** 1290 miles

One of Alaska's great adventures, this is an epic road trip past tundra, rushing rivers and rolling mountains that unfurl as you head north across the Arctic Circle. To drive the gravel highways on this itinerary, rent from a specialty outfit such as Alaska 4x4 Rentals in Anchorage.

❶ ANCHORAGE ⏱ 1 DAY

See the city's wilder side on a 3-mile round-trip hike up **Flattop Mountain** (p146). It's a rite of passage that offers stunning views over Cook Inlet and the Alaska Range (weather permitting). Afterwards, head to the **Alaska Native Heritage Center** (pictured; p154), where you can learn all about Alaska's First Peoples. End the day with food, drinks and live music at **Chilkoot Charlie's** (p154). 🚗 6½hr

❷ MCCARTHY ⏱ 3 DAYS

The drive is a big part of the adventure, particularly along the rugged, 60-mile **McCarthy Rd** (pictured; p338). You'll pass over lofty bridges, with viewpoints and trails along the way. Once in McCarthy, celebrate with drinks at the **Golden Saloon** (p337), then spend two days immersed in **Wrangell-St Elias National Park** (p334), with glacier hikes, scenic flights, rafting and tours of the old mining town. 🚗 6hr

❸ TOK ⏱ ½ DAY

Refuel in tiny Tok. Stop in the **visitors center** (p330) for details on the road ahead, and leave time for **Mukluk Land** (pictured; p331), a whimsical slice of Alaskan quirkiness with vintage games, oversized sculptures and vintage machinery. 🚗 1¼hr

🚗 *Detour: Tack on another two days (round trip) for the challenging drive along the Taylor Hwy to the old gold-mining settlements of **Chicken** (p331) and **Eagle** (p333).*

④ DELTA JUNCTION ⏱ ½ DAY

Moving north on the Richardson Hwy, green tundra contrasts with the sparkling Delta River. Amid the vast wilderness, you'll find **Big Delta State Historical Park** (pictured; p328), which has a collection of beautifully preserved buildings from the early 1900s. A few miles up the road, the **Sullivan Roadhouse** (p329) is also packed with curiosities from bygone days. Dine at **Buffalo Center Drive-in** (p329) next door. 🚗 *2hr*

⑤ FAIRBANKS ⏱ 1 DAY

Take a stroll through the old-time exhibits at **Pioneer Park** (pictured; p321) or take a journey along the Chena aboard the **Riverboat Discovery** (p326), a vintage paddle wheeler. Later, look for sandhill cranes and other migratory birds on the trails of **Creamer's Field** (p325). 🚗 *12hr*

↪ *Detour:* It's a scenic 70-minute drive out to **Chena Hot Springs** (p328), where you can unwind in a steaming outdoor pool.

⑥ DALTON HIGHWAY ⏱ 2 DAYS

You'll need to be doubly prepared for a journey on the remote **Dalton Hwy** (p383). You'll cross the Arctic Circle some 200 miles north of Fairbanks. Turn back here, or keep going another 300 miles, passing tiny settlements in the mountain-studded wilderness and over the continental divide. The road ends in **Deadhorse** (p385), where you take a shuttle to reach the Arctic Ocean.

FROM LEFT: LOGAN BUSH/SHUTTERSTOCK, TOMASZ WOZNIAK/SHUTTERSTOCK, FOTOGRO/SHUTTERSTOCK

WHEN TO GO

Alaska is evolving into a year-round destination, but most visitors still arrive between May and early September.

In the land of the midnight sun, summer is the most obvious time to visit. From June through August, you'll find the broadest array of outdoor activities on offer, plus lively festivals and easy access to trails and nature preserves. It's wise to plan well ahead to avoid paying a premium (on top of the already high summer prices) when booking last-minute accommodations and car rentals. If you hope to see the northern lights and want to enjoy some wintertime activities (cross-country skiing through snowy forests, ice-skating on frozen lakes), schedule a trip for December through March.

Want to Save Money?

Plan your trip for the off-season, which is roughly late September to early May. You can save as much as 50% on hotel prices and car rentals. Keep in mind that activities and tours are more limited or non-existent – some excursions are available only from late May to early September.

I LIVE HERE

FAMILY FUN IN ANCHORAGE

Sara Dykstra, director, SEL at Anchorage School District

There are so many things I love about raising my kids in this special place! Whether it's playing in the snow, after-dinner hikes in the endless summer light, spotting a moose, salmon fishing or cheering on sled-dog teams on our neighborhood trail during the Fur Rendezvous festival – I love that my kids are learning to explore nature their own way, learning about the Indigenous people of Alaska and learning to respect the wildness and beauty of this great state.

SUMMER DAYS

June through August brings long, lingering daylight with lots of extra sunshine. Be sure to pack sunscreen and apply liberally, even if temperatures don't feel that warm, and especially if you're on water or a snowfield, where reflections can burn skin quickly.

Lupine flowers in summertime, near Anchorage (p137)

Weather through the Year: Anchorage

	JANUARY	FEBRUARY	MARCH	APRIL	MAY	JUNE
Avg. daytime max:	23°F	27°F	34°F	44°F	56°F	64°F
	Days of snowfall: 7	Days of snowfall: 6	Days of snowfall: 7	Days of rainfall: 4	Days of rainfall: 5	Days of rainfall: 7

DRAMATIC FLUCTUATIONS

Alaskans know how weather patterns shift depending on the region. A warm day in one area may mean wet and windy in another. Dress for conditions in the destination, and be ready for anything, including snow in June or temperatures topping 90°F in the Interior.

Summertime Celebrations

Fairbanks celebrates the longest day of the year with panache during the **Midnight Sun Festival** (p371). Catch live performances, craft vendors and food stalls, then see a late-night baseball game (p323), no lights required. **June**

Cheer on the brave (insane?) runners making the near vertical ascent up Mt Marathon during Seward's **Fourth of July Festival** (p247). There's also a boat parade, fireworks and whimsical games for all. **July**

Temperate rainforest is the backdrop to the **Girdwood Forest Fair** (p141), with three stages for live music, as well as dance, art installations and kids' games. **July**

At the **World Eskimo Native Olympics** (p317), see extraordinary feats of skill, such as the blanket toss (jumpers reach 30ft in the air), or the superhuman four-man carry. There's also dancing, drumming and other cultural performances. **July**

THE MAGIC OF WINTER

KattiJo Deeter, professional dog musher and kennel owner at Black Spruce DogSledding. @blacksprucedogsledding

If you've ever wanted to be in a snow globe, visit Fairbanks in the winter. Every tree, twig and fence post is covered in snow and hoarfrost. We've also got this alpenglow, where the sun comes up but then immediately starts going down. So you just get this warm golden light on the white snow – this perpetual sunrise and sunset during the day. It's magnificent.

Winter landscape near Fairbanks (p316)

Off-Season Revelry

The **Cordova Iceworm Festival** (p203) is a 'winter-blues buster', with a parade, Miss Iceworm competition, bazaar and survival-suit race, honoring the seaside community's commercial fishing and boating. **January**

Cheer on fleet-footed canines during the **Iditarod** (p369), the world's most famous sled-dog race. The 1000-mile competition begins near Anchorage and ends 10 days later in Nome. Be prepared for yipping, yowling sled dogs and a host of cheering locals. **March**

Don your fur tunic and horned helmet and join other costumed revelers during Petersburg's big springtime gathering at the **Little Norway Festival** (p81). There's a parade, Norwegian dancing, dog fashion show and a seafood bake and barbecue. **May**

Homer shows off its creative side during the **Alaska World Arts Festival** (p274), featuring a globe-trotting lineup of music, film, theater, comedy and storytelling. **September**

GREENER PASTURES

The state's latitude means a later spring and shorter summer and fall. Look for what Alaskans call 'green up' and leaves on trees in late May, and observe the dramatic color changes to a fall landscape by the end of August.

JULY	AUGUST	SEPTEMBER	OCTOBER	NOVEMBER	DECEMBER
Avg. daytime max: **66°F**	Avg. daytime max: **65°F**	Avg. daytime max: **55°F**	Avg. daytime max: **40°F**	Avg. daytime max: **28°F**	Avg. daytime max: **25°F**
Days of rainfall: **11**	Days of rainfall: **15**	Days of rainfall: **15**	Days of snowfall: **11**	Days of snowfall: **8**	Days of snowfall: **7**

Mountain ranger, Denali National Park & Preserve (p303)

GET PREPARED FOR ALASKA

Useful things to load in your bag, your ears and your brain.

Clothes

Forget fashion Function trumps fashion, especially while outdoors. Plan for a variety of weather patterns and swift changes. Follow the Alaska adage of 'There's no bad weather, just bad clothing!'

Layers Dress in layers of non-cotton clothing. The most consistent thing about Alaska weather is its inconsistency. Be prepared with layers that can be easily removed or added.

Warmth Winter starts early and ends late. October through April means winter, so bring hardy cold-weather gear.

Sturdy shoes You'll need shoes suitable for walking on uneven terrain. While some Alaskans can and do wear sneakers or sandals, it's advisable to have shoes with tread. It's customary to remove shoes when entering someone's home.

Accessories Always pack a warm hat, gloves and sunglasses, especially if you're planning water-based activities.

Manners

Alaskans are a casual and friendly lot, so **a smile and conversation goes a long way**. Be curious about their unique lifestyle and ask questions about everything, *except* a favorite fishing hole or berry patch.

The phrase 'Alaska Native' is reserved for the Indigenous First People who have lived here for centuries. It's better to ask if one was 'born and raised in Alaska' rather than 'Are you an Alaska native?'

📖 READ

The Last Stand of the Raven Clan (Easter & Vorhees; 2024) Story of the Tlingit people, who thwarted imperial Russia and greatly impacted the continent's history.

Two Old Women (Velma Wallis; 1993) Two elderly Athabascan women show remarkable survival skills after their tribe abandons them in winter.

The Great Alone (Kristin Hannah; 2018) A tale of community and resilience as a troubled family moves to a remote Alaskan settlement.

The Cruelest Miles (Gay & Laney Salisbury; 2003) Sled dogs and their mushers make an epic journey to Nome during a devastating 1925 diphtheria outbreak.

Words

Alaska Marine Highway System State-run ferry system that links various destinations in the Southeast, Southcentral and Kodiak Island.

Alpenglow The pinkish or orange-hued glow on the mountains around sunrise or sunset.

Borough Alaska is divided not into counties but 19 sizable boroughs.

Break-up The early spring season when river ice breaks apart, and slushy puddles, dirty cars and muck is omnipresent.

Cheechako A new arrival to Alaska who has a lot to learn.

Freeze-up The day lakes and rivers are officially frozen for the winter, not melting until spring.

Frost heaves Cold-weather damage to roads that leave undulating waves in the pavement.

Lower 48 Anywhere else in the contiguous United States that is *not* Alaska.

Mukluks Fur boots.

Muskeg Spongy, waterlogged wetland, much like a bog.

Permafrost Deep layer of earth that stays frozen all year.

Permanent Fund Dividend (PFD) The annual payment (born of the oil boom) awarded to every Alaskan residing continuously in the state for at least one year.

Sourdough A longtime Alaskan (derived from the early gold miners who carried their sourdough starter with them).

Termination dust The first snowfall on the mountain peaks, signifying the arrival of winter.

Tundra Treeless expanse of low shrubs and plants. Present in the north and at higher elevations.

📺 WATCH

Call of the Wild (pictured; Chris Sanders; 2020) Recent version of the classic Jack London novel set in the late 1890s near Skagway.

Frozen Ground (Scott Walker; 2013) Anchorage in winter is the moody backdrop to this suspenseful crime thriller based on a true story.

Into the Wild (Sean Penn; 2007) Visually stunning adaptation of Jon Krakauer's book about the travels of Christopher McCandless.

30 Days of Night (David Slade; 2007) Vampires invade Utqiaġvik (Barrow) during the sunless days of deep winter.

Grizzly Man (Werner Herzog; 2005) This darkly incisive documentary follows Timothy Treadwell's life (and death) among grizzlies.

🎧 LISTEN

Sisters of White Chapel (Annie Bartholomew; 2023) Theatrical album showcasing the stories of women who were part of the Klondike gold rush.

A Lovely Place to Die (Blackwater Railroad Company; 2024) Channels bluegrass and string music in its feel-good Alaska-centric medleys.

Woodstock (Portugal. The Man; 2017) Grammy-winning band from Southcentral Alaska, known for the blockbuster tune 'Feel It Still.'

Drums of the North (Pamyua; 2005) A soulful Yupik-Inuit band that melds traditional rhythms with uplifting chant-like choruses.

Cruise ship by a glacier, the Inside Passage

TRIP PLANNER

CRUISING ALASKA

Alaska's southern coastlines are riddled with large and small islands, deep fjords and ancient glaciers. Nearly all of the area is roadless, so seafaring vessels, including cruise ships, provide a popular way of reaching these pristine areas. Traveling by sea also affords some magnificent wildlife-watching opportunities.

Why Cruise?

A cruise offers a chance to glimpse a vast natural wilderness once available only to those with ample time or funds to visit hard-to-reach places. On an Alaska cruise, anyone can travel in relative comfort and convenience to some fascinating destinations. Larger cruise ships typically stop at three or four ports, where you'll have plenty of options to experience Alaska culture, see wildlife or enjoy some outdoor activities. Excursions give a fine overview of Alaska, but don't offer much of a personal touch.

Smaller vessels may not stop in local ports, instead anchoring at night and offering guests the chance to hike a remote shoreline, whale-watch in a kayak, or see a presentation by Indigenous artisans. More boutique cruise lines strive to immerse their guests in the wild Alaska and stop at smaller communities such as Petersburg, Wrangell or Haines.

Cruising isn't for every traveler. If you enjoy all-inclusive resorts and rigid excursions, a typical cruise may be a good fit. If you like to explore on your own without the time constraints of a cruise itinerary, you might be better off planning an independent trip.

WHEN TO GO

Depending upon the cruise line, sailings begin in late April and continue through early October. The most dependable weather typically appears in July and August, but that's also the most popular (and expensive) time, so for cheaper tickets and shore excursions, pick a trip earlier or later in the season.

For spring and fall passengers, know that temperatures will be cooler than you might expect, with variable types of precipitation, including snow showers, occurring during the trip. In summer, it's still cool on deck and near glaciers, so don't expect a lot of outdoor pool time or sunbathing onboard.

Where Will You Sail?

Large cruise ships sail Alaska's Inside Passage from Seattle, Washington or Vancouver, British Columbia, sailing through the Gulf of Alaska to Seward or Whittier. In between, passengers usually stop in Ketchikan, Juneau and Skagway, and then sail up College Fjord to see glaciers stretching their icy fingers into the sea en route to Whittier. You'll see plenty of stunning scenery along the way. Smaller cruises max out at around 200 passengers and have the ability to nose into Southeast Alaska's nooks and crannies, launching skiffs and kayaks from their lower decks to visit less-trammeled shores. If any ports are visited, they're likely to be smaller communities such as Wrangell, Sitka, Petersburg and Yakutat.

Additionally, with the Northwest Passage now open to marine traffic, the northwestern city of Nome is a regular port of call for higher-end, midsize cruise lines, giving passengers access to more remote parts of Alaska.

Cruise ship by the Hubbard Glacier, near Yakutat

WHAT TO BRING ON AN ALASKA CRUISE

Packing appropriate clothing and gear is essential for an enjoyable cruise experience. Alaska's weather patterns are nothing if not variable, swinging from sunny to cloudy to rainy in a matter of hours, depending on the location. Plus, the outer decks of cruise ships are notoriously chilly while ships are on the move, even when the weather is great. To be prepared for anything, pack the following items.

Layers
● Layers of non-cotton clothing that will keep you warm and dry as you explore ports of call and participate in outdoor activities.

Hats & Gloves
● Both a warm hat for colder climates, and a hat with a brim for sunny days and glacier visits. Gloves are useful on cold, rainy days.

Outerwear
● A fleece or woolen sweater that traps body heat.
● Waterproof rain jacket and pants for excursions.

Shoes
● Sturdy sneakers, hiking shoes or boots that allow for long days of walking and will keep feet dry no matter the conditions. Make sure to break in footwear before your trip for maximum comfort.

Backpack
● Handy for extra clothing, water bottle, camera, binoculars and other items during shore days.

Tote Bag
● Stuff a small tote bag in your backpack when heading ashore so you'll have extra carrying capacity for crafts and other items purchased at town shops.

Sustainable Cruising

While all travel causes environmental and cultural impacts, cruising leaves its mark to varying degrees on Alaska's fragile ecosystems. The average large cruise ship can have a carbon footprint greater than 12,000 cars, and produce up to a ton of trash each day. While there can be a positive economic impact on ports of call, a small community visited by 15,000 people a day during sailing season can intrinsically change. The industry's trade group Cruise Line International Association (CLIA) touts a desire for 'conscious cruising.' It's instilled guidelines for water conservation and upgrades to heating, air-conditioning and ventilation, with a goal for ships to be net zero by 2050, along with expectations about paying more attention to the cultural traditions of a destination through cooperative regenerative tourism that preserves a community's unique history, culture and values.

WHAT YOU CAN DO

If you're considering an Alaska cruise, you should find out about the strategies different cruise lines employ as a commitment to cleaner energy and conservation practices, then choose accordingly. Be aware of the cruise line's impact on the pristine land and sea it visits, and consider what you can do to help reduce your impact as you sail.

● **Reduce use of single-use plastics** by packing your own water bottle and refilling onboard, and bring reusable shopping bags for port visits.

● Ask about **recycling stations** onboard, and look for locations in the communities you visit.

Kayaking, Kenai Fjords National Park (p245)

Popular Shore Excursions

GLACIER & WILDLIFE TOURS
Cruise for a few hours aboard a smaller vessel to sight whales, otters, seals and icy glaciers.

DOGSLEDDING
Learn about mushing, huskies and the operations of sled-dog kennels before taking a spin behind a team.

BEAR VIEWING
Book a small-group tour by float plane from Juneau to Pack Creek, where you can often spot bears.

● Read up on the **impacts of climate change** on Alaska's sensitive environments, where glacial melt, coastal erosion and a loss of permafrost present real-time issues to wilderness, ocean and communities around the state *(nps.gov/glba)*.

● **Friends of the Earth** *(foe.org/cruise reportcard)* gives out letter grades to cruise lines for environmental impact, with an 'A+' as the highest rating.

Booking Through the Ship

If you sail aboard a larger ship, the company will direct you to their selected shore excursions. This is because the company receives a hefty portion of the fee for every excursion booked through the cruise line. Also, should the excursion be delayed in returning passengers, the ship will wait to sail. Additionally, if you're traveling with a large group, it can be logistically easier to book through the ship.

Exploring Independently

Breaking away from the dock and port crowds can provide a wealth of insight into a city. It's also a chance to book your own adventures without the added cruise-line markup. Check how much time you have in port, stop by the visitor center for a map (often, representatives are at the disembarkation point) and be on your way. Make sure you're back onboard at least 30 minutes before the ship is due to depart, and ask about exact times with tour operators to avoid being left behind at your own expense.

EXTENDING THE ADVENTURE

Many cruise companies offer pre- or post-cruise tours to provide visitors with options to explore other regions of Alaska such as Anchorage, Talkeetna, Denali National Park or Fairbanks. Typically, these tours are part of a package involving motor-coach transfers and accommodations at large, cruise-line-owned properties. Like cruises themselves, these tours are usually large (up to 50 people) and skim the surface of other Alaska destinations over the course of seven to 10 days. That said, you can enjoy some memorable activities, particularly in Denali, with the possibility of rafting, hiking, flightseeing or visiting a sled-dog kennel. Some lines also offer cruise–rail combos allowing you to experience Alaska's grandeur while riding its famous railway (p38). While you can also book these activities on your own, package tours generally offer decent value since they're booked in tandem with the sailing.

Humpback whale

FLIGHTSEEING
See Alaska's landscapes in a unique way, spotting wildlife and ogling glaciers and mountain ranges from far above.

ALASKA NATIVE TRADITIONS
Learn the ways of Alaska's many tribal groups, with demonstrations of dancing, drumming and totem-pole carving.

RIDE A HISTORIC TRAIN
Skagway's White Pass & Yukon Route Railway (p130) climbs over Chilkoot Pass for a hands-on gold-rush history tour.

PADDLE POWER
Hop in a raft or kayak and explore Alaska's beautiful coastlines and its rushing mountain rivers.

Coastal Classic train, Seward (p245)

TRIP PLANNER

THE ALASKA RAILROAD

Going strong for over 100 years, the Alaska Railroad travels from the southern tip of the Kenai Peninsula all the way up to Fairbanks, deep in the interior. The plush 470-mile journey takes you past dramatic views of coast, mountains and tundra, with ample wildlife-watching opportunities along the way.

The Onboard Experience

The eye-catching blue-and-yellow train is professionally run, and employees take pride in operating America's northernmost, year-round rail line. Big windows afford expansive views of the landscape, and conductors do much more than simply validating tickets. They provide commentary throughout the journey, describing key places you'll pass along the way – historic small towns, river systems and mountain peaks, along with forays into natural science (permafrost, wildfires, glaciers) and history (the gold rush, the Iditarod, the railroad's creation). Looking for Alaskan species big and small is a key part of the experience, and when animals are spotted, the train will slow and details will be relayed throughout the cars so everyone can try to catch a glimpse. Keep an eye out for moose, bald eagles, Dall sheep, otters, whales and the occasional bear, among other creatures.

DENALI STAR

The most popular route, and the Alaska Railroad's flagship line, is the *Denali Star*, which runs between Anchorage and Fairbanks. It's a roughly 12-hour trip if you ride straight through, but you can get more out of the experience by breaking up your journey. The charming town of Talkeetna (p292) makes a great base for a night or two, with jet-boat rides,

RAIL KNOWLEDGE

The Season
Denali Star and *Coastal Classic* run daily from mid-May to mid-September.

Tickets
Purchase tickets online (alaskarailroad.com) several weeks ahead. Seats sell out during the summer, especially around the Fourth of July.

Winter Travel
The Anchorage to Fairbanks route is called the *Aurora Winter Train* from mid-September to mid-May. It runs northbound on Saturdays and southbound on Sundays, plus a few additional days in February and March.

Other Trains
The *Glacier Discovery* runs from Anchorage via Girdwood and Whittier to Spencer Glacier Whistle Stop (p178), where rangers lead guided hikes to a glacier viewpoint. There's also the *Hurricane Turn Flagstop* from Talkeetna (p299) and the White Pass & Yukon Route Railroad (p130).

---

scenic flights and bike rides, though leave time to stroll the shops and stop in the eateries and drinking spots of this tiny arts-loving settlement. You'll also want to stop off in Denali for adventures in the national park – the train station is handily located within walking distance of the main visitor center.

COASTAL CLASSIC

Possibly even more scenic than the *Denali Star* is the memorable route linking Anchorage with Seward. The *Coastal Classic* travels along the Turnagain Arm with views of towering summits and sparkling waterways, where you might spy beluga whales or see the bore tide (p226) roll in. The trip takes 4¾ hours, but it's worth stopping off in Girdwood (p172) for a wide range of nature activities, plus access to the mountain resort of Alyeska (p174).

Goldstar Service class, Alaska Railroad train en route to Denali National Park & Preserve (p303)

CLASSES & PRICES

The train offers two different classes and both have comfortable, roomy seats. Charging outlets are available (but not in every seat).

Goldstar Service
The top-notch Goldstar Service has a glass-dome ceiling and an outdoor upper-level viewing platform. There's also a dining car, where meals (and two alcoholic drinks) are included with your ticket. The menu is similar between the two trains, though *Denali Star* has more options. Dishes lean toward elevated northern comfort fare: cream of barley with blueberry-peach compote for breakfast, burgers or quesadillas for lunch. For dinner, there's baked Alaska cod, reindeer penne bolognese and slow-braised pot roast.

Adventure Class
Adventure Class seats lack the dome ceiling, though there is a public Vista Dome car, with a glass ceiling that gives an elevated view over the terrain. No meal is provided, but both trains have food counters where you can purchase ham-and-cheese croissants, sandwiches, vegetable curry, chips, cookies and other snacks, as well as drinks, including cocktails, beer and wine. *Coastal Classic* passengers also have access to a dining room, with a small menu featuring the likes of breakfast plates, burgers (meat or veggie), chickpea masala and pot roast.

Ticket Prices
Anchorage to Fairbanks (one way)
- Adventure Class: $294/147 (adult/child)
- Goldstar Service: $553/315

Anchorage to Seward (one way)
- Adventure Class: $133/67
- Goldstar Service: $277/162

Caribou, Denali National Park & Preserve (p303)

TRIP PLANNER

ALASKA'S PARKS & WILDLIFE

Alaska residents take outdoor recreation seriously, be it a casual stroll or a multiday adventure deep in the wilderness. Thankfully, public parks and preserves cover a wide swath of the state, encompassing mountains, rivers, lakes and parts of the Pacific Ocean's bays and coves.

A Wealth of State Parks

Alaska has 156 state-park units. Two of them – Wood-Tikchik in the Southwest, and Chugach near Anchorage – are among the three largest US state parks. State parks are broken down into six distinct regions: Southeast, Chugach, Mat-Su Valley, Kenai Peninsula, Northern and Southwest (including Kodiak Island). Each features miles of trails for hiking and exploring, public-use cabins for rustic accommodations, and campgrounds if you want to pitch a tent or park a RV. Most of Alaska's state-park units and facilities are accessible by road but some, particularly those in Southeast, require a boat or floatplane to reach. Thus, visitors can find plenty of opportunities for recreation, ranging from kayaking and canoeing to skiing and mountain biking.

National Parks & Preserves

Parks and outdoor spaces take center stage in Alaska, which is home to about 60% of the total national-park land in the US, with eight parks covering 56 million

📅 WHEN TO GO

Bear Viewing
If you have your heart set on seeing bears in action (fishing and gorging on salmon) at Brooks Falls and other viewing spots (p45), try to plan your trip for July or August, when there are more bears in the area.

Northern Lights
Seeing the northern lights is a possibility from late August to early April, with better chances from December to March. There's no guarantee to see them, so build in extra days to increase your odds.

Winter Activities
November through March is the cross-country ski season. Skating on frozen lakes and ponds typically happens from December through March.

---

acres. Some parkland also features preserves, with extra restrictions on hunting, fishing, camping and other recreational pursuits to protect animals, birds or sensitive environments.

Denali National Park & Preserve (p303) is accessible by road and headlined by its namesake mighty mountain, Denali, the Great One. It's also a popular location for spying Alaska's 'Big Five' animals: moose, bears, wolves, caribou and Dall sheep.

Gates of the Arctic National Park (p386) attracts the adventurous visitor who understands the challenges and joys of exploring this roadless, remote piece of Alaska. At 8.4 million acres, it's a park to be traveled with great respect for its harsh but beautiful environment.

Glacier Bay National Park & Preserve (p109) brings thousands of cruise-ship visitors to its icy fjords each summer, but it's also a valuable ecosystem for tracking climate change. Take time to explore the quiet coves and bays by kayak or small boat from the park headquarters in Bartlett Cove.

> ### KNOW BEFORE YOU GO
>
> #### Costs
> Some public lands in Alaska are free to visit, while some parks charge parking fees. It usually costs $5 to $7 for a day pass at Alaska State Park trailheads, picnic areas and lakeside recreation spots. If you're doing a multiday hike, you'll need to pay for every day you're parked at the trailhead. Nightly rates for campgrounds range from $20 to $35.
>
> Denali National Park is the only national park in Alaska to charge a formal entry fee, payable at the main visitor center. Some US Forest Service visitor centers, such as **Mendenhall Glacier Visitor Center** (p100) in Juneau and Begich-Boggs Visitors Center in Portage (p179) charge a nominal admission fee.
>
> #### Permits
> Permits are not required for recreational activities in Alaskan state parks. Only two national parks require permits – if you're backpacking in Denali or heading off on a multiday kayaking trip in Glacier Bay, you'll need to apply in person for the free permit from each park's backcountry office.
>
> #### More Information
> For more detailed information about parks or public lands, visit the following websites:
> - **Chugach National Forest** (fs.usda.gov/chugach)
> - **Tongass National Forest** (fs.usda.gov/tongass)
> - **Alaska State Parks** (dnr.alaska.gov/parks)
> - **National Park Service, Alaska Region** (nps.gov/orgs/1840/index.htm)
> - **Alaska Public Lands Information Centers** (Anchorage, Fairbanks, Tok, Ketchikan; alaskacenters.gov)

Gates of the Arctic National Park (p386)

Katmai National Park & Preserve (p358) is the place to find Alaska's enormous coastal brown bears fishing for salmon from June to September. Access is by small plane or a water taxi from King Salmon, and it's a backcountry experience with few luxuries available.

Kenai Fjords National Park (p245) can be reached from the small town of Seward, but to see its magnificent glaciers and marine wildlife, book a boat tour or a guided kayaking excursion.

Lake Clark National Park & Preserve (p278) is west of the Kenai Peninsula, across Cook Inlet. Tiny Port Alsworth serves as the hub and the launchpad to bear viewing, fishing, camping and paddling. Must be accessed by float or wheeled small aircraft in summer only.

Wrangell-St Elias National Park & Preserve (p334) is the nation's largest national park and gateway for climbing, hiking, camping, fishing and other active pursuits. It's also home to Kennecott Mines National Historic Landmark, a restored copper mine and company town near the village of McCarthy.

The Wild Lives in Alaska

It's no secret that a major reason people visit Alaska is to witness the animals that have given the state its popularity. Depending on where and when you visit, look for the following wildlife.

Bears inhabit nearly every region of Alaska. Black bears are found in the rainy Southeast up to Anchorage and the Southcentral region. Coastal brown bears live wherever the salmon run: rivers, coastlines and the occasional lake. Grizzly

Exit Glacier (p252), Kenai Fjords National Park

Alaska's Most Popular Parks

DENALI NATIONAL PARK & PRESERVE
In the Interior region, home to the tallest mountain in North America (p303).

KENAI FJORDS NATIONAL PARK
Near Seward on the Kenai Peninsula, famous for glaciers and wildlife (p245).

GLACIER BAY NATIONAL PARK
A major draw in the Southeast with towering tidewater glaciers and abundant wildlife viewing by ship or kayak (p109).

bears inhabit the Interior and far north, while the polar bear, technically a marine mammal, lives on the ice of Arctic areas. Look for bears in all national-park areas. Get the complete lowdown on p45.

Moose are the largest members of the deer family and thrive in Southcentral and Interior Alaska, and some areas of Southeast. Tall and gangly, they are excellent swimmers and fast runners and can be terribly vicious during calving in the spring and mating season (the rut) in the fall.

Caribou travel in herds and spend their days in the Interior and Arctic regions, nibbling lichens for food and raising their young. Spy caribou in Denali National Park & Preserve or Gates of the Arctic.

Wolves have increased in number over the past few years – up to 10,000 or so – but it's hard to know exactly because these pack animals live a hidden life far from humans. Wolves inhabit approximately 85% of Alaska, but are rarely seen, so any sighting is lucky, indeed! Look for them in Denali National Park & Preserve or Katmai National Park & Preserve.

Dall sheep are relations of the bighorn sheep of the mountain west, and can be distinguished by the males' curled horns. Known for thriving on rocky, steep slopes and mountainsides, sheep will spend the summer in grassy areas when they can, and rocky ledges eating lichen and small plants in other seasons. Find Dall sheep along Anchorage's Turnagain Arm section of the Seward Hwy, in Kenai Fjords National Park and Denali National Park & Preserve.

CAMPING ESSENTIALS

If you'll be camping or renting a cabin (p393) in one of Alaska's parks or public lands, keep in mind that wildlife play an important role in planning and activities.

- Keep food and fragrant items separate from other supplies. This includes personal and sanitary products. If in the backcountry, use a bear-resistant food container, available at sporting-goods stores or the land management agency.
- If you can, store food and scented products in a hard-sided vehicle or cabin at night. If backcountry camping, cook, wash and brush your teeth in an area at least 50yd from sleeping quarters.
- Don't sleep in the same clothing you wore to prepare food. Store this clothing away from sleeping areas.
- Educate yourself and everyone in your party about bears, moose and other wildlife present in Alaska's wild spaces. Know how to respond to an encounter and carry bear spray for all remote activities.

Dall sheep, the Alaska Range

KACHEMAK BAY STATE PARK
Near Homer, with stellar kayaking, hikes to glacial lagoons, and halibut or salmon fishing (p280).

KATMAI NATIONAL PARK & PRESERVE
In Southwest Alaska, where coastal brown bears congregate to feed on salmon (p358).

CHUGACH STATE PARK
In the greater Anchorage Bowl, with miles of hiking, biking and skiing (p161).

SITKA NATIONAL HISTORICAL PARK
Home of a major Russian/Native Alaskan battle and the location of stunning displays of totem poles (p92).

Polar bears off Alaska's northern coast

TRIP PLANNER

BEARS, BEARS, BEARS

Meeting a mighty bruin in the wild can be a terrific or terrifying experience – or both. For animal lovers, seeing this magnificent creature in its natural habitat is sure to be a highlight of a trip to Alaska. Here's the scoop on how to get a glimpse (and stay safe).

Bears of Alaska

BLACK BEARS

The most abundant bear species in Alaska is the black bear *(ursus americanus)*, inhabiting most parts of the mainland (except the extreme north) and many islands in Southeast Alaska. They are the smallest of the bear species, standing about 30in high and weighing up to 200lb.

BROWN BEARS

Brown bears *(ursos arctos)*, by contrast, can stand up to 60in tall and weigh as much as 1500lb. Coastal brown bears tend to be larger than their 'grizzly' cousins in the interior due to abundant food resources and milder climate, but they are the same species. The brown bears of Kodiak Island – the largest specimens – are a distinct subspecies *(ursos acrtos middendorfi)*, having been isolated since the last ice age.

POLAR BEARS

Polar bears *(ursos maritimus)* rival brown bears for size. They are limited to the northern and northwestern coast of Alaska, as they never range far from the pack ice. It is possible to see polar bears near Kaktovik and Utqiagvik, but opportunities are limited and the chance of a sighting is far from certain.

Bear Safety 101

The number-one rule of bear safety: respect the bear. Bears are not usually aggressive

📅 WHEN TO GO

Follow the Fish
Although bears are solitary in nature, they often converge on feeding spots, especially salmon-spawning streams. The predictability of the annual salmon runs creates optimal conditions for observing black and brown bears, as they gorge on fish in preparation for their winter hibernation.

Peak Months
The precise timing of salmon runs depends on the species of salmon and local weather patterns, but they generally occur between June and September. Peak bear viewing is usually in July and August, with some variation by location.

---

unless they feel threatened. Avoid startling bears, invading their personal space, or coming between a sow and her cubs.

ON THE TRAIL
- If possible, hike with a friend or a guide.
- Carry bear spray and know how to use it – but don't be jumpy.
- Talk, sing or wear a bear bell on the trail to alert bears of your presence, especially in dense foliage or around blind corners.
- Don't run away from bears, as this stimulates their chase instinct. Instead, remain calm and slowly back away to allow the bear to proceed.
- Pack out all food and trash.

AT A VIEWING SITE
- Always use established trails and viewing locations.
- Do not approach or pursue a bear. Always leave plenty of room for them to get around you.
- Never use food or fish to distract or lure a bear.

Coastal brown bears, Katmai National Park & Preserve (p358)

HOW TO SPOT A BEAR

It's not unusual to spot a bear on the trail, or even from the road, in many parts of Alaska. These encounters are exciting, however fleeting (and hard to plan). If you want to get a good long look at your ursine friends, plan to visit a dedicated bear-viewing site. Located in protected wilderness areas, these are known places where bears congregate, usually with viewing platforms and safety protocols in place. Rangers are usually on hand to answer questions. Sightings are all but guaranteed, and you'll have plenty of opportunities for great wildlife photos. Bring your binoculars!

These remote spots are accessible only by boat or floatplane, so the excursions can be pricey.

Bear-Viewing Sites
- **Kodiak National Wildlife Refuge** (p346) Kodiak Island is the only place to see the largest of the brown bears.
- **Katmai National Park & Preserve** (p358) Brooks Falls is home to Alaska's most famous bears, thanks to its popular bear cam.
- **Lake Clark National Park** (p42) With three different viewing areas, Lake Clark offers premier bear viewing out of Homer.
- **Anan Creek Wildlife Observatory** (p78) This site near Wrangell is the only place where black and brown bears are often seen fishing together.
- **Admiralty Island National Monument** (p107) Bear activity is less concentrated at this wilderness area, accessible from Juneau.

Alaskan crab

THE FOOD SCENE

The land and sea provide a bounty central to the regional and cultural traditions of Alaskans past and present.

From the Arctic to the Southeast, gathering for a meal takes many forms in Alaska, and residents recognize their good fortune when it comes to partaking in the state's most famous edible resources. Food is central to a larger story of cultural and social traditions dating back centuries, be it a community gathering to celebrate the annual harvest of fish, or foraging for wild berries with family in an expanse of tundra. For outsiders, food is also the gateway to adventure, at least when it comes to seafood. You can head off on deepwater fishing adventures in search of monster-sized halibut, or join locals at teeming fishing spots on the Kenai Peninsula during salmon season.

Food and drink also play a large role in Alaska's social scene. Over recent years, microbreweries and local distilleries have popped up in just about every major Alaskan city, often with kitschy food trucks parked outside serving specialty nosh, making for a festive atmosphere that cheers up even the darkest winter evening.

Legendary Seafood

Alaska is home to America's most valuable fishing industry (generating over $5 billion of economic activity) so it's no surprise that seafood plays a starring role on both restaurant menus and in home kitchens. Salmon is justly famed here, and you'll find five species of Pacific salmon, from aptly named king (or Chinook) salmon to the humble chum salmon. Other fish to look out for include halibut, which boasts a white flaky meat that's ideal for

---

Best Alaska Dishes

SALMON
Grilled, smoked or baked, Alaska's favorite food practically swims to the table.

BERRIES
From huckleberries to cranberries, find these tiny fruits in jams, pies and syrups.

CRAB
Caught and eaten the same day with lots of butter, crab is king in coastal areas.

PILOT BREAD
This quirky Alaska-favorite cracker is suitable for dips, spreads and butter.

high-end beer-battered fish and chips; rockfish, which also has a white flaky texture, plus a mild, slightly sweet flavor; and black cod or sablefish, with a silky, buttery texture that goes particularly well with a miso marinade. When it comes to crustaceans, Alaska boasts delectable king crab, a true luxury at more than $100 a pound in most places. There's also snow crab, which has a more delicate flavor than king crab, and Dungeness crab, with tender sweet meat often used to make crab cakes.

Diverse Influences

Depending on where you're visiting and, in some cases, when, ingredients will vary. Alaska is a culinary melting pot, with Indigenous, Russian and Scandinavian influences as well as the masses of miners during the gold-rush era. Still, there are longtime favorites, even if each group adds a particular twist to the recipe. In the Southeast, Southwest and much of Southcentral Alaska, look for seafood 'right off the boat,' meaning the salmon, halibut or shrimp on your plate was swimming not that long ago. In the Interior, dive into reindeer sausage, smoked and dried salmon, and pilot bread, a flatbread-cracker combination that packs well and has a long shelf life. In all regions during the growing season, try local foraged greens and berries, often infused into beverages, salads or sides for a unique flavor twist. There's even fireweed ice cream (and jams), made of

Alaska State Fair (p167), Palmer

FOOD & DRINK FESTIVALS

Kodiak Crab Festival (*kodiakcrabfest.com;* May) Going strong since 1958, this fest celebrates the leggy crustaceans and related foods from the sea.

Nalukataq festival (p380; June) Held in Iñupiat communities, including Utqiaġvik, after a successful whale hunt, when the whole town gathers for celebration and feasting.

Taste of Homer (p274; late May–early June) This weeklong fest is a showcase of the vibrant waterfront town (and the seafood harvested offshore), with special restaurant menus, a big food-truck event and chef competitions.

Ketchikan Blueberry Arts Festival (p71; first week August) Includes a plethora of fine arts, entertainment and blueberry-themed menu items.

Alaska State Fair (p167; August) Food steals the show at this huge two-week event in Palmer with dozens of vendors selling everything from deep-fried halibut chunks to fresh peach pies.

Wild berries

SOURDOUGH BREAD, PANCAKES & MUFFINS	REGIONAL VEGETABLES	MUKTUK	REINDEER SAUSAGE
Baking without yeast for an addictive tang.	Fresh local produce is abundant from June to October.	Wild-harvested whale meat and blubber, served in the Arctic. Restricted to Alaska Natives.	A popular street food in Anchorage, especially in summer; available commercially.

Alaskan wild salmon

those outlandishly bright flowers that grow all across the state in the summer.

Vegetarians & Vegans

While places catering to vegans are rare throughout Alaska, you will find at least one health-food store in most midsize towns and cities, as well as a number of restaurants advertising 'vegetarian options.' Alternatively, search out Thai and other Asian restaurants for the best selection of meatless dishes – just be sure they hold the fish sauce.

Another place to find ready-to-eat meals without meat is at Safeway, Fred Meyer and other large supermarkets. Head to the well-stocked salad and prepared-food bar where you can dish up (self-serve style) hot and cold dishes charged by weight.

Bread of the Ancestors

Many Alaskans carry on the tradition of using sourdough for baked goods, augmenting the high cost at local groceries. Sourdough is a traditional method of baking without yeast that requires 'feeding' a starter of flour and water on a regular basis. In some families, sourdough starter is passed down through generations and is a worthy part of pancakes, biscuits, bread and other baked goods.

Raise a Glass

Alaskans are creative, and that goes double for drinks. From beer made with spruce tips to wild-blueberry vodka, craft breweries and distilleries are popping up across the state. A town walking tour can pair nicely with stops at local purveyors of fine adult beverages. Scores of locals can be found at the same places, so it's easy to strike up a conversation and learn more about the community.

Cafes & Food Trucks

The mainstay of Alaskan restaurants, particularly in small towns, is the main-street cafe. It opens early in the morning serving bagel sandwiches, breakfast burritos or perhaps heartier plates of eggs, bacon, pancakes and oatmeal. By lunchtime, the menu morphs into sandwiches and perhaps hamburgers and grilled items.

Some small towns have a food truck or two. These can be a hamburger hut – a small shack or trailer with picnic tables

LIVING OFF THE LAND

Newcomers are often surprised they need extra storage for the wealth of harvested meat, garden produce and foraged fruits they've accumulated over the short season of plenty. Under special-use subsistence or personal-use permits, Alaska residents can fill freezers with proteins like caribou, moose, salmon and halibut. In the far north, an entire Iñupiat village shares in the bounty after a successful whale hunt – the responsibly harvested animals have sustained their community since time immemorial.

Backyard gardens flourish under the midnight sun. Plants grow quickly, and berry bushes have plenty of fruit. Canning jars and pressure cookers are hot commodities to ensure nothing edible is wasted, and kids are raised to understand the sweat equity of harvesting produce. Anyone who doubts the power of Alaskan growers (or at least the long daylight hours) should attend the Alaska State Fair in Palmer when farmers compete for top prizes for their gargantuan cabbages, some even topping 80lb.

outside – serving burgers, hot dogs, wraps or fried fish. Increasingly, you can find top-notch ethnic fare, especially Thai food served at food trucks.

Local Specialties

Meats & Fish

Grilled meat and fish Alaskans love to throw food on the grill, any time of year.
Jerky Jerky or dried and smoked meat or fish are staples of those needing a preserved, portable protein.
Smoked fish Usually referred to as 'candy' for its sweetness.
Sausage Often made from caribou, reindeer (domesticated reindeer), or moose (not available commercially).

Fruits of the Land

Wild-berry cobblers and pies Made with fresh berries or canned for desserts later in the year.
Fiddleheads The tendrils of a young fern, still coiled, are cooked or pickled as an early spring treat.
Beach greens Harvested along the shorelines and cooked up like spinach.

Snacks

Salmon dip Comes in many forms (often with secret recipes) and can be easily spread on crackers, pilot bread or toast.
Sushi Big business in Alaska, with locally sourced fish and seaweed.

Sweet Treats

Ice cream Features such flavors as rhubarb, blueberry, birch syrup and even fireweed blossoms.
Spruce-tip-infused baked goods The tang (and high vitamin C content) of spruce tips make for a unique coffee partner.
Aqutak, or Eskimo ice cream An Indigenous favorite made with whipped animal fat, berries and sometimes ground fish.

MEALS OF A LIFETIME

Seven Glaciers Restaurant (p175) Take the tram up Mt Alyeska for a multicourse event that ranks among Alaska's best dining experiences.

SALT (p106) Run by a chef born and raised in Juneau, SALT serves elevated Alaskan seafood (and juicy steaks) with Asian accents.

The Cookery (p247) Feast on fresh oysters, perfectly cooked halibut or spicy fried chicken, along with a good wine selection at this Seward gem.

Pump House (p322) Tuck into grilled reindeer medallions while enjoying the views over the Chena River in this always-lively Fairbanks spot.

The Kannery (p274) Homer's best restaurant has a creative, eclectic menu with numerous standouts and imaginative cocktails.

THE YEAR IN FOOD

SPRING

Spring ushers in delicate greens such as nettles and fiddleheads (pictured) as ground thaws and gardeners eagerly await planting time. It's a time to use up last year's salmon or halibut, making way for summer's fresh fish.

SUMMER

The short but bright summer growing season brings overflowing produce markets and home-garden plots. Salmon (pictured) fishing begins in early June and ends with the silver salmon run in late August.

FALL

From late summer until first frost, berry pickers flock to patches. Hunters get permits and head to remote hunting camps. At home, it's time to can, smoke or preserve the foods harvested all summer.

WINTER

This is the season for hearty soups and stews, so look for seafood chowders on local menus. Coffee huts do a brisk business in nearly every community, with lattes and mochas produced from local roasters.

Guided hike, Matanuska Glacier (p160)

THE OUTDOORS

Alaska's wildly diverse terrain offers adventures for all experience levels, from easygoing guided kayaking excursions along the coast to multiday treks amid snow-covered peaks in the interior.

Mountains, forests, rivers and glacier-backed shorelines set the stage for unrivaled adventures in Alaska. In summer, national parks and preserves bustle with activity, from the Inside Passage to the Brooks Range in the Arctic. Whether you're out for a short hike or a multiday trek, you won't lack for options all across the state. Paddlers and rafters also have plenty of variety in this great rugged wilderness, including leisurely floats, Class V rapids and kayaking on glacial lagoons.

Walking & Hiking

From paved urban paths to remote alpine trails, Alaska has terrain for all abilities, with mostly year-round access. One of the classic hikes near Anchorage is the short (3-mile round trip) but challenging (1350ft of elevation gain) ascent up **Flattop Mountain** (p146) for a stupendous view. Memorable trails dot the southeastern islands, and you can find outstanding hikes through rainforest in Ketchikan (try the **Deer Mountain Trail**; p70), Wrangell (**Rainbow Falls Trail**; p80), Petersburg (**Raven Trail**; p85), Sitka (**Mt Verstovia**; p94) and Juneau (**Perseverance Trail**; p104).

Other regions have equally impressive trails. In Denali National Park, you can tackle the **Savage Alpine Trail** (p307) for plenty of variety and great views throughout. Hikes across glaciers are popular (such as the route across **Root Glacier** (p335) in Wrangell-St Elias National Park) and you

---

Alternative Adventures

CYCLING
Enjoy forest and water views (and possible moose sightings) while pedaling the **Tony Knowles Coastal Trail** (p152) in Anchorage.

RAFTING
Hold on tight as you bounce through Class V rapids during a thrilling white-water trip on **Six Mile Creek** (p224).

BEAR VIEWING
Save up for the once-in-a-lifetime trip to see large groups of bears swatting and biting for salmon at **Brooks Falls** (p358).

FAMILY ADVENTURES

Head to Homer and book an excursion with the **Center for Alaskan Coastal Studies** (p275), which runs fun hikes, tide-pooling and boat trips.

Spend a day rafting along the **Nenana River** (p311) as it winds through a canyon near Denali National Park.

Walk the trails of **Sitka National Historical Park** (p92), home to totem poles, verdant forest and an artifact-filled visitor center.

Step back in time aboard the **White Pass & Yukon Route Railway** (p130) as it chugs past forests, waterfalls and mountain views.

Feed and interact with Santa's favorite herbivores at the **Reindeer Farm** (p168) near Palmer and go on a short reindeer trek.

Enjoy close encounters with friendly dogs of all sizes at the **Husky Homestead** (p312) near Denali.

---

can climb above **Exit Glacier** (p252) for top-of-the-world views at Kenai Fjords National Park. You can also combine train travel with a short glacier hike near Girdwood (p178) and Skagway (p131).

Backpacking Alaska

Multiday trail adventures can be a once-in-a-lifetime experience, but only with proper preparation. Unlike many popular Lower 48 destinations, Alaska's hiking trails are often in remote areas with few options for access should you need assistance. Backpackers must be fully prepared with adequate gear, plenty of food, bear and bug spray and a trip plan. A handy resource is the **Alaska Public Land Information Center** *(nps.gov/anch/index.htm)*, which has maps, weather and trail conditions, alerts and directions to campgrounds and trailheads. Reach out online, or through its offices in Anchorage, Fairbanks, Ketchikan and Tok.

Popular overnight destinations include the 40-mile **Resurrection Pass** (p227) from Hope to Cooper Landing on the Kenai Peninsula, with public-use cabins available for rent. The popular **Chilkoot Trail** (p126) between Dyea and Bennett Pass is 33 miles of rugged hiking. In Denali National Park, you can make a two-day (or longer) outing along the **Triple Lakes Trail** (p308), or go deeper into the park by creating your own adventure (p308).

Kayaking & Canoeing

The paddle is a way of life in Alaska, especially in the Southeast, Prince William Sound and the Kenai Peninsula, all of which offer spectacular backdrops for kayaking. You can paddle amid icebergs in **Resurrection Bay** (p250) off Seward, paddle the forest-lined shores of **Kachemak Bay State Park** (p280), explore the glaciers and fjords of **Blackstone Bay** (p213) and look for bald eagles and sea stars near **Ketchikan** (p71). For an adventurous outing right from downtown Fairbanks, you can hop in a canoe and make the easygoing trip along the **Chena River** (p321). A shuttle will take you back to your starting point at journey's end.

Skier, Alyeska Resort (p174)

ALPINE SKIING
Get your fill of magnificent powder while carving your way down dozens of runs at the **Alyeska Resort** (p194).

JET BOATING
Roar up the **Susitna River** (p294) over massive rapids, stopping for insight into Athabascan tradition along the way.

BIRDWATCHING
Look for sandhill cranes and other avian summer migrants amid the diverse backdrops of **Creamer's Field** (p325) in Fairbanks.

FISHING
Cast your line into the deep as you hunt for massive halibut on a fishing trip off **Homer** (p276).

ACTION AREAS

Where to find Alaska's best outdoor activities.

Kayaking/Canoeing
1. Ketchikan (p71)
2. Auke Bay (p105)
3. Blackstone Bay (p213)
4. Kachemak Bay (p280)
5. Resurrection Bay (p250)
6. Eklutna Lake (p161)
7. Chena River (p321)

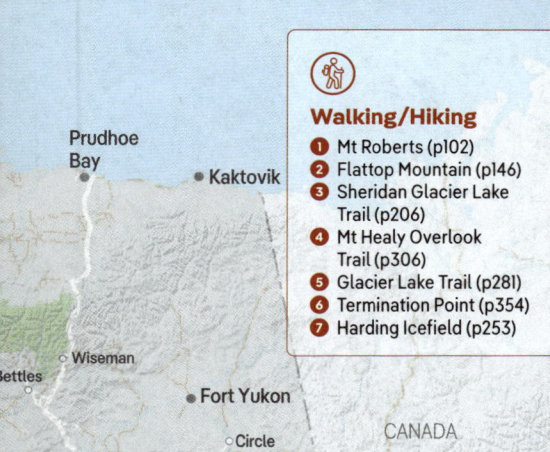

Walking/Hiking

1. Mt Roberts (p102)
2. Flattop Mountain (p146)
3. Sheridan Glacier Lake Trail (p206)
4. Mt Healy Overlook Trail (p306)
5. Glacier Lake Trail (p281)
6. Termination Point (p354)
7. Harding Icefield (p253)

Animals/Wildlife

1. Brooks Falls (p358)
2. Frazer Lake (p355)
3. Lake Clark National Park (p278)
4. Creamer's Field (p325)
5. Glacier Bay (p112)
6. Alaska Wildlife Conservation Center (p179)
7. Chilkat Bald Eagle Preserve (p119)

Skiing

1. Alyeska Resort (p194)
2. Valdez Heli Skiing (p194)
3. Chena Hot Springs (p328)
4. Slikok Multi-Use Trails (p264)
5. Tsalteshi Trails (p220)
6. Kincaid Park (p153)

National Parks

1. Glacier Bay National Park (p109)
2. Kenai Fjords National Park (p245)
3. Denali National Park & Preserve (p303)
4. Wrangell-St Elias National Park & Preserve (p334)
5. Sitka National Historical Park (p92)
6. Klondike Gold Rush National Historical Park (p123)
7. Katmai National Park & Preserve (p358)

PLAN YOUR TRIP THE OUTDOORS

ALASKA

THE GUIDE

Nome & the Arctic p364

Denali & the Interior p286

Anchorage & Around p137

Kenai Peninsula p217

Prince William Sound p182

Juneau & the Alexander Archipelago p56

Kodiak & Katmai p343

Chapters in this section are organised by hubs and their surrounding areas. We see the hub as your base in the destination, where you'll find unique experiences, local insights, insider tips and expert recommendations. It's also your gateway to the surrounding area, where you'll see what and how much you can do from there.

Kayakers, Kenai Fjords National Park (p245)
DAVIDHOFFMANN PHOTOGRAPHY/SHUTTERSTOCK

Researched by
Mara Vorhees

Juneau & the Alexander Archipelago

RAINFORESTS, GLACIERS AND TOTEM POLES

Stunning scenery, wildlife-watching on land or sea, and vibrant Indigenous culture: Southeast Alaska is a destination that inspires curiosity and wonder.

If you imagine Alaska as a treeless expanse of barren land and permafrost, the Alexander Archipelago will quickly destroy this notion. Stretching for some 300 miles along the state's southeastern panhandle, these 1100 islands are home to ice-blue glaciers, rugged snowcapped mountains and some of the most verdant wilderness on the planet. In fact, the entire region lies within the vast Tongass National Forest, the largest remaining temperate rainforest on Earth.

Long before the first European sailors arrived on the scene in the 18th century, Alaska Natives flourished in small interwoven communities scattered across the archipelago. The Tlingit, Haida and Tsimshian tribes still have a strong presence here, with artfully wrought clan houses and impressive totem poles still rising over forested ancestral homelands.

Before WWII, the Southeast was Alaska's heart and soul, and Juneau was not only the capital but the state's largest city. Today, the region is characterized by old-growth forests and small towns. Each community here has its own history and character – from Norwegian-influenced Petersburg to Russian-tinted Sitka. You can feel the gold fever in Skagway and see a dozen glaciers near Juneau. Every town in this region is unique. And none of them is connected to another by road.

Travel here might mean kayaking through dramatic fjords, hiking up craggy mountaintops or discovering Indigenous culture. And at day's end, some of Alaska's best seafood awaits.

STEVE ESTVANIK/SHUTTERSTOCK

THE MAIN AREAS

KETCHIKAN
Totem poles in the wild. **p62**

WRANGELL
Bears on view. **p76**

PETERSBURG
Norwegian history and glacial scenery. **p81**

SITKA
Alaska Native culture and Russian heritage. **p87**

For places to stay in Juneau & the Alexander Archipelago see p134

Left: Totem Bight State Historical Park (p67); Above: Harbor seals near LeConte Glacier (p84)

JUNEAU
Political capital with nature appeal. **p96**

GLACIER BAY NATIONAL PARK & PRESERVE
Scenic glacier and wildlife cruise. **p109**

HAINES
Small town with big nature. **p115**

SKAGWAY
Gold-rush history on display. **p122**

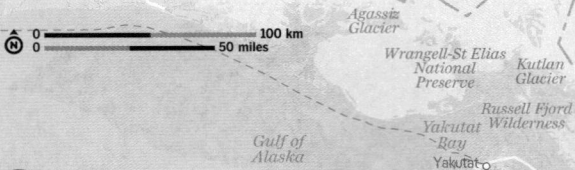

CAR

Although you can take a vehicle on the ferry, the sporadic schedule makes this impractical. You may not need a vehicle at all, but rentals are available in every town, if you want to visit attractions outside the main hubs.

Haines, p115
The tranquil arts-loving settlement is the place for wildlife-watching, hiking and water adventures. There's also an important Tlingit heritage center nearby.

FERRY

The Alaska Marine Highway System ferries connect the main islands. Service is sporadic from Ketchikan up to Juneau – and even less frequent to Sitka – but boats run daily between Juneau, Haines and Skagway, and three times a week to Glacier Bay.

Glacier Bay National Park, p109
Take a ranger-led boat excursion through an icy, watery world of hump-back whales, sea otters and puffins.

PLANE

Alaska Airlines operates daily flights throughout the region, island-hopping from Ketchikan to Sitka to Juneau, or from Ketchikan to Wrangell to Petersburg to Juneau. There are also daily flights to Gustavus (gateway to Glacier Bay National Park & Preserve). Floatplanes provide access to more remote areas.

Sitka, p87
Russian architecture and totem-filled forests attest to the rich history of this picturesque city. Hiking trails lead right from town.

Find Your Way

The panhandle of Alaska's Southeast is an island-studded wilderness set with small towns wedged between narrow straits and verdant rainforest. Travel is by plane and boat since you can't drive between the islands.

Skagway, p122
This vibrant town has historic buildings that bring the past to life, a scenic railroad line and lots of outdoor activities, including hiking and cycling.

Juneau, p96
Alaska's photogenic capital has museums and excellent dining, plus forested trails, gold-mining ruins and a famous glacier outside of town.

Petersburg, p81
A hardworking town with Norwegian roots, Petersburg makes a great base for glacier viewing, kayaking excursions, and hiking trips in the rainforest.

Wrangell, p76
Gateway to some of the best bear-watching in the Southeast, Wrangell also offers rainforest hikes, petroglyphs and wilderness golf.

Ketchikan, p62
This forest-covered island has a wealth of totem poles outside a charming town of museums, craft shops and seafood restaurants.

Plan Your Time

Juneau makes a great base for exploring. Alternatively, you can work your way north from Ketchikan to Skagway, stopping at various islands to admire Indigenous carvings, observe burly bears and hike rainforest trails.

White Pass & Yukon Route (WPYR) Railway (p130)

Pressed for Time

● If you only have time for one destination, Juneau offers a lot of bang for the buck, with easy access to the stunning **Mendenhall Glacier** (p100), scenic hiking and gold-rush history on the **Perseverance Trail** (p104) and fantastic museums and dining in downtown Juneau (p96). Your day (or days) will be packed, even if you never leave town.

● With more time, there are also fantastic opportunities for a scenic cruise through Tracy Arm Fjord (p106), whale-watching in Auke Bay (p105), bear-viewing on Admiralty Island (p107) and other Alaskan adventures, reachable by boat or floatplane.

Seasonal Highlights

The region caters to cruise ships from May to September. At other times of year, tours and services are limited and many restaurants and hotels close.

APRIL
Skagway welcomes (slightly) warmer days with live music, craft fairs and community clean-up at the **Skagway Spring Festival** (p129).

MAY
Petersburg's **Little Norway Festival** (p81) features food, folk dancing and a whimsical parade, while Haines has fun at the annual **BeerFest** (p120).

JUNE
At **Gold Rush Days** (p103) in Juneau you'll find crafts, food and live music, along with jackleg drilling, spike driving and other mining-era competitions.

While Away a Week

● After a few days in Juneau, board a plane or ferry to Gustavus, the gateway to **Glacier Bay National Park & Preserve** (p109). Take the full-day **boat tour** (p112) for a look at glaciers, cerulean seas and mountainous backdrops, along with an impressive cast of wildlife characters.

● Alternatively, use your extra days to catch a ferry to **Skagway** (p122). Ride the scenic **White Pass & Yukon Route Railway** (p130) for memorable mountain vistas. Or, even better, disembark at one of the cool glacier hiking trails (p131). In any case, you can't leave Skagway without visiting the well-preserved **national park sites** (p123) to learn about gold-rush history, followed by drinks and a guided tour at the historic **Red Onion Saloon** (p130).

Island-Hopping

● Start the adventure in **Ketchikan** (p62), home to one of the world's best collections of totem poles. See soaring works at **Totem Bight State Historical Park** (p67) and hike the temperate rainforest to summit lookouts (p69).

● Next, fly or ferry to **Wrangell** (p76) for bear-watching at **Anan Creek** (p78). Continue north to **Petersburg** (p81), a charming town with Scandinavian roots. Take your pick from kayaking, whale-watching or scenic glacier cruises (p83), before continuing to **Juneau** (p96).

● Your final destination is **Sitka** (p87), a fine stop for local history at Russian sites (p87), Indigenous arts and heritage at **Sitka National Historical Park** (p92) and many other island adventures (p93).

JULY
Towns everywhere host big celebrations for the **Fourth of July**, especially Wrangell (p76). This month also brings spawning salmon, hungry bears and binocular-wielding naturalists to Anan Creek (p78) and Pack Creek (p107).

AUGUST
Haines hosts the **Southeast Alaska State Fair** (p120), with live music and lumberjack competitions, while Ketchikan celebrates its favorite foodstuffs at the **Blueberry Arts Festival** (p71).

OCTOBER
On the anniversary of the US–Russia transfer, Sitka hosts the **Alaska Day Festival** (p90) with a reenactment ceremony, a period costume ball and a parade.

NOVEMBER
The Earth's largest gathering of **bald eagles** (p119) takes place in Haines, which hosts tours, seminars and arts events to coincide with the migration.

Ketchikan

RAINFOREST HIKES | TOTEM POLES | LEGENDARY SEAFOOD

☑ **TOP TIP**

Ketchikan is striped with stairways climbing its steep hills. The reward for your exertion is the view from the top. Edmond St is often called the **'Street of Stairs'** for reasons that will become obvious when you get there.

Wedged between densely forested mountains and the placid waters of the Tongass Narrows, Ketchikan is a dramatic gateway to southeastern Alaska. Heavy rainfall transforms the landscape into a backdrop of every shade of green, and the town's famous Haida- and Tlingit-carved totem poles are visible across town.

The town occupies a narrow strip of coastline on Revillagigedo Island and has a large commercial fishing fleet. However, these days tourism plays an even more prominent role in filling the city's coffers. From mid-April through to October, Ketchikan welcomes around 1.5 million cruise-ship passengers who come to view totem poles, embark on boat tours, or board seaplanes out to the Misty Fjords National Monument. Despite the seasonal frenzy, Ketchikan hasn't lost its charming small-town vibe, especially evident in the jumbled clapboard facades of Creek Street and the picturesque harbor at Thomas Basin.

Creek Street

Get a glimpse of early Ketchikan

Old Ketchikan still stands along **Creek Street**, a historic row of wooden walkways and buildings perched on pilings along the creek. A gathering spot for loggers, fishermen and goldminers, the colorful wood-paneled houses served as Ketchikan's infamous red-light district until 1954. Signs proudly claim

GETTING AROUND

Ketchikan's public bus system has two main lines. The Green Line runs from downtown into the hills above, then north past the airport ferry. The Silver Line heads south past Saxman Native Village to Rotary Beach, and north all the way past Totem Bight State Historical Park. Both run hourly.

There's also a free downtown bus loop, which goes from the Plaza Mall/Safeway to the Totem Heritage Center.

Alaska Marine Highway System ferries dock near 3501 Tongass Ave, about two miles north of the town center. This dock is near the terminal for ferries to the airport.

Creek Street

Ketchikan as the only place where both fish and fishermen went upstream to spawn.

Get a glimpse of the era inside the green dollhouse known as **Dolly's House** *(admission $10)*, once a parlor for one of Ketchikan's most famous madams, Dolly Arthur. Tours include a look at the brothel, including its bar, which was placed over a trapdoor to the creek for quick disposal of bootleg whiskey. Further along the boardwalk, **Married Man's Way** was a backdoor route up the hill, allowing discreet getaways from the bars and brothels.

Nowadays, Creek St is lined with galleries and shops. The wooden boardwalk continues all the way up the creek to a salmon ladder, which helps the fish get over the white water as they migrate up the river to spawn.

BEST SHOPPING STOPS

Parnassus Books: When the weather sours, Parnassus is a delightful place to browse Alaska books, cards and local art.

Star Gallery: This gem showcases eclectic works by several contemporary Ketchikan artists, including the beloved (but punny) Ray Troll.

Main Street Gallery: A small gallery showcasing the work of local artists, operated by the Ketchikan Area Arts & Humanities Council.

Crazy Wolf Studio: Owned by a Tsimshian artist, Crazy Wolf stocks authentic crafts, including drums, baskets and jewelry.

Sam McGee's: A Creek St classic packed with one-of-a-kind items that are made in Alaska.

 ### DRINKING IN KETCHIKAN: MADE LOCALLY

Bawden Street Brewing Co: Ketchikan's favorite microbrewery is this hole-in-the-wall, serving up unique flavors and friendly vibes. *10am-8pm*

Uncharted Alaska Distillery: Housed in a former fire station, this distillery and cocktail bar serves cocktails with housemade whiskey, gin and vodka. *9am-9pm*

Alaska Legends Cider & Wine: Cozy space with games and armchairs, perfect for lingering and sampling the ciders and wines, made on-site. *9am-9pm*

Baleen Brewing Co: This tiny brewhouse goes for quality over quantity, with just four tasty beers on tap, all made in-house. *9am-8pm*

KETCHIKAN

Naha Bay (20km)

Water St
Tongass Ave
Chapman St
Schoenbar Rd
Harding St
Warren St
Bayview St
Hopkins Al
Bauer Way
Main St
Cedar St
Front St
Revilla St
Pine St
Water St

Harbor View Park

Waterfront Promenade

Cruise Ship Berth 3

Tongass Narrows

Cruise Ship Berth 2

Greater Ketchikan

Second Waterfall Creek
First Waterfall Creek
Revillagigedo Island
Coon Island
Georges Inlet
White River
Talbot Lake
Whipple Creek
Connell Lake
Upper Mahoney Lake
Mud Bay
Ward Lake
Ward Cove
Perseverance Lake
Upper Ketchikan Lake
Tongass Narrows
Tongass National Forest
Carlanna Lake
Lower Ketchikan Lake
Blue Lake
Gravina Island
Totem Heritage Center
See main map
Whitman Lake
Saxman Native Village & Totem Park
Pennock Island
Herring Bay
Annette Island (5mi)

0 — 5 km
0 — 2.5 miles

★ HIGHLIGHTS
1. Saxman Native Village & Totem Park
2. Totem Heritage Center

● SIGHTS
3. Creek Street
4. Dolly's House
5. Potlatch Park
6. Southeast Alaska Discovery Center
7. Street of Stairs
8. Tongass Historical Museum
9. Totem Bight State Historical Park

● ACTIVITIES
10. Baranof Fishing Excursions
11. Bering Sea Crab Fishermen's Tour
12. Deer Mountain Trailhead
13. Dude Mountain Trailhead
14. Family Air Tours & Hook Up Fly Shop
15. Ketchikan Kayak Company
16. Married Man's Way
17. Perseverance Trail
18. Rainbird Trail
19. Southeast Exposure
20. Ward Lake Nature Walk

● SLEEPING
21. Black Bear Inn
22. Cape Fox Lodge
23. Gilmore Hotel
24. Inn at Creek Street
25. Ketchikan Hostel
26. My Place

● EATING
27. Alaska Crepe Co
28. Alaska Fish House
29. Alava's Fish-n-Chowder
see 23 Annabelle's Keg & Chowder House
30. Asian Garden
31. Barn Door
32. Burger Queen
33. Bush Pilots' Lounge
34. Dock Street Yard
see 22 Heen Kahidi Restaurant
35. Just Dandy Apothecary & Cafe
36. Ketchikan Crab & Go
37. New York Cafe
38. Pioneer Café

● DRINKING & NIGHTLIFE
39. Alaska Legends Cider & Wine
40. Asylum
41. Baleen Brewing Co
42. Bawden Street Brewing Co
43. Green Coffee Bean Company
44. Hole in the Wall Bar & Marina
45. Island Brew Cafe
46. Potlatch Bar
47. Totem Bar
48. Uncharted Alaska Distillery

● ENTERTAINMENT
49. Great Alaskan Lumberjack Show

● SHOPPING
50. Crazy Wolf Studio
51. Main Street Gallery
52. Parnassus Books
53. Sam McGee's
54. Star Gallery

Totem Bight State Historical Park

UNDERSTANDING TOTEM POLES

Totem poles are unique to the Pacific Northwest, carved for centuries by the Haida, Tlingit and Tsimshian peoples. Usually fashioned from mature cedars, totem poles have a natural lifespan of around 75 years before the damp climate takes its toll. Progressive deterioration is seen as part of the natural life cycle. Ideally, they are left to rot and return to the earth.

Totem poles were never intended as objects of worship. They serve several nonreligious functions: 'welcome poles' greet visitors to houses and communities; 'memorial poles' honor the dead; 'mortuary poles' contain ancestral remains; 'house poles' have a structural function, and 'shame poles' ridicule public figures for wrongdoing.

Nature & Culture on Display
Browse Ketchikan's best museums

Large totems greet you in the lobby of the **Southeast Alaska Discovery Center** (fs.usda.gov/r10/tongass/offices; adult/child $5/free), a fascinating museum run by the United States Forest Service (USFS). A school of silver salmon suspended from the ceiling leads you toward a slice of recreated temperate rainforest. Upstairs, the exhibit halls highlight Southeast Alaska's ecosystems, Alaska Native traditions and Alaska's natural resources. The 18-minute introductory film gives an impressive overview of the natural and human-made wonders of the Tongass rainforest.

Just across the creek, the small **Tongass Historical Museum** (ketchikanmuseums.org; adult/child $6/free) houses a collection of local and Alaska Native artifacts, many dealing with Ketchikan's fishing industry. The impressive totem near the entrance tells the Tlingit creation story of Raven stealing the sun.

EATING IN KETCHIKAN: QUICK BITES

Burger Queen: Ketchikan's favorite roadside burger joint also serves a mean halibut sandwich. *11am-7pm Tue-Sat* $

Barn Door: Great option for burgers and shakes, chicken sammies or fish and chips. Order at the window and sit at a picnic table. *6.30am-7pm Thu-Tue, 11am-4pm Tue & Sat* $

Dock Street Yard: Food truck in a beer garden: what's not to love? The rotating menu ranges from fish tacos to pork banh mi. *11am-3pm Thu-Sun* $

Alaska Crepe Co: Crispy crepes are stuffed with sweet and savory fillings (think wild berries or smoked salmon) for a satisfying snack. *7am-6pm* $

Soaring Symbols of Tlingit & Haida Culture

Totem poles and clan houses

With a 16% Alaska Native population, Ketchikan proudly touts its Indigenous heritage – not least through its extensive collection of totem poles, the largest in the country. You can get a crash course in carved artwork at the **Totem Heritage Center** *(ketchikanmuseums.org; adult/child $6/free)*, where at least 16 poles – some more than 100 years old – are on display. The center's almost spiritual setting accentuates the reverence Alaska Natives attach to them.

To see totems in a natural setting of forest and shoreline, hop on a bus to **Totem Bight State Historical Park** *(dnralaska.gov; $5)*, located 10 miles north of downtown Ketchikan. This 11-acre seaside park contains more than a dozen restored totem poles, a colorful clan house and a viewing deck overlooking Tongass Narrows. Interpretive boards explain the importance of this site, which was one of the earliest attempts to revive the dying art of totem-carving in the 1930s. Pick up a free guide to the totem poles on display. Among the highlights is a Haida mortuary pole representing the mythical thunderbird and its prey, the killer whale. Towering above the clan house is a totem pole that represents several key Tlingit stories. Perched at the top is Raven, holding a box that he stole to bring light into the world.

Next door to Totem Bight, the less manicured **Potlatch Park** *(potlatchparkalaska.com; free)* shows off an impressive collection of totem poles, one of which is 42ft high. There are also beautiful tribal houses and an on-site carver who may be working in the carving shed. A nearby garage houses a collection of vintage cars, while the main building contains impressive taxidermy and a collection of antique firearms.

Another important Native site lies 2.5 miles south of Ketchikan. **Saxman Village** is an incorporated Tlingit village of about 350 residents. On site is a **Totem Park** *(capefoxtours.com; $5)* with two dozen totems from abandoned villages around the Southeast, restored or recarved in the 1930s. Among them is a replica of the Lincoln Pole (the original is in the Alaska State Museum in Juneau), which was carved in 1883 using a picture of Abraham Lincoln as a reference, to commemorate the first sighting of white people. (Carvers apparently had no idea how tall he was.) You can wander around Saxman Totem Park on your own or reserve in advance to join an Alaska Native–led two-hour village tour. Tours are largely geared toward the cruiseship crowd and may include a traditional drum-and-dance

CARVING AS A WAY OF LIFE

One of Alaska's living legends, master carver **Nathan P Jackson,** describes a lifetime of carving.

Way back in 1962 is when I got going, and I've been carving for over 60 years. It all started with my great uncle's stepson who used to carve with a pocketknife. When I receive a commission, say two totem poles that are 14ft tall, I say to the client, 'Now you're going to have to tell me a story,' but sometimes they leave it to me. A lot of these ideas begin with sketching out all the possible ideas. Drawing becomes a way that you can figure out what needs to be done. Nowadays, my son is also a carver, so the tradition continues.

 EATING IN KETCHIKAN: SEAFOOD

Alava's Fish-n-Chowder: Carry-out fish sandwiches, tacos and fantastic chowder served up at a shack in the Safeway parking lot. *11am-6pm Mon-Sat* **$**

Alaska Fish House: Casual waterfront spot for outstanding fresh catch of the day served in fish-and-chips, tacos or over rice. *10am-8pm* **$$**

Asian Garden: Alaska does not immediately scream 'sushi,' but maybe it should. The interior isn't inspiring, but the fish is as fresh as it gets. *11am-8pm Mon-Sat* **$$$**

Ketchikan Crab & Go: Guests rave about halibut fish and chips, crab and clam chowder and massive (but pricey) king crab legs. *hours vary* **$$$**

BEST FISHING CHARTERS

Chick Charters: This fun woman-owned operation caters especially to families and novice fishers.

K-Seas: A Ketchikan native, Captain Casey takes guests out on the Toni Lee.

Hook Up Fly Shop: Jim Davis and his team of guides are the go-to guys for fly fishing (especially fly-in fly fishing).

Alaska Strike Zone: One of the state's oldest charter fishing companies. Captains Nolan and Logan are expert fish finders.

Baranof Fishing Excursions: After fishing, your guides will take you to a remote beach campsite to cook and eat the catch.

performance, in addition to a narrated tour of the totem poles and a visit to the carving shed.

Gone Fishing
Experience the salty life

Sometimes called the 'salmon capital of the world,' Ketchikan is the only city in Alaska that has healthy runs of all five kinds of salmon, not to mention populations of halibut, cod, rockfish and more. Fishing is the very heart and soul of this town. If you want to get a taste of the salty life, this is the place to do it. **Fishing charters** give novices and experts alike the chance to hook their own fish, whether salmon, halibut or both. Charters run $300 to $350 per person for a five-hour trip. Most companies can arrange for your catch to be cleaned, filleted, frozen, and packed for you to take home, for an extra charge.

If you're curious about the life of a commercial fisher, sign up for the popular **Bering Sea Crab Fishermen's Tour**. On an authentic crab-fishing boat called the F/V *Aleutian Ballad*, the team of old sailors demonstrates fishing techniques and recounts incredible stories from the tempestuous waters of the Bering Sea. No actual fishing takes place on this tour, but an onboard touch tank allows for up-close observation of different kinds of crabs. The veteran crabbing boat may look

EATING AND DRINKING IN KETCHIKAN: CUTE CAFES

Green Coffee Bean Co: Locals agree this is the best coffee (and cookies) in Ketchikan, despite the location 7 miles out of town near Ward Cove. *6am-5pm* **$**

Island Brew Cafe: The friendliest place in town for hot coffee, fresh-baked pastries, breakfast burritos and lunchtime sammies. *7am-4pm* **$**

Just Dandy Apothecary: Salads and grain bowls for something healthy. Great choice for those with dietary restrictions. *10.30am-3pm* **$**

Pioneer Cafe: Hearty no-frills cooking served in a traditional diner with fast service and free coffee refills. *6am-10pm* **$$**

Ward Lake Nature Walk

familiar: the *Aleutian Ballad* featured on season 2 of the Discovery Channel's *Deadliest Catch* series.

Grand Views From the Trail
Hiking the island's rainforests

Ketchikan's excellent trail system winds through verdant rainforests and up to lofty heights. You'll find several trails in the Ward Lake area, around 9 miles northwest of the town center.

The easy 1.5-mile **Ward Lake Nature Walk** is a favorite with local dog owners. The interpretive loop begins near the north-end parking lot and encircles the peaceful lake. Beavers, birds and the occasional black bear might be seen. The trailhead is about 7 miles north of downtown Ketchikan. Turn right on Revilla Rd and continue up 1.5 miles to Ward Lake Rd.

From Ward Lake, the moderately easy, well-trodden 2.4-mile (one-way) **Perseverance Trail** passes through mature coastal forest and muskeg and terminates at Perseverance Lake. The view of the lake, with its mountainous backdrop, is spectacular. The trailhead is on Ward Lake's east side, just past a campground.

Dude Mountain Trail is a rewarding alpine trek that begins in stands of old-growth spruce and follows a narrow ridge to the 2848ft peak. It's a 1.5-mile trek with a gain of 1500ft to the

TONGASS NATIONAL FOREST

In many ways, Southeast Alaska is the Tongass, the largest national forest in the US, dedicated in 1907 by President Theodore Roosevelt. The **Tongass National Forest** encompasses most of the Alexander Archipelago's 1110 islands, as well as some mainland areas. This is the largest temperate rainforest in the world, packed with Sitka spruce, western hemlock and red cedar. However, some 40% of the Tongass isn't exclusively forest, but also comprises wetlands, ice and high mountain terrain. For adventurers, rustic off-the-grid accommodations are available in 13 campgrounds and 150 scattered USFS cabins, most of which are only accessible by boat or floatplane.

 EATING IN KETCHIKAN: BEST RESTAURANTS

New York Cafe: Historic joint good for excellent coffee, a satisfying meal or delicious after-dinner drinks. *8am-8.30pm Tue-Sat, to 2pm Sun* **$$**

Annabelle's Famous Keg & Chowder House: Tuck into first-rate seafood, including Ketchikan's best chowder, amid 1920s decor. *9am-10pm* **$$**

Bush Pilots' Lounge: Stylish spot for high-end seafood, steaks and creative vegetarian-friendly fare with water views. *4-10pm Tue-Sat* **$$$**

Heen Kahidi: Wonderful views, food and service make Cape Fox Lodge's restaurant a special-occasion spot. Take the funicular up from Creek St. *7am-9pm* **$$$**

TSIMSHIAN COMMUNITY

In 1887, Anglican missionary William Duncan left Metlakatla, British Columbia, due to a dispute with church authorities, and arrived at **Annette Island** with 823 Tsimshian Natives. Their community at Metlakatla, Alaska, became a federally recognized Indian Reservation – the only one in the state. This means that the 20-mile-long island is reserved for Tsimshian Natives (and other Alaska Natives who wish to join the community). It is the only Tsimshian settlement in the US.

The village (population 1454) is the antithesis of Ketchikan, with nary a cruise ship in sight. Fishing is the economic mainstay of the island. Tsimshian culture is on display at a community art center, a totem park and a traditional longhouse that hosts Native dance performances. The island is located due south of Ketchikan. Ferries run between Ketchikan and Anette Bay five times a week.

Great Alaskan Lumberjack Show

top. Once there, you're in open alpine country and can easily ridge-walk to Diana Mountain (3014ft) or Brown Mountain (2978ft). The trailhead is around 9 miles inland from Ward Cove, 6 miles up the scenic but slow-going Revilla Rd, then another 3 miles on Brown Mountain Rd.

The **Deer Mountain Trail** is a popular option that can be reached from downtown Ketchikan on foot. This well-maintained trail features a 2.5-mile climb up to the 3001ft summit of Deer Mountain. Overlooks provide panoramic views all along the way. Toward the top of the mountain, more trails extend into the alpine region and to a free-use shelter. Beyond the shelter, the hike becomes steeper and more challenging, with few markers. Get to the trailhead by taking the Green Line bus to the corner of Deermount and Fair Sts, and then heading south on Ketchikan Lakes Rd.

Blazed a little over a decade ago, the 1.3-mile (one-way) **Rainbird Trail** is just outside of Ketchikan. This delightful trail winds through a rainforest along a bluff before giving way to striking views of the city and Tongass Narrows below. You can ride to the western end of the trail by bus (get off near the University of Alaska-Southeast campus off 7th Ave). From there, hike your way eastward back into town.

Lumberjack Festival

Witness feats of strength and skill

Is it hokey? Yes, it sure is. But the **Great Alaskan Lumberjack Show** *(alaskanlumberjackshow.com; $45)* is also entertaining and pretty darn impressive, as athletes show their strength and skill in competitive pole-climbing, log-rolling, axe-throwing and various methods of wood-chopping. The show celebrates Ketchikan's logging history (and takes place on the site of the former Ketchikan Spruce Mill, which closed in 1993). Back in the day, timber teams from around the region would come to Ketchikan to compete for the title of 'King of the Woods'. The show re-creates such a contest. In addition to the feats of strength, the family-friendly show includes lots of corny jokes and much hooting and hollering from the audience.

Paddle Among the Wild Things
Short and multi-day excursions

Scattered with dozens of islands and islets, Ketchikan's waterways are ripe for exploration by kayak. Possible trips range from an easy paddle around the islands north of town to a weeklong trip in Misty Fjords National Monument (p72).

Several companies offer easygoing but scenic guided paddling trips, operating out of Clover Pass, about 15 miles north of town. The **Ketchikan Kayak Company** *(ketchikankayakco.com; per person $150)* takes visitors through the waterways of Clover Pass, circumnavigating an island or two and taking in the magnificent scenery. Along the way, paddlers often spy sea lions, seals, starfish, bald eagles, Sitka deer and even humpback whales, as well as plentiful sea stars in the tidal zone. Tours have a maximum of six paddlers per guide. **Southeast Exposure** *(southeastexposure.com; per person $100-165)* also does paddle tours in this area, with loops around Eagle Islands or the more distant Tatoosh Islands.

Experienced paddlers might opt for a multi-day DIY adventure. One option is the 8-mile trip from Settlers Cove State Recreation Site (at the end of N Tongass Hwy) to **Naha Bay**. From the bay, you can paddle through the narrow outlet to Roosevelt Lagoon (at high slack tide only). Alternatively, leave your kayak at the floating dock at the bay's head, and hike down the 5.4-mile Naha River National Recreation Trail. The scenic hiking trail follows the river up to Jordan and Heckman lakes, both of which have United States Forest Service (USFS) cabins. **Southeast Exposure** *(per day from $45)* rents both plastic and fiberglass sea kayaks for independent paddlers.

BEST BERRIES FOR PICKING

Sweet and tart berries grow wild along trails and throughout the forests of Southeast Alaska. Here are the best berries for picking – and one to avoid.

Salmonberry: The most prolific and delicious trailside berry looks like a big red or orange raspberry – or salmon roe, which is how it got its name.

Blueberry: Taste the best of Ketchikan's crop at the local Blueberry Arts Festival, held every year in early August.

Strawberry: Small but sweet 'beach strawberries' are often found in coastal areas.

Black Huckleberry: A shrubby bush with shiny, dark purple berries that are tart and tasty.

Baneberry: Highly poisonous, these red or white berries grow in clusters on a leafy bush. All parts of the plant are toxic!

DRINKING IN KETCHIKAN: LOCAL FAVORITES

Hole in the Wall Bar & Marina: 8 miles south of town, this much-loved spot has a prime waterfront setting and occasional live music. *noon-10pm*

Potlatch Bar: A local favorite overlooking Thomas Basin, popular among the fisherfolk. *10am-2am*

Asylum: Good times are all but guaranteed at this old-timey bar, with pool, darts, pinball and 30 beers on draft. *8am-2am*

Totem Bar: Doesn't get more local than this dark dive, owned by the same family for five decades. Trivia, karaoke and open-mic nights draw regulars. *9am-2am*

Beyond Ketchikan

The seascape around Ketchikan is an outdoor adventurer's dreamscape, with a vast island to the west and stunning fjords to the east.

Places

Misty Fjords National Monument p72

Prince of Wales Island p73

GETTING AROUND

The **Inter-Island Ferry** makes the three-hour trip between Prince of Wales Island and Ketchikan, departing Hollis at 8am and returning from Ketchikan at 3.30pm. **Taquan Air** also flies scheduled floatplanes to 10 different destinations on the Island. Unless you're staying at a full-service lodge, you'll need a car. Rent from DJ's Alaska Adventure Rentals or Rainforest Auto Rentals (book ahead). Bring your car on the ferry, though some rental agencies prohibit this.

Outside of Ketchikan, you'll find some of the most dramatic scenery in southeastern Alaska. One of the biggest draws is the aptly named Misty Fjords National Monument, which naturalist John Muir compared to the Yosemite Valley for its similar geology and grandeur. Though most people fly or boat in for a quick glimpse of this glacially carved region, adventurers can make a multi-day kayaking trip through the national monument.

Prince of Wales Island is another lure for the adventurous: a rugged place of tiny villages, hiking trails, canoe routes, remote cabins and fishing opportunities. The 990-mile coastline meanders around countless bays, coves and protective islands, while its 1300 miles of roads are ripe for exploring.

Misty Fjords National Monument

TIME FROM KETCHIKAN: 2 HRS OR 30 MINS

Marvel at the misty magic

The spectacular 3570-sq-mile **Misty Fjords National Monument** is a natural mosaic of sea cliffs, steep fjords and rock walls jutting 3000ft straight up from the ocean. Brown and black bears, mountain goats, Sitka deer, bald eagles and a multitude of marine mammals inhabit this drizzly realm, located some 40 miles east of Ketchikan.

The monument receives 150in of rainfall annually, and many people think Misty Fjords is at its most beautiful when the granite walls and tumbling waterfalls are veiled in fog and mist.

The most picturesque areas are Walker Cove, Rudyerd Bay and Punchbowl Cove. They are accessed via the Behm Canal, the long inlet separating Revillagigedo Island from the mainland.

The most common way to view the Misty Fjords is on a sightseeing flight or day cruise. The five-hour **catamaran cruise** can be good for spotting wildlife in the cove, but most of the time is spent on the open water, traveling to/from the destination (two hours each way). **Flightseeing trips** take about 90 minutes, including a lake landing. This is a big seller for cruise ship passengers: when the weather is nice, there is

Misty Fjords National Monument

an endless stream of floatplanes flying to Rudyerd Bay and Walker Cove. Also, be aware that floatplane crashes are not unheard of, so refrain from flying in poor weather conditions.

Prince of Wales Island

TIME FROM KETCHIKAN: **3 HRS**

Learn about Native culture

On the east side of Prince of Wales Island, a 50-mile drive east from Craig, tiny Kasaan is one of only two Haida villages in all of Alaska. It is also home to a **Totem Historic District** – one of the most important Haida cultural centers in the state. In a beautiful bayside setting, a forested trail meanders past numerous totem poles (both Haida and Tlingit) and the centerpiece Chief Son-I-Hat Whale House. Check out the 52ft Yáadaas clan pole, a carving that was removed from Kasaan more than a century ago and returned in 2022. The complex also contains a couple of Native cemeteries, one of which guards the remains of Chief Son-I-Hat (1829–1912).

On the western side of the island, the impressive collection of totems at **Klawock Totem Park** is a source of community pride. Situated on a hill overlooking the town's cannery and harbor, Klawock's 21 totem poles comprise one of the largest

MISTY FJORDS OPERATORS

Family Air: One pilot, one plane. Reliable local operator Jim Davis runs 1½-hour trips to the fjords in a five-seat Cessna.

Island Wings: Pilot Michelle Madson has more than 20,000 flight hours on the books. She offers fly-out hiking, fishing and bear-viewing, in addition to Misty Fjords.

Seawind Aviation: Flights to Misty Fjords, as well as Prince of Wales Island, Anan Creek and Traitor's Cove.

True Alaska Tours: Runs a popular 4½-hour boat trip to Misty Fjords, as well as a wildlife cruise and a half-day trip to Meklakatla.

Alaska Hummer Adventures: Charter a 30ft aluminum boat (six people max.) for a customized trip to Misty Fjords, with wildlife-watching and optional stops along the way. Other custom tours on offer include bear viewing and marine wildlife-watching.

EATING ON PRINCE OF WALES ISLAND: SEAFOOD & SAMMIES

Klawock Totem Cafe: The only place to eat in Klawock is this old-school roadside diner, with sandwiches and milkshakes on the menu. *8am-7pm Tue-Sun* $

Annie Betty's Bakery: A family-owned local favorite spot in Craig, makes fresh pastries, frothy coffee drinks, sandwiches and wraps. *7am-2pm* $

Dockside Cafe: Tuck into fruity French toast and reindeer sausage while enjoying the small-town charm of this friendly old-fashioned diner in Craig. *7am-7pm* $

Papa's Pizza: When you're hungry after 7pm, Papa's thin-crust pizza, calzone and salads do the trick. Located in Craig. *11am-8pm to 9pm Fri & Sat* $

NATIVE PEOPLES OF SOUTHEAST ALASKA

Southeast Alaska is home to three different Alaska Native groups. The largest is the Tlingit, resident in these parts since time immemorial and occupying the area from the Dixon Entrance (south of Ketchikan) all the way up to Yakutat. The Kaigaini Haida migrated from British Columbia and settled on Prince of Wales Island in the early 1700s, while a group of Tsimshian people arrived in 1887 and settled on Annette Island (Metlakatla). Despite the geographical proximity, the three groups are unrelated to each other, and their languages are distinct.

These people do share many cultural similarities, including a matrilineal social structure based on clans. Tlingit and Haida clans are organized into moieties (Eagle vs Raven), while Tsimshian clans are divided into four phratries. Other cultural similarities include the carving of totem poles and the practice of potlatch to commemorate important events.

Staircase leading to the El Capitan Cave

single-site collections in Alaska. Some totems are originals from the former village of Tukekan. The totem park is 7 miles north of Craig, just west of the Klawock town center.

Hike, bike or paddle on POW

The USFS maintains over a dozen hiking trails on Prince of Wales Island. In the south, the **One Duck Trail** is a good option, beginning just off the road to Hydaburg, 2 miles south of the Hollis Hwy junction. The steep trail climbs 1400ft in 1.2 miles, but it ends at an open alpine area with panoramic views of the Klawock Mountains. There is a three-sided free-use shelter (sleeps four) at the summit.

To the north, the mostly flat, 2.8-mile **Balls Lake Trail** circles around the lake. Start at Balls Lake picnic site or Eagle's Nest Campground. Another favorite is the **Sunnahae Mountain Trail**, a 7-mile round-trip hike that climbs more than 2500ft to the summit. The trailhead is just outside of Craig, off the Craig-Klawock Hwy. Bring a mapping system and be prepared for wet and marshy conditions.

Bikers have 260 miles of scenic byways to explore, with gorgeous scenery and few cars. Unfortunately, there are no bike rental facilities on the island, so you'll need to bring your own two wheels. Rent a bike in Ketchikan from Southeast Exposure's **Ketchikan Town Bike Rental** *(southeast exposure.com; per day $40)*. **Sandy Beach Rd** (also known as Forest Rd 30) – from Coffman Cove to Thorne Bay – is a 36-mile ride along the narrow, winding dirt road that skirts

Clarence Strait. Along the way is **Sandy Beach Picnic Area**, an excellent place for beachcombing and whale-watching.

Opportunities for paddlers are also rewarding. At the north end of the island (off Forest Rd 20) is the **Sarkar Lakes Canoe Route**, a 15-mile loop of five major lakes and portages, along with a USFS cabin and excellent fishing. For a day of kayaking, depart from Klawock and paddle into **Big Salt Lake** (part of Klawock Inlet), where the water is calm and the birding is excellent. Be mindful of the inlets at mid-tide as they can hold treacherous white-water conditions. **DJ's Alaska Adventure Rentals** *(djsalaskaadventurerentals.com; per day from $65)* rents kayaks and canoes.

Navigate a network of caves

At the northern end of the island, the lush old-growth forest and muskeg bogs conceal an intriguing geological feature – intricate and expansive karst formations beneath the Earth's surface. Over the millennia, the limestone layer has eroded, creating underground streams and caverns, including more than 850 grottos and caves. It's worth the 2½-hour journey (70 miles) from Craig to explore some of the more accessible caves and karst formations.

Stop first at the **Beaver Falls Karst Trail** (on the main road FS 20 between the two turn-offs for Whale Pass). This trail offers an above-ground experience, as its 1.4-mile boardwalk loop leads past sinkholes, pits, underground rivers and other typical karst features.

A further 6 miles northwest, **El Capitan Cave** is the longest mapped cave in Alaska. You can see a section of it on a free, two-hour ranger-led cave tour (Wednesday through Saturday, seasonally). Contact the Thorne Bay USFS Ranger Station for reservations (907-828-3304) at least two days in advance. (No children under seven allowed). If the tours are not running due to funding cuts, you can still go into the first room of the cave system to look around the cool darkness. The hike to the cave is short but steep, with 200 steps carved out of the limestone.

THE CREATION OF A CAVE SYSTEM

Muskeg – a peat bog-like wetland with poor drainage and low oxygen levels – has wet, acidic soil that contributes to the formation of karst and caves. The muskeg sits on top of a vast layer of limestone bedrock. The acidic moisture of the muskeg seeps down into the limestone, causing erosion. When the water encounters clay or other nonporous surfaces, it may stop the downward flow. The water then pushes sideways, over time creating cave systems that can extend underground for miles. Karstlands may include above-ground features, such as spires, pinnacles, and mountains, in addition to sinkholes, streams, and caves below the Earth's surface.

DRINKING ON PRINCE OF WALES ISLAND: BOOZE & BREWS

| **JT Brown's Store:** Best coffee on the island at the general store in Craig. Also, fishing gear. *7am-3pm* | **Locked & Loaded Coffee Co:** Good coffee and breakfast nibbles by folks who cherish their Second Amendment rights. Located across from the Klawock airstrip. *6am-5pm Mon-Sat, from 8am Sun* | **Craig Inn:** The friendliest bar in Craig has a couple of pool tables and Alaskan microbrews on tap. There's also food available at the restaurant in the back. *11am-10pm Tue-Sat, to 6pm Sun & Mon* | **Hill Bar:** 'The Hill' is the oldest bar on the island and a favorite local hangout in Craig. *noon-9pm Sun-Thu, to midnight Fri & Sat* |

Wrangell

BEAR VIEWING | PETROGLYPHS | NATIVE HERITAGE

GETTING AROUND

Wrangell Airport is about a mile north of town, and most lodging provides transfers. The ferry terminal is a short stroll northwest of the center. Wrangell's heart is compact, with a few eateries and cafes sprinkled around near Front St. For hiking or camping trips out of town, you can rent cars from various outfits, including Island Escape. With little traffic in the area, biking is also an excellent option.

☑ TOP TIP

The **Nolan Center** hosts events throughout the year, including a monthly Community Market, when local makers sell their creations. Takes place one Saturday per month.

Wrangell is Southeast Alaska's unpolished coastal outpost, a small boom-bust fishing community colored by centuries of Tlingit settlement and more recent incursions by the Russians and British. Lacking the fishing affluence of Petersburg or the cruise-ship-oriented economy of Ketchikan, the town nurtures a tough outback spirit more familiar to Alaska's frigid north than its drizzly panhandle. A collapse in the lumber industry in the 1990s hit the town hard, a blow from which it has only recently recovered.

Wrangell attracts only a handful of visitors, who are drawn to its incredible natural attractions, namely some outstanding wildlife-watching, fishing in the nearby Stikine River Delta, and adventures in the countryside outside of town. The mishmash of boggy muskeg and tree-covered mountains offers fine hiking, a fact not lost on Scottish-born American naturalist John Muir, who decamped here in 1879 on the first of four Alaska visits.

Native History & Artistry
Wrangell's Tlingit heritage

Wrangell's Tlingit culture has deep roots, with some 20% of the town identifying as Alaska Native. A stroll around town reveals the rich culture and strong commitment to preserving it.

The most significant Tlingit landmark is the **Chief Shakes Clan House** *(wcatribe.org/shakes-house)*, a precise replica of the Naanyaa.aayi, or Killer Whale, clan house. Chief Shakes was not one person, but rather a title given to successive Naanyaa.aayi clan leaders in the 19th and 20th centuries. Located on a tiny island in the harbor known as Shakes Island, the house was recreated by the Civilian Conservation Corps (CCC) in 1940. It is looking fine after an extensive restoration in 2013. The clan house is not normally open unless you make advance arrangements with

the Wrangell Cooperative Association *(907-874-4304)* or book a tour through a cruise line. But you can admire the various totems – several of which are newly carved – scattered about the grounds.

Heading back into town, there is a small **totem park** on Front St, with half a dozen poles, each recounting its own story. And two blocks further north is the **carving shed**, where you can sometimes see the carvers at work. Some of the older totems from Shakes Island are now housed here.

The last stop is the impressive **Wrangell Museum** *(wrangell.com/museum; admission $12)*, a fitting tribute to the colorful history and characters of this town. Throughout

TOP EXPERIENCE

Anan Creek Bear Watch

Thirty miles southeast of Wrangell on the mainland, Anan Creek is the site of one of the largest pink salmon runs in Southeast Alaska. From the platforms at Anan Creek Wildlife Observatory, you can watch eagles, black bears and brown bears fishing and feasting on the spawning humpies. It's one of the few places in Alaska where black and brown bears coexist at the same run.

Brown bear, Anan Creek

TOP TIPS

- The **Anan Wildlife Observatory calendar** (*anancalendar.com*) allows you to see which tour operators have permits available for which days.

- Bring drinking water and binoculars.

- Don't miss the riverside blind, which allows visitors to spy on the bears at water's edge, sometimes just a few feet away.

PRACTICALITIES

- *fs.usda.gov/r10/recreation/epic-adventures/anan-creek-wildlife-viewing-area*
- Season July 5 to August 25
- Permit $30-50

Permits

Permits are normally provided by your tour operator. If you're arriving independently, you can reserve a permit through *recreation.gov* starting on February 1.

Tours

Anan Creek is located within Tongass National Park, about 30 miles south of Wrangell on the Alaska mainland. Tours start with a one-hour boat ride to the site. Upon arrival, an armed ranger gives a safety presentation, then accompanies the group from the boat dock to the viewing platform, which overlooks the creek on three sides.

Anan Bay Cabin

A great option for adventurous types is to overnight at the USFS Anan Bay Cabin, which is a 1-mile hike from the observation area. The rental includes four permits. Reserve six months in advance.

Black vs Brown

Park rangers and guides are on a first-name basis with many of the bears at Anan Creek. It's not unusual to see more than a dozen black bears swimming, fishing, eating and sometimes fighting. Brown bears also come to this site – especially sows and cubs hoping to avoid aggressive boars, who tend to be protective of their fishing grounds.

the museum, an audio tour narrates the various chapters of Wrangell's past, from Tlingit culture to the gold rush era. Among other interesting exhibits, you can see the intricately carved house posts from the original Chief Shakes clan house, considered the oldest existing house posts.

A Story in Stones
Ancient rock carvings

A one-mile walk north of Wrangell's center, **Petroglyph Beach State Historic Site** has a surprising collection of rock art, including some pieces carved more than a thousand years ago. A viewing deck has interpretive displays and replicas, so you know what you're looking for. There are nearly 50 petroglyphs on the beach. Many are submerged at high tide, so be sure to consult the charts before you come.

After descending the deck, turn right and walk north on the beach for about 50yd. Before you reach the wrecked fishing vessels, look for faint carvings of spirals and faces on the large rocks.

Nine Holes, Alaska-Style
Golfing in the wild

Completed in 1998 on sawdust and wood chips from local sawmill operations, Wrangell's nine-hole **Muskeg Meadows Golf Course** *(muskegmeadows.com; 9 holes $30)* is the first certified course in the Southeast. Surrounded by wilderness, the course is uniquely Alaskan, with narrow fairways and tangled roughs of spruce and muskeg. Members are rarely alarmed when a bear comes bounding across a fairway.

Don't forget the Raven Rule: if a raven steals your ball, you may replace it with no penalty.

Lush Forests, Lovely Views
Hiking and biking around Wrangell

Wrangell has a handful of rewarding hikes, from short hill climbs to more challenging full-day excursions. With limited time, your best option is the **Mt Dewey Trail**. This 1-mile, out-and-back hike takes you to a scenic forest-backed overlook with views over the town and harbor, and out to the spruce-covered islands off in the distance. John Muir fans will appreciate the fact that the great naturalist climbed the mountain in 1879.

BEST TOUR OPERATORS

All of these tour operators offer bear watching at Anan Creek, trips to LeConte Glacier and excursions up the Stikine River.

Breakaway Adventures: Breakaway is the oldest of Wrangell's tour operators, also providing a handy water-taxi service and bike rental.

Alaska Vistas: This reputable outfitter rents out sea kayaks and canoes and offers guided paddling tours.

Muddy Water Adventures: Located at the Stikine Inn, Wrangell-native Zach Taylor offers wildlife tours and water taxi services.

Alaska Waters Inc: Offers an island heritage tour and a forest walk, in addition to boating adventures.

Alaska Charters & Adventures: Unique for its birding and whale watching tours, in addition to the regulars.

 EATING IN WRANGELL: OUR PICKS

Stik Cafe: Delicious Alaskan-roasted Heritage coffee and tasty sandwiches for the trail. Located in the Stikine Inn lobby. *6am-4pm* **$**

Sweet Tides Bakery: Charming spot with the island's best pastries (and coffee), plus sandwiches and pasta dishes. *7am-2pm Mon-Fri, 9am-1pm Sat* **$**

Wolf Shack: Friendly snack shack serving A+ burgers, chicken sandwiches, and a few Mexican specials to keep things spicy. *11am-2pm Sun-Fri* **$**

Stikine Inn: Enjoy a solid line-up of international favorites, along with sunset views from the Stik patio. *4-8pm* **$$$**

FLYING THE MILK RUN

On the bucket list of many aviation lovers, the so-called 'milk run' is a daily Alaska Airlines flight between Seattle and Anchorage that stops at Ketchikan, Wrangell, Petersburg and Juneau en route. What the milk run lacks in directness, it makes up for in flightseeing opportunities. Since the airports are located in close proximity to one another, airplanes don't have time to gain much height, meaning (weather permitting) you can look down with silent awe on the arboreal beauty of the Tongass National Forest (p69) spread out like a satellite map beneath you. Grab a window seat for close-up views of the braided Stikine River Delta and the frigid **LeConte Glacier** (p84).

Petroglyph Beach State Historic Site (p79)

You'll need a car or bicycle to reach the other trails, which lie outside Wrangell. Rent an e-bike from **Breakaway Adventures** (*breakawayadventures.com; bikes per hour/day $25/75*) or Wrangell Extended Stay and ride south out of town for magnificent vistas across the Inner Passage. The **Shoemaker Bay Recreation Area**, 4.7 miles south of town, is a good stop for a picnic with a view.

There are also several hiking trails in this area, namely the popular **Rainbow Falls Trail**, which starts just across the street. It's about 0.7 miles of moderate uphill walking to reach the waterfalls. Most of the path is on a narrow wooden walkway and stairs are fitted with wire mesh for better grip.

Beyond the falls, you can continue along the **Institute Creek Trail**. This leads ever upward (also via wooden walkways), climbing some 1500ft over 2.8 miles (one way) to the Shoemaker Bay Overlook Shelter. Or, branch off and hike along the **North Wrangell Trail** up to a stunning overlook.

Petersburg

GLACIAL MAGNIFICENCE | MARINE LIFE | SCANDINAVIAN VIBES

At the northern tip of Mitkof Island, Petersburg is a unique and appealing destination, where Norwegian flags fly alongside the Stars and Stripes, and wide, unhurried streets exude a distinctly Scandinavian sense of tidiness and order.

Petersburg was founded in 1897 by Norwegian immigrant and homesteader Peter Buschmann, starting with a cannery, a sawmill and a dock. Other folks followed – mostly from Scandinavia – to fish the waters and work in the canneries. And the rest is history. Petersburg's enduring prosperity is largely a result of its steely independence, built around a self-contained fishing industry and the four canneries that abut the busy harbor. The shallow port is inappropriate for large cruise ships, so there is no massive summer invasion of tourists here. Instead, Petersburg attracts a more intrepid cross section of travelers, who are keen to explore its glacial waters and sample its small-town charms.

☑ TOP TIP

The biggest event of the year is the famed Little Norway Festival. The four-day event in May features live music, street food, arts and crafts and roaming Vikings. Local residents don their Norwegian *bunader* (traditional costumes) and parade through the streets. See *petersburg.org* for other local events.

Downtown Petersburg

Walk the historic waterfront

The first, best introduction to this fish-oriented town is the **North Harbor**. Near the Harbormaster's Office, a wooden deck provides a picturesque overview of the commercial fleet, while some interpretive panels give insights into fishing techniques.

GETTING AROUND

Most lodgings will pick you up from the airport, which is about one mile southeast of Petersburg's center. Once in town, it's easy to get around on foot with restaurants, shops and cafes scattered along Nordic Dr and Sing Lee Alley. Beyond Petersburg, you'll find many miles of scenic, barely traveled two-lane roads in good condition. Unfortunately, there are no bicycle rental outfits in town, but several hotels rent vehicles, including the Tides Inn and Scandia House.

PETERSBURG

SIGHTS
1. Bojet Wikan Fishermen's Memorial Park
2. Cannery Park
3. Clausen Memorial Museum
4. North Harbor
5. Outlook Park
6. Petersburg Fisheries
7. Sandy Beach Park
8. Sing Lee Alley
9. Sons of Norway Hall
10. Totem Park

ACTIVITIES
11. City Creek Trail
12. Hungry Point Trail
13. Mountain View Boardwalk
14. Petersburg Lake Trailhead
15. Petersburg Mountain Trailhead
16. Raven Trailhead
17. Viking Travel

SLEEPING
18. Scandia House
19. Tides Inn

EATING
see 19 ¡Fire! Bistro
20. Coastal Bear's Pizza
21. Coastal Cold Storage
22. Compass Cookery
23. El Zarape
24. Helse
25. Inga's Galley
26. Salty Pantry
27. Studebaker's Pizza

DRINKING & NIGHTLIFE
28. Common Grounds
29. Glacier Express
30. Harbor Bar
31. Kito's Kave

SHOPPING
32. Blomster Hus
33. Cedar Box
34. Lee's Clothing
35. Sing Lee Alley Books

One block north of here on Nordic Dr, **Cannery Park** has a small display on the history of Petersburg and the fish processing industry. Here there is also a map of the town's 'Historical Cans' – a dozen trash cans that feature vintage labels from the local canneries. The nearby **Petersburg Fisheries** is the original outfit founded by Peter Buschmann in 1900 and the oldest operating seafood plant in Alaska.

You'll gain a deeper insight into Petersburg at the **Clausen Memorial Museum** *(clausenmuseum.org; adult/child $5/ free)*, with a 25-minute film about the town's history. The museum's small collection features a range of curiosities, mostly fishing artifacts. Look for the largest king salmon ever caught (126lbs) and several sculptures by local artists.

Back on the waterfront, take a stroll through **Sing Lee Alley**, an ensemble of vintage wooden buildings dating from the 1910s. Around this time, an influx of Chinese immigrants worked the canneries and opened restaurants. Sing Lee was one such transplant – a merchant who ran a general store for 23 years. The alley was named for him after he was brutally murdered in his shop in 1932.

Much of Sing Lee Alley is built on pilings over Hammer Slough. The centerpiece is **Sons of Norway Hall**, dating to 1912. Here is the center for Petersburg's Norwegian culture, not to mention the cutthroat bingo games on Friday nights. Next to the hall, **Bojet Wikan Fisherman's Memorial Park** contains an impressive 9ft statue of a fisherman, honoring his fellow crew members lost at sea. Also on display is a replica of the Viking ship *Valhalla*.

Adventures on the Water

Whale watching, kayaking and glaciers

Whether you want to spot giants of the deep or immerse yourself in the icy wilderness, Petersburg has some unrivaled opportunities to get out on the water. All tour operators offer whale-watching and glacier trips; **Viking Travel** is a broker that works with local tour providers.

Boat trips here offer some of the best whale watching in Southeast Alaska, also with chances to see orcas, sea lions and seals. From mid-May to mid-September, humpback whales migrate through and feed in Frederick Sound, 45 miles northwest of town. Among many excursions available, **Seek Alaska Tours** *(seekak.com; per person $350)* offers the full-day 'whiskers and whales' tour for spotting breaching humpbacks and lazing sea lions. They also have

> **GROWING UP IN PETERSBURG**
>
>
>
> **James Valentine**, co-owner of Viking Travel, reminisces about growing up in Petersburg.
>
> There are things you do here that are not considered 'normal' in the Lower 48. During 8th grade, you'd take a class called Southeast Survival. For the final, they took our whole class of 30 or so and dropped us off at a beach. In order to be picked back up, you had to make a fire, make a shelter and then create some kind of an SOS. During high school, we'd travel by ferry to team sporting events, which might be 30 hours away in Skagway. Our teachers were also our coaches, so in a sense, we had this traveling school, and it was really fun.

 EATING IN PETERSBURG: OUR PICKS

Salty Pantry: Trendy cafe with creative food concoctions and inviting outdoor seating overlooking the Middle Harbor. *5.30am-3pm Mon-Sat* **$**

Coastal Bear's Pizza: Thick, generously topped pizzas are worth the sometimes long wait at this friendly spot. *noon-7pm Mon-Sat* **$$**

Inga's Galley: Outdoor tables, diverse and delicious food, and craft beer make for a great time. *7am-8pm Mon-Sat* **$$**

Helse: Iconic spot on Sing Lee Alley offering an eclectic mix of sandwiches, milkshakes and Chinese dishes. *10.30am-4pm Sun-Thu, to 7.30pm Fri & Sat* **$$**

LeConte Glacier

SHOPPING IN PETERSBURG

Sing Lee Alley Books & Gifts: Stocks a carefully curated selection of reading material, in addition to thoughtful Alaska art and souvenirs.

Cedar Box: This little gallery has a small but excellent assortment of jewelry, clothing and art pieces, created by Alaska Native artists.

Blomster Hus: It's a florist-cum-art gallery, showcasing pieces by some 40 regional artists.

Lee's Clothing: Unique and useful things to wear, from handmade Norwegian sweaters and hats, to shirts and shoes by Alaskan designers.

Coastal Cold Storage: For a taste of Alaska at home, pick up some local seafood, packed and frozen and ready to ship.

a hydrophone, so you can listen to the whales while you watch them.

Located some 24 miles southwest of Petersburg, the **LeConte Glacier** is the southernmost tidewater glacier in the Northern Hemisphere. Boat trips journey deep into the photogenic fjord, cruising amid floating berglets and lounging seals. LeConte is known for its frequent calving, much of which takes place below the water's surface. The result is 'shooter' icebergs, which break off underwater, then shoot out of the water due to their buoyancy.

Tongass Kayak Adventures *(tongasskayak.com; per person half-day/full-day from $150/450)* runs an immersive full-day trip to LeConte Glacier. After cruising out to the fjord by boat, you can paddle amid the icy, otherworldly scenery in LeConte Bay. Tongass Kayak Adventures also leads other trips, including half- and full-day paddles in Frederick Sound.

Before the Norwegians
Discover Tlingit history and heritage

Long before Peter Buschmann started a cannery and named a town after himself, the Mitkof and nearby Kupreanof

EATING IN PETERSBURG: QUICK BITES

Studebaker's Pizza: Open late (by Petersburg standards) for pizza; carryout or delivery only. *11am-9pm Wed-Mon* **$**

Compass Cookery: Friendly food truck offering a rotating menu of global fare. Sunday brunch is full of surprises. *11am-7pm Fri, Sat & Mon, 10am-3pm Sun* **$$**

El Zarape: Add some spice to your stay in Petersburg with Mexican favorites from this semi-permanent food truck (with shaded seating area). *8am-8pm* **$$**

¡Fire! Bistro: A hot spot at the Tides Inn, with an interesting lineup of gourmet sandwiches, smoothies and ramen. *11am-7pm Thu-Fri, to 5pm Sat* **$$**

Islands were home to the Tlingit people, and likely others before them. You can see relics of this early history at **Sandy Beach Park**, about 2 miles east of downtown. It's not much of a swimming beach, but the coastline here has a few petroglyphs and the remains of a 2,000-year-old fish trap, which is visible in the mud flats at low tide.

The focal point on the beach is the more recent **Hutli pole**, carved by artist Fred Fulmer Sr. The thunderbird at the top represents Thunder Bay (LeConte Bay), named by the Tlingit for the thunderous sound of the calving glacier. The pole depicts five species that are integral to Tlingit culture: halibut, wolf, killer whale, harbor seal and salmon.

Sandy Beach Park is also the starting point for one of Petersburg's loveliest short hikes, the **City Creek Trail**. A 2000ft boardwalk through coastal forest takes in moss-draped branches and scenic views, including regular glimpses of Frederick Sound. Additional signage will highlight the ongoing relationship between the local Tlingit and their natural environs.

Happy Trails
Hiking the shores and trails

Petersburg has an appealing range of trails, some of which are easy to reach from the main waterfront. In addition to the **City Creek Trail**, the more difficult **Raven Trail** also begins near Sandy Beach Park. The first mile takes you across muskeg on a raised gravel path before plunging into the forest, where the trail gets steeper. You'll ascend around 1800ft in just under 3 miles (one way). There are some fine viewpoints along the way before the trail's end at the USFS **Raven's Roost Cabin**. The cabin is above the tree line, providing sweeping views of Petersburg, Frederick Sound and Wrangell Narrows.

For a shorter and flatter jaunt, the Hungry Point trail system is a series of paths and boardwalks that lead one mile across the island, through muskeg and woodlands. Surrounded by stunted trees, you have a clear view of Petersburg's mountainous skyline, including the foreboding Devils Thumb. From the Mort Freyer sports fields, the **Hungry Point Trail** crosses the muskeg for 1.25 miles to its terminus at Sandy Beach Rd. Turn right and walk a quarter-mile to reach **Outlook Park**, a marine wildlife overlook where you can peer across Frederick Sound in search of humpback

RAVEN VS EAGLE

The Tlingit have a complex societal structure. The main economic, social and political unit in Tlingit society is the clan. Traditionally, local clans hosted ceremonies, engaged in trade, organized hunting parties, cooperated or fought with other clans and controlled resources. Power was held by the clan leader, a role that was (and still is) inherited. All clans belong to one of two groups, or moieties, identified as Raven or Eagle. There is an emphasis on balance between moieties that extends to all important ceremonies and rituals, including marriage.

The **totem park** in front of the USFS regional office features two totems representing the two moieties – Raven and Eagle. The figures on the poles represent the Petersburg clans within each moiety.

DRINKING IN PETERSBURG: MORNING TO NIGHT

Common Grounds: Serves locally roasted coffee by Alaska Island Coffee, as well as fresh pastries and prepared sandwiches. *7am-5pm Mon-Fri, 9am-2pm Sat & Sun*

Glacier Express: Petersburg's 'other' coffeehouse is a basic affair with sweet coffee drinks and smoothies. *6am-5pm, to 3pm Sun*

Kito's Kave: Legendary dive bar that's been around for eons. Jon Krakauer mentions it in his book *Eiger Dreams*. *10am-2am*

Harbor Bar: A classic domain of deckhands and cannery workers, with pool tables, free popcorn and occasional live music. *10am-2am*

DEVILS THUMB

On clear days, the sharp, glacier-encrusted peaks of the Alaska Coast Range are clearly visible from Petersburg on the opposite side of Frederick Sound. Of the rocky behemoths, none is more disquieting than 9077ft **Devils Thumb**, an imposing mass of granite that thrusts skywards over the wild border between Alaska and British Columbia in Canada. Although far from being the state's highest mountain, the 'Thumb' is arguably one of its most dangerous. The northwest face – an intimidating 6700ft-high wall of sheer rock – has never been successfully climbed, though several experienced alpinists have died trying. Instead, the mountain is usually tackled via its east ridge, a route pioneered by legendary US climber Fred Beckey in 1946.

Raven Trail (p85)

whales, orcas and sea lions. Walk back to town on the **Mountain View Boardwalk**, accessible from 14th St.

Peeler's Alaskan Experience *(peelersalaskanexperience.com; per person from $150)* offers some unique guided hiking tours.

Island Hop
Explore Kupreanof Island

Across the Wrangell Narrows is a rambling, roadless Kupreanof Island. The largest population center is the village of Kake, on the west side of the island, but the small community of Kupreanof sits directly across from Petersburg. This is the gateway to the Petersburg Creek Wilderness, which is part of Tongass National Park. Hire a water taxi to make the 12-mile trip across the narrows to explore this pristine wilderness.

The hiking trails on Kupreanof are difficult but rewarding. From the state dock, the 3.5-mile (one-way) **Petersburg Mountain Trail** ascends to a 2750ft summit, which offers views of Petersburg, the Coast Mountains, glaciers and Wrangell Narrows. The longer but less strenuous **Petersburg Lake Trail** is a 10.5-mile trail that leads to the USFS Petersburg Lake Cabin. All hikers should contact the Petersburg Ranger District to inquire about trail conditions before tackling the lake trail.

Sitka

NATIVE ARTS | RUSSIAN HISTORY | MOUNTAIN TRAILS

It's not always easy to uncover evidence of Alaska's 135-year dalliance with the Russian Empire – until you dock in Sitka. This sparkling gem of a city, which kisses the Pacific Ocean on Baranof Island's west shore, is one of the oldest non-Indigenous settlements in the state. It was the former capital of Russian Alaska, once known as Novoarkhangelsk (New Archangel).

As a bonus, Sitka mixes its wonderfully preserved history with outstanding natural beauty. Looming on the horizon across Sitka Sound is Mt Edgecumbe, an extinct volcano with a graceful cone visible on rare, clear days. Closer in, small forested islands turn into beautiful, ragged silhouettes at sunset, competing for attention with the snowcapped mountains and granite peaks flanking Sitka to the east. Around town, picturesque remnants of Sitka's Russian heritage are tucked around every corner, along with soaring totem poles and other reminders of Sitka's even older Alaska Native heritage.

Sitka's Russian Roots
Double-headed eagles and onion domes

Sitka's waterfront shows off original architecture and interesting exhibits about its Russian foundation. Begin your explorations at **Totem Square**, home to the famous Baranov Totem. This unusual pole features a double-headed eagle, the symbol of the Russian Empire, along with a carving of Alexander Baranov at the top.

Nearby, Baranof Castle State Historic Park – better known as **Castle Hill** – rises above the south end of town. Rich in historical significance, this was once the site of the Kiks.ádi village of Noow Tlein. Later, Alexander Baranov oversaw the construction of the Russian governor's mansion on this prominent spot. In 1868, it became the site of the ceremony

Continues on p90

GETTING AROUND

Sitka's public bus system, The Ride Sitka, runs on three color-coded lines and serves most places of interest to visitors. Crescent Harbor is the terminus for all three lines – one heading north, one heading south and one looping around downtown. Unfortunately, The Ride does not go to the airport. The buses also don't run on weekends. If you need a taxi, try calling Hank's Taxi (907-747-8888) or Baranof Taxi (907-738-4722).

☑ TOP TIP

Sitka's best and most affordable dining is the street food from trucks and street vendors all around town. Find some great options right on Lincoln St near the Lake St intersection, on Harbor Dr, and at the Sawmill Pkwy roundabout.

SITKA

★ HIGHLIGHTS
1. Russian Bishop's House
2. Sitka National Historical Park

● SIGHTS
3. Alaska Raptor Center
4. Castle Hill
5. K'alyáan Pole
6. Sheldon Jackson Museum
7. Sitka Historical Museum
8. Sitka National Historical Park Visitor Center
9. St Michael's Cathedral
10. Totem Square

● ACTIVITIES
11. 907
12. Gavan Hill Trail
13. Indian River Trail
14. Mt Verstovia Trail
15. Sitka Cross Trail
16. Sitka Sound Science Center
17. Tlingit Sea Tours
18. Totem Trail

● SLEEPING
19. Aspen Suites Hotel
20. Cascade Creek Lodge
21. Longliner Lodge
22. Southeast Resort
23. Tillie Paul Hostel

EATING	31 Sitka Pel'meni	37 Ernie's Old Time Saloon	43 WinterSong Soap Co
24 Ashmo's	32 The Fresh Fish	38 Harbor Mountain Brewing Co	44 X'útaa Hidi
25 Beak Restaurant	33 WildFlour Café & Bakery		TRANSPORT
26 Blanco Burger	34 Ye-TacoLoco	39 Pioneer Bar	45 Yellow Jersey Cycle Shop
27 Chocolate Moose	DRINKING & NIGHTLIFE	SHOPPING	
28 Highliner Coffee		40 Alaska Pure Sea Salt Co	
29 Ludvig's Bistro	35 907 Beer Garden	41 Island Artists Gallery	
30 Mean Queen	36 Back Door Café	42 Old Harbor Books	

ALASKA DAY

In October 1867, hundreds of American soldiers arrived in Sitka for the official transfer of Alaska from the Russian Empire to the United States. Soldiers from both nations paraded in front of the governor's house on Castle Hill, then formally lowered the Russian flag and raised the US flag. Music played and cannons fired in celebration.

This event is reenacted each year on October 18 during the **Alaska Day Festival** *(alaskadayfestival.com)* in Sitka. The multiday festival also includes a celebratory parade, historical ball and other themed events. In recent years, the Tlingit community has held a simultaneous mourning ceremony, reminding celebrants that the transfer occurred between two colonial powers – without the consent of the Tlingit or any Indigenous people.

Continued from p87

transferring ownership of Alaska from Russia to the United States. Admire the views and see if you can catch a glimpse of Mt Edgecumbe.

St Michael's Cathedral occupies a central spot at the opposite end of Lincoln St. Originally built in the 1840s, the church stood for more than 100 years as Alaska's finest Russian Orthodox structure. It was the state's oldest Russian-era building until it was destroyed by fire in 1966. Fortunately, heroic residents saved most of the priceless treasures and icons, and the church was quickly rebuilt. The interior is rich in detail and iconography, including an 18th-century depiction of *Our Lady of Sitka* by Vladimir Borovikovsky.

Located in Harrigan Centennial Hall, the **Sitka Historical Museum** *(sitkahistory.org; admission $5)* has exhibits on all parts of Sitka's history, with plenty of artifacts from the Russian period. Several displays focus on daily life in Novoarkhangelsk, including a scale model of the settlement.

Across the street, the **Russian Bishop's House** *(nps.gov/sitk)* was built in 1843 and is one of only four Russian colonial structures in North America. It has been restored to its 1853 appearance, when it served as a school and residence for Bishop Innocent (Ivan Veniaminov). The downstairs exhibit gives an excellent overview of Russia's North American experiment, while free ranger-led tours show the upstairs living quarters and private chapel of Bishop Innocent.

Anthropology Collection
Exploring Alaska Native cultures

Sheldon Jackson College was founded in 1878 as a 'training' school for Tlingit boys, teaching technical skills, English, and Christian doctrine. The college became the state's oldest institution of

THE HISTORY OF RUSSIAN AMERICA

Russia's cultural impact in Alaska is still evident throughout the state, especially in **Kodiak** (p347), **Kenai** (p258) and around **Homer** (p267). Learn more about this history at p412.

St Michael's Cathedral

higher education before closing in 2007. Presbyterian missionary and amateur anthropologist Sheldon Jackson supported the school through significant fundraising and later donated his collection of Native American artifacts to establish the **Sheldon Jackson Museum** *(museums.alaska.gov/sheldon_jackson; adult/child $9/free)*. It still stands as Alaska's oldest museum.

The unusual octagonal building houses a small but excellent collection of artifacts from all of Alaska's Indigenous groups. Look for finely woven Chilkat textiles (made partly from shredded cedar bark), Inupiat bone armor and whaling suits, colorful Chugach masks, Athabascan quill necklaces and Yupik ceremonial objects. The showpiece is the raven helmet worn by the Tlingit warrior Chief K'alyáan during the 1804 Battle of Sitka.

Island Kayaking

Paddle scenic waters

The mini-archipelago of tiny islets that crowd Sitka's harbor makes the surrounding waters ideal for kayaking. **SEAK Adventure** *(seakadventuresitka.com; adult/child from $200/150)* offers some unique one-day paddling experiences, such as a 'war bunkers and wildlife' tour. Alternatively, spend the day

BEST FOR ANIMAL LOVERS

Alaska Raptor Center: A bird sanctuary where you can get up-close looks at eagles, hawks and owls, as they regain their ability to fly.

Sitka Sound Science Center: Contains five aquariums and three touch tanks for lots of hands-on interactions.

Fortress of the Bear: A rescue facility where you can observe brown and black bears that were orphaned as cubs. Take the Blue Line bus approximately 5.5 miles south of Sitka.

Tlingit Sea Tours: This father-son team takes out small boats of six people, in search of whales, sea otters, sea lions and harbor seals. Upgrade to a 'premium tour' to see the puffins at Saint Lazaria Island.

 EATING AND DRINKING IN SITKA: CAFES & BAKERIES

| **Back Door Café:** Behind a bookstore, this cozy spot whips up Sitka's best coffee and enticing pastries. *7am-3pm Mon-Fri, to 1pm Sat* $ | **Highliner Coffee:** Spacious, light-filled coffeehouse with a wide variety of drinks, plus bagels and breakfast burritos. *6am-6pm Mon-Fri, to 5pm Sat & Sun* $ | **WildFlour Café & Bakery:** Flaky croissants, acai bowls and yummy sandwiches pair well with frothy lattes and smoothies. *6am-2pm Tue-Sat* $ | **Chocolate Moose:** Partly florist and partly chocolatier, but totally romantic. They also make a mean espresso. *10am-5pm Mon-Sat* $ |

TOP EXPERIENCE

Sitka National Historical Park

Southeast of the town center, Sitka National Historical Park is a mystical juxtaposition of towering hemlocks and totem poles, with walking trails winding along and across the Indian River. The park marks the historic site where the Tlingit were defeated by the Russians in the devastating 1804 Battle of Sitka (p412).

K'alyáan Pole

TOP TIPS

● Visit the carving shed behind the visitor center to see master carvers at work.

● Every totem tells a story: download the NPS app for a Totem Trail walking tour.

● Cross the Indian River Bridge for a view of spawning salmon (late July to mid-September).

PRACTICALITIES

● nps.gov/sitk ● visitor center 9am-5pm, grounds dawn-dusk ● free

Visitor Center

Start your visit at the Sitka National Historical Park **visitor center**, beginning with the 15-minute film, *Voices of Sitka*. The film provides an overview of Sitka's diverse cultural heritage, touching on age-old Tlingit traditions and life under Russian rule. You can also peruse a small but excellent collection of Indigenous artwork, including drums, regalia and other ceremonial objects, including some very cool contemporary pieces. The historical artifacts are a highlight, such as the hammer used by Chief K'alyáan in the 1804 battle. Finally, duck into the totem hall to gain insight into different carving styles, techniques and significance.

Totem Trail

Follow the mile-long **Totem Trail** through the dense rainforest and along the scenic seashore past 18 totem poles, often enveloped in mist. The most poignant is the moving **K'alyáan Pole**, a memorial to the Tlingit ancestors who resisted the Russians in the 1804 battle. The figure at the bottom of the totem is a frog, representing the Kiks.ádi clan, holding the sacred raven helmet, which was worn by the warrior K'alyáan. Prominently placed in a clearing, the pole marks the site of the Tlingit fort known as Shis'g'i Noow.

island-hopping and wildlife-watching, then end with a salmon bake on the beach.

Sitka Wild Coast Kayaks (*sitkawildcoastkayak.com; 5-day trip $1840*) specializes in multi-day excursions, including trips to the crystalline waters around Chichagof Island, tidal rapids at Surgis Rapids or the healing waters of Goddard Springs. The owner, Michael, can also help you plan and get equipped for an independent paddling adventure, whether you want to go out for an afternoon or for a week.

Adventures By Boat
Volcanoes, birds and hot springs

The waters around Sitka are dotted with islands begging to be explored. Ten miles west of Sitka, **Kruzof Island** is a popular destination for hiking, thanks to the many logging roads that crisscross the island. **Iris Meadows Rd** is a popular route for a 7-mile hike across the island from Mud Bay to Shelikof Bay. Once on the Pacific Ocean side, you'll find a beautiful sandy beach for beachcombing and the USFS **Shelikof Cabin**. Also enticing is the hike up Mt Edgecumbe (3210ft), a dormant volcano that (some say) resembles Mt Fuji. The challenging 6.7-mile **trail** to the crater rim takes at least five hours one-way, beginning at the USFS **Fred's Creek Cabin**. Views from the summit are spectacular on a clear day.

Just below Kruzof, the island of **Saint Lazaria** is a **wildlife refuge**, protecting the habitat of half a million nesting seabirds. Some of the more charismatic species include the tufted puffin and its cousin, the rhinoceros auklet, as well as black oyster catchers, ancient murrelets, common murres and pelagic cormorants. The island is off-limits to people, but the bird-watching is excellent from the boat. Bring your binocs.

About 16 miles south of Sitka, **Goddard Hot Springs** is located on Hot Springs Bay, on the outer coast of Baranof Island. These mineral springs have long drawn local residents for their natural healing properties. Nowadays, the water is pumped into hot- and cold-water pools, which are covered by rustic, open-air shelters. This is a popular destination for picnicking and camping (and soaking).

A few specialized tour agencies offer these trips: **Sitka Alaska Outfitters** (*sitkaalaskaoutfitters.com; 3hr charter $900*) and **Sitka Wildlife Adventures** (*sitkawildlifeadventures. com; 4hr charter $1500*). Alternatively, local boat captains will gladly take you to any of these destinations. Try **Baranof**

PEAK PRANK

Mt Edgecumbe is the photogenic stratovolcano that looms over Sitka from its position on Kruzof Island. The volcano has been dormant for millennia. But on April 1, 1974, Sitka residents awoke to see smoke billowing from the mountain. The islanders were terrified, considering they had nowhere to escape the imminent explosion.

The Coast Guard sent a helicopter to investigate, only to find 'April Fool!' spray-painted in humongous letters in the snow at the summit. Smoke was spewing from a massive pile of burning tires. The stunt was the work of Porky Bickar, a proud prankster who had waited years for a clear April 1 morning to pull it off. Porky has passed, but his legacy endures in this beloved local history.

EATING IN SITKA: FOOD TRUCKS

Ashmo's: Solid choice for fish tacos, fish and chips, and other fresh, wild and local dishes. *11am-4pm Sun-Fri* **$**

Blanco Burger: Burgers, dogs and grilled cheese, hot off the grill, with fancy fixin's. *hours vary* **$**

Ye-TacoLoco: Not just tacos, but also burritos, bowls and chilaquiles. And not just fish! *11am-9pm Sun-Thu, to 2am Fri & Sat* **$**

Fresh Fish: Same catch, now served in poke bowls, po' boys and ceviche. Can't decide? Try the Sitka Sound Flight for the 'holy trinity' of fish. *11am-4pm Sun-Thu* **$$**

BEAR SAFETY

Alaina Brown is a hiking guide and owner of **Tongass Treks**, tongasstreks.com.

When hiking in Southeast Alaska, bear safety is essential. Before hitting the trails, stop by the visitor's center to get the latest bear activity report and current trail information. Or talk with a local; they are generally happy to help! It's advised not to hike alone. Be sure to make noise, especially on blind corners and in dense bushy areas to avoid surprising them. Carry bear spray and know how to use it, and never leave trash or food behind. You don't need to hike in fear, but being bear-aware is crucial for enjoying the outdoors safely.

Water Taxi *(baranoftours.com)* or **High Ridge Expeditions** *(highridgesitka.com)*.

Mountains & Forests
Sitka's diverse hiking trails

Sitka offers superb hiking in the beautiful and tangled forest surrounding the city. Check out **Sitka Trail Works** *(sitkatrailworks.org)* for detailed trail information. **Tongass Treks** *(tongasstreks.com)* leads private guided hikes on these (and other) routes.

The **Gavan Hill Trail** is a great option for hikers without a vehicle, as the trailhead sits at the end of Baranof St. You'll ascend some 2500ft over 1.6 miles, mainly via wooden staircases. The trail breaks into alpine terrain higher up, offering excellent views of Sitka and the surrounding area. It's 3 miles (three to four hours) from the trailhead to an emergency-use shelter, which marks a junction with the Harbor Mountain Trail.

North of town, the 3-mile **Harbor Mountain Trail** ascends a series of switchbacks to alpine meadows, knobs and ridges with spectacular views. It follows the tundra ridge to the shelter, where you can pick up the Gavan Hill Trail. To reach the trailhead, take the Harbor Mountain Bypass Rd, hooking up with the National Forest Service road. There's a parking lot at the road's end: the unmarked trail begins on the lot's east side.

The 2.5-mile (one-way) climb along the **Mt Verstovia Trail** is a challenging but iconic hike. It takes about two hours to ascend some 2550ft to a compact summit called Picnic Rock. This 'shoulder' is the turnaround point for most hikers, yielding incredible views that take in the summit itself. It's possible to continue climbing, following the ridgeline for another hour to the summit of Mt Verstovia (3349ft), but the trail is not maintained beyond Picnic Rock. The trailhead is 2 miles east of Sitka along Sawmill Creek Rd. Look for the sign across from Jamestown Bay.

For something with lower elevation, consider the **Indian River Trail**. This 9-mile out-and-back takes you along a clear salmon stream to **Indian River Falls**, an 80ft cascade at the base of the Three Sisters Mountains. The hike takes you through typical Southeast rainforest, replete with deer, bald eagles and brown bears (bring bear spray). Plan on four

EATING IN SITKA: OUR PICKS

Sitka Pel'meni: Serves up piled-high Russian dumplings topped with dollops of sour cream. Comfort food at its finest. *11.30am-midnight Sun-Thu, to 2.30am Fri & Sat* **$**

Beak Restaurant: James Beard semifinalist chef Renee Trafton crafts creative dishes with Alaskan ingredients at this sustainable, gratuity-free restaurant. *11am-8pm Wed-Sat* **$$**

Mean Queen: The wide-ranging menu features deep-dish pizza and locally harvested oysters, all served with a fabulous view. *8am-midnight, bar to 2am* **$$**

Ludvig's Bistro: A classy and cozy spot for Mediterranean fare with an local twist, such as wild Alaskan paella and pasta with elk and truffles. *5-9pm Wed-Sat* **$$$**

Indian River Falls

to five hours round-trip to the falls. The trailhead is about a mile walk from town at the end of Indian River Rd.

Mountain Bike Mania
Exploring on two wheels

Ditch the crowds and the cars and cruise on Sitka's many miles of gravel roads and trails. The **Sitka Cross Trail** is a gravel road that skirts the downtown area, running 3.8 miles from the Indian River to Harbor Mountain Rd. It's an easy mountainside route, passing at least one waterfall on the way. The Cross Trail provides access to the **907**, a one-way single-track trail that winds through forest and hills. Other popular routes include the scenic Green Lake Rd along the shore of Silver Bay, and the strenuous (but rewarding) climb up Harbor Mountain Rd. Rent a mountain bike from **Yellow Jersey Cycle Shop** *(yellowjerseycycles.com; rental 2hr/day $35/45)*.

BEST SHOPPING

Old Harbor Books: Fantastic collection of books with Alaska themes, many by local authors, with an enticing cafe attached.

Island Artists Gallery: An artist cooperative, showcasing the work of local painters, sculptors, beaders, jewelry makers and fashion designers.

X'útaa Hidi: Unique jewelry, fashion, paintings and other artistic offerings by Alaska Native creatives.

Alaska Pure Sea Salt Co: Feeling salty? Add some flavor to your cooking with hand-crafted Sitka Sound flake salt, bath products and other goodies.

WinterSong Soap Co: Lather up with soapy scents from Alaska, such as salmonberry, fireweed and luscious Alaska rose.

 DRINKING IN SITKA: BEER BARS

Harbor Mountain Brewing Co: Chill spot serving a dozen creative kinds of beer and cider, plus tasty pies provided on site by Campfire Pizza. *11am-9pm*

Pioneer Bar: The P-Bar is Sitka's classic maritime watering hole. Don't ring the ship's bell over the bar unless you're ready to buy a round for the house. *8am-2am*

Ernie's Old Time Saloon: Head to this friendly dive to shoot pool and swill duck farts (Kahlúa, Baileys and whiskey) with the fun-loving seasonal workers. *8am-2am*

907 Beer Garden: A spacious beer tent serving drinks from Alaskan Brewing Co. Eats provided by on-site food trucks. *hours vary*

Juneau

EXCELLENT MUSEUMS | GLACIER HIKES | DRINKING & DINING

D'you know the capital of Alaska? Or should we say, Juneau, the capital of Alaska? Yes!

One of the country's most unusual state capitals is also one of its most captivating. You can't drive anywhere from here, but you can hike from downtown into mountainous wilderness in under half an hour. During the winter, the city is a hive of legislators, aides and lobbyists locked in perpetual political disputes. Come summer, more than 1.6 million cruise-ship passengers arrive to explore some of Southeast Alaska's finest cultural and natural attractions. Driving into town from the airport or the ferry terminal, you're likely to see black bears grazing in the meadows.

Adventure comes in many forms in Juneau. Boats and seaplanes depart from the waterfront for nearby salmon fishing, bear viewing and whale watching. Meanwhile, just a few miles out of town, a massive glacier calves into a lake, with forested National Park Service (NPS) trails offering mesmerizing views of the action.

GETTING AROUND

Capital Transit buses depart from the downtown transit center, serving Douglas Island and Mendenhall Valley. Note: the bus does not go to the ferry terminal at Auke Bay, nor does it reach the Mendenhall Glacier. If you're heading to the airport, disembark at Glacier Hwy and Shell Simmons Dr, which is a 5-minute walk to the terminal. Nearby hotels offer airport and ferry transfers, as do **Glacier Taxi & Tours** *(907-796-2300)*.

☑ TOP TIP

Sample Juneau's art scene on the first Friday of every month. The Juneau Arts & Humanities Council hosts a reception at the **Juneau Arts and Culture Center**, while the Alaska State Museum and Sealaska Heritage Institute host special events and exhibits too.

Cultural Wanders

MAP P99

Browse museums, mansions and churches

Juneau is definitely the state capital, with the official buildings to show for it. Most interesting, the **Alaska State Museum** *(museums.alaska.gov/asm; adult/child $14/free)* displays one of the country's finest collections dedicated to Alaska Native culture and the state's history. There's a wealth of extraordinary artifacts on display, including artistic pieces by Alaska Native artists from all regions, including items originating from the Tlingit, Athabascan, Yupik, Inupiat and more.

Other halls feature displays on the Russian period, the transfer of Alaska to the US in 1867, the gold rush days of the late 19th century, and the dreadful period of American

JUNEAU

SIGHTS
1. Last Chance Mining Museum
2. Mendenhall Glacier Visitor Center
3. Mendenhall Viewpoint
4. Sandy Beach
5. Savikko Park
6. Treadwell Mine Historic Trail
7. Takhu, the Alaska Whale Sculpture

ACTIVITIES
8. Above & Beyond Alaska
9. Amalga Trail
10. East Glacier Loop
11. Herbert Glacier Trail
12. Juneau Tours
see 12 Mendenhall Glacier Transport/M & M Tours
13. NorthStar Helicopters
14. Nugget Falls Trailhead
15. Perseverance Trail
16. Rainforest Trail
17. Steep Creek Trailhead
18. Trail of Time Trailhead
19. True Alaskan Tours
20. West Glacier Trail

SLEEPING
21. Juneau Hotel
22. Mendenhall Campground

EATING
23. Breeze In
24. Canton Asian Bistro
25. Garvie's Lunchbox
26. Island Pub

DRINKING & NIGHTLIFE
27. Alaskan Brewing Co

ENTERTAINMENT
28. Perseverance Theatre

TRANSPORT
29. Cycle Alaska
30. Ward Air

missionaries and boarding schools. Various exhibits showcase the Alaska Natives' fight for civil rights. You can also learn about the state's role in WWII after Japan invaded the Aleutian Islands when Alaska was suddenly on the front lines.

It's a short walk from the museum up to Calhoun Ave for a look at the **Governor's Mansion of Alaska**. Built and furnished in 1912, this mansion has 26 rooms across some 14,400 sq ft. It is not open to the public.

BENNY'S FLAG

In 1926, the Governor of Alaska Territory, George Parks, initiated a contest among Alaskan students to design a territorial flag. Some 142 pupils submitted entries, including Benny Benson, a 13-year-old student of Aleut and Swedish heritage. Benny turned his gaze skyward, drawing the Big Dipper and the North Star. As Benny later explained his design inspirations, 'The blue field is for the Alaska sky and the forget-me-not, an Alaska flower. The North Star is for the future of the state of Alaska, the most northerly in the Union. The dipper is for the Great Bear – symbolizing strength.' The territorial legislature unanimously adopted Benny's flag in 1927, and it also became the official state flag when Alaska joined the union in 1959.

By contrast, you can go inside the **Alaska State Capitol** *(alaskacapitol.gov)* to check out the legislative chambers, the governor's office and committee rooms. In summer, free one-hour guided tours are offered in the afternoon (from 1.30pm to 3pm), or you can take a self-guided audio tour whenever the building is open. Keep an eye out for artwork, elaborate carvings and historical displays.

Across the street, the **Juneau-Douglas City Museum** *(juneau.org/library/museum; adult/child $7/free)* showcases key events in city history, with a focus on Tlingit culture, mining and politics. There are 3D photo viewers, timelines, interactive exhibits and film clips, not to mention a 7ft-long relief map of the city. The 26-minute video *Juneau: City Built on Gold* gives an overview.

It's a steep climb up to the **Wickersham State Historic Site** *(dnr.alaska.gov; adult/child $5/free)*, but worth the effort for the views alone. The garden-fringed house-museum was once the residence of pioneer judge and statesman James Wickersham. The 1898 home is set with period furnishings, as well as curios acquired from Wickersham's many years of traveling in Alaska.

Heading back into downtown Juneau, stop for a peek at the 1893 **St Nicholas Russian Orthodox Church**. Etched against the backdrop of Mt Juneau, this diminutive onion-domed church is the second-oldest Russian Orthodox church in Alaska.

Native Heritage in Juneau

MAP P99

Discover Tlingit, Haida and Tsimshian culture

All three of Southeast Alaska's Indigenous groups have a strong presence in the state capital. It is most noticeable along the waterfront, where a dozen **totems** line the channel. Most of them portray Tlingit clans, while a few represent the Haida and Tsimshian people. Download the **Totem Pole Trail guide** *(sealaskaheritage.org/shi-juneau-alaska-totem-pole-trail-guide)* to learn more.

The most distinctive totem is the Sealaska Cultural Values Pole, which honors all three tribes and their shared values. It stands in front of the **Sealaska Heritage Institute** *(sealaskaheritage.org; adult/child $7/free)*, an organization dedicated to preserving and celebrating Alaska Native culture. The photogenic building is a work of art itself, with beautiful panels framing the entrance. Inside, a small museum explores aspects of Alaska Native culture, from spiritual beliefs to fishing techniques. The centerpiece of the building is a full-scale replica of a clan house, with photos and descriptions of Tlingit, Haida, and Tsimshian traditions.

SOUTHEAST ALASKA NATIVES

The Tlingit, Haida and Tsimshian peoples have distinct languages and lineages, but they do share some cultural similarities. See p74 to learn more about the Indigenous tribes of Southeast Alaska.

JUNEAU CITY CENTER

★ HIGHLIGHTS
1. Alaska State Museum

● SIGHTS
2. Aak'w Village
3. Alaska State Capitol
4. Gajaa Hit
5. Governor's Mansion of Alaska
6. Juneau-Douglas City Museum
7. Sealaska Heritage Institute
8. St Nicholas Russian Orthodox Church
9. Totem Pole Trail
10. Wickersham State Historic Site

● SLEEPING
11. Alaskan Hotel
12. Alaska's Capital Inn
13. Driftwood Lodge
14. Juneau Hostel
15. Silverbow Inn

● EATING
16. Alaskan Crepe Escape
17. Bernadette's
18. Deckhand Dave's
19. Hangar on the Wharf
20. In Bocca Al Lupo
21. Pel'Meni
22. Rainbow Foods
23. Rookery Cafe
24. SALT
25. Sandpiper Café
26. Spice
27. Tracy's King Crab Shack
28. V's Cellar

● DRINKING & NIGHTLIFE
see 11 Alaskan Bar
29. Amalga Distillery
30. Crystal Saloon
31. Devil's Club Brewing Co
32. Griz Bar
33. Heritage Coffee Co & Café
34. Imperial Bar
35. Red Dog Saloon

● SHOPPING
36. Foggy Mountain Shop
37. Juneau Artists Gallery
38. Juneau Arts and Culture Center
39. Rainy Retreat Books
40. Treetop Tees

Mendenhall Glacier viewpoint

TOP EXPERIENCE

Mendenhall Glacier

Part of the massive, 1500-sq-mile Juneau icefield, Mendenhall Glacier is an impressive remnant from the last ice age. Sitting in a mountain valley, the glacier flows some 13 miles from its source. It ends at Mendenhall Lake, where it has a half-mile-wide face and a shimmering waterfall nearby.

DON'T MISS

- View from the Visitor Center
- Film *Landscape of Change*
- Nugget Falls
- Salmon in Steep Creek
- Paddling trip to the glacier's edge

Visitor Center

Start your visit at the **Mendenhall Glacier Visitor Center**, which houses various glaciology exhibits, including a fabricated ice face of the glacier and a relief map of the ice field. Nearby is a time-lapse of the glacier's startling retreat over an eight-year span. The theater shows a 15-minute film about the glacier, its formation and other key features in the Tongass National Forest.

PRACTICALITIES
- *alaska.org/detail/mendenhall-glacier* ● adult/child $5/free
- 8am-7.30pm

Viewpoint Trails

Outside the visitor center, several trails offer views of the glacier and the surrounding environs. For starters, you can take a quick stroll along the Photo Point Trail to the **viewpoint**, where you'll have a panoramic view of the glacier off in the distance.

The busy **Nugget Falls Trail** is an easy, 1-mile (one-way) walk out to a huge churning waterfall that empties into the lake near the face of the glacier. You can't actually see the glacier from here, but the waterfall is impressive.

On the far side of the parking lot, the **Steep Creek Trail** is an easy but rewarding walk on a short boardwalk loop, winding past viewing platforms along the creek. From July through to September, you might see sockeye and coho salmon spawning beneath the viewing decks (and maybe even brown and black bears feasting on them). This is Southeast Alaska's most affordable bear-viewing site, though it is often closed in summer due to heavy bear traffic.

Hiking Trails

Several trails lead away from the glacier and into the surrounding forest. The **Trail of Time** is a 1-mile loop that winds through the forest, with interpretive panels shedding light on features from the past. You'll pass a 1930s Civilian Conservation Corps (CCC) cabin, which was once within viewing distance of the glacier (giving you an idea of how much Mendenhall Glacier has receded). Nearby, the ruins of an old drinking fountain (also from the 1930s) once channeled water from Steep Creek. You can also visit the spot where US President Warren G Harding stood in 1923, and see vestiges from an old 1914 mining operation.

Leave the crowds behind when you follow the more challenging **East Glacier Loop**. This 3.5-mile loop takes you on a well-maintained path through spruce and hemlock forest, past ferns and moss, with around 750ft of elevation gain. Black bears are occasionally spotted here. There are some fine views too, though you'll find better glacier overlooks on the other trails. Find the trailhead by walking south of the visitor center along the Trail of Time.

Getting to the Glacier

The cheapest way to get to Mendenhall Glacier is to hop on a Capital Transit bus (numbers 3, 4, or 8) for $2. Strangely, the bus drops you 1.5 miles from the visitor center. Follow the paved path north along the Glacier Spur Rd. Alternatively, you can book Uber or Lyft for about $40, but you'll have trouble getting a return trip due to a lack of cell service. **Juneau Tours** *(juneautours.com; adult/child $65/45)* and **M&M Tours** *(mmtoursofjuneau.com; adult/child $79/49)* offer round-trip transportation from downtown Juneau, with two hours for self-guided exploration at the glacier.

IMMERSIVE GLACIER ADVENTURES

Paddle a canoe 2½ miles across Mendenhall Lake, passing the gushing Nugget Falls, before stepping ashore at the base of the glacier. Book with **Above & Beyond Alaska** (p105; *beyondak.com; hike/paddle $209/349 per person*).

Take a helicopter flight over the Juneau Icefield, landing on the glacier for a guided trek or ice climbing. No experience required. Book with **NorthStar Helicopters** (p105; *northstartrekking.com; trek/climb from $479/589*).

TOP TIPS

● Mendenhall Glacier is beautiful against blue skies and snowcapped mountains, but it's also photogenic on a cloudy afternoon, when the ice turns to shades of deep blue.

● There is no food for sale at Mendenhall Glacier, and picnicking is forbidden from April to November due to bear activity.

● The visitor center is wheelchair accessible, as are the Photo Point Trail and Nugget Falls Trail.

Goldbelt Tram

AAK'W VILLAGE

The area between Willoughby St and Gold Creek is known as Aak'w Village. This was traditionally the summer village of the **Aak'w Kwáan** Tlingit, until many of them moved here permanently to be closer to the mines. There are still some original village houses along Village St. Nowadays, the district is a sort of tribal campus for Tlingit and Haida groups, with different services for their members. Particularly interesting is **Gajaa Hít**, a community center with two totem poles honoring the Raven and Eagle clans of the Aak'w Kwáan.

Majestic Mt Roberts
Summit by trail or tram

Mt Roberts is the city's most prominent peak, towering 3819 feet over downtown Juneau and the Gastineau Channel. The summit provides a sweeping panorama of the Gastineau Channel, Douglas Island, the Chilkat Mountains and the lofty peaks on Admiralty Island off in the distance. It's worth a trip up the mountain, whether you hike or ride.

The **Goldbelt Tram** (*goldbelttram.com; adult/child $60/45*) whisks you from sea level up to the timberline, which is not the summit, but is still some 1800 feet above the rooftops of downtown Juneau. Apart from admiring the view, there are a handful of activities at the upper tram station. Inside the 120-seat Chilkat Theatre, you can watch *Seeing Daylight*, a short and scenic film that explores Tlingit history and culture. The **Timberline Bar & Grill** serves fairly average food with exceptional views.

If you prefer to hike up (for free), the **Mt Roberts Trail** begins on Basin Rd, just north of town. It's a steep 1.2 miles through the forest to the tramway station, and a further (and steeper) 2.8 miles to the summit. Of course, there's no reason you can't take the tram up and then continue on foot, which many people do.

EATING IN JUNEAU: SNACKS & STREET FOOD

MAPS P97 & P99

Pel'meni: The only eatery open late serves delicious, piping-hot Russian dumplings filled with either potato or beef. *11.30am-1.30am* $

Rainbow Foods: Iconic community store with Earth-friendly groceries, baked goods, and salads and sandwiches for your picnic. *9am-7pm* $

Bernadette's: Much-loved waterfront food stall doling out Filipino barbecue, sandwiches and *dinuguan* (pork stew). *11am-7pm* $

Garvie's Lunchbox: Parked at the Nugget Mall (near the airport), Garvie has you covered if you're craving a juicy, made-to-order burger. *noon-5pm* $

A half-mile beyond the tramway, you'll reach the holy spot known as Father Brown's Cross, named after a Jesuit priest and keen hiker who blazed an early trail up the mountain. This alone is a rewarding add-on, especially for the flower-bedizened alpine meadows immediately above the tram station.

Above the cross, the going gets tougher. You'll ascend high alpine terrain and may encounter snow as the path narrows, traversing a ridge that connects to Mt Gastineau (3666ft). Beyond that, the path drops into a saddle before ascending again to Mt Roberts (3818ft). Be aware that the uphill climbs are grueling after the cross. The ridge in particular can be a bit of a scramble and quite hazardous in the snow and mist.

In any case, you can recharge over snacks and drinks at the Timberline: spend $20 or more, and your tram ride down is free of charge.

Douglas Island's Gold-Mining Remains MAP P97
Old mines and ghostly ruins

It's hard to imagine today, but the Treadwell Mine was once the largest gold mine in the world, spurring Juneau's growth and facilitating the development of other local industries. The mining complex on Douglas Island was set up like a small town, with its own stores, dormitories, blacksmith, and even a baseball diamond. The mine reached its zenith in the 1880s, when the surrounding population grew to 15,000. The mine was subsequently abandoned after part of it slid into the sea in 1917.

Today, spooky reminders of Juneau's prosperous mining past poke through the forest on the well-marked **Treadwell Mine Historic Trail** (alaska.org/guide/treadwell-mine-historic-trail-walking-tour). Interpretive boards explain what remains of the machinery and buildings, including the handsomely restored office building, the 1917 slide site, a 'glory hole,' and a restored pump house that stands like a beached tower just offshore.

Treadwell is 3 miles south of the Douglas Bridge, adjacent to Savikko Park; take bus 1 from downtown Juneau. If the ruins alone don't do it for you, try the innovative tour **Treadwell: Alaska's Last Mine** (treadwelltour.com; adult/child $95/85), which enhances the experience with augmented reality.

For two days each June, Juneau's gold-rush history comes back to life when **Savikko Park** hosts **Juneau Gold Rush Days** (juneaugoldrushdays.com). Summon your inner miner and try your hand at jackleg drilling, spike driving, hand mucking, and (of course) gold panning. Or, just come for the live music and good times.

Early Gold-Mining Operations MAP P97
A hike through history

Treadwell's rival across the channel was the Alaska–Juneau Gold Mining Company, established by the so-called 'Last

DOUGLAS ISLAND

Taylor Vidic, musician and producer shares recommendations for visiting lesser-known places in her hometown.
@taylordallasv

Island Pub: With its views across the water and good pizzas, the Island Pub has a loyal local following.

Perseverance Theatre: Juneau's most professional theater productions.

Sandy Beach (Savikko Park): Walk on the beach for a sandy stroll (also good for dog spotting) or along the path to see the Treadwell Mine ruins.

Rainforest Trail: If you have a car, head to Douglas' north side for ocean views and a far-off peek at the Mendenhall Glacier. Land at the Rainforest Trail – it delivers on its namesake.

Breeze In: As local as a convenience store can be. Swing by before your Douglas adventure for daily-made donuts (before they run out!)

JUNEAU'S GOLDEN HISTORY

In 1880, Tlingit clan chief Kowee led prospectors Joe Juneau and Richard Harris to a sparkling river, now known as Gold Creek, where they found gold 'lumps as large as peas and beans.' They soon staked their mining claims and established the town site nearby. Many hopeful miners followed them to the shores of the Gastineau Channel.

This was the foundation of Juneau, but it was the later development of larger hard-rock mines that fueled the city's economic growth. At Silverbow Basin, the Alaska Juneau Gold Mining Company employed 1000 workers at its peak. Across the channel on Douglas Island, the Alaska Mill & Mining Co became the largest gold-mining operation in the world, employing 2000 workers across five mills and four mines, including the Treadwell Mine.

THE HUNGARIAN SAILOR/SHUTTERSTOCK

Chance Group' in 1881. Today, the former mining complex houses the **Last Chance Mining Museum** *(facebook.com/lastchanceminingmuseum; adult/child $5/free)*. Here, you can see remains of the compressor house and examine tools and other relics from the operation. A 3D glass map of the shafts shows just how large it was. For an additional fee, you can purchase a kit and try your luck at panning for gold in the river. The museum is 1 mile east of town on Basin Rd.

From the museum parking lot, the **Perseverance Trail** follows the route used to reach the mines in the Gold Creek Valley, including the Alaska–Juneau Mine. Popular with mountain bikers and trail runners, the 6-mile, out-and-back route follows the rushing creek, offering views of waterfalls and snow-covered mountaintops. The trail leads into Silverbow Basin, an old mining area that still has hidden adits and shafts. The final stretch to the mining camp ruins is narrow, steep and poorly marked, so take extra care.

Vast Mountain Vistas

MAP P97

Summit Juneau's namesake mountain

The hike up Mt Juneau (3576ft) is a steep and difficult climb that ascends more than 3400ft over the course of the 3.5-mile (one-way) route. The switchback trail starts near the

EATING IN JUNEAU: BREAKFAST

MAP P99

Alaskan Crepe Escape: A fun food truck offering sweet and savory crepes all day long. *8am-8pm* $

Rookery Cafe: This bustling diner serves scratch-made bennies, burgers and plenty of other delicious, creative fare. *7am-2pm Mon-Sat* $$

Heritage Coffee Roasting Co: Community-minded local Juneau chain with a spacious coffeehouse on Front St. *6.30am-6pm* $

Sandpiper Cafe: Juneau's best breakfast joint serves up a mind-boggling array of omelets, eggs Benedict and irresistible French toast. *7am-2pm* $$

View from Mt Juneau

Perseverance Trailhead, ascending rapidly over the city and crossing several waterfalls. The section near the summit – across the Juneau ridgeline – yields glorious, top-of-the-world views. Keep your eyes peeled for mountain goats, ptarmigan, porcupines, marmots, bald eagles and black bears.

To avoid the significant elevation gain, you can also get a helicopter ride up to the summit and hike down. Call **NorthStar Helicopters** *(northstartrekking.com; per person $150)* and inquire about a 'deadhead'. Note that booking in advance is difficult, as they only take deadheads if an empty copter is available.

Adventures on the Water

MAP P97

Whale watching and glacier gawking

From Auke Bay Harbor, there are myriad opportunities to get out on the water and explore the surrounding channels and inlets, taking in marine wildlife and magnificent scenery. Paddle around this stunning seascape on a kayak tour with **Above & Beyond Alaska** *(beyondak.com; kayak/whales $119/449)*. Even better, they can take you out to Channel Islands Marine Park, an abundant feeding ground for humpbacks, for an incredible adventure kayaking with whales.

TAKHU, THE ALASKA WHALE SCULPTURE

With keen eyes, you can get a good, long look at a breaching humpback whale right from the Juneau waterfront. Check out Takhu, the Alaska Whale Sculpture *(alaskawhalesculpture.com)*, a striking installation near the bridge to Douglas Island. Created by the Alaskan artist RT Wallen, the life-sized behemoth (at 6 tons and 25ft long) emerges from its shallow surrounding pool against the backdrop of the Gastineau Channel and distant peaks. The fountain's cascading water and splash effects make it appear as if the animal has just breached the surface, and by night, LED lights illuminate the whale in changing colors.

EATING IN JUNEAU: INTERNATIONAL FLAVORS

MAPS P97 & P99

V's Cellar: Creative Korean-Mexican fusion, such as braised short ribs and tacos to light your tongue on fire (in a good way). *11am-9pm* **$$**

In Bocca Al Lupo: Handmade pasta and wood-fired pizza, with some wild Alaskan ingredients thrown in for authenticity. Reservations recommended. *5-9pm Mon-Sat* **$$**

Spice: Follow the scent of aromatic curries into this elegant spot for authentic Indian cuisine. *11am-9pm* **$$**

Canton Asian Bistro: Generous portions of Chinese favorites, Thai curries and sushi, for a satisfying meal near the airport. *11.30am-9pm, from 4pm Mon* **$$**

DO SOMETHING DIFFERENT

Juneau Food Tours: Eat your way around Juneau, and learn about the city's storied past along the way.

Cycle Alaska: The signature tour – Bikes, Views & Brews – includes a visit to Mendenhall, a bike ride through the Valley and a stop at a local microbrewery. (Or just rent a bike or e-bike and do the same excursion independently for a fraction of the cost.)

NorthStar Helicopters: The Helicopter Glacier Dogsled Adventure takes you to a dog camp to meet the sled dogs, learn the basics of mushing and go for a ride in the snow.

Taku Glacier Lodge: Flightseeing, glacier viewing and salmon bake, all in one, at the rustic yet luxurious Taku Lodge. Operated by Wings Airways.

Kawanti Adventures: Operates the seven-line Alpine Zipline Adventure through the rainforest canopy at Eaglecrest Ski Area on Douglas Island.

If you prefer to do your wildlife-watching from the comfort of a covered and enclosed motor boat, regular whale tours also head out from Auke Bay in search of humpbacks. Boat captains share information about the location of their favorite marine mammals, so sightings are all but guaranteed. (It's also possible – though less likely – to see fast-moving orcas passing through.) **Harv & Marv's Outback Alaska** *(harvandmarvs-juneau-whale-watching.com; from $169)* is a favorite.

For a change of scenery, **True Alaskan Tours** *(truealaskantours.com; adult/child $359/289)* offers an all-day cruise to Tracy Arm-Fords Terror Wilderness, a spectacular 653,000-acre preserve of glaciers, fjords and waterfalls. Normally, the boats travel through Tracy Arm Fjord, one of two long, deep fjords in the preserve. Flanked by 2000ft cliffs, Tracy Arm is fed by the Twin Sawyer Glaciers, which create a stunning seascape.

Glacier Trails

MAP P97

Hike to the ice

Juneau's glacier hikes are relatively challenging, but reward trekkers with super *cool* destinations.

The shortest and most accessible is the 7-mile, out-and-back along the **West Glacier Trail**, which hugs the mountainside beside the famous Mendenhall Glacier (p100). The trail provides exceptional views of glacial features before ending at a rocky outcrop. The last section of the trail, unmaintained and marked by cairns, heads toward the face of the glacier. The trailhead is off Montana Creek Rd, past Mendenhall Campground.

The **Herbert Glacier Trail** extends 5 miles along the Herbert River to the eponymous glacier, a round-trip of four to five hours. The first 3.5 miles are wide and easy, with little climbing (good for mountain biking), though it can be wet in places. The trail begins just past the bridge over Herbert River at Mile 28 of Glacier Hwy, north of Juneau.

Nearby, the **Amalga Trail** (also known as the Eagle Glacier Trail) is a mostly level route that winds 5.5 miles to Eagle Glacier Cabin, with stunning glacier views. It's another 2 miles to reach the impressive glacier itself. Plan on seven to eight hours for the 15-mile round trip. The trailhead is at Eagle Beach State Recreation Area.

EATING IN JUNEAU: SEAFOOD

MAP P99

Deckhand Dave's: Happening outdoor spot with counters for fish tacos, craft beer, oysters and champagne. *11am-9pm* **$$**

Tracy's King Crab Shack: Feast on crab served with butter and slaw. The second location (Shack 2) has a laidback vibe and outdoor seating. *11am-8.30pm* **$$$**

SALT: This high-end restaurant specializes in creative renditions of Alaskan fare in a swanky setting. Reservations recommended. *5-9pm* **$$$**

Hangar on the Wharf: Housed in Merchant's Wharf, it's a nice setting for seafood, plentiful beer and channel views, with seaplanes buzzing overhead. *11am-9pm* **$$$**

Bald eagle

Fortress of the Bears

MAP P97

Bear viewing at Pack Creek

Just 15 miles south of Juneau, **Admiralty Island National Monument** is a 1493-sq-mile preserve, of which 90% is designated wilderness. The monument has a wide variety of wildlife, from Sitka black-tailed deer and nesting bald eagles to harbor seals, sea lions and humpback whales. Most notably, the 96-mile-long island has one of the highest concentrations of bears in the world, with an estimated 1600 brown bears. It's the reason the Tlingit called the place Kootznoowoo, or 'Fortress of Bears.'

Pack Creek flows from the 4000ft mountains before spilling into Seymour Canal on the island's east side. The extensive tidal flats at the mouth of the creek draw a large number of bears in July and August to feed on salmon. Floatplanes bring visitors for bear-viewing at **Stan Price State Wildlife Sanctuary**, named for an Alaskan woodsman who lived here for almost 40 years. Rangers meet visitors on arrival to explain the safety rules: movement on the island is fairly restricted. The main viewing area overlooks the creek and flats. There is also a shady 1-mile trail that leads to an observation tower further inland.

BEST SHOPPING STOPS

Juneau Artists Gallery: A co-op of local artists features an array of paintings, etchings, glasswork, jewelry and pottery.

Rainy Retreat Books: Indeed, a great (anytime) retreat with a well-curated selection of new and used books – especially Alaska-themed books – and records too.

Treetop Tees: Unique designs on t-shirts and hoodies that embrace Alaska's nature, wildlife and the great outdoors.

Foggy Mountain Shop: Juneau's premier shop for clothing and gear for hiking, backpacking and Nordic skiing.

Sealaska Heritage Institute: The gift shop here is a one-stop shop for beautiful craftwork, jewelry, paintings and books by Indigenous artists.

DRINKING IN JUNEAU: HISTORIC DIGS

MAPS P97 & P99

Red Dog Saloon: Iconic spot with swinging doors, sawdust floors and country-and-western crooning (plus ribs and beer-battered cod). *11am-10pm, to 11pm Fri-Sun*

Alaskan Bar: Historic, dimly lit bar drawing crowds, especially on Wednesdays (karaoke) and Thursdays (open mic). *noon-1am, to 3am Fri & Sat*

Imperial Bar: Juneau's oldest bar is a cozy drinking option, with a good selection of beer and whisky and a local vibe. *11am-1am, to 3am Fri & Sat*

Alaskan Brewing Co: Alaska's largest brewery has a tasting room 5 miles north (free shuttle) and a downtown public house near the ship terminals. *11am-7pm*

WHY I LOVE JUNEAU

Mara Vorhees, Lonely Planet writer

What can I say? I am a city girl. Juneau has everything a real city should have (albeit on a smallish scale): museums, food, art. Juneau's population of Alaskan Natives is not huge – it's less than 10% – but the community and culture are vibrant and proud, as showcased by impressive artistic displays like the Totem Trail. There's also a significant Asian population here – mostly Filipino – so the city has a real multicultural vibe. Despite all these characteristics of a 'real' city, Juneau is surrounded by lush mountains and stunning glaciers, life-filled waterways and uninhabited islands. The wilderness is literally steps away.

Brown bear, Admiralty Island National Monument (p107)

The months for bear viewing are from May to mid-June (during the mating season) and from July to August (when salmon are running). Unlike some other bear-viewing destinations, the bear population on Admiralty Island is dispersed. So despite the large numbers, there is no guarantee of spotting many (or any) of them, even during peak seasons.

The USFS and Alaska Department of Fish and Game *(recreation.gov; permit $64)* operate a permit system for Pack Creek, which allows only 24 people per day from June to mid-September. You can get your own permit and book a charter plane through **Ward Air** *(wardair.com; from $1116)*. Or book a tour through **Above & Beyond Alaska** (p105; *beyondak.com; per person $989*), who will make all the arrangements for you.

DRINKING IN JUNEAU: OUR PICKS — MAP P99

Amalga Distillery: A microdistillery serving up creative drinks (including mocktails) from a family-friendly tasting room. *noon-9pm*

Devil's Club Brewing Co: Housemade craft beer goes well with smoked-salmon platters and stacked sandwiches at this inviting microbrewery. *11am-9pm*

Crystal Saloon: Beautiful space for lingering over drinks while catching live music or playing pool, pinball or vintage video games. *11.30am-1am, to 3am Fri & Sat*

Griz Bar: Warm up by the fire with a cocktail in hand at this outdoor waterfront bar. Featuring Alaskan-made spirits, cider and craft beer. *11am-11pm, to midnight Fri & Sat*

Glacier Bay National Park & Preserve

WILDLIFE-WATCHING | GLACIAL PANORAMAS | EPIC KAYAKING

Glacier Bay is the crown jewel of cruise ship destinations and a dream destination for anybody who has ever paddled a kayak. Seven tidewater glaciers spill from the mountains and fill the sea with icebergs of all shapes, sizes and shades of blue – making Glacier Bay National Park and Preserve a world-renowned icy wilderness.

Beyond its high concentration of tidewater glaciers, Glacier Bay is a dynamic habitat for humpback whales, sea otters and puffins. Other wildlife commonly seen here includes orcas and porpoises, harbor seals and Steller's sea lions, brown and black bears, wolves, moose and mountain goats – and you're likely to spot (almost) all of the above from the boat.

Travelers who spend more than a day can also enjoy hiking, camping and maybe even cold-water swimming, with the tiny settlement of Gustavus as a charming base for exploring the area.

> ☑ **TOP TIP**
>
> Bartlett Cove is home to the Glacier Bay National Park headquarters, visitor center and Glacier Bay Lodge. This is where the ferry docks and day boats depart. The tiny town of Gustavus, 8 miles southeast, has the airport as well as some restaurants and lodgings. See *gustavusak.com* for more info.

Nature & Traditional Culture
Browse the National Park exhibits

The best first introduction to Glacier Bay National Park is the **visitor center** *(nps.gov/glba)*, located on the second floor

GETTING AROUND

It's a short but scenic flight between Juneau and Gustavus, with both Alaska Airlines (once daily) and Alaska Seaplanes (four to five daily) making the 25-minute journey. The Alaska Marine Highway ferry also runs three times a week in summer (twice weekly in winter), typically departing Juneau at 7am and departing Gustavus at 12.30pm or 1.30pm for the 4½-hour journey.

Most lodges provide free transportation to and from the airport or ferry terminal. Local taxi services include Strawberry Point Courier (907-697-2150) and TLC taxi (907-697-2239), the latter with room for groups, gear and kayaks.

GLACIER BAY NATIONAL PARK & PRESERVE

● SIGHTS
1 Gustavus Dray
2 Huna Tribal House
3 Strawberry Point History Museum
4 Whale Skeletons

● ACTIVITIES
5 Bartlett River Trail
6 Forest Loop Trail
7 Spirit Walker Expeditions

● SLEEPING
8 Bartlett Cove Campground
9 Bear Track Inn
10 Cottonwood Lodge
11 Glacier Bay Lodge

● EATING
see 9 Excursion Restaurant
12 Fairweather Restaurant
13 Red Rooster

● DRINKING & NIGHTLIFE
14 Fireweed Gallery, Coffee & Tea House

● INFORMATION
15 Glacier Bay National Park Visitor Center

---

of Glacier Bay Lodge. Exhibits explain the geology of the glaciers and ecology of the area, with photographs, models and stuffed examples of the local flora and fauna. At 6pm, rangers lead an evening program, which typically features a talk about a specific curiosity of the park's landscape or ecology.

Down on the Bartlett Cove waterfront, an open-sided pavilion contains one of the largest humpback **whale skeletons** on display in the United States. The 45ft whale named Snow had been a regular visitor to Glacier Bay since 1975, when she was tragically struck by a cruise ship in 2001.

Follow the shoreline northeast to reach Xunaa Shuká Hít, aka the **Huna Tribal House** (open 1pm to 3.30pm Tuesday to Saturday). The elaborate interior references the four historical Huna Tlingit clans in Glacier Bay. The clan house remains a gathering spot for tribal members, but it's also used for presentations by the National Park Service (NPS), which manages it jointly with the Huna Tlingit.

Forest Loops & River Walks
Hiking around Bartlett Cove

Most Glacier Bay activities take place on the water, but it's worth exploring the surrounding landscape if you have a few extra hours to spare. The mile-long **Forest Loop Trail** winds through the pond-studded spruce and hemlock forest near the campground. Start at the Bartlett Cove dock, or join a daily ranger-guided walk.

The **Bartlett River Trail** is a 2-mile route that begins near Bartlett Cove and ends at the Bartlett River estuary. On the way, it meanders along a tidal lagoon – a good place to spot spawning salmon and hungry bears (in season). Plan on two-plus hours for the 4-mile round-trip. A more challenging route branches off for the 8-mile, out-and-back trail to Bartlett Lake.

Homesteading History
Exploring Gustavus, then and now

The base for visiting Glacier Bay National Park is **Gustavus**, a tiny settlement with a year-round population of around 400 people. There's no 'downtown' in Gustavus, aside from the main intersection, known as Four Corners. You'll know you're there when you see **Gustavus Dray**, a photogenic gas station from the 1930s (which is still operational and, in fact, the only gas station in town). Take a peek inside to see the century-old pumps and other artifacts.

A half-mile west of Four Corners, the **Strawberry Point History Museum** provides an intimate glimpse into the early history of Gustavus. Starting in 1914, a few intrepid families settled in a wild landscape, originally named Strawberry Point for the berries that grew on the flats. The museum's walls are crammed with more than 1000 artifacts related to the lives of early homesteaders, gold mining in Glacier Bay, the one-room schoolhouse, and more. The museum is open by appointment: to arrange a visit, call Linda Parker (907-209-2673), who will recount stories about the interesting, inventive and independent people who lived here.

Paddling Adventures in Glacier Bay
Kayaking the national park

Paddling a kayak is an ideal way to explore Glacier Bay, since there are few hiking trails or roads in the national park. **Glacier Bay Sea Kayak** (GBSK; *glacierbayseakayaks.com; half/full-day tour from $105/165*) runs guided paddle tours, in addition to renting kayaks for independent exploration. One-day excursions stay in Bartlett Cove, a protected cove surrounded by rainforest-covered islands. Seals, sea lions, porpoises and even sea otters are sometimes spotted in these waters. Equipment and rain gear are provided.

Continues on p114

LOCAL LORE

In November 1957, 11 National Guardsmen were traveling from San Francisco to Anchorage in a Douglas C-47 'Gooney Bird.' High winds prevented a planned fuel stop near Ketchikan, so the crew had to stop in Gustavus. Tragically, heavy snowfall impeded visibility, causing the pilot to miss the runway and crash into the forest two miles north of the airport. All four crewmen died. The seven passengers survived thanks to local residents who mounted a rescue effort when they heard the crash, trudging through the snowstorm and carrying the wounded out on makeshift branch stretchers. The wreckage still rests in the forest as a memorial. Look for the trail on the east side of Mountain View Rd, about a half-mile north of Wild Alaska Inn.

Margerie Glacier

TOP EXPERIENCE

Glacier Bay Day Boat

Spectacular tidewater glaciers and snow-capped mountains set the scene for a fantastic day on board the Glacier Bay Day Boat, a seven-hour excursion from Bartlett Cove. The high-speed catamaran makes the 65-mile journey to the north end of Glacier Bay, with chances to see abundant wildlife including some rare marine mammals.

DON'T MISS

- Puffins and sea lions at South Marble Island
- Mountain goats on Gloomy Knob
- Margerie Glacier
- Harbor seals on the growlers
- Sea otters all around
- Breaching humpback whales

Wildlife Stops

After departing Bartlett Cove, the boat motors (slowly) through whale waters, often offering glimpses of orcas and humpbacks. Thousands of sea otters are swimming in these waters, and sightings are practically guaranteed.

The first wildlife viewing stop is the birding paradise of **South Marble Island**, where tufted and horned puffins, pigeon guillemots, surf scoters and pelagic cormorants are often seen. Near the shoreline, Steller sea lions bask on rocky ledges and watch idly as boats glide past.

PRACTICALITIES
- *visitglacierbay.com* • adult/child $266/139
- board 6:50am, depart 7:15am, return 3.30pm; late May-Aug

Further along, the captain will slow the boat when sailing alongside **Gloomy Knob**, a barren rock face with steep cliffs where mountain goats are frequently spotted. Brown bears are also occasionally seen walking along the shoreline.

Fairweather Range

The excursion offers dramatic views of the high peaks of the Fairweather Range, home to some of the world's highest coastal mountains, including **Mt Fairweather**, which tops out at 15,266ft. The landscape changes as you draw nearer to the ice field, with steeper mountains and sparser vegetation. Soon, the color of the water changes as well, with a milky blue-green hue from the silt and sediment of the massive glacial flows.

Tarr Inlet

Boats will typically take the narrow passage of **Tarr Inlet**, which dead-ends near one of the national park's most spectacular glaciers. You know you're getting close when you see growlers and bergy bits (small and medium-sized icebergs) floating in the water.

At the northwest end of the inlet lies **Margerie Glacier**, a stunning and iconic tidewater glacier that stretches nearly a mile wide and towers some 250ft above the waterline (and another 100ft extending below the surface). Its terminus is just a small piece of this 21-mile-long river of ice that originates in the Fairweather Range. The snowy white surface appears blue in places, and its colors are more vivid on cloudy days. The boat will linger in hopes of possibly seeing calving, when huge icebergs shear off the glacier and plunge into the water.

Next to Margerie is the **Grand Pacific Glacier**, which is thickly covered by debris and lies just a mile south of the Canadian border.

Apart from the striking backdrop – icebergs in the foreground, the wide glacier, and chiseled mountains off in the distance – Tarr Inlet is also a good place to spot wildlife. Look for harbor seals stretched out on the ice, sea otters in the water, and black-legged kittiwake gulls flying past.

More Glaciers

You'll pass other glaciers as you make the return journey, including the **Lamplugh Glacier**, a photogenic formation at the terminus of the ever-shrinking Brady Icefield. Nearby is the small, slow-moving **Reid Glacier**, which was once the backdrop to a cabin built by the Ibachs, a pioneering family that, in the 1920s, searched for gold in the nearby mountains. The foundations are still there, along with several trees that they planted.

ALL GLACIER, NO BAY

As recently as 1750, Glacier Bay was covered in ice up to 5000ft thick in the north and 300ft thick at Bartlett Cove. During the Little Ice Age (16th to 19th centuries), the northern glaciers advanced as far as Icy Strait, destroying villages and transforming landscapes. The Tlingit communities evacuated and relocated 30 miles south to present-day Hoonah. In the late 18th century, the massive glacier began its retreat, which continues to this day.

TOP TIPS

● The boat ride is narrated by a NPS ranger, who can answer questions about the geology and ecology of Glacier Bay.

● The excursion includes coffee and doughnuts for breakfast, a mid-morning snack, and a decent lunch. Additional snacks and drinks are available for purchase.

● Window seats are recommended, but the best view is from the deck. Binoculars are available to borrow for the duration of the cruise.

WILDLIFE OF GLACIER BAY

Sea otters: Extremely rare in the 1980s, today sea otters are the most abundant marine mammal in the bay.

Bears: Brown and black bears inhabit the region. Look for the latter near Bartlett Cove, and grazing in beach meadows.

Moose: A relative newcomer, moose can sometimes be spotted off Park Rd and on the Bartlett Cove seaside trail.

Mountain goats: Scan the cliffs for these agile, white-coated creatures, who recolonized the region after the glaciers retreated.

Porcupines: One of North America's largest rodents, these prickly animals are sometimes spotted near cottonwood trees.

Humpback whales: Look for these giant mammals from the boat and from the shoreline, near the entrance to Bartlett Cove.

Kayaking, Glacier Bay (p111)

Continued from p111

For a more immersive kayaking and camping adventure, the Beardslee Islands are a popular destination for a two- to three-day trip. The islands are accessed at high tide only through a corridor at the end of Bartlett Cove. The entire area is closed to motorized vessels, which makes for a uniquely peaceful and wildlife-rich experience.

Longer multiday excursions allow paddlers to delve deeper into the 65-mile-long bay, exploring the well-protected arms and inlets where the glaciers are located. The Glacier Bay Day Boat (p112) provides a drop-off and pick-up service for kayakers, who typically spend four to ten days camping and paddling in the upper reaches of the bay.

Rent kayaks from GBSK (*glacierbayseakayaks.com; per day from $70*). Alternatively, GBSK and **Spirit Walker Expeditions** (*seakayakalaska.com*) run guided trips to all of these destinations.

EATING IN THE GLACIER BAY AREA: OUR PICKS

Fireweed Gallery Coffee & Teahouse: At Four Corners, stop into this cafe, gallery and shop for crepes, biscuit sandwiches and good coffee. *8am-5pm Mon-Sat* $

Red Rooster: Sandwich shop by day, pub by night, serving burgers, sandwiches and drinks, plus Tuesday-night karaoke. *11am-9pm Mon-Thu, to 11pm Fri & Sat* $$

Excursion Restaurant: The Bear Track Inn kitchen specializes in Alaskan fare such as seafood, game and made-from-scratch sides. *6.30-9pm* $$$

Fairweather Restaurant: Glacier Bay Lodge guests dine here for pricey but satisfying meals with views overlooking Bartlett Cove. *6am-9am, noon-3pm & 6-9pm* $$$

Haines

TLINGIT CULTURE | BALD EAGLES | RIVER RAFTING

Snow-capped peaks tower above Alaska's longest fjord, Lynn Canal, its blue-green waters lapping at the edge of one of Southeast Alaska's most captivating small towns. This area was long known to the Tlingit as Deishú, or 'End of the Trail.' White settlers began arriving in 1880 – first Presbyterian missionaries, then cannery workers, and later the US Army. Nowadays, the tranquil streets are dotted with all the essentials of good living in Alaska: curio-filled museums, chef-driven restaurants, house-roasted coffee, craft brews and spirits, and a good bookstore. Not to mention a disproportionate number of art galleries, thanks to the high density of creative types.

Haines is also the gateway to spruce and hemlock forests, alpine meadows and rushing rivers. Come summer, the streams are teeming with salmon (beloved by brown bears), and Alaska's densest concentration of bald eagles fills the skies. Though just an hour away by ferry, Haines sees only a fraction of Skagway's cruise traffic and retains a low-key, local vibe.

GETTING AROUND

The ferry arrives 5 miles north of town. Your lodging may give you a lift, or you can make arrangements with **Haines Pick-up** *(907-314-0812)* or **Miss Lucy** *(907-314-2060)*.

Haines is small and walkable. For venturing out, rent a car from **Hotel Halsingland** or **Lynn View Lodge**, or rent a bike from **Sockeye Cycle** *(sockeyecycle.com)* or an e-bike from **Ebike Haines** *(ebikehaines.com)*.

Chilkoot Lake

Marvel at a mountain lake

About 10 miles north of town, **Chilkoot Lake State Recreation Site** is a super scenic destination for a bike ride, paddle, fly-fishing outing – or even just a drive. The namesake turquoise lake is surrounded by mountain cliffs, with eagles perched in Sitka spruce along the shore, keeping an eye out for their next meal. The Ferebee Glacier is visible at the northern end, and the panorama is gorgeous enough to warrant the trip from town to take a photo. From here, the Chilkoot River flows out to the Lynn Canal, a great place to see salmon runs in summer – not to mention the occasional brown bear family.

Continues on p118

☑ TOP TIP

Stop by the **Haines Farmers Market** *(10am-1pm Sat, Jun-Sep)* at the Southeast Alaska State Fairgrounds for local produce, baked goods, handmade arts and crafts, and live music.

HAINES

BEST SHOPPING STOPS

Wild Iris: Enter through the garden to reach this impressive gallery with original jewelry, prints and local art.

The Bookstore: Literary and cultural hub with lots of Alaska-themed books and works by local authors.

Fairweather Ski Works: Gorgeous handmade skis and boards, crafted from local wood and adorned with artistic graphics. Located at the State Fair Grounds.

Wildhaven Wools: Adorable, colorful, and comfortable merino-wool clothes for kids, in clever 'grow-with-me' styles that fit the kiddos longer.

Alaska Rod's: Beautiful hand-crafted knives for hunting, filleting, cooking and more. Also carries deluxe body products by Great Alaska Soap Co.

Haines Sheldon Museum

Continued from p115

Rent a bike or e-bike from **Sockeye Cycle** (*cyclealaska.com; 4hr $29*) or join one of their tours to enjoy superb views of the Lynn Canal as you pedal from town. Greg Schlachter and his team at **Fly Guides** (*hainesflyfishing.com; half/full day from $275/325*) can set you up for fly fishing on the river. Or contact **SEAK Expeditions** (*seakexpeditions.com; kayak only/bike-kayak combo $164/259*) to paddle around the lake.

Rainy Day Destinations

Visit Haines' eclectic museums

When the weather is grey – or even if it's not – you'll appreciate the odd assortment of museums in town. At the bottom of Main St, the **Haines Sheldon Museum** (*sheldonmuseum.org; adult/child $10/free*) houses a small but beautifully curated collection of Indigenous artifacts. You'll find bentwood boxes, spruce root baskets and a fascinating array of rare Chilkat blankets. The rest of the museum is devoted to the pioneer and gold rush days, as well as other key moments in Haines' history.

One block west of the museum, you'll reach a 20ft hammer, a sure sign that you've arrived at one of Alaska's weirdest exhibits. The extravagantly esoteric **Hammer Museum**

EATING IN HAINES: OUR PICKS

Bamboo Room: A long-running classic with a colorful history and an extensive menu, famed for its halibut fish and chips. *7am-8pm Fri-Mon, 10am-4pm Tue* **$$**

Alpenglow: A cozy setting to nosh on wood-fired pizzas or tasty soup and sandwiches. *11am-8pm Wed-Sun* **$$**

Deer Heart: Named for an edible forest floor green, this spot creatively uses local ingredients, whether farmed, fished or foraged. *5-9pm Thu-Sat, 9am-1pm Sun* **$$$**

Taste of Deishú: Tlingit-owned waterside gem with a small, ever-changing menu featuring local ingredients. *7.30am-2pm Mon-Fri, plus 5.30-8.30pm Tue-Wed* **$$$**

(*hammermuseum.org; adult/child $7/free*) showcases more than 2500 hammers, from a Neolithic hammer used to build the Pyramids of Giza in Egypt to the heavy-duty tools of erstwhile dentists, shoemakers and blacksmiths. The five mannequins, all busy hammering things, were donated by the Smithsonian.

Heading south of Main St, you can learn about Alaskan wildlife at the **American Bald Eagle Foundation** (*baldeagles.org; adult/child $25/15*). This nonprofit organization functions as a sanctuary for injured birds of prey, although there are only a few in residence. The on-site museum has numerous taxidermic exhibits.

Age-Old Tlingit Traditions
Artistic carvings in the Eternal Village

Part of a welcome renaissance in Tlingit art and culture in Alaska, the **Jilkaat Kwaan Cultural Heritage Visitor Center** (*jilkaatkwaanheritagecenter.org; admission $15*) is located in the ancient Alaska Native settlement of Klukwan, which means 'Eternal Village' in the Tlingit language. Located 22 miles north of Haines, the center includes some of the most prized heirlooms of Alaska Native culture, namely four elaborate house posts and a rain screen (the legendary 'whale house collection') carved by a Tlingit Michelangelo over 200 years ago. It became available for public viewing only in 2016.

Apart from carvings and the clan house, the museum features impressive Chilkat weavings, including robes and blankets. The center is also home to a studio used by contemporary carvers, and it offers classes to aspiring Indigenous artists to carry on the rich traditions that date back centuries. Call ahead to book a private tour.

There's no regular transportation out to Klukwan, so you'll need to rent a car or book a tour with **Miss Lucy's Taxi & Tours** (*907-314-2060; tour $99*).

Local Military History
Explore Fort Seward

Alaska's first permanent military post was right here in Haines, thanks to an early-20th-century border dispute with Canada. **Fort William Seward** was constructed and completed in 1904. Over the years, it served as a recruitment station and training center until it was finally decommissioned after WWII.

VALLEY OF THE EAGLES

The **Chilkat Bald Eagle Preserve** in Haines protects the largest known gathering of bald eagles in the world. Each year from October to February, more than 4000 eagles congregate to feed on spawning salmon. Eagles come to the area because an upwelling of warm water prevents the river from freezing, thus encouraging the late salmon run. It's a remarkable sight – hundreds of birds sitting in the bare trees lining the river, often six or more birds to a branch.

The best time to witness this wildlife phenomenon is in November, during the four-day **Alaska Bald Eagle Festival**, which features wildlife workshops, raptor presentations, and naturalist-led tours to the Chilkat River to observe the eagles.

 DRINKING IN HAINES: MADE IN HAINES

Haines Brewing Company: Tasting room pouring local favorites like Captain Cook's Spruce Tip Ale or the Black Fang imperial stout (8.2%). *noon-7pm Mon-Sat*	**Port Chilkoot Distillery:** Inside Fort Seward's former bakery, creative cocktails feature house-made bitters and syrups and seven signature spirits. *2-9pm Mon-Sat*	**Three Northmen:** This rustic tasting room serves meads, ciders and hard sodas made from hand-harvested ingredients. *2-8pm*	**Fogcutter Bar:** Locals congregate at this old-timey bar to play pool, swill drinks and spout off. Serves locally crafted beer and spirits. *10am-close*

FESTIVE EVENTS IN DALTON CITY

Haines is at its most festive during special events hosted at the **Southeast Alaska State Fairgrounds**. Bet you can't guess what one of them is? That's right, in late July or early August, the **Southeast Alaska State Fair** *(seakfair.org; day pass adult/child $25/10)* promises four days of live music, logging contests, fisherman's rodeo, and lots of food and arts and crafts. Brewers and drinkers take over the fairgrounds for **Beerfest** *(seakfair.org/beerfest)* during the last weekend in May.

The fairground feels straight out of the Gold Rush era, with its faded clapboard houses lined up on a dusty street. In fact, the street and houses were constructed to replicate Dawson City for the 1991 movie *White Fang*, starring Ethan Hawke.

Head uphill from the waterfront to wander around this National Historic Landmark, with more than a dozen original buildings scattered around the parade grounds. The former recreation hall is now the **Chilkat Center for the Arts** *(chilkatcenter.org)* for theater, concerts and other performances. The former hospital now houses the **Alaska Indian Arts Center** *(alaskaindianarts.com)*. Both are open to the public. The line of handsome houses on the west side of the parade ground was known as **Officers Row**, while the buildings of **Hotel Halsingland** (p115) housed the Captain and the Commanding Officer.

The log cabin at the center of the parade grounds is **Noow Hít**, a tribal house of the Chilkoot Indian Association. This traditional gathering place was built in the mid-20th century, as a part of an ongoing renewal and rediscovery of Tlingit arts and culture.

Coastlines & Mountaintops

Hitting the trails

Haines offers enticing hiking opportunities, including two major trail systems within walking distance of downtown, plus several rewarding hikes on the Chilkat Peninsula, located just south of Haines. **SEAK Expeditions** *(seakexpeditions.com;*

EATING IN HAINES: CAFES & BAKERIES

Mountain Market & Cafe: This keystone of the community is equal parts health-food store, deli, cafe and coffee roaster. *cafe 8am-3pm, store to 6pm* $

Rusty Compass Coffeehouse: Locally loved spot with breakfast burritos, sandwiches and expertly pulled espresso. *6.30am-2.30pm Mon-Fri, to noon Sat, to 10am Sun* $

Chilkat Restaurant & Bakery: Stop in for fresh-baked goods or grab a seat for something heartier like American breakfasts or Thai curries. *7am-2pm & 5-8pm* $$

Olerud's Market: This friendly local market stocks pies, pastries and other homemade goodness from Gunick's Bakery. *8am-7pm* $

Mt Riley Trail

per person from $148) leads guided hikes along some of these routes.

If you have limited time, the **Battery Point Trail** is a pleasant, flat walk along the shore to Kelgaya Point. After winding through the forest, cut across to a pebble beach and follow it to Battery Point for excellent views of Lynn Canal. The 2-mile (one-way) trail begins at the end of Beach Rd.

For something more challenging, tackle the **Mt Riley Trail**. The 1760ft summit provides good views in all directions, including vistas of Rainbow and Davidson Glaciers. One trail up the mountain begins at a junction off the Battery Point Trail, about a mile out of Portage Cove State Recreation Site. From here, you hike 3 miles over Half Dome and up Mt Riley.

Even loftier, the 3600ft summit of **Mt Ripinsky** yields a sweeping view of Lynn Canal and the land stretching from Juneau to Skagway. The **trailhead** is less than a mile from Haines town center. Follow 2nd Ave north, branch onto Young Rd, and then head up the hill. You can camp in the alpine area between Mt Ripinsky and the South Summit, then continue the next day west along the ridge to Peak 3920. From there, descend to 7 Mile Saddle and then to the Haines Hwy, putting you 7 miles northwest of town. The entire route is about 10 miles and requires eight to 10 hours of hiking.

A lower-elevation trail that takes in some lovely shores is the 6.8-mile (one-way) **hike to Seduction Point**, which marks the point dividing Chilkoot and Chilkat Inlets. Starting near the **Chilkat State Park Campground**, this sometimes swampy, rooty trail swings between forest and beach, offering blue-chip views of Davidson Glacier. Check the tides before departing, as the final stretch along the beach after David's Cove should be done at low or mid-tide. The entire round trip takes nine to 10 hours.

TOURS & ADVENTURES IN HAINES

SEAK Expeditions: Leads cycling, kayaking and rafting trips from half-day to week-long adventures. The Klehini River excursion lets the current do the work as you spy bald eagles and other wildlife.

Sockeye Cycle: Rents bikes and runs one-day and multiday bike tours. Hike, Bike and Brew is a favorite.

Alaska Nature Tours: This husband-wife team leads hikes and nature tours, focusing on wildlife observation and appreciation of the natural world.

Alaska Mountain Guides: Various one-day guided hikes and kayak trips, as well as a two-day rafting trip on the Upper Tsirku River.

Haines Rafting Co: The local rafting specialists offer day trips to the Chilkat Bald Eagle Preserve, as well as a variety of exciting longer (one-week and multi-week) expeditions.

Skagway

GOLD RUSH LORE | SCENIC TRAIN | FABLED HIKING

☑ TOP TIP

Dating to 1899, the outlandish **Arctic Brotherhood Hall** was the fraternal hall and club for prospectors. It has nearly 9000 pieces of decorative driftwood covering the facade. Today, it houses the Skagway Visitor Information Center.

At first sight, Skagway appears to be an amusement park for cruise ship day-trippers, a million of whom disembark onto its sunny boardwalks every summer. But, haunted by Klondike ghosts and beautified by a tight grid of handsome turn-of-the-century buildings, this is no northern Vegas. Skagway's history is very real.

During the 1898 Klondike gold rush, 40,000 stampeders passed through the nascent settlement. They were a sometimes unsavory cast of characters who lived against a backdrop of brothels, gunfights and debauched entertainment, wilder than the Wild West. From here, they took their chances on the perilous journey north to the Klondike, in hopes of striking it rich. Today, Skagway's main actors are seasonal workers and storytelling park rangers; indeed, most of the town's important buildings are managed by the National Park Service (NPS). This colorful history – along with Skagway's location on the cusp of a burly trail-laced wilderness – makes for a unique and rewarding destination.

GETTING AROUND

Most of Skagway is walkable. Cruise ships, as well as the Alaska Marine Highway ferry to Haines, dock at the main terminal, just a few minutes' walk into town (the Skagway Small Boat Harbor with fast ferries from Haines is also in the same area). If you don't want to hoof it, the city runs the SMART bus, which goes from the cruise ship docks up Broadway St as far as 8th Ave. You can also call for **on-demand service** *(907-612-0902)* to Dyea or the White Pass Summit. Note that several companies rent e-bikes, including Klondike Electric Bicycles.

Klondike Gold Rush National Historical Park

Gateway to the Klondike
Revisit the gold rush days

Skagway's buildings and streets comprise the **Klondike Gold Rush National Historical Park**, which recalls the days when tens of thousands of stampeders passed through town on their way to seek their fortune. The NPS has restored many of the historic buildings and designed exhibits to share this somewhat strange moment in history.

Begin your journey into the past at the **Klondike Gold Rush National Historical Park Visitor Center** *(nps.gov/klgo)*, set in the original 1898 White Pass & Yukon Route depot. The center features a few exhibits, with a particular focus on the two routes out of Skagway: Chilkoot Pass and White Pass. In the theater, a 25-minute film provides an overview of gold rush history. There is also tons of information about free walking tours, ranger talks, hikes, and attractions around town.

Get a (free) ticket at the Visitor Center for **Jeff Smith's Parlor**, which is probably the oldest tourist attraction in Skagway, as it opened as a museum in 1935. The original 'parlor' was in fact the hangout of one of the town's biggest outlaws. Back in 1898, so-called 'Soapy' Smith would meet with his fellow conmen here, devising schemes to swindle stampeders

Continues on p129

THE STAMPEDER'S DREADFUL DILEMMA

Two rugged mountain barriers faced stampeders on their way to the Klondike gold fields in 1897–98. One feverish prospector who had tried both described them as 'hell' and 'damnation'.

White Pass, at 2864ft, is the lower of the two, but the 44-mile route is significantly longer – and notoriously muddy, narrow and treacherous. Though accessible by horse, which was both a blessing and a curse: so many packhorses were worked to death by their owners that it became known as 'Dead Horse Pass.'

The 33-mile **Chilkoot Trail** (p126) is steeper than White Pass, but as a long-established Tlingit route, it was the more popular option. It quickly fell out of favor in April 1898 after an avalanche killed more than 60 people.

 EATING IN SKAGWAY: FOOD TRUCKS

Starfire: Spicy and satisfying Thai fare, served from a food truck at 'Crow's Corner.' Portions are generous, to say the least. *11am-5pm Tue-Sat* **$**

Peppers Street Fusion: A school bus serving tacos, burritos and bowls with Mexican flavors and several vegan options. *11am-8pm Mon-Fri, to 6pm Sat & Sun* **$**

Skagway Weenie Wagon: All-beef hot dogs and reindeer sausages served on a stick or in a bun, plus some wild daily specials. *11am-5pm Mon-Fri, noon-4pm Sat* **$**

Benny's Bonanza Bites: Folks go berserk for Benny's Bonanza Bites, which are irresistible, fresh-made mini donuts. Served with coffee or hot chocolate. *9am-5pm* **$**

Wooden church, Bennett (Mile 33; p128)

TOP EXPERIENCE

Hiking the Iconic Chilkoot Trail

The **Chilkoot Trail**, the epic trek undertaken by over 30,000 gold-rush stampeders in 1897–98, is sometimes known as the 'Last Great Adventure.' Nowadays, the storied route draws adventure-seekers who spend three to five days traversing the forbidding terrain. And the trail is still dotted with the remnants of one of the 19th century's most incredible journeys.

> **DON'T MISS**
>
> Before starting the trail, all hikers must pick up permits and attend an orientation session at the **NPS Trail Center** in Skagway.

 Dyea

The trailhead is at Dyea, 9 miles northwest of Skagway, site of a once-rambunctious gold-rush town that rose and fell within just six years (1897-1903). Explore the **Dyea National Historic Site** (p133) before commencing the historic trek.

PRACTICALITIES
- nps.gov/klgo/planyourvisit/planning-your-hike.htm
- permits + reservation fee for US/Canadian side CA$39/54
- open Jun–mid-Sep

After an initial ascent, the trail is mostly flat and parallels the Taiya River, with boardwalks aiding passage through the swampy Beaver Pond area.

❷ Canyon City (Mile 7.8)

In 1898, Canyon City was a burgeoning village, with two tramway powerhouses and many services for prospectors. Nowadays, a narrow 0.7-mile spur trail leads to the old townsite, where you can see some structural remains and the ruins of an old boiler.

The trail gains about 1000ft en route to Pleasant Camp and Sheep Camp beyond.

❸ Sheep Camp (Mile 13)

Sheep Camp was a large congregation point during the gold rush, with thousands of temporary residents and many businesses, including hotels, restaurants, stores and even dance halls. Nowadays, it is the last campground before the summit, with a ranger station (and a nightly ranger briefing about conditions).

An early departure from Sheep Camp is recommended. From here the going is difficult, ascending the excruciating Long Hill and emerging above the tree line.

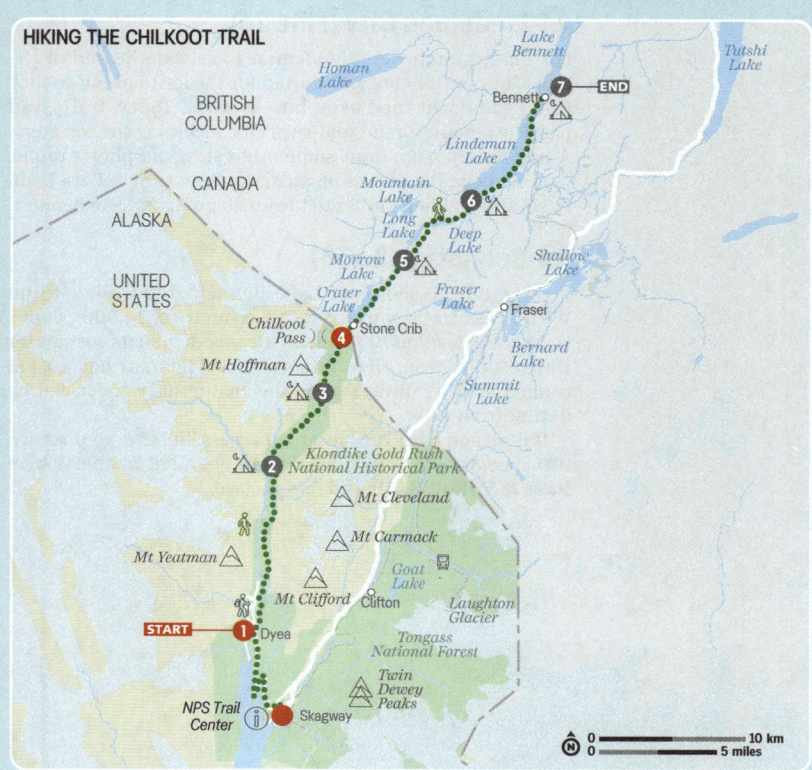

> **PLANNING YOUR HIKE**
>
> Attention! The international border at Chilkoot Pass was closed in 2025 – hopefully temporarily – making the Chilkoot Trail impossible to hike in its entirety in one go. The route here assumes the border will reopen in the near future.
>
> Purchase permits and reserve campsites through **Parks Canada** *(reservations.pc.gc.ca)* even if you are hiking only on the US side.

❹ Chilkoot Pass (Mile 16.5)

At mile 15.8, the Scales was a small outpost where packers had to reweigh their supplies. It was also (and still is) a last resting place before the push to the summit. From here, the rough trail climbs a 45-degree, 1000ft-high scree slope to 3525ft Chilkoot Pass. The summit is often misty, windy and snow-covered, but there is a warming hut on site. As long as the US–Canadian border remains closed, Chilkoot Pass is the turnaround point for the return to Dyea. If you're able to continue into British Columbia, the trail descends to Cascade Lakes and then skirts through high alpine terrain past several smaller lakes to Happy Camp.

❺ Happy Camp (Mile 20.5)

Prospectors were so relieved to arrive after crossing the pass, that this outpost (however humble) was dubbed Happy Camp. It is the only alpine campsite on the trail.

Continuing north, you'll duck under the tree line again soon after Deep Lake. Then proceed atop the north side of a deep gorge that carries an angry river down to placid Lindeman Lake.

❻ Lindeman City (Mile 26)

For many stampeders, Lindeman Lake was the end of the line. They built boats and waited for the ice to break so they could sail down the Yukon into Dawson. Today, trails lead past the remains of the gold-rush city, including the cemetery. A tent museum contains some interesting old photographs.

From here, it's 3 miles on an undulating trail to Bare Loon Lake, and another 4 miles to the finish point on Lake Bennett.

❼ Bennett (Mile 33)

Finally, on the shores of Lake Bennett, the Chilkoot and White Pass trails converged in a tent city of 10,000 people. In May 1898, some 700 homemade wooden boats set sail for Dawson City from the southern shore. Bennett has a good campground, a railway station and an unusual wooden church dating from 1898.

It does not, however, have road access. Reserve your return transportation on the hikers' train operated by the **White Pass & Yukon Railroad** *(wpyr.com)*.

Red Onion Saloon (p130)

Continued from p123

out of their money. Years later, collector and Skagway booster Martin Itjen converted the building into a museum to tell Soapy's story and to show off his collection of curiosities. Many of these are still on display, from taxidermy animals to Skagway's first telephone to an animatronic Soapy Smith.

Further along Broadway is the **Mascot Saloon** – the only saloon in Alaska that doesn't serve booze. But it did during the gold rush, and plenty of it. Now the building has been restored, and it contains a small museum with a mock bar.

The oldest structure in town is the **Historic Moore Homestead**. On a hunch, savvy Captain William Moore arrived in the area in 1887 and built himself a small log cabin in the uninhabited woods. Beside the cabin is Moore's newer homestead, which was built on the eve of the gold rush in 1897. Inside, the rooms are meticulously set with period furnishings that provide a glimpse into life in the early 1900s.

At the north end of town, the **Skagway Museum** contains the city's best collection of historic artifacts. It occupies the 1st floor of the venerable century-old McCabe Building, a former college, and is devoted to various aspects of local history, including Alaska Native baskets, beadwork and carvings, and, of course, the Klondike Gold Rush.

BEST NIGHTLIFE & ENTERTAINMENT

Days of '98: Going strong for over 100 years, this family-friendly show mixes comedy and high-kicking dancing in a vaudevillian comedy.

Happy Endings Saloon: A true local favorite, with thematic cocktails, live music, and a competitive cornhole arena. Good times.

Red Onion Saloon: There's always something going on at the Red Onion, from live-music Mondays to art exhibits to the occasional burlesque show.

Lumberchaun Axe-Throwing: Test your aim, flex your muscles and learn how to wield your weapon like a true Alaskan. Closed-toe shoes required.

Skagway Arts Council: Hosts music and art events throughout the year, such as the Skagway Spring Festival in April and the Blues, Brews & Barbecue in July.

EATING AND DRINKING IN SKAGWAY: CUTE CAFES

Lucy's Bakery: Lucy's pastries are to-die-for, especially the decadent cinnamon roll. For savory, the breakfast taco is perfection in a tortilla. *7am-5pm* $

Glacial Coffeehouse: A great anytime spot, this spacious cafe whips up good coffee, hot breakfasts and lunch sandwiches. *6am-2pm* $

Sittin' Sasquatch: Comfy cafe for breakfast and lunch, while the standalone coffee shop serves 'legendary' caffeine drinks. *8am-4pm* $

Cafe on 5th: Sweet little spot for coffee and pastries, plus fresh-made sammies. *6.30am-3.30pm Mon-Sat* $

BUILDING THE RAILROAD TO WHITEHORSE

At the height of the gold rush, Michael J Heney, an Irish contractor, convinced a group of English investors that he could build a railroad over the White Pass Trail to Whitehorse in Canada. The construction was one of the great engineering challenges of the day. Upwards of 2000 men worked in relays over the summer, when near-constant daylight allowed for continuous work. Local timber degraded too easily, so all the wood for ties and bridges had to be imported, along with 450 tons of dynamite that was used to blast through seemingly impenetrable rock faces. The railroad was completed in just 27 months, a remarkable accomplishment given that everything was done by hand. Sadly, 35 workers lost their lives in the process.

White Pass & Yukon Route (WPYR) Railway

Skagway's Working Women
Historic brothel and street-walking tours

Occupying a prominent corner on Skagway's main drag, the **Red Onion Saloon** *(redonion1898.com; brothel tour/walking tour $20/50)* harks back to the era when it operated as an acclaimed bordello. Downstairs, the historic saloon still buzzes with activity. Throughout the day, the so-called 'madams' – decked out in period dress and dropping innuendos in every sentence – give interesting and entertaining tours of the restored brothel rooms upstairs. This so-called 'Quickie' tour covers the history and operation of the brothel, as well as the lives of the working girls.

For a more in-depth look at the lives of Skagway's women of yore, 'Ghosts and Good Time Girls' is a walking tour of Skagway's infamous haunts. You'll see a 'House of Negotiable Affection,' or crib, where sex work occurred. You'll also learn the story of Harriet Pullen, an entrepreneur and amateur historian who ran a long-operating (and respectable) rooming house. The tour ends with a visit to the brothel and a champagne toast.

Scenic & Historic Train Ride
Riding the gold-rush railway

The epic **White Pass & Yukon Route (WPYR) Railway** gives visitors a taste of a bygone era, riding in restored or replica train carriages, along the same route that gold rush stampeders followed more than a century ago. More than just a history lesson, it is also an awesome show of jagged peaks, gushing waterfalls, forested hillsides and otherwise stunning vistas.

The classic experience aboard the WPYR Railway is the 2.5-hour **White Pass Summit Excursion** *(adult/child $150/75)*, a 40-mile round-trip journey that follows the rushing Yukon River, winding up forest-lined slopes and chugging past grand overlooks. A highlight is the shimmering Bridal Veil Falls, which drops into the Skagway River. Dramatic trestle bridges and horseshoe curves yield photogenic views of the train itself. The train slows as you reach the sub-alpine tundra zone of White Pass and the border between Canada and the US. From here, the White Pass Summit Excursion trains return to Skagway. No passport required for this trip.

The 'premier' trip is the all-day **Bennett Scenic Journey** (adult/child $270/135), which continues beyond the pass, traveling a total of 68 miles to Carcross, Yukon. This epic trip includes a stop in Bennett, British Columbia, a gold rush ghost town, where the 1903 train station has been restored. In Carcross, travelers disembark and return to Skagway by bus. The return route follows along the scenic Klondike Hwy, also showing off lake, waterfall and mountain views. Note that you'll need to bring your passport.

Both journeys are narrated by tour guides, who share fascinating details on the history of the railroad line. They also make sure you have your camera ready for the most photogenic moments. Trains run frequently throughout the day between mid-April and late October.

Train to Trail

Ride the rails to a glacier hike

Does an all-day (or even a half-day) scenic train ride sound like too much sitting still? You might opt to disembark at one of two trailheads and spend the day hiking instead. Book special (cheaper) round-trip tickets for the White Pass & Yukon Route 'hiker service.' Trains with dedicated hiker cars run twice a day in each direction. The trails each take about 3½ hours round trip, less if you turn around at the viewpoint.

Note that passengers using the hiker service must bring a passport, even though they don't cross the border.

The **Denver Glacier Trail** (wpyr.com; adult/child $60/30) begins at Mile 6 of the WPYR, where USFS has renovated an old train carriage into the Denver Caboose, a rental cabin of sorts. The trail heads up the east fork of the Skagway River for 2 miles, through old-growth hemlock forest and past Denver Falls. It then swings south and continues another 1.5 miles up the glacial outwash to Denver Glacier. Most of the trail is overgrown with brush, and the second half is particularly tough hiking.

> **BEER FROM TREES**
>
>
>
> **Doug Williamson**, chief tasting officer at Lucy's Bakery (facebook.com/lucysbakeryak), provides insight into one of Skagway's most famous concoctions.
>
> In the 1970s, Dennis Corrington came into town and opened a microbrewery. He found an 18th-century recipe by Captain Cook for spruce-tip beer, something the famous explorer developed to prevent scurvy in his men. Corrington took that recipe, put it into play and it became a huge hit. Years later, this beer still plays an important role in the community. Every spring locals go into the woods, collect spruce tips and bring them to Skagway Brewing Company, where they're brewed into this fantastic beer. It's an amazing thing: a beer that's made from trees.

 EATING IN SKAGWAY: BEST SEAFOOD

Woadie's Southeast Seafood: Sit outside, feast on fresh seafood and drink local beer. A+ for local oysters. *11am-4pm Sun, 10am-7pm Mon-Fri* **$$**

Salty Siren Eats & Tap Room: Creative local seafood, from smoked salmon rillette to peppered prawns, in a waterside setting. *11am-7pm Mon-Fri* **$$$**

Olivia's Bistro: Not just seafood, but also wild game and garden-fresh veggies and herbs. Delightful garden seating. *10.30am-8pm* **$$$**

Skagway Fish Company: A true seafood shack with no-nonsense service and fantastic harbor views. *11am-8pm, to 4pm Sun* **$$$**

BEST TOURS

Sockeye Cycle: Travel out to White Pass Summit by bus or train, then cycle (coast) 15 miles back into town, descending nearly 3300 feet.

Skagway Float Tours: Popular scenic river floats can be combined with a guided hike on the Chilkoot Trail. Located at the Golden North Hotel.

Packer Expeditions: Skagway's oldest trekking company, Packer, offers guided (and catered) 5-day hiking trips on the Chilkoot Trail.

Klondike Tours: Klondike's two popular tours are geared towards the cruise-ship crowd, with a 3-hour scenic bus trip to White Pass and a 5-hour version with dog sledding and gold panning.

An even better option is the **Laughton Glacier Trail** *(wpyr.com; adult/child $100/50)*, which starts at Mile 14. The trail follows the roaring river to its source. It's a 1.5-mile hike through spruce and hemlock forest to the USFS Laughton Glacier Cabin, then another mile to Laughton Glacier, with fantastic alpine scenery all around. This impressive glacier hangs between the 3000ft walls of the Sawtooth Range, and you can hike right up and fill your water bottle with the glacial ice water.

Waterside Treks
Hiking Skagway's trails

Many hikers come to Skagway to tromp across the legendary **Chilkoot Trail** (p126), but Skagway has other rewarding (and more accessible) excursions on foot. Pick up a Skagway trail map from either visitor center.

A short walk from town, the **Dewey Lakes Trail System** leads to a handful of alpine and subalpine lakes and waterfalls. The trailhead is off Spring St, between 3rd and 4th Ave, across the railroad tracks. Plan on a one-hour round trip for the hike to Lower Dewey Lake (1 mile one way to the water's edge), where there are picnic tables, camping spots, and a 2.5-mile trail circling the lake.

From the north end of the lake, an alpine trail ascends steeply to Upper Dewey Lake, 3.5 miles from town. The route then turns south and continues another 1¼ miles further to Devil's Punch Bowl. This is an all-day trip. Alternatively, make reservations to spend the night at the **Upper Dewey Lake cabin** *(skagwayrecreation.org)*.

The Skagway River footbridge, at the foot of the airport runway on 1st Ave, leads to a couple of easy strolls. To reach **Yakutania Point**, turn left at the far side of the bridge and follow the mile-long trail to picnic areas with lovely views. Sheltered Smuggler's Cove lies a quarter mile further on. You can make a loop by hiking up a dirt road behind the cove and descending through the woods to a pet cemetery before heading back to the bridge.

Ghosts of Dyea
Ruins of a gold rush town

In 1898, the town of **Dyea** (die-YEE) was the trailhead for the **Chilkoot Trail** (p126), the shortest route to Lake Bennett, where stampeders began their float to Dawson City. Gold fever

DRINKING IN SKAGWAY: KEEPING IT CRAFTY

Skagway Brewing Co: An iconic brewery and restaurant with a wide variety of beers on offer, including the famous Spruce Tip Blonde Ale. *10am-9pm*

Klondike Brewing: Super cozy spot for delicious craft beers and good vibes, with a sweet beer garden out back. *noon-6pm*

Skagway Spirits: Worth the stroll for brilliant cocktails using house-distilled gin and vodka. Try the rhubarb Collins. *noon-7pm Mon-Thu, to 8pm Fri, to 6pm Sat & Sun*

Kone Kompany: Serving the most refreshing drinks in town: fruit smoothies, specialty shakes and lotus-plant energy drinks. *10am-7pm Mon-Sat, 11am-5pm Sun*

Slide Cemetery

transformed the tiny settlement into a boomtown of 8000 people in the course of months. The glory days were short-lived, however. After the White Pass & Yukon Route railroad was completed in 1900, Dyea quickly died. By 1903, the population had plummeted to just three year-round residents. Today, there are a few crumbling foundations and the remains of Dyea Wharf, but the forest and river have taken over.

The 1-sq-mile **National Historic Site** *(nps.gov/klgo/learn/historyculture/dyea.htm)* is 1½ miles past the Chilkoot Trailhead. It includes five or six 'blocks' from the former town. Signs indicate and show pictures of the buildings that used to stand here, so you can imagine Dyea as a bustling boomtown. The site feels less like a ghost town and more like an empty campsite, but the history is interesting and the setting on the Taiya River is gorgeous. Nearby, **Slide Cemetery** is the final resting place for 47 men and women who perished in an avalanche on the Chilkoot Trail in April 1898.

A half-mile past the historic site, the **Dyea Flats** are a vast and beautiful stretch of tidal flats, where the Taiya River meets the inlet from the Lynn Canal. In summer, the salmon run in the river and the flats are abloom with wildflowers, making this a wonderful place to explore.

Dyea is a 10-mile drive from Skagway along Dyea Rd, with numerous hairpin turns. Pull off to admire the views at the **Skagway Overlook**, a viewing platform 2.5 miles from Skagway. If you don't have a vehicle, you can catch a lift from the SMART taxi service for $15 each way.

You can also get to Dyea by bicycle (or e-bike). And you'll appreciate the wheels as you explore the spread-out sights and attractions. Rent your ride from **Sockeye Cycle** (p118) or **Klondike Electric Bicycles**.

THE TLINGIT CHILKOOT TRAIL

Long before anybody discovered gold in the Yukon, the Tlingit used the Chilkoot Trail as a route for trading with interior tribes. When Russian, British and US merchants arrived on the coast, the Tlingit had almost exclusive access to European products. The Chilkoot Tlingit did not allow others to use their trail, so they became the middlemen in the lucrative fur trade.

At the start of the gold rush, the US Navy reached an agreement with the Chilkoot Tlingit allowing miners to use the trail, as long as they did not interfere with trade. The industrious Chilkoot Tlingit then used their experience and control of the trail to create a packing monopoly, transporting the miners' equipment and goods over the pass.

Places We Love to Stay

$ Budget $$ Midrange $$$ Top End

Ketchikan MAP p64

Ketchikan Hostel $ Located in a Methodist church, this clean, safe (and cheap!) hostel has room for 19 guests in single-sex dorms. No frills, but plenty friendly.

Inn at Creek Street $$ Delightful boutique hotel, showing off 1920s elegance and modern amenities. Located in several different properties along the creek.

Gilmore Hotel $$ A century-old hotel with small but modern rooms, some facing the water. Excellent central location.

My Place $$ Set up for extended stays (with kitchens and laundry), this convenient spot with decent rooms and helpful service is a solid choice for short stays too.

Black Bear Inn $$$ Wonderful waterfront inn with six elegant suites, located 7.5 miles north of town.

Cape Fox Lodge $$$ This opulent hilltop lodge has amenity-filled rooms and an acclaimed restaurant overlooking the city. Alaska Native–owned.

Prince of Wales Island

Great Blue Heron Inn $ Four cozy rooms overlook South Cove harbor in Craig.

Dreamcatcher B&B $$ On the Craig beachfront, Dreamcatcher offers three attractive rooms, homemade breakfast and a wraparound deck with views.

Klawock River Inn $$ Comfortable and affordable, but rather anonymous, this roadside inn overlooks the estuary in Klawock.

Fireweed Lodge $$$ This all-inclusive place on the Klawock River gets rave reviews for its water-view suites, delicious meals and superb fishing.

Wrangell MAP p77

Wrangell Extended Stay $$ Centrally located rooms (with kitchenettes) offer super service and good value.

Stikine Inn (p79) $$$ Rooms are fairly spartan for the price, but 'the Stik' is the center of the action in Wrangell.

Grand View B&B $$$ Ocean- and mountain-view lodging that lives up to its name, with three guest rooms sharing a large kitchen and deck. Breakfast is a highlight.

Petersburg MAP p82

Scandia House $$ Petersburg's most prominent lodging is this light-filled locale, offering cheerful service and complimentary coffee and muffins in the morning.

Tides Inn $$ Sparse but spotless rooms and self-service continental breakfast are the hallmarks of this centrally-located motel.

Sitka MAP p88

Tillie Paul Hostel $ Well-run hostel in a historic building near the Sheldon Jackson campus, offering dorms and private rooms with shared kitchen and bath.

Aspen Suites Hotel $$$ A reliable option for businesslike suites with big windows and well-equipped kitchenettes, all within striking distance of town.

LongLiner Lodge $$$ Excellent accommodations on the working waterfront (which starts to bustle at 4am). Wake up to gorgeous views over Sitka Harbor.

Southeast Resort $$$ Renovated and rebranded in 2025, this central hotel has all the amenities you need, if not a lot of soul.

Cascade Creek Lodge $$$ Two miles north of town, this classy fishing lodge has 10 handsome rooms with private balconies overlooking the ocean.

Juneau MAPS p97, 99

Mendenhall Campground $ USFS campground on the namesake lake, 14 miles north of town. Many sites have views of floating icebergs or the glacier itself.

Juneau Hostel $ An old-school, volunteer-run hostel with bunk beds and cozy common spaces. Beware the daytime lockout.

Driftwood Lodge $ Juneau's best bargain, this Alaska Native-owned motel in Aak'w Village has dated decor but clean rooms and attentive service.

Alaskan Hotel $$ Lots of character at this historic gold rush–era hotel, with both shared-bath and en-suite rooms. The downstairs bar gets rowdy.

Juneau Hotel $$ Suites at this handsome hotel are equipped with a full kitchen, washer and dryer, set on the channel near Tahku the Whale.

Alaska's Capital Inn $$$
Period details mingle with modern comfort inside the gorgeous 1906 home of prospector John Olds.

Silverbow Inn $$$ This charming boutique inn has just 16 rooms, all done up in quirky, contemporary style. The rooftop Jacuzzi is definitely a bonus.

Glacier Bay National Park & Preserve   MAP p110

Bartlett Cove Campground $ Free camping (though you do need a permit) at this NPS facility, just south of the lodge.

Cottonwood Lodge $$
Attractive rooms and several freestanding cabins are set amid forest, about a mile west of Four Corners in Gustavus.

Glacier Bay Lodge $$$ The national park lodge has cozy, wood-paneled rooms, a good restaurant, and easy access to the day boat and Bartlett Cove activities.

Bear Track Inn $$$ This luxurious log-cabin lodge has spacious rooms, a highly-rated restaurant, and its own roster of activities on offer.

Haines   MAP p116

Sheltered Harbor $ A warm welcome is guaranteed at this sweet B&B near Fort Seward. Generous homemade breakfast ensures you will not leave hungry.

Aspen Suites $$ Guests love the comfort and convenience of this modern, all-suite hotel. The whole operation exudes a polished sheen.

Hotel Halsingland (p115) **$$** Historic hotel on the grounds of Fort Seward, with old-fashioned rooms and atmospheric touches like fireplaces and claw-footed tubs.

Beach Roadhouse $$ About a mile out of town, this forest-bound B&B includes spacious rooms and rustic cabins, offering easy access to Battery Point Trail.

Skagway   MAP p124

Morning Wood $ Handsome hotel with plain but comfortable digs – some with shared bathrooms – in a location just a few blocks away from the buzz.

Chilkoot Trail Outpost $$ Hitting the 'Koot? Sleep in a cozy Sitka spruce cabin, followed by a satisfying breakfast, and you're just a half-mile from the trailhead.

At the White House $$ Antiques and remembrances of the Klondike fill the large, historic nine-room inn.

Historic Skagway Inn $$$ An 1897 Victorian original and former brothel, this inn's small but lovely vintage rooms are named for women from gold-rush history.

Historic Skagway Inn

Above: Snowboarder, Mt Alyeska (p174); Right Anchorage Museum (p148)

Researched by Kevin Raub

Anchorage & Around

LOCALLY ROOTED URBAN PLAYGROUND, INCREDIBLE NATURE

Alaska's biggest city offers the state's best urban respite, surrounded by some of North America's most astonishing natural scenery and attractions.

British explorer Captain James Cook sailed past what is current-day Anchorage as far back as 1779 in his pursuit for the elusive Northwest Passage. A century later, optimistic gold prospectors descended on Ship Creek, which today runs just off the city's compact downtown, in hopes of striking it rich. But it wasn't until 1915, when the Alaska Railroad settled in and the 'Great Anchorage Lot Sale' was held, that a tent city of 2000 leapt to life faster than a salmon runs. Today, locals like to say that Anchorage is only 30 minutes from Alaska: wedged between 5000ft peaks and an inlet filled with salmon and whales. While more of a jumping-off point for further exploration north towards Denali National Park or east towards Prince William Sound and Seward and beyond for most folks, there's no shortage of thirst-quenching breweries, excellent restaurants and quirky 'Alaskana' kitsch to kill time between outdoor adventures. Right on nature's doorstep, it's a wonderful spot to play hard. Outside town, kayaking, biking and hiking opportunities abound, especially around the stunning glacier-and-peak-ringed Eklutna Lake, the largest body of water in Chugach State Park, America's fourth-largest state park. Midwestern-farmer-settled Palmer, 43 miles northeast of town, throws a bit of history and culture into the mix, while Girdwood, 40 miles southeast, serves up Alaska's only destination ski resort.

THE MAIN AREAS

ANCHORAGE
Nature-surrounded urban hub, Alaska's biggest. **p142**

PALMER
Historic agriculture colony unique to Alaska. **p163**

GIRDWOOD
Charming ski resort off Turnagain Arm. **p172**

Find Your Way

Just under 300,000 people call Anchorage Municipality home, but it encompasses a massive 1961 sq miles that's home to 40% of Alaska's population. Girdwood and Palmer are both under an hour's drive from the city.

BUS

Anchorage's public transport, known as **People Mover** *(muni.org)*, is decent but won't be winning any innovative transport awards. Cash fares are $2 (or $5 for a day pass). Girdwood and Palmer can be reached by limited public transport and charter bus services.

CAR

Having your own wheels greatly enhances Anchorage exploration opportunities, though car-rental rates are extremely high, so it's important to factor that into your budget. Avoid an extra 25-30% in airport rental fees by renting in town; or consider Turo *(turo.com)* to (possibly) help ease the pain.

TRAIN

The celebrated **Alaska Railroad** (p157) stops at Girdwood along its Coastal Classic Route from Anchorage to Seward, but fares are stiff if you are just using it as transport *(adult/child from $100/50)*. You're better off in a rental car.

Anchorage, p142

Built on the back of the great Alaska Railroad, Anchorage offers urban respite (great restaurants, fun breweries, stylish shopping) against epic alpine scenery.

Palmer, p163
Distinctive agriculture colony fashioned by President Franklin D Roosevelt's 1930s New Deal – historic farming buildings, fine food and drink and astonishing mountain landscapes.

Girdwood, p172
Small hamlet in a scenic valley that's home to Alyeska, Alaska's only destination ski resort, and a handful of excellent bars and restaurants.

THE GUIDE

ANCHORAGE & AROUND

Plan Your Time

Home to Alaska's biggest international airport and a Southcentral travel hub, Anchorage is a place most travelers pass through, but consider holing up awhile to discover its more inconspicuous virtues. It's also a good base for rewarding day trips.

Tony Knowles Coastal Trail (p152)

In & Out

● For a perfect day in **Anchorage** (p142), start off with a 'crabby' omelet or a salmon cake Benedict at **Snow City Café** (p143) before either hopping on a bike to track moose along the **Tony Knowles Coastal Trail** (p152) or hike **Flattop Mountain** (p146).

● For lunch, indulge in halibut tacos at downtown favorite **Humpy's Great Alaskan Alehouse** (p143) or one of the world's most memorable halibut sandwiches at **White Spot Cafe** (p143). In the afternoon, devote a solid few hours to catch up on Alaska Native culture at the world-class **Anchorage Museum** (p148).

● Come happy hour, don't miss excellent craft beers on the panoramic rooftop at **Forty-Ninth State Brewing** (p143) then set your sights on salmon: **Glacier Brewhouse** (p143) or **Simon & Seafort's** (p151) are standouts.

Seasonal Highlights

Long dark winters and summers under the midnight sun characterize Anchorage's extreme seasonality.

JANUARY

Beery festivities makes light of dark winter days – Anchorage and elsewhere host craft-beer events. Otherwise, light is in short supply (daily sunlight: 5–6.5 hours) and temperatures barely creep into the teens most days. Brrrr!

MARCH

The **Iditarod Trail Sled Dog Race** officially kicks off near Wasilla after its ceremonial start in Anchorage the day before. Daily temperatures still hover below freezing most days but folks around Anchorage begin to see the light.

MAY

Tourism roars to life alongside the Salmon run! King salmon (Chinook) and silver salmon (coho) speed through Anchorage's **Ship Creek** late May through July; tourism starts up while crowds and prices remain relatively tolerable.

A Few Days to Linger

● Spend a day or two absorbing **Anchorage's** greatest hits (p151), discovering its fantastic craft-beer scene, wonderful seafood restaurants and incredibly close nature. Don't miss the halibut sandwich at downtown's **White Spot Café** (p143).

● Rent some wheels and head northeast towards **Eagle River** (p159) and **Eklutna** (p161). Drive the scenic Eagle River Road to the **Eagle River Nature Center** (p159) and go for a walk in the woods. Nearby, **Thunderbird Falls** (p161) is an easy, family-friendly hike with a big payoff. Eagle River evenings must begin at **Odd Man Rush Brewing** (p161).

● Set aside some time for kayaking on gorgeous **Eklutna Lake** (p161) as well, stopping to take in the fascinating **Eklutna Village Historical Park** along the way – one of the area's few cultural offerings.

A Week to See It All

● Venture out of downtown Anchorage to explore the artsy charms of neighborhoods like **Spenard** and **Midtown**, home to scores of independent, locally run businesses. Cool galleries/shops like **Dos Manos** (p155) and **Hulin Alaskan Design Clothing Co** (p155), restaurants/bars like **Arctic Roadrunner** (p155) and **Chilkoot Charlie's** (p154) and pilgrimage-worthy taprooms all warrant exploration.

● Spend a few days in pleasant **Palmer** (p163), soaking up the town's interesting history and wonderful restaurants like **Feather & Flour**'s fantastic farm-to-table **Slow Day Café** (p165) and some of the best ice cream in Alaska at **Big Dipper** (p165).

● Drive the **Turnagain Arm** (p162) to **Girdwood** (p172) for either the state's finest meal at **Seven Glaciers** (p175) and/or the best skiing infrastructure at **Alyeska Resort** (p174).

JUNE
Summer Solstice Festival (along with pride and history in the Anchorage region) highlight the most festive month. Weather can be unpredictable (cold one day, record-setting heat advisory the next) and big crowds have yet to arrive.

JULY
The year's highest average temps – 62°F (17°C) – spur festivities: arts, music and bohemian vibes at the **Girdwood Forest Fair**; music, cultural events and the famed Slippery Salmon Olympics at Eagle River's **Bear Paw Festival** (p161).

AUGUST
Food and fun galore – including big-name musical acts - highlight Palmer's famed **Alaska State Fair** (p167) from late August to early September. Mild weather makes for a fine time for hiking and other outdoor activities.

DECEMBER
Slopes open at Girdwood's **Alyeska Resort** (p174); day and night runs are available, though it's mostly night all day (there are lights)! The **Alaska Native Heritage Center Holiday Bazaar** features over 60 Native artisans.

Anchorage

MUSEUMS | FOOD & DRINK | OUTDOOR ADVENTURES

☑ TOP TIP

The **Flattop Mountain Shuttle** *(US$25)* travels to and from the Glen Alps trailhead daily from late May to early September, departing **Downtown Bicycle Rental** *(alaska-bike-rentals.com)* at 12:15pm, returning at 4.30pm. There are plenty of scenic Anchorage views to take in along the way.

Alaska's biggest city shares few traits with elsewhere. Enveloped by the extraordinary peaks of the Alaska Range on the northern horizon, the Chugach Mountains on its eastern doorstep and the Gulf of Alaska's Cook Inlet and its outstretched Arms to the west and south, its incredible surroundings are undeniable. What is less obvious are the charms of the city itself. Anchorage isn't easy on the eyes. From an architectural standpoint – save a handful of historic buildings and the modern Anchorage Museum, of course – the rambling city is mostly a microcosm of some of America's least-innovative ideas: strip malls, monotonous office buildings, suburban sprawl. But a closer look reveals an interesting twist. The typical chains that would normally anchor such architecture (Target, Subway, Pizza Hut) are far harder to stumble across here, instead replaced by a cavalcade of locally owned, independent businesses running on the state's free-spirited nature.

Anchorage Away!

MAPS P144 & P147

An Alaska big city best-of

Anchorage's bricks-and-mortar aesthetic harbors restaurants serving the world's best salmon and halibut, breweries churning out fantastic craft beer, a wealth of both

---

 GETTING AROUND

Downtown Anchorage is walkable but otherwise the city spreads far and wide (perhaps surprisingly, it actually clocks in as the fourth-largest city in the US by area). The **People Mover** (p138; *muni.org*) city bus system covers it decently, but you really need a car (or at least a bike) for efficient mobility.

Over 120 miles of paved bike and multiuse trails canvas the municipality, connecting many parks and neighborhoods and allowing for traffic-free, two-wheel movement around parts of the city. In winter, add 130 miles of plowed winter walkways and 105 miles of maintained ski trails to the mix as well.

Snow City Café

frontier and **Alaska Native** culture, and a fiercely local-driven ethos. Start at **Snow City Café** *(snowcitycafe.com)*, an artsy, award-winning destination-breakfast joint for purveyors of finer morning things. Go for a 'crabby' omelet ($23) or a salmon cake Benedict ($21).

Downtown Anchorage is a walkable delight of scenic overlooks and locally run businesses inhabiting a compact grid rubbing up against the shores of **Cook Inlet**. Take a gander at the **Oscar Anderson House** *(oscarandersonhouse museum.org)*, the city's oldest wooden-framed home (1915). Though closed indefinitely for renovations, the house museum was the humble abode of Anchorage's 18th settler, a Swede who turned right at Seattle and headed northwest.

Need a pick-me-up? The **Fire Island Rustic Bakeshop** *(fireislandbread.com)*, inside the trendy **K Street Market**, is a local staple doing scrumptious things with artisan baked goods, including incredible scones. For something more substantial, indulge in Alaska's fine seafood at downtown favorites **Humpy's Great Alaskan Alehouse** *(humpysalaska.com; main courses $16–30)* or **Glacier Brewhouse** *(glacier brewhouse.com; main courses $16–57)* – both do wonderful things with salmon, king crab or halibut, chased with a bounty of local brews. And whatever you do, don't miss lunch at the **White Spot Café** *(facebook.com/thewhitespotcafe)*, a bygone-era diner serving an Alaska-famous monster of a halibut sandwich, fried to golden brown perfection ($24). In the evenings, it's all about excellent craft beer, great pub food and outstanding patio views at **Forty-Ninth State Brewing** *(49thstatebrewing.com)*. There are 18 (repeating) taps on every floor and a newly added streetside patio with food trucks.

BAKED JAZZ

Duke Russell (@papaduke123, dukerussell.com), a tried-and-true Alaskan and man-about-Anchorage, shares his tips on the city. A local artist and musician, his quirky and colorful prints, stickers and cards decorate restaurants all over the city.

When you feel like taking a break from the bar scene, head to **Monday Night Jazz** from 6.30pm to 9.30pm at **Fire Island Rustic Bakeshop** at the **K Street Market** downtown. When the bakery shuts down, the jazz turns up with a house band and guest performers lighting up the stage. During the day, K Street Market is a one-stop shop for coffee, lunch at **That Feeling Co** (p156), desserts at Fire Island and specialty beer, wine and liquor at **La Bodega** *(labodegastore.com)*.

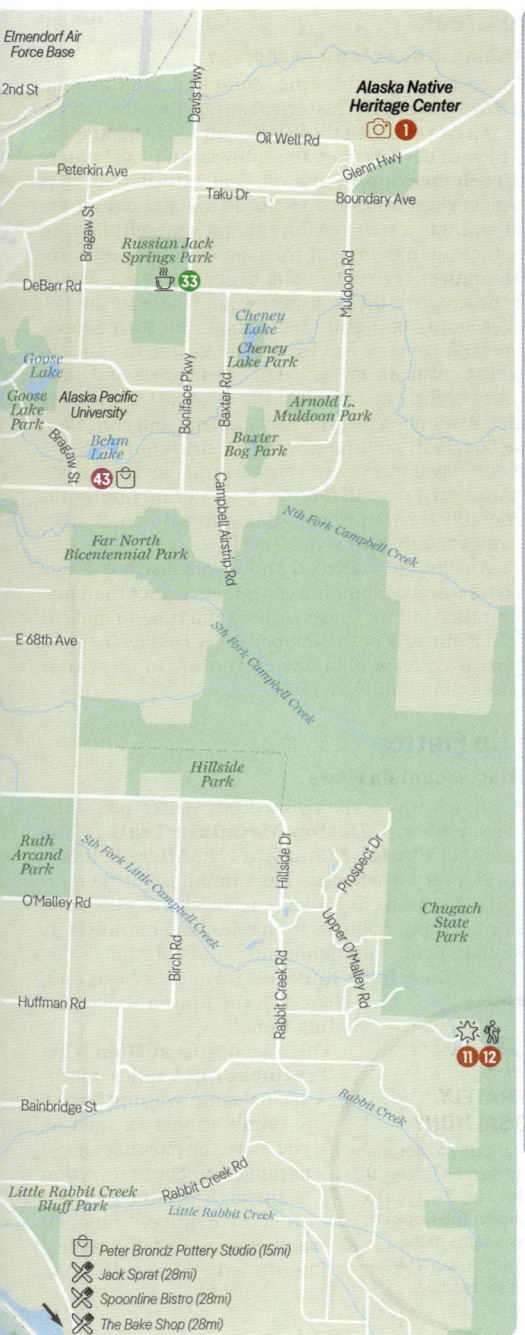

HIGHLIGHTS
1. Alaska Native Heritage Center

SIGHTS
2. Alaska Aviation Museum
3. ANC Viewpoint
4. Downtown Anchorage Viewpoint
5. Earthquake Park
6. Kincaid Park
7. Point Woronzof Overlook
8. Spenard Beach Park
9. Westchester Lagoon

ACTIVITIES
10. Alaska Photo Treks
11. Flattop Mountain Trail
12. Glen Alps Trailhead
13. Regal Air
14. Rust's Flying Service

SLEEPING
15. Aloft
16. Base Camp Anchorage Hostel
17. Lake Hood Inn

EATING
18. Arctic Roadrunner
19. Bear Tooth Grill
20. Charlie's Bakery
21. Fromagio's Artisan Cheese
22. Middle Way Cafe
23. Moose's Tooth Brewpub
24. PHOnatik
25. Rustic Goat
26. Spenard Roadhouse
see 17 The Deck at Lake Hood
27. Tommy's Burgers
28. Wild Scoops
29. Wooden Spoons

DRINKING & NIGHTLIFE
30. Anchorage Brewing Company
31. Anchorage Distillery
32. Black Cup Coffee
33. Caffé D'Arte
34. Chilkoot Charlie's
35. Cynosure Brewing
36. King Street Brewery
37. Midnight Sun Brewing Company
38. SteamDot
39. Turnagain Brewing

SHOPPING
40. Alaska Mountaineering & Hiking
41. Dos Manos
42. Hulin Alaskan Design Clothing Co
43. The Craft Shop at ANMC

INFORMATION
44. Visit Anchorage Visitor Information Center

TRANSPORT
see 17 Lake Hood Bike Rentals
45. Lake Hood Seaplane Base
46. Ted Stevens Anchorage International Airport

BEST TOUR AGENCIES

Alaska Photo Treks: *(alaskaphototreks.com)* Year-round, day/multiday professional photographer-led safaris that frame Alaska's stunning natural beauty for budding wildlife paparazzi.

Alaska Trail Guides: *(alaskatrailguides.com)* Go-to agency for getting out and about on two wheels, especially the Tony Knowles Coastal Trail.

Salmon Berry Travel & Tours: *(salmonberrytours.com)* A popular choice for a day of snow and ice on Matanuska Glacier, the largest roadside glacier in Alaska.

Rust's Flying Service: *(flyrusts.com)* Offers three-hour Denali flights, including magnificent 40-mile-long Ruth Glacier ($525), as well as tours around Anchorage and Prince William Sound.

Regal Air: *(regal-air.com)* Flying from Lake Hood, Regal Air specializes in scenic flights (Denali, Knik Glacier, among others) and backcountry bear-viewing excursions.

Up Ship Creek

MAP P147

Salmon fishing in downtown Anchorage

From mid- to late summer, king, coho and pink salmon spawn up **Ship Creek,** the historical site of Tanaina Indian fish camp. You can cheer on those love-starved fish humping their way toward destiny from the spillway and fish ladders at **Ship Creek Overlook Park** off East Whitney Rd, but when in Anchorage, do as the locals do and get out on the water and wrangle a trophy king salmon yourself! During high tide, these banks just off the heart of downtown are lined with anglers trying to hook dinner in what has to be one of the greatest urban fisheries anywhere in the US.

Ship Creek's only bait-and-tackle shop, the **Bait Shack** *(thebaitshackak.com)*, is run by salmon evangelist Dustin Slinker, whose enthusiasm has led to day-trippers and business travelers reeling in a trophy king after just 15 minutes in the water. A complete fishing package (rod and reel, waders, tackle box, bait, landing net and all the required State of Alaska one-day nonresident sport-fishing licenses) costs $120 for those aged over 16 for a 24-hour period (under 16s pay considerably less). Once you snag your salmon, Slinker can fillet and vacuum seal it for travel.

As this is Anchorage's railroad and warehouse basin, the scenery skews towards shipping containers rather than majestic mountains, but for those without the time to make it to the Kenai Peninsula or the Copper River Delta, it's tough to beat for convenience. And fine craft beers to toast your catch are less than a mile away!

Falling Up Flattop

MAP P144

Urban hiking, mountain views

If there's a quick way to bag your first Alaska peak, the three-mile round-trip **Flattop Mountain Trail** to the 3510ft summit of **Flattop Mountain** is it. After all, this is the first peak every Anchorage kid summits. But be forewarned: this is not an easy hike (and these are kids from Alaska we're talking about!). Its namesake summit is as big as a football field, with panoramic views of Anchorage, Cook Inlet, Knik and Turnagain Arms and, on a clear day, the Alaska Range, including Denali.

The hike begins at **Glen Alps Trailhead**, 15.5 miles southeast of downtown, and begins to climb almost as soon as you leave the parking lot ($5 parking fee). The first section is through a wind-twisted grove of hemlock, but you soon emerge to talus slopes. There's a brief respite at a

DESPERATELY SEEKING SALMON?

Ship Creek is a great place to get your feet wet with a bit of salmon fishing 101, but head to **Cordova** (p204) if you're a more serious angler. The **Copper River** produces some of the world's best salmon, aka 'The Wagyu of seafood.'

ANCHORAGE CITY CENTER

★ HIGHLIGHTS
1 Anchorage Museum

● SIGHTS
2 Oscar Anderson House
3 Ship Creek Overlook Park

● ACTIVITIES
4 Bait Shack
5 Salmon Berry Travel & Tours

● SLEEPING
6 Copper Whale Inn
7 Historic Anchorage Hotel
8 Oscar Gill House
9 Salted Roots Basecamp
10 Susitna Place
11 Wildbirch Hotel

● EATING
12 Club Paris
13 Fire Island Rustic Bakeshop
14 Humpy's Great Alaskan Alehouse
see 6 Simon & Seafort's
15 Snow City Cafe
16 Whisky & Ramen
17 White Spot Cafe

● DRINKING & NIGHTLIFE
18 Bernie's Bungalow Lounge
19 Crow's Nest
20 Forty-Ninth State Brewing
21 Glacier BrewHouse
22 La Bodega
23 Tent City Taphouse
24 That Feeling Co.

● SHOPPING
25 Oomingmak Musk Ox Producers Co-op
26 Sevigny Studio

● TRANSPORT
27 Downtown Bicycle Rental
28 Flattop Mountain Shuttle
see 28 Tony Knowles Coastal Trail

THE GUIDE ANCHORAGE & AROUND ANCHORAGE

147

TOP EXPERIENCE

Anchorage Museum

Striking architecture, fascinating homegrown art and thoughtful, often tongue-in-cheek temporary exhibits highlight Anchorage's cultural jewel, a world-class museum that does anything but blend into Anchorage's downtown landscape. Dating to 1966 but dramatically expanded by award-winning architects over the years, its conspicuous glass-facade now reveals something different, including the state's largest Alaska Native collection.

Exhibit, Anchorage Museum

TOP TIPS

● Extended hours on the first Friday of the month (6-9pm) offer free admission.

● Don't saunter past the museum shop – it's one of the best you'll see, featuring unique jewelry, art and foodstuffs.

● Don't miss the **Alaska Exhibition Gallery**, a contemporary showcase highlighting Alaska life and history.

PRACTICALITIES

● *anchoragemuseum.org*
● adult/child $25/12
● 10am-6pm

A Skyline Redefined

While much of Anchorage's downtown architecture counts khaki-hued utilitarian as its standout feature, Alaska's largest museum – with a shimmering, fritted glass-facade stacked in varying heights designed by award-winning David Chipperfield Architects – seemingly blends into the city's soaring surrounds, at once both reflecting the Anchorage cityscape and, when seen from the air, almost melding to the greater mountainous panorama that flanks the city. Admiring this striking work from the museum's birch-forested garden is an experience in itself.

Treasures of Alaska

Start on the 4th floor and work your way down towards the museum's flagship exhibit (2nd floor), **Living Our Cultures, Sharing Our Heritage: The First Peoples of Alaska** (part of the Smithsonian Arctic Studies Center and the largest and longest loan ever made by the Smithsonian Institution). It beautifully displays more than 600 Alaska Native objects, including some incredible parkas hewn from ground squirrel, caribou, wolf and wolverine furs, crested auklets and guillemot skin, and mountain sheep skin depending on the tribal entity (Yup'ik and St Lawrence Island Yupik are our favorites). Traditional Yup'ik masks are also a highlight.

saddle before your final push to the summit. You'll need to scramble the last few hundred feet; the trail here is marked by spray-painted rocks.

Give yourself 90 minutes to climb the short but steep trail (1350ft altitude in 1.7 miles) and an hour to get back down. Bring sturdy shoes, plenty of water and a hat and jacket. Always be wary of wildlife (moose and bears in summer).

The trail is closed in winter, and snow and mud can be rampant even in June, so novice and/or casual hikers should reconsider in these conditions (the easy 1.5-mile Blueberry Loop circles Flattop at a lower elevation and bags many of the same astonishing views).

Beers in the Last Frontier

MAPS P144 & P147

An Anchorage brewery pilgrimage

Nearly 60 craft breweries call Alaska home – the state ranks an impressive 4th in the USA for breweries per capita, according to the independent craft-brewing advocacy group the Brewers Association. Expectedly, Anchorage's beer and brewery scene pulls the preponderance of those pints – 13 breweries call this hophead heaven home. It would be unwise to attempt them all on a short visit, so here's a curated list of favorites.

Bear in mind, Alaska taproom laws are strict: 36oz per person per day (so, three beers), no entertainment is allowed (no TVs, no games) and last call is a frighteningly early 9pm (breweries with restaurants and full liquor licenses are a different story).

If you want to simply plant yourself in one convenient place and sample your way though the scene, downtown's **Tent City Taphouse** (*facebook.com/tentcitytaphouse*) dedicates all of its 24 taps to Alaska microbreweries and boasts an updated drinking patio as well.

Big Swig Tours (*bigswigtours.com*) offers an Anchorage Brews tour ($169) Wednesday to Sunday year-round. Owner/hoperator Bryan Caenepeel has spent a decade cultivating relationships with local beer geeks; as a result, his behind-the-scenes access and camaraderie with local brewers makes for a world-class suds sojourn. You'll hit at least three breweries (they vary), kicking off at the perky hour of 2.30pm.

THE GOLDEN SPIKE RETURNETH

One of the newest and most remarkable acquisitions of the **Anchorage Museum** (p148) is the 2025 return of the Alaska Railroad's **Golden Spike**, originally gifted to one of the railway's chief engineers, Colonel Frederick Mears, in 1923. That same year, it was lent to US President Warren G. Harding, who drove this final spike into the rails near Nenana, 305 miles north of Anchorage (the only time a sitting US president has driven a railroad spike). It remained in the private ownership of the Mears family and numerous private collectors over the years. In 2025, the Anchorage Museum acquired the spike for $201,600 via auction, allowing its return to its rightful home in the museum's Alaska Exhibition.

The go-to place after conquering Flattop Mountain!

 EATING IN ANCHORAGE: BEST OF THE REST — MAP P144

Fromagio's Artisan Cheese: Gourmet cheesemonger and specialty sandwich café. Perfect stocking up for a hike picnic. *10.30am-6pm Mon-Fri, 9.30am-5pm Sat, 11am-4pm Sun* $

Rustic Goat: Loft-evoking bistro; seasonal comfort fusion and creative pizzas with occasional local nod (Kodiak Weathervane scallops, reindeer sausage). *4-9pm Thu-Mon* $$

Bear Tooth Grill: Wildly popular hangout attached to converted theaterpub. Burgers, Alaska seafood, globally inspired fusion. *11am-9pm Mon-Thu, to 10pm Fri, 10am-10pm Sat, 10am-9pm Sun* $$

Moose's Tooth: Midtown brewpub commanding crowds for gourmet pizza (fantastic crust!), oven-baked sandwiches and 20 taps of local craft beer. *10.30am-11pm Mon-Fri, from 11am Sat & Sun* $$

A BEER BOSS' FAVORITES

Cindy Drinkwater, co-owner of **Cynosure Brewing** in Anchorage, highlights a few of her favorite things about Alaska's biggest city. *@cynosurebrewing*

Trails! That's one thing I love about Anchorage. In the winter, you can access 170km of groomed cross-country ski trails connecting the mountains to Turnagain Arm. In the summer, the options for biking and running are similarly fabulous. Visitors should check out the **Tony Knowles Coastal Trail** (p152), easily explored by foot or rental bike from downtown. My favorite post-workout stops are **That Feeling Co.** (p156) for coffee (and plants!) or **Fromagio's Artisan Cheese** (p149) for a fab avocado melt. Plus, Fromagio's shares space with the Georgia Blue Gallery showcasing beautiful and intriguing artwork.

Don't be too concerned about day drinking; in Alaska, at least in summer, you're always day-drinking anyway!

Before exploring breweries further afield, there's no better starting point than wildly popular **Forty-Ninth State Brewing** *(49thstatebrewing.com)*, downtown Anchorage's top craft-beer destination occupying a former 1917 Elks Lodge building near Ship Creek. The brewery's famed Solstice IPA started it all, but founder David McCarthy especially shines when he calls on Alaska's local bounty (the fantastic Spruceplosion IPA, for example, is a Mosaic and Citra hop bomb accented by Alaska Sitka spruce tips).

Like a proper microbrewery should be, **Cynosure Brewing** *(cynosure.beer)* is appropriately tucked away (and signless) in an unremarkable industrial area two miles east of Spenard. If you're indifferent to the IPA brigade, you'll find haven in its intimate, 12-draught taproom. German and Belgium styles dominate (there's an excellent Rauchbier made with smoked beechwood, Helles Bocks, Saisons and Tripels) and they go down steps from the tanks. Further south, several worthwhile breweries congregate in an industrial area about six miles below downtown, affectionately referred to as the 'Beermuda Triangle' by enthusiasts.

Similarly positioned in industrial surrounds, **Midnight Sun Brewing** *(midnightsunbrewing.com)* is Anchorage's oldest brewery, dating to 1995. Its loft taproom features 16 taps and two handpumps and is the best bet, both geographically and gastronomically, for a food stop – serving green chili hummus, Ancho beef dip and

ANOTHER ROUND?

Head 43 miles northeast out of Anchorage along the Knik Arm to **Palmer** (0000), the other great drinking town in the Anchorage metropolitan area.

Forty-Ninth State Brewing

more. They were pouring a white stout on our visit (Snow Went Down to Georgia) that might be Anchorage's most perfect beer.

Don't miss a pint with former general surgeon Ted Rosenzweig, who hung up his medical scrubs in favor of wrangling his own wild yeasts at tiny **Turnagain Brewing** (*turnagainbrewing.com*), Anchorage's destination brewery for sours, wild ales and other results of Rosenzweig's mad scientist-like experimentation. At **King Street Brewery** (*kingstreetbrewing.com*), brewer Max Crutch unleashes classics, including an outstanding Czech-style pils, Bavarian-style hefeweizens and an enormous imperial stout that will set you straight in Alaska's dark winter. With pours starting at $6.50, this is some of the state's best-value drinking. Next door, **Anchorage Brewing Company** (*anchoragebrewing.company*) excels at double hazy IPAs and other hop-forward styles among giant foeders as scenic drinking backdrops.

Sidenote: there are an estimated 1500 moose in Anchorage, and sharing your beer with one is illegal in Alaska.

WHERE TO HAVE 'ONLY IN ALASKA' MOMENTS

James Beard semi-finalist **Laile Fairbairn** is the owner of **Snow City Café** (p143) and several other go-to Anchorage restaurants. She reveals her perfect day off.
@snowcitycafe

For a perfect day off in Anchorage, drive to **Girdwood**, get breakfast at **The Bake Shop** (sourdough pancakes!), hike the beginning of **Crow Pass** then get dinner at **Spoonline Bistro** (p177) or **Jack Sprat** before calling it a night. On the way back, be sure to stop at **Peter Brondz Pottery Studio** in **Bird Creek**. Here you can experience one of those unique, 'only in AK' moments. The studio is always open, you pick something out and then leave your money in the box.

Creative schmears include smoked salmon and spicy kimchi!

 EATING IN ANCHORAGE: BEST OF THE REST — MAPS P144 & P147

| **Middle Way Café:** Cozy and casual café serving hearty (or healthy!) breakfasts, organic salads, soups and sandwiches. *7am-5pm Mon-Fri, from 8am Sat & Sun* $ | **Simon & Seafort's:** Classic surf and turf standout; expensive but wonderful king/sockeye salmon and absolutely divine panko-crusted halibut cheeks. *11.30am-10pm Mon-Sat, to 9pm Sun* $$$ | **Whisky & Ramen:** Unanimous superstar; rich, authentic ramen and superb mixology accented by minimalist décor. Reserve! *5-10.30pm Sun-Thu, to midnight Fri & Sat* $$ | **Wooden Spoons:** Locals claim these are Alaska's best bagels. That might be too limiting – they rival bagels anywhere! Fat, detour-worthy breakfast sandwiches. *7.30am-2pm Tue-Fri, 8am-noon Sat* $ |

CYCLING TOUR

Cruisin' the Coast

The two-hour, 11-mile **Tony Knowles Coastal Trail** hugs Knik Arm as it unravels through moose-heavy birch forest on its way to Kincaid Park. Fantastic views abound: of Cook Inlet and the Alaska Range. Choose your adventure: hire a bike to cycle out and back or go with **Alaska Trail Guides** (p146; *alaskatrailguides.com*; adult/child $119/105), who begin at Kincaid Park and take a leisurely, mostly downhill route back to Anchorage, allowing you to soak up the scenery.

1 Westchester Lagoon

Margaret Eagan Sullivan Park, 1.5 miles southwest of the downtown trailhead at 2nd and H St, is home to the waterfowl haven also known as **Westchester Lagoon**. Moose sightings here aren't uncommon and all manner of waterbirds (ducks, mallards, geese, wigeons) congregate. It's a popular spot for family picnics, canoodling couples and leisurely kayakers.

The Ride: From Westchester Lagoon, follow the trail southwest for 2.9 miles to the western end of Northern Lights Blvd on the Knik Arm.

2 Earthquake Park

When the 9.2 magnitude Good Friday earthquake rocked Anchorage in 1964, a massive landslide known as the Turnagain Heights Slide wiped out an entire residential neighborhood, taking down 75 homes and four lives along with it. For decades, the apocalyptic aftermath remained a barren

Bull moose, Kincaid Park

moonscape; today, it's memorialized as the 134-acre **Earthquake Park**.

The Ride: Follow the trail 0.7 miles northwest as you begin to ascend above Cook Inlet, taking in Anchorage skyline views along the way.

3 Downtown Anchorage Viewpoint

On a clear day, this **viewpoint** frames vistas of Anchorage's modest skyline for several miles along the coastal trail. The 22-story, 296ft Conoco-Phillips Building – Alaska's tallest – dominates the view.

The Ride: The roar of jet engines will guide you 0.8 miles northwest along the trail towards Ted Stevens Anchorage International Airport.

4 Plane-spotting ANC

Depending on flight patterns of the day, this popular **viewpoint** serves up intensely close and thunderously loud plane-spotting opportunities as aircraft take off or land at Alaska's busiest airport. It's an especially crucial entertainment stop for those traveling with little people.

The Ride: From here the coastal trail curves south around Pt Woronzof, a 0.4-mile ride from the airport.

5 Point Woronzof Overlook

Named after 19th-century Russian ambassador Count Simon Romanovitch Woronzof, **Point Woronzof Overlook** isn't much more than a parking lot, but offers spectacular views of coastal tidelands and the mountain ranges north of Cook Inlet.

The Ride: It's 4.9 miles south to the coastal trail's turnaround point at Kincaid Park.

6 Kincaid Park

The 1516-acre **Kincaid Park** is one of the city's best for both wildlife and outdoor adventuring. Moose sightings are extremely common, and there are bald eagles and black bears. There are 40 miles of groomed ski trails (some of which are illuminated in winter).

COFFEE CHRONICLES

While not uncommon throughout the Pacific Northwest, free-standing **coffee huts** (small, drive-thru/walk-up kiosks peddling jitter juice) are definitely next level in Anchorage. Coffee huts blanket the city's landscape (along with brick-and-mortar, an estimated 170 at last count). Climate is a factor – with temperatures averaging well below zero during Alaska's harsh winter months, nobody wants to leave the confines of their well-heated vehicle – but the real reason may be more to do with food safety regulations. In Alaska, food service establishments with a capacity of fewer than 12 people are not required to connect to a water line (rules in the Lower 48 are generally stricter). As a result, coffee huts have sprung up virtually anywhere!

Visit Anchorage Visitor Information Center

Alaska Native History and Culture MAP P144

Explore Anchorage's Alaska Native Heritage Center

To gain a broader understanding of Alaska Native culture and history, Anchorage's **Alaska Native Heritage Center** *(alaskanative.net; adult/child $30/20)*, 7 miles east of downtown, is a pricey but unmissable excursion from the city center. The entire facility is a language, art and cultural knowledge bank of incalculable value. Spread over 26 acres, it does a wonderful job of recreating life in the interior and offers fascinating insight into Alaska Native traditions. It feels notably unforced – it's not a show for tourism purposes but rather a vehicle to educate visitors on the history, issues and customs of Alaska's Indigenous peoples. A shuttle ($25) leaves from the **Visit Anchorage Visitor Information Center** six times a day from 9am to 3pm from mid-May to mid-September.

As long as the shades are not drawn!

DRINKING IN ANCHORAGE: OUR PICKS   MAPS P144 & P147

Bernie's Bungalow Lounge: See-and-be-seen venue; large outdoor patio is the city's best for live music. *11am-10pm Tue-Thu, to 1.30am Fri, 3pm-1.30am Sat, 3-11pm Sun*

Chilkoot Charlie's: Rambling local drinking den with live music and log cabin-esque nooks and crannies across 10 or so different spaces. *11-2.30am Sun-Thu, to 3am Fri & Sat*

Anchorage Distillery: Modern distillery south of downtown for cocktails craft-distilled with glacial water, Alaska-grown barley, etc. *3-8pm Wed-Thu & Sun, to 9pm Fri & Sat*

Crow's Nest: Million-dollar Cook Inlet views pair fantastically with award-winning cocktails at the top of Hotel Captain Cook. Also Anchorage's fanciest restaurant. *5-9pm Tue-Sat*

Check ahead for the daily schedule and time your visit for two captivating demonstrations: Alaska Native Games, which sees Alaska Native young adults showcase village games like the one-hand reach, Alaskan high kick and, our favorite, the seal hop (the knuckle version is brutal!); and the Alaska Native dance featuring traditional Yupik dancing with detailed explanations of the meaning of various moves and how they correspond to the song and dance storytelling.

Then explore the main building, which houses the newly added Hall of Cultures, home to small but extremely well-done temporary exhibitions on Alaska Native history and culture. Through 2027, the poignant 'Education in Alaska: Disruptions to Our Traditional Teaching' exhibition details painful but necessary insight into the 19th and 20th century forced removals and assimilation of Alaska Native and Native American children around the state by a unified conspiratorial assembly of numerous Catholic and Protestant religious groups. Browse the ever-changing selection of artisans hawking art, jewelry, Ulu knives and other Alaska Native handicrafts.

Finish off outdoors circulating picturesque Lake Tiulana, lined with fascinating village structures from the Aleut, Yupik, Tlingit and other tribes – a few members of each community provide further insight and field whatever questions you may have.

Awash in 'Alaskana'

MAPS P144 & P147

Soaking up Rage City's quirkier side

Americana, the word typically thrown around for quirky items associated with the history and culture of the US, doesn't quite cut it for Alaska. The state needs its own word; here's where to immerse yourself in 'Alaskana'. Lovingly referred to as 'Koots' by locals, the hallowed, rambling halls at **Chilkoot Charlie's** *(koots.com)*. Next door, born-and-bred Alaskan artist Brett Hulin Connor designs and prints unique hoodies, T-shirts and art prints at **Hulin Alaskan Design Clothing Co** *(hulin.shop)*, all of which are inspired by Alaska's wilds.

Popular diner **Arctic Roadrunner**, deeply entrenched in the 'Best Burgers in Anchorage' war, sits idyllically alongside

> Cajun seasoning gives these meaty beasts their edge!

EATING IN ANCHORAGE: BEST ON A BUDGET

MAP P144

Wild Scoops: Alaska-sourced ingredients (birch syrup, fireweed, Yukon Gold potato chips, rhubarb, sea salt) give Anchorage's best ice cream its addictive oomph. *noon-10pm* $

PHOnatik: Southside joint serving up Alaska-sized bowls of excellent pho, great for warming up after a chilly hillside hike. *11am-9pm Mon-Sat, noon-8pm Sun* $

Charlie's Bakery: Spicy pulled chicken, kong bao shrimp, hot and spicy beef, beloved dim sim – quite simply Alaska's best Chinese food. Always packed. *11am-8.30pm Mon-Sat* $

Tommy's Burgers: Spenard's award-hogging burger hut. No daintiness – just sloppy, perfectly chargrilled creations fulfilling your quintessential American burger dreams. *10.30am-9.30pm Mon-Fri, 11am-9pm Sat, noon-6pm Sun* $

BEST SHOPS IN ANCHORAGE

Alaska Mountaineering & Hiking: Staffed by local experts who've already done what you're setting out to do.

Dos Manos: 'Funktional' art gallery dealing in locally crafted art and jewelry, hip Alaska-themed tees/hoodies and other worthwhile souvenirs.

Sevigny Studio: Local artist-owned downtown gallery/gift shop. Art prints, hand-painted coffee mugs and so on, from over 40 Alaska artists.

The Craft Shop at ANMC: Some of the finest publicly available Alaska Native arts and crafts; at Alaska Native Medical Center. Cash only.

Oomingmak Musk Ox Producers Co-op: Pricey knit hats, headbands ($170) and tunics hand-knitted in Inupiaq villages from hyper-warm arctic musk ox wool.

CLIMATE CATASTROPHE?

In 2025, the National Weather Service issued heat advisories in Alaska for the first time in recorded history. The potential disastrous effects of climate change are of particular concern to Alaska, and Anchorage is sitting in the hot seat. The rise in ocean temperatures is already altering migration and foraging habits of critically endangered Cook Inlet beluga whales. Rising temps have also unleashed unprecedented bark beetle outbreaks, affecting two to three million acres of southcentral Alaska forest, much of which encircles Anchorage. And then there's the fires. Anchorage hit 90 °F (32 °C) in 2019 – the highest temperate ever recorded in the city – and spats of wildfires have broken out in alarmingly high rates compared to the past.

gurgling Campbell Creek (it has a fantastic creekside patio in summer). Occupying a rustic, cabin-like wood-and-stone building, it's chock-full of Alaska Native art, animal carvings and historic photos dating to the 1960s. Cash only.

At **Spenard Roadhouse** *(spenardroadhouse.com)* in the heart of Spenard, Alaska kitsch meets the fiercely locally driven cuisine from the same owners as beloved Snow City Café. Local art, an arsenal of Alaska license plates and faux taxidermy set the scene for diners knocking back elevated comfort food (halibut and chips, gourmet grilled cheeses on sourdough) without coming off as too cluttered.

A pink neon sign summons passersby at splurge-worthy **Club Paris** *(clubparisrestaurant.net)*, Anchorage's oldest (and best!) steakhouse (steaks are market price, around $37 to $72 on our visit), an atmospheric downtown throwback with a 1950s-era wood and Formica-top bar and historic memorabilia galore.

Jetlagged & Caffeinated

MAPS P144 & P147

Exploring coffee huts, specialty cafes

Unless you have come to Alaska from the North American West Coast, chances are you have come a long way indeed. With its own time zone (Alaska Standard Time or AKST, which covers everywhere but the Aleutian Islands) and nearly 20 hours of daylight during the summer high season, normal sleep patterns require significant recalibration. For coffee drinkers, caffeine will be required! Luckily, Anchorage takes coffee very seriously; so seriously, in fact, that almost nowhere else in the US has more coffee shops per capita than here. The city is absolutely peppered with coffee huts (drive-thru temples of caffeine that often open earlier than standard coffee shops). If you're up early, huts from award-winning local roaster **Caffé D'Arte** *(caffe dartealaska.com)* open at 5am but it's a haul (the Boniface Pkwy location, 4.7 miles east of downtown, is the closest). Otherwise, look for any huts serving coffee from Anchorage's favorite local roaster, **Kaladi Brothers** *(kaladi.com)*.

For a more traditional specialty coffeehouse experience, **SteamDot** *(steamdot.com)* begins pulling its single-origin espressos from a coveted Slayer Espresso machine at 6am in Midtown. Nearby, **Black Cup Coffee** *(blackcupak.com)*, Alaska's inaugural local roaster dating to 1975, opens at the same time.

If you're (not) sleeping downtown, you'll need to wait until 7am for part plant nursery/part specialty coffeehouse **That Feeling Co** *(thatfeeling.co)*, which does excellent espresso inside the exhaustingly hip K Street Market, to get your fix.

All Aboard!

Riding Alaska's historic rails

Anchorage's roots as Alaska's biggest city were planted in 1914, when a hurriedly erected railway construction camp at Ship Creek roared to life to extend an existing 50-mile rail

Alaska Railroad train

line from Seward to Fairbanks. Today, the famed all-weather **Alaska Railroad** *(alaskarailroad.com)*, inaugurated by President Warren G Harding shortly before his death in 1923, shuffles more than 400,000 passengers and 5.11 million tons of freight along 656 miles of track. Rides are a glorious, nostalgic way to traverse the state's incredible landscapes.

From its downtown depot, departing train buff-coveted journeys include the *Denali Star,* which heads north daily between May and September to Talkeetna *(adult/child $123/62)*, Denali National Park *($199/100)* and Fairbanks *($285/143)*; The *Coastal Classic*, calling at Girdwood *($100/50)* and Seward *($129/65)*; and the *Glacial Discovery*, connecting Anchorage with Whittier *($111/46)*, among others.

Festivals Under the Midnight Sun

Outdoor fun, live jazz

Anchorage loves a summer festival. The **Summer Solstice Festival** (usually June 20-22), celebrates the longest day of the year – 22 hours of sunlight – with an arsenal of outdoor events and cultural festivities around the city. Plant yourself with a pint in various beer gardens, browse art and crafts vendors or try your luck at catching the fattest salmon in Ship Creek. Another favorite is the **Spenard Jazz Fest** *(spenardjazzfest.org; May/June),* a week of cool, trendy and local jazz musicians staging concerts and workshops throughout Anchorage.

Bikes in the Hood

MAPS P144 & P147

Plane-spotting on two-wheels

You don't need to be an aviation buff to appreciate the unique urban setting of Lake Hood, home to the massive, extremely busy **Lake Hood Seaplane Base**. It's a wonderful spot for

SPLASHDOWN ANC!

The **Lake Hood Seaplane Base**, part of Anchorage's **Ted Stevens Anchorage International Airport** *(dot.alaska.gov/anc)* and located just east of the airport terminals, is the largest and busiest seaplane base in the world. It's quite a spectacle as both a massive floatplane parking lot (some 1000 single-engine aircraft are based here) and an active water-based taxiway (there are between 200 and 500 takeoffs/landings per day, depending on the season). The base dates to 1938, when a gravel runway was constructed along with a channel connecting Lake Hood and Lake Spenard (pre-dating the traditional airport by over a decade). If you're looking to dock your own seaplane, be prepared to settle in for the long haul – there's a 13-year waiting list for a floatslip.

Seaplane on Lake Hood

plane-spotting as you meander around the lake. Grab a bike at the **Lake Hood Bike Rentals** station near the Lakefront Anchorage Hotel *(download the Movatic app; 6hr $20)* and set out counterclockwise on a combination of a pedestrian/bike path that (very) intermittently encircles the lakes (it's technically Lake Spenard at this point) and airport roads. Be wary of restricted areas, which are plentiful, and always watch out for planes – active taxiways cross the road at various points. Along the way, the **Alaska Aviation Museum** *(alaskaairmuseum.org; adult/child $18/11)* makes for an interesting stop, but it's really about watching the floatplane action. The best spot for watching takeoffs is around **Spenard Beach Park** on the lake's northeast shore. In addition to the air action, there's plenty of waterfowl and no shortage of Bald Eagles. Give yourself a few hours to soak up the atmosphere. There are picnic tables off Lakeshore Dr if you want to bring along provisions; or park yourself at Lakefront Anchorage Hotel's **The Deck at Lake Hood** for an alfresco meal with a perfect view towards Takeoff Lane. It's a fascinating glimpse into Alaska life – one out of five Alaskans can fly a plane, after all!

Beyond Anchorage

Hiking, biking and paddling adventures await day-trippers around Eagle River and Eklutna, while the Turnagain Arm dazzles on road trips southeast.

It's patently evident from any vantage point in Anchorage that the great outdoors beckons mere steps from the city. Driving northeast out of town, you'll soon be parallel to Knik Arm, while the Chugach Mountains stay to your right. The wilds await. Both the larger community of Eagle River and tiny, 350-year-old Alaska Native village of Eklutna, 12 miles further northeast along the Knik Arm, offer access to the mountains and day trip–friendly Chugach State Park; at 773 sq miles, it's one of the four largest state parks in the US. To the southeast, the stunning Turnagain Arm and its Seward Highway Scenic Byway is a bonanza of nature reserves, extraordinary wildlife and scenery fit for a postcard.

Places
Eagle River p159
Matanuska Glacier p160
Eklutna Lake p161

Eagle River

TIME FROM ANCHORAGE: **20 MINS**

Eagle River flyby

The small community of **Eagle River**, northeast of Anchorage in the heart of the Chugach Mountains, is an easy day trip from the city. Grab some wheels and head out on scenic **Eagle River Road**, which hugs the winding Eagle River for 13 miles from the town of the same name to the log cabin **Eagle River Nature Center** *(alaska.org/detail/eagle-river-nature-center; day use $5)* inside **Chugach State Park** (p161).

Several worthwhile hikes commence here, including the easy 0.75-mile **Rodak Nature Trail**, which loops through stunning scenery to lovely beaver- and salmon-viewing platforms; and the **Albert Loop Trail**, a 3-mile jaunt through boreal forest to the bank of the river (closed from August through October to allow bears to feast on salmon uninterrupted). For a bigger day out, the **South Fork Valley Trail** follows the South Fork of Eagle River through a valley filled with wildflowers to Eagle and Symphony Lakes. To reach the trailhead, take the Eagle River Loop/Hiland Dr exit off the Glenn Hwy. Follow Hiland Dr 7.5 miles, take a

GETTING AROUND

Public transportation is scarce in both Eagle River and the village of Eklutna – you'll need a rental. Eagle River is pretty spread out and definitely not foot-friendly, while Eklutna is a tiny village that's little more than one point of interest. If you don't want to paddle Eklutna Lake in a round trip, **Lifetime Adventures** *(lifetimeadventures.net)* offers a paddle-and-pedal combo ($149). Kayak in, bike out!

TOP EXPERIENCE

Matanuska Glacier

Matanuska Glacier, 104 miles northeast of Anchorage, stretched all the way to the north end of the city some 22,000 years ago. Today, it remains one of Alaska's most accessible ice tongues and exploring this behemoth of brilliant blue-streaked snow and ice makes for one of Anchorage's best days out.

Glacier guides, Matanuska Glacier

TOP TIPS

- Tours from Anchorage run $300-350, including lunch. Save by booking directly and driving yourself.

- For deeper exploration, book a heli-tour with Mark Fleenor at **Sheep Mountain Lodge** *(sheepmountain.com; from $299)*. He's a former NGO pilot who worked in Afghanistan.

- **Long Rifle Lodge** frames the icy beast perfectly from its dining room.

PRACTICALITIES

- tours hourly 9am-5pm Jun-Sep; 10am, 11am, 1pm & 2pm Oct-May
- adult/child $150/30
- *glacier-tours.com*

The Mighty Matanuska

Matanuska Glacier's terminus currently unravels from the Chugach Mountains about a mile and a half from Glenn Highway. Though it's estimated to be retreating at a startingly 655 feet per year, it remains a staunch layer cake of compacted snow and ice clocking in at 27 miles long and four miles wide.

Spectacular Glacial Playground

The glacier's terminus sits on private land, controlled by one entrepreneurially minded family. Access is by licensed and insured guides only. Glacier treks are the most popular activity. You'll trounce across the meltwater on a floating modular foot bridge, slip on microspikes (which act as a sort of 4WD for your feet!) and ramble about this beautiful outcrop of ice, peering into moulins, sipping on water from small waterfall spouts and peering over mini-summits for spectacular Chugach views (in winter, a designated route is pre-determined for safety reasons). You'll get up close with the Cathedral, Matanuska's terminal wall, where medial moraine has created an intensely beautiful Carrara marble effect. Besides the concessionaire, only Salmon Berry Travel & Tours (p146; *salmonberrytours.com*), **Nova** *(novalaska.com)* and **Greatland Adventures** *(greatlandadventures.com)* have licensed guides.

left onto South Creek Rd and then a right onto W River Dr, where you'll see the trailhead.

If you spend a day hiking in the area, reward yourself with local brews among the liberal hardwoods, cassette tape–covered walls and an old hockey scoreboard at atmospheric **Odd Man Rush Brewing** *(oddmanrushbrewing.com; beers $8)* followed by a carb reload at **Pizza Man** *(pizzamanak.com; pizza from $15)*, an Eagle River mainstay.

If you're around mid-July, it's well worth traipsing out this way for the good-time **Bear Paw Festival** *(bearpawfestival.org)* and its 'Slippery Salmon Olympics,' a relay race involving pink flamingos, hopscotch, serving trays and large, dead fish!

Eklutna Lake
TIME FROM ANCHORAGE: **45 MINS**

Outdoor adventures around stunning blue lake

Eklutna Lake, 15 miles southeast, is a glassy, mountain-bound glacial reservoir within **Chugach State Park** *(dnr.alaska.gov; day use $5)* that provides Anchorage with most of its drinking water (and brewers with their secret ingredient!). The 7-mile-long lake can be tackled on the excellent 25.7-mile out-and-back **Lakeside Trail**, or **Lifetime Adventures** (p159; *www.lifetimeadventures.net*) rents kayaks *(half-/full day $75/100)* and mountain bikes *(half-/full day $50/65)*. For an overview, the **Twin Peaks Trail** steeply climbs 2.6 miles from the parking lot through lush forest into alpine meadows presided over by the imposing eponymous peaks. Nearby, **Thunderbird Falls** *(day use $5)* is a rewarding 2-mile round-trip walk along a deep gorge with a gorgeous little waterfall for the grand finale.

EKUTNA ECLETIC

The blink-and-you've-missed-it Dena'ina Athabascan village of **Eklutna**, northeast of Anchorage, is the last of eight villages that existed prior to the arrival of American colonists who came to build the Alaska Railroad in the early 20th century. An uneasy marriage of the **Athabascan** and **Russian Orthodox** cultures is enshrined at **Eklutna Village Historical Park** (p141), where the small **St Nicholas Church** (interior modeled after Noah's ark) was constructed of hewn spruce logs by Russian missionaries in the 1840 (a newer, more overtly obvious Russian Orthodox church was built next door in the 1960s). Both churches rub elbows with the **Dena'ina Athabascan Eklutna Cemetery**, home to 80 brightly colored spirit boxes.

Eagle River's most sophisticated dining/drinking option.

EATING & DRINKING IN EAGLE RIVER: OUR PICKS

Jitters: Community hub Jitters serves baked goods, to-go breakfast burritos and the best coffee between Anchorage and Palmer. *5.30am-5pm Mon-Fri, from 6am Sat, from 7am Sun* **$**

Eagle River Alehouse: ERA serves satisfying bar fodder (wood-fired pizza, burgers) and has 32 taps of (mostly) craft beer. *11am-10pm Mon-Fri, from 10am Sat & Sun* **$$**

LimeLeaf: Somewhat upscale Asian mainstay doing excellent creative sushi rolls, Chinese stir-fries and Thai curries; partly Thai-owned. *4-9pm Mon-Fri, noon-9pm Sat & Sun* **$$**

Corks & Hops: Extensive by-the-glass wine list (plus local taps) fuel this elevated pub grub destination with large three-sided centerpiece bar. *noon-10pm Tue-Fri, 11am-10pm Sat, 11am-8pm Sun* **$$$**

TURNAGAIN ARM – ANCHORAGE TO GIRDWOOD

Turnagain Arm, a narrow branch of the Gulf of Alaska harboring incredible wildlife, spectacularly unravels on this driving tour southeast of Anchorage. For the Girdwood to Portage Valley section see (p179).

START	END	LENGTH
Anchorage	Girdwood	40 miles/2 hours

The first 40 miles of the 127-mile Seward Highway Scenic Byway to Girdwood hugs Turnagain Arm, a narrow branch of the Gulf of Alaska and one of two such arms that straddle Alaska's biggest city (the other being Knik Arm). Give yourself a few hours (viewpoints and gawking turnoffs are considerable) and be on the lookout for wildlife (beluga whales, Dall sheep) and the bore tide, a neat trick of geography that requires a combination of narrow, shallow waters and rapidly rising tides.

Heading out of Anchorage, your first glimpse of water comes just before ❶ **Potter Marsh Wild Viewing Boardwalk**, a fantastic 1500ft boardwalk created in 1916. ❷ **Chugach State Park Headquarters** (p161) serves up good mud flat views and train buffs will appreciate the rotary snowplow on display, a real life snowpiercer! Wildly beautiful ❸ **Beluga Point** is next up. Whales can be seen mid-July and August but it's also a favorite spot to catch the bore tide. At Mile 102, ❹ **Bird Ridge Trail** starts with a wheelchair-accessible loop, then continues with a steep, popular and well-marked path that reaches a 3500ft overlook at Mile 2.

Before reaching Girdwood, make a pitstop at ❺ **Bird Creek**. The bore tide is your soundtrack if you camp at nearby ❻ **Bird Creek State Campground**.

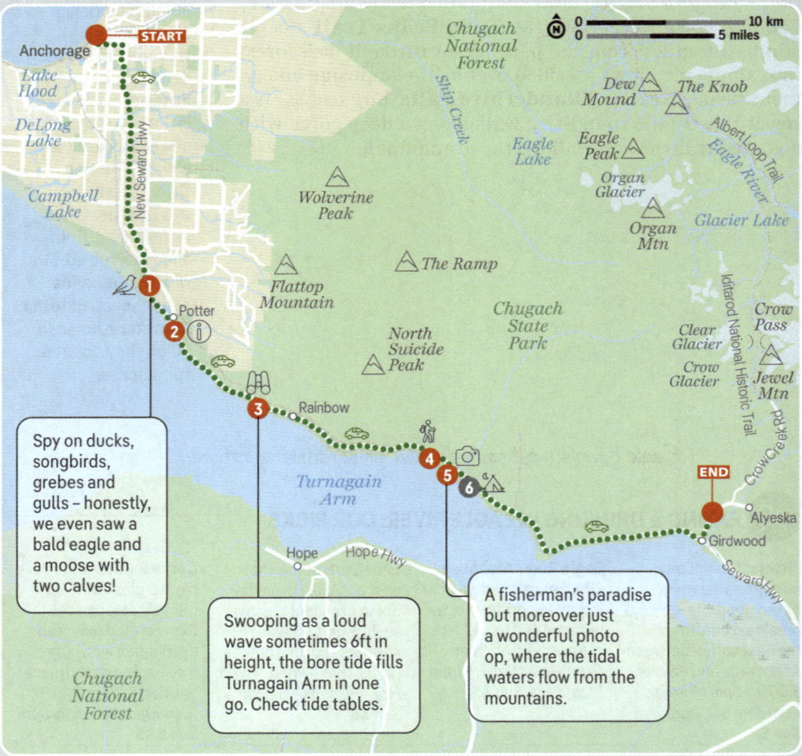

Spy on ducks, songbirds, grebes and gulls – honestly, we even saw a bald eagle and a moose with two calves!

Swooping as a loud wave sometimes 6ft in height, the bore tide fills Turnagain Arm in one go. Check tide tables.

A fisherman's paradise but moreover just a wonderful photo op, where the tidal waters flow from the mountains.

Palmer

COLONIAL HISTORY | CRAFT BEER | STATE FAIR

It doesn't take long to fall for Palmer; it's immediately evident something different this way comes. Born of a 1935 New Deal social experiment spearheaded by President Franklin D Roosevelt, Palmer saw the transplant of 203 farming refugees from the Depression-era Dust Bowl (the worst agricultural disaster in US history) to Alaska, where they would cultivate a new agriculturally driven society known as the Matanuska Colony. These transplants, known as Valley Colonists, farmed the land and built the city, turning it into Alaska's only settlement founded on agriculture. Today, historic farming-related buildings pepper the town, juxtaposing 1930s ambience with antique furniture, wood floors, modern restaurants and flowing craft-beer taps. It's all ringed by some of the region's most dramatic mountains. Palmer's unique history and living agricultural community make for an ideal escape from the city hassles and high prices of Anchorage. There's a lot to love here.

☑ TOP TIP

The Mat-Su (Matanuska-Susitna) Valley, including Palmer, likes its festivals year-round – not only in summer – and doesn't let a cold and dark winter spoil the fun. Consider visiting for the Jr Iditarod Sled Dog Race, Iron Dog Snowmobile Race, Iditarod Restart Golf Tournament and Colony Christmas, which all take place in winter.

Mat-Su Moments

Small-town culture, dramatic mountain scenery

Carved by glaciers and surrounded by 25,000 sq miles of pure Alaska wilderness dominated by the Chugach Mountains and the Matanuska, Knik, and Susitna Rivers, the Matanuska-Susitna Valley (Mat-Su for short), 35 miles north of Anchorage, is

GETTING AROUND

Palmer's historic points of interest are walkable; otherwise **Valley Transit** *(valleytransitak.org)* serves nine 'zones,' or communities, in the area, including Palmer and Wasilla. A bus ride is $3 per zone. This is an on-demand service based on availability, so you must call ahead. Taxis services are also available – try **Alaska Cab** *(alaskacabllc.com)* or **A Cab** *(acabak.com)*. However, having a rental car is really the way to go. Parking is plentiful and you'll definitely need it if you plan on visiting the farms outside of Palmer proper.

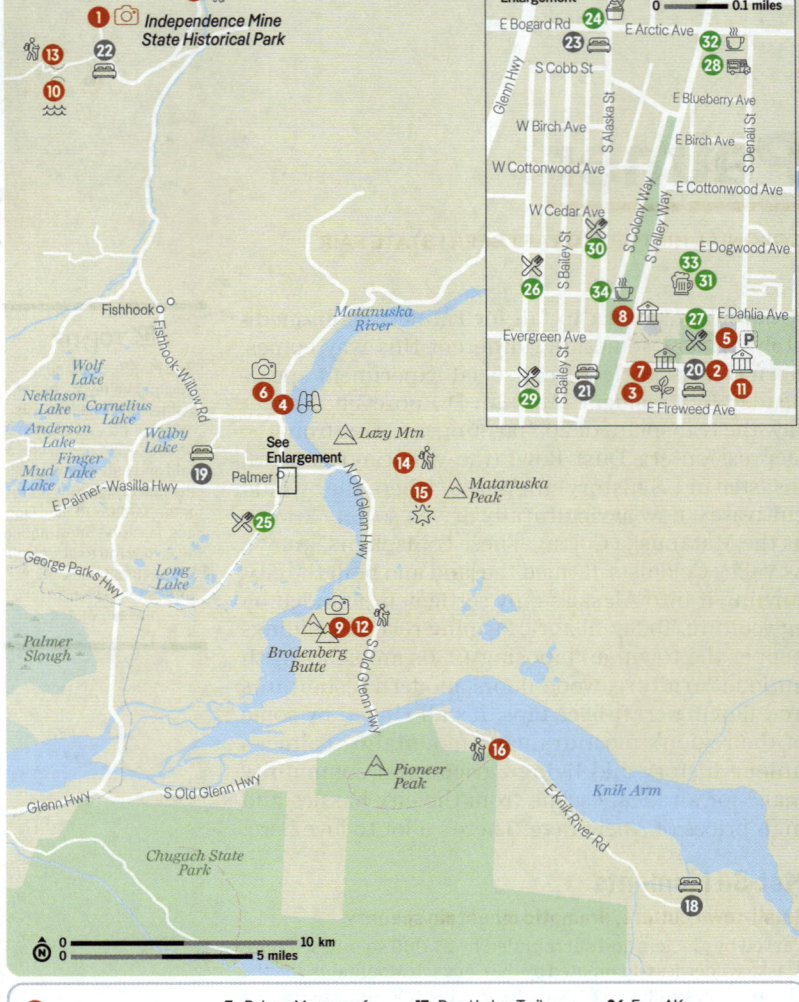

HIGHLIGHTS
1 Independence Mine State Historical Park

SIGHTS
2 Colony House Museum
3 Matanuska Valley Agricultural Showcase
4 Matanuska Valley Lookout
5 Matanuska-Susitna Borough Building
6 Musk Ox Farm
7 Palmer Museum of History & Art
8 Palmer Train Depot
9 Reindeer Farm
10 Summit Lake
11 United Protestant Presbyterian Church

ACTIVITIES
12 Bodenburg Butte Trail
13 Hatch Peak Trail
14 Lazy Mountain Trail
15 Matanuska Peak Trail
16 Pioneer Ridge Trail
17 Reed Lakes Trail

SLEEPING
18 Alaska Glacier Lodge
19 Alaska's Harvest B&B
20 Colony Inn
21 Eagle Hotel
22 Hatcher Pass Lodge
23 Pioneer Motel

EATING
24 Big Dipper
25 Colony Kitchen/Noisy Goose Café
26 Fern AK
27 Palmer Alehouse
28 Reuben Haus
29 Slow Day Cafe
30 Turkey Red

DRINKING & NIGHTLIFE
31 Bleeding Heart Brewery
32 Lekker Coffee and Baking Co.
33 Matanuska Brewing Company
34 Vagabond Blues

Alaska's fastest-growing region, its most accessible natural area and a superb spot for respite.

Mingle with locals over massive cookies and a wealth of sandwiches at **Vagabond Blues**, the town's de facto community center. Their coffee is certainly decent, but you'll want to head to the new **Lekker Coffee and Baking Co.** *(@lekker coffeeandbakingco)* for the best espresso in all of the Anchorage area. And it better be – at $4 a pop, it's considerably more expensive than other specialty coffee shops in the area. The small batch, light-to-medium offerings from local roaster **Farm Loop** *(farmloopcoffee.com)* pull beautifully from their Italian La Marzocco machine. Lunch at fiercely local farm-to-table restaurant **Feather & Flour** *(featherandflour.com)*. It's operating a scaled-down menu now as the pop-up **Slow Day Café** and could potentially be sold, but it's still the best restaurant for miles and miles. Sufficiently fueled and caffeinated, spend some hours taking in the town's historic frontier atmosphere, admiring original colony buildings. If you have your own wheels, head out on Archie Road near Musk Ox Farm – nearby the turnoff for the farm is a mostly unmarked roadside pull-off. Here, a **Matanuska Valley Lookout** affords incredible views of the valley and surrounding mountains.

Looking for a happy ending? **Big Dipper** *(ilovebigdipper. com)* does to-die-for ice cream, often calling on the Alaska wild for flavor inspiration (fireweed, lingonberries and birch toffee, for example). You'll need to travel 2221 miles to Seattle for a sweeter experience!

Drink in Historic Surrounds

Beers and breweries in historic Palmer

One of the coolest things about Palmer is that a chunk of its original colony space has been resurrected by atmospheric craft breweries and restaurants. Drink your way through Palmer's colonial 'Matanuska Maid' block – named after the colony's dairy cooperative – and you'll quicky see why Palmer is the best beer town in the area outside of Anchorage proper. Head to veteran-run **Bleeding Heart Brewery** *(bleeding heartbrewery.com)*, which perfectly blends experimental craft brews forged from the local bounty and an eclectic hang space in the co-op's former cold storage facility. Both co-founders, Stefan Marty and Zack Lanphier, grew up on colonial farmlands and they often call on local provisions in their brewing process (Alaska-grown beets flood their famed Beet IPA, locally roasted coffee is often used in their porters, stouts and so on). Here it's all about the prosciutto mac and cheese *($16)* and the Beet IPA above (though there's smash burgers outside in summer). Sneak out the back door for a shortcut to **Matanuska Brewing Company** *(matanuskabrewing company.com)* inside the colony's former grain mill. You'll find 22 taps and, though the excellent burgers are the top seller, locals swear by the tacos. Another 44 taps await around the corner at **Palmer Alehouse** *(palmeralehouse.com)* occupying the colony's signature building, the former trading post. Its sun-catching patio is Palmer's ultimate people-watching party spot.

ESCAPE TO HATCHER PASS

Zack Lanphier, cofounder of Palmer's **Bleeding Heart Brewery** *(@bleeding_ heart_brewery; bleedingheartbrewery.com)* recommends heading north.

I suggest escaping to **Hatcher Pass** for a breath of fresh air above the 'noise'. While most flock to **Independence Mine State Historical Park** (p170), **Hatcher Pass Lodge**, or **Summit Lake**, the sneakier go-to is the charming **Hatch Peak hike**. Not a guidebook star, but a local favorite. Who needs fame when you've got hidden splendor? Day or night, novice or pro, it suits all and can easily be done with a beer or two in your bag. There's no beer like a summit beer! Throw in a snack, a buddy, and some questionable decision-making, and you've got yourself the perfect outing!

A NEW DEAL DAWDLE

Soak in Palmer's distinctly Midwestern atmosphere on this roundtrip stroll taking in numerous original Matanuska Colony buildings peppered around town.

START	END	LENGTH
Palmer Visitor Center	Palmer Visitor Center	1 mile; 30min

Many of Palmer's historic colony buildings have been refurbished and maintain their rustic wooden looks. Start off by perusing the small exhibits on the town's agricultural past at the ❶ **Palmer Museum of History & Art** within the Palmer Visitor Center. Walk one block east along E Elmwood Ave, passing the bell of St Mihiel (the ship that transported the colonists from San Francisco to Seward), on your left to ❷ **Colony Inn**, constructed in 1935 as the Matanuska Colony Teacher's Dormitory.

Pop into the ❸ **Colony House Museum** across the street, run by enthusiastic colony descendants. A further block east, the log cabin ❹ **United Protestant Presbyterian Church**, built in 1936, is still in use today. Cut across the large parking lot just north and look left at the massive whitewashed ❺ **Matanuska-Susitna Borough Building**, originally built as Palmer's first schoolhouse.

Next, walk a block north to the best brewery in town, ❻ **Bleeding Heart Brewery** (p165), once the cold storage for the colony produce co-op. One block south is the ❼ **Palmer Alehouse** (p165), occupying the colony's colorful former trading post, shooting range and only restaurant. Head another block west and you'll see the colony's former train depot, now the ❽ **Palmer Community Center**. It's 200yd south on S Valley Way to return to the Palmer Visitor Center.

In August, see the area's famous oversized vegetables at Matanuska Valley Agricultural Showcase garden in the same complex.

Constructed in 1935, the most historic accommodations in town, chock-full of antiques and historic charm.

Admire the industrial epicenter of the colony over delicious IPAs with Alaska beets, or stouts made with local artisanal coffee.

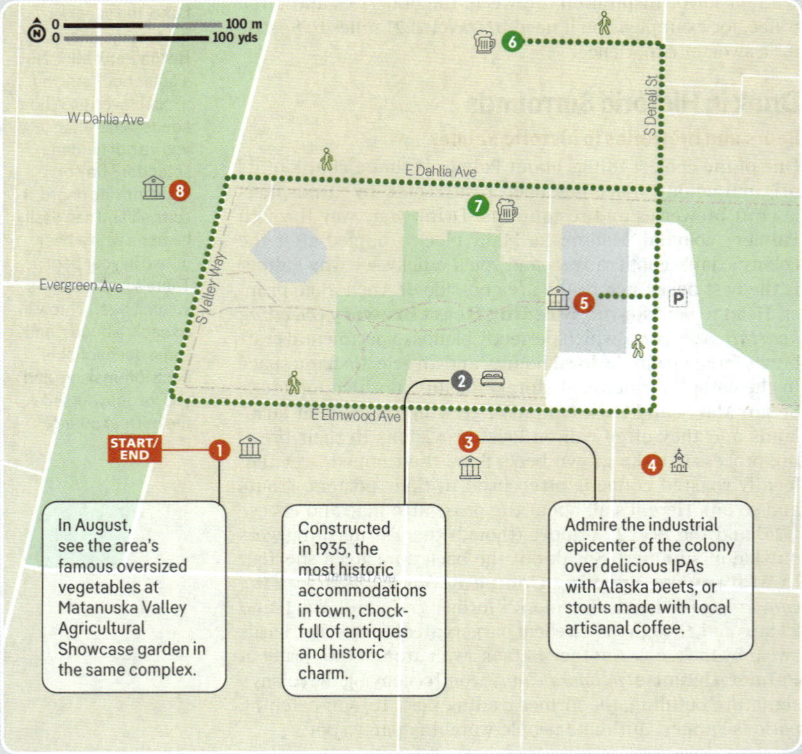

A Fair in Palmer
An Alaska state-fair romp

In the grand tradition of many Midwestern states from which much of Palmer's population descended, one of the most rollicking good times of the year closes out the summer for the state's annual **Alaska State Fair** *(alaskastatefair.org; adult/child from $16.50/9.50)*. The fair, first held in 1936 by a fraternal organization of colonists, takes place over 12 days from late August to Labor Day and is well worth planning a visit around (though, to be fair, while big for Alaska, it's small compared to some Lower 48 state fairs). Still, the event draws some 300,000 people annually from throughout the municipality of Anchorage, and Alaska far and wide. There's live music from national acts (2025 drew the Beach Boys, Wiz Khalifa and Weird Al Yankovic, for example); prized livestock from the surrounding area, as well as amusement rides (Alaska's only rollercoaster!), horse shows and a rodeo.

One of the fair's biggest attractions is the giant cabbage weigh-off to see who grew the biggest one in the valley. In 2012, a world record was set: 138lb! – to get an idea of just how big that is, there's a model at the **Matanuska Valley Agricultural Showcase** *(palmermuseum.org/showcase-garden)* next to the Palmer Visitor Center. As at all state fairs, food is a major draw: expect scallops, shrimp, and crab plucked fresh from Alaska waters, Prince William Sound oysters, deep-fried halibut chunks and Alaska salmon quesadillas, among other treats.

Still not convinced? There's an apple pie cook-off – ain't nothing more American than that!

A Farmin' Good Time!
Farm visits, animal encounters

Palmer has long flirted with farming – it's one of Alaska's only communities founded on an agricultural lifestyle. Farming-related buildings around town evoke a Midwestern crossroads; that is, until the surrounding Talkeetna and Chugach Mountains give it away as about as far-flung as possible from the corn belt. Pretty farms dot the back roads in these parts, several of which make for family-friendly excursions from town.

Three miles north of Palmer proper, **Musk Ox Farm** *(muskoxfarm.org; tours adult/child $14/8)* is home to the

BEST PALMER HIKES

Pioneer Ridge: A 5.7-mile route that climbs the main ridge, extending southeast from Pioneer Peaks (6400ft). Climb through forest until reaching alpine tundra at 3200ft.

Matanuska Peak Trail: The 8-mile trail is steep, traversing the south slope of Lazy Mountain.

Lazy Mountain Trail: The 2.5-mile climb to the top is very steep at times, but ends in an alpine setting with pleasant views.

Reed Lakes Trail: A moderately difficult 7-mile climb at Hatcher Pass, taking in mountain lakes, waterfalls and towering walls of granite.

Bodenburg Butte Trail: Short (1.5 mile) but steep step/switchback climb to a 900ft-high Palmer panorama.

EATING IN PALMER: OUR PICKS

Fern AK: Acai bowls are the highlight, but the coffee, smoothies and people-watching are great, too. *8am-6pm* $

Reuben Haus: Fabulous food truck: Reubens, buttermilk fried chicken sandwiches and burgers. There's kale salad but you don't want that - get zesty fries! *11am-7.30pm Wed-Sat* $

Colony Kitchen/Noisy Goose Café: Heaped servings of Southern-fried breakfast staples served beneath stuffed birds suspended from the ceiling. *7am-3pm Sun, Wed & Thu, to 8pm Fri & Sat* $

Turkey Red: Colorful cafe serving Med-influenced fare, wonderful fresh-baked breads and desserts. Some dishes can be ordered in smaller servings. *7am-9pm Tue-Sun* $

Aerial view of Palmer in winter

WHY I LOVE PALMER

Kevin Raub, Lonely Planet writer.

I found Palmer's unique historical feel (by Alaska standards) immediately captivating as I drove into town. There's a frontier feel to its charming downtown streets and a distinct sense of community. It's a great place to hang your hiking shoes out to dry and take in some urban therapy (ok, urban is a stretch, but in comparison to the boundless outdoor adventures in its vicinity, it's downright city-like!). There are historic buildings to admire (the old train depot and former trading post are especially easy on the eyes), and past-life farm-production facilities have regained relevance as excellent destination craft-beer breweries and for great food – all surrounded by one of the most dramatic mountain backdrops you'll ever see.

largest captive herd of these big, shaggy beasts in the world (some 80 or so live out a stress-free lifestyle in harmony with the farm's gentle sustainable agriculture philosophy). These ice-age critters are intelligent enough to have evolved a complex social structure that allows survival under incredibly harsh conditions. Qiviut (kiv-ee-oot), the incredibly warm, soft and pricey material ($110 for an ounce of yarn or $249 for a 100% qiviut headband), is tenderly handcombed from the musk ox's undercoat. This is a year-round working farm, so visits are guided only. The tour lasts about 45 minutes and is best booked in advance.

Reindeer Farm (*reindeerfarm.com; self-guided tours adult/child $19/17*), eight miles south of Palmer, is one of the original colony farms and a great place to bring the kids. Here they will be able to pet and feed the reindeer and are encouraged to think the reindeer are connected to Santa. There are also moose and Highland cattle, among other fun farm animals, and pony rides. A small food trailer serves burgers, reindeer dogs and famed fireweed milkshakes. You can easily spend a few hours here, especially if you're toting little ones.

FEELING FESTIVE?

Palmer is one of the most festival-friendly cities around Anchorage, but **Girdwood** (p172) holds its own at least once a year, when a beautiful forest setting welcomes arts, crafts and music for the **Girdwood Forest Festival**.

Beyond Palmer

Some of the Mat-Su Valley's most dramatic landscapes sit on Palmer's doorstep – the massive Knik Glacier and the scenic Hatcher Pass.

It's not easy to tear yourself away from Palmer proper, what with all those brews and views on offer, but you'd be remiss not to venture into the wild from here. Highlights throughout the Mat-Su Valley are plentiful, but two destinations hog the spotlight. Hatcher Pass, which cuts a deeply gorgeous path across the Talkeetna Mountains between Palmer and Willow, is home to some of Southcentral Alaska's best alpine hiking and the kind of mountain scenery that needs no filter. Then there's Knik Glacier, best accessed by a spectacular boat ride along the Knik River – avoid ATVs, please! – a monstrous ice field of impeccable beauty less than 30 minutes by car southeast of Palmer.

Places
Knik Glacier p169
Knik/Wasilla p171

Knik Glacier

TIME FROM PALMER: **30 MINS**

River trip to the glacier

Acute awareness of his surroundings and a bit of geographical luck in the mid-'90s allowed Tom Faussett to lay down roots near the extraordinary **Knik Glacier**, 22 miles or so southeast of Palmer as the crow flies, and harbor a monopoly on the most magical three-hour journey to its mesmerizing presence at the northern end of the Chugach Mountains. Though on public land, one must trespass his private property to safely launch a boat on the cinematic Knik River, an absolutely breath-stealing route to see this wondrous ice field in all its glory. **Knik Glacier Tours** *(3hr tour adult/child $125/65)* was born.

GETTING AROUND

On-demand **Valley Transit** *(valleytransitak.org)* serves numerous communities in the area (Houston, Big Lake, Meadow Lakes, Wasilla, Knik Goose Bay, Fairview, Port MacKenzie, Palmer and the Butte) Monday to Saturday, but the most coveted locales, Knik Glacier and Hatcher Pass included, require your own set of wheels. The road to Independence Mine State Historic Park is often closed well past what you might think of as winter. Check ahead.

HIT THE ROAD TO HATCHER

Meadows, ridges and glaciers highlight the Hatcher Pass, Matanuska-Susitna's alpine wonderland in the Talkeetna Mountains on this easy driving tour.

START	**END**	**LENGTH**
Palmer	Independence Mine State Historical Park	20 miles; 30min

Impassable in winter and often closed well into summer, the Hatcher Pass carves a picturesque, 60-mile track through the Talkeetna Mountains from Palmer to Willow. This scenery-saturated drive sticks to the Palmer side, which is more accessible for more of the year than the entire pass. Head out Fishhook-Willow Rd/N Palmer-Fishhook Rd out of Palmer, parallel with scenic ❶ **Little Susitna River**, which tumbles down the mountain in a whitewashed flurry of photogenic moments.

You'll pass ❷ **Government Peak Recreation Area** to the west. A pit stop here might include mountain biking or a steep hike. If overnighting in winter, you can ski in to the Recreation Area from ❸ **Mountain Streams Lodge**, a few miles west. Continue climbing for 8.5 miles to Mile 14, where the easy, 16-mile round-trip ❹ **Gold Mint Trail** follows the Little Susitna River into a gently sloping mountain valley.

The rustic ❺ **Hatcher Pass Lodge** (p165) is three miles ahead, dramatically perched near the turnoff for Hatcher Pass Rd and completely enveloped by stunning mountain scenery. Open year-round, it offers cabins and an on-site restaurant. A final push leads to ❻ **Independence Mine State Historical Park** *(parking $5)*, home to a huge 272-acre gold mine, abandoned since 1955, sprawled out in a gorgeous alpine valley.

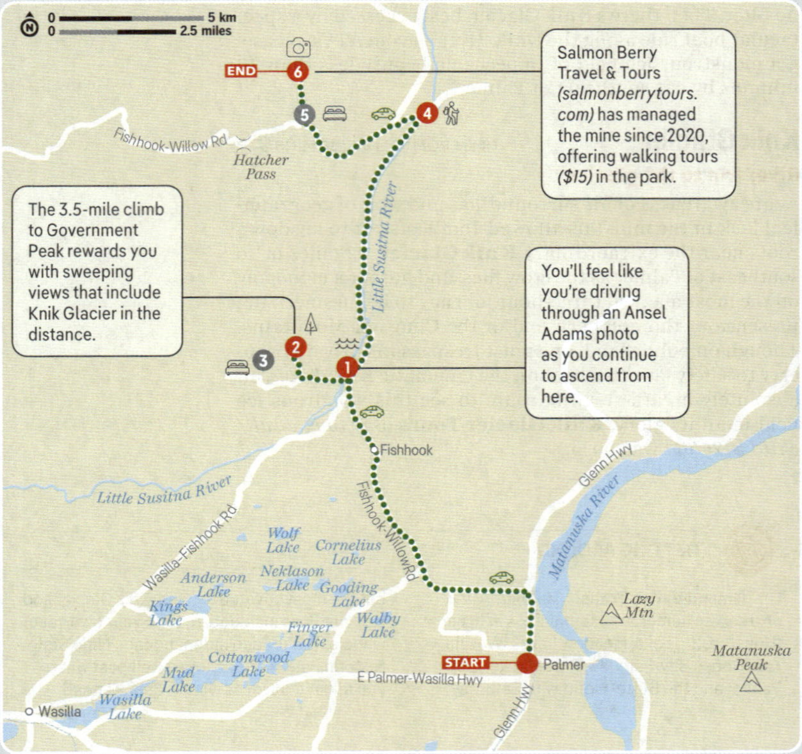

> Salmon Berry Travel & Tours *(salmonberrytours.com)* has managed the mine since 2020, offering walking tours *($15)* in the park.

> The 3.5-mile climb to Government Peak rewards you with sweeping views that include Knik Glacier in the distance.

> You'll feel like you're driving through an Ansel Adams photo as you continue to ascend from here.

Board Faussett's military issued, 6WD truck for a 4-mile, 30-minute ride through near-desertscape scenery bound by Chugach Mountains to the shores of the Knik River. Pay attention: the glacier eventually makes itself known on the horizon. Once riverside, you'll embark in custom-built extremely shallow jet boats for an epic 20-minute ride along the snaking, silty-green Knik River. And then it happens. The boat rounds a bend in the river and the big reveal arrives in an instant, redefining 'wow'. A sanctuary of glassy, snow-white and turquoise ice cubes bob across a postcard-perfect pool of glacial melt. Beyond the blue, the massive Knik Glacier (6 miles across, 28 miles long) bound by the incredible peaks of Mt Marcus Baker (13,176ft), Mt Gannett (9629ft), and Mt Goode (10,610ft) form a panoramic backdrop.

Trekkies take note: Knik Glacier is best known as the setting where a portion of *Star Trek VI: The Undiscovered Country* was filmed. But Hollywood does it no justice.

Knik/Wasilla

TIME FROM PALMER: **25 MINS**

History of the Iditarod Trail

Near Wasilla, the town of Knik has a rich sled-dog history as the home of many Alaskan mushers. There is a small **Knik Museum and Mushers Hall of Fame** *(adult/child $3/free)* along the **National Historic Iditarod Trail**, the National Trails System's only winter footpath as well as Alaska's only Congress-designated National Historic Trail. The 1000-mile main trail stretches between Seward and Nome (some 1400 additional miles of trail unravel from the main trail, linking communities and other historic sites). But the real reason to come out this way is 13 miles east in Wasilla proper; the **Iditarod Trail Headquarters** *(iditarod.com)* and its small museum, where famous sled dogs Togo and Andy are immortalized. Outside, you can take a short sled-dog ride ($10) and mingle with adorable Siberian huskies and Alaskan malamutes.

RUN FOR THE RIVER

Anne Thomas owns a collection of athletic-shoe stores (Aktive Soles; *shop.aktivesoles.com*) and organizes a year-round Monday night 'Happy Run' that ends at **Palmer Alehouse** (p165).

Runners should head straight for The Butte. Surrounded by gigantic mountains, the views are stunning. The summer view: Two towering peaks, Matanuska and Pioneer (each amazing climbs), and the Knik river, where, with binoculars, you might catch sight of beaver, swans, moose or bear and at the end of the valley the **Knik Glacier** (p169) standing sentinel. Winter view: a beautiful array of stars and occasionally the northern lights. Both views are not only of beautiful landscape but also an area rich in cultural history of the Ahtena and Dena'ina peoples.

LOOKING FOR GLACIERS?

Another monstrous ice tongue easily accessed from Palmer is the **Matanuska Glacier** (p160), which nearly kisses Glenn Hwy about 61 miles northeast of the city.

Girdwood

SKIING | FINE FOOD | HIGH-ALTITUDE ESCAPADES

☑ TOP TIP

Alyeska Resort is a part of the Ikon Pass *(ikonpass.com)* network, offering money-saving unlimited/restricted access at some 60 domestic and international ski resorts, including heavy hitters such as Mammoth Mountain, Big Bear Mountain Resort, Sun Valley, Chamonix Mont-Blanc Valley (France), Zermatt Matterhorn (Switzerland) and Valle Nevado (Chile), among others.

Girdwood is the kind of charming mountain hamlet that only a ski resort could build. Some 37 miles south of Anchorage, the Alyeska Hwy splits off at Mile 90 of the Seward Hwy and rolls 3 miles east to Girdwood. Historically home to a mining community set on searching for gold around the Turnagain Arm (historic mines, both ruined and intact, are scattered about), Girdwood remained a haven of residential quiet encircled by mighty peaks brimming with glaciers until Alyeska Resort was built by Japanese investors in 1994. Today, the Canadian-managed resort is destination number one for powder in Alaska. It remains small – just a few commercial streets, all of which vie for resort runoff dollars – but is a dog-and-kid kind of town, with excellent hiking, fine restaurants and a feel-good vibe that will have you staying longer than anticipated.

Glacier City's Greatest Hits
Off-piste alpine best-of

Girdwood is 3 miles northeast from the Seward Highway Scenic Byway, tucked away in a stunning valley crammed with Sitka spruce – you can admire its textbook beauty most

Continues on p176

 GETTING AROUND

Girdwood is small and its compact village is walkable. If you're without wheels and need to get to the lifts, **Glacier Valley Transit** *(glaciervalleytransit.com)*, known simply as 'The Shuttle,' is Girdwood's bus service. It operates from Alyeska Resort to the Seward Hwy (Coast Plaza) by donation ($1 recommended), making all important stops. Extra services run into the wee hours on Saturday nights in summer. **Powder Hound** *(powderhoundak.com)* rents summer bikes (per day $100) and winter fat bikes (per day $50).

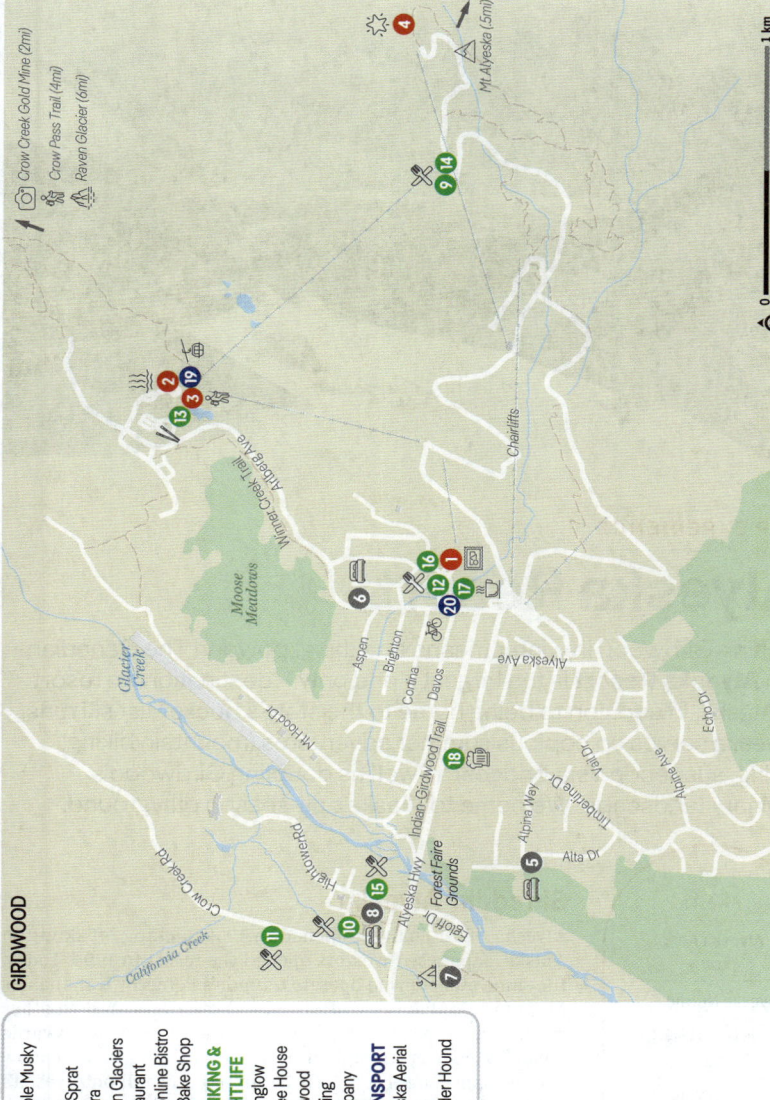

GIRDWOOD

SIGHTS
1. Girdwood Center for Visual Arts

ACTIVITIES
2. Alyeska Nordic Spa
3. North Face Trail
4. Veilbreaker Skybridges

SLEEPING
5. Alyeska Hostel
6. Alyeska Resort
7. Girdwood Campground
8. Ski Inn

EATING
9. Bore Tide
10. Chair 5
11. Double Musky Inn
12. Jack Sprat
13. Sakura
14. Seven Glaciers Restaurant
15. Spoonline Bistro
16. The Bake Shop

DRINKING & NIGHTLIFE
17. Alpenglow Coffee House
18. Girdwood Brewing Company

TRANSPORT
19. Alyeska Aerial Tram
20. Powder Hound

THE GUIDE

ANCHORAGE & AROUND GIRDWOOD

TOP EXPERIENCE

Alyeska Resort

Visiting Girdwood in winter means one thing: powder! The Canadian-run **Alyeska Resort** is the largest – and only – destination ski resort in Alaska. In addition to being home to the state's bucket-list ski runs, Alyeska serves up copious summer adventures (mountain biking, hiking, suspended skybridges) as well as doubling Girdwood's culinary landscape. Welcome to Alaska's all-season playground.

- Mt Alyeska
- Alyeska Aerial Tram
- Alyeska Nordic Spa
- Seven Glaciers Restaurant
- Bore Tide
- Veilbreaker Skybridges
- Sakura

Shreddin' Alyeska

Alyeska's first chairlift opened in 1959, kicking off skiing in Alaska. Japanese investors opened the resort in 1994. Today, the same owners who operate Canada's Pomeroy Kananaskis Mountain Lodge are running the show. Compared to other mountains in North America, Mount Alyeska leans towards advanced/expert (though all levels are catered to) and snow is in no short supply – nearly 700in per year fall on Alyeska's 1610 skiable acres and 76 named trails. Alyeska's famed North

PRACTICALITIES
- *alyeskaresort.com*
- ski season: late Nov–late Apr
- lift tickets: adult/child from $119/69

Face is home to North America's longest continuous double black diamond, where gate flips and rope drops on runs such as Christmas Chute, Ragdoll, Chuck's and Sundeck serve up some of the best inbound turns in the industry. A total of seven lifts (two high-speed quads, two fixed quads, two magic carpets and a 40-passenger Aerial Tram) elevate skiers to a vertical rise of 2500ft, where steep lines, vertical faces and family friendly groomed runs await, blanketed in Alaska's famed snow. Full-day lift tickets range from $119 for adults ($69 for kids) midweek to $149 ($89 for kids) on weekends. Nonskiers pay $48 to take the Aerial Tram as sightseeing. Select runs are available for night skiing. Pro tip: Save $5 on lift/tram tickets by booking online.

Walk on Air

The **Veilbreaker Skybridges** *(per person from $150)*, opened in 2023, connect several peaks (Alyeska, Mighty Mite and Glacier Bowl). You'll be suspended 2500ft in the air as you traverse a high-mountain circuit over the course of two to three hours. You'll need a drink afterward, so pop into **Bore Tide** *(alyeskaresort.com/bore-tide-deli-bar)* for a well-earned libation – brews from Girdwood, King St and Denali Brewing, among others, go down even faster after this high-adrenaline excursion.

Dinner with a View

Alaska is not typically thought of as a fine-dining destination – more of a halibut and chips and grilled salmon kind of place. But the state does offer a handful of epicurean experiences that draw foodies from far and wide, none more so than a night lit in alpenglow at **Seven Glaciers Restaurant**, the signature fine-dining restaurant at Alyeska Resort.

Located at the top of the **Alyeska Aerial Tram** (tram tickets are included with dinner reservations), its remarkable mountain setting is unparalleled in Alaska, to the extent that you might not even notice if the food isn't up to snuff (which of course it will be). Tables throughout the restaurant frame incredible Chugach Mountain views, so close to your plate vertigo isn't out of the question. On certain summer nights, the alpenglow never wavers, casting a reddish-orange radiance over your meal that puts candlelight to shame.

Alaska's most memorable dinner setting is paired with a multicourse tasting menu ($139; reservations essential, vegan available). Expect starters like scallop bisque with brown butter croutons and paddlefish caviar before moving on to main courses like wakame steamed salmon with duck yolk mousse, *salmorejo*, caviar and sherry vinegar. Save room for dessert!

FOREST REFUGE

The **Alyeska Nordic Spa**'s incredible outdoor hydrotherapy circuit is the best $115 to $145 you might ever spend. A series of hot and cold pools evoke a spirit of Scandinavian wellness, but the intimacy and stunning Sitka spruce rainforest backdrop of the Forest Loop is where you'll want to beeline. Banya and Finnish saunas and near-private wood hot tubs await – an absolutely gorgeous setting for rejuvenating after a day in the mountains.

TOP TIPS

● More affordable Seven Glaciers alternative: An abbreviated **Night Cap** option (7-9pm) that includes a drink and bar snack (but no tram ticket).

● Expert skiers should tune in to Alyeska's **daily mountain report** for exciting outer area openings.

● **Sakura**'s creative sushi and other modern Asian specialties are a surprisingly worthwhile Japanese experience, even if not staying at the resort.

● **Ted's Express** (Chair 4) and **Bear Cub Quad** (Chair 3) give you access to the resort's intermediate/advanced single-track downhill Bike Park in summer *(noon-6pm Sat & Sun)*.

● Hike the advanced 2.2-mile **North Face Trail** up and ride the aerial tram down for free.

Continued from p172

clearly while taking a ride on the Swiss-designed **Alyeska Aerial Tram** (p175; *adult/child $43/33*) to Mt Alyeska (2300ft). From here, you also get extraordinary views of Turnagain Arm, Chugach Mountain peaks and, in summer, some outrageous outdoor adventures.

On **Crow Pass Trail**, you'll be swarmed by spruce forest, thick willow, glacial lakes, waterfalls and wildflowers. Dall sheep are often seen on the slopes above. Along the route, you'll encounter the rusted mining ruins of the Monarch Mine as well. It's four miles to **Raven Glacier**, the traditional turnaround point, and three miles to a USFS cabin. The trailhead sits 5.8 miles north of Alyeska Hwy on Crow Creek Rd. If you want to move a little faster, Alyeska Resort (p174) offers a guided e-bike tour *($135)* to Bird Point along forested sections of the Lower Iditarod Trail. Unobstructed views of the Chugach and Kenai Mountains and Turnagain Arm are highlights.

If you're looking for something less active, poke your head into the **Girdwood Center for Visual Arts** *(gcvagallery. org)*, a nonprofit cooperative art gallery filled with the work of those locals who get inspired by the majestic scenery that surrounds them. The work of over 30 local artists is represented, though you'll have to pop into Bake Shop to see the epic jewel-toned acrylics and graphic prints of our favorite, **Meg Smith Art + Design** *(megsmithdesign.com)*.

Bakes & Brews
Dining and drinking in Glacier City

Hurry up and wait at the Bake Shop (p151; *thebakeshop. com; mains $8.50-18)*, which is almost too popular for its own good, but it's hard to fault its old-school grilled-cheese sandwiches on house-made sourdough. It also does a wealth of other cold and hot sandwiches and draws hordes for breakfast (sourdough pancakes).

Nocturnal diversions abound in Girdwood, but a few hot spots are not debatable. Enjoy hop-heavy IPAs and NEIPAs under the lip of the mountain at **Girdwood Brewing Company** *(girdwoodbrewing.com)*, where ski bums and beer nerds share benches forged from skis surrounding year-round firepits. If brewery gear is your thing, GBC serves up some particularly tempting designs. Then head for always packed **Double Musky Inn** *(doublemuskyinn. com; mains $40-65)*. Folks drive down from Anchorage

---

BIKES & BITES WITH A METAL (P<OV>)

Self-proclaimed 'Metal Princess,' artist/fisherwoman **Alexandra Cronquist** *(@cronmonster)* is a Girdwood-based metal artist. Here are her biking and dining tips.

My top biking trails are **Lower Iditarod** – the trail runs through the Girdwood Valley and makes you feel like you are experiencing several forests in one trail – and the **Indian-Girdwood Trail** which travels through the coast from Girdwood to Indian with beautiful scenic pull outs along the way. Both double as great hikes! Powder Hound (p172) has bike rentals for all season and cross country/ downhill ski rentals. For an all-time dinner, go to Spoonline Bistro and get the keto flatbread and Caesar salad. Then head up the street to Jack Sprat (p151) for their King Dong cake and an espresso.

HOOKED ON HELI-SKIING?

Girdwood offers Alaska's only destination ski resort, but who needs a resort? Or even a ski lift for that matter? Some of North America's gnarliest heli-skiing awaits in **Valdez** (p193) for those who've graduated well beyond the bunny slopes.

for the French pepper steak – a brick-sized New York strip encrusted in cracked pepper and covered with a spicy burgundy sauce – but don't discount the Dijon/panko-crusted salmon in season, either. The Cajun-accented destination restaurant – and its ever-present cast of characters – is everything that's great about Girdwood.

Fun in the Forest

Arts, crafts and live music

The first weekend of July brings the good times to Girdwood for the **Girdwood Forest Fair** *(girdwoodforestfair.com)*, an annual Alaska music, arts and crafts fair in a gorgeous wooded setting. There's a beer garden that backs onto a glacial stream, and three stages of music (jazz, funk, folk, rap, Irish, country and more). Artists and performers come from all over Alaska. The festival has been going strong since 1975, when a few local artisans set up shop in the woods to move their craft. It's fun for the whole family as well – some sort of kids' game happens hourly throughout the festival. There are only three rules: No Dogs, No Politics, No Religious Orders. If you can't snag/afford a place to stay in Girdwood, there's a special commuter bus to the fair five times daily leaving from **University Center** in Anchorage (one-way/return $5/10).

Rush for Gold!

Mining history, panning for gold

Girdwood gets its name from James Girdwood, a real-life gold digger who hit pay dirt around the Crow Creek area in 1896. At its peak, **Crow Creek Gold Mine** *(crowcreekgoldmine.com; adult/child $13/6)* was producing 700 ounces per month. It remains a working mine today, but also an atmospheric, Gold Rush-evoking treasure trove of historic mining buildings and rare mining equipment. You can wander the grounds on your own and even learn how to pan for gold yourself *(adult/child $35/26)*. Stake your claim!

THE TOWN THAT SKIING BUILT

Girdwood's original townsite, founded as a supply camp for placer gold miners, was located on the Turnagain Arm, where today little exists beyond a gas station and a small strip mall with a bakery and other services. The devastation suffered from the 1964 Good Friday Earthquake pushed the town 2.5 miles further into the valley, closer to the original chairlift and day lodge at Alyeska, which had been operating for five years prior. But it wasn't until Alyeska opened its resort in 1994 that Girdwood grew into a proper town, prompting the birth of amenities (bars, restaurants, a mercantile, a brewery) and additional infrastructure needed (and desired) by incoming powder hounds.

EATING & DRINKING IN GIRDWOOD: OUR PICKS

Alpenglow Coffee House: A good place for an espresso hit, breakfast sandwiches and burritos, and a tasty selection of pastries. *7am-5pm* **$**

Chair 5: Local après-ski of choice; 10 craft beer taps (more classics in bottles) plus pizza, tacos, pasta, steak and burgers. Serious billiards action. *noon-2am* **$$**

Spoonline Bistro: Cozy, wine-centric spot serving well-rounded New American cuisine. Good weekend brunch (tasty vegan oyster mushroom burritos!). *5-9pm Mon-Wed, 9am-2pm & 5-9pm Sat & Sun* **$$**

Jack Sprat: Fantastic globally inspired comfort cuisine in cozy cabin-like environment (p151). The King Dong cake is local legend. *4-9pm Sun, Wed, Thu, to 10pm Fri & Sat* **$$$**

Beyond Girdwood

Glaciers – some unreachable by road, some more easily accessible – highlight Girdwood's environs, along with roadside wildlife and plenty of wild hiking.

GETTING AROUND

Once you leave Girdwood's compact environs you'll need your own wheels. This is pristine alpine territory and the best bits await off the main arteries. Further off the grid, Alaska Railroad's Spencer Glacier Whistle Stop service on the Glacier Discovery route is the only way to access Spencer Glacier. Unless you're heading on to Whittier, the road ends at Begich, Boggs Visitor Center. Be on the lookout for moose!

Girdwood sits in prime position for exploring further south along the Turnagain Arm. The Seward Highway Scenic Byway passes just 3 miles southwest of town; between there and the Anton Anderson Memorial Tunnel (which controls access to Whittier), an abundance of hiking and wildlife viewing unfolds on both sides of the highway. Beluga whales are regularly spotted once the salmon get up and running in summer, and the Alaska Wildlife Conservation Center is a feel-good rehabilitation sanctuary for a list of animals that may have eluded you in the wild. Then there's the glaciers: pretty Portage Glacier south of the byway; and backcountry Spencer Glacier, accessed by the Alaska Railroad's Spencer Glacier Whistle Stop service only.

Spencer Glacier

TIME FROM GIRDWOOD: **20 MINS**

Ride the rails to Spencer Glacier

If you don't have time for a longer trip on the famed **Alaska Railroad** (p157), the **Spencer Glacier Whistle Stop** service is a perfect half-day train/hike/glacier adventure from Girdwood. Catch the *Glacier Discovery* at **Portage Depot**, 14 miles southeast of Girdwood, at 1.30pm. From there, the ride to **Spencer Glacier** takes about 25 minutes. Upon arrival, hook up with United States Forestry Service Ranger for a guided, 2.6-mile round-trip jaunt to the glacier viewpoint. If you move briskly, you can also hike a 6-mile round-trip trail to the face of the glacier on your own (some folks opt to bring a pack-raft and hit the water as well). Whistle Stop hikers have from 1:45pm to 4:40pm to complete the hike and meet the train for the return. Or you can camp overnight at a group campsite. Round-trip fares from Portage Depot are cheaper *(adult/child $91/46)*; you can also catch the train from Anchorage or Girdwood *(adult/child $149/75)*.

Glacial recession is the hike's hot topic – in 1914, the Spencer Glacier came right up to the Whistle Stop station. According to the rangers, the glacier has receded 1.4 miles since 1890 (or about 70ft per year). The pleasant, easy hike is relatively flat through willow, cottonwood and spruce forest and you can

TURNAGAIN ARM – GIRDWOOD TO PORTAGE VALLEY

Glaciers, backcountry beauty and wildlife await on a driving tour of the Turnagain Arm along the Seward Highway Scenic Byway from Girdwood to Portage Valley.

START	END	LENGTH
Girdwood	Portage Valley	18 miles; 25min

About five miles south of Girdwood is ❶ **Chugach National Forest**, the second largest national forest in the US. Waterfalls tumble down the hillside before the wonderful ❷ **Alaska Wildlife Conservation Center** *(adult/child $27/22)*, a nonprofit haven where injured and rescued animals are rehabilitated. The USA's only herd of wood bison is of particular interest, but you'll see moose, reindeer, musk ox and brown bears – a great consolation if you missed them in the wild.

At the tip of the Turnagain Arm at Mile 79, head east on Portage Glacier Rd (Seward Hwy continues south for 78 miles to Seward) into the ❸ **Portage Valley** where fields of wildflowers flank silty rivers fed by glaciers hanging on for dear life.

The ❹ **Begich-Boggs Visitors Center** sits on the edge of Portage Lake at the valley's end. Ironically, the glacier hasn't been seen from here since 1994. To see it now, you'll need to venture out on **Portage Glacier Cruise**'s *MV Ptarmigan (adult/child $49/29)*, which traverses Portage Lake five times daily from the nearby dock (if you're lucky, you might see some calving ice); or continue on to the far end of the Whittier tunnel and hike the four-mile roundtrip ❺ **Portage Pass Trail**.

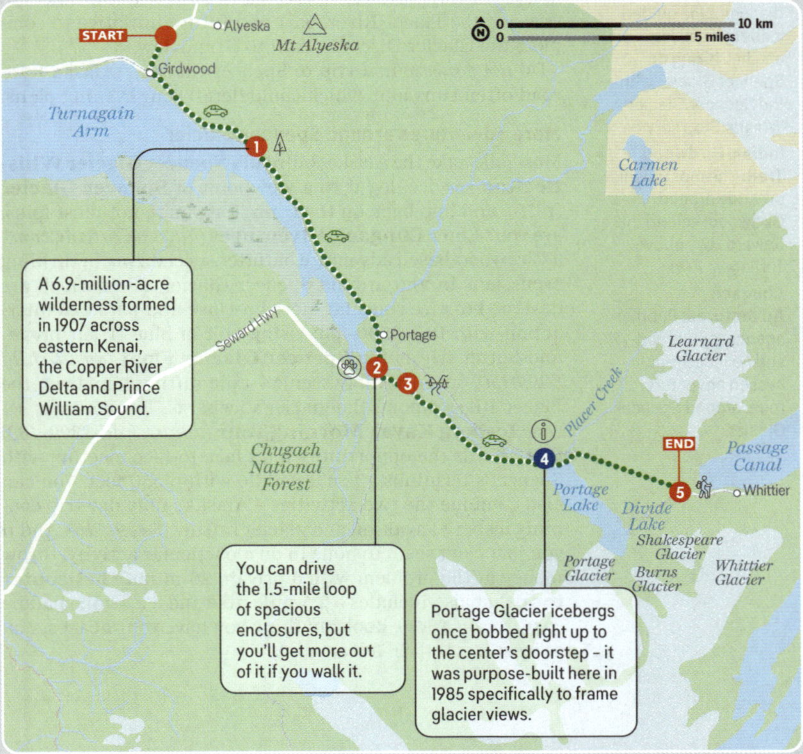
START
Alyeska
Mt Alyeska
0 10 km
0 5 miles
Girdwood
Turnagain Arm
Carmen Lake
A 6.9-million-acre wilderness formed in 1907 across eastern Kenai, the Copper River Delta and Prince William Sound.
Seward Hwy
Portage
Learnard Glacier
Placer Creek
END
Passage Canal
Whittier
Chugach National Forest
Portage Lake
Divide Lake
Shakespeare Glacier
Portage Glacier
Burns Glacier
Whittier Glacier
You can drive the 1.5-mile loop of spacious enclosures, but you'll get more out of it if you walk it.
Portage Glacier icebergs once bobbed right up to the center's doorstep – it was purpose-built here in 1985 specifically to frame glacier views.

BEST DISTRACTIONS OFF THE SLOPES

Crow Creek Gold Mine: James Girdwood staked the first claim on Crow Creek in 1896. Today you can still see some original buildings and sluices at this working mine.

Winner Creek Trail: Easy hike winding 5.5 miles (round-trip) through lush forest, ending in a dramatic gorge.

Ascending Path: This climbing-guide service has tours that combine guided iceberg kayaking and heli hiking on Spencer Glacier with the Spencer Glacier Whistle Stop service.

Indian-Girdwood Trail: The most scenic bike ride around Girdwood – along the Seward Hwy above Turnagain Arm.

Chugach Adventures: Popular agency for railroad- and helicopter-accessed adventure tours around Spencer Glacier.

Rafting near Spencer Glacier

see the vegetation gradually change as it has become more exposed, due to the glacier's retreat. Don't miss snapping a photo of the 'longest single span glue-laminated wooden truss bridge' in North America, erected in 2013 to allow hikers to traverse the Placer River, part of a future initiative to complete the Glacier Discover Trail to Grandview.

Do not *squeeze* in a trip to Spencer Glacier – Alaska Railroad often runs late, which could derail your evening plans.

More adventures around Spencer Glacier

Most folks take the Alaska Railroad's **Spencer Glacier Whistle Stop** service, leg it to a viewpoint of **Spencer Glacier** (p178), and hop back on the train. But you're not most folks, are you? Enter **Chugach Adventures** *(alaskanrafting.com)*, a Girdwood-based adventure outfitter specializing in thrilling excursions in and around Spencer Glacier, all of which are designed to give you a far more up-close-and-personal interaction with this 3500-foot-rising bolt of blue. Their bread-and-butter trip is the **Spencer Glacier Float** *(adult/child $299/150)*, an incredibly scenic 7-mile rafting trip down the Placer River among the glacier's icebergs. But it's their serene **Iceberg Kayak Morning Tour** *(adult/child $399-439)* that affords the opportunity for a face-to-face meeting with Spencer's terminus – you'll paddle within 350 feet. You can also combine the two activities – Alaska's only day trip coupling iceberg kayaking and glacier rafting *($499-546)*. And if you just can't seem to hone in on a particular activity, throw money at the problem with a private 20-minute **helicopter tour** that also includes a 2.5-mile hike and a 2.4-mile paddle *(per person $849)*. Book anything you have your heart set on at least a month in advance.

# Places We Love to Stay

$ Budget $$ Midrange $$$ Top End

Anchorage   MAPS p144, p147

Base Camp Anchorage Hostel $ Amid Midtown's action, this community-driven hostel has uncrowded dorms, a private queen with shared bath and a wood-fired sauna.

Oscar Gill House $$ Old fashioned three-room B&B occupying a historic 1913 clapboard home relocated from Knik by a former Anchorage mayor.

Susitna Place $$ View Alaska Range from this 4000 sq ft, five-room home perched on a downtown bluff. Suites have various bonus touches: soaking tubs, fireplaces, private patios.

Copper Whale Inn $$ Ideal downtown location, elegant interiors and two relaxing waterfall courtyards at this top-choice inn.

Lake Hood Inn $$ Airplane artifacts fittingly adorn this upscale home on Lake Hood, where you can ogle floatplanes landing and taking off to your heart's content. Lakeside rooms start at $189.

Salted Roots Basecamp $$$ Modern studios, 1- and 2-bedroom apartments/lofts that aren't cheap, but far less worse for wear than many downtown options.

Historic Anchorage Hotel $$$ Established one year after Anchorage itself, this distinguished, 26-room icon is rich in historic elegance.

Wildbirch Hotel $$$ In a downtown building that used to be a homeless shelter, this stylish boutique hotel has a cool bar and mid-century-modern vibes.

Aloft $$$ A welcoming, 146-suite chain boutique hotel for modern travelers in Midtown.

Beyond Anchorage

Alaska Chalet B&B $ European-style B&B tucked away deep into a residential neighborhood 1.1 miles east of the main drag. Host speaks German.

Eagle River Campground $ Coveted walk-in sites ensure at least half are reserved up to a year in advance. The river runs closest to the shady sites in the 'Rapids' section. At Glenn Hwy Mile 11.5.

Eklutna Lake State Recreation Area $ Popular 50-site campground at the west end of the lake with water, latrines, picnic tables and firepits.

Chugach State Park Cabins $$ Offers several cabins around Eklutna Lake (Dolly Varden, Kokanee, Rainbow Trout, Yuditna); wood stoves, off the grid.

Palmer   MAP p164

Pioneer Motel $ Historic road motel with 18 newly refurbished rooms in the heart of Palmer; with queen rooms starting at $165, it's good value.

Eagle Hotel $ Centrally located, old-style road hotel with particularly spacious rooms for the money (from $150). It's no frills, but you're steps from everything, including their own diner.

Alaska's Harvest B&B $$ This cozy, 6-room B&B frames uninterrupted views of Pioneer Peak from 15 wooded acres two miles outside town.

Alaska Glacier Lodge $$$ Clean and cozy one-room elevated cabins facing the Knik River, spruced up in recent years by new owners. Whir of helicopters from their tours are constant presence.

Girdwood   MAP p173

Girdwood Campground $ Eighteen mostly unmaintained walk-in sites in the woods near the action; $10 per night on honor system. Moose roam regularly.

Alyeska Hostel $ Bunks ($30) and private options (room, cabin, studio) in residential neighborhood one mile from Alyeska Hwy.

Ski Inn $$ Seven-room boutique B&B with both private and shared bathrooms on Girdwood's 'town square.' With rooms from $129, it's Girdwood's best deal. Mountain views.

Alyeska Resort (p174) **$$$** The mega ski resort that built Girdwood. Eight bars and restaurants serve 299 rooms, of which floors 6,7, and 8 have been modernized. Doubles from $289.

Researched by
Kevin Raub

Prince William Sound

IMPOSING GLACIERS AND ISOLATED FISHING PORTS

Snowcapped mountains, endearing wildlife, thrilling outdoor escapades and enormous glaciers highlight adventures launched from Prince William Sound's far-flung and funky fishing ports.

The second-largest national forest in the USA envelopes this island-speckled sound named for an 18th-century British prince. Chugach National Forest, surprisingly enough, is a temperate rainforest, but a bit of drizzly weather can't stop the good time the incredible scenery and nature affords those who venture here. The list runs deep and wide and tall: precipitous fjords, sheer-sided coastal mountains, numerous boom-crashing tidewater glaciers and remarkable bird and animal life shock and awe from bay to beautiful bay.

The sound clocks in at some 3800 miles of coastline, most of which is untarnished save three very unique 'villages' that guard the gates to endless adventure possibilities. Military-manufactured Whittier, the smallest of the bunch (everyone in town lives in one of two apartment blocks!), is popularly reached on a day trip from Anchorage and offers the largest concentration of tidewater glaciers within an hour of Alaska's biggest city. Valdez, by contrast, is the sound's 'cosmopolitan' fishing village, with good restaurants, breweries and hotels, and unmatched access to bucket-list glaciers like Columbia and Meares. Finally, there's Cordova, unreachable by road and all the more raw, authentic and uncrowded for it. Like three distinctive siblings, each of these seafaring towns relishes in its own distinct personality and offers unprecedented outdoor escapades. Local cruise-ship traffic among them is light, lending the region a genuine remoteness.

THE MAIN AREAS

VALDEZ
Epicurean-pleasing glacier and heli-ski haven. **p188**

CORDOVA
Wetlands-surrounded fishing town unreachable by road. **p198**

WHITTIER
Tiny and quirky military-built fishing village. **p208**

> For places to stay in Prince William Sound, see p215

Left: Sea otter, Columbia Glacier (p190); Above: Kayaking near Shoup Glacier (p192)

Find Your Way

At 70 miles wide and 30 miles long, Prince William Sound is an enormous body of water bound by majestic mountains and the Gulf of Alaska. Whittier, Valdez and Cordova, the sound's three biggest settlements, are all rather isolated.

CAR
Car hire is the preferred method of travel around Prince William Sound, especially considering you can take it on the ferry and use it in Cordova, where transport is an issue. Whittier and Valdez are 357 miles apart by road.

FERRY
The Alaska Marine Highway links Whittier, Valdez and Cordova by ferry a few times a week. Traveling by ferry in this region is an experience in itself – albeit a slow one – and an amazing way to see the sound for those who are unhurried.

PLANE
Cordova is connected with Anchorage and Yakutat by Alaska Airlines at least once a day; otherwise, charter flights and the ferry are the only ways to reach this isolated eastern Prince William Sound fishing depot.

> **Whittier, p208**
>
> Quirky fishing port originally built by the United States Army Corp of Engineers as a strategic Cold War outpost. Popular day-trip destination from Anchorage.

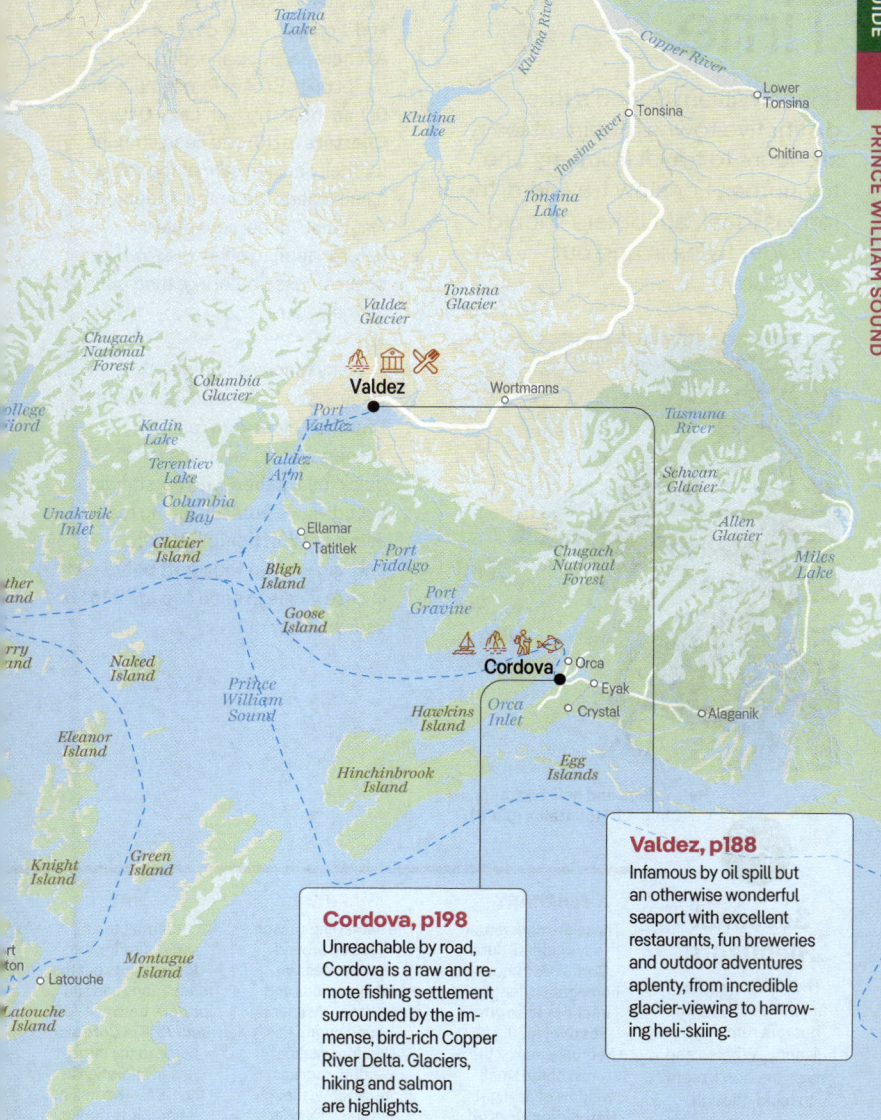

THE GUIDE

PRINCE WILLIAM SOUND

Cordova, p198
Unreachable by road, Cordova is a raw and remote fishing settlement surrounded by the immense, bird-rich Copper River Delta. Glaciers, hiking and salmon are highlights.

Valdez, p188
Infamous by oil spill but an otherwise wonderful seaport with excellent restaurants, fun breweries and outdoor adventures aplenty, from incredible glacier-viewing to harrowing heli-skiing.

Plan Your Time

Prince William Sound's three distinctive towns require at least six hours to travel from any one to another. For slow travelers, the ferry is ideal, but others should consider flying in and out of Cordova.

Heli-skiiers and heli-boarders, Chugach Mountains (p200)

In a Rush

● **Whittier** (p208) is the most easily reached of the three towns and works as a fine day trip from Anchorage. Book ahead to secure a seat on a 'Best of Prince William Sound' boat trip with **Lazy Otter Charters** (p210) and head straight for their seaside cafe of the same name (check the Anton Anderson Memorial Tunnel schedule beforehand!) to enjoy the town's best espresso before getting out on the water.

● Enjoy glaciers, humpback whales, sea otters and incredible **Chugach Mountain** (p200) scenery before returning for a quick meal paired with outstanding sound views from the dining room at **Inn at Whittier** (p212) – the only gig in town with draft beers, in case you're in need of a toast to your wild day out.

Seasonal Highlights

The driest months are June to August, but rain remains a nuisance. Whales and sea otters don't seem to mind, though.

FEBRUARY
These are dark winter days indeed, but Cordova's famous homegrown, tongue-in-cheek **Iceworm Festival** (p203) in February makes the most of the small window of daylight. **Heli-skiing** kicks off in Valdez.

APRIL
The heli-skiing season wraps up around Valdez; massive bird migrations and pre-season discounts abound during this shoulder season. Weather remains unpredictable, though, and some tourism services remain shuttered.

MAY
Warmer temps start settling into double digits but the fluctuations can still be brutal – between 33°F and 75°F in **Cordova**, home to the largest avian migration in the USA – five million shorebirds throng the delta.

A Few Days to Hang Out

● Given its proximity to Anchorage, a day trip to **Whittier** (p208) is a given, but then you'll need to choose between two far-flung fishing villages with contrasting personalities. **Valdez** (p188), reachable by a road swarmed with incredible scenery, is a heli-skiing and glacier-viewing hot spot with the sound's best restaurant and 'nightlife' scene (nightlife used lightly, but there are some fun local breweries!)

● **Cordova** (p198) is privy to no such land connection and is all the better for it, a place whose novel regenerative tourism initiatives promote a holistic partnership between the community and visitors. It's a spot to spend a few days outside the lines, soaking in local color, enjoying small-boat fishing and wildlife-viewing trips, and hiking and biking in unadulterated nature.

A Week to See It All

● Spend at least one night in **Whittier** (p208) to absorb the town's quirky military history and fun seaside restaurants that fill up with locals after the tourist boats have docked for the night.

● Take the long way round by car from Whittier to **Valdez** (p188), a six-hour-and-some-change road trip that delivers everything you want to see in Alaska: idyllic alpine scenery, roadside wildlife, idiosyncratic roadside stops and numerous glaciers. Be sure to pull over for a refreshing spray from **Bridal Veil Falls** (p195), a roadside waterfall 18 miles west of town.

● Then cross the sound via the great Alaska Marine Highway ferry to **Cordova** (p198) and while away some time taking in raw Alaska at its finest before returning to Whittier on the ferry.

JUNE
Early June visits bypass Alaska's biggest crowds and highest prices. Boat trips in Prince William Sound aren't yet full. Whittier celebrates the **summer solstice** (June 20 or 21) with playful festivals.

JULY
Whale-watching picks up, salmon are running and the sun shines; the driest month in Whittier sees 7.1in of rain. Highs in the low to mid-60°F range means pleasant days (when it's not raining!).

AUGUST
High-season tourism is in full swing – high prices, big crowds and full cruise ships are the norm. The majority of people descend on Whittier and Valdez, while Cordova is less cruise ship–focused.

SEPTEMBER
Shoulder season's fewer crowds and some sinking prices pair well with lingering days still great for hiking. Sound cruises out of Valdez can get a closer look at **Columbia Glacier** than June and July.

Valdez

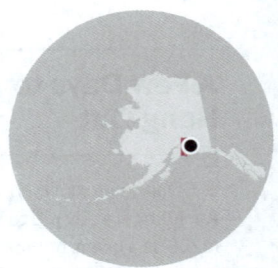

GLACIER VIEWING | WILDLIFE-SPOTTING | OUTDOOR ADVENTURES

GETTING AROUND

Valdez is small and walkable, with most exploration further afield involving a boat. Many tour operators, restaurants and bars face the water along North Harbor Dr. Most hotels, museums, the **Visitor Information Center** and a few other points of interest are spread among several blocks west and north from the harbor toward the **Ferry Terminal**. Nothing is more than a 15- to 20-minute walk. **Valdez Stay and Play** *(valdezstayandplay. com; rental per 2/3/4hr $45/60/75)* rents a variety of e-bikes.

Though infamous for being the departure point of one of history's worst oil-spill disasters (and the inconvenience of the doomed *Exxon Valdez* bearing its name), Valdez persevered and survived long before the environmentally catastrophic incident of 1989 that killed marine life, disrupted ecosystems and ruined livelihoods. In fact, the adventure-sport-loving and culturally conscious town of today is Valdez 2.0. The original version was located 5 miles to the east pre-1964, before the second-strongest earthquake in recorded history sent its docks sliding into the sea. The town was quickly rebuilt on more stable ground (it remains one of the few towns in North America to ever be completely relocated), a testament to Valdez' feisty Alaska spirit. Today, this quaint harbor town is a cool, inclusive city by the sea, with excellent museums, good restaurants and outdoor adventures aplenty – especially its iceberg-punctuated seas and heli-skiing in the razor-sharp peaks standing sentinel over town.

Glacier Getaway

Glacier-viewing, wildlife-spotting

If Valdez has a main event, it's glacier gawking on the **Prince William Sound**. But don't fret about repeating experiences if you've already been chasing ice in Whittier, for example – due to its mammoth size, this side of the sound offers a completely different set of glaciers. Columbia steals the spotlight – it's the second largest tidewater glacier in Alaska, after all (Eastern Alaska's Hubbard Glacier is the biggest) – you might consider visiting the less famous but every bit as spectacular Meares Glacier instead.

The best way to see the glaciers around Valdez is on a boat tour. **Stan Stephens Glacier & Wildlife Cruises** *(stephens cruises.com)*, the biggest tour operator in town, runs wonderful and comfortable catamarans for up to 149 people to **Columbia Glacier** *(adult/child $169/84.50)* and 7½-hour trips to **Meares Glacier** *(adult/child $189/94.50)*. Staff is extremely friendly

PRINCE WILLIAM SOUND VALDEZ

VALDEZ

HIGHLIGHTS
1 Columbia Glacier
2 Maxine & Jesse Whitney Museum
3 Meares Glacier
4 Valdez Museum

SIGHTS
5 Robe Lake
6 Valdez Marine Terminal
7 Valdez Museum Annex

ACTIVITIES
8 Anadyr Adventures
9 Lu-Lu Belle Glacier Wildlife Cruises
10 Pangaea Adventures
11 Stan Stephens Glacier & Wildlife Cruises

SLEEPING
12 Bear Paw RV Campground I
13 Best Western Valdez Harbor Inn
14 Chugach Naswik Suites
15 Downtown B&B Inn
16 Eagle's Rest RV Park
17 Keystone Hotel
18 Robe Lake Lodge
19 Totem Hotel & Suites
20 Valdez Glacier Campground

EATING
21 Fat Mermaid
22 Nat Shack
23 Old Town Diner
24 Poor Betty's
25 Roadside Potatohead Too
26 Rogue's Garden

DRINKING & NIGHTLIFE
27 Growler Bay Brewing Co.
28 The Coffee Co.
29 Valdez Brewing

INFORMATION
30 Valdez Visitor Information Center

TRANSPORT
31 Ferry Terminal
32 Valdez Stay and Play

OUT & ABOUT IN VALDEZ

Lisa Cronk is the General Manager at **Valdez Brewing** (p192). When she's not pulling pints, you'll find her around Prince William Sound. *(@ak.fishergirl)*

Nothing beats those sunshine days where you can get outside in Valdez. I personally recommend being out on the water whenever you can. You'll love kayaking on the ocean or nearby **Robe Lake**. Getting to see the wildlife from the boat is a bonus. We also have an amazing trail system here and you can see the mountains and ocean from many of them. If you want a taste of the Sound, **Poor Betty's** *(poorbettys.com)* outside of Valdez Brewing makes their own fish fry and use local halibut for their halibut po' boy! And, of course, they make their own tartar sauce. Delish!

and eager to please, and knowledgeable captains maintain an open bridge, so you can visit and chitchat at your leisure. Both tours incur a $1 per person Valdez Harbor Fee. **Lu-Lu Belle Glacier Wildlife Cruises** *(lulubelletours.com; tours per person $181)* also runs recommended glacier trips. Now which glacier to choose?

Columbia Glacier is undoubtedly the big daddy of Prince William Sound's glaciers and is one of the world's fastest moving, though, like many ice floes in Alaska, it's rapidly retreating – peeling back an estimated 15 miles since 1980. Spilling forth from the Chugach Mountains, it ends with a face as high as a football field. The rub? Columbia is calving an unprecedented amount of ice by Alaska standards – up to 8 million tons of ice falls daily from its face. While boats aim to get as close as half a mile from Columbia's terminus, the sheer amount of ice and icebergs can sometimes prevent boats from giving passengers the up close and personal look they came to Alaska to get. According to one captain, boats sometimes cannot get any closer than 2 to 6 miles from May through July (August and September trips fair better).

Meares Glacier, on the other hand, is one of Alaska's only stable glaciers (some even claim it's advancing though that is unlikely). Due to its distance from Valdez, it's less visited than Columbia, but no less awe-inspiring. In fact, the moment the boat rounds the northeastern corner of Unakwik Inlet for the grand unveiling of Meares is arguably Prince William Sound's most breath-snatching moment. An enormous, spiky-topped wall of burning blue evoking an impenetrable security fence for an otherworldly ice fortress imposingly stares you down

SEA LIONS, OTTERS & WHALES

On the hunt for more wildlife in Prince William Sound? **Whittier** (p208), reachable via ferry or road from Valdez, is another excellent launching point for boat trips into the sound.

Kayaker, Prince William Sound (p188)

– insert *Game of Thrones* anecdote here – and the boat can get as close as a quarter-mile from the face. That's far closer than Columbia. Additionally, the two extra hours required to visit Meares generally translates into far more wildlife-viewing opportunities, so take that into consideration if gaggles of sea otters, harbor seals and the occasional humpback whale are on your to-see list.

Valdezian Outdoor Exploits

Alfresco adventures around Valdez

There are (almost) as many distractions in and around Valdez for culture hounds, hopheads and gastronauts as there are for thrill-seekers and outdoor enthusiasts, though the latter is certainly the main draw. Over the course of a few days here, adventures in the wild should dominate your day, though rest assured there's plenty of culinary and craft-beer pursuits to come back to in the evenings.

For outdoor adventuring, choices are vast (if you've come to Valdez thinking there's nothing to see here besides the Columbia Glacier, you'll need to recalibrate that train of thought). Sea-kayaking adventures abound. Recommended outfitter **Anadyr Adventures** *(anadyradventures.com)* takes on full-day trips to Columbia Glacier ($375) or, for those pressed for time, a wonderful half-day trip to Valdez Glacier ($175). **Pangaea Adventures** *(pangaeaadventures.com; day trips $89-375)*, under enthusiastic ownership by a relocated Minnesotan, is also highly recommended.

For day-hikers, set out on the **Mineral Creek Trail**, a 12.2-mile round trip to the old Smith Stamping Mill, built by WL Smith in 1913, notable for only requiring two men to operate it (using mercury to remove the gold from the ore). Mind the bears and mountain goats! The **Shoup Bay Trail** (Section A) is also worth consideration, a 6.5-mile coastal-hugging round

EXXON VALDEZ DISASTER

The *Exxon Valdez* crashed into Prince William Sound's Bligh Reef in 1989, spilling 11 million gallons of oil. Numbers are staggering: $2.8 billion (estimated economic loss), $2 billion (cleanup), $1.8 billion (habitat restoration) and $1.1 billion (civil and criminal damages). Industry changes include the mandating of double-hulled oil tankers, tugs must escort tankers in Prince William Sound, and mandated oil-spill response facilities have been constructed in Chenega and Tatitlek with another on the way in Cordova. The *Exxon Valdez* itself, which was initially repaired and renamed *Exxon Mediterranean*, was sold for scrap in 2012. As for the oil, some remains in the beaches to this day and the ecosystem is still recovering.

☑ TOP TIP

Come hoping for sun but be prepared for rain: Prince William Sound sits in a temperate rainforest. It rains a lot around here. Packing in layers is best, avoiding cotton as much as possible – synthetic materials are much better at insulating.

THE 1964 GREAT ALASKA EARTHQUAKE

The 9.2 Good Friday Earthquake devastated the first incarnation of Valdez in 1964. The disaster was the most powerful earthquake ever recorded in North America (and the second largest worldwide – only Chile's 1960 Valdivia earthquake was bigger). The ground shook for an unimaginable 4½ minutes, terrorizing the citizens of Valdez right around 'rush' hour (5.36pm). Thirty people were killed when a massive underwater landslide took out the city harbor and docks (and a ship docked at the time). A 27ft-high tsunami was unleashed on the nearby village of Chenega, killing scores more. Nearly 140 deaths were recorded in total, the majority from tsunamis in Alaska, Oregon and California.

trip that takes in stunning views of **Port Valdez**, **Shoup Glacier** and the impressive **Gold Creek Delta**.

If you just want to take in the seafaring air, Valdez' small boat harbor is about as picturesque as it gets, with an incredible backdrop of serrated Chugach peaks visible on a clear day. Settle in on a bench along the boardwalk and take in soaring gulls and bald eagles weaving in and out all manner of vessels – often manned by lucky anglers weighing in 100lb or 200lb halibut!

Prince William Sound's Best Museums
Settler artifacts, fascinating town history

Valdez packs in a good deal of culture for a town with a population that barely squeaks above 3800. Don't miss the most fascinating museum in the Sound, **Maxine & Jesse Whitney Museum** *(pwsc.alaska.edu/maxine-and-jesse-whitney-museum)*, which houses the mesmerizing private collection of an American couple who settled in Alaska in 1947 and became enthusiastic hoarders of Alaska Native art, artifacts and taxidermy. The family's story is captivating, to say nothing of highlights such as ivory and baleen artwork, colorful Athabascan footwear, an extraordinary collection of parkas and *mukluks*

Beautiful epoxy resin bar by artist Jess Crow!

 DRINKING IN VALDEZ: OUR PICKS

Valdez Brewing: Wonderful patio and art-supporting interior are perfect backdrops to this 12-tap brewery. Bring your own food. Save money for epic gear. *noon-9pm*

The Coffee Co.: Best espresso in town and bits and bobs for breakfast (burritos, protein-stuffed English muffins) in a space doubling as a plant nursery. *6am-4pm*

Fat Mermaid: The harborfront outdoor deck is the spot for tale swapping, adventure prep or mountain gazing paired with 18 taps of Alaska craft. *8am-11pm*

Growler Bay Brewing Co.: Owner-operated nanobrewery inside a lovely historic teal house relocated from Old Valdez. Rousing good time on cruise-ship days. *noon-9pm Fri & Sat*

Pinzon Bar, Valdez Museum

(Indigenous soft hide boots) as well as Alaska Native dolls and an incredible taxidermy collection (which includes what once was the largest fully-mounted moose in the world). It's all extremely well put together and curated. It's only open from May 5 to Labor Day (September 1) and, for now, remains free.

Equally well done is the **Valdez Museum** (*valdezmuseum.org; adult/child $12/7*), which is chock-full of town-centric exhibits shedding light on Valdez and what makes it tick. So much so, in fact, it needed the **Valdez Museum Annex** nearer the water to hold it all. Highlights in the main exhibit include a gorgeous Ahrens Steamer fire engine dating to 1907; the old timey **Pinzon Bar**, a social hub with pieces manufactured in the late 1880s relocated in its entirety from Old Valdez; and a deep dive to the *Exxon Valdez* oil spill that includes a damaged piece of the ship's hull. At the annex, you'll find a scale model of the original town – essential to fill in the blanks if you are visiting Old Valdez.

Holy Heli!

Heli-skiing above Valdez

Valdez is home to some of the steepest, deepest, gnarliest and burliest snow-riding terrain anywhere in the world. At inland

THE END OF THE LINE

If you take a boat cruise out of Valdez, you'll depart the Port of Valdez, passing the **Valdez Marine Terminal** (VMT), the southern terminus of the **Trans Alaska Pipeline System**, on the boat's port side. Each of the 14 crude-oil holding tanks (seven are visible from the boat) hold 510,000 barrels of oil. It was from here that the doomed *Exxon Valdez* departed on that faithful night in 1989 before running aground on nearby Bligh Reef. The site once welcomed visitors, but since September 11, 2001, stricter security protocols have closed it to the public (though it doesn't stop bevvies of RVing looky-loos from trying to get a closer look from the end of the Dayville Rd).

 EATING IN VALDEZ: OUR PICKS

Take out only as closing time nears.

Roadside Potatohead Too: Valdez's must-stop street-food stall; globally inspired – black-bean corn salad breakfast wrap, pulled pork po' boys. *7am-9pm* $

Nat Shack: Lines don't lie: Worth-the-wait Cal-Mex food truck. (Banh-mi crunch wrap or halibut tacos. Trust us!) Service is slow but worth it. *11am-8pm* $

Rogue's Garden: Lovely organic supermarket and local-farm-supporting sandwich deli; daily soup and sandwich combo or build your own. *9am-6pm Tue-Fri, to 5pm Sat* $

Old Town Diner: Down-home diner easily serving the best burgers in town coupled with good value and…disappointing service. *11.30am-7.30pm Wed-Sun* $

SEEKING THE SLOPES?

If you're looking to hit the slopes the old-fashioned way (via a comfortable ski lift rather than a helicopter), **Alyeska Resort**, Alaska's top ski resort, is 339 miles by road west of Valdez.

ski resorts in, say, Colorado, dry powder barely clings to 50-degree inclines; here in the coastal Chugach Mountains, the sopping-wet flakes glue to angles of 60-plus-degrees, creating ski slopes where elsewhere there'd be cliffs. Factor in 1000in of snow per winter and mountains that descend 7000ft from peak to sea, and you've got a ski bum's version of Eden. For advanced skiers, the February to April season is legend. If you've got the skills (and the cojones) **Valdez Heli-Ski Guides** (*valdezheliskiguides.com*), the most experienced heli-ski operation in Alaska, can drop you from a chopper. Weekly packages ('Memberships') start at $9850.

Rafting Through Keystone Canyon

Class III rapids, mountain scenery

The glacial Lowe River flanks Richardson Hwy 12 miles outside Valdez, providing a stunning pairing for the soaring mountains all around. It's one to thing ogle it from your car, of course, but quite another to raft it. Cutting through the impressive **Keystone Canyon**, you'll navigate relatively easy class III rapids, but sheer canyon walls, cascading waterfalls and superb views of the magnificent Thompson Pass replace thrills and spills with vistas and hills! Pangaea Adventures (p191) is the go-to agency in town; their three-hour raft down the river (*$110*) also includes a stop at Bridal Veil Falls.

Skier, Valdez region

Beyond Valdez

Valdez marks the eastern end of the sound's accessible roadways; driving here takes in some of Alaska's most prize-winning scenery.

Richardson Hwy (Hwy 4) ends at Valdez, but not before unveiling plummeting waterfalls (Horsetail and Bridal Veil Falls) along the Keystone Canyon just outside town and the site of Old Valdez, destroyed in the 1964 earthquake. Further afield, glaciers both near and far can be viewed from Hwy 1 west of Glennallen. On clear days, a postcard-panorama of the Chugach Mountains looms to the south. The massive, 4-mile-wide Matanuska Glacier practically unravels right onto the playground of the appropriately named Glacier View School in Glacier View, nearly making its way onto the highway. Bear- and moose-spotting often accompany the views. In short, road-tripping to/from Valdez is a beautiful thing indeed.

Old Valdez

TIME FROM VALDEZ: **10 MINS**

A town relocated

Before it was decimated in 1964 by the largest earthquake the United States has ever seen, **Old Valdez** was located 4 miles southeast of the current town. In 1964, 4.38 minutes of shaking started, and now, like a wilder, starker, less-trampled version of Italy's Pompeii, there isn't much left to see, bar some street signs, a few overgrown foundations and a smattering of interpretive boards. Free, one-hour guided walking tours of the site are organized by the Valdez Museum (p193) on selective days throughout the summer; otherwise they offer a QR-coded self-guided tour. Bring your imagination.

Bridal Veil & Horsetail Falls

TIME FROM VALDEZ: **30 MINS**

Get sprayed by roadside waterfalls

For a quick and easy excursion from Valdez, head to **Keystone Canyon**, a steep-sided 3-mile-long slit between miles 14 and 17 of the Richardson Hwy, 18 or so miles from Valdez. Here, two impossibly photogenic, kitty-corner waterfalls spray the highway (and you!). First up, **Bridal Veil Falls**, which drops 900ft from the canyon walls, and then **Horsetail Falls**, a 328ft descending waterfall that freezes in winter.

Places

Old Valdez p195

Bridal Veil & Horsetail Falls p195

GETTING AROUND

The beautiful mountain and glacier-blanketed expanse radiating out from Valdez is prime road-trip territory – having your own wheels will greatly enhance your experience and you won't exactly be spoiled for choice. If you want to see the incredible landscapes that surround the sound, you'll need wheels. Make sure to gas up whenever you can. Besides Valdez, Glennallen and Palmer, gas stations are scarce. Moose love to saunter across Hwys 1 and 4, so watch out!

DRIVING TOUR

Long Way Round the Sound

With Cordova unreachable by road, circumnavigating Prince William Sound by car isn't possible, but you can *almost* do it, which is far from a disappointing consolation. There's no moment on this epic 360-mile, 6½-hour road trip from Valdez to Whittier where you're not flabbergasted by Chugach scenery. Raging glacial rivers, majestic mountains, eye-popping waterfalls and imposing glaciers – it's all here on the Alaska open road.

1 Blueberry Lake State Recreation Site

The small alpine **Blueberry Lake** is pretty enough, but the real reason to stop here is to absorb the incredible scenic surrounds of the **Thompson Pass**. This 2600ft-high breach cuts through the **Chugach Mountains**, which almost seem to envelope you as you drive through. Blanketed in snow even in summer, it's jarringly beautiful.

The Drive: It's a 15 mile or so drive northeast through the often thick-clouded Thompson Pass to the Worthington Glacier State Recreation Site.

2 Worthington Glacier

A National Natural Landmark since 1968, the rapidly retreating, 9-sq-mile **Worthington Glacier** once practically sideswiped your vehicle as you passed by. Now, you'll need to park ($5) and walk 0.4 miles to a viewing platform, where you can just see the glacier's terminus peering over the edge of the mountain.

Worthington Glacier

The Drive: Take Hwy 4 (Richardson Hwy) 59 miles north to Willow Creek.

3 Willow Mountain View Station

On a clear day, this highway **lookout** affords expansive views across Wrangell-St Elias National Park & Preserve (p334), the largest national park and designated wilderness area in the US, with several towering Wrangell Mountain peaks forming a cinematic backdrop, including Mt Wrangell (14,163ft) and Mt Blackburn (16,390ft). From here, it's a straight shot 160 miles north to the next road, Canada's Alaska Hwy.

The Drive: Hwy 4 ends 28 miles north at Glennallen. Take Hwy 1 west for 84 miles to Glacier View.

4 Matanuska Glacier

After jaw-dropping **Nelchina Glacier** views south (if it's clear) on the drive, the mighty **Matanuska Glacier** comes spilling out of the Chugach Mountains like a snow tsunami heading for the highway. The best and most complete view is just after Caribou Creek Recreational Mining Area between Miles 106 and 105, but you can see this giant ice tongue from numerous vantage points for the next several miles.

The Drive: It's 115 miles southeast through stunning mountain scenery to Turnagain Arm, passing worthwhile stops Palmer and Anchorage along the way.

5 Turnagain Arm

The landscape completely changes south of Anchorage, where the Seward Hwy Scenic Byway parallels the **Turnagain Arm** for 50 miles southwest. Along the way, wildlife-spotting possibilities include beluga whales in the water and Dall sheep along the mountainside. It's an incredibly scenic ride all the way through the Portage Glacier Rd turnoff for the final 11 miles to Whittier.

Cordova

FISHING VILLAGE | COPPER RIVER SALMON | GLACIER HIKES

☑ TOP TIP

Don't make the mistake of assuming Cordova is walkable from the airport by looking at Google Maps, where **Cordova Municipal Airport** (CKU) is just 1.5 miles from the harbor. Alaska Airlines flies into **Merle K (Mudhole) Smith Airport** (CDV) – 11.5 miles southeast.

If you're searching for raw Alaska, isolated Cordova is as unadulterated as it gets. With no road access, this small, eccentric fishing village has managed to stave off mass tourism. Its newly adopted regenerative tourism model is best described as a 'conscious untouristing,' at least from the high-dollar, quick-fix cruise tourism that Whittier and Valdez have embraced (only five expedition-style cruise ships call here each year). Buzz words like authenticity come to mind, but without the usual ironic accompaniment. Think of the village as a choose-your-own-adventure port of call that wants its eco-altruistic tourism goals to not only benefit the local community without leaving a footprint but improve the destination as a whole. This is why Cordova deserves a place on your itinerary, but there's no shame in enjoying the trail-accessible glaciers, plentiful well-marked hiking trails and the strikingly beautiful Copper River Delta while you're here.

Sailing the Sound
Ferrying across Prince William Sound

Anyone can hop on a blink-and-you-missed-it Alaska Airlines flight from Anchorage or Yakutat to Cordova – if the weather cooperates, the views are flabbergasting and it's indeed an

GETTING AROUND

Compact Cordova can be easily explored on foot – just a few main streets and a beautiful harbor area. For points further afield, there's **Chinook Auto Rentals** (*chinookautorentals.net; per day from $85*), but renting a bike from **Cordova Gear** (*cordovagear.com; bike/e-bike rentals from $65/80*) is a rewarding way to transport yourself. For Cordova's Merle K. (Mudhole) Smith Airport there's a **shuttle** (*907-424-2277; $20*). Reserve ahead or walk outside the airport terminal to the red building on the left.

CORDOVA

HIGHLIGHTS
1. Small Boat Harbor

SIGHTS
2. Cordova Historical Museum
3. Ilanka Cultural Center
4. Prince William Sound Science Center

ACTIVITIES
5. Mt Eyak Ski Area

SLEEPING
6. Alaskan Hotel & Bar
7. Bear Country Lodge
8. Odiak Camper Park
9. Orca Adventure Lodge
10. Prince William Motel
11. Reluctant Fisherman Inn

EATING
12. Baja Taco
13. Jen's Hella Good Pizzeria
14. Little Cordova Bakery
15. Powder House Bar & Grill

see 11 Reluctant Fisherman

DRINKING & NIGHTLIFE
16. Copper River Brewing

see 11 Reluctant Fisherman Bar

ENTERTAINMENT
17. Cordova Center

SHOPPING
18. Copper River Fleece
19. Cordova Gear
20. Drifters Fish

TRANSPORT
21. Chinook Auto Rentals

see 19 Cordova Gear

22. Cordova Municipal Airport
23. Merle K Smith Airport

48 HOURS IN CORDOVA

Cordovan **Katrina Hoffman** is the president and CEO of the Prince William Sound Science Center (p203) and co-owner of **Webber Wild Seafood** (webber-wildseafood.com).

Head to **Alaganik** for wetland views from the boardwalk. On your way back to town, take Sheridan Glacier Rd to the end to see the active **Sheridan Glacier** (p205). Hit up the **Cordova Historical Museum** (p202). The next day, visit the **Ilanka Cultural Center** (ilankaculturalcenter.com) to learn about the culture of the region. Grab treats at one of the coffee shops or the bakery before strolling the breakwater or hiking up ski hill. Relax with dinner and drinks at **Reluctant Fisherman Inn** while looking over the commercial fishing fleet.

experience in itself. But time-permitting, the **Alaska Marine Highway** (dot.alaska.gov/amhs) from Whittier offers a slow-boat journey across the Prince William Sound, one of Alaska's most cinematic landscapes.

AMH sails the M/V Aurora ($72, 6½ hours) from Whittier to Cordova on Sunday and Thursday, with return trips sailing on Monday, Wednesday and Friday (you can also reach Cordova from Valdez via Whitter as well as Chenega Bay). Bicycles, kayaks and inflatables cost $30 extra per item.

The vessel carries 250 passengers as well as 33 vehicles (not a bad idea when heading to Cordova, where local transport can be an issue).

While no luxury cruise (this is state of Alaska public transport after all), the M/V Aurora is equipped with a cafeteria-style restaurant, a covered heated solarium (popular with those pitching tents), a movie lounge, showers and observation lounges with comfy chairs. It's the latter where you'll want to plant yourself – both the surrounding scenery of the **Chugach Mountains** and an incredible array of potential wildlife opportunities (sea otters, sea lions and humpback and orca whales highlight the list) should distract from the lack of wifi. You are welcome to bring your own food aboard (alcohol is prohibited).

Doing the trip one-way only and flying out is worth considering, especially since ferry timings might not gel with your particular travel plans.

Cordova Calling

Isolated fishing village, outdoor escapades

Cordova is the kind of place you don't stumble upon – if you're here, you've come with purpose. That purpose has traditionally been fishing, be it commercial or recreational. Tourism is an emerging concept here, which is precisely what

Cordova

gives the town its authentic Alaska ethos. A few days spent here is hard to shake from your wanderlust consciousness.

If you bed down at rustic Orca Adventure Lodge (p215), 3 miles northeast of the harbor, you'll benefit not only from choosing Cordova's top option, but you'll get access to one of the best restaurants in town (guests only), the best coffee shop/cafe in town (the **Whale's Tail**; open to the public) and Cordova's principal adventure outfitter. Basic but comfortable rooms offer patios with outstanding sea views and the entire property is located within a historic cannery ecosystem built by the Pacific Steam Whaling Company in 1886 that predates Cordova by 30 years. It's isolated and wonderful.

Guest or not, Orca is the go-to operator for guided adventures. They can get you out on the water for fishing or wildlife tours, sea kayaking at Sheridan Glacier (p205) and photo safaris.

Cordova itself is small. Take an afternoon to wander in and out of the main street offerings - if you can tear yourself away from the picturesque **Small Boat Harbor** and the dramatic 360-degree views on offer by walking the harbor's short **Breakwater Trail**.

Harbor views from the outdoor patio are spectacular.

WHY I LOVE CORDOVA

Kevin Raub, Lonely Planet Writer

I have always been intrigued by off-the-grid places; what you find there is usually a version of something at its most raw. Cordova is raw Alaska, where a brawny, sea-hardened population (just 2300 or so) self-sustains on moose, deer and salmon against an isolated, impossibly scenic backdrop of the Copper River Delta and the Chugach Mountains. There's no road in or out, which protects its unbowing to tourism and sustains its way of life; and only one real road of note in town as well. It houses just a handful of locally owned establishments and is full of characters like Andrew Smallwood, a once-nationless British-Kenyan who bush piloted alongside the man the airport is named after. Brilliant.

 EATING IN CORDOVA: OUR PICKS

Baja Taco: Sockeye salmon tacos, burritos and other Mex-leaning treats served seasonally out of an aged red school bus. Good breakfast. *7am-9pm* **$**

Jen's Hella Good Pizzeria: Year-round pizzeria doing wood-fired pies as well as a wealth of burgers, pitas, tacos and bowls. No alcohol (for now). *11am-10pm* **$**

Powder House Bar & Grill: Local's haunt overlooking Eyak Lake. Burgers (with egg), Reubens and seafood specials. *11am-9pm Tue-Thu, to 10pm Fri & Sat, noon-8pm Sun* **$**

Reluctant Fisherman Restaurant: *The* spot in town. Commendable burgers, fish and chips, pot roast, global fusion, fantastic views. *11am-2pm & 4-9pm Tue-Sun* **$$**

THE ART OF RETREAT

Be on the lookout for the captivating oil-on-linen/oil-on-board paintings of Cordova-based landscape artist **David Rosenthal** *(907-424-5613; antarcticpaintings.com)*. Calling on decades of eyewitness account as well as historical research, Rosenthal's ongoing exhibition, *Painting at the End of the Ice Age*, chronicles changes in glacial landscapes in remarkable technicolor. The vibrant works illustrate the remarkable retreat of the Cordova's surrounds, including Sheridan, Miles, Childs, as well as Prince William Sound glaciers further afield, such as Columbia. Call ahead for a personal viewing of this constantly-evolving, socially-imperative project, which often depicts the same stunning Cordova landscapes you might have seen on a visit here. Rosenthal also offers drawing, watercolor or painting classes in his home studio.

Aerial view of Cordova

Be sure to visit the modern **Cordova Center** *(cityofcordova.net/the-cordova-center)*, a wonderful cultural center that houses a library, a 206-seat theater that attracts traveling acting groups and film festivals, and the **Cordova Historical Museum** *(cordovamuseum.org)*, featuring well-done exhibits on the city's history and revolving local artwork.

Rise and shine at 5.30am and head to the **Little Cordova Bakery** *(tlcbakerycdv.com)*, too, not only for cheddar biscuits and gravy as good as anything in Georgia (along with divine caramel pecan sticky buns and commendable kolaches), but to sit on the harborview bench with your coffee and watch gaggles of town characters come in for their morning caffeine fix. There is a sea otter that likes this spot, too; you might see him down in the water.

Until 2022, nocturnal diversions in Cordova were of the drinking den variety, places for fisherman to unload after a day at sea, the kind of places you see in Hollywood films about far-flung fishing villages unaccustomed to outsiders. **Copper River Brewing** *(copperriverbrewing.com)* has given Cordova a civilized drinking establishment, where 'artists, skiers, knitters, fishermen, pilots, welders, biologists and desk jockeys' can mingle over brewer Micah Renfeldt's excellent IPAs, stouts and often locally driven experimental beers (a Berliner Weisse with local kelp, for example). Call it a night!

Cordova's Small but Historic Ski Hill
Single chairlift skiing

The **Mt Eyak Ski Area** *(mteyak.org; lift ticket adult/child $35/15)* offers good-value winter skiing – you'll be lifted up by one of only two single chairlifts in North America! The relic 1939 American Steel and Wire single chairlift from Sun Valley, Idaho, was transferred to Cordova in the 1970s. Along its 800ft vertical drop, you'll encounter around 30 different trail options for all skill levels on this ski 'hill'. There's an easy trail down the hill for those looking for less thrills and spills; as well as a rope tow on the bunny hill.

The Iceworm Cometh!
Winter escapades, festival fun

Cabin fever in these parts ain't no joke, but locals have one of the sound's most unique antidotes: Cordova's famous homegrown, tongue-in-cheek **Iceworm Festival** *(iceworm festival.com)*, held on the first weekend in February. Alaska's oldest community festival, it includes the crowning of a Miss Iceworm, a Survival Suit Race that sees participants don survival suits and plunge into the harbor, a parade that culminates with a 100ft-long iceworm float and a hotly-contested paper-airplane contest. The raucous event was dreamed up in 1961 and is one of Alaska's best times during its long, hard winter.

Shops in the Sound
Browse homegrown shops for unique souvenirs

Cordova is home to fewer than 2500 people, but they're a determined, independently minded bunch. That translates into some very cool businesses around town. Locals swear by the high-quality, unique fleece jackets, vests and hats at **Copper River Fleece** *(copperriverfleece.com; hoodies from $109)*. Colorful trim is the company's signature, and most of the sewing is done upstairs above the shop (there's a 24-hour turnaround on custom designs). It's one of the best and most functional mementos from town. If you want to take home some indulgent Alaska salmon, **Drifters Fish** *(driftersfish.com)* sustainably harvests wild salmon and prawns from their small boat, flash freezes it and ships it to your home; or pick up some smoked sockeye ($16) or coho ($30) in a tinned can. In addition to being the town go-to for bike and gear rental, **Cordova Gear** *(cordovagear.com)* has a smorgasbord of uniquely designed proprietary products (hoodies, blankets, neck tubes etc) printed and sewn only in Cordova.

THE RAVEN AND THE EAGLE

The striking architecture of the **Prince William Sound Science Center** *(pwssc.org)*, constructed in 2023, beautifully assimilates into the surrounding landscape 2 miles north of Cordova proper yet looks like nothing else in town. A closer look reveals its entrance flanked by two magnificent totems, the work of lifelong Cordovan and Alaska Native salmon fisherman and carver Mike Webber. A representation of a raven and an eagle, the totems represent Prince William Sound's two main Alaska Native communities and are well worth a closer inspection. PWSSC is the only organization committed to tracking the oceanography of Prince William Sound, rounding out its research with fisheries ecology, bird colony studies, monitoring the ongoing effects from the *Exxon Valdez* oil spill and more.

Food truck? More like a food bus!

DRINKING IN CORDOVA: OUR PICKS

Copper River Brewing: Cordova's top drinking establishment; brew-friendly sandwiches on house-baked bread with up to 16 taps of fine swig. *noon-10pm Mon-Sat*

Reluctant Fisherman Bar: Notably less divey hot spot pairing harbor views (that patio!) with rotating microbrews and decent cocktails. *11am-2pm & 4-9pm Tue-Sun*

The Alaskan Bar: Hardened day drinkers and rowdier night crowds converge along the lengthy, historic bar. You're not drunk – the sign is upside down! *noon-1am Sun-Thu, to 3pm Fri & Sat*

Baja Taco: Besides being the only Mexican offerings for miles, this Cordova icon (p201) carries local craft brews on draught and in bottles. Harbor views. *7am-9pm*

Fishers, Copper River

A Copper River Fishery Tour
Observe salmon fishing with locals

One of Cordova's best days out is an up close and personal view of the action in the **Copper River Fishery** dreamed up by local upstart adventure agency **Explore Cordova** *(explorecordovaak.com; 6 people $2400; May-Aug)*. Fishing fleet veteran Mike Mahoney hung up his fishing nets after 25 years and now takes up to six folks for a full day out in the Copper River 'flats' - the world's best waters for salmon. You'll head out along the shores of **Orca Inlet** (home to seals, sea otters and abundant bird life) and round **Point Whitshed**, where you'll enter the network of channels that make up the protected inside waters behind the barrier islands. Wild and breathtaking scenery awaits, including expansive views of the towering Chugach Mountains and the Gulf of Alaska. The trip culminates in a firsthand look at some 400 permitted fishing vessels canvassing the vast fishery (a 40-mile range from the Western end of the flats at Hook Point to the Eastern end at the Martin Islands), harvesting the Copper River's famed salmon as they go. In addition to the unique perspective on Cordova's sustainable fishing trade, Mahoney's exciting stories add plenty of local color. Prior to the tour, Explore Cordova will connect you with fishermen selling their catch direct to customers, so guests may see their own fish being caught. Meals include Copper River smoked salmon dip!

MUSEUMS OF THE SOUND

If you're looking for more cultural breaks between outdoor adventures, both **Whittier** (p208) and **Valdez** (p192) are home to museums and historic attractions for killing time between whale-watching and glacier stalking.

Beyond Cordova

The bird- and wildlife-rich Copper River Delta unfurls east of Cordova; tidewater glaciers, braiding waterways, glacial lakes and numerous hikes await.

As Cordova's defiant slogan embraces, there's 'No Road' connecting the fishing town with other parts of Alaska, so reaching anything beyond Cordova requires a flight or an Alaska Marine Highway ferry ride. Except the massive Copper River Delta, North America's largest contiguous Pacific Coast wetlands – it brushes up against town limits and surrounds Cordova's Merle K (Mudhole) Smith Airport. It's from the Copper River's waters that some of the world's most coveted salmon are plucked to the delight of diners globally. In addition to the abundant waterbirds expected of a wetland of this size (it drains an area of more than 24,000 sq miles), hiking, glacial viewing and moose- and seal-spotting highlight the Delta's greatest hits list.

Sheridan Glacier
TIME FROM CORDOVA: **30 MINS**

Glacial pursuits

One of Alaska's most accessible glaciers sits just outside Cordova along the Copper River Hwy. **Sheridan Glacier**, a 15-mile-long, 2-mile-wide expanse of bolting blue that unravels from the Chugach Mountains into Sheridan Lake, which perfectly reflects the glacier and its floating icebergs and smaller bergie bits. Head out on the Copper River Hwy by car or bike; at Mile 13.7, turn north on Sheridan Mountain Rd for around 4 miles until it dead-ends at two trails. On the right, an easy, 1.5-mile hike through spruce-hemlock forest leads to the glacier, which makes its stunning debut in the foreground a few minutes in. From there, spectacular views frame the glacier as it folds into the silky lake. It's a striking scene that makes for an easy half-day out from town. Pick up a car from Chinook Auto Rentals (p198) or a bike from Cordova Gear (p203) and make a full day out of it. You can also explore the glacier by kayak – contact **Orca Adventure Lodge** (orcaadventurelodge.com; per person $250).

GETTING AROUND

There is one road out of Cordova, the Copper River Hwy (Hwy 10), which begins after the intersection of 1st St and Railroad Ave just south of downtown. It's 49.5 miles in total, but impassable by cars beyond Mile 36 thanks to a 2011 bridge washout that has closed the road beyond permanently. The road is cyclable by bike or e-bike but it's a big day out even for ambitious or advanced cyclists – contact **Cordova Gear** (p203).

DRIVING TOUR

Head out on the Highway

The 49.5-mile Copper River Hwy traverses the extraordinary Copper River Delta, an outrageously beautiful wetlands that's home to a cavalcade of bird and wildlife plus coveted Copper River wild salmon. The last 13.5 miles are unreachable due to a bridge collapse, but bird- and wildlife-watching and the wildly beautiful (and accessible) Sheridan Glacier feature in the road's accessible part. This 35-mile drive hits the highlights.

1 Copper River Delta Entrance Pavilion

Heading east out of Cordova on Lake Rd toward the airport, the road is paved as it passes Eyak Lake and Mt Eyak to the north. The Copper River Delta begins shortly after crossing the Eyak River. This **entrance gazebo** has info panels and offers views to spy beaver lodges and trumpeter swans across the delta. It's also a sublime spot for a bit of contemplation.

The Drive: Continue east on Hwy 10 (Scott Glacier is visible between Miles 8 and 9 on clear days) to Sheridan Glacier Rd. Head north for 4 miles to the trailhead

2 Sheridan Glacier Lake Trail

This 4-mile detour off the Copper River Hwy provides the drive's can't-miss moment. Just a few minutes into this easy, 1.5-mile hike, Sheridan Glacier (p205) appears in the foreground, a stunning blue-veined ice tongue spitting frozen bergs into a silty lake. The glacier, as is commonplace, is

Million Dollar Bridge

receding, but you can walk right up to the glacial lake shoreline. Incredible!

The Drive: You'll enter Eyak Corporation Land before heading south on un-Googleable Alaganik Slough Rd and travel 3 miles to the end.

❸ Pete Isleib Memorial Boardwalk

This middle-of-nowhere **boardwalk**, 3 miles off Mile 17, is not only wonderful for contemplative bird- and wildlife-watching across the Alaganik Slough, but it's a great rest stop if you've brought along provisions or a beer or two. Dusky Canada geese, bald eagles and even moose congregate here. If you're on a bike, you likely won't be able to linger long, but those driving will want to while away a bit of time here.

The Drive: Road conditions take a turn for the worse; if the road hasn't been recently graded, it's slow going to Mile 27, but several excellent trails offer respite.

❹ Flag Point

Your first glimpse of the 290-mile Copper River and its heavily braiding channels comes at Mile 27's **Flag Point**. During the famed Copper River salmon run, seals sometimes shop for dinner at the glacial lunarscape here. There's no compelling reason to go on from here, but check if anyone is transporting visitors to the **Million Dollar Bridge**, where both Miles and Childs glaciers are visible (it's only accessible by boat nowadays). If you're interested in further exploration, inquire locally about possible tours.

Whittier

WILDLIFE-WATCHING | GLACIER VIEWING | MILITARY HISTORY

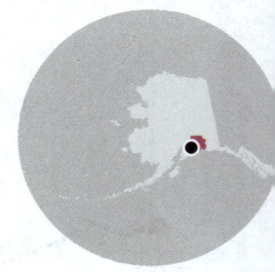

☑ TOP TIP

Don't even think about showing up in Whittier without rain gear! The city's precipitation clocks in around 196in of rain per year (just slightly under maximum Amazon numbers!).

Whittier doesn't take itself too seriously – one of the town's catch phrases is, 'It's Prettier in Whittier,' which is a self-depreciating nod said with a wry smile. Truth be told, Whittier is both beautiful and ugly, a wonderfully weird Cold War anachronism set on the edge of some sublime coastal wilderness where rugged fjords dispatch tumbling glaciers into Prince William Sound. Even by Alaska standards, this is a bizarre outpost. Founded in 1941 as an intake military base for US soldiers deployed to Alaska, Whittier was heavily fortified in the early years of the Cold War (the military pulled out in the 1960s). Ghost-town status loomed, but Whittier persevered. Today, it's a popular cruise-ship port and day-trip destination from Anchorage, revered for its kayaking, fishing and glacier-viewing. It also sort of feels like it survived the zombie apocalypse because the access tunnel was closed and everyone was out fishing.

Prince William Sound Safari
Wildlife-spotting, glacier-gawking

Quirkiness aside, most folks wind up in Whittier to take in the incredible sights of the western end of Prince William Sound. Rain or shine, boat tours from here are a fantastic

---

GETTING AROUND

When driving to Whittier check the schedule for the **Anton Anderson Memorial Tunnel** – North America's longest highway tunnel. The controlled, one-way thoroughfare, shared by cars and trains, runs from 5.30am to 11:15pm May 1 to September 30 and only opens once per hour in either direction ($13 round trip). Whitter is very small – you can walk from one end of the harbor to the other in around five minutes and all the town's bars, restaurants and tourism outfitters are along this route.

WHITTIER

PRINCE WILLIAM SOUND WHITTIER

★ HIGHLIGHTS
1 Lu Young Park
2 Portage Glacier
3 Prince William Sound Museum

● SIGHTS
4 Begich Towers
5 Buckner Building
6 Cold Storage Facility
7 Gymnasium
8 P-12 Motor Pool Building
9 U.S. Army Headquarters
10 U.S. Army Signal Corps Building

● ACTIVITIES
11 Lazy Otter Charters
12 Portage Glacier Cruises
13 Portage Pass Trail
14 Whittier Boardwalk

● SLEEPING
15 Anchor Inn
16 Inn at Whittier
17 June's Whittier Condo Suites

● EATING
see 16 Inn at Whittier Restaurant
18 Lazy Otter Café
19 Swiftwater Seafood Cafe
20 Whittier Ice Cream & Pizza
21 Wild Catch Cafe

PERFECT DAY IN WHITTIER

Decades-long Whittier resident **Kelly Bender** is the owner of **Lazy Otter Charters** and the cafe of the same name. @lazyottercharters

For a short and easy hike, walk behind **Begich Towers** to the line of trees, take 10 steps into the woods and there is a raging river and waterfall. It's sensory overload with the sound of roaring river, lush green forest, and the mist from the water. Pop into the **Prince William Sound Museum**, which is dedicated to Whittier, military and earthquake history. Impressive by any measure but especially for our small town. And don't miss strolling the **boardwalk** overlooking the boats. Grab an ice cream at **Whittier Ice Cream & Pizza** to maximize your walking enjoyment!

day out on the water, and wildlife is the main event (hard to fathom considering how jaw-dropping the glaciers are on this side of the sound). **Lazy Otter Charters** *(lazy otter charters.com)* operates out of a very pleasant cafe on the harbor and offers all the adventurous water activities you could hope for, including a grand eight-hour 'Best of Prince William Sound Cruise' (per person $330) limited to just six passengers.

Are you into sea lions and sea otters? You'll be tired of them by the end of the tour. If you've come to Alaska in search of humpback whales, it's not uncommon for them to breach near the boat throughout the day between May and July. The tour also takes in an astounding **black-legged kittiwake rookery**, where thousands of these coastal birds cling to the cliffside amid a half-dozen tumbling waterfalls; a colony of tufted puffins near the Dutch Group islands and nesting bald eagles. You might even catch a black bear or two, hobbling along the shoreline in the Esther Passage.

Depending on the weather and sea conditions, you'll take all of this in enroute to/from a variety of astonishing tidewater glaciers such as the massive **Harvard** and **Yale Glaciers** (45 or so nautical miles from Whittier); or the smaller but no less spectacular glaciers of Blackstone Bay (p213). Here, amid glacier slush and a smattering of vibrant-blue icebergs, the **Beloit** and **Blackstone Glaciers**, both flanked by numerous waterfalls, are absolutely staggering. And they are just the sideshow.

Picnic in Paradise

Serene scenery, mountain backdrop

Whittier is home to a few of the sound's most stunning, easily accessed locales, 99% of which visitors never see as they tend to hover around the harbor. For a secluded moment away from the hubbub, grab a boxed lunch from Lazy Otter Café (p212) or takeaway fish and chips from nearly anywhere and head to **Lu Young Park**, a wildly beautiful retreat just a 1.3-mile walk from the harbor. Here you'll find a few picnic tables overlooking a secluded bay. An impossibly gorgeous, absolutely raging stream comes tumbling out of a forest inundated with Sitka spruce, western hemlock, alder and cottonwood alongside it, emptying into the sound. Breathtaking. And you'll likely have the place to yourself.

Portage Pass Trail

Family-friendly hiking with glacier views

While the water-based excursions no doubt hog the spotlight in Whittier, the town is home to one USFS-maintained trail, the **Portage Pass Trail**, a 4-mile-long, family-friendly out and back walk that provides an immediate wilderness fix and great views just 2 miles outside of town. It's the only way to see the **Portage Glacier** (where Alaska Natives once portaged goods between Turnagain Arm and Prince William Sound) on foot. There are boat tours available on Portage Lake

A WALK IN WHITTIER

Founded as a deep-water military base, the Whittier Army Port Historical District is a fascinating, Cold War–era step back in time.

START	END	LENGTH
Lazy Otter Café	Hodge Building	1.9 miles; 45min

Fuel up on Whittier's best coffee at ❶ **Lazy Otter Café** (p212) then head through the pedestrian tunnel to the teal ❷ **P-12 Motor Pool Building**, once used to service the fleet of army vehicles needed to make Whittier hum. Next door, the ❸ **Cold Storage Facility** was once a gigantic refrigerator for perishable foods being shipped to Interior Alaska army bases.

Continue along Whittier St a few steps to ❹ **U.S. Army Headquarters**, a former Cold War command center, now a supermarket, Anchor Inn hotel rooms and the well-done ❺ **Prince William Sound Museum**. Next door, Anchor Inn's bar and restaurant was once the ❻ **U.S. Army Signal Corps Building** and the only surviving WWII construction in town. Head uphill on Blackstone Rd to the ruins of the massive ❼ **Buckner Building**, a Brutalist-evoking construction that once housed 1000 troops. The building was mothballed when the army jumped ship in 1960.

Back down the hill to Billings St, the army's ❽ **Gymnasium** is now a boat and kayak shed. One block south, you can't miss the gigantic ❾ **Hodge Building**. Known locally as BTI (Begich Towers Inc), it's home to almost all of Whittier's population plus a grocery store, post office and community center. An underground tunnel links it to the local elementary school.

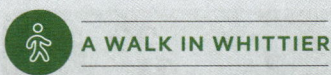

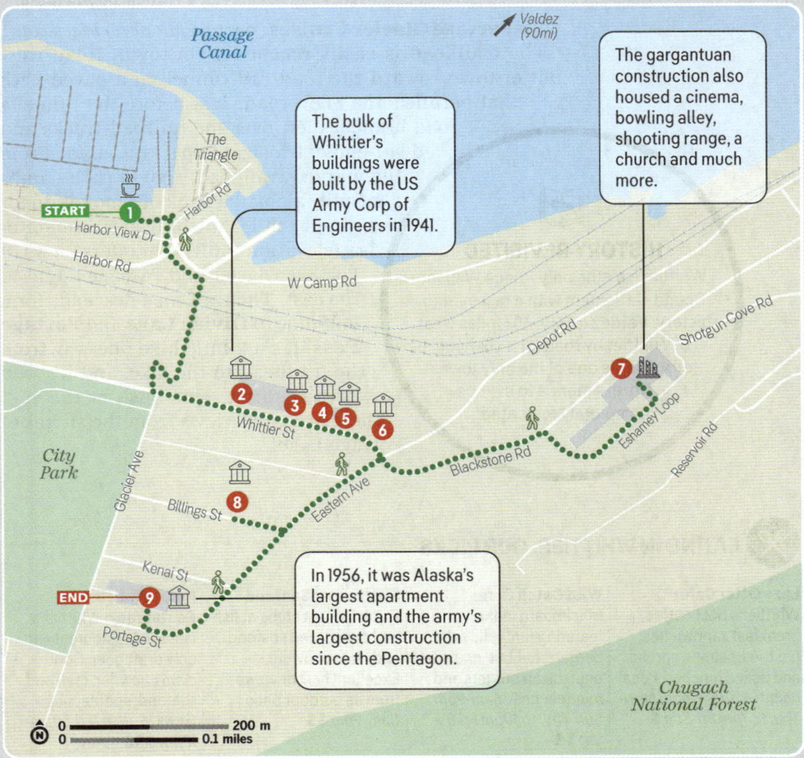

The bulk of Whittier's buildings were built by the US Army Corp of Engineers in 1941.

The gargantuan construction also housed a cinema, bowling alley, shooting range, a church and much more.

In 1956, it was Alaska's largest apartment building and the army's largest construction since the Pentagon.

Steller sea lions, Prince William Sound (p188)

with **Portage Glacier Cruises** (*portageglaciercruises.com*). The trailhead is easily reached from town. Head west out of town toward the road/rail tunnel on a paved path that parallels the main road. Just before the tunnel a road branches left over the railroad tracks and dead-ends at a sizable parking area. From the marked trailhead, a good path climbs steadily along the flank of a mountain for around a mile, finishing at a promontory (elevation 750ft) that offers views of Portage Glacier and Passage Canal to the east. The trail then descends for a half-mile to **Divide Lake** and **Portage Pass**. It's a 2-mile hike one-way from the trailhead to the lake, and it's well worth bashing some bush at the end. There are great views from the shores of Portage Lake!

HISTORY REVISITED

Whittier isn't the only Prince William Sound settlement with a fascinating history. **Valdez** (p188), 357 miles west of Whittier by road (or a six-hour ferry ride), is one of the only towns in North America to ever be completely relocated.

 EATING IN WHITTIER: OUR PICKS

Lazy Otter Café: Whittier's best coffee, breakfast sandwiches, pastries, salmon spread and boxed lunches. Local haunt. *6.30am-6pm Mon-Thu, to 7pm Fri-Sun* **$**

Wild Catch Café: Blackboard menu featuring fantastic salmon burgers, halibut, grass-fed beef/bison burgers and reindeer chili. *6am-9pm Sun-Thu, to 10pm Fri & Sat* **$$**

Swiftwater Seafood Cafe: Decent stabs at fish and chips, fried seafood and clam chowder. Excellent harbor views from its outdoor patio. *11am-9pm* **$$**

Inn at Whittier Restaurant: Whittier's classiest restaurant and only draft beer. Good clam chowder, crab and seafood; spectacular views. *6-11am & 11.30am-10pm* **$$$**

Beyond Whittier

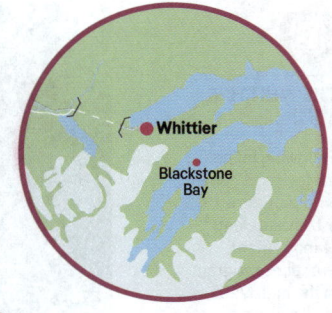

Whittier's location on the doorstep of Prince William Sound comes with a cavalcade of glacier and wildlife wow – namely in neighboring Blackstone Bay.

Whittier is little more than a tiny harbor – just over 300 residents call the town home on a year-round basis – with a quirky history. Most folks don't spend the night, choosing to visit instead as a launching pad for day trips around the real reason to come: Prince William Sound, encompassing some 3800 miles of coastline. Fortunately, one of the sound's premiere destinations sits just over the Kenai Mountains from Whittier, reached by an hour-long boat ride around Decision Point. Blackstone Bay looms, a 15-mile-long fjord teeming with glaciers and wildlife best seen by kayak.

Blackstone Bay

TIME FROM WHITTIER: 1 HR

Kayaking in Blackstone Bay

On the western edge of Prince William Sound, reached via a one-hour, glacier-viewing boat ride along the Passage Canal from Whittier, sits beautiful **Blackstone Bay**, a glacier-hogging fjord that's a haven for sea kayakers. The bay is home to seven (count 'em, seven!) cliff-hugging glaciers, two of which still embrace the glacier waters below. If you want to see chucks of ice calving into the bay like artisanal ice cubes falling into an already slushy cocktail, this is the place. **Alaska Sea Kayakers** (alaskaseakayakers.com) and **Paddlers' Realm** (paddlersrealm.com) can get you out on the water with guides. Full-day tours run from $400 to $435. If you just need kayaks, head to **Sound Paddler** (pws kayakcenter.com; per day single/double/triple $70/120/150). The trip is designed for novices, though it's a high-stamina outing involving 7 to 10 miles of paddling over the course of five to six hours.

As soon as you round the corner from Whittier, you'll see the mighty **Tebenkof Glacier** as you enter Blackstone Bay. Deeper into the bay, **Northland Glacier** stands perched on the cliffs above – its beautiful waterfall rains down below. Kayak tours usually paddle within 500yd of **Blackstone**

GETTING AROUND

Excursions from Whittier are sea-based – unless you have your own boat, you'll be along for the ride. Water taxis to Blackstone Bay run $493 one-way, for example, but organized tours make more sense unless you're sharing expenses or multinight camping. For shorter excursions, you can rent kayaks in town (single/double per day $70/120). Stand-up paddleboards (SUP) can also be rented (per day $65) from **Sound Paddler**. Parking is scarce – arrive early to secure a spot.

Calving ice, Blackstone Glacier

THE WHITTIER TBMP

Following in the footsteps of Juneau, who pioneered a Tourism Best Management Practices program in the mid-1990s, Whittier has adopted its own set of sorely needed pledges to minimize the community impacts of tourism. Limited by space and access, Whittier's situation was particularly delicate, but when the town's new **Chugach Glacier Gateway Cruise Terminal**, built in partnership between Huna Totem Corporation (a for-profit Alaska Native village corporation) and Norwegian Cruise Line, opened at the head of the bay in late 2024, it was time to act. The cooperative effort among tour operators, cruise lines, transportation providers, the City of Whittier and its residents have agreed to a set of five overarching values, including Keep It Clean and Prevent Overcrowding.

Glacier, an actively calving glacier (the thunderous rumble of huge slabs of ice dropping into the sea is a common soundtrack on a day in the bay). After lunch on a deserted beach, the afternoon continues to the biggest glacier of the bunch, **Beloit Glacier**, a tidewater glacier with its terminus dipping below the sea. Weather and time permitting, a brief hike to the terminus of landlocked **Lawrence Glacier** is in the cards. Expect to share the sea with harbor seals, sea otters, black-legged kittiwakes and, if you're lucky, you might spy a bald eagle's nest as well!

Places We Love to Stay

$ Budget $$ Midrange $$$ Top End

Valdez
MAP p189

Valdez Glacier Campground $ Part-owned by the military (a firing range next door means occasional noise), this spot has 101 pleasant wooded sites, dry cabins and a foaming waterfall. Located 6 miles out of town.

Bear Paw RV Campground I $ Mega-popular, family-friendly campground that dominates much of a big barren parking lot behind the small-boat harbor. Clean showers, strong wifi, friendly management.

Eagle's Rest RV Park $ Well-equipped RV park with showers and laundry in a gravel lot on the edge of town. Wooden cabins and glamping tents as well.

Keystone Hotel $ Utilitarian Valdez container hotel distinctly evocative of pipeline boom years. Clean rooms, if old-fashioned; friendly staff.

Robe Lake Lodge $$ Built to last from full scribe logs with massive beams crossing vaulted ceilings, this four-room, six-cabin lodge 6 miles outside Valdez boast views of absurdly pretty Robe Lake from its hot tub.

A Place on Coho B&B $$ Three rooms with shared bathroom, massive living room and kitchen, above-and-beyond touches (delightful pastries, bathrobes) highlight this great-value neighborhood B&B.

Downtown B&B Inn $$ Dressed in glacier blue, this gabled house wouldn't stand out whatsoever in alpine Austria, but here in Valdez, it makes a statement. Threadbare rooms are cheap for Valdez ($125 for a double).

Best Western Valdez Harbor Inn $$$ Independently run waterfront comfort. Business-savvy rooms to Best Western standards. It's overpriced, of course, but it's one of the few completely full-service hotels.

Totem Hotel & Suites $$$ Rebuilt and refocused post-destructive fire; newer, modern hotel suites plus older but cozy cabins.

Chugach Naswik Suites $$$ The sound's best new hotel, featuring 37 extremely modern, clean-lined studio and two-bedroom suites with full kitchens. Very friendly management.

Cordova
MAP p199

Odiak Camper Park $ Popular with seasonal salmon fishers, this small campground is little more than a gravel lot (with an outstanding view) and a restroom. Twelve RV sites ($35) and four tent platforms ($20). Book through City of Cordova (*cityofcordova.net*).

Prince William Motel $$ Utilitarian but perfectly comfortable and friendly motel. The 14 rooms (with/without kitchenette from $180/$160) are popular with fisherman. Wifi is $2 extra.

Reluctant Fisherman Inn $$$ Cordova harbor views and a great bar-restaurant make up for the motel-basic rooms at this town focal point. Can get noisy when live music is on, but there's no better views.

Bear Country Lodge $$$ Two lodges (cedar log house and chalet-style home) in serene surrounds on Eyak Lake. Great choice for families, groups and those looking for a more natural setting.

Orca Adventure Lodge $$$ This end-of-the-road, 40-room adventure lodge is Cordova's best in show, artfully encased in the erstwhile Orca Cannery 2 miles north of downtown. Incredible views, a ravishing on-site restaurant and myriad water adventures beckon.

Whittier
MAP p209

Anchor Inn $$ Industrial, austere, quintessential Whittier. Think aged motel run with exotic flair. Rowdy bar on cruise-ship night.

June's Whittier Condo Suites $$ Hospitality veteran June Miller has three one- and two-bedroom condos on the 14th and 15th floor of Begich Towers.

Inn at Whittier $$$ Cape Cod–stylized inn with postcard-perfect harbor view, historic tavern and excellent restaurant. Rooms expected to return (after a devastating flood) for 2026 season.

Above: Tour boat, Kenai Fjords National Park (p248); Right: Seward (p245)

Researched by
Regis St Louis

Kenai Peninsula

ADVENTURES ON LAND AND SEA

Kayak iceberg-dotted lagoons, hike to lofty overlooks, and fish for salmon and halibut in this captivating region of mountains, glaciers and rainforests.

The Kenai Peninsula offers some of the most accessible wilderness adventures in Alaska. There are hikes to alpine lakes through the snowcapped Kenai Mountains and otherworldly paddles through the glaciated fjords of a dazzling national park. You can camp (or stay in a cabin) on serene coves in remote corners of Kachemak Bay State Park, and battle some of the biggest fish around. In every forgotten corner, you'll be immersed in the natural world: the mountains, lakes, rivers – and the people – that make Alaska wild.

Approximately the size of Belgium, the peninsula is a top pick for first-time Alaska explorers simply because it has everything: abundant adventures and wildlife-watching amid stunningly diverse scenery. The eastern peninsula is dominated by large ice fields, the jutting Kenai Mountains and the icy waters of Resurrection Bay. To the west it flattens out, with rolling hills, mirror-like lakes and a long coastline.

Wilderness aside, the peninsula is home to seaside towns and riverside settlements. In Homer, you'll find an arts-loving community with intriguing museums and galleries, and a long spit dotted with shops, restaurants and adventure operators. Seward's historic downtown is a delight to wander with its beautifully sited waterfront, while the sleepy settlement of Hope preserves its gold-mining glory in log cabins and historic trails.

Elsewhere you'll find vestiges of the region's Indigenous past, its Russian colonizers and the early homesteaders who are still fondly remembered today.

THE MAIN AREAS

HOPE
Historic mining town with epic rafting. **p222**

COOPER LANDING
'Combat' fishing on turquoise waters. **p232**

SEWARD & KENAI FJORDS NATIONAL PARK
Hiking, boating and kayaking amid mountains and glaciers. **p245**

KENAI & SOLDOTNA
Salmon fishing with rich Indigenous history. **p258**

HOMER
Nature adventures off an artist enclave. **p267**

Find Your Way

Spread across 25,000 sq miles, the Kenai Peninsula has a limited road network to take you to the key oceanside and riverfront communities. Beyond the pavement, you can explore mountains, glaciers and fjords by boat, foot or bush plane.

BUS

Without a car, a bus from Anchorage is your best bet for reaching the region. This is a good way to reach Cooper Landing, Soldotna, Homer and Seward. Just keep in mind that schedules are limited and prices are high.

TRAIN

The Alaska Railroad travels to and from Seward (daily mid-May to mid-September), with impressive scenery along the way. Trips can begin at the main depot in Anchorage or at a stop nestled between Portage and Girdwood.

BOAT

Book a private water taxi or a boat tour to see abundant marine life and access alluring coastline off Seward and Homer. You can also catch a ferry from Homer to either Seldovia or, less frequently, Kodiak (p346).

Kenai & Soldotna, p258

Don't miss the rich salmon runs into the Kenai and Kasilof rivers that make these two towns bucket-list destinations for world-class sport and subsistence fishing.

Homer, p267

With a vibrant local art scene, and land and sea adventures in Kachemak Bay, there is plenty to do at this end-of-the-road destination.

KENAI PENINSULA

Hope, p222
An old off-the-beaten-path gold-mining town, this quiet community offers world-class rafting, as well as hiking amid stunning views of the Turnagain Arm.

Cooper Landing, p232
Tucked against the azure waters of the Kenai River, this bustling town draws anglers in search of the world's tastiest salmon.

Seward & Kenai Fjords National Park, p245
It's all about the mountains, glaciers and ocean in Seward – the gateway to hiking, ocean fishing, kayaking, wilderness treks and more.

Plan Your Time

The reasonably compact size of the peninsula allows you to travel to several different areas and enjoy some diverse activities (hiking, rafting, fishing, kayaking, wildlife-watching) over a relatively short time span.

Puffin, Alaska SeaLife Center (p247)

An Action-Filled 36 Hours in Seward

● Start the day bright and early at the small boat harbor, where you'll meet your guide and head off on a half-day adventure of **wildlife-watching** (p248), **kayaking** (p250) or **fishing** (p251). After your return, visit the fascinating collections covering homesteaders, Iditarod champs and earthquake survivors at the **Seward Community Library & Museum** (p245). Nearby, watch diving puffins and massive stellar sea lions at the **Alaska SeaLife Center** (p247).

● Take an early evening stroll along the **waterfront** (p249), then have dinner at the **Cookery** (p247), followed by drinks at **Yukon Bar** (p253).

● The next morning, motor out to the Kenai Fjords National Park for a walk to the **Exit Glacier overlook** (p252) – or, if time allows, make the challenging ascent to **Harding Ice Field** (p253).

Seasonal Highlights

Travel peaks during salmon runs, and June and July; at other times, enjoy holiday celebrations, bird migrations and winter sports.

FEBRUARY
Break out the cross-country ski gear and hit the **Tsalteshi Trails** groomed ski area in Kenai for some winter fun (there are also winter bike trails). Nearby, ice skaters can get their fix on frozen **Arc Lake** (p264).

MAY
Homer throws Alaska's largest wildlife celebration, during the annual **Kachemak Bay Shorebird Festival** (p274). Attend talks, visit birding hot spots with naturalists and learn to spot a diverse array of migrating species on your own.

JUNE
Enjoy small-town life at its liveliest during the **Summer Solstice Festival** (p157) in Moose Pass. You can catch live music, browse craft stalls and enjoy some barbecue and brews. The money raised helps support the community.

Weekend in Homer

● Get the lay of the land at the **Pratt Museum** (p267), which explores the human history of Homer and the surrounding area. Afterwards stop by the **Alaska Islands & Ocean Visitor Center** (p271) to learn about the diverse wildlife all along the coast. Check out the **art scene** at a gallery or two (p272), then cap the day with dinner and drinks at the Cannery.

● On your second day, book a trip across the water. Make your destination Kachemak Bay State Park, where you can hike to a jewel-like **glacial lake** (p280). Alternatively, ferry across to **Seldovia** (p277) to visit a tiny settlement backed by rugged forests and pristine shoreline. Later, take a stroll along the **Spit** (p270) and raise a glass at **Homer Brewing Company** (p275).

Five Days to Travel the Peninsula

● After hitting the highlights in Seward and Homer, head up to Soldotna, Kenai and Cooper Landing. If the salmon are running, join the crowd for world-class **'combat fishing'** (p232) or, if you're not a fisher, make the hike up to **Russian River Falls** (p235) to look for salmon and possibly the brown bears that love (to eat) them.

● Take in the cultural heritage of the upper peninsula, walking in the footsteps of the Kenaitze Indian Tribe at the **K'Beq' Cultural Heritage Interpretive Site** (p237), perusing the Indigenous arts and crafts at the **Kenai Visitor Center** (p263) and stepping into the past at **Russian Orthodox churches** (p282).

● End the journey with a bang, by going for a thrilling white-water rafting trip on **class V rapids near Hope** (p222).

JULY

Seward is one of the best places in Alaska to celebrate Independence Day. You can cheer on runners during a grueling 5k, watch whimsical competitions (fish toss) and catch fireworks at midnight on July 4 eve.

AUGUST

The temperatures are starting to cool and the mosquito populations dip a bit. It's a great time for outdoor activities, especially hikes in Kachemak Bay State Park and nearby Seldovia, where it's prime blueberry-picking season.

SEPTEMBER

Head to Homer for the **Alaska World Arts Festival** (p274), a two-week event that features a wide-ranging lineup of cultural fare from indie films to experimental dance, along with nights of storytelling, old-time radio theater and more.

DECEMBER

Get into the spirit of the season by attending Seward's **Holiday Arts & Craft Fair** (p254), held early in the month. Seward is also the best place to be at the end of the month, for fireworks to ring in the New Year.

Hope

WHITE-WATER RAFTING | GOLD PANNING | VILLAGE LIFE

☑ TOP TIP

Time your visit around live music at the Creekbend Cafe or Dirty Skillet, and salmon fishing at Resurrection Creek in late August for a fun weekend of sport and entertainment. If visiting in a large RV, book a campsite early for easy access from either spot.

Perched along a stunning stretch of Turnagain Arm, Hope is a tiny settlement backed by the spruce-covered slopes of the Chugach National Forest. A few dirt lanes wind through the community, which has a population that barely reaches three digits. For those looking to escape the stress of modern life, Hope is the perfect antidote: you can hike forested trails to lofty overlooks and little visited mountain lakes, or simply soak up the tranquility of a welcoming little community.

Years prior to the infamous 1896 Klondike gold rush in the Yukon, gold was discovered in Resurrection Creek in 1888 just outside modern Hope. You can learn about its past in a complex of old log cabins – including a former one-room school – or even try your hand at gold panning on a public access site off Resurrection Creek. For more intensity, book a rafting trip with one of Hope's adventure operators, who will take you on a roller-coaster ride over class V rapids along roaring Six Mile Creek.

Raft Legendary Six Mile Creek
Thrilling class IV and V rapids

One of North America's most thrilling white-water adventures, the rafting trip along Six Mile Creek takes you through churning class IV and class V rapids throughout the heart-pumping

GETTING AROUND

While it's possible to get dropped at the junction of the Hope Hwy and Seward Hwy by the Seward Bus Line or Red Eye Rides 17 miles outside Hope, this isolated town is best accessed by car. The two-lane Hope Hwy is long and winding, but well maintained.

Drivers and walkers may need to navigate puddles and potholes in old-town Hope, and the unpaved roads spurring off the Hope Hwy can be even more bumpy. RVs are not recommended on unpaved roads outside the old-town area.

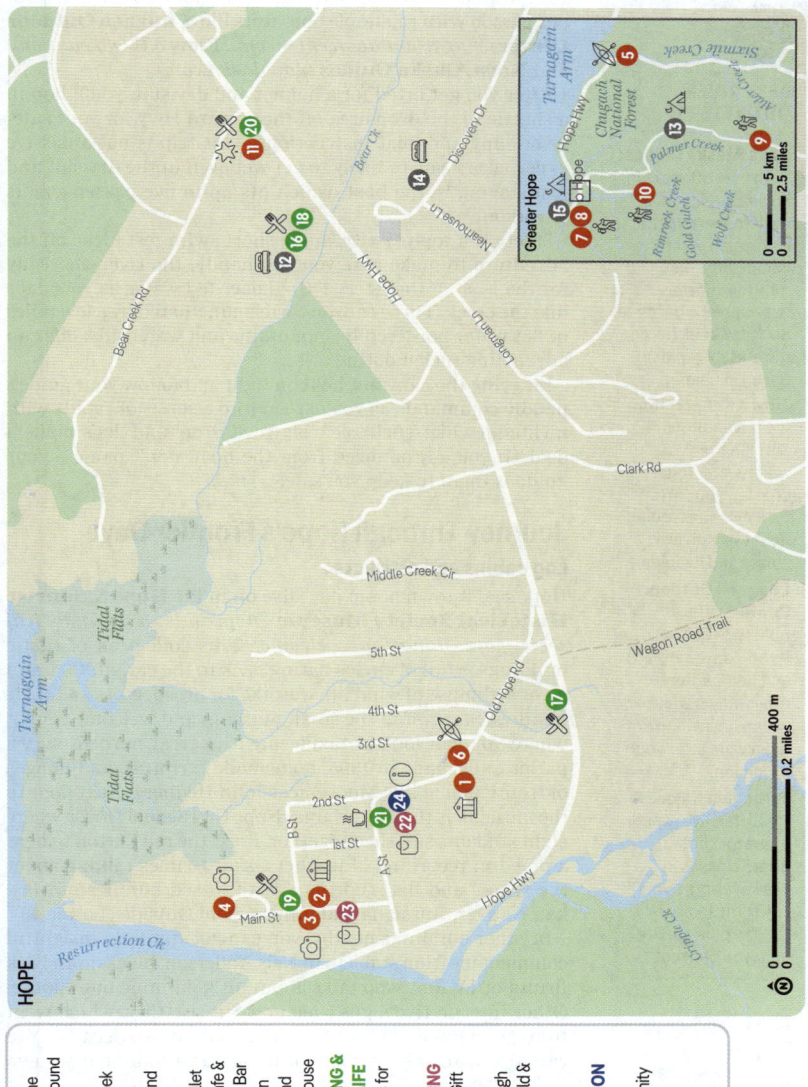

HOPE

SIGHTS
1. Hope & Sunrise Historical Society Museum
2. Hope Social Hall
3. public parking & restroom
4. tidal flats

ACTIVITIES
5. Chugach Outdoor Center
6. Flow AK
7. Gull Rock Trail
8. Hope Point Trailhead
9. Palmer Creek Lakes Trail
10. Resurrection Pass Trail
11. Turnagain Kayak

SLEEPING
12. Bear Creek Lodge
13. Coeur d'Alene Campground
14. Discovery Cabins
15. Porcupine Campground

EATING
16. Bear Creek Lodge
17. Creekbend Cafe
18. Dirty Skillet
19. Hope Cafe & Seaview Bar
20. Turnagain Kayak and Coffeehouse

DRINKING & NIGHTLIFE
21. Grounds for Hope

SHOPPING
22. Library Gift Shop
23. Sourdough Dru's Gold & Gifts

INFORMATION
24. Hope Community Library

BEST RIVER OUTFITTERS

Nova Alaska Guides: With over 50 years in business, Nova is a well-known outfitter in the Alaska rafting community. Also runs the shorter two-canyon stretch of Six Mile Creek (to skip the class V rapids). Based in Palmer.

Flow AK: Apart from the adventurous Six Mile Creek white-water roller coaster, you can opt for a more easygoing float trip with just class I and II rapids.

Chugach Outdoor Center: Offers both two- and three-canyon trips and gentler float trips with no white water. An inviting hot tub awaits after your excursion.

Turnagain Kayak: A small, family-owned operator that offers classes in sea kayaking, river kayaking and pack rafting, plus quality gear you can rent.

11-mile descent. The current rate for this four-hour trip is $225 per person with reputable operators like **Chugach Outdoor Center** *(chugachoutdoorcenter.com)*, **Flow AK** *(flowak.com)* and **Nova Alaska Guides** *(novalaska.com)*.

After you get fitted for a helmet and dry suit, you'll hop in a shuttle to the drop area off the Seward Hwy for your safety briefing and boat instructions. This trip is not a passive experience – you're likely to get wet even in the dry suit and just staying in the boat, which fits up to five passengers, is a workout.

Safety is a top priority, and a short swim test kicks off the adventure to make sure you can handle the river. Be ready for the rush of the 34°F (1°C) glacier-fed water as your face hits the creek. Three canyons, each punctuated by a few miles of flat water bordered by mountains and waterfalls, offer an adrenaline-fueled outing.

Entering the canyons, hold on tight and follow your guide's paddle commands as you careen into a series of rapids with nicknames like 'suckhole,' 'big rock drop' and 'let's make a deal.' If you get bounced from the boat, don't panic – your guide is there to keep you safe.

Journey Through Hope's Frontier Days
Log cabins and artifacts

Hope's gold-town boom days live on in the **Hope & Sunrise Historical Society Museum** *(hopeandsunrisehistoricalsociety.org; donations welcome)*. This collection of rustic buildings is full of curios dating back to the early 1900s, and gives a glimpse of what life was like for prospectors and their families. Start off in the small museum and welcome center, where you can look at taxidermy (the great horned owl), a parlor quilt made in 1895, homemade furniture and images of frontiersmen like Moosemeat John Hedberg. Next door to the museum is the tiny original Hope City School House where eight students smashed together. Press the red button to hear a piped-in recording of teacher Oskar Grimes talking about the school and his students – with mixed families of Alaskan Natives, Russians and miners from Outside (Lower 48).

In other buildings nearby, you can get similarly insightful commentary from stableman Nels Anderson, blacksmith Nick Bruhn or LV Ray, who talks about his gold-mine bunkhouse. Other interpretive signs touch on Sunrise City, which went from boomtown to ghost town in less than two decades. You can also learn about some of the area's prominent women

 EATING IN HOPE: OUR PICKS

Dirty Skillet: Varied menu of Indian-inspired rice bowls, curries and famous burgers, plus local beers on tap and live music on Friday and Saturday. *3-9pm Tue-Sun* **$$**

Turnagain Kayak & Coffeehouse: Hope's only roastery pours out frothy lattes, as well as smoothies, breakfast sandwiches and delicious baked goods. *9am-2pm Sat-Wed* **$**

Bear Creek Lodge: Full espresso bar in a cozy lodge setting. Hang out and read or play one of the games stashed nearby. *8am-4pm* **$**

Creekbend Cafe: Creative and delicious brunch, burgers and seafood paired with a beer menu and periodic summer concerts. *9am-3pm Thur, Sun & Mon; to 11pm Fri & Sat* **$$**

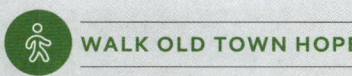

WALK OLD TOWN HOPE

This easy stroll takes you past tidal flats and historic buildings from Hope's early 20th-century boom days.

START	END	LENGTH
Main St	Hope & Sunrise Historical Society Museum	0.5 miles; 45min

Start at the **1 public parking & restroom** on Main St. Visit the official public bulletin board, see what's happening in Hope and read a little history posted there by locals.

Then, head down Main St, noting the photogenic **2 Hope Cafe & Seaview Bar**, built in 1906 for the manager from the Alaska Commercial Company, a grocer and mercantile. Walk toward the grassy **3 tidal flats**, and enjoy the great view of Bird Ridge across the Arm. The 1964 earthquake lowered Turnagain Arm about 6ft, and this grassy wetland today stays largely dry. It's safe to walk out on these grasses, but stay away from the deadly mudflats, which can trap you. Head back toward the buildings, and see **4 Hope Social Hall**. Built in 1902, the hall still hosts music, weddings and even funerals. Follow Main St to A St, where you will take a left quarter-mile past privately owned historic buildings and find the **5 Hope Community Library**. This building was used as the city's small schoolhouse between 1938 and 1985 before a new, larger one was constructed nearby. Today this independent library offers a cozy, dry spot to all visitors Monday through Saturday.

Taking a right on 2nd St, find the **6 Hope & Sunrise Historical Society Museum** with static displays and interpretive signs free to peruse, even if the museum is closed.

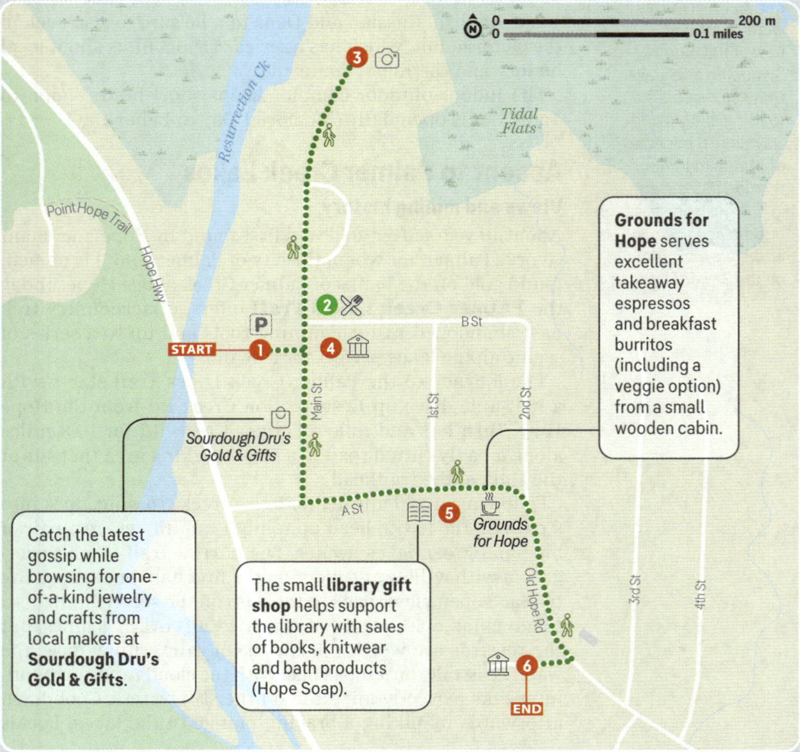

Grounds for Hope serves excellent takeaway espressos and breakfast burritos (including a veggie option) from a small wooden cabin.

Catch the latest gossip while browsing for one-of-a-kind jewelry and crafts from local makers at **Sourdough Dru's Gold & Gifts**.

The small **library gift shop** helps support the library with sales of books, knitwear and bath products (Hope Soap).

THE DRAMATIC BORE TIDE

Turnagain Arm has some of the world's most dramatic tidal fluctuations – a 27ft differential, in fact, between low and high tides. This is also the place to witness Alaska's most impressive bore tide – a rush of seawater that returns to the narrow inlet when conditions are right. These tend to happen after extreme minus low tides are created by a full or a new moon – look for them during the five-day window around new or full moons. Swooping as a wave that can reach 6ft to 10ft in height and traveling at speeds of 10mph to 15mph, the tide fills the arm in one go. Hope is a good place to see it, as are viewing spots on the Seward Hwy.

Mudflats during low tide, Turnagain Arm

pioneers, like Polly Renner (1869–1927), a prospector and talented seamstress who made her own fashionable clothes based on magazines she came across. She served as an interpreter in local courts owing to her linguistic talents – she spoke English, Russian and Dena'ina. Be sure to also peek in the Quonset hut, which has a series of short films about local history and the Kenai Peninsula.

The indoor-outdoor complex keeps short hours (noon to 4pm), but is open daily (Memorial Day to Labor Day).

Ascent to Palmer Creek Lakes

Views and mining history

About 10 years after gold was first found in Hope, merchant George Palmer, for whom the city of Palmer (p163) is named, found gold on the banks of Palmer Creek above Hope. Today the **Palmer Creek Lakes Trail** offers a backcountry trek past abandoned historic mining tools and up to a series of scenic alpine lakes perfect for a swim.

The journey to the Palmer Creek Lakes Trail starts with a half-mile drive up Resurrection Creek Rd from the Hope Hwy. Turn left and follow Palmer Creek Rd for 10.8 miles along a badly rutted road to a small parking area that sits at the start of the trailhead.

Following an old mining road to a creek crossing, duck into a path on the left to head up to high tundra, where a pair of blue and green lakes awaits. The narrow trail is a bit overgrown with willow and alder on the first half, but keep going to reach open views back to the pass on the second half. It's a tough climb, with a gain of nearly 1000ft over 1.4 miles, but the rewards are worth the effort. On calm, sunny days, the waters can take on a topaz hue, with the clouds and surrounding peaks perfectly mirrored on the still waters. Cool down afterwards by taking a bracing plunge in the lakes. Locals sometimes haul pool toys to these lakes, so don't be surprised to find a plastic unicorn taking an alpine lake cruise. Allow two to 2.5 hours to make the 2.8-mile return hike.

Pan for Gold on Resurrection Creek
Fun public access spot

A short drive up Resurrection Creek Rd, you'll reach the parking lot for the famed **Resurrection Pass Trail**. From the trailhead, cross the wooden pedestrian bridge over the creek and turn left. The easement for gold panning here follows the creek south for about a half-mile from the bridge – it's a 20-acre claim owned by the USFS and allows amateur prospectors to try their luck. This creek was the site of the second Kenai Peninsula gold rush back in the late 1800s. Over the years, some 35,000 oz of gold have been taken out of the creek at many different sites. You'll see evidence of past mining amid the now-forested tailing piles just over from the trail.

The Climb to Gull Rock
Forest and ocean views

With so many of the vast forests around Hope inaccessible to vehicles, visitors typically turn to other ways of getting to the top sites: on foot or by bicycle. Both are excellent methods of visiting Gull Rock, a popular destination for day trips and backing out of Hope.

Although the **Gull Rock Trail** gains about 800ft over the course of 5.7 miles (one-way), this is a jewel among Alaska hikes because it pairs a wilderness experience with gentle grades and only some steep sections, instead of the constant stark climbs common elsewhere.

Start your trek from the trailhead parking lot (and toilet) at the end of Bob Mathewson Ln. Look for the lane off to the left just before you reach Porcupine Campground and the end of the Hope Hwy.

Walk among dense spruce and birch trees, before a climb takes you up to occasional glimpses of Hope and the Turnagain Arm between the sometimes high brush. If it's a windy day on the Turnagain Arm, you won't notice until you leave the shelter of the trees. Spot a series of bent trees at about Mile 5. If you do encounter high winds here, you'll feel the same force that makes some of their branches shorter than others. If you have them, bring hiking poles to navigate some of the occasional steep sections plus a small scree field just after the 3-mile mark. In July and August, keep an eye out for wild berry snacks along this stretch.

Travel another 0.2 miles to find Gull Rock and take in the stunning views of the Cook Inlet, the same vista seen over thousands of years by the Alaska Natives who call this place home. It takes around 6 hours to make the complete round trip (11.4 miles), but if the trail is overgrown, some hikers hike only 3 miles to enjoy some decent views before turning around.

WATCH THE ROAD

Like many parts of the state, unpaved roads in and around Hope may not be open year-round, receive regular maintenance or be appropriate for RVs. For example, Palmer Creek Rd is gated through the winter and is often closed until early July, and Resurrection Creek Rd can be deeply pitted. It's a good idea to give the **USFS Seward office** *(907-224-3374)* a call to check their status. Palmer Creek Rd becomes narrow at the 6.7-mile mark, and then includes a shallow creek crossing. Passenger vehicles traveling carefully and with good clearance are unlikely to run into any trouble, but with no usable turnaround spots, RVs should skip this drive.

UNMARKED CAMPGROUNDS

As in other regions of Alaska, free camping is permitted on most public lands even if it is not a designated campsite, unless posted otherwise. While some areas, such as national parks, have rules on how far off the trail you must stake your tent, most places allow camping in plain sight. When using these campsites in and around Hope, avoid building a fire, always practice good 'leave no trace' principles, bury human waste and keep your food locked safely in your car away from wildlife. In and around Hope, watch for these unofficial primitive campsites along the Gull Rock Trail, at the Resurrection Pass Trail Head, along the Hope Hwy and on Palmer Creek Rd.

Gull Rock Trail (p227)

Challenging Hike to Hope Point

Wildflowers and panoramas

The **Hope Point Trailhead** begins at the same spot as the Gull Rock Trail (p227), near the Porcupine Campground. This one is much more challenging, though, as you'll be ascending some 3400ft over the course of 4.2 miles (8.4 miles round trip). The steep climb takes you past dazzling stretches of wildflowers and up to a ridgeline where you'll have jaw-dropping views of Turnagain Arm and the Resurrection Creek Valley. Except for an early-summer snowfield, you'll find no water after Porcupine Creek. Take it slowly as the trail can be slick, and quite dangerous amid the steep drop-offs after a recent rainfall. Budget around six hours for the day's outing. As elsewhere, mosquitoes and flies can be fierce on the trail, so be prepared.

HIKING RESURRECTION PASS

The finishing (or starting) point of the 38.4-mile **Resurrection Pass Trail** is just outside of Hope, and ranks among the best long-distance trails on the Kenai Peninsula.

Beyond Hope

Towering mountains flanked by wildflower meadows in the summer make the entrance into the Kenai Peninsula a stunning travel corridor.

The Upper Kenai Peninsula makes an impressive gateway to this adventure-filled playground. You'll find spots for hiking (and skiing in winter), fishing lakes and scenic overlooks as you drive south from Turnagain Arm toward the center of the peninsula. Much of the hiking located just off this road includes sections of the Iditarod National Historic Trail, which stretched 1000 miles from Seward to Nome. It is infamous for its use during the gold-rush era, but its first travelers were Alaska Natives traveling to fishing and hunting grounds. The geography here predates even those ancient users. Spot the moraine at the top of 900ft Turnagain Pass, the highest point on the Seward Hwy. These low mounds are the mineral-rich deposits left behind thousands of years ago by a glacier.

Kenai Mountains – Turnagain Arm National Heritage Area   TIME FROM HOPE: 25 MINS

Geocache along the National Heritage Area

In partnership with the **Kenai Mountains – Turnagain Arm National Heritage Area** (KMTA), the Geocache Alaska geotrail (p231) combines the thrill of the hunt with plenty of education and insight on this special region of the Kenai Peninsula. There are 23 caches in total, stretching from **Girdwood**, just north of the Peninsula and an hour from Hope, into Cooper Landing (p232), 55 minutes from Hope, and down to Seward (p245), 90 minutes from Hope. Seven of those are in or just beyond Hope.

The trail combines 16 traditional, four multi, two mystery, one adventure lab and one earth cache to create a hunt with plenty of variety. But with a difficulty rating typically below two and never above 2.5 out of five, the hides are designed to be beginner-friendly and are hidden in large green metal boxes known as ammo cans. Each cache description contains a chance to learn something about the area.

Places

Kenai Mountains – Turnagain Arm National Heritage Area p229
Summit Lake p231

GETTING AROUND

This region is broadly used as a travel corridor between Anchorage to the north and the main towns farther south along the Kenai Peninsula, including Cooper Landing, Seward and Homer. Buses pass along the highway but don't stop here, so you'll need your own wheels to experience this section. Speaking of driving, be careful when pulling off the highway to admire the scenery. Traffic moves quickly, and fog and rain can limit visibility, making for particularly hazardous conditions.

DRIVE THE KENAI MOUNTAINS – TURNAGAIN ARM HERITAGE AREA

On this scenic stretch along Highway 1, you'll pass dramatic views, churning waterways and historic log cabins. Driving from Girdwood? See p179.

START	END	LENGTH
Welcome Sign, Seward Highway	Summit Lake Lodge	30 miles; 1½ hours

You'll know you've entered the famed peninsula when you spot the ❶ **wooden sign** on your right reading 'Welcome to Alaska's Kenai Peninsula.' Just under 4 miles up the road on the right, you'll pass the ❷ **Seward Highway Falls**, a small cascade just off the road. The highway glides past fine views, sometimes opening onto mountain vistas to north or south.

On the left, pull off to stretch your legs at ❸ **Turnagain Pass Rest Area**. There you can see evidence of the glaciers that 10,000 years ago covered this area with 2000ft of ice. Around 4.5 miles south of there, turn (left) to the ❹ **Johnson Pass Trail**. Here you can walk a piece of history: the trail was first blazed in the 1890s when gold seekers made the arduous northbound journey from Seward to Nome. Seven miles further, pull off at ❺ **Canyon Creek Rest Area**. Here you can follow a trail down to the confluence of Canyon Creek with the Six Mile Creek, once known as The Forks by early prospectors heading to seek riches in the area.

Another 5 miles south, you'll reach another ❻ **pull-off to Canyon Creek**. Word of gold claims on Canyon Creek and nearby Mills Creek brought a rush of 3000 prospectors to the area in 1896. End your journey 5.5 miles south at ❼ **Summit Lake Lodge**, where you can recharge over a coffee.

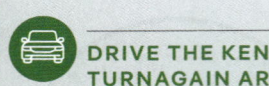

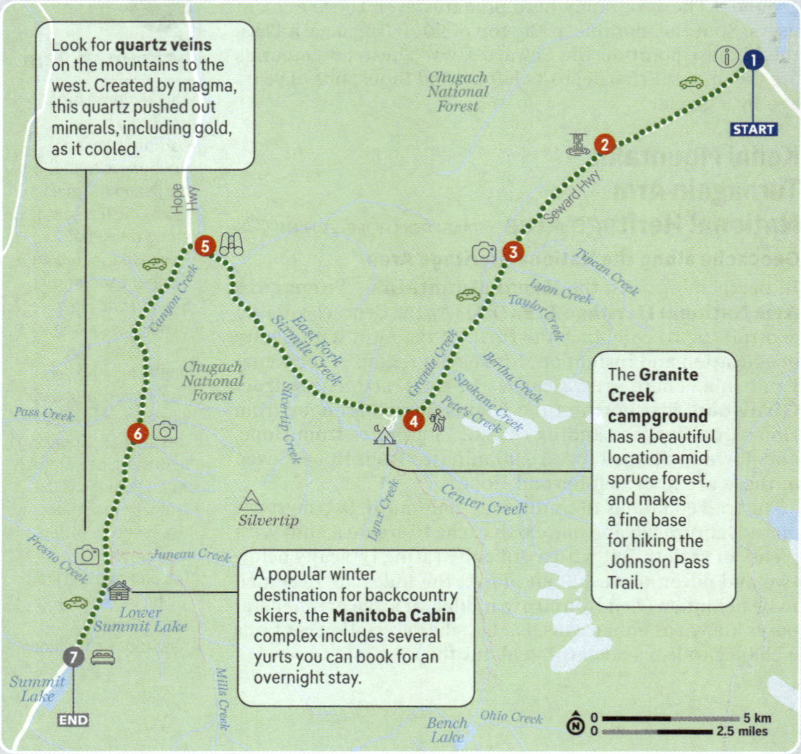

Look for **quartz veins** on the mountains to the west. Created by magma, this quartz pushed out minerals, including gold, as it cooled.

The **Granite Creek campground** has a beautiful location amid spruce forest, and makes a fine base for hiking the Johnson Pass Trail.

A popular winter destination for backcountry skiers, the **Manitoba Cabin** complex includes several yurts you can book for an overnight stay.

Organizers want to make the trail as friendly to visitors as possible, which is why each site includes a parking area that can accommodate up to a 20ft RV. But be prepared to go tromping off road and onto the side of the highway in pursuit of this chase.

Each cache also contains a code word to be filled into a passport available on KMTA's website (kmta-geotrail.gcak.org). Users who log and submit at least 20 cache code words on the passport are eligible to purchase a special Geocoin to commemorate this GeoTrail.

Summit Lake

TIME FROM HOPE: **35 MINS**

Fishing, hiking and camping

The picturesque **Summit Lake** offers a scenic base camp for lake fishing, boating, hiking and camping right off the Seward Hwy about 35 minutes south of Hope.

The road climbs from the **Seward Hwy** and **Hope** junction to reveal high ridgelines on either side. It's here that **Summit Lake** sits with a private lodge on one side and USFS campground on the other.

The **Summit Lake Lodge** *(summitlakelodge.com)* restaurant and parlor, which are open seasonally, are the only place you'll find for food or drinks along this stretch of highway. That makes it the perfect place to stop for a bite before hitting the lake. The parlor section offers a welcome break on warm days for ice cream and a cold drink, or coffee on the rainy and chilly ones that can sweep across the area in the summer, while the restaurant has sit-down service.

Use a boat or kayak from the lodge for a pleasant day exploring the lake, or bring your own. Like many lakes in this region, Summit Lake is stocked annually with fingerling rainbow trout, and has a natural population of Dolly Varden and lake trout thanks to the **Canyon** and **Tenderfoot creeks**, which feed it from the east. While fishing for trout and Dolly Varden is typically open with limits, it's always a good idea to check the **Alaska Department of Fish & Game** website for the latest rules *(adfg.alaska.gov)*.

DIVE INTO GEOCACHING

Growing steadily in popularity since the advent of personal handheld GPS devices in 2000, geocaching is a hobby beloved worldwide for its ability to connect curious seekers via caches or hidden containers. Today players can use a GPS device or their phones with downloaded GPS maps in locations without cell service to read clues and find the sites. Add some extra fun by keeping handy some small tokens to trade out for those left in the cache by previous visitors, known as 'swag.' Sign the logbook to let others know you were there and log your find in the app or online with a note of what you saw or where you were visiting from. Find out more at *geocaching.com*.

Cooper Landing

SALMON STREAMS | FLOAT TRIPS | PROSPECTING

☑ TOP TIP

All but the most experienced anglers will benefit from a guide service on the upper Kenai and Russian rivers thanks to the intense crowds during the hottest runs and complicated state fishing regulations. Staying bear-aware here is also incredibly important – humans aren't the only creatures who love salmon.

While the settlers who first founded Cooper Landing came for gold, visitors today are drawn to a different natural wonder: world-class salmon runs. At the confluence of the emerald-green Russian River and turquoise-blue upper Kenai River, Cooper Landing offers access to multiple mega salmon runs where thousands of anglers bag their limits mere feet from each other in a fishery so hot it's known as 'combat fishing.' The Dena'ina people who first lived here also understood its richness. This area is known by their descendants as 'Sqilantnu,' which translates as 'ridge place river,' and you can walk in their footsteps at the ancient K'Beq' Cultural Heritage Interpretive Site.

While only about 500 people call Cooper Landing home year-round, thousands of visitors from all over the world head here for recreation (namely fishing). Off its two-lane road that winds for miles along the banks of the river, incredible hiking, river day trips and gold-rush history sit at the ready.

Fish the Kenai & Russian Rivers
The thrill of sportfishing

Salmon and trout fishing are the main attractions in Cooper Landing for the thousands of visitors from across the state and all over the world who annually flock here to subsistence and sportfish. When the salmon are running, parked cars line

GETTING AROUND

With no train service on the Cooper Landing side of the Kenai Peninsula, the best way to get to and explore Cooper Landing is by car or by bus. If you're coming from Anchorage or Homer, get dropped off in Cooper Landing by **Alaska Bus** *(alaskabuscompany.com; from either city $99)*. If you're drift fishing on the Kenai without a guide service, use **Wildman's** (p237) shuttle service to move your car to your end point. Once you're in Cooper Landing, expect a narrow, two-lane road with no pavement and minimal maintenance anywhere outside town.

COOPER LANDING

SIGHTS
1. Cooper Landing Historical Society Museum
2. K'Beq' Cultural Heritage Interpretive Site

ACTIVITIES
3. Alaska River Adventures
4. Alaska Rivers Company
5. Cooper Landing Fishing Guide
6. Kenai River Drifters Lodge
7. Prospector John's
8. Russian River Falls

SLEEPING
9. Eagle Landing Resort
10. Kenai Princess Wilderness Lodge

see 6 Kenai River Drifters Lodge

11. Russian River Campground

EATING
12. Cooper Landing Brewing Company
13. Gwin's Lodge

see 10 Rod & Reel

14. Two Brothers Roadhouse

SHOPPING
15. Wildman's

the highway here, as anglers walk into or take the river ferry across the confluence of the **Russian** and **Kenai rivers** for flossing off the bank. Bears are also a common sight here as they look to feast on the same fish that have beckoned you.

If you don't like the press of crowds, instead join your guide for a drift-boat fishing trip down the turquoise-blue upper Kenai River. Drop your line for king or coho salmon, also known as silvers, and wait patiently for a bite; when the time is right, switch to fly-fishing, targeting silvers only. Bask in the pristine quiet of this wilderness area as you watch bald eagles soar overhead – the upper Kenai River is open to non-motorized boating only.

When the runs are hot, you may easily reach your bag limit for salmon within the first few hours of your trip. If that happens, finish out your adventure fishing for mammoth rainbow trout. Depending on when you're visiting, you could be in for a trophy-class catch – August and September are known for their monster, 30in trout.

FIND A RAFTING ADVENTURE
Looking for a more intense river adventure in the region? Head up to Hope for thrilling class IV and V white-water rafting on **Six Mile Creek** (p222).

FIVE SPECIES OF SALMON

Alaska's infamous salmon runs bring in five distinct species of salmon over the course of the summer. What type you target will depend on when the fish are running, current state restrictions and your personal preferences. Chinook or king salmon are large, fatty fish valued for their taste. They require immense patience to catch all season long. Coho or silver salmon have firm, bright orange-red meat. Red or sockeye salmon are prized for their flavor and deep red color. Pink salmon have a tender texture and are only open for fishing in even-numbered years. Finally, chum or dog salmon are generally not targeted for sportfishing, largely thanks to their unappealing appearance.

A Scenic Rafting Trip
Floating the Kenai River

Start your trip down the Kenai River from the moment its beautiful blue-green water leaves Kenai Lake on its 82-mile journey to the sea. With its property just above the launch area, your guide with **Alaska River Adventures** *(alaskariveradventures.com; half-day rafting adult/child $75/38)* will suit you up with a light rain suit and boots – just enough to keep you from getting you wet from the 38°F (3.5°C) waters flowing out of the snow glacier.

Board the raft with your guide and up to nine other guests, then start down your 8-mile journey to the confluence of the Kenai and Russian rivers.

While your guide paddles by drift fishing and navigates through two minor class II rapids, take the time to enjoy the many views the river has to offer and learn about the glacial silt that makes this river so very blue. Spot bald eagles nesting high above the banks, common merganser ducks diving for their dinner, and swallows swooping onto the water chasing mosquitoes.

As the river winds, note **Cecil Rhode Mountain** towering 4400ft above you. Keep your eyes out for moose and bears

EATING & DRINKING IN COOPER LANDING: OUR PICKS

Two Brothers Roadhouse: Delicious barbecue smoked on-site, along with pizzas, halibut tacos and decadent brisket-topped nachos. Order craft beers from the bar in back. *noon-9pm* **$$**

Gwin's Lodge: Hearty American-style breakfasts and food with hamburgers, smash burgers and beer-battered halibut and chips, plus rich carrot cake for dessert. *8am-8pm* **$$**

Cooper Landing Brewing Company: Sit on the patio while enjoying a golden ale and other microbrews, plus burgers and hot chicken sandwiches. *noon-9pm* **$$**

Rod & Reel: Inside the chalet-style dining room of Kenai Princess Lodge, enjoy high-end cooking with a stunning view of the Kenai River. *7-11am & 5.30-9pm* **$$$**

Fly-fishing, Russian River

along the banks – sightings that are most common on morning and evening trips.

End your journey with a shuttle bus back to the start about two hours later, after exiting the river at a popular crossing point for anglers fishing the hot salmon runs here.

If you want to spend more time on the river, opt for the full-day rafting trip *(adult/child $185/93)*, which takes you on a few more class II rapids as you venture deeper into the Kenai National Wildlife Refuge and into the Kenai River Canyon. The seven- to eight-hour journey ends in Skilak Lake.

See the Salmon Leap

Hike to Russian River Falls

The **Russian River Falls** hike is an easy way to see the spectacular show of salmon as they make their last mad dash upstream – and maybe even witness some bears hunting for their own lunch.

Enter via the staffed entrance at the busy **Russian River Campground**, pay a $14 parking fee in cash (no charge if you've booked/paid for a campsite), and follow the directions to the assigned parking lot. Expect crowds at the gate – this is a popular fishing spot during salmon season.

Outside the major salmon runs in mid-June and July, this hike offers a pleasant walk through the woods to a small waterfall. But when the fish are running, the waterfall viewing deck is the place to be as you witness one of nature's greatest journeys.

From the trailhead, travel 2.4 miles along the wide, gravel trail as it gently follows the river upstream. You'll have minimal elevation gain (around 450ft) as you go. Be sure to make plenty of noise so you don't surprise any bears – they also use this route to access the river.

BEST AQUATIC ADVENTURES

Alaska Rivers Company: Runs both half- and full-day fishing trips to a peaceful stretch of the upper Kenai River. Also offers leisurely rafting and paddleboarding trips.

Kenai River Drifters Lodge: Fishing experts run memorable excursions, including hike-in wade fishing on the Russian River, and small-plane fly-in trips. Runs rafting trips too.

Kenai Kayak Company: Look for moose, bald eagles and other wildlife on a three-hour paddling tour on Kenai Lake or go for a scenic rafting trip on the Upper Kenai River.

Cooper Landing Fishing Guide: Expert guides take you on half-, three-quarter- or full-day adventures seeking the prime species from May to October.

Alaska River Adventures: In addition to rafting, leads single- and multiday fishing trips.

Follow signs at the fork for the Russian River Falls. Hear the sound of rushing water as you go downhill onto one of the viewing platforms. No humans fish here, but you can be witness to the magic of these massive fish, flinging themselves upstream to spawn. Bears fishing here are also sometimes spotted – you'll need patience and a bit of luck to see one.

If you're not ready to call it a day, you can extend your hike by walking 0.6 miles back down the trail and take the fork off to the right toward Lower Russian Lake. From the fork it's another mile to the Lower Russian Lake, a lovely spot with a public-use cabin (Barber Cabin) perched along the shore. The trail keeps going (some 21 miles total) and also links up with the Kenai's prime backpacking route, the 38-mile Resurrection Pass trail.

Watch the Fishing Action
Fishers and wildlife

The **Russian River Campground** (p235) is also a big draw for anglers. Apart from making the hike to the waterfall, you can take the level paths along the river itself. Boardwalk trails are cleverly designed to allow enough light for vegetation to grow underneath, and you might spot ptarmigans and other birdlife in the area. There's also the possibility of seeing bears, particularly when the fish are running. Along the river, sets of stairs lead right down to the water, where fishers from far and wide come during the salmon season (June through September).

Strike It Rich off Kenai Lake
Feel the rush of gold mining

There's reading about gold fever and the intense labor that goes into working a gold claim, and then there's the rush of stepping into mining for yourself.

That's the journey you'll take when you visit **Prospector John's** *(goldpan-alaska.com)* for a half-day of mining out at his claim on **Kenai Lake**. Start your trip donning rented hip waders (or bring your own), then hop into his boat for a 20-minute ride across windy Kenai Lake, keeping an eye out for wildlife along the shore. For the **Gold 'n Boat tour** *($99, 2 hr)*, you'll get a tour of the mining camp, followed by the chance to try your hand at gold panning – you can keep whatever you find.

For a more hands-on day, consider booking the **Section Dredge Adventure** *(4/6hr $269/369)*. After that boat ride to Devil's Canyon Mining Camp, get ready to work. This is far from a passive lesson – you're about to become a real miner. As you plunge your gloved hands into the creek's pay dirt to operate the dredge motor, which functions like a high-powered vacuum sucking up water, rocks and black sand from the creek floor, your partner will watch the line for clogs and the sluice box for signs of gold. Swap places to warm up your

COMBAT FISHING

In a place that's mostly natural and wild, there are few sights more unnatural than what happens each summer wherever Alaska's best salmon rivers meet a busy road. When the fish are running, the banks become a human frenzy – a ceaseless string of men, women and children hip-to-hip, hundreds of fishing rods whipping to and fro, the air filled with curses and cries of joy. This is combat fishing. There are subtle rules that guide the chaos: don't wade out in front of other anglers, give your neighbor space (and don't foul your line with theirs), and if you get a bite, shout, 'Fish on!' so others can reel in their lines and give you room to wrestle your catch.

FISH ACROSS THE KENAI

While Cooper Landing is a top destination for salmon fishing, guides based in Kenai and **Soldotna** (p262) also frequently target the same river areas.

Kenai Lake

hands and comb over rocks, constantly wondering if you've struck it rich or simply just found more rust.

After a few hours of tough work, step back to watch magic unfold as your guide opens up the sluice box, revealing your haul, panning it out and carefully placing it in a vial for you to take home. Bonanza! Wrap up your time on the claim in the warming tent hearing wild stories about prospecting in Alaska.

If you have kids in tow and just want a taste of prospecting, Prospector John's offers **Roadside Adventures** *($65)*, where you get to shovel, scoop and sluice through the running water, then pan for gold while separating out the fine silt.

Learn About Indigenous Heritage

Exploring the K'Beq' Cultural Heritage Interpretive Site

The **K'Beq' Cultural Heritage Interpretive Site** *(kenaitze .org/culture/kbeq-cultural-site; by donation)* is the region's most-often mentioned destination for learning about and understanding Kenai-area Indigenous history and culture. It's operated by the Kenaitze Indian Tribe, which is based in Kenai, and sits directly across the street from the Russian River Campground. Get oriented at the small log cabin welcome center, and take a peek at the small model of a traditional dwelling, which gives details on wall construction, roof thatching and sleeping platform. Next door is the Darien-Lindgren Cabin, built in 1937 by a Dena'ina elder and used for trapping and living off the land. It was originally near the traditional village of Stepanka, and was moved here log by log to save it from a 2012 wildfire.

A short tree-lined boardwalk leads through the centuries-old site known as 'Sqilantnu', meaning 'ridge place river.' It was used for preserving and storing salmon, which were harvested from the river just below. Panels give insight into the plant and animal life and Kenaitze ways of living. You can also ask

TRAVEL ESSENTIALS AT WILDMAN'S

Wildman's *(wildmans. org; 6am-8pm)* has been an essential stop for travelers traversing the Sterling Hwy ever since it opened in 1997. Located just east of the Cooper River Bridge, Wildman's has a convenience store with a little of everything: snacks, clothing, groceries, beer, ice cream and bear spray. There's a food counter where you can order breakfast or lunch sandwiches, French fries and espresso drinks. Those who are camping can take advantage of the showers and self-service laundromat. There's also a shuttle service for hikers, fishers and campers, where staff can move your vehicle so it's waiting for you at the end of your one-way journey. Lastly, Wildman's prides itself on its clean bathrooms.

Brown bear, Kenai River (p233)

FISHING WITH BEARS

The presence of bears is not uncommon during the salmon season, so you'll need to follow safe practices to avoid an unpleasant encounter. Splashing fish can attract bears, so if a bear becomes interested while you have a fish on the line, give it slack or cut the line. Immediately kill your catch and bleed into the water (not onto the bank). When cleaning fish, cut at a designated site (or off-site), chop the carcass into small pieces and throw into fast-moving water. Store fish on ice in a proven bear-proof container, and keep it close. Carry bear spray and know how to use it. And obviously don't ever feed a bear.

for a free guided tour, which will help bring the past to life. Check on the K'Beq' Cultural Heritage Interpretive Site Facebook page for upcoming volunteer opportunities and special events – including beading, plant and berry harvesting, fur presentations, and drum and dance ceremonies.

Enter Cooper Landing's Past

Historic curios and photos

The **Cooper Landing Historical Society Museum** (*cooper landingmuseum.com; free*) is less like a museum and more like a collection of local lore and community heirlooms. Staffed by friendly volunteers over limited hours in the summertime (1pm to 5pm Wednesday to Monday), the museum has a wide-ranging collection of printed oral history, newspaper clippings and an array of home goods and supplies, starting with the gold-rush era, interspersed over two buildings.

You can study images of homesteaders of the 1920s and '30, see devastating wildfire photos from decades past, and check out a slab taken from a massive 400-year-old Sitka spruce harvested on Montague Island. There is taxidermy, including a 65lb king salmon caught on the Kenai River and several ptarmigans in winter plumage. The crown jewel of the museum is a large bear skeleton assembled by local elementary school students in 2002 and now kept in a large glass case.

Next door to the museum and with the same small parking area, the visitor center hosts information about local services. Stop in here to find helpful advice on fishing guides and more.

GOLD PANNING IN THE WILD

Take your new-found gold-panning and mining skills to the accessible public claim on the Resurrection River near the **Resurrection Pass trailhead** in **Hope** (p227) to try your hand at solo gold mining.

Beyond Cooper Landing

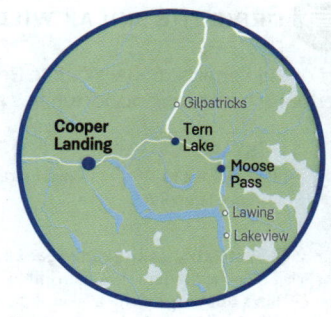

Just outside Cooper Landing, you'll find fabulous hikes, dramatic lakes and one-of-a-kind adventures, including flight-seeing, multiday treks, and kayaking and hiking excursions.

Whichever way you head from Cooper Landing, you can quickly immerse yourself in the wilderness, amid boreal forests and jewel-like lakes. To the west, take a dive into the far reaches of the Kenai National Wildlife Refuge and the state's top backpacking destination: the Resurrection Pass Trail. To the south, tiny Moose Pass was originally a station on the Alaska Railroad. Today you can arrange some memorable adventures on Upper Lake Trail (pontoon plane flights, kayaking excursions) or enjoy a festive solstice celebration if you time your visit right.

Like so many of the wilder stretches on the Kenai Peninsula, this scenic corridor is often overlooked by travelers hurrying to reach Seward. Linger here to experience Alaska's vast beauty away from the crowds.

Places
Moose Pass p239
Tern Lake p244

GETTING AROUND

If coming from Anchorage (p142) or Seward (p245) to Moose Pass, use Red Eye Rides for a drop-off or pass by on the Seward Bus Line. Otherwise, your only option for accessing the area beyond Cooper Landing is by private car. While the Seward Hwy is paved, expect a bumpy, unpaved and at times teeth-chattering drive on Skilak Lake Loop Rd. The road is well worth the extra hour in the car. Don't skip it!

Moose Pass

TIME FROM COOPER LANDING: **25 MINS**

Adventures on glacial lakes

Blink and you might just miss tiny Moose Pass, most noticeable on a drive between Cooper Landing (p232) and Seward (p245) due to its drastically reduced speed limit. But it's worth stopping for a meal, a bit of history or the opportunity for some off-the-beaten-path adventure.

Moose Pass Adventures *(moosepassadventures.com)* offers varied excursions from its base overlooking Trail Lake in Moose Pass. One of the best full-day outings is the **Grant Lake Guided Hike & Kayak Tour** *(per person including lunch $229)*, where you'll paddle across the emerald lake, the surrounding mountains reflected on its surface. On the other side, you'll set out on foot to hike along a section of the Iditarod National Historic Trail, gaining about 600ft as you climb to stunning blue-green glacial Grant Lake. You'll stop there for lunch, then do some more kayaking in the afternoon

DRIVE THE SKILAK WILDLIFE RECREATION AREA

Part of the Kenai National Wildlife Refuge, this drive takes you past lakes and overlooks, with hiking opportunities galore.

START	END	LENGTH
East Entrance to Skilak Lake Loop Rd	West Entrance to Skilak Lake Rd	19 miles; 1½ hours

Begin at ❶ **East Entrance to Skilak Lake Loop Rd** at Mile 58 on the Sterling Hwy. Turn left to reach ❷ **Jim's Boat Launch** for a view of the startling blue Kenai River. Back on the main road, note the wildfire burnout zone, remnants of the 2019 Swan Lake Fire. On the left, you can stop for a hike along the ❸ **Upper Kenai River Trail** or, a little further, climb upward into the burned zone along the ❹ **Hideout Trail**.

The road descends, passing interpretive signs on bald eagles and wildfires. Take the turnoff for ❺ **Hidden Lake Campground** where you can see the lush shores of Hidden Lake, a popular spot for boating and fishing. Back on the loop road, note how the trees change to a mix of live birch and cottonwood, then pause at the ❻ **scenic overlook** for a spectacular view of Skilak Lake. From here, drive on for a steep, winding descent, making your way to the ❼ **Upper Skilak Lake Campground** or ❽ **Lower Skilak Lake Campground**. Both offer a boat launch, picnic tables and fabulous views.

Round out your journey watching for birds of prey soaring overhead and wildlife in the brush by driving 6 miles to the ❾ **West Entrance to Skilak Lake Rd** to reunite with the Sterling Hwy.

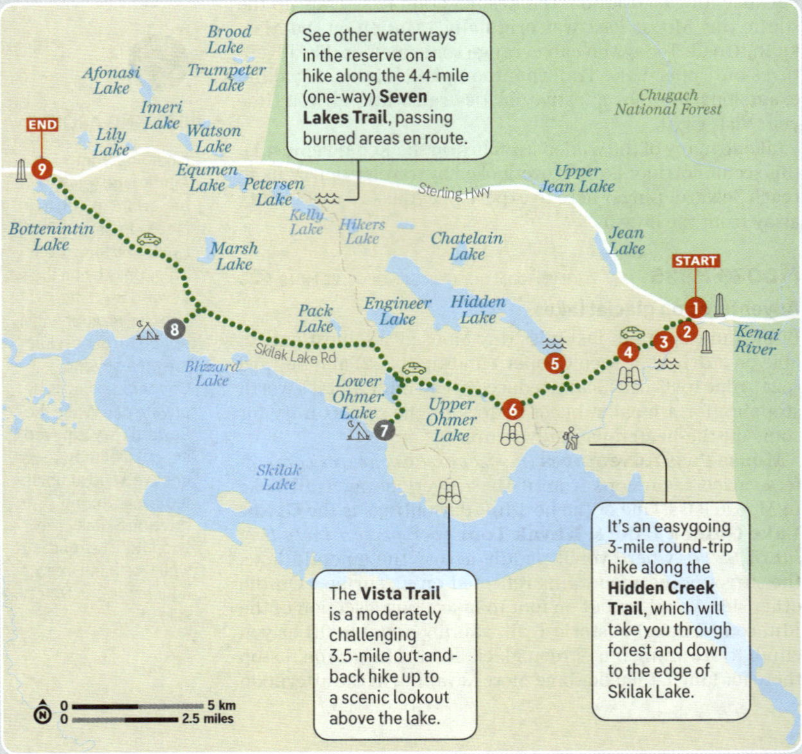

See other waterways in the reserve on a hike along the 4.4-mile (one-way) **Seven Lakes Trail**, passing burned areas en route.

The **Vista Trail** is a moderately challenging 3.5-mile out-and-back hike up to a scenic lookout above the lake.

It's an easygoing 3-mile round-trip hike along the **Hidden Creek Trail**, which will take you through forest and down to the edge of Skilak Lake.

on this sparkling body of water, before hiking back down the trail and back to Moose Pass.

With more time on your hands, you can consider booking an overnight adventure, combining the two-lake kayaking and hiking trip with a stay in a backcountry yurt. You'll have a good frontier-style dinner, then awake the next morning to birdsong on the lake. After breakfast, you'll return to Moose Pass by kayak. It's also possible to make this a three-day, two-night trip, with the second day spent looking for wildlife on Grant Lake.

If you just want to explore Trail Lake, you can rent a kayak for a bit of DIY adventure during a morning, afternoon or evening **paddling session** (*per kayak for 3½hr $90*).

Take a panoramic flight

One of the best ways to see the peaks and glacial lakes of the Kenai Peninsula is from the air. **Scenic Mountain Air** (*scenicmountainair.com*) runs floatplane tours that take off from Trail Lake. On a one-hour tour (*$299*), you'll fly over emerald lakes, vast forests, snow-covered mountains and ice fields, with the possibility of spotting moose and other wildlife. Shorter flights are also offered, from 15 minutes (*$119*) and up, and you can book customized trips – to get you to prime backcountry for fishing, backpacking or staying at a remote cabin.

Have a meal at the lodge

Opened in 1949, the **Trail Lake Lodge** (*traillakelodge.com*) is a handy place to stop for a meal when traveling the Seward Highway. The cozy, wood-paneled dining room has salads, sandwiches and burgers (including a vegetarian option) for lunch, with creative pub fare (curry, fish and chips, meatloaf mozzarella) for dinner. Afterwards, you can walk off your meal with a lakeside stroll.

Snacks and a bit of history

Though it doesn't look like much from the outside, **Estes Brothers Grocery** (*facebook.com/estesbros*) is an Alaskan landmark. It was rolled on logs from the railroad tracks to its present location back in 1938 and it's been in the same family for four generations. You can pick up snacks and groceries in the store, order espresso drinks, or grab a bite from the takeout counter – including tasty breakfast burritos or grab-and-go deli sandwiches. Be sure to peer in the back room, which is full of photos and old newspaper clippings from the early days of Moose Pass. It's open most days from 7am to 8pm (from 8am on weekends).

A few paces north of the store (same side of the street) is an old water wheel, which today powers a grinding stone. As the sign says, 'Moose Pass is a peaceful little town. If you've got an axe to grind... Do it here!'

CELEBRATE THE SUMMER SOLSTICE

Every year, Moose Pass draws visitors from distant corners of the Kenai Peninsula to the Summer Solstice Festival. It usually happens on the third weekend in June, with live music on Friday night at the Trail Lake Lodge, followed by a packed two days of activities: more live music, barbecue, a beer garden, bake sale, games for kids, and a craft market with 20 or so different vendors. Much of the action happens outdoors and in the nearby Community Center. Profits from the fest help fund the Moose Pass community – including its library, volunteer fire department and children's programming. The event has been around since 1978.

HIKING TRIP
Backpack the Resurrection Pass Trail

First carved by prospectors in the late 1800s, the 38.5-mile Resurrection Pass Trail is the most popular hiking route on the Kenai Peninsula. You'll reach into high alpine tundra as you go from Cooper Landing to Hope, with jaw-dropping views and trail infrastructure – campsites every few miles and several popular public-use cabins. It's often tackled over four days. If you're not going out and back, have your car shuttled to your end point by Wildman's (p237).

1 Resurrection Pass South Trailhead

Start your hike at the South Trailhead near Cooper Landing, at Mile 53.2 of the Sterling Hwy. Head through spruce and aspen forest as you steadily climb, leaving sounds of the highway in the distance.

The Hike: From the South Trailhead, hike up 4.2 miles through a clearing of wildflowers to Juneau Creek Falls. Find the falls via a 50yd side trail to the right, near a posted brown tent graphic sign.

2 Juneau Creek Falls

Listen for the roar, then get a perfect view of the falls just off the trail. Enjoy the mist, then head back up the trail to cross a bridge over Juneau Creek.

The Hike: A 5.2-mile mix of climbing and easy walking leads from the falls to Juneau Lake. Stop for the night at one of three nearby campsites or cabins.

Juneau Creek Falls

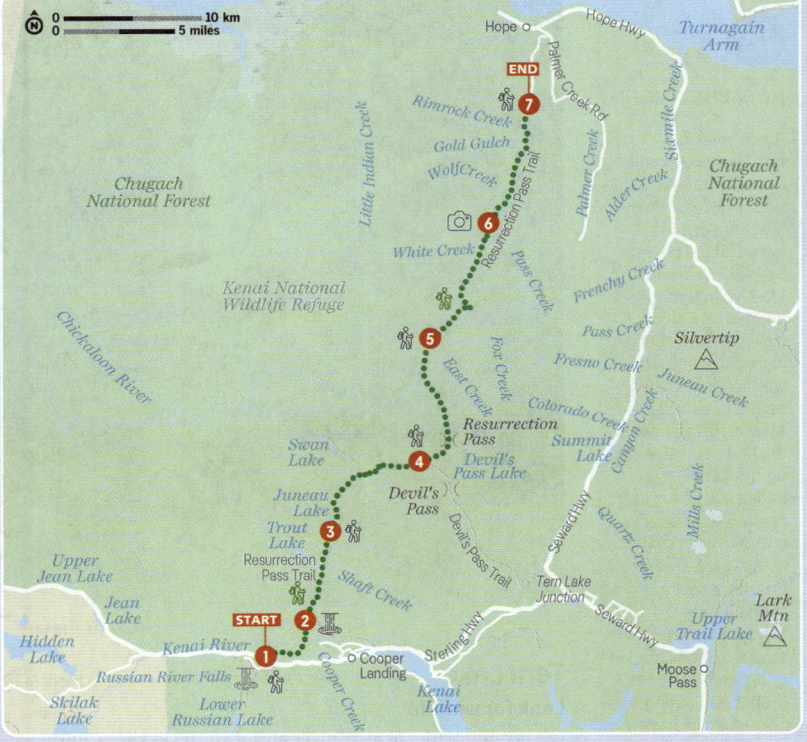

3. Juneau Lake

Traversing up forest-boarded switchbacks, arrive at an area damaged by the 2019 Swan Lake fires. Take in the fields of purple fireweed as you approach and follow the shoreline along the glassy and stunning Juneau Lake.

The Hike: Move through a creek drainage, up steep switchbacks and over tundra 7.2 miles to the Devil's Pass trail junction. Cabin, campsites and pit toilet available.

4. Devil's Pass

Stay bear-aware as you hike through the bushy devil's club to the high alpine tundra, where sweeping views of rolling green and yellow stretch as far as you can see.

The Hike: Travel 7 miles from Devil's Pass to East Creek, a sometimes-steep descent punctuated by short climbs. Cabin and campsite available.

5. East Creek Cabin

Follow an easy climb to the highpoint of Resurrection Pass, enjoying wildflowers. Snap a photo near the sign – elevation 2600ft – and start your descent.

The Hike: Go 7.4 miles past multiple campsites and cabins to the Caribou Creek bridge.

6. Caribou Creek Cabin

Slow down for the stunning vistas as you head to Caribou Creek, winding up and down between drainages before hitting this rushing creek and long bridge.

The Hike: Trek a final and mostly flat 7.1 miles over bushy paths and back into forest to finish out the journey.

7. Resurrection Pass North Trailhead

Your trip is almost over as you travel along Resurrection Creek, keeping a close eye out for both wildlife and wild berries. End by crossing Resurrection Creek, an active public gold-mining site (p227).

MOOSEMEAT JOHN

Adventurers, fortune seekers and iconoclasts have long been drawn to Alaska. Moosemeat John ticked all the boxes. Born in Sweden in 1865, John Hedburg hopped on a ship to New York as a young man, and worked his way across the US before heading up to Alaska. He built one of the first homesteads on the Kenai Peninsula, where he prospected, fished, and delivered mail by dog sled. He and his wife, Anastasia Nutnal'tna, had 11 children. He often stopped to talk to people on the street – friends and strangers alike – and he gave unsparingly to those in need. According to some accounts, he earned the nickname Moosemeat after providing sustenance to suffering, snowbound residents of Kenai during the 1918 flu epidemic.

Arctic tern

Tern Lake

TIME FROM COOPER LANDING: **15 MINS**

Look for wildlife

Glassy and wide, beautiful **Tern Lake** sits at the 'Y' intersection of the Seward and Sterling Hwys, offering an exciting and perfectly accessible stop for wildlife viewing. Tucked between meadow and forest, this lake was created by the construction of the highways. Today, it serves as a perfect stopover point for birds and wildlife.

Headed toward Anchorage from Cooper Landing, pull off the highway into the Tern Lake parking lot and viewing area.

Grab your binoculars and birding book and get ready to look for the remarkable Arctic tern. Stark white with a black cap, this long-distance migratory bird annually travels around 25,000 miles as part of its pole-to-pole pattern.

Keep your eyes peeled for soaring bald eagles, then spot the common loons floating among the lake's grassy mats of cotton grass, bog rosemary and sundew. Listen closely to hear songbirds flitting among the trees and alders.

Otters and muskrats are also a common sight here as they dip under the lake's cold, shallow water. Linger on the shoreline for a chance to see moose traveling along the tree line, or look up to the mountains to spy Dall's sheep and mountain goats.

Although bird-watching cools here in the winter, wild ice skating heats up. Join the locals in a favorite pastime, taking Nordic ice skates out to glide over the lake's clear, frozen surface.

Seward & Kenai Fjords National Park

WILDLIFE-WATCHING | ADVENTURE TOURS | ALPINE HIKING

Perched on the edge of Resurrection Bay, Seward offers jaw-dropping views of water, sky, mountain and forest. The picturesque downtown area, with its photogenic waterfront, is home to an aquarium and marine research center, as well as a worthwhile collection of artifacts tracing the town's history over the last century.

A quick jaunt from town – whether by land or sea – the Kenai Fjords National Park offers a wide array of adventures. On the water, you can spend the day sea kayaking across sapphire-blue glacial lagoons, or cruise out to remote fjords while spotting an extraordinary array of wildlife along the way. By road, it's a short drive to the Exit Glacier area for easy hikes to overlooks of the retreating glacier, or more challenging ascents along wildflower-strewn switchbacks up to mountain overlooks high above the Harding Ice Field. Seward is also a big draw for its fishing, multiday treks and alpine adventures.

☑ TOP TIP

You can stock up on groceries, including baked goods, deli items and prepared foods, at the **Safeway** (6am-10pm) on the way into town. The store is also near the **Seward Visitor Center**, a handy information point.

Travel into Seward's Past
Exhibits and films

One of the best places to learn about Seward's past, the **Seward Community Library & Museum** *(cityofseward.us; adult/*

GETTING AROUND

The Alaska Railroad offers a memorable way to travel from Anchorage, with gorgeous views throughout. Several bus companies also link Seward with Anchorage: Alaska Cruise Transfer has daily service, as does Park Connection, which also continues up to Denali (10 hours, including a stop for lunch in Anchorage). If you're driving from Anchorage, it's a scenic 2½-hour journey, but delays (from traffic and construction) are not uncommon, especially on summer weekends when the roads can get packed. Once in town, you can get around easily with the free Seward Shuttle, with half-hourly services looping around the historic downtown and out to the cruise terminal.

SEWARD & KENAI FJORDS NATIONAL PARK

● SIGHTS
1. Jujiro Wada statue
2. Kenai Fjords National Park
3. Seward Community Library & Museum

● ACTIVITIES
4. Alaska SeaLife Center
5. Exit Glacier Guides
6. Glacier Overlook Trail
7. Fish House
8. Harding Icefield Trail
9. Ididaride
10. Kenai Backcountry Adventures
11. Liquid Adventures
12. Major Marine Tours
13. Sunny Cove Kayaking

● SLEEPING
14. Exit Glacier Lodge
15. Harbor 360 Hotel
16. Hotel Seward
17. Resurrection Campground
18. Safari Lodge

● EATING
19. Chinooks
20. Coho Joe's
21. Cookery
22. Firebrand BBQ
23. Miller's Landing
24. Resurrect Art Coffee House
25. Tidewater Taphouse
26. Zudy's Cafe

● DRINKING & NIGHTLIFE
27. Flamingo Lounge
28. Primrose Provisions
29. Seward Brewing Company
30. Yukon Bar

● SHOPPING
31. Safeway

● INFORMATION
32. Seward Visitor Center and Chamber of Commerce

child $5/free) is packed with fascinating exhibits that shed light on key events and prominent figures of the 20th century. You can see old photos of the well-dressed Lowell Family, who were the first homesteaders in the area when they settled in Resurrection Bay in 1884. Read about tough frontier folk – like Nellie Lawing, who became so famous that a letter simply addressed to 'Nellie, Alaska' would find its way to the roadhouse she operated. There are wooden road signs, a cross-cut of a 353-year-old tree, and flying gear from ace pilots like Hank Rosiness. The section on the Iditarod is another highlight: check out the Yupik-made fur-trimmed *kuspuk* (parka) and *mukluks* (boats) made for Dan Seavey in one of the first Iditarod races.

A faded 1927 flag pays tribute to Benny Benson, the Alaska Native student who, in Seward at age 14, designed what later became the Alaska state flag. Equally moving are the photos of young pupils at the Jesse Lee Home, which Benny Benson attended. The boarding school operated in Seward from 1925 to 1964, and was home to Indigenous children from the Aleutian Islands who were sent there (sometimes forcibly). Don't overlook the small nook at the end, where you can learn about the devastating 1964 earthquake, and hear eyewitness stories from survivors. You can watch video footage on demand by selecting the options from a touch screen. For more insight, you can catch **Movies@2** *(suggested donation $5; 2pm Tue-Sat)*, with the back-to-back screening of two 25-minute films about the Iditarod and the 1964 earthquake. It takes place in the Community Room.

The staff are enthusiastic and knowledgeable, and worth engaging. The library (upstairs) is a good place to relax on a rainy day (and entrance is free).

Explore a Cold Water Aquarium
Sea birds, touch tanks and marine mammals

After the 1989 *Exxon Valdez* 11-million-gallon oil spill damaged 1500 miles of Alaska coastline and its wildlife, spill settlement funds were given to Seward to establish a public aquarium and marine wildlife research and rescue facility. Today the **Alaska SeaLife Center** *(alaskasealife.org; adult/child $35/21)* welcomes visitors to its 115,000-sq-ft facility for an immersive experience of exhibits, tanks, touch pools and behind-the-scenes tours.

WORLD'S TOUGHEST 5K

Held on July 4, Seward's **Mt Marathon Race** *(mountmarathon.com)* is often called the world's toughest 5k. The race takes 750 runners up and down a soaring near-vertical mountain, which gains a whopping 2675ft in just under 1 mile. The slope averages 34°, and the ascent traverses a muddy-root-laden pitch, jagged rock face and a scree field – followed of course by the perilous descent (described as more of a 'controlled fall' by those who've done it). Top adult racers finish this race in under 48 minutes, with fastest racers descending in an unbelievable 11 minutes. Those eager to experience this punishing but unforgettable race can try their luck in the lottery in March.

EATING IN SEWARD: OUR PICKS

Cookery: Seward's best restaurant spreads wide-ranging temptations: briny oysters, decadent halibut dishes, and spicy fried chicken, plus good wines by the glass. *5-9.30pm Tue-Sun* **$$$**

Chinooks: Big windows overlook the harbor at this minimalist space for fresh-off-the-boat seafood with creative accents, and hearty clam chowder. *4-8pm* **$$$**

Tidewater Taphouse: The buzzing two-story space has many hits, including snow-crab dip, halibut sandwiches and miso-marinated sablefish. Great craft-beer selection. *11am-9pm Tue-Sun* **$$**

Firebrand BBQ: This outdoor Texan-run barbecue spot serves up juicy brisket, ribs and pork belly with seating at picnic tables. *7am-8pm* **$$**

> **TRAIL RUNNING IN ALASKA**
>
> Southeast Alaska is home to a vibrant and welcoming trail- and mountain-running community. The region is remote and with little to no on-trail support, and races here are small and inclusive. Competitors range from top, record-setting athletes to amateurs who simply enjoy a great day in the mountains. **Alaska Mountain Runners** *(alaskamountain runners.org)* keeps a statewide annual calendar of the best trail and mountain races, with distances ranging from 5km to more than 100 miles. While some of these runs are lottery or invite-only or require an application, others have open registration for everyone. Jump in on one of these events, but be prepared for a uniquely Alaska experience complete with technical trails, tough conditions and a robust required gear list.

Thoughtfully designed multi-story aquariums allow you to see animals both above and below the water line. You can come nose-to-nose across the glass with Steller sea lions in their 185,000-gallon tank. In the bird habitat, colorful horned puffins and common murres show off their dazzling aquatic abilities as they dive down and rocket through the water like torpedoes.

Don't miss the tide-pool touch tank for a chance to feel the bumpy texture of starfish and soft, squishy anemones, or take a break at the octopus tank where a giant Pacific octopus stretches its long tentacles against the glass.

Before leaving, discover the fascinating, stingray-type skate and its so-called mermaid's purse, then get a primer on the five types of salmon that swim through Alaska's waters. A fine finale is the small tank of delicate jellyfish, moving gracefully in the darkness like creatures from the beyond.

The center also offers **private experience tours** *(per group depending on size $275-475)*. Get up close and personal with puffins, sea lions or the giant octopus, and learn firsthand what it's like to feed these magnificent creatures.

Boating into an Otherworldly Landscape
Wildlife and glaciers amid the fjords

Kenai Fjords National Park *(nps.gov/kefj; free)* stretches across more than 600,000 acres, with 545 miles of coastline and steep, narrow inlets known as fjords that were created by glaciers long ago. Home to gigantic whales, photogenic tufted puffins and many other marine species, the park has an impressive variety of wildlife. One of the best ways to understand its natural wonders is to head out on a full-day wildlife cruise (p34).

Boarding your boat at the Seward Boat Harbor, stand on deck as it moves slowly through the bay, passing the stunning, snowcapped mountains. As the boat pauses at various coves and rocky outcroppings, witness nesting common murres, watch for colorful puffins bobbing along the water and catch a view of seals basking in the sun.

Head inside for lunch and a view out the window, but don't get too comfortable. Your captain is in constant contact with other boats in the area as they all watch for signs of humpback and orca whales. The captain will take you where they've been spotted so you, too, can see these creatures leap from the water.

Hang on as your cruise goes from the relatively calm waters

EATING & DRINKING IN SEWARD: CAFES

Resurrect Art Coffee House: Join the line for outstanding espressos and heavenly pastries inside a former church turned cafe and crafts gallery. *7am-5pm* **$**

Coho Joe's: Tiny woman-owned coffee spot with first-rate espresso drinks; has a few outdoor seats facing the small boat harbor. *6am-7pm* **$**

Zudy's Cafe: Stop in for breakfast plates, lunch (sandwiches), espresso or delicious slices of cake in a historic building facing Resurrection Bay. *9am-3pm Mon-Sat* **$$**

Miller's Landing: Sit on the deck over the water while enjoying breakfast fare, top-notch fish and chips, frothy cafes and local microbrews. *7am-8pm Mon-Thu, 7am-10pm Fri-Sun* **$$**

WALK SEWARD'S HISTORIC STREETS AND WATERFRONT

Panoramic backdrops, murals and historical insight are all part of the allure of a wander through Seward's photogenic downtown.

START	END	LENGTH
Alaska SeaLife Center	238 4th Ave	1½ miles; 1¼ hours

Start at the free parking next to the ❶ **Alaska SeaLife Center** (p247) with a statue honoring ❷ **Jujiro Wada**, a Japanese immigrant who helped establish the National Historic Iditarod Trail. Stop to admire the view of ❸ **Resurrection Bay** as you head to the ❹ **Iditarod Trail Mile Marker Zero**, the starting point for the 1000-mile historic trail to Nome. Look for bald eagles in the trees above the ❺ **skate park and playground**, and scan the water for otters and humpback whales.

Passing the tent campground on your left, step off the trail to walk along the rocky shore. During low tide, you can spot ❻ **timber pilings** – remnants of the once industrial shoreline destroyed by the 1964 earthquake. Further along, the ❼ **Japanese Toro** is a stone lantern presented to Seward in 1973 as a token of friendship from Hokkaido, Japan. Stop here and stroll back south, turning onto Jefferson St.

A few blocks uphill, take a left onto 4th Ave where you'll spot the ❽ **Qutekcak Mural**, which pays homage to Seward's Indigenous roots. One block down, you'll reach ❾ **Kawabe Park**, named in honor of a Japanese-American businessman who made substantial contributions to Seward. End your walk at the nearby ❿ **alley dotted with murals**, including a montage of photo-like figures (and a spectacled dog!) from Seward's past.

The mural **Remembering Exit Glacier** shows the gargantuan size of this river of ice in years past.

The view west of town takes in the soaring peak of **Mt Marathon**, where runners test their endurance on July 4 (p247).

4th Ave is dotted with eateries, though you'll also find food trucks in this gravel lot, like **Los Chanchitos** for excellent Mexican fare.

THE GUIDE

KENAI PENINSULA SEWARD & KENAI FJORDS NATIONAL PARK

THE SCIENCE OF GLACIERS

Even without climate change, there is no such thing as a glacier that never changes. For starters, all glaciers are either moving forward, known as 'advancing,' or getting shorter, known as 'retreating.' Glaciers grow or shrink in another way, too, as they thicken or grow thinner, a process known as 'downwasting.' As a glacier moves, large cracks known as 'crevasses' form without warning across the top, while the heavy ice grinds apart the rocks and debris, producing a mineral-rich dirt known as 'glacial silt' and leaving behind icy rock fields known as 'moraine.' The warming planet has sped up the process of retreat or, in other cases, slowed down the natural growth or advance of those that are moving forward.

FIND MORE ALASKA KAYAKING

Love kayaking? Hit the water in **Kachemak Bay State Park** (p280), **Whittier** (p208) or **Valdez** (p188) for more Alaska ocean adventures.

of the bay and over the bumpy open ocean. You're headed now to Aialik Bay and the stark blue tidewater of Bear Glacier where it descends into the ocean. Bundle up against the cold air here, watching ancient glacial ice float through the water near the boat. As you return to port, linger over the magnificent landscape just outside the boat.

Kayak Amid Glaciers
Cinematic paddling excursions

The ocean and coastline of Kenai Fjords National Park are best experienced from the water, and touring by kayak is the most immersive way to do it. Kayak travel offers the most direct contact with this place and its astonishing beauty. Two different day trips here are worth your time, and which you pick depends on which you value more: time near a glacier or time journeying on the water.

Glacier enthusiasts should join **Liquid Adventures** *(liquidadventures.com)* for their popular full-day adventure in Aialik Bay, home to an active tidewater glacier (full-day tour per person $509). After whale-watching and seabird spotting from the shuttle boat on the two-hour ride from Seward, you'll land on a beach with your guide to start your 3½-hour kayaking journey. You'll navigate safely around ice floes and enjoy unique perspectives of the glacier, before pulling onto a rocky beach for a lunch break. The views and wildlife-watching opportunities are exceptional, including on the boat ride back to Seward. For a shorter outing, consider the five-hour **Rainforest and Waterfall excursion** *(per person $149)* in Resurrection Bay.

Another reputable outfitter, **Sunny Cove Kayaking** *(sunnycove.com)* runs a paddle trip to Fox Island in Resurrection Bay *(per person $259)*. After a one-hour shuttle to the island, follow your guide

Humpback whale breaching, Kenai Fjords National Park (p248)

around the island's perimeter on your seven-hour adventure, visiting a magical array of coves and cliffs. Pause on the shore for lunch, explore a waterfall, then beach at a petrified forest to walk among the ghostly natural history created by the 1964 tsunami. Afterwards, you'll boat to the harbor, arriving around 5pm.

Both of these outfitters run a wide range of other tours, including a combo kayaking and helicopter tour offered by Liquid Adventures, and a kayaking and hiking experience run by Sunny Cove.

Pull in Halibut & Salmon

Spectacular fishing trips

Like much of the Kenai Peninsula, Seward is a top destination for sport and subsistence fishing for both Alaskans and visitors. Summer days here bring throngs of anglers looking for a fresh ocean catch via private or charter boat.

Start your own Seward fishing experience bright and early with a reputable outfitter like the **Fish House** *(thefishhouse. net)* on a full-day trip for either salmon *(per person $350)* or halibut *(per person $400)*. Setting out from the small boat harbor, travel up to four hours out of Resurrection Bay to the deep ocean where halibut is found. Pass by the towering fjords and keep an eye out for wildlife as you head out for deep-sea fishing – harbor seals, whales, sea birds, including puffins, and Dall's porpoise are common sights out here.

Dropping lines from heavy poles into the sea, wait for a bite and then fight these monster fish onto the boat – some weigh more than 90lb. Feel the excitement of reeling in other fish species that you're not specifically targeting, including

BEST OUTDOOR ADVENTURES

Exit Glacier Guides: Famed operator offering naturalist-led walks, ice climbing and glacier hikes, plus fly-in adventures and mountaineering courses.

Major Marine Tours: The gold standard for wildlife-watching boat cruises in Kenai Fjords National Park.

Liquid Adventures: Offers memorable paddling excursions out to Bear Glacier and Aialik Bay, with multiday options.

Ididaride: Travel by helicopter to Punchbowl Glacier, where you'll then go dogsledding. Or skip the flight and go for a ride through the woods (on a dogsled-driven cart).

Kenai Backcountry Adventures: Runs a huge array of summer and winter tours: hiking, rafting, scenic flights and bear-viewing, from four-hour excursions to eight-day expeditions.

MORE HALIBUT FISHING

Halibut fishing from Seward requires a journey of several hours, but in **Homer** (p276) the halibut fishing is found closer to the harbor.

THE HUMPBACKS OF RESURRECTION BAY

Ryan Fisher, owner of Exit Glacier Guides and Liquid Adventures *@liquid_adventures*

Lately in the summers, we've had really incredible whale-watching. If you've never experienced it, bubble netting is when a pod of humpbacks work together to feed on a school of fish. They circle around them underwater, blowing bubbles to make a tighter bowl and get their prey closer to the surface, and then in unison the whales rush to the surface. It's just an explosion as they burst out of the ocean, fish falling out of their mouths and the birds going crazy. Seeing it live is like watching from inside of a National Geographic IMAX movie. It's one of the most incredible things to see.

rockfish and lingcod, before starting your return journey for salmon fishing in the bay.

Swapping equipment for lighter rods that are good for the comparatively small salmon, get ready for the fun of battle and the cry of 'fish on' around the boat as you pull in your limit of silvers before heading back to the harbor.

Admire your catch and snap photos with it next to the infamous 'Caught at Seward Alaska' sign before handing it off to Captain Jack's Seafood Locker for processing, flash freezing and, if needed, shipping.

Seward Gateway to the National Park
Exhibits at the visitor center

The Kenai Fjords National Park visitor center just off Seward's small boat harbor offers an in-depth view of the park's wildlife, fjords, coastline, Harding Ice Field and Exit Glacier. Combining immersive static displays with a 20-minute educational video, the center and small gift shop are an ideal start for any Kenai Fjords adventure. You can also chat with park rangers and get insight into less-visited hiking trails and the latest travel conditions.

FIND MORE GLACIERS
The Exit Glacier isn't the only place to explore the ice in Alaska. Other trekking options include the **Matanuska Glacier** (p160), the **Root Glacier** (p335) and the **Worthington Glacier** (p196).

Gaze Across the Exit Glacier
Witness climate change in action

While the vast majority of Kenai Fjords National Park is on the coast and in the water, its 680,000 acres also include the **Harding Icefield** and the 40 glaciers it feeds, including the **Exit Glacier**. Few other places in Alaska offer such clear evidence of the rate of glacial retreat in the face of a warming planet. On the drive here from Seward, you'll pass small brown road signs with numbers like

Exit Glacier

1815. The number corresponds to a particular year, which notes the glacier's location at that time. You'll encounter more of these year-marker signs as you walk the scenic **Glacier Overlook Trail**, an easy 2-mile loop that takes you past various viewpoints of the glacier and the outwash plain below.

For more context on the glacier and the surrounding national park, join a ranger-led walk up to the **Glacier Overlook**. These happen daily at 10am and 2pm and depart from the Exit Glacier Nature Center.

Hike to the Harding Icefield

Climb to the glacier's source

The park's most challenging day hike is the ascent on the **Harding Icefield Trail**, an 8.2-mile round-trip hike (out-and-back) that moves through forest, meadows and high alpine. You'll also pass avalanche shoots, icefall zones and river outwashes, and it's important to be prepared. Some years, the mountain gets hit with such heavy winter storms that snow on the trail persists at the higher elevations well into August. Hiking poles are recommended, and you may also need crampons. Talk with a ranger about the current conditions in the visitor center before setting out. Despite the difficulty level, the hike

KENAI FJORDS NATIONAL PARK PRACTICALITIES

Fees: Admission is free.

Visitor Centers: In addition to the visitor center in Seward, the park has a post in the Exit Glacier area with maps, info and some exhibits.

Ranger Programs: Rangers lead informative walks twice daily (10am and 2.30pm) to the Glacier Overlook, plus less frequent Junior Ranger Walks.

Camping: A half-mile from the visitor center, the park has 12 free walk-in tent-only sites; first-come first-served.

Trails: There are two trails here: an easy walk to a glacier overlook), and a challenging 8-mile (round-trip) ascent.

Getting There: It's a 12-mile drive from Seward. If you don't have a car, various companies offer transport, including **Exit Glacier Shuttle** *($20 round-trip).*

 DRINKING IN SEWARD: OUR PICKS

Flamingo Lounge: Sip Seward's most imaginative cocktails while sinking into a plush chair in a retro-chic space. There's also seafood, steaks and sharing plates. *5-10pm*

Seward Brewing Company: The family-owned brewpub has creative housemade craft beer and elevated pub fare – loaded fries, Asian tacos and wood-fired pizzas. *4-9pm Wed-Mon*

Primrose Provisions: Delightful spot for wine, cheese, charcuterie boards and imaginative sandwiches, with fine views over the bay. *11am-9pm*

Yukon Bar: A friendly dive with a regular lineup of live music, karaoke and open-mic nights, along with weekly DJ dance parties. *noon-2am*

OTHER TOP EVENTS IN SEWARD

Polar Bear Jump: A favorite of costumed masochists who plunge into frigid Resurrection Bay in mid-January, all to raise money for kids with cancer.

Mermaid Festival: One weekend in mid-May, the harbor area fills with mermaids, mermen, pirates and assorted ocean creatures during a fest featuring live music, food trucks and craft vendors.

Silver Salmon Derby: Held in August, one of Alaska's oldest fishing tournaments features a week of competition for cash prizes and daily awards.

Holiday Arts & Craft Fair: Dozens of vendors sell their artwork and finely made crafts at this large indoor fair that takes place in early December.

New Year's Eve: Ring in the new year by catching the fireworks show over Resurrection Bay from Seward Waterfront Park.

Harding Icefield Trail (p253)

is quite popular. Set out early, and avoid going on weekends to beat the crowds.

Once you get underway, you'll be ascending over 3100ft over the course of 4 miles, sometimes along steep switchbacks. But the rewards are worth the effort, especially when you reach the the edge of the 700-sq-mile Harding Icefield. Backed by mountains, the views are dazzling – you might see small planes landing on the ice cap. Along the hike, you'll pass high above the Exit Glacier's terminus zone, and wind your way past colorful thickets of wildflowers – purple-blue hues of lupine and white dwarf dogwood. Keep an eye out for thick-furred marmots as well as mountain goats peeping out from the vegetation above you. Once at the top, pause for a snack near the rustic national park cabin shelter before starting the steep hike back down. Allow six hours to complete the hike.

Celebrate July 4 Seward-Style
A famous race and much more

After pushing through the long months of winter darkness, Alaskans go all in for celebrations under the midnight sun of summer. July 4 is best known for its incredible 5km mountain foot race (p247). Grab a spot near the finish line on 4th Ave to see these world-class runners and hometown favorites cross the finish line, many of them bleeding thanks to the mountain's sharp shale rocks paired with the steep descent. Apart from the 5k, there are lots of other fun events over several days, like the fish toss, grease-the-pole competition, seagull call and tug of war. Plenty of kids activities draw families from across the region, and there's live music, food vendors and an 11pm boat parade, followed by some midnight fireworks – the lingering twilight allows just enough darkness to see the fiery display.

Beyond Seward

Hike through temperate rainforest past untrammeled coastlines, or head into the hills on rewarding climbs to glimmering mountain lakes.

For more than 7500 years, the Alutiiq/Sugpiaq people lived here using the ice-free port and harvest-rich coast for sustenance and trading. In the 18th century, Russian fur traders forever altered that way of life. They were followed by early American settlers in 1890, who founded the terminus of the Alaska Railroad.

Nowadays the region beyond Seward beckons visitors with its excellent trail network. To the south, Lowell Point State Recreation Site offers miles of hiking and access to the abandoned Fort McGilvary at Caine's Head, accessible by foot only at low tide. To the north, there is the popular mountain-biking and hiking Lost Lake trail, stunning views of Kenai Lake from the south, and access to the mirrored blue-green Ptarmigan Lake.

Places
Primrose p255
Lowell Point State Recreation Site p256
Ptarmigan Lake p257

GETTING AROUND

The two-lane Seward Hwy that snakes south to terminate in Seward offers easy, paved access to the area north of the city. Reaching Lowell Point requires following the unpaved and, at times, narrow Lowell Point Rd along the coast south of the city. Prone to landslides, this road is periodically closed or narrowed as crews work on slide mitigation. Don't skip the chance to take in the unbelievable view of Kenai Lake from the Primrose Campground parking lot, just five minutes off the Seward Hwy.

Primrose

TIME FROM SEWARD: **25 MINS**

Hike or bike the Lost Lake trail

On this trail you can hike or bike from temperate rainforest to alpine lakes. One of the most popular mountain-biking, hiking and running trails in Southeast Alaska, Lost Lake is a don't-miss trek on a summer day. For the best hiking views, do this point-to-point or out-and-back starting at the Primrose trailhead 25 minutes north of Seward. For excellent mountain biking, start at the Lost Lake trailhead in town. No matter your method, the nearly 15-mile journey makes a fabulous day trip or overnight backpacking expedition.

Starting from the **Primrose Campground & Trailhead**, climb 5 miles to the tree line through hemlock and Sitka spruce. Keep an eye out for blueberries, plentiful on this trail in late summer. Ascending to the rolling tundra, take in 360-degree mountain views and vibrant colors with Kenai Lake to the north. Continue to **Lost Lake**, enjoying the purple of lupine flowers against its blue expanse. Pitch a tent or stop for a snack on the USFS forest service sites, but avoid trampling the tender tundra off trail. Plan to linger at the lake? Carry bug spray and a head net – the small black flies here can often be incessant.

If mountain biking, start your journey at the southern Lost Lake trailhead closer to town, renting from Seward Bike Shop and, if necessary, cycling the 5 miles to the trailhead. This

THE TEMPERATE RAINFOREST

The timberline around Seward is a temperate rainforest, a unique ecosystem of towering trees protecting the vegetation-rich ground below. Sitka spruce, cottonwood, alders and some mountain hemlocks make up 70% of the forest's rooftop in this region, sheltering the forest floor from the rain, which can accumulate as much as 75in annually. Blanketed with lichens and moss, it's also a perfect environment for foraging fiddlehead ferns and a wide variety of berries, including blueberries and orange salmonberries. But watch out for the prickly and towering devil's club with its large, green leaves. While the inner bark is used by herbalists for salves, direct contact with the leaves and stem can cause irritation to your skin and eyes.

rocky trail is a steady uphill climb able to be pedaled by experienced riders. The trail leads to a wide plateau to the south of Lost Lake, where you can take in the stunning views of the mountains and distant ocean. Make a fast descent back to your vehicle or the road to town.

Lowell Point State Recreation Site

TIME FROM SEWARD: **10 MINS**

Hike through a coastal forest

Accessed just 3 miles south of town at the true end of the road, Lowell Point offers remote ocean views from the trees and rocky coastline. This trail is frequented by both day hikers and overnight backpackers headed to **Caines Head** and the abandoned WWII outpost **Fort McGilvary**, which can only be accessed at low tide.

Head out for a 3-mile day hike from the recreation site parking area, trekking through the forest to a series of switchbacks down to the coast. Cross a bridge, watching for spawning salmon, before heading back into the forest to walk the trail boardwalks, then hit the broad beach at **Tonsina Point** for some more ocean views.

If the tides work in your favor, extend your adventure out to the fort, a 5-mile hike from the parking area. Perched on a headland 650ft above the bay, Fort McGilvary served as a strategic spot for defending Seward during WWII, even as enemy forces occupied portions of the Aleutian Chain.

Pack a flashlight, then climb through the fort's maze of underground tunnels and chambers accessible in its depths. Imagine what it was like to be stationed for months at a time in this gorgeous yet isolated place. But keep an eye on the time. Unless you plan to stay the night, you'll need to head back before the tide rises, trapping you on the point.

Ptarmigan Lake

Another hike that can be accessed from the Lowell Point State Recreation Site is the **Cathedral Falls Trail**. This moderately difficult 8.9-mile out-and-back trail is lined with wild berry bushes. You can get to this trail from the Tonsina Point trailhead.

Ptarmigan Lake
TIME FROM SEWARD: **30 MINS**
Backcountry backpacking with a view

While many backpacking or hiking destinations in the area beyond Seward are major undertakings, a journey to **Ptarmigan Lake** over the **Ptarmigan Creek Trail** offers a moderate, family-friendly hike with a big reward. The rolling trail offers plenty of variety over 6.8-miles out-and-back, and only gains about 800ft on the journey to the glassy, green-blue lake. A hike to the lake is great on a warm summer day for a perfect picnic spot and a swim. Watch out for wild blueberries and stay bear-aware while on this hike. Take in the fireweed along the lakeshore and the stunning reflection of the surrounding peaks before beginning your journey back to the trailhead.

If you don't want to head out as far as Ptarmigan Lake, or want to tackle another hike on the way there and back, the **Bear Lake Trail** can be found about 10 minutes from downtown Seward in the same direction as Ptarmigan. **Bear Lake** is a popular summer swimming hole. As the name suggests, bears are common on this easy 4.3-mile out-and-back trail, so remain bear-aware.

Alternatively, the **Grayling Lake Trail** is a family-friendly 3-mile out-and-back trail. It's part of the National Historic Iditarod Trail, located just 15 minutes outside Seward and accessed directly off the highway.

THE GOOD FRIDAY EARTHQUAKE

Before 1964, Seward had a bustling waterfront complete with fish-processing plants, warehouses and oil tanks. Railroad tracks ran along the shore, near the present-day Alaska SeaLife Center. Everything changed on March 27, 1964, when an 8.3-magnitude earthquake struck. After the earth finally stopped churning, oil tanks exploded, and a powerful tsunami, some 30ft high, swept nearly a mile inland. Thirteen people died and five were injured; 86 houses were completely destroyed and hundreds badly damaged. With the bridges, railroad and boat harbor gone, Seward was suddenly cut off from the rest of the state. Repairing the city took six years, and some parts of the waterfront were never rebuilt.

Kenai & Soldotna

SALMON FISHING | INDIGENOUS HERITAGE | HOMESTEADERS

✅ TOP TIP

In July, dip-netting draws hundreds of Alaskans to the beach near the mouth of the Kenai and Kasilof rivers. Open to residents only, this is a sight worth seeing and a window into the rich salmon runs that sustained Alaska Natives on this very spot for thousands of years.

Sitting against the lower Kenai River as it flows into the Cook Inlet, Soldotna and its neighbor Kenai carry a distinctive industrial feel. But hiding just beyond is a close-knit community welcoming to outsiders who want to experience one of the top salmon fisheries in the world. Anglers flock here to fish the summer salmon runs, while Alaskans hit the beach for residents-only dip-netting in crowds so thick the event is known as combat fishing.

Kenai has been home to Alaska Natives as far back as 1000 BCE, and Russian fur traders established one of their first mainland Alaska outposts here in 1791. After WWII, the area was opened to military veteran homesteaders who flocked here for a fresh start. Modern Kenai and Soldotna link both their success and decline to the oil industry. It was 20 miles northeast of here that oil was first discovered in Alaska in 1965.

Gateway to Soldotna
Information and animal insight

A handy place to get your bearings when you arrive is the **Soldotna Visitor Center** *(visitsoldotna.com)*. A volunteer on hand can advise on Soldotna attractions and events, hikes and other activities in the area. While it's more exciting to see

GETTING AROUND

Kenai and Soldotna are both easily accessible by road and are located just off the two-lane Sterling Hwy between Homer and Anchorage. The **Alaska Bus Company** route connects Soldotna with Anchorage *($119, 3½ hours)*, Cooper Landing *($79, 1¼ hours)* and Homer *($79, 1½ hours)*.

There's no bus service to Kenai, though you can arrive by plane. Both **Grant Aviation** *(flygrant.com)* and **Kenai Aviation** *(kenaiaviation.com)* run regularly scheduled small passenger planes between Anchorage and Kenai.

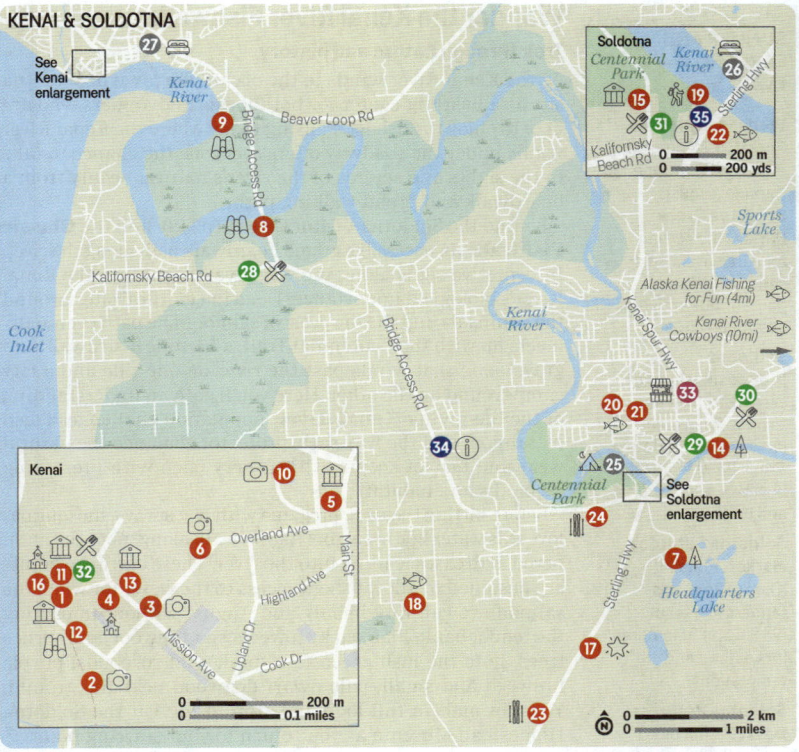

KENAI & SOLDOTNA

SIGHTS
1. cabin built in 1898
2. dirt path
3. Fort Kenay
4. Holy Assumption of the Virgin Mary Russian Orthodox Church
5. Homesteader's Cabin
6. Kenai Moose Range
7. Kenai National Wildlife Refuge Headquarters & Visitor Center
8. Kenai River Flats Overlook
9. Kenai River Viewing Platform
10. Kenai Visitor Center
11. Oskolkof/Dolchok Cabin
12. Overlook
13. Parish House Rectory
14. Soldotna Creek Park
15. Soldotna Homestead Museum
16. St Nicholas Chapel

ACTIVITIES
17. Arc Lake
18. Chadwicks Fishing Guide Service
19. Classic Fishwalk
20. Eric Loomis Fishing
21. Kenai Fish Company
22. Ken's Alaskan Tackle
23. Slikok Multi-Use Trails
24. Tsalteshi Ski Trails

SLEEPING
25. Centennial Park Campground
26. Kenai River Lodge
27. Uptown Motel

EATING
28. Flats Bistro
29. Odie's Deli
30. St Elias Brewing Company
31. Tanner's
32. Veronica's Old Towne Cafe

SHOPPING
33. Soldotna Saturday Market

INFORMATION
34. Alaska Department of Fish & Game
35. Soldotna Visitor Center

them in real life, the taxidermy animals on display allow you to get a close-up view of prime Kenai wildlife, including a mountain goat, a wolverine, a king crab and various bird species. You can also see the largest king salmon ever caught – a 97lb behemoth fished out of the Kenai River in 1985.

SUMMER AND EARLY FALL EVENTS

Wednesdays in the Park: On Wednesday evenings from June through August, **Soldotna Creek Park:** is the setting for a free live music series, with beer garden, kids activities and food vendors.

Soldotna Wednesday Market: Weekly from 11am to 6pm, the market (also held in Soldotna Creek Park) features baked goods, veggies and crafts.

Soldotna Saturday Market: Running 10am to 2pm, this farmers market at 193 E Coral St features lots of food and craft temptations.

Soldotna Progress Days: It's fun times during the fourth weekend of July with a parade, rodeo, livestock show, pie-eating contest, mustache/beard contest and block party.

Kenai River Marathon: In late September, you can join the action during a scenic race along the Kenai River.

Wander the Kenai River Fishwalk
Trek through nature and history

As the Kenai River winds to the ocean, the town of Soldotna sits as a bustling center for both locals and anglers who are here to enjoy the fishery. Pausing today where the Kenai River winds under the roadway offers everyone the chance to take in the sights and sounds of the river's natural beauty from a boardwalk and broad walking path.

Behind the Soldotna Visitor Center (p258), find the **Classic Fishwalk**, an accessible grated boardwalk path along the river. Interpretive signs along the way give insight into the Kenai River's biological importance, Dena'ina cultural sites around the peninsula and the life cycle of salmon. The path eventually meets up with the Centennial Trail, a 1.5-mile boardwalk and gravel loop that winds past the river on one side and a city campground on the other. Here you'll gain an understanding of the life-giving **Kenai River**, population challenges faced by salmon, and the way their protectors balance the natural wear and tear of keeping this fishery open with preserving its banks and habitat.

Before hitting the trail, pregame with bug spray – mosquitoes love this waterside area, too. As you walk along, note the numbered staircases leading into the river. These entrance points are designed to allow fishers access to the water for when the salmon are running in July and August without impacting the tender bank. Flanked by towering cottonwood and spruce trees, note the lush green fern, pink wild rosebuds, purple fireweed and small, pale dwarf dogwood near the ground. You can make a full loop and stop in to visit the Soldotna Homestead Museum as you return to your starting point.

The Life of a Homesteader
Early-20th-century history

Before or after hitting the Classic Fishwalk, stop by the **Soldotna Homestead Museum** *(soldotnamuseum.com)* to get a taste for how people lived in the area in the early 20th century. Because WWII veterans were given preference for homesteading in this region in the late 1940s, many of the earliest American residents here traveled in with army-issued gear – and the museum's collection reflects that. It includes a classic pair of 'bunny boots' – so named because of their white, oversized appearance – used during the Korean War.

EATING IN KENAI & SOLDOTNA: OUR PICKS

Odie's Deli: Delicious made-to-order hot and cold sandwiches, soups and salads, and there's a guitar and piano free for the playing. *8am-4pm Mon-Fri, 9am-2pm Sat* $$

Flats Bistro: Enjoy grand views of the Kenai River Flats as you sup on fresh Alaska seafood, spicy gumbo or local greens. *3-8.30pm Wed-Sun* $$$

Veronica's Old Towne Cafe: In a 1918 log building, Veronica's serves espressos and healthy sandwiches, and you can sit outside by the flowers. *10am-4pm Tue-Sat* $$

St Elias Brewing Company: The family-owned Soldotna brewpub serves up satisfying stone-fired pizzas and quality beers (try the Williwaw IPA). *noon-10pm* $$

WALKING OLD TOWN KENAI

Glimpse Kenai's past while taking in the coastal beauty of this tranquil walk through Old Town.

START	END	LENGTH
Kenai Visitor Center	Overlook	0.5 miles; 1 hour

Start at the 1 **Kenai Visitor Center** (p263) on Overland St. Take a peak at the historic 2 **Homesteader's Cabin**, once belonging to the colorful 'Moosemeat' John Hedberg. Taking a right on Overland St, you'll soon pass four historic buildings on your right, the original headquarters of the **Kenai National Wildlife Refuge** (p263), then known as the 3 **Kenai Moose Range**. Continue down the block to the corner of Overland St and Mission Ave and find a replica of the surprisingly small 4 **Fort Kenay**, originally built near here by the US in 1869.

Turn right onto Mission Ave and find yourself transported into a different era, as you approach the historic blue-and-white onion-domed 5 **Holy Assumption of the Virgin Mary Russian Orthodox Church**, built in 1894. Directly across from it, you'll see the 6 **Parish House Rectory**, believed to be the oldest original building on the Kenai Peninsula. Services are still held at the church, which is one of the oldest Russian Orthodox houses of worship in Alaska.

Follow this road to a final Russian Alaska stop at the 7 **St Nicholas Chapel**, built in 1906. The first missionary, Father Nikolai, helped bring the smallpox vaccine to Kenai, saving many lives. End your walk at an 8 **overlook** gazing out onto the Cook Inlet where the Kenai River meets the ocean.

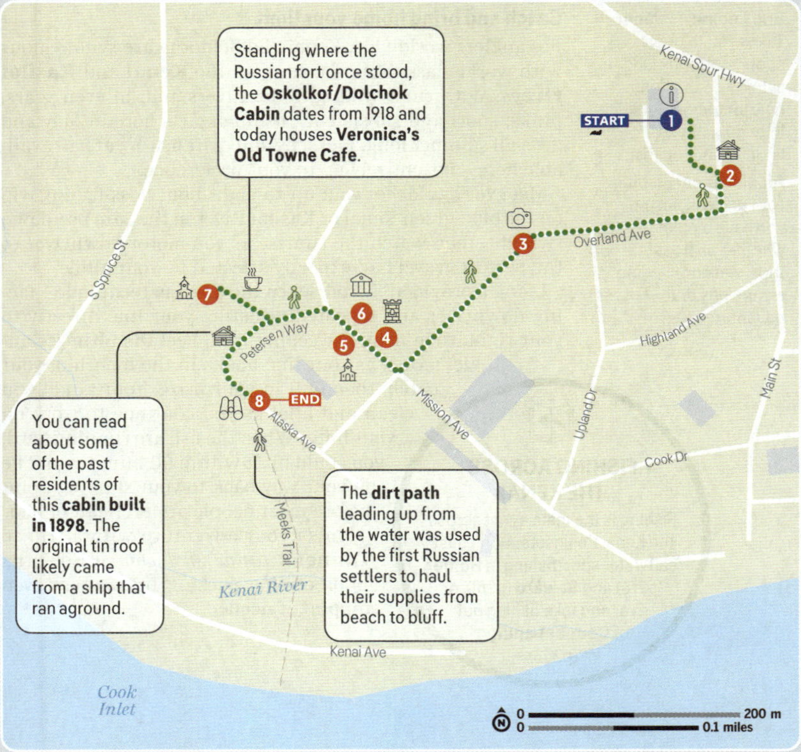

Standing where the Russian fort once stood, the **Oskolkof/Dolchok Cabin** dates from 1918 and today houses **Veronica's Old Towne Cafe**.
You can read about some of the past residents of this **cabin built in 1898**. The original tin roof likely came from a ship that ran aground.
The **dirt path** leading up from the water was used by the first Russian settlers to haul their supplies from beach to bluff.
START
END
Kenai Spur Hwy
Overland Ave
Highland Ave
Main St
Upland Dr
Cook Dr
Mission Ave
Alaska Ave
Petersen Way
S Spruce St
Meeks Trail
Kenai River
Kenai Ave
Cook Inlet
0 200 m
0 0.1 miles

BEST KENAI AREA FISHING GUIDES

Kenai River Cowboys: Full guiding service for salmon and trout in small groups over the summer and fall.

Chadwicks Fishing Guide Service: Half- and full-day rates vary by season for salmon and trout fishing along the Kenai and Kasilof rivers.

Kenai Fish Company: Family-friendly charters on the Kenai and Kasilof rivers or in the ocean off the Kenai Peninsula.

Eric Loomis Fishing: Takes you to prime spots for trophy king salmon on the Kenai river, or out on Cook Inlet for halibut, lingcod and rockfish.

Alaska Kenai Fishing for Fun: Will ensure you have a great time, whether on float trips, walking-wading excursions or fly-out adventures.

A series of rustic timber buildings here offers an immersive perspective on what life was like for the homesteaders. Unlike some local museums, which only allow you to pop your head into a recreated room, the Homestead Museum lets you walk fully in, feeling the true confines and challenges of this musty, isolated lifestyle in small, close-built cabins. Among the curios on display are the wood carvings of practical items and figurines made by Ed Ciechanski, a homemade bassinet passed from family to family when a new baby in the community arrived, an early Alaskan flag signed by Benny Benson (the young student who designed it) and some amusing quotes by wilderness residents ('We canned a lot of moose...' said Mickey Faa Carver).

It's easy to feel as though you've stepped back in time, walking into the Skilok Valley School. Dating from the 1950s, it was the last log school built during Alaska territorial days, and has the original gas lanterns and blackboard used until its closure in 1960.

There's also an Alaskan cache – a small wooden building on stilts used to dry fish and protect food supplies from roving animals. Volunteers at the museum are happy to shed more light on the collection and the intriguing residents from the past.

Fish the Renowned Kenai Salmon Runs

Catch and bring home your limit

For anglers worldwide, Kenai and Soldotna are synonymous with world-class salmon fishing on the **Kenai** and **Kasilof rivers**. With runs of king, reds, silvers and, in even years, pinks, sport and subsistence fishing starts here in May and goes all summer long. Floss, fly and drift fishing are all available here – it's entirely up to your preference.

Meet your guide for your up-to-eight-hour floss-fishing trip on the blue-green Kenai or Kasilof River in the 3am pre-dawn twilight, then watch the sunrise as you motor downriver to the perfect gravel bar, expertly selected by your guide.

Using a provided fly rod, learn the flossing technique – facing downriver and repeatedly casting your line directly to your right, then firmly sweeping it in. Feel the ultimate angler's rush as your line hooks in the mouth of your catch, then pull in your prize. Your guide will clean and fillet as you continue to work on your limit. When the fish are running hard, you could hit it within 90 minutes and be on your way back to your starting point before most people are even out of bed.

Finish your adventure with a trip to **Tanner's** *(tannersfish.com)* in Soldotna for processing, packing, freezing and even shipping if needed.

FISHING ACROSS THE KENAI

Fishing is the main event across the Kenai Peninsula. Don't miss saltwater sportfishing in **Homer** (p276) and **Seward** (p251), or river and lake fishing out of **Cooper Landing** (p232).

Kenai National Wildlife Refuge

Launchpad to the Kenai National Wildlife Refuge
Exhibits and trip planning

A few minutes' drive south of the Soldotna Visitor Center, you'll find the beautifully designed **Kenai National Wildlife Refuge Headquarters & Visitor Center**. Known as 'Alaska in miniature' thanks to its broad array of wildlife and topography, the **Kenai National Wildlife Refuge** stretches across nearly 2 million acres. It spans ice fields, glaciers, mountains, tundra, forest and coastal wetlands in a parade of opportunities for solitude and awe. Get an understanding of this unique region by exploring the interactive exhibits here. You can listen to different types of bird song, see nighttime footage of creatures spotted on trail cams, and learn about the different habitats where life flourishes in the *Icefield to Ocean* exhibit. Park rangers can give tips on exploring the refuge beyond these walls. A good place to start – for hiking, scenic views and wildlife-watching – is the Skilak Wildlife Recreation Area (p240).

If time is limited, you can walk one of the short trails that begin here – the quarter-mile Keen-Eye Nature Trail leads down to an observation deck overlooking Headquarters Lake, which is a fine spot to look for loons and other waterbirds.

Indigenous Arts & Crafts
Exhibits on Kenai history and heritage

One of the main attractions in town, the **Kenai Visitor Center** *(kenaichamber.org; free)* has a small but beautifully curated collection of local Indigenous artifacts, clothing and tools,

CAST YOUR LINE

While hiring a guide all but guarantees you'll hit your limit after a day at Kenai's infamous salmon runs, it is possible to drop a line on your own. A boat is needed to access the best gravel bars, but many anglers instead choose to fish from the bank. Bring your own equipment or rent in Soldotna from **Ken's Alaskan Tackle**. You can also borrow a rod from the **Alaska Department of Fish & Game** *(adfg.alaska.gov)*. On the Kenai River, join the crowds on the fish walk just off the Soldotna Visitors Center. To fish the Kasilof, visit a half-mile section known as 'the people hole' just off Crooked Creek Campground.

LEARN ALASKA NATIVE HISTORY

You'll find other impressive collections devoted to Alaska Native heritage at the **Anchorage Museum** (p148), the **Alaska State Museum** in Juneau (p96) and the **University of Alaska Museum of the North** (p322) in Fairbanks.

TOP WINTER ACTIVITIES

Tsalteshi Ski Trails: Soldotna has an outstanding cross-country ski area, with 15 miles of groomed trails, plus 6 miles of single-track winter bike trails.

Frozen RiverFest: Sip craft brews by open bonfires while listening to live music at this one-of-a-kind beer fest in March.

Ice Skating: Nothing compares to ice skating on frozen **Arc Lake** in the winter; it's liveliest on Saturday afternoons.

Kenai National Wildlife Refuge: From the headquarters (p263) in Soldotna, you can head off on the trails for cross-country skiing or snowshoeing.

Slikok Multi-Use Trails: Just south of Arc Lake, you can head off on 3 miles of cross-country ski trails, with another 3 miles of bike-friendly single track.

Loons, Kenai National Wildlife Refuge (p263)

as well as models of Dena'ina dwellings – like the Nichil, a subterranean gabled house used in winter. You'll see finely made basketry from across Alaska, one-of-a-kind folk art like Emil Dolchok's handcrafted chair made of moosehide lacing, Mike Sausedo's animal tableaux carved in shed antlers or the Kenai bicentennial quilt featuring key scenes from the region's history.

Outside on the grounds, you can have a good look at a steam donkey (used to pull fishing boats out of the water), see the faded painted door of a 1920s cannery, and try to make sense of the rocket-like fixture dating from the discovery of oil in the region in 1957.

Views Across the Estuary
Bird-watching and scenic backdrops

A five-minute (2.5-mile) drive south of the visitor center, the **Kenai River Viewing Platform** offers a fine vantage point over the estuary. This is a great spot for bird-watching. Depending on the season, you might see sandhill cranes, Arctic terns, bald eagles, godwits or many other species. Land animals, including caribou, sometimes make an appearance, while offshore, you might spy beluga or harbor seals. You can visit another enticing viewing platform, the **Kenai River Flats Outlook**, 0.8 miles to the south just off the Bridge Access Rd. This one has a viewing telescope and overlooks the Kenai River Flats. Like the platform to the north, this boardwalk viewpoint offers an impressive glimpse of Mt Redoubt, the conical 10,197ft stratovolcano soaring above the water on the western side of Cook Inlet. Assuming the weather is cooperating, of course!

Beyond Kenai & Soldotna

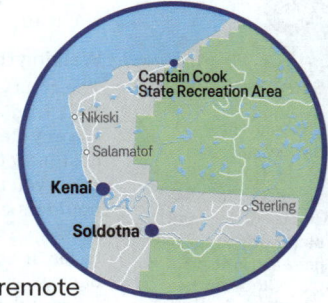

Vast, protected wildlife reserves meet a remote and stunning state park to create a wilderness backdrop ideal for reconnecting with nature.

While Kenai and Soldotna revolve today around their rich salmon fisheries, the areas just beyond them are a playground of a different sort thanks to the Kenai National Wildlife Refuge and the coastal Captain Cook State Park. Together they cover about 2 million acres from mountain to sea for beach combing, hiking, camping and even a renowned canoe trail. Like most of this area, these lands were originally home or hunting grounds for Alaska Natives before their settlement by homesteaders. Today it's easy to find solitude here as you wander off the main roads, spotting bald eagles soaring over the low wetlands bordered by black spruce trees, topaz-blue lakes and the rocky Alaska coast.

Captain Cook State Recreation Area

TIME FROM KENAI & SOLDOTNA: **30 MINS**

Exploring rugged coastline

Bluffs looking over the **Cook Inlet** and out to the **Tordrillo Mountains** along with secluded, rocky beaches ideal for agate hunting, an interpretive trail, lakes and streams, all make **Captain Cook State Recreation Area** a worthy side trip. Tucked 25 miles north of Kenai on the Kenai Spur Hwy, it is the only public destination in that direction after a not particularly scenic drive, passing multiple working and defunct industrial plants.

As you enter the park, watch for **Swanson Lake** to the east. Surrounded by cottonwood and thick and prickly devil's club, the lake offers chilly swimming and pleasant boating. Just down the road, the clear **Swanson River** flows toward the ocean and is a popular take-out point for trips down the 22-mile **Swanson River Canoe Trail**, which starts in the Kenai National Wildlife Refuge (p263). It's at the end of the paved road that you'll find this area's top destination: **Discovery Beach**. Park at the day-use area and head down the bluff to the rocky beach, keeping an eye out for bald eagles in the sky and beluga whales in the water. Wander the

GETTING AROUND

Like so much of the Kenai Peninsula, access to both the Captain Cook State Recreation Park and the Kenai National Wildlife Refuge is a mix of two-lane, sometimes rough highways and unpaved, deeply pitted roads. The roads into the developed portions of these areas, including to the designated campgrounds, are suitable for RVs, but you'll need to watch closely for potholes.

coastline, which is popular with agate hunters, and look for your own rocks as you watch the dramatic, 30ft tides come and go.

Walking the forests and beaches

The reserve's hiking trails are short but rewarding. A short walk from the **Captain Cook State Recreation Area Discovery Campground**, you'll find the start of a nature trail designated 'This Land Through Time.' The 1-mile route takes you through northern boreal forest, past out-of-place boulders carried here by glaciers thousands of years ago. Pick up an informative brochure at the start of the trail to learn about the Dena'ina connection to the land dating back at least 1000 years. Be prepared for fierce mosquitoes.

Around 3.5 miles west of there (on the road to Kenai), the **Bishop Creek Day Use Area** has an easygoing half-mile trail, which passes through mature birch forest and past a shallow creek where you can sometimes spot red salmon swimming upstream in the summer. The trail ends at the beach, where you can explore a rarely visited shoreline.

Hunting for agate

Found in a wide variety of colors worldwide, this common gemstone is known for its durability and is said to contain healing properties. No matter how you plan to use it, trying your hand as a rock hound along the Captain Cook State Recreation Area is a delightful way to spend an hour or more wandering the beach. To identify agate, look for color banding on stones that appear translucent. They are easier to spot when wet thanks to their bright colors, which makes hunting for them along the coast ideal. Need help understanding what you're looking for? Swing by the Soldotna Homestead Museum (p260) on your way to the park to see a small display of polished and unpolished agate.

Another prime spot for agate hunting is **Nikiski Beach** (also called 'Agate Beach'). Find it by heading 12 miles north of Kenai along the Kenai Spur Hwy. Look for the turnoff down the gravel road off to your left. There's just enough room to park and turn around right before you hit the beach. From there, you can head in either direction to find some unique specimens of agate, as well as sea glass.

FLYING BLOODSUCKERS

Everyone knows the *real* state bird of Alaska is the mosquito. There are around 30 different bloodsucking species here, and in some places they can be relentless, swarming you the second you leave your car. The mosquitoes are at their worst from early June to late July. A few tips to avoid attracting them: wear light-colored clothing; mosquitoes are attracted to certain colors like black, red and orange. Avoid using scented lotions, soaps or shampoo. For longer forays in the wilderness, consider wearing a head net. Tighter weave cotton clothing is more protective than porous synthetics. DEET-based repellents are the gold standard, though you can also buy permethrin-treated clothing or treat your own garments with a permethrin spray like Sawyer.

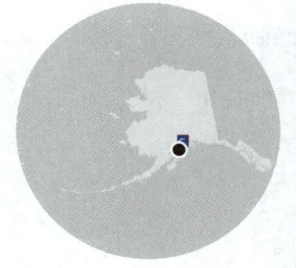

Homer

NATURE IMMERSION | ART GALLERIES | SPORTFISHING

Sweeping views across mountain-backed Kachemak Bay welcome you to Homer, a town at the end of the road that is equal parts adventure gateway and creative hub for artists and freethinkers.

At first glance, the narrow 4.5-mile-long Homer Spit jutting into the ocean can feel like it's crawling with tourists, but don't let the RV parks and boat-filled marina stop you from journeying down this scenic shoreline thoroughfare, where you can arrange all manner of boating and flightseeing activities. Nearby marshes and meadows play host to an array of shorebirds and wildflowers, while galleries in the nearby downtown area display imaginative work of local artists.

Used as a camp by the Sugpiaq, Homer became a coal-mining town in the late 1890s through WWII, then later an important port for goods coming into the state. Today this self-proclaimed 'halibut-fishing capital of the world' benefits heavily from both the commercial and sportfishing industries.

> ☑ **TOP TIP**
>
> Though Homer lacks formal mountain-biking trails, the dirt roads in the hills above town lend themselves to some great rides, especially along Diamond Ridge Rd and Skyline Dr. You can rent bikes (including e-mountain bikes) from **Cycle Logical** *(cyclelogicalhomer.com)*.

Natural & Human History in Kachemak Bay

Interactive exhibits at the Pratt Museum

Though relatively small, the **Pratt Museum** *(prattmuseum. org; adult/child $15/9)* is packed with interactive exhibits focusing on Kachemak Bay and the coastline beyond. You can read

Continues on p271

 GETTING AROUND

Homer is at the literal end of the road. You can get here either by catching a bus with the Alaska Bus Company or by air from Anchorage via Alaska Airlines or Aleutian Airways. Homer is also a port for the Alaska State Ferry, traveling roughly three times per week to both Seldovia *($34, 1½ hours)* and Kodiak *($91, 10 hours)*. If you're heading down to the Spit (departure point for many boat tours), you'll find some free parking lots, as well as places that charge by the day *(typically $10)*. Be sure to verify before leaving the lot.

HOMER

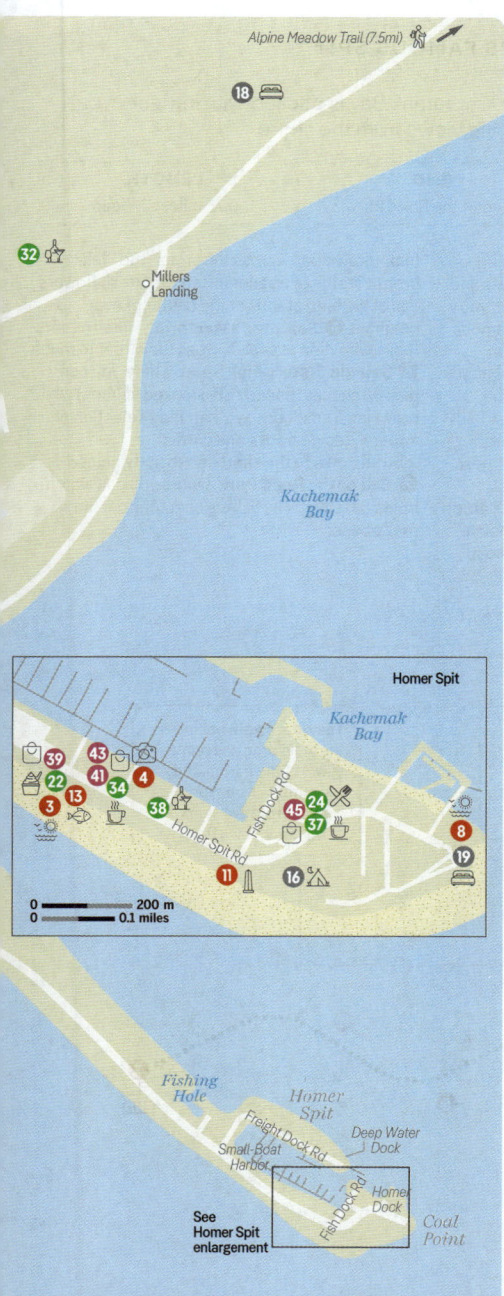

★ HIGHLIGHTS
1. Alaska Islands & Ocean Visitor Center
2. Pratt Museum

● SIGHTS
3. beach
4. boardwalk
5. Bunnell Street Arts Center
6. Carl E Wynn Nature Center
7. Center for Alaskan Coastal Studies
8. End of the Road Park
9. Homer Council on the Arts
10. Mariner Park
11. Seafarer's Memorial

● ACTIVITIES
12. Calvin & Coyle
13. North Country Halibut Charters
14. Reber Trail

● SLEEPING
15. Driftwood Inn
16. Homer Spit Campground
17. Homer Stay & Play
18. Juneberry Lodge
19. Land's End Resort
20. Pioneer Inn

● EATING
21. Alibi Bar & Cafe
22. Carmen's Gelato
23. Fat Olives
24. Johnny's Corner
25. Mike's Alaskan Eatery
26. River Cafe
27. The Kannery
28. Two Sisters Bakery
29. Wild Honey Bistro

● DRINKING & NIGHTLIFE
30. Alice's Champagne Palace
31. BB's Bakery
32. Bear Creek Winery
33. Captain's Coffee Roasting Co
34. Coal Town Coffee & Tea
35. Grace Ridge Brewing Company
36. Homer Brewing Company
37. Salmon Sisters Mug Up Coffee
38. Salty Dawg Saloon

● SHOPPING
39. AK Starfish Co
40. Art Shop Gallery
41. Brown Bear Products Gallery
42. Fireweed Gallery
43. Homer Clayworks
44. Homer Farmers Market
45. Salmon Sisters Fish Shop

● TRANSPORT
46. Cycle Logical

WALK DOWN HOMER'S FAMOUS SPIT

The iconic strip of land jutting into Kachemak Bay is packed with intrigue, from one-of-a-kind shops to jaw-dropping views from the shore.

START	END	LENGTH
AK Starfish Co	End of the Road Park	0.75 miles; 1½ hours

Start off at the 1 **AK Starfish Co**, an inviting store with high-quality T-shirts, colorful hats and jewelry made of mammoth ivory. Next door, you can join the line at 2 **Carmen's Gelato**, famous for its handmade gelato – among the best in Alaska. Try the wild Alaskan rose with local honey or the fig and rum. Cross the street to reach 3 **Brown Bear Products Gallery**, the go-to for new reading material. It has an excellent selection of new and used Alaska-related titles, plus artwork and craft items.

Set in an 1897 cabin, the 4 **Salty Dawg Saloon** (p275) has been a railroad station, schoolhouse and family home, but today it's the Spit's most famous dive bar. Across the street, the lifelike bronze statue of a sailor (often with fresh flowers lain at his feet) stands at the center of the poignant 5 **Seafarer's Memorial**, which honors those who died at sea. Recross the street to reach 6 **Salmon Sisters Fish Shop**, where you can pick up snacks (tinned fish, smoked salmon) while browsing a small but eye-catching selection of apparel, recipe books and cards.

Stroll down to the shoreline to aptly named 7 **End of the Road Park**, where you can watch boats passing by as fishers cast off from the rocky beach.

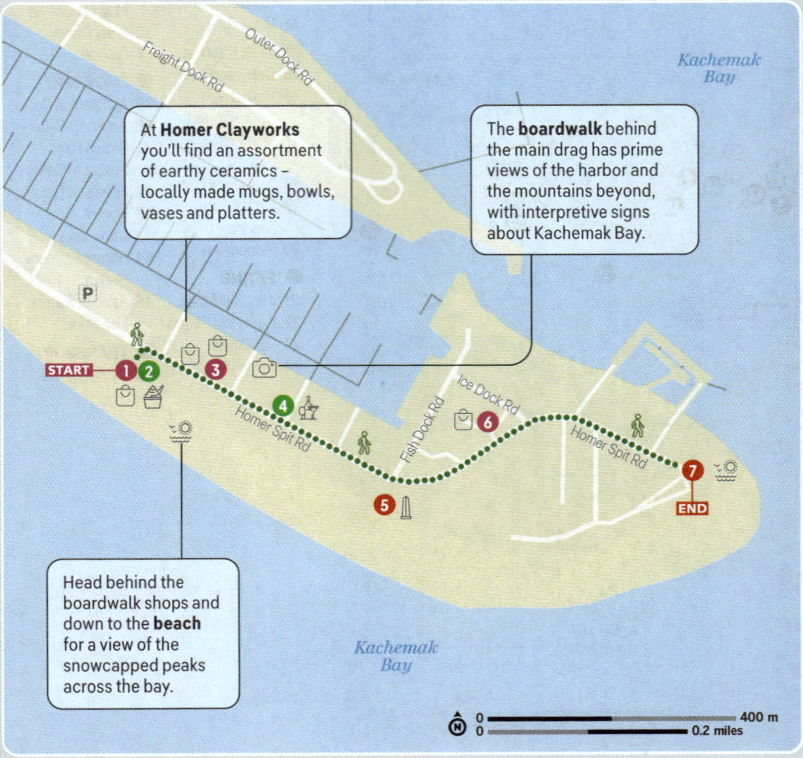
Kachemak Bay
Freight Dock Rd
Outer Dock Rd
At **Homer Clayworks** you'll find an assortment of earthy ceramics – locally made mugs, bowls, vases and platters.
The **boardwalk** behind the main drag has prime views of the harbor and the mountains beyond, with interpretive signs about Kachemak Bay.
P
START
1
2
3
4
5
6
7
END
Homer Spit Rd
Fish Dock Rd
Ice Dock Rd
Homer Spit Rd
Head behind the boardwalk shops and down to the **beach** for a view of the snowcapped peaks across the bay.
Kachemak Bay
N
0
400 m
0
0.2 miles

Continued from p267

about historic volcanic eruptions and peer through a microscope at different ash samples; see photos of the Good Friday earthquake while learning about the dynamic geological forces at work in this region; and see specimens of Alaskan wildlife – from tufted puffins to a complete beluga whale skeleton, along with a rather philosophical-looking brown bear.

In the 'Living by the Tides' exhibit, you can read about harrowing storms, learn about cliff-nesting seabirds on Gull Island and see detritus disguised as art pieces in a display of Japanese glass floats used by the fishing industry that washed onto Alaskan beaches. There's also coverage of the impact of the *Exxon Valdez* oil spill on the region.

Other exhibits revolve around Kachemak Bay's human history, from Indigenous clothing and crafts to industrial objects transformed into household objects by 20th-century homesteaders (a bellows made from a car muffler, metal fuel containers converted into saddlebags). You can pick up an old phone to listen to a homesteader reminisce about living in the wilderness. Don't miss the small image of ancient rock art depicting people in a large skin boat with mystical overtones (for more on petroglyphs, check out p272).

Museum admission includes access to the nearby Historic Harrington Homestead, a log cabin built in the 1930s, with its knickknacks from the early 20th century. There's also a two-seater outhouse from 1929 – apparently, the oldest in town.

Gateway to the Alaska Maritime National Wildlife Refuge

Connect with wildlife and conservation

Spanning across the islands in the Aleutian Chain, over the Bering Sea and far north past Kotzebue in an area equivalent to the space between California and Georgia, the Alaska Maritime National Wildlife Refuge protects habitat for marine life and seabirds in 2500 coastal spots including islands and headlands. Its Homer headquarters, known as the **Alaska Islands & Ocean Visitor Center**, offers a window into this far-reaching space, with a focus on its seabirds, conservation and Alaska Natives who have long called it home.

Start with a walk through the interpretive center, where you'll encounter an immersive perspective on the human uses of the refuge, including many Alaska Native artifacts, how modern users have impacted the wildlife and what conservationists are doing today to mitigate that. Interactive exhibits and beautifully shot films give fascinating insight into this remote region. The best is a room that's a replica seabird colony, complete with clifflike formations, cacophonous bird calls and surround-view flocking. The center also hosts guided hikes, discovery labs (where you can chat with naturalists) and other activities.

GETTING ORIENTED IN HOMER

Homer lies at the end of the Sterling Hwy, 225 road miles from Anchorage. For visitors, there are two distinct sections of town. The 'downtown' area, built on a hill between high bluffs to the north and Kachemak Bay to the south, lies along – or near – busy Pioneer Ave. Heading eastward, Pioneer Ave becomes rural East End Rd, with a number of other lodging and eating options. The second section of Homer, and certainly the most famous, is the Homer Spit, a skinny tongue of sand licking halfway across Kachemak Bay. There's lots going on both in town and on the spit, with a mix of restaurants, shops, galleries, drinking spots and even theater in each area.

MORE SMALL TOWN CHARM

Love local museums and markets? Head to **Palmer** (p163) and check out the small museum and weekly summer Friday Fling market and festival.

ANCIENT INHABITANTS OF KACHEMAK BAY

Native people have lived in the Kachemak Bay Area for over 3000 years. They fished, gathered mollusks and hunted for caribou, moose, bears and marine mammals. Housing structures evolved over the centuries, from dwellings of stone and whale vertebrae to half-subterranean log structures in later periods. Domesticated dogs were kept, which is not surprising given the tradition existed in Alaska for at least 4000 years. Early Native people also left behind prehistoric pictographs, which have been found in rock shelters on four different sites, including Chugachik Island, Bear Island and Peterson Bay. The ancient artwork depicts sea and land animals, anthropomorphic figures and abstract shapes, and they may have served a ritual function.

The refuge is a paradise for bird-watchers, and the 1.2-mile Beluga Slough trail just outside the center offers a chance to dive in firsthand. It's a stopover point for migrating seabirds in the spring and fall, and sandhill cranes often spend the summer here, as well as many other species. Extend your wanderings with a walk just beyond the trail to Bishop's Beach with its flat, gray rocks, or linger among the tide pools at low tide.

The Homer Art Scene
Galleries featuring local artists

After decades as a place mostly for homesteaders and fisherfolk, Homer in the late 1960s and early 1970s became a magnet for back-to-land and hippie culture. Today, the legacy of that shift is the vibrant Homer art scene, known for being friendly to emerging artists.

A good place to begin the deep dive into Homer's art scene is at the **Bunnell Street Arts Center** *(bunnellarts.org)* near Bishop's Beach. Going strong for more than three decades, this gallery hosts top-notch exhibitions from local and regional artists, and stages the occasional live music event. Don't skip the shop, where you'll find beautifully crafted jewelry, hand-carved bowls, and bold notecards created by Alaskan makers. The center supports and promotes public art around town

 EATING IN HOMER: BREAKFAST & LUNCH

River Cafe: Cozy spot with a few tables inside and picnic tables outside for hearty breakfasts, rice bowls and burritos. *7am-4pm Mon-Sat, 8am-3pm Sun* **$$**

Two Sisters Bakery: A local favorite for its excellent coffee paired with mouthwatering baked goods. Go early before they sell out. *10am-3pm* **$**

Wild Honey Bistro: Delicious sweet or savory crepes and sourdough croissants, plus soup and hearty sandwiches for lunch. *9am-2pm Tue-Sun* **$$**

Mike's Alaskan Eatery: Small takeaway spot known for its satisfying, well-stuffed sandwiches, and you can head next door for ice cream and milkshakes. *10.30am-4pm* **$$**

Alaska Islands & Ocean Visitor Center (p271)

(including eye-catching installations, murals and even poetry) like the nature-themed poems you'll encounter on the Beluga Slough trail (p271).

A half-mile northwest of there, the **Homer Council on the Arts** *(homerart.org)* has roots dating back to the 1950s, and each month a new exhibition is staged, which typically focuses on an emerging artist from Homer or the Kenai Peninsula.

Homer Council on the Arts lies near the south end of Pioneer Ave, which is sprinkled with shops, restaurants and two other creative spaces. At **Art Shop Gallery** *(artshopgallery.com)* you can browse for Alaskan-themed watercolors, prints, photography and Native crafts, including carvings made from walrus ivory. Further up the street, Ptarmigan Arts is a local co-op featuring the work of dozens of artists. You'll find paintings, photos, jewelry, pottery, woodwork, clothing made from recycled garments, and works in mixed media. Next door, **Fireweed Gallery** *(fireweedgallery.com)* is another cultural icon of Homer, with a wealth of works by Indigenous artists.

Stroll the Galleries on First Fridays

Special exhibitions

If you're in Homer for the first Friday of the month, be sure to pay a visit to the art galleries around town. During the evening

SAILING THE ALEUTIAN CHAIN

The largest ship in the US Fish and Wildlife Service, the 120ft R/V *Tiĝlax̂* plays a vital role in managing the Alaska Maritime National Wildlife Refuge. Ever since 1987, the research vessel has sailed the Aleutian Chain, covering some 20,000 nautical miles each year while ferrying biologists and supplies out to field camps strung across the volcanic archipelago. Named after the Aleut word for 'eagle', the *Tiĝlax̂* (tehk-lah) is also the floating base for researchers studying marine ecosystems, oceanic change and critical seabird colonies. It has even hosted the occasional artist, like Kim McNett who served as artist-in-residence on a 900-mile voyage in 2022 and helped bring the marine wilderness to life through her writing, sketches and watercolor paintings.

DRINKING IN HOMER: BEST COFFEE SPOTS

Coal Town Coffee & Tea: On the Spit, this log-cabin espresso bar is the perfect stop before a morning boat trip. Excellent lattes. *6am-6pm* **$**

Captain's Coffee Roasting Co: A family-owned place with in-house roastery and delicious housemade baked goods. *7am-3pm* **$**

Salmon Sisters Mug Up Coffee: Near the end of the Spit, you can order an excellent takeaway espresso and go for a waterfront stroll. *7am-3pm* **$**

BB's Bakery: Handily located on Ocean Drive, BB's has frothy coffee drinks, biscuits and gravy, donuts and other morning essentials. *7am-2pm* **$**

Sea otter and pup, Homer region

TOP EVENTS IN HOMER

Kachemak Bay Shorebird Festival: In early May, Homer celebrates the spring migration with naturalist talks, boat trips to nesting sights and art workshops.

Alaska World Arts Festival: This two-week fest in September features a diverse lineup of live music, film, dance, visual arts, puppetry and more.

Burning Basket: In early September, the whole Homer community comes together for this big annual bonfire on the beach at **Mariner Park**.

Taste of Homer: The late-May showcase of food, wine and brew culminates in the Homer Harborfest, a one-day shindig of music, art and food trucks.

Kachemak Bay Highland Games: One Saturday in early July, you can catch Celtic-inspired competitions including a kilted foot race, hammer toss and tug-of-war.

(5pm to 7pm), new exhibitions are unveiled, and you can meet the artists while enjoying refreshments (cookies, coffee, punch, tea).

Browse for Crafts & Picnic Fare

Homer's twice weekly farmers market

If you're lucky enough to be in Homer on a Wednesday (2pm to 5pm) or Saturday (10am to 3pm), don't miss the **Homer Farmers Market** *(homerfarmersmarket.org)*. Packed with local vendors peddling vegetables, arts and crafts, baked goods, flowers, espresso drinks, ice cream and fresh seafood, this stop is part market, part community-gathering space.

Forest Walks & Nature Activities

Beloved nature reserve trails

Situated on the bluffs above Homer, the **Carl E Wynn Nature Center** *(akcoastalstudies.org/wynn-nature-center; adult/child $10/8)* is home to 5 miles of hiking trails amid boreal forests favored by moose. It's a great spot for families and anyone interested in the area's ethnobotany.

On the interpretive nature trails – one of them a boardwalk and wheelchair accessible – you can learn which plants can be

EATING IN HOMER: OUR PICKS

Alibi Bar & Cafe: Famous for their wings (try the birch bourbon variety), plus halibut tacos, burritos and Alaskan craft beers on tap. *4-9pm Tue-Sat* **$$**

Fat Olives: Upscale and very popular Italian spot with good pizzas, piping-hot calzones, Greek salads and rich seafood pastas. *11.30am-9pm* **$$$**

The Kannery: This stylish but unpretentious spot serves Homer's best cooking: pan-seared rockfish, summer risotto and smoked game hen, alongside creative cocktails *4-9.30pm* **$$$**

Johnny's Corner: Head to the end of the Spit for delicious sticky rice and kimchi bowls topped with salmon, halibut, pork belly or tofu. *noon-5pm Thu-Tue* **$$**

used to heal a cut, condition your hair or munch for lunch. **Naturalist programs** *(adult/child including admission $20/10)* happen daily (except Mondays) during the summer, and feature everything from bird or fungi walks to insight into edible plants and wild-craft making.

Naturalist-Led Excursions
Immersion in Homer's unique ecosystems

The non-profit **Center for Alaskan Coastal Studies** *(akcoastalstudies.org)* runs well-loved excursions that immerse you in the natural beauty in the wilds above Homer and in Kachemak Bay. It runs properties on both sides of the bay, plus a yurt on the Spit – all great places to learn about the region's diverse ecosystems and its abundant life on land and in the sea.

Five different tours are offered, with knowledgeable naturalists and hands-on activities an important part of the experience (and one reason why they're popular with kids): The **Living Ocean Tour** *(adult/child $175/95)* is a three-hour boat tour where you'll visit seabird rookeries, look for otters and other marine mammals, stop at a local oyster farm to talk with farmers (while sampling the fruits of their labor), and explore intertidal zones to learn about the unique species there.

At the Carl E Wynn Nature Center or the nearby Inspiration Ridge Preserve on the bluff above Homer, meet up with a staff naturalist for a **90-minute guided tour** *(adult/child including reserve admission $20/10)* through woods, fields and marsh to gain detailed insight into the plants and animals you see around you. Learn to recognize the signs of a booming snow-hare population, hear about the traditional uses for flowers and bushes, and witness the impact of climate change on the forest. Down on the Spit, the **Creatures of the Dock** *(adult/child $15/10)* is a family-friendly one-hour tour that offers hands-on encounters with tidal creatures.

There's also the seven-hour **Sea to Tree tour** *(adult/child $195/125)* which includes a boat trip across the bay to the center's Peterson Bay Field Station. This stunning spot sits on the bluffs just outside Kachemak Bay State Park and offers an immersive journey into the tide pools and meadows behind the center. Spend time exploring tidal pools to observe creatures like crabs and starfish, then take a hike through little visited coastal forests before heading back to Homer.

BEST TRAILS IN HOMER

Alpine Meadow Trail: In the Eveline State Recreation Area, this 1.4-mile loop traverses open meadows, with distant views of glaciers across Kachemak Bay.

Diamond Creek Trail: The 4.6-mile out-and-back trail takes you through forests, over meadows and down to a lovely stretch of beachfront.

Homestead Trail: Drive 4 miles northwest of town to Rogers Loop for the start of this 6.5-mile out-and-back venture with fine views over fields and hills.

Reber Trail: Follow the fireweed-lined switchbacks up to an overlook with impressive views of Kachemak Bay (0.4 miles one-way).

Calvin & Coyle: An easy 1.4-mile loop through meadows with an overlook onto the Beluga Wetlands. Good birding and possibly moose spotting.

 DRINKING IN HOMER: OUR PICKS

| Homer Brewing Company: The Kenai Peninsula's first brewery has a buzzing taproom where you can sample its traditional country ales. *1-7pm Sun-Thu, 1-8pm Fri & Sat* | Salty Dawg Saloon: The iconic, cash-only Homer Spit dive bar where the ceilings and walls are lined with $1 bills. *11am-1am* | Grace Ridge Brewing Company: The small family-owned brewery has a taproom (and outdoor seating) for enjoying their in-house brews. *noon-8pm* | Alice's Champagne Palace: With its country saloon interior, Alice's has a huge draft-beer menu and hosts open mic and live music nights. *noon-9pm* |

THE VOLCANIC HORIZON

During cloudless days, the Kenai Peninsula makes a fine vantage point for spotting active volcanoes rising above the surface of Cook Inlet. On a boat tour from Homer, **Mt Augustine** looms some 70 miles southwest of the Spit. The perfectly conical 4134ft volcano sits on its own small island and has erupted nine times since the 1930s – most recently in 2006. Another nearby volcano is **Mt Redoubt**, a 10,197ft peak some 50 miles west of the Kenai River mouth; it last erupted in 2009. There's also **Mt Iliamna**, a 10,016ft mountain located 49 miles west of Ninilchik. Every few years it rumbles and ejects steam, though it hasn't erupted since 1867.

Welcome sign, Homer

Sportfish for Halibut

'Halibut-fishing capital of the world'

The hefty halibut is the largest species of flatfish, and it's found in deep water off the coast of Alaska. Swimming sideways with both eyes on the top of its head, the halibut, which can live up to 50 years and weigh more than 90lb, is unlikely to win any beauty contests. But its tender white meat is prized for its flavor – and there's nothing like hauling in a fish so large it's sometimes called a 'barn door.'

A number of reputable outfitters lead trips, including **North Country Halibut Charters** (northcountrycharters.com; half-day/full-day per person $205/310), a family-owned operation with over 40 years of experience. The day starts around 7am, at the small boat harbor, where you'll meet your captain before heading out on a 90-minute ride to the deep waters where the halibut live. The ocean can be rough out here, so be prepared for rocking seas as you drop your line. Sit back and gaze at stunning views of the active volcanoes visible off Homer on a clear day – **Mt Augustine**, **Mt Iliamna**, **Mt Redoubt** and **Mt Spurr**.

MORE ALASKA SEA FISHING

While Homer is a top destination for halibut fishing in Alaska, it isn't your only option. Check out **Seward** (p251) and **Valdez** (p188) as alternative ports.

Watch your line bounce, then work with the captain or deck hand to haul in your catch. If your fish is especially huge, don't be surprised if your crew member pulls out a small shotgun or pistol and shoots the fish in the head before bringing it onboard – this is a safety measure for both passengers and crew who can easily be injured by such a large animal coming onboard alive. Pulling in a live, moving fish this big could also damage the boat. The fish will be filleted on the boat; back on the dock, fish processing is available, so you can send home your fresh catch.

Beyond Homer

Book a boat trip to reach memorable hiking in a state park or off-the-beaten-path village rambles in waterfront Seldovia.

Some of the best reasons to come to Homer are outside the city limits. Kachemak Bay State Park has outstanding scenery you can reach only by boat and walking trail – including a glacial lake dotted with jewel-like ice formations. Another draw is Seldovia, where you can get a taste of life in a remote village, and explore more forested trails and virgin coastline. Homer's charter pilots run trips to Lake Clark and even Katmai, for unforgettable up-close bear encounters.

Like much of the Kenai Peninsula, this area with its rich salmon runs was originally visited by Alaska Natives during harvest season. Russian traders also settled here, and their legacy lives on in the region's historic churches.

Places

Anchor Point p277
Seldovia p277
Kachemak Bay State Park p280
Ninilchik p282
Nikolaevsk p283

Anchor Point
TIME FROM HOMER: **20 MINS**

Forest-fringed gallery

For something completely different, make the 12-mile journey north of Homer to the **Norman Lowell Gallery of Alaska** *(normanlowellgallery.org; free)*, just off the Sterling Hwy. The spacious gallery features works by the late self-taught homesteading painter, Norman Lowell, though you'll also see permanent works he accumulated over the years from other artists and craftmakers. Many of Lowell's paintings focus on the Alaskan wilderness, with mountains, glaciers and rugged coasts playing a starring role in his unique works. After taking in the landscapes, go for a stroll along the woodland paths and have a look at the outside of the original log cabin homestead, which the artist built back in 1958.

Seldovia
TIME FROM HOMER: **45 MINS**

Explore a historic waterfront village

Tucked just out of sight across Cook Inlet, Seldovia is a charming village of about 300 residents and home to a scenic boardwalk, spectacular hiking and a rich history. Seldovia is compact and picturesque, founded by Russian settlers in the late 18th century on the traditional homeland of the Sugpiaq people,

GETTING AROUND

For adventures in Kachemak Bay State Park, many Homer operators offer boat service: a round-trip costs $90 to $110 (Ashore Water Taxi offers some of the best rates). You can arrange to get dropped off in one area and picked up in another. If you're heading to Seldovia, one-way rates are $50 with **Seldovia Bay Ferry**. **Alaska Marine Highway Ferries** are cheaper *($34)*, but slower and less frequent (three times a week).

TOP EXPERIENCE

Lake Clark National Park & Preserve

Just across Cook Inlet from the Kenai Peninsula, this 6300-sq-mile national park is a near composite of Alaska: tundra-covered hills, mountains, glaciers, coastline, vast lakes and two active volcanoes. With no access by road, most visitors fly in on short flightseeing or bear-viewing tours, though you can extend your stay by basing at a campground or backcountry lodge inside the park.

Brown bear, Lake Clark National Park & Preserve

TOP TIPS

- Air taxis connecting Port Alsworth in Lake Clark National Park & Preserve to other locations such as King Salmon can be arranged – useful for hopping straight over to other national parks in Alaska, like Katmai (p358).

PRACTICALITIES

- nps.gov/lacl
- lodging & tours Jun-Oct
- 7hr flight excursion from Homer $1200

Bear Viewing

It would be nearly impossible to visit from June to September and not see a bear. Small-plane operators out of Homer and other Kenai Peninsula towns typically make the one-hour flight across the Cook Inlet, then land on the beach, where it's just a short walk to see the prime attraction: bears out on the mudflats digging for (and gorging on) mussels and clams.

Kayaking & Canoeing

Kayaking and canoeing are popular ways to explore Lake Clark itself, the shores of which range from craggy horizons to low tundra. In the park's main settlement, Port Alsworth, **Tulchina Adventures** *(tulchinaadventures.com)* will rent out kayaks or set up an unguided kayaking/camping trip.

Backpacking

The hiking is phenomenal, but Lake Clark is best suited to the experienced backpacker. Highlights include the Telaquana Trail Route, a historic Dena'ina Athabascan route running from Telaquana Lake to Kijik Village, and Twin Lakes, where dry tundra slopes provide easy travel to ridges and great views.

Guided Adventures

If you prefer not to go alone, book a trip with experienced operators like Alaska Alpine Adventures, which leads a one-week paddling trip as well as seven- to 10-day backpacking trips.

then used as a regional supply center until the highway extended to Homer across the bay.

After arriving by boat from Homer, it's an easy stroll into the village past a few shops and restaurants. You'll pass the stairs leading up to Seldovia's most photogenic building: the **St Nicholas Orthodox Church**, an 1891 landmark with an octagonal belfry. Perched on a hill just above Main St, the church opens only during services.

You can learn more about the the human presence on Seldovia, the plant and animal life of the region, and key events that shaped history (like the Good Friday earthquake in 1964) at the **Seldovia Village Tribe Visitor Center** *(svt.org; free)*. Unique objects on display at the small museum here include drum-like herring floats, artfully carved stone tools and bone implements, a beautifully painted Aleut-style hunting visor, an 1894 Russian Orthodox icon, and various objects (including a barnacle-encrusted teapot) uncovered from a wreck offshore. The gift shop sells crafts and clothing as well as a book entitled *Sharing Recipes*, describing favorite dishes gathered from the community.

Keep walking along the main street to reach Seldovia's **historic boardwalk**. Overlooking the slough, this atmospheric collection of weathered buildings (mostly private homes) and flower beds has scenic views across the water to stilted houses backed by forests.

Hike the Otterbahn Trail

The best way to enjoy a bit of nature outside of Seldovia is to hike the cleverly named **Otterbahn Trail**. Created by local high-school students, the easygoing path takes you through lush forest, past dense thickets of salmonberry bushes. After about 1 mile, you'll cross a boardwalk bridge that spans a marsh (keep an eye out for moose and beavers), and soon reach the coastline. From there you can explore the coast. When the tides are low enough (below 17ft), you can make your way up to Outside Beach, around 0.3 miles from trail's end. There's a tidal chart posted at the trailhead. You'll find the start of the Otterbahn behind the Susan B English School, off Winifred Ave (a 10-minute walk from the ferry dock).

Bike the forested roads

With little traffic, and forest-backed scenery lining the mostly gravel roads, Seldovia makes a memorable setting for a spin. Those looking for a fairly leisurely ride can pedal the 10-mile Jakolof Bay Rd, which winds along the coast nearly to the head of Jakolof Bay. Along the way, you'll pass the turnoff to **Outside Beach** (roughly 1.4 miles from town). This rocky shore is an excellent place for spotting eagles, seabirds and possibly even otters. At low tide, you can explore the sea life among the rocks, and on a clear day the views of Mt Redoubt and Mt Iliamna are stunning.

For a more rigorous ride, keep going past Jakolof Bay for another 6 miles beyond the end of the maintained road, climbing 1200ft into the alpine country at the base of Red Mountain.

BERRY PICKING IN SELDOVIA

Seldovia is known best for its berries – particularly its blueberries, which grow so thick just outside town that, from late August to mid-September, you often can rake your fingers through the bushes and fill a two-quart bucket in minutes. If you visit then, you'll likely share the ferry over with berry pickers who have their buckets in tow. Other delicacies to seek out include watermelon berries: these dark red, jelly-bean-sized berries with a faint taste of their namesake ripen in August. There are salmonberries, which resemble raspberries and ripen in July and August. Low-bush cranberries are also prevalent, with peak season in August and September. Be mindful of where you gather: harvest only on public lands.

CABIN IN THE WILDERNESS

The Kenai Peninsula has scores of public-use cabins, including more than a dozen in Kachemak Bay State Park. These dwellings vary from simple yurts to spruce cabins with bunk beds, a wood-heating stove, table and benches. All have an outhouse. Some are set on lakes and even come with a rowboat for your use. You'll need to bring sleeping bags and pads, food, water purification, toilet paper and garbage bags (you must pack out whatever you bring). Getting there is an adventure – requiring you to hike or ski in, take a boat or fly in via bush plane. The price: $45 to $80 per night. Alaska has many other cabins sprinkled across the state. You can book these online at *recreation.gov*.

You can bring mountain bikes over from Homer, or rent them at **Seldovia Outdoor Rentals** *(seldovia.fun; 4hr/day rental $25/45)* on the main street.

Climb Rocky Ridge

Seldovia's steepest hike is the **Rocky Ridge Trail**, where 800ft of climbing will be rewarded with remarkable views of the bay, the town and Mt Iliamna. There's some fine berry picking along the way. The trail starts (or ends) off Rocky St and loops back to the road to the airport, covering about 3 miles.

Kachemak Bay State Park

TIME FROM HOMER: **30 MIN – 1 HR**

Hike to a Glacier Lake

By far the most rewarding day hike in Kachemak Bay State Park is the journey to **Grewingk Glacier Lake**. Several trails take you through forest full of towering cottonwoods and Sitka spruce before ultimately reaching the edge of a stunning lake. Leave ample time to enjoy this serene shoreline with its view of chiseled ice formations floating in the mirror-like waters, and a backdrop of snowy peaks and the long expanse of **Grewingk Glacier** feeding into the lake. A few hardy souls even go for a swim in the frigid waters.

EATING IN SELDOVIA: OUR PICKS

Jack & Aiva's: Pleasant views over the water, and thoughtfully prepared dishes: battered Alaskan cod, chicken sandwiches, salads. *11am-4pm daily & 6-9pm Thu-Sat* **$$**

Linwood Bar & Grill: A family restaurant with a large deck and a relaxed atmosphere that serves up tasty burgers, clam chowder and pizzas. *noon-midnight* **$$**

Seldovia Roasting: Enjoy house-roasted coffees and sweet or savory crepes in a cozy spot that makes a fine retreat when the rain arrives. *8am-5pm Mon-Sat* **$**

Otter Cove Ice Cream: Attached to the Boardwalk Hotel, Otter Cove scoops up creamy salted caramel, Bordeaux cherry and other hits. *11am-4pm* **$**

Grewingk Glacier, Kachemak Bay State Park

There are several ways to reach the lake. One popular option is to take the **Glacier Lake Trail**, which starts at the Glacier Spit. It's easy to miss the start of this trail – especially during low tide, when your boat operator may drop you some distance down the shore – so look carefully for the marker just above the beach: an orange triangle painted with a black 'T'. Once you find the start, it's well marked and easy to follow along a fairly flat trail some 3.3 miles to the lake. Another way to reach the lake is via the **Saddle Trail**, which starts at Halibut Cove. This route is shorter (2 miles one-way to the lake), but a bit more strenuous with around 350ft of elevation gain. You can also combine the hikes – reaching the lake via the Grewingk Lake Trail and returning via the Saddle Trail, for instance – which is a common strategy. Just make sure you and your boat operator have an ironclad understanding of where you'll meet for your return boat ride back to Homer.

Reach the summit of Grace Ridge

For a more challenging hike with alpine scenery, set your sights on the **Grace Ridge Trail**, which leads you to a 3105ft peak affording jaw-dropping views in every direction (on clear days). The entire length of the trail is 8.9 miles along a roughly north–south axis, and you can make it an out-and-back hike (around 8 miles) by going just up to the peak and back, starting at a shoreline trailhead at either end. The easiest access is at Kayak Beach, a 30-minute water-taxi ride from Homer. From there, it's a steady and sometimes muddy incline through a boreal forest for 1.4 miles to a rocky outcropping, where you'll have fine views of the bay. Call it a day here, or continue up to Mile 2.9, where an alpine knob (elevation 1745ft) affords even more striking vistas. If you keep going, it's another mile to the high alpine through bushy alders and over tundra. The ridgeline offers the reward of a nearly unbelievable vast blue expanse flanked by the green curves of land against the water.

TOP TOURS FROM HOMER

Ashore Water Taxi: This family-owned place has excellent service, and experienced paddlers can rent kayaks for multiday trips.

Mako's Water Taxi: A local institution, Mako's operates year-round and will drop you at trailheads, or take you on a tour.

True North Kayak Adventures: Rewarding excursions begin with a boat ride from Homer to either Yukon Island or Halibut Cove, followed by a kayaking trip.

Emerald Air Service: This floatplane operator will fly you out to see the bears in Katmai National Park (p358), either at Brooks Falls or a more remote location.

Cook Inlet Adventures: Runs flight tours to Katmai National Park or Lake Clark National Park & Preserve (p278), for cinematic viewing of coastal brown bears.

CLAMMING ON THE ALASKA COAST

You might have read or heard about digging for razor clams along the coast of the Cook Inlet north of Homer or even driven by the suggestively named Clam Gulch. But accessible personal clamming here has long been closed by the state owing to overharvesting and winter storms that have destroyed the clam population near Ninilchik. In 2023, a four-day clamming season opened here for the first time in more than a decade. Visitors who are eager for access to clamming can coordinate with an outfit like **Ninilchik Charters** *(ninilchik. com)*, which will transport diggers during certain low tides across the inlet to the western shore where clamming has remained open.

If you're hiking the whole length, once you travel the ridgeline, you'll follow an equally steep path – this time downhill to the southern terminus of the South Grace Trailhead on Tutka Bay.

A few caveats: check weather forecasts carefully before setting out and consider postponing or cutting your hike short if the clouds move in, when it can make trail finding difficult – and hazardous with steep drop-offs. This is also prime black bear country, so make ample noise when hiking here.

Ninilchik

TIME FROM HOMER: **45 MINS**

Village rambles and pristine coastline

Directly off the Sterling Hwy, Ninilchik is a quiet gem on the coast 38 miles north of Homer. The Dena'ina were the first inhabitants in the region who fished in the abundant waters at Deep Creek and the Ninilchik River. In 1847, Russian colonists came and put down roots, leaving evidence of their presence in the **Old Ninilchik Village**.

Start your exploration into Ninilchik at the southern end of the township with a stop at the Deep Creek Recreation Area beach. From here you can watch fishing boats launch straight into the waves via tractors and witness bald eagles feasting on cast-off fish bones as you walk the beach.

Then, journey up the road to the Old Ninilchik Village. Find a series of historic homes and shanties in a postcard-perfect setting against the shoreline. On the bluff above stands the photogenic **Transfiguration of Our Lord**, a Russian Orthodox Church built in 1901. A white picket fence rings the mini-domed, gabled structure, and the adjoining cemetery is full of colorful wildflowers in the late summer.

In August, Ninilchik is the base for the small **Kenai Peninsula Fair** *(kenaipeninsulafair.com)* with a family-friendly lineup featuring a rodeo, folk bands, magic shows and pig

Transfiguration of Our Lord, Ninilchik

races. Ninilchik is even better known for hosting **Salmonfest** *(salmonfestalaska.org)*, also held in August. With an eclectic mix of local and national artists, this festival's headliners have included everyone from the Revivalists to Jewel, who keeps a home just outside Homer.

Nikolaevsk

TIME FROM HOMER: **35 MINS**

Dine at a Russian settlement

It's a trip well off the beaten path to find the tiny community of Russian Orthodox Old Believers and their town of Nikolaevsk. Heading north along the Sterling Hwy, you'll turn onto the little-traveled North Fork Rd and drive 11 winding miles to reach a relatively modern village, which was established in 1968 by a tiny sect of Orthodox Russians who were looking to shut themselves off from the influences of the modern world. The onion-domed **Church of St Nicholas** sits on the far edge of town, but the central attraction here is the **Samovar Cafe** and its proprietor and personality, Nina Fefelova.

Call or text ahead, so Nina can be prepared *(907-227-5566)*. The menu is classic Russian fare with an Alaskan twist: delicious borscht (beet soup), fireweed bread, piroshki (meat dumplings) and her housemade tea blends (also featuring fireweed). She sometimes whips up profiteroles for dessert. Everything is made with care, and Nina enjoys interacting with visitors who make the effort to visit. You'll dine at the picnic table outside.

VILLAGE OF OLD BELIEVERS

Nina Konstantinovna Fefelova, owner of Samovar Cafe

The exodus of Old Believers toward religious freedom began in the 1920s, after the arrival of communism in Russia. Yet the struggle dates back centuries, when their ancestors refused to accept the reform of the Russian Orthodox Church and were excommunicated as a result. Russian-speaking Old Believers fled to various countries and some ended up in the western US. In 1967, four bearded Russian immigrants from an Old Believer community in Oregon found their way to the Kenai Peninsula. They surveyed and purchased a square mile of wilderness and formed a village they called Nikolaevsk. More families soon arrived, and the town grew to became the largest Old Believer settlement in Alaska.

Places We Love to Stay

$ Budget $$ Midrange $$$ Top End

Hope MAPS p223

Porcupine Campground $
Waterfront campground with remarkable coastal views and excellent hiking nearby. Hope's old town is just 1 mile south.

Coeur d'Alene Campground $ A serene tents-only campground *(free)* at the end of a narrow, winding back road set high in an alpine valley.

Bear Creek Lodge $$ Stay in a hand-hewn log cabin (most with shared bathroom) surrounding a small pond. There's a sauna, cafe and restaurant.

Discovery Cabins $$ On a forested bluff above gurgling Bear Creek, this cozy collection of spruce cabins immerses you in forest. Shared bathrooms.

Beyond Hope MAP p230

Granite Creek Campground $
Lovely spot just off the highway and tucked against a rushing glacial creek at the bottom of Turnagain Pass. Reserve ahead.

Summit Lake Lodge $$$ A mix of new and historic rooms and cabins in a striking lakeside setting. Included breakfasts, a fire pit, restaurant, and kayaks and canoes (p231).

Cooper Landing MAP p233

Russian River Campground $
Some 83 sites are just a stroll to the banks of the Russian River with guaranteed access to world-class fishing (p235).

Kenai River Drifters Lodge $$ Stay in a cozy cabin or apartment, and enjoy the river-facing sauna and nightly campfires.

Eagle Landing Resort $$$
Large and small modern cabins with great views of the Kenai River; guided fishing trips available.

Kenai Princess Wilderness Lodge $$$ The resort complex perched above the river has bungalow-style rooms with wood-burning stoves and porches. Nature trail, lounge and restaurant on-site.

Beyond Cooper Landing

Trail Lake Lodge $$
Overlooking its namesake lake in Moose Pass, this friendly lodge has tidy rooms, wood-paneled restaurant and unique tours on-site (p241).

Inn at Tern Lake $$$
Photogenic B&B outside Moose Pass with home-cooked breakfasts and stunning views.

Seward MAP p246

Resurrection Campground $
One of several city-managed campgrounds with coveted bayside RV and tent spots. Book via *cityofseward.us* well in advance.

Hotel Seward $$ The historic 1905 hotel has simple rooms and a great downtown location within walking distance of restaurants and bars.

Harbor 360 Hotel $$$ Modern and comfortable waterfront rooms with free breakfast plus an indoor pool and hot tub – a Seward rarity.

Exit Glacier Lodge $$$
Around 2½ miles north of the harbor, the lodge has pleasant, well-equipped rooms overlooking greenery, and a good seafood restaurant next door.

Safari Lodge $$$ Adjacent to the small boat harbor, with waterfront-facing patios for each room. Run by Saltwater Safari, which runs fishing charters.

Beyond Seward

Miller's Landing $$ Private campground on Lowell Point with wooded sites, beach cabins and spacious yurts. There's shuttle transport to town, water taxis, kayak rentals and tours.

Renfro's Lakeside Retreat $$
Tucked off topaz-blue Kenai Lake, these forest-backed cabins are well equipped (kitchens, bathrooms), and there's also an RV park.

Kayakers Cove $$ Accessed by water taxi, this bayfront spot has rustic cabins backed by forest with hiking trails nearby. BYO food and sleeping bag.

Orca Island Cabins $$$
Private yurts in a stunning, immersive glamping setting accessed by water taxi.

Shearwater Cove $$$
Comfortable, private yurts with boat tour and kayaks included in the price tag.

Salted Roots Cabins $$$
These boutique-style A-frame cabins with huge windows onto the forest are located just off the beach on Lowell Point. There's a sauna, fire pit and outdoor kitchen.

Kenai & Soldotna MAP p259

Centennial Park Campground $ City-run, first-come, first-served spot with boardwalk access to Kenai River fishing and downtown Soldotna.

Uptown Motel $$ Comfortable, relatively affordable rooms in a central Kenai location. Good-value steak and seafood restaurant on-site.

Kenai River Lodge $$$ This Soldotna place has a good mix of suites and rooms, all with river views, and you can relax at the waterside lounge.

Beyond Kenai & Soldotna

Captain Cook State Recreation Area Discovery Campground $ Some 27 miles north of Kenai, this wooded 53-site campground puts you near a lovely, little visited shoreline (p266).

Johnson Lake Campground $ Tucked in the wildlife refuge 16 miles south of Soldotna, 48 reservable sites are set around a lake that's ideal for boating and fishing.

Homer MAP p268

Homer Spit Campground $ A wide variety of sites with hot showers, laundry and unbeatable views of the bay.

Driftwood Inn $$** Offers a mix of European-style chambers with shared bathrooms, roomier ensuites, cabins, cottages and an RV park. Good location just steps to Bishop's Beach. **$$

Pioneer Inn $$ Cheerfully furnished rooms, mountain views and a good town location within strolling distance of several restaurants.

Homer Stay & Play $$ B&B on a peaceful property with incredible bay views, delicious homemade breakfasts and kind, knowledgeable proprietors.

Juneberry Lodge $$ The sustainably run log-and-stone home has three sunny rooms, with hand-hewn wooden bed frames topped with quilts. Good breakfasts and heartfelt hospitality.

Land's End Resort $$$ The resort at the end of the Spit has attractive rooms, and there's a sauna, indoor pool and two outdoor hot tubs, plus a seafood restaurant.

Bear Creek Winery $$$ In a serene setting at the Bear Creek Winery, you'll find a spacious apartment and two suites (each with a kitchenette), plus a hot tub, nature trail and fire pit.

Beyond Homer

Kachemak Bay State Park Yurts $ Each of eight yurts is located on a scenic beach and accessible by kayak or water taxi. BYO supplies (sleeping bag, food, cookware, water).

Kachemak Bay State Park Camping $ Tent camping is permitted across the park, with tent pads, fire rings and picnic tables near yurts and cabins.

Seldovia Boardwalk Hotel $$ Seldovia's best option has bright and cheery rooms with expansive windows, welcoming hosts, and on-site rentals of mountain bikes and golf carts.

Kenai Princess Wilderness Lodge

Researched by
Regis St Louis

Denali & the Interior

TOWERING PEAKS AND CREATIVE TOWNS

The Alaskan Interior is about many things, from rare Indigenous artifacts in Fairbanks to wilderness adventures in Denali National Park.

The Aleut word for Alaska – the Great Land – aptly describes the vast Interior: a wild expanse of boreal forest, alpine tundra and jagged peaks flanked by braided rivers and serpentine stretches of frost-white glaciers. It's a place of climactic extremes, where you can catch a midnight baseball game in the summer or watch the aurora borealis light up the frigid night sky in an otherworldly display during the winter.

In a region larger than the state of California, adventure comes in many forms. You can raft through narrow canyons on class IV rapids, strap on crampons for a cinematic walk across a glacier, or join a ranger-led hike heading deep into the trackless wilderness. You can have a close canine encounter by holding an armful of husky puppies on a visit to an Iditarod sled dog kennel, or look for the big five – grizzlies, moose, caribou, Dall sheep and wolves – while taking a naturalist excursion through a national park.

Humans seem a small consideration in a place so sparsely inhabited (current population around 115,000), and yet the ancestors of the present-day Athabascans have been here for at least 6000 years. Vestiges of their ancient presence live on in artifacts and carvings amid one of Alaska's finest Indigenous museums. The Interior is also home to historic mining camps, early homesteads and tiny arts-loving villages that showcase the latest generation of Alaskan ingenuity.

THE MAIN AREAS

TALKEETNA
Captivating small town and Denali gateway. **p292**

DENALI STATE PARK
Escape the crowds on wilderness trails. **p300**

DENALI NATIONAL PARK & PRESERVE
Epic hiking, trekking and wildlife-watching. **p303**

For places to stay in Denali & the Interior, see p340

THE GUIDE

DENALI & THE INTERIOR

Left: Chilkat weaving, University of Alaska Museum of the North (p322);
Above: Bull caribou, Denali National Park & Preserve (p303)

FAIRBANKS
Historic sites and river lore. **p316**

TOK & THE TAYLOR HIGHWAY
Off-the-beaten-path travel and mining history. **p330**

WRANGELL-ST ELIAS NATIONAL PARK & PRESERVE
Rugged drives, glacier hikes and village life. **p334**

Find Your Way

The majority of the Interior is made up of tundra, rolling mountains and few services, which makes it important to plan ahead before traveling through the region, especially if you're visiting outside the summer months.

Fairbanks, p316

More town than city, Fairbanks has some impressive museums and a pioneer village, plus botanical gardens, river activities and wintertime allure (the northern lights).

Denali National Park & Preserve, p303

Amid river valleys and snowcapped summits, experience Alaska's untamed wilderness while hiking, camping, trekking or taking a naturalist-led tour.

Denali State Park, p300

The lesser known little sister to the national park offers memorable hikes and backpacking adventures, plus panoramic views of the great mountain.

Talkeetna, p292

The arts-loving community makes a great base for scenic flights, paddling trips, whistle-stop train rides or just enjoying the quirky, small-town charm.

CAR
Driving yourself is the simplest mode of transportation, with good highways (George Parks Hwy) to reach Denali and Fairbanks. There are plenty of rugged roads as well (Taylor Hwy and McCarthy Rd), where you'll need to hire a 4WD from a specialty outfit.

BUS
The Park Connection Motorcoach provides daily summer service linking Seward, Anchorage, Talkeetna and Denali National Park (and reverse), with morning and afternoon departures. Transfers from Denali to Fairbanks are also available via the Parks Hwy.

TRAIN
The Alaska Railroad (p38) offers daily summer service between Anchorage and Fairbanks, with stops in Talkeetna and Denali. Reservations are a must. In winter, the schedule is drastically cut, with only one train traveling north on Saturday, and south on Sunday.

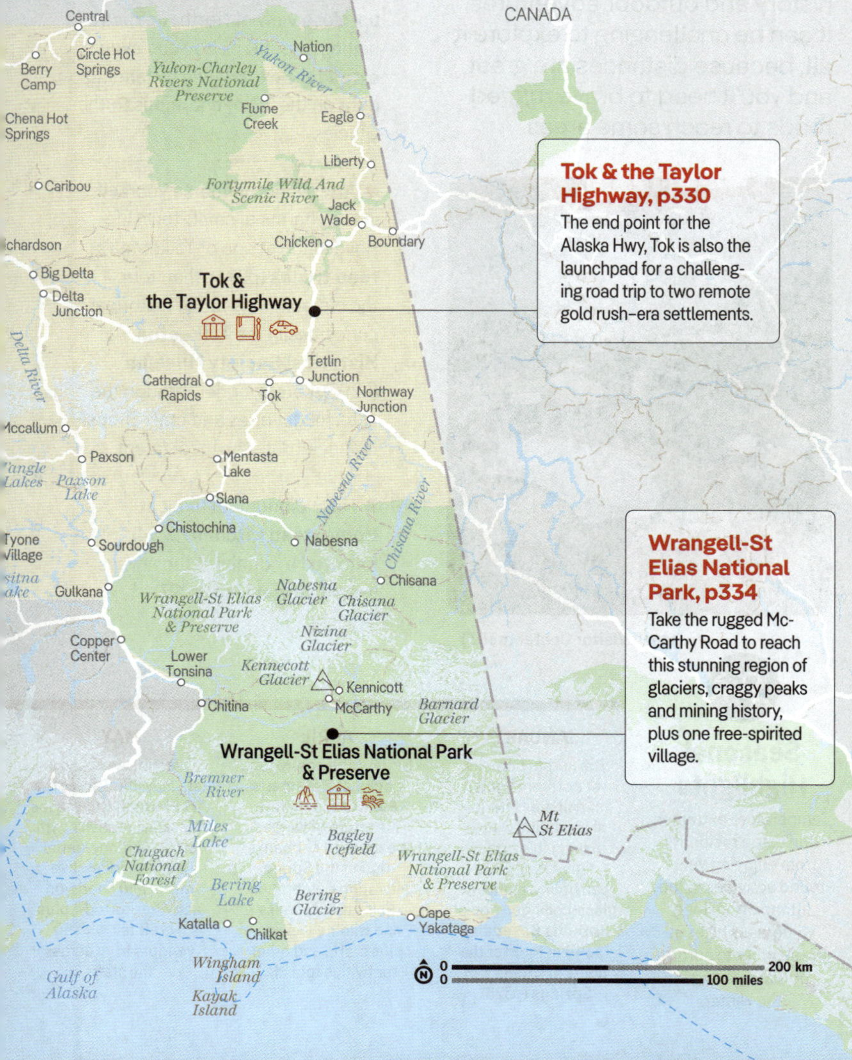

THE GUIDE

DENALI & THE INTERIOR

Tok & the Taylor Highway, p330
The end point for the Alaska Hwy, Tok is also the launchpad for a challenging road trip to two remote gold rush–era settlements.

Wrangell-St Elias National Park, p334
Take the rugged McCarthy Road to reach this stunning region of glaciers, craggy peaks and mining history, plus one free-spirited village.

Plan Your Time

Sweeping across the heart of Alaska, the Interior is rich in history and outdoor adventures. It can be challenging to explore it all, because distances are great, and you'll need to brave rugged roads to reach some areas.

Denali Visitor Center (p303)

An Epic Day in Talkeetna

● Start the morning with a trip to the town airstrip for a once-in-a-lifetime **flightseeing adventure** (p298). Aboard a small plane, you'll soar over the vast wilderness of Denali National Park and get an up-close view of North America's highest mountain. You can even extend the experience by landing right on the ice of enormous Ruth Glacier.

● Afterwards, immerse yourself in the charms of small-town life. Have lunch at one of Talkeetna's **food trucks** (p296), then tour the old buildings full of historical curiosities in the **Talkeetna Historical Society Museum** (p292). Later wander through the colorful galleries and craft shops that celebrate the local talent.

● Have dinner that night at **Homestead Kitchen** (p294), followed by drinks at the always lively **Fairview Inn** (p297).

Seasonal Highlights

Temperature extremes don't stop residents from enjoying year-round activities in the Interior, from long wilderness hikes in the summer to aurora-borealis gazing in the winter.

JANUARY

The aurora borealis, or northern lights, illuminates Interior skies during winter, making this a prime time to visit. You can book a night in a glass-ceilinged pod at **Borealis Basecamp** (p341) or look for the lights at **Chena Hot Springs** (p328).

APRIL

Birders and nature fans gather at **Creamer's Field** (p325) to fete the return of winged beauties to Fairbanks during the Spring Migration Celebration. Enjoy nature walks and wildlife viewing, plus crafts and other activities for kids.

MAY

Over one weekend in late May, the **Talkeetna Art Festival** showcases Alaskan creativity with art exhibitions, aerial performances, live music and hands-on activities for kids, plus a craft fair with 50 vendors from across the state.

Two Days in Denali National Park & Preserve

● Getting to Alaska's most famous national park is part of the adventure: take a **scenic train ride** (p38) from either Anchorage or Fairbanks. Once you reach the park, head to the **Denali Visitor Center** (p303) to see exhibits covering natural history, wildlife and the park's connection to Alaska Natives. Pay a visit to the much-loved canine rangers at the **Sled Dog Kennels** (p305), then head off on a rewarding hike – either ascending **Mt Healy** (p306) or tackling a trail near the **Savage River** (p306).

● On day two, head deeper into the park with a ranger on an adventurous, off-trail **Discovery Hike** (p307); for something more low-key, take one of the naturalist-led **bus tours** (p307). End the day with a **ranger talk at the campground** (p309).

A Week to Travel the Interior

● After getting a taste of Talkeetna and Denali, head to Fairbanks. Visit the **University of Alaska Museum of the North** (p322) for a look at Alaska Native treasures, then see vintage motor cars at the **Fountainhead Museum** (p325) and look for sandhill cranes in **Creamer's Field Migratory Waterfowl Refuge** (p325).

● Take a day trip to **Chena Hot Springs** (p328) for a soak in a natural geothermal pool.

● Head south to a slice of homesteading history at the **Big Delta State Historical Park** (p328), then continue to Wrangell-St Elias National Park. Explore the old mining town of **McCarthy** (p336), take a tour of the **Concentration Mill** (p336), then enjoy some nature time with a hike across **Root Glacier** (p335) or the challenging climb along the **Bonanza Mine Trail** (p336).

JUNE
Celebrate the longest day of the year with locals during the Midnight Sun Festival, with live performances throughout the day, and food and craft vendors. This is also the time to catch the famous **Midnight Sun Game** (p323).

JULY
One of Fairbanks' biggest events commemorates the city's glittering past during **Golden Days**. You'll see whimsical events like the rubber-ducky race, watermelon-eating contests and log splitting, along with a parade and street fair.

SEPTEMBER
See **Denali National Park** without the crowds by coming in mid- or late September. Park Rd is open to self-sufficient visitors until snow closes access. The fall colors are stunning – and aurora viewing is a possibility.

DECEMBER
The subzero temperatures can't dampen the good cheer. During **North Pole Winterfest** (p327), you can browse a holiday bazaar, join in Christmas sing-alongs and catch evening fireworks. Talkeetna also hosts the lively **Talkeetna Winterfest** (p296).

Talkeetna

ARTS & CRAFTS | HOMESTEADING HISTORY | SCENIC FLIGHTS

> ☑ **TOP TIP**
>
> Time your visit to coincide with one of many community events. There's a **Live at 5** *(facebook.com/liveatfivetka)* concert series every Friday (5pm to 7pm) in the **Talkeetna Village Park**, and live music each weekend at Fairview Inn. Check other listings via the **Denali Arts Council** *(denaliartscouncil.org)*.

One of Alaska's most captivating small towns, Talkeetna is home to mix of creative artisans and outdoor adventurers (often one and the same) who are happy to share their tightly knit, free-spirited community with those who make the trip here, whether by road or rail. Plenty of tourists fill the streets on summer days, though it's easy to find quieter parts of town after wandering the buzzing shop- and restaurant-lined main street or taking in the must-see view of Denali (when the weather gods cooperate) from the riverside. Talkeetna is also the best place to arrange a scenic flight over the fabled national park, book a jet-boat ride on the Susitna River or rent a bike for some DIY exploring.

Talkeetna proudly wears its badge of honor for Alaska bush aviation; famous pilot Don Sheldon settled here in the 1940s to establish Talkeetna Air Service, flying scores of mountaineers to and from Denali and nearby peaks for climbing and scientific exploration.

Learn all about Talkeetna (and Denali)
Exhibitions and films

One place not to miss on a visit to town is the **Talkeetna Historical Society Museum** *(talkeetnamuseum.org;*

 GETTING AROUND

In the summer, there is one train daily traveling north from Anchorage *(from $123, 2¾ hours)* and another traveling south from Fairbanks *(from $169, nine hours)* via Denali *(from $115, 4½ hours)*. Trains generally run weekends only in the winter.

Buses arrive and depart near Talkeetna Historic District. There are two buses a day to both Anchorage and Denali National Park. Purchase **tickets online** *(alaskatravel.com/bus-lines; from $75)*.

Talkeetna has a compact center. It's about a 1-mile walk from the train station to town. If you need transport, call **Charlie** *(251-747-2300)*, who charges $10 per person ($30 maximum) for rides of up to 5 miles.

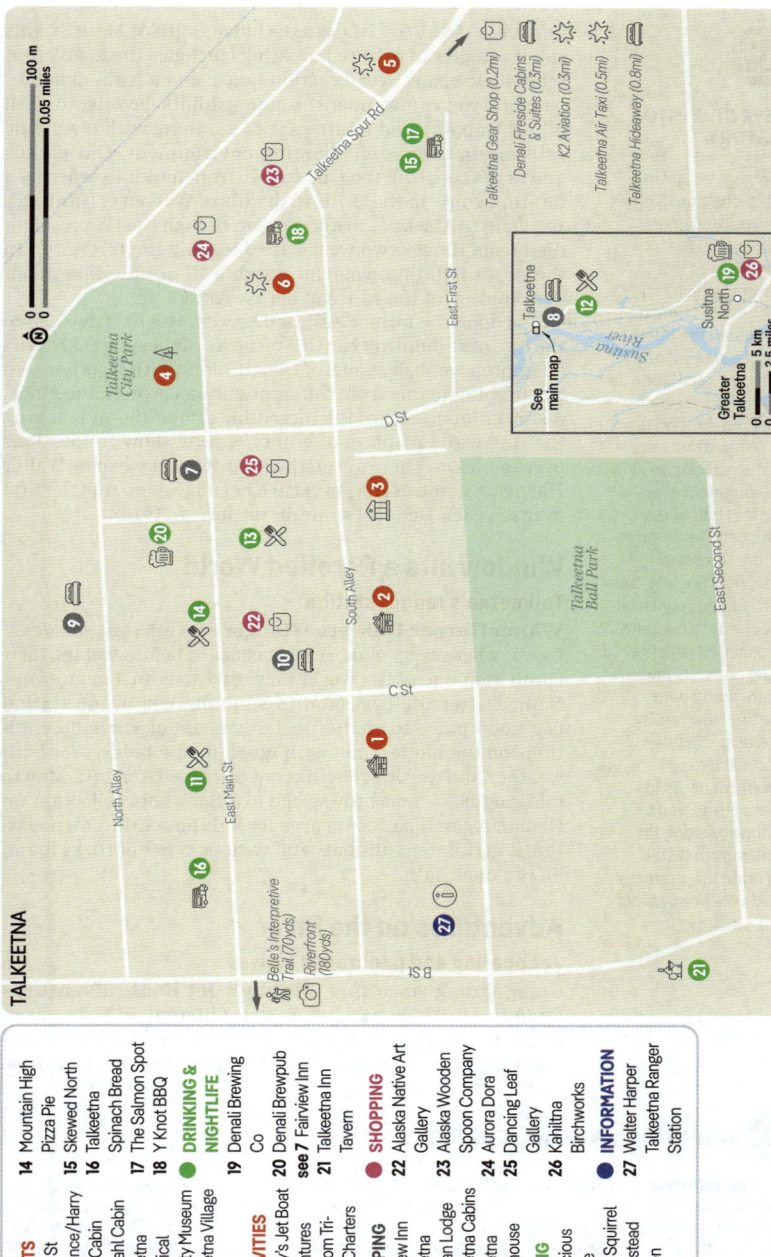

TALKEETNA

SIGHTS
1. David St Lawrence/Harry Robb Cabin
2. Ole Dahl Cabin
3. Talkeetna Historical Society Museum
4. Talkeetna Village Park

ACTIVITIES
5. Mahay's Jet Boat Adventures
6. Phantom Tri-River Charters

SLEEPING
7. Fairview Inn
8. Talkeetna Alaskan Lodge
9. Talkeetna Cabins
10. Talkeetna Roadhouse

EATING
11. Conscious Coffee
12. Flying Squirrel
13. Homestead Kitchen
14. Mountain High Pizza Pie
15. Skewed North
16. Talkeetna Spinach Bread
17. The Salmon Spot
18. Y Knot BBQ

DRINKING & NIGHTLIFE
19. Denali Brewing Co
20. Denali Brewpub
see 7 Fairview Inn
21. Talkeetna Inn Tavern

SHOPPING
22. Alaska Native Art Gallery
23. Alaska Wooden Spoon Company
24. Aurora Dora
25. Dancing Leaf Gallery
26. Kahiltna Birchworks

INFORMATION
27. Walter Harper Talkeetna Ranger Station

DENALI & THE INTERIOR TALKEETNA

DEEP DIVE INTO HISTORY

For more insight into Talkeetna's past, pick up a walking-tour brochure at the front desk of the Talkeetna Historical Society Museum, or download the free **Talkeetna Historic Tour** app for iPhone or Android, then proceed through town to 19 important sites that shed light on its development over the first half of the 20th century. Created by the Talkeetna Historical Society, this self-guided tour is a great way to become acquainted with the early pioneers and learn more about the tiny town's role in Alaska's history. Allow at least a couple of hours for your self-guided tour of town, visiting the buildings that still emulate the character of Alaska's early days as a territory.

adult/child $10/free). Located a block south of Main St, this small complex of restored buildings includes the town's first schoolhouse, a railroad section house and a train depot.

Inside, you can wander through exhibits devoted to bush pilots, trapping and mining artifacts, along with laying the railroad in such a challenging environment. Old photos and artifacts bring the past to life, from mukluks worn by a hunting guide in the 1970s to details of Warren G Harding's 1923 trip to Alaska (a historic event, though the US president died from illness two weeks after leaving the territory). In the depot building, you can watch a 19-minute film about the building of the railroad across Alaska.

Next door, the former Railroad Section House is devoted to the lore of summiting North America's highest peak. There's an impressive scale model of Denali, along with flags donated by climbing teams from different nations around the globe. A short film describes the incredible difficulties of reaching the top, while displays of climbing gear show innovations over the years. There's even the type of outfit worn by Walter Harper, a guide of Alaska Native heritage, who was the first ever to reach Denali's summit, on June 6, 1913.

Window into a Rarefied World

Talkeetna's ranger station

Walter Harper Talkeetna Ranger Station *(nps.gov/dena; free)* is where every climber must check in before making their climb atop one of the world's most treacherous mountains. Named after the first man to summit Denali, the station is a good place to chat with rangers about current conditions on the mountain – with up-to-date forecasts for both weather and aurora viewing (not possible from mid-May to mid-August) – and browse the excellent book selection on Denali. A small hands-on area for kids has children's books, skulls of different animals and various types of rocks found on the mountain.

Adventures on the River

Jet boating and panoramic views

Going strong since 1977, **Mahay's Jet Boat Adventures** *(mahaysriverboat.com)* offers four different jet boat adventures. Journeying up pristine rivers is a big draw, as are the spectacular panoramas of the Alaska Range on clear days.

EATING IN TALKEETNA: OUR PICKS

Homestead Kitchen: With an inviting patio, Homestead features fancier twists on the usual fare, like seafood gumbo pot pie and refreshing spritzers. *8am-8pm* **$$**

Mountain High Pizza Pie: The year-round institution serves satisfying pizzas and big salads best enjoyed on the terrace. Live music most weekends. *11am-9pm* **$$**

Flying Squirrel: Great coffee, pastries and artisan breads (and weekend pizza nights) in a spacious coffeehouse setting 3 miles south of town. *8am-4pm Tue-Thu & Sun, 8am-9pm Fri & Sat* **$**

Conscious Coffee: Sit in rustic furniture outside the small cozy interior while enjoying Talkeetna's best coffees, crepes and bagels. *7am-3pm* **$**

TALKEETNA'S HISTORIC HIGHLIGHTS

Step into the early 1900s on a stroll that takes in log cabins, forest and riverfront.

START	END	LENGTH
Talkeetna Historical Society Museum	Fairview Inn	0.6 miles; 1 hour

Start your tour at the 1 **Talkeetna Historical Society Museum** (p292). This original one-room schoolhouse operated from 1936 to 1971, and began with a class of just 11 students. Turn left and you'll soon spot the 2 **Ole Dahl Cabin**, a trapper-style log cabin from 1916 that gives a fair idea of the rustic simplicity required to live in Talkeetna a century ago.

A few paces farther along South Alley, the 3 **David St Lawrence/Harry Robb Cabin** from 1920 is larger than most of the era, and it contains clothing, canned goods and other personal items from Harry Robb, who lived here until 1975.

Head up to Main St and turn left at the white archway onto 4 **Belle's Interpretive Trail**. Lined with ferns, this short forested path takes you past the ruins of a trading post started by the pioneering businesswoman Belle Grindrod in the 1920s.

A short spur leads out to the 5 **Riverfront**, where the Talkeetna and Chulitna rivers join the Susitna, which flows 100 miles south to the Cook Inlet, west of Anchorage. On rare clear days, you can spot the snowcapped peaks of Denali from here (look northwest). Back on Main St, continue to the 6 **Fairview Inn**. Long the heart of town, this 1920s building has a bar lined with old photos and upstairs guest rooms that are allegedly haunted.

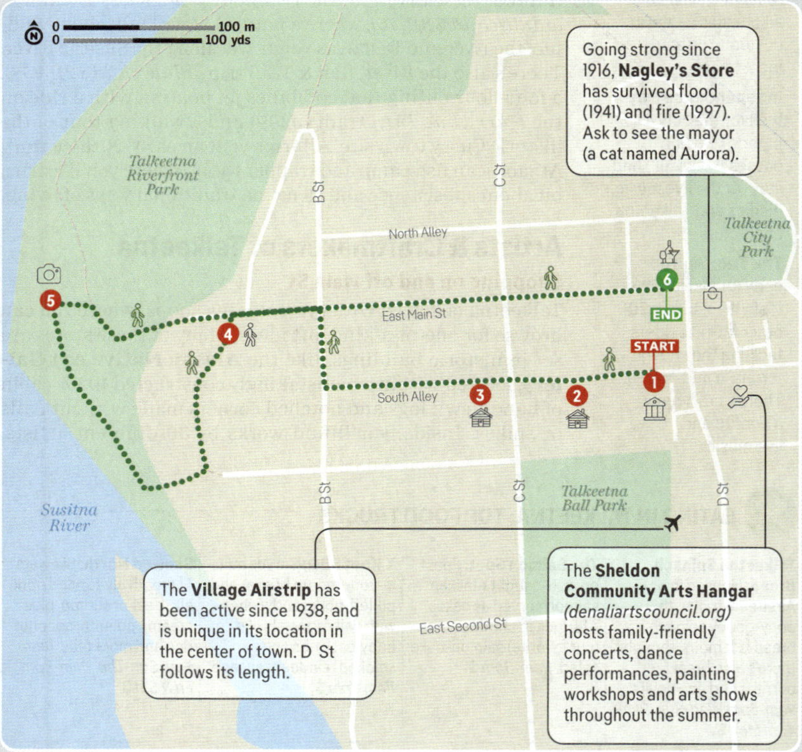
0 100 m
0 100 yds
Going strong since 1916, **Nagley's Store** has survived flood (1941) and fire (1997). Ask to see the mayor (a cat named Aurora).
Talkeetna Riverfront Park
B St
C St
North Alley
Talkeetna City Park
East Main St
END
START
South Alley
1
2
3
4
5
6
Susitna River
Talkeetna Ball Park
D St
The **Village Airstrip** has been active since 1938, and is unique in its location in the center of town. D St follows its length.
East Second St
The **Sheldon Community Arts Hangar** *(denaliartscouncil.org)* hosts family-friendly concerts, dance performances, painting workshops and arts shows throughout the summer.

TOP TALKEETNA EVENTS

Talkeetna Art Festival: On Memorial Day weekend (late May), catch live performances, craft vendors and hands-on kids activities.

Winterfest!: An early December fest featuring tree lighting, and decorating and caroling, plus a Wilderness Woman competition and a Bachelor Auction.

Oosik Classic Ski Race: Popular early March cross-country race, with skiers of all abilities (some in costume) hitting local trails.

Independence Day: Visit for the July 4 parade ('So fine it passes by twice!') and stay for the live music, picnics and Talkeetna characters.

The Trio: Sign up early (or just join the festivities) to join 200 other fat-bike riders tackling the snowy terrain in mid-March. There's craft brew, a bonfire and live music.

Storefronts, Talkeetna

The top excursion is the wild (but surprisingly smooth) ride blasting through class V rapids into Devil's Canyon, a five-hour 130-mile round-trip *(adult/child $228/171)*. If time is limited, you can opt for the two-hour Wilderness Excursion *(adult/child $101/76)*, where a naturalist will talk about wildlife, the river and Denali as you travel along the Susitna River. There's also the River, Rail & Trail trip *(adult/child $211/158)*, a four-hour outing that combines jet boating with a ride on the *Hurricane Turn* train (p299) and a walking tour of the historic Curry town site. All trips visit an early-20th-century Athabascan fish camp and trapper cabin, where you'll learn a bit about subsistence and Dena'ina traditional ways of living.

Artists & Craftmakers of Talkeetna
Shopping on and off Main St

Talkeetna is dotted with eye-catching shops, where you can browse for one-of-a-kind gift ideas. Many of these stores are set in historic buildings, like the **Alaska Native Art Gallery**, located within a painstakingly constructed 1920s cabin of hand-hewn logs and notched corners made without nails or spikes. Inside, you'll find works by 30 different artists,

 EATING IN TALKEETNA: TOP FOOD TRUCKS

Talkeetna Spinach Bread: Housed in an Airstream trailer, the ooey-gooey spinach bread is famous, though there's also breakfast burritos and rice bowls. *9am-6pm Wed-Sun, 9am-4pm Mon* $

The Salmon Spot: Feast on wild-caught Alaskan salmon served as cakes, a burger, in chowder or (our favorite) salmon-cake salad. *11am-8pm* $

Y Knot BBQ: Serves melt-in-your-mouth brisket and pulled-pork sandwiches, with daily specials like baby back ribs and smoked reindeer sausage. *11am-7pm* $

Skewed North: Skewers of creatively topped pork, elk, beef or shrimp, plus creamy polenta, coconut rice and mocktails. *11am-3pm Sun-Thu, 11am-8pm Fri & Sat* $

including carvings by many Alaska Natives, as well as jewelry, notecards and Indigenous-themed books.

The same owners run the **Dancing Leaf Gallery** *(facebook.com/thedancingleafgallery)* a few doors down, and you'll find here a wider selection of jewelry, along with paintings and ceramics. Also on Main St, near the riverfront, an open-air market features a variety of vendors selling their wares, including birchbark baskets, handmade knives, hats, leather items and more.

At the opposite end of Main St (opposite the Talkeetna Village Park), **Aurora Dora** *(auroradora.com)* features the exquisite images of Dora Redman, who's been photographing the aurora borealis since 2001. The vibrant colors of the northern lights, printed on scratchproof and waterproof aluminum, look otherworldly, and the staff can give insight into the creation process – of both the photography and the natural phenomenon captured on camera.

A short hop from Aurora Dora, the **Alaska Wooden Spoon Company** *(alaskawoodenspooncompany.com)* sells exactly what you'd imagine: well-honed kitchen implements made by hand from birch or occasionally maple. In addition to stirrers, skillet spoons and spurtles (a long thin rod of Scottish origin), you'll also find cutting boards and serving bowls.

Further south (and across the railroad tracks), the **Talkeetna Gear Shop** stocks new T-shirts, hats and hoodies, as well as used gear for wide-ranging outdoor adventures: camping mats, sleeping bags, down jackets, sunglasses and other essentials. You'll also find some quality craft items created by local makers as well as paintings, jewelry, incense and tins of smoked salmon.

Get Active with Talkeetna Gear Shop

Art workshops, gear rentals and tours

In addition to the shop selling outdoor gear, crafts and artwork, the **Talkeetna Gear Shop** *(talkeetnagearshop.com)* also hosts events throughout the year, including cyanotype and other art workshops, blueberry bike rides, film screenings and bike polo tournaments. This is also the best place in town to rent bikes (including electric mountain bikes) as well as bear spray, SUP and, in winter, snowshoes. For something a little different, book one of their excursions – like the **Bike & Brew tour** *(bike rental, half pizza & 2 beers*

FLYING OVER DENALI

Marne Sheldon, co-owner Sheldon Chalet
@sheldonchalet

Taking a scenic flight up to Don Sheldon Amphitheater and landing on the glacier can be a life-altering, spiritual experience. You depart Talkeetna and fly over beautiful river valleys carved out by glaciers millennia ago. You're spotting wildlife and you're flying next to these sheer granite cliffs, and then flying above and around these giant peaks. And then you'll land on the glacier, which the pilots handle so skillfully. You'll step outside and have a beautiful view of the summit. It's a spectacular place that doesn't exist anywhere else in Denali. Depending on the time of year, you might be the only people landing on the glacier and you get to marvel in the silence.

 DRINKING IN TALKEETNA: OUR PICKS

Denali Brewing Co: Worth the 12-mile drive south of town for the top-quality brews and excellent wood-fired pizzas, plus occasional live music. *11am-9pm*

Denali Brewpub: Denali Brewing Co's buzzing in-town option has a prime Main St location and offers table service and hearty pub fare. *11am-10pm*

Fairview Inn: Opened in 1923, the Fairview is the liveliest spot in town (sometimes rowdy!) and adorned with historic knickknacks. *2pm-1.30am*

Talkeetna Inn Tavern: A cave-like retreat for bad-weather days, this welcoming dive bar with a full-sized pool table is set in a vintage A-frame building. *noon-9pm*

SCANDALOUS PRESIDENTIAL VERSES

In 1923, Warren Harding became the first US president to set foot in Alaska during a visit celebrating the completion of the 470-mile Seward–Fairbanks railroad. Not in attendance was Carrie Fulton Phillips, a married woman with whom Harding (also married) carried on a decade-long amorous affair. Harding wrote her over 100 letters, which were unsealed in 2014, and they reveal a surprisingly explicit side of the president: 'Wouldn't you like to get sopping wet out on Superior – not the lake – for the joy of fevered fondling & melting kisses?' he wrote in 1913. You can read more about Harding and his titillating poetry by stopping by the Fairview Inn, which is decorated with mementos from the past.

Flightseeing tour, Denali National Park & Preserve (p303)

$150), where you'll join a 12-mile ride followed by beer and pizza at Denali Brewing Company.

Epic Flight in the Mountains
Soaring above Denali

There's no doubt that the presence of Denali, the mountain, influences much of Talkeetna's visitor numbers, today. If you're not attempting the climb to Denali's 20,310ft summit, the best way to enjoy those top-of-the-world views is on a scenic flight. All summer long, the buzz of small planes taking off and landing can be heard over town as travelers make their way over the rivers and toward the glaciated flanks of North America's highest peak.

The typical Denali flightseeing tour operated by companies like **Talkeetna Air Taxi** *(talkeetnaair.com; 1hr flight adult/child $275/200)* and **K2 Aviation** *(flyk2.com; 1hr flight adult/child $350/255)* flies over town and across the muskeg and tundra of the Susitna Valley before traversing the Great Gorge of the Ruth Glacier, with mile-high granite walls and a 4000ft river of ice. Also part of the tour are Mt Huntington, Moose's Tooth and Broken Tooth peaks, and, if you add it on *(another $130 or so per person)*, a landing upon the Ruth Glacier itself in the heart of the Sheldon Amphitheater. For the complete experience, you can opt for a two-hour summit flight *($495, $620 with glacier landing)*.

Making Birch Syrup
Tour and tasting

On a short tour at **Kahiltna Birchworks** *(alaskabirch syrup.com; tour adult/child $10/free)*, you can learn about the rare and unusual making of birch syrup. Only white paper birch grown in northern boreal forests can be harvested, and a mere 5000 gallons are produced worldwide. This small mom-and-pop outfit (actually owned by two brothers) produces 20% of that global supply. At the end, you'll get to taste several varieties of birch syrup, which range in sweetness and complexity from early to late harvest. The shop sells a wide range of birch goodies, from syrups and drinks to ice cream, along with other goods made by Talkeetna makers.

Casting a Line
Fishing in the wilderness

Those wanting to drop a fishing line in the water will be pleased to know that all five species of salmon, rainbow trout and grayling may be found in the waters around Talkeetna, and freshwater angling is an exciting option for visitors. Try **Phantom Tri-River Charters** *(phantomtri rivercharters.com; 3hr charter per person $238)*, which offers three-hour fishing charters as well as loads of other options, including half- and full-day float trips and backcountry fishing reached by helicopter.

Take a Train to Hurricane
America's last flag-stop service

The **Alaska Railroad** (p38) has been a force for development along the so-called rail belt between Seward and Fairbanks since its construction in the mid-1900s. As such, many homesteaders and miners of the Talkeetna area used the train's conveyance to establish and maintain cabins and claims within striking distance of the railroad. When it came time to resupply or visit 'civilization,' people would stand along the tracks and wave a flag or item of clothing to stop the train. This 'Flag Stop Service' is still routinely used along the **Hurricane Turn** route, a 60-mile day trip offered during the summer season to accommodate fishers, campers, and cabin or homestead owners. It runs Thursday to Monday, mid-May to mid-September, and once monthly the rest of the year. Round-trip fares are $121 ($62 for children).

Visitors aboard the Hurricane Turn will be treated to a shorter train with an engine on either end, and one passenger and baggage car. Traveling along some of the most scenic Alaska landscapes, the train follows rivers full of fish, and quaint communities like Chase, Sherman and Curry, before traversing the deep Hurricane Gulch gorge and reversing its course for the return to Talkeetna. It is a bare-bones trip with no food or beverage service, but for those with an adventurous spirit, the Hurricane Turn makes for a memorable day.

KING OF MUSHROOMS

Jocelyn Stewart, sales associate at Kahiltna Birchworks, sheds light on one of the world's most medicinal mushrooms. @alaskabirchsyrup

The chaga mushroom is found only on the white paper birch. It has a symbiotic relationship with the tree and will grow on wounds in the bark, protecting and healing it, much like a bandage. Chaga has one of the highest levels of antioxidants among all of the mushrooms. It can also help lower blood sugar levels, making it beneficial for those with diabetes. In shops, you may not recognize it as a mushroom – it looks like a chunk of dark wood – but its popularity is growing. It's great as a hot tea with cinnamon and oat milk.

Denali State Park

RIDGELINE TRAILS | GRAND VIEWS | WILDLIFE

GETTING AROUND

Visitors to Denali State Park should be aware that the only way to access and get to or from trailheads, campgrounds or cabins is by private vehicle. **Alaska Nature Guides** *(alaskanatureguides. com)* does offer transportation from McKinley Princess Lodge in Trapper Creek a few miles south.

Take it slow on your drive here – especially early or late in the day, when wildlife are more likely to wander onto the highway. It's worth pulling off at the signed scenic overlooks, such as those anchoring each end of the park: Denali View South (Mile 135) and Denali View North (Mile 162).

Most Alaska visitors pass right on by Denali State Park on their way to Denali National Park further up the George Parks Hwy. But they're missing something extraordinary: some of the trails in this state park are actually much closer to Denali than those near the national park entrance – which means on clear days, you'll have spectacular views of the famed mountain.

Established in 1970, this quiet park encompasses some 508 sq miles. With excellent campgrounds, diverse hiking trails and those splendid views, it's worth at least a few hours to explore without the crowds of the national park. Dominated by white spruce and paper birch trees, the park is also a haven of wildflowers, particularly wild rose, lupine and dwarf dogwood. In late summer, find a plethora of blueberries around the lakes and streams. Come winter, Alaskans flock to the park on skis, snow machines or snowshoes to several public-use cabins for a cozy getaway off the grid.

Hike the Curry Ridge Trail
Denali views from the ridge

One of the best day hikes in Denali State Park, the **Curry Ridge Trail** *(day parking pass $5)* – blazed back in 2016 – takes you up to a lofty ridgeline where you'll have spectacular views over the Alaska Range and Denali – assuming the weather is cooperating. The 6-mile journey is an out-and-back hike, and it's worth adding on the short spur (half-mile one-way) down to Lake 1787 once you reach the overlook. This small body of water is surrounded by brush, but it's a fine spot for photos – or just stopping to enjoy the mesmerizing serenity of the landscape. Find the trailhead near the K'esugi Ken campground. From there, you'll gently ascend some 1030ft over the next 3 miles, as you pass a few bridged stream crossings and make your way around bushy

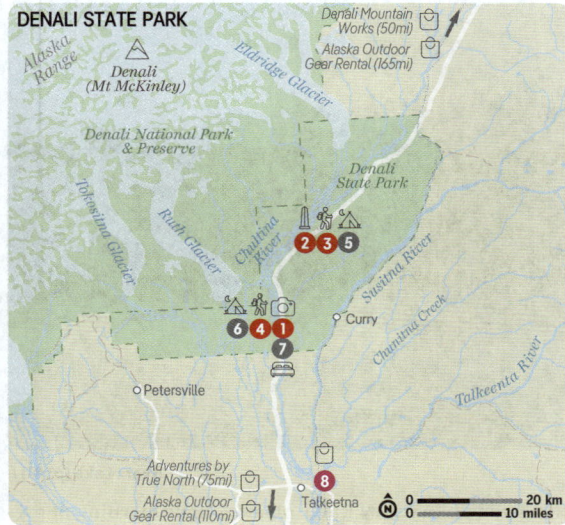

- **SIGHTS**
  1 K'esugi Ken Interpretive Center
  2 Veterans Memorial
- **ACTIVITIES**
  3 Byers Lake Loop Trail
  4 Curry Ridge Trail
- **SLEEPING**
  5 Byers Lake Campground
  6 K'esugi Ken Campground
  7 Mt McKinley Princess Wilderness Lodge
- **SHOPPING**
  8 Talkeetna Gear Shop

switchbacks (this is prime blueberry picking in August). At the top, you'll reach Rocky Knob, which is the perfect spot for a picnic on a sunny day.

Always be bear-aware on this trail, which receives a smattering of other hikers on summer weekends, but is fairly quiet even then.

Walking Byers Lake
Easy hike and wildlife

If you only have a few hours, but want to get away from it all, head out on the level 4.8-mile hike on the **Byers Lake Loop Trail** *(day parking pass $5)*. The path begins at **Byers Lake Campground**, passes along sometimes overgrown paths and loops back to the starting point after a bridge crossing. Keep an eye out for abundant birdlife.

Take a Guided Hike or Multiday Trek
Naturalist-led excursions

For a more enriching experience in Denali State Park, book an excursion with **Alaska Nature Guides** *(alaskanatureguides.com)*. This Talkeetna-based ecotourism outfit offers several guided nature walks, including the 2.5-hour Byers Lake Nature Walk *(adult/child $75/55)*. The focus of this is spotting wildlife (possibly loons, trumpeter swans or even bears) and also learning about native plants and some of the extraordinary pioneers who once lived in the area. It's an easygoing, level stroll over 2 miles.

Those seeking a bit more challenge can sign up for their longer Denali Wilderness Hike *(adult/child $122/104)*, which

☑ TOP TIP

Just north of the turnoff to Byers Lake, the **Veterans Memorial** is a poignant tribute to Alaskan veterans who've served in all military branches (army, navy and air force). It's located in a wild but peaceful setting and dates back to 1983.

NO GEAR? RENT SOME!

Anchorage: Alaska Outdoor Gear Rental has a full line of equipment, with kayaks, tents and fishing poles for summer, and boots, ice-fishing gear and skis for winter.

Wasilla: Adventures by True North near Palmer rents everything from sleeping bags to kayaks.

Talkeetna: Talkeetna Gear Shop (p297) rents mountain bikes, fat bikes, skis or snowshoes, stand-up paddleboards, and more. It also sells a wide range of used gear.

Denali: Denali Mountain Works, a short drive north of the national park entrance, has rentals including tents, sleeping bags, packs, cook stoves and bear-resistant canisters.

Fairbanks: Alaska Outdoor Gear Rental's second store has all the essentials, with an extra inventory of extreme-cold-weather gear.

Byers Lake (p301)

takes you up to Curry Ridge on a 4.5-hour morning or evening hike and offers insightful commentary along the way.

If you have more time on your hands, the four-day, 18-mile backpacking trip along Kesugi Ridge offers deep immersion in the wilderness. You'll need your own personal gear (backpack, sleeping bag, pad), though they provide the tent and cooking equipment.

Explore the K'esugi Ken Interpretive Center
Insight into natural history

Meaning 'Ancient One' in the traditional Tanaina language, the **K'esugi Ken Interpretive Center** *(day parking pass $5)* was designed in partnership with local tribal members, and offers visitors the chance to experience the area in a hands-on way. An open pavilion contains interpretive information about Denali State Park and the Alaska Range, and from here you can take a short walk along the Glacier View Trail past signposts about geology, plant life and animals while you take in views over the landscape. For a slightly longer outing, walk the easy half-mile Moose Flats Loop Interpretative Trail, which takes you past wildflowers, a pond, and along a boardwalk over muskeg (a bog).

Denali National Park & Preserve

WILDLIFE-WATCHING | HIKING AND TREKKING | SLED DOGS

Alaska's most famous national park is a parcel of land both primeval and easily accessible. Here, you can head off into the trackless wilderness amid 6 million acres of tundra, boreal forest and ice-capped mountains. Alternatively, you can hike Denali's handful of established trails along meandering riverbeds, over mountain passes or up to alpine lakes. An even easier way to experience Denali is by taking a wildlife-minded bus tour in search of moose, caribou and bears along the only road into the park. With more time, you can join a ranger-led hike or enjoy quality time with Denali's furry rangers – the only working sled dogs in the national park system.

All of these attractions lie in the shadow of the 20,308ft (6190m) summit known to native Athabascans as the Great One (and officially renamed Mt McKinley by the US government in 2025). You can learn about the deep Indigenous connections to this region while exploring the visitor center's well-curated exhibits.

> ☑ **TOP TIP**
>
> Plan your day around the weather. If the skies are clear, hit the trail (and get an early start). Come back to explore the exhibitions and films in the visitor center when rains or cloudy skies appear.

Delve into All Things Denali
Exhibits and films

The best place to learn about the park is at the **Denali Visitor Center** *(nps.gov/dena; free)*, which has thoughtfully designed displays and short films that explore wildlife, geology and

 GETTING AROUND

You can get to Denali National Park & Preserve via the George Parks Hwy north or south from Anchorage or Fairbanks. The Alaska Railroad offers service daily in the summer and weekly in the winter. Motorcoach transportation is available from either Seward or Anchorage, and van transfers are available from Fairbanks.

Within the park itself, access beyond Mile 43 remains closed until 2027 due to landslides. There are several different buses (p306) operating through the park, including a free service up to Mile 17, and transit buses and camper buses out to Mile 43.

DENALI NATIONAL PARK & PRESERVE

● SIGHTS
1. Mountain Vista Area

● ACTIVITIES
2. McKinley Station Trail
3. Mt Healy Overlook Trail
4. Oxbow Loop Trail
5. Savage Alpine Trail
6. Savage River Loop Trail
7. Sled Dog Kennels
8. Triple Lakes Trail

● SLEEPING
9. Camp Denali
10. Riley Creek Campground
11. Savage River Campground
12. Teklanika River Campground

● EATING
13. Morino Grill

● INFORMATION
14. Backcountry Information Center

15. Denali Visitor Center
16. Murie Science & Learning Center

● TRANSPORT
17. Denali Bus Depot
18. Savage River Parking Area

human history. There's insight into rock formations, a replica gold miner's cabin, flower displays and animal feet that show their adaptations for winter survival. Perhaps most fascinating are the exhibits on the Athabascans, which illuminate just how much the seemingly inhospitable land provides: tanned moose for coats and gloves, sinew for thread, spruce pitch for waterproofing and chewing game, and birchbark for baskets, canoes and cradles. You can also check out an impressive bear spear (on loan from the Starr family) and see some of the plants used in native medicine, like fireweed – with stems used on cuts, and the leaves and flowers infused into a tea to relieve stomach aches, coughs and asthma.

Films play in the theater every half-hour. The beautifully photographed 18-minute *Heartbeats of Denali* is a perennial favorite and shows the region throughout the seasons. You might also catch the 22-minute *The True Heart of Winter*, which focuses on Denali's sled dogs and the magic (and challenging conditions) of winter.

SCENIC FLIGHTS

Flying over the soaring peaks and vast ice fields of **Denali National Park** is not something you're likely to forget. Scenic flights depart from Talkeetna, and you can also add on a glacier landing (p298).

Go for a Guided Nature Walk
Short ranger-led excursions

During the summer (sometimes twice a day), rangers lead free short (typically two-hour) **guided walks** that travel slowly and make several stops to take in the scenery. Along the way, you'll learn about some of Denali's plant and animal life, permafrost, human settlers to Denali and the dramatic forces that created these mountains and valleys. These walks depart from the visitor center; no reservation is necessary. Stop in – or check the signpost out front – to see when the next one departs.

Explore the Past on a Front Country Hike
Walking the McKinley Station Trail

A rewarding, 1.6-mile (one-way) hike, the **McKinley Station Trail** takes you from Denali Visitor Center to Riley Creek Campground. You'll pass historic signposts and a few remains of former buildings from the park's early days in the 1920s and '30s. The trail winds past the former sites of the once iconic (but quite rustic) Mount McKinley Park Hotel, the original park headquarters, the railroad trestle (although the steel bridge remains, the 1922 wooden structure was replaced by an artificial embankment), a fox-farming ranch and a roadhouse that was quite the den of vice in the 1920s (bootlegging, gambling, sex work). You'll have to use your imagination to visualize some of these settings 100 years ago. Forest has reclaimed once-cleared lands.

See the Sled Dogs in Action
Denali's canine rangers

Denali is the only US national park where rangers conduct winter patrols with dog teams. In summer the huskies serve a different purpose: amusing and educating the legions of tourists who sign up for the park's free daily tours of the **Sled Dog Kennels** and dog demonstrations. These popular gatherings typically happen three times daily (10am, 2pm and 4pm), and you need to line up early to get a spot on the free shuttle bus (these depart 40 minutes in advance). Alternatively, it's a 2-mile walk from the visitor center along the roadside trail.

Once there, a park ranger will describe the important work the dogs perform and talk about the Alaskan huskies (they aren't actually a recognized breed) who have been a presence in the park for over a century. The best part is seeing the dogs excitedly pull a ranger on a four-wheeled cart around a short oval-shaped course. Then each dog is introduced before being sent back to the doghouse. Afterwards, you can wander through the kennels and admire the puppies along with the more reserved older dogs.

Alternatively, you can visit at any other time when the kennels are open (9.30am to 4.30pm), and freely wander the kennels and chat with rangers who may be on hand.

DENALI ESSENTIALS

Admission: Adult/child $15/free

Park Info: Stop by the **Denali Visitor Center** (nps.gov/dena), which is open daily in summer (8.30am to 6pm). From late September through April, visit the Murie Science and Learning Center (9.30am to 5pm).

Food: Next door to the visitor center, the **Morino Grill** is the park's only sit-down restaurant with burgers, grilled sandwiches, premade salads, fish and chips, and good coffee. Healy, 11 miles north, has many options.

Camping & Lodging: There are six developed campgrounds in the park. Experienced backpackers can overnight nearly anywhere with a backcountry permit (p308). There are more options outside the park in Healy and Cantwell (29 miles south), plus backcountry lodges within the park, reachable only by air.

BUS TRANSPORTATION 101

Private vehicles without a permit are prohibited beyond Mile 15. There are buses within the entrance and along open sections of the Park Rd (to Mile 43).

Narrated Tour Buses: Certified driver-guide provides commentary on five-hour excursions ($117 to $145). Reservation only (denaliparkvillage.com). Tan-colored buses.

Non-Narrated Transit Buses: Service beyond Mile 17. Buses depart and arrive at **Denali Bus Depot**. Reservation only (reserve at least 24 hours ahead). Green buses. $34 per person (free under age 16).

Camp Buses: For accessing a campground or backcountry unit further in the park with space for gear and bikes. $34 per person (free under age 16).

Free Shuttle Buses: Savage River, Riley Creek Loop and Sled Dog Demonstration; tan or green shuttles (free for park visitors).

Sled-dog demonstration (p305)

Hike the Mt Healy Overlook Trail
Top-of-the-world views

One of the most rewarding hikes near the park's entrance area, the 5.5-mile (round trip) **Mt Healy Overlook Trail** is proof that you needn't go deep into the park to find some great wilderness hiking. One of the steepest official hikes in the park, it yields some fantastic views from the top of Mt Healy. Plan on the route taking three to five hours. You'll start off on the Horseshoe Lake Trail before beginning the ascent on the intersecting trail toward Mt Healy. It's a gentle climb (200ft elevation gain) for the first 1.5 miles through spruce, alder and aspen, but gets steeper as you ascend another 1500ft over the next 1.2 miles. As you go higher, you enter alpine tundra – a world of moss, lichen and wildflowers – along with some incredible views. Keep an eye out for the large hoary marmots (a northern cousin of the groundhog) and pikas (a small relative of the rabbit). From the overlook (3425ft), hardy hikers can climb another mile to the high point of Healy Ridge (4217ft) or another 2 miles to the summit of Mt Healy (5714ft).

Hit the Trails near Savage River
River life and dramatic views

The Savage River parking area, near Mile 15, is a trailhead for two popular hikes: the **Savage River Loop Trail** and **Savage Alpine Trail**. For the loop portion, hike along either side of Savage River through a scenic canyon, Healy Ridge and Mt Margaret. The trail winds along meadows and scrub brush – keep an eye out for ptarmigans – for about a mile before crossing the river at a bridge (an excellent spot for photos) and continuing back on the other side. Of course, you needn't turn around at the bridge. You can keep going off trail (permitted in Denali) and explore to your heart's content.

The Savage Alpine Trail is tougher, traveling between Savage River Campground (next to Mountain Vista) at Mile 13 and the Savage River Canyon, traversing a high section of what's called the Outer Range. The 4-mile (one-way) excursion ascends some 1300ft, but it's well worth the (often windy) climb for the sweeping views of the valley, surrounding peaks and Park Rd. Whichever way you hike this trail, you can hop on the free **Savage River Shuttle** (running in the summer only) to return to your starting point.

Take a Ranger-Led Discovery Hike
Off-trail with a naturalist

National Park Service (NPS) rangers lead moderate to strenuous adventures known as **Discovery Hikes** deep into the heart of the park on a daily basis during summer. The location varies from day to day, and hikes go rain or shine. Stop in the visitor center to get details on the hike, which can include stream crossings, elevation gain, crossing bogs and bushwalking through alder thickets – all of which make for an adventure-filled, one-of-a-kind outing (every hike is different). The hike is free, but you'll need to reserve a spot in person at the visitor center one or two days in advance and then reserve (and pay for) a transit ticket at the Denali Bus Depot.

Shuttles leave at 8am. Note that hiking is off trail, so be sure to have sturdy, waterproof footwear and to pack rain gear, food and water (a trekking pole or two is also recommended). Rangers will turn away unprepared hikers. This is an all-day affair; the bus ride to the hiking departure point can take up to four hours, to hike for three to five hours, and then a similar-length bus ride back to the park entrance. Anyone aged eight and older can participate.

Motor Through Denali with a Naturalist
Narrated bus tours

Those seeking a deeper understanding of the park, who may not have the time or desire to hit the trail, should consider booking one of Denali's narrated bus tours. On a day's outing, you can learn more about the history, flora and fauna of the park, and perhaps see some wildlife. This is an excellent option for those with limited mobility. Hopping on a bus, whether taking a narrated tour or just a transit bus, is one of the best ways to see bears (both black bears and grizzlies) – as you're more likely to see them between Mile 20 and Mile 60 of the Park Rd, where private vehicles are prohibited.

There are two trips available to Denali National Park visitors, offered between late May and early September. The five-hour **Denali Natural History Tour** *(denaliparkvillage.com; adult/child $117/51)* travels from the entrance area to Primrose Ridge at Mile 17. Passengers will stop at several points along the way, with an hour of free time to

DENALI ROAD CLOSURE

A landslide at Pretty Rocks area near Mile 45.4 on the only road through the park has kept half of the park inaccessible since 2021. In 2023, the park began work on a 475ft bridge to span the landslide at an estimated cost of $100 million (nothing comes cheap in Alaska!). The road in its entirety is expected to open for the entire season in 2027. Until then, no one can pass beyond Mile 43, which means some of the most popular sections of road are impossible to reach. For the few backcountry lodges near Wonder Lake at Mile 90 and beyond, aircraft is the only way in and out.

OTHER ALASKA NATIONAL PARKS

Try other road-accessible national parks like **Wrangell-St Elias** (p334) southeast of Fairbanks and northeast of Valdez; or **Kenai Fjords** (p248) near the city of Seward, about three hours south of Anchorage.

BACKPACKING IN DENALI

The park is divided into 87 backcountry units, with a limited number of overnighting backpackers allowed in at one time. Permits are needed if you want to camp overnight and you can obtain these at the **Backcountry Information Center** (at the Denali Bus Depot). Permits are issued only a day in advance. The next step is to watch the required backcountry orientation video, followed by a brief safety talk that covers, among other things, proper use of the bear-resistant food containers (BRFCs) the park will loan you. Finally, after receiving your permit, buy the topographic maps for your unit and purchase a ticket for a camper bus *($34)* to get you out to the starting point of your hike.

explore off the bus. The first stop is at the Denali Bus Depot with the film *Across Time and Tundra* explaining the natural history of this unique environment. Then, buses stop at the historic Savage Cabin to learn how the cabin was once used for housing, and how it continues to be used today by Denali's sled-dog teams and mushers. Finally, the bus will stop at Primrose Ridge, where you will experience a memorable Alaska Native presentation that provides a background into how the First People have used this land for nearly 10,000 years.

The **Tundra Wilderness Tour** *(denaliparkvillage.com; adult/child $145/65)* is the longest-running tour (in various forms since 1923) in the park. This is a 5½-hour trip traveling along the open sections of the Park Rd corridor, looking for wildlife and seasonal shifts in landscapes. A highlight is a stop at the Murie Cabin near the East Fork River (Mile 43) to experience where Adolph Murie lived while conducting his famous research inside what was then known as Mt McKinley National Park.

Reserve these tours a week or more in advance (they sometimes sell out) at *reservedenali.com*. Tours depart from various locations at different times depending on the day, so be sure to confirm the details when booking. Wheelchair-accessible buses are available, too, and all stops are wheelchair accessible.

Tackle the Triple Lakes
Denali's longest established trail

The longest official trail in the park, the **Triple Lakes Trail** offers varied terrain and vegetation, and there's a palpable feeling that you've truly entered the wilds. Allow four to five hours to travel the length of the 9.5-mile (one-way) trail.

From the McKinley Station Trail, the path begins after a bridge crossing of Hines Creek, followed by an even more photogenic crossing (via suspension bridge) over Riley Creek

Bus tour (p307), Denali National Park & Preserve

another quarter-mile further along. The trail is flat at first and the forest cover unusually lush. In about a mile you begin to climb switchbacks, eventually reaching a ridgetop affording yodel-inspiring views of the Alaska Range and the valleys formed by Hines Creek and the Nenana River. After a long run along the ridgeline, the path begins to descend, first to the Triple Lakes and then to George Parks Hwy. Since the park shuttle doesn't run along the highway, you'll have to either retrace your steps or arrange for transport through one of the area hotels (Denali Park Village, for instance, lies near the southern terminus of the trailhead, and runs a courtesy shuttle for guests to the visitor center).

Another option is to hike northward from the southern end of the trail (there's parking near the **Oxbow Loop Trail**, Mile 231 of the George Parks Hwy). You can make the lakes your focus for a shorter day by hiking under the highway bridge, later crossing railroad tracks and reaching your first lake after about 1 mile from the trailhead. It's another 0.6 miles to the next lake, and another 1.4 miles to the third lake – making for a round-trip outing of 6 miles (and 1200ft elevation gain) – as you return to your starting point.

Attend a Science Talk

Rangers and wildlife specialists

During the summer, the amphitheaters at **Riley Creek Campground** and **Savage River Campground** host free evening talks given by the park's deeply knowledgeable park rangers. These 45-minute presentations (typically starting around 7.30pm) cover a wide range of topics: grizzly bears, wolves, wilderness trekking, glacier formation and the sound of science.

On Tuesdays (usually starting at 7pm), the **Murie Science & Learning Center** hosts a summer evening speaker series

BIRTH OF A NATIONAL TREASURE

The Athabascan people used what is now Denali National Park & Preserve as hunting grounds, but it wasn't until gold was found near Kantishna in 1905 that the area really began to see development. With the gold stampede came the big-game hunters, and things weren't looking very good for this amazing stretch of wilderness until a noted hunter and naturalist, Charles Sheldon, came to town.

Sheldon, stunned by the destruction, mounted a campaign to protect the region. From this, Mt McKinley National Park was born. Later, as a result of the 1980 Alaska National Interest Lands Conservation Act, the park was enlarged by 4 million acres, and renamed Denali National Park & Preserve.

BE BEAR-AWARE

Bear-safety preparation: Watch bear-safety videos at the Denali Bus Depot.

Travel in groups: The more the merrier (five or more is ideal).

Make noise: Sing, clap loudly, or wear large 'bear bells' on trails or in the backcountry. If near running water, increase your volume and be extra vigilant.

Carry bear spray: Firearms are prohibited in national parks. Bear spray, when used correctly, has been proven more effective in deterring a charging bruin. Make sure you know how to use and store bear spray safely.

Signs of bear activity: Look for scat (poop), tracks, carrion or animal carcasses partially buried. If you see the latter, leave immediately, with bear spray out and ready to deploy.

Triple Lakes Trail (p308)

(also free) featuring wildlife researchers, biologists and geologists who lead insightful discussions about science and natural history.

Mountain Vista Meditation
Exploring the dramatic transition zone

Denali offers epic beauty and you needn't even venture far into the park to discover it. The **Mountain Vista Area** is a fine spot for a picnic or a walk on the Mountain Vista Loop Trail. Though short (just 0.6 miles), the trail is ideal for catching a view of Denali on a clear day. Along the way, signposts featuring old photos from the 1930s show how much the area has changed over the years. Be sure to take the spur trail down to the rushing Savage River, with a jaw-dropping view over the river valley to the south and Mt Healy to the north. This is another fine spot to head off trail for a wander along the meandering river.

This area is set amid a transition zone found at elevations sandwiched between taiga or boreal forests, and tundra. Only shrubs and smaller trees grow here, and this open scape allows for the far-off views. Note: during the summer months, the Mountain Vista parking lot fills up quickly, so the Savage River Shuttle (p307) is the best bet for accessing this popular trailhead.

Beyond Denali National Park & Preserve

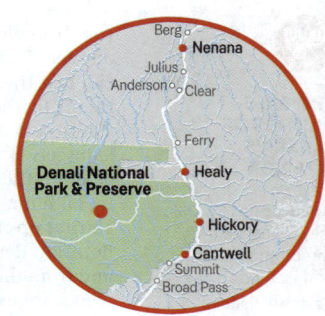

Go white-water rafting, take a rugged scenic drive or visit a famous sled-dog kennel while exploring the wild landscapes outside Denali.

The lands around Denali have been inhabited by the Athabascan people, and before that, their ancestors, for over 12,000 years. Once miners, trappers and then railroad workers began migrating here from the late 1800s, homesteaders soon followed. They were drawn to a life removed from the humdrum affairs of modernity. These homesteaders still exist, albeit with satellite internet and motorized conveyances instead of dog teams. But the free spirit of Alaska looms large here, and it's a big draw to visitors wanting more than a typical 'check-the-box' experience. From cuddling sled-dog puppies at an Iditarod racing kennel to driving the rugged and remote Denali Hwy or rafting class III and class IV rapids, this is the place for uncommon adventures.

Places
Healy p311
Hickory p312
Cantwell p314
Nenana p314

Healy
TIME FROM DENALI NATIONAL PARK & PRESERVE: **10 MINS**

Raft the Nenana River
The Nenana River runs along Denali National Park & Preserve's edges and travels near access points with the Parks Hwy, so it's easy to take advantage of the many opportunities offered by local rafting companies.

For a family-friendly day of adventure along the scenic Nenana, opt for the Wilderness Wave Raft Tour *(adult/child $140/90)* offered by **New Wave Adventures** *(newwaveadventures.com)*.

 GETTING AROUND

Exploring beyond Denali National Park & Preserve's boundaries can be challenging if you don't have a vehicle – though some lodges and hotels in the area do run shuttles to and from the park. There are no taxis or ride-share services available, though you can book transport around the area with **Denali Transit** *(denalitransit.com; one-way $15)*, which runs shuttles to/from the park entrance within a 20-mile radius. If you're only stopping in Nenana, you can visit it by train from Anchorage or Fairbanks.

THE 'BIG 5' ANIMALS OF ALASKA'S INTERIOR

Moose: Brushy areas; they prefer willows, shrubs and grasses, as they feed all day.

Caribou: Feed on lichens and other low-lying plants of the tundra areas. Can sometimes be seen from roadways along the Denali corridor northward.

Dall sheep: Live along rocky slopes and hillsides where they have protection from predators and a ready food source.

Wolves: Elusive creatures but savvy hunters, roaming the entire Interior in packs. Their scat or prints are often seen more than the actual animal.

Grizzly bears: Grizzlies can run up to 40mph and have a keen sense of smell, so be bear-aware (p94).

Suitable for those aged five and above, the 11-mile journey takes you through glacially carved canyons with class I and II (and one set of class III) rapids along the way. Adrenaline junkies can test their mettle against the class III and a few class IV rapids further down the river on the Canyon Wave Raft Tour *($140)*, a heart-pumping 11 miles that passes through turbulent sections with names like 'Coffee Grinder' and 'Razorback.' Open to those aged 12 and up. Each tour lasts around three to 3.5 hours (two hours spent on the water), which includes suiting up in the provided dry suit, booties, PFD (personal flotation device) and helmet, followed by transportation to and from the launch site. You can opt to paddle or not. Those who want even more time on the river combine the two trips into a 5.5-hour New Wave Combo Raft Tour *(adult $240)*, rafting some 22 miles total.

Denali Raft Adventures *(denaliraft.com)* is another reputable operator that runs similar tours on the Nenana: 11-mile trips *(adult/child $140/100)* of either churning white water (the Canyon Run) or gentler class I and II rapids. Likewise, you can combine the two for a 5.5-hour outing (four hours spent on the water) in the Healy Express Run *($240)*.

Hickory

TIME FROM DENALI NATIONAL PARK & PRESERVE: **15 MINS**

Meet athletes of the Iditarod

Mushing is Alaska's official state sport, and it's not uncommon to see teams of dogs and their human partners enjoying a run down the trail, especially on cold winter days. During the summer months, however, mushers and dogs take it easier, running carefully crafted workouts to keep up on training plans and, in the case of many kennels, becoming ambassadors for their vocation.

After you've visited Denali National Park's **sled-dog kennels** (p305), take a look at the life of a racing dog who has or will tackle what is billed the 'Last Great Race,' the Iditarod. If you're staying in the general vicinity of Denali National Park & Preserve during the summer months, **Husky Homestead** *(huskyhomestead.com)* is located at Mile 228 of the Parks Hwy, around 10 miles south of the park entrance. Here, Iditarod champion Jeff King and his handlers provide an indepth look at the history of mushing, training strategies and the characteristics of champion teams. A highlight is seeing the corral of puppies and witnessing a team hooked up to a dryland 'sled' for a training run, their raw power on full display on a 50ft treadmill. Tours happen three times daily in the summer *(adult/child $64/54)*.

From February to April, Husky Homestead offers two-hour winter tours *(adult/child $185/120)*, which includes a visit with the animals as well as a ride with the main sled-dog team. For a more immersive experience, the homestead offers private, customizable tours, including three-day, two-night adventures where you'll learn to mush your own dog team.

DRIVE THE DRAMATIC DENALI HIGHWAY

The original connecting road to Denali National Park, 135-mile Denali Hwy is home to mountain vistas, rushing rivers and pristine trails.

START	END	LENGTH
Cantwell	Paxson	135 miles; 8 hours

Before setting out, make sure you have a reliable 4WD vehicle (such as those offered by Go North or Arctic Outfitters). Traditional rental companies prohibit their cars being driven on this gravel road. Alternatively, join Denali Jeep Tours *(denalijeep.com)* for a guided four-hour excursion (you drive in a convoy).

If you're driving, proceed from ❶ **Cantwell** past an excellent ❷ **Denali viewpoint** (Mile 124), where you'll have a stunning panorama on clear days. Up at ❸ **Brushkana Creek** (Mile 105), stop to look (or fish) for grayling running through the crystal-clear streams. You'll soon draw away from the Susitna River Valley into the foot of the Clearwater Mountains, where you'll find remnants of ❹ **Old Valdez Creek Mine** (Mile 85), Denali's own gold-rush site that began in 1903. At ❺ **Clearwater Creek Wayside** (Mile 55), you'll find a great spot for birding, with warblers, dippers and swallows regularly spotted.

Stretch your legs on the ❻ **MacLaren Summit Trail** (Mile 37), a 3-mile, mostly dry route that runs north across the tundra to MacLaren Summit. The easy, 3-mile ❼ **Landmark Gap Trail North** (Mile 24) passes through the heart of the Tangle Lakes Archaeological District, a vast swath of land home to hundreds of archaeological sites. A ❽ **pullout** (Mile 13) yields impressive 360-degree views, including a glimpse of the Wrangell Mountains to the southeast. At the intersection of the paved Richardson Hwy, you'll reach journey's end at the settlement of ❾ **Paxson**.

This stretch (Mile 59) travels atop an **esker** – ridge of gravel, silt and sand deposited by melting glaciers eons ago.

The so-called **Crazy Notch** (Mile 46) was formed by the Maclaren Glacier, which flowed through the valley.

The 8-mile **Osar Lake Trail** (Mile 37) leads to the eponymous lake and offers wide views of the MacLaren River Valley.

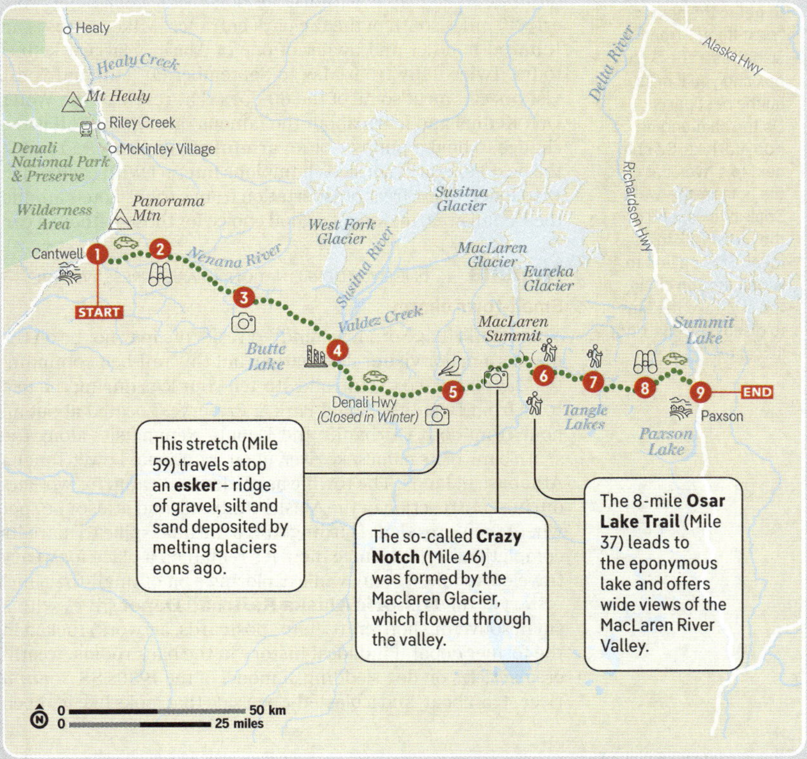

MAKING THE MOST OF DENALI

Vanessa Jusczak, Executive Director of Discover Denali @discoverdenali

Vanessa lives and works in Healy, a small community just north of the Denali National Park boundary. She was born and raised in this mining town and tourist hub, and has advice for first-time visitors.

'Slow down. Soak it in. Nature isn't meant to be sped through to get to the next "best thing". Treat Denali as a checked box and you'll miss all the best parts. Do the challenging (for you) hike. Sit still next to a river. Eat at the hole-in-the-wall. Soak in the sound of the birds. Talk to a local. Stay up late to watch the sun circle the sky. Take the time to discover Denali, not just see it.'

Cantwell

TIME FROM DENALI NATIONAL PARK & PRESERVE: **35 MINS**

Snuggle with puppies

Similar to Husky Homestead, **DogGoneIt** *(doggoneittours.com; adult/child $65/55)* is paradise for dog lovers. On a huge property 30 miles south of the the park entrance, Mike Santos is an Iditarod handler and owner of one of Alaska's largest kennel tours. Twice daily from May to September (at 8am and 7pm), visitors can meet some of the 60 dogs that reside at the Wolf's Den Kennel and learn about the famous race. Best of all is the chance to hold a puppy – or an armful of puppies – and watch the next generation of sled champions interact with each other. DogGoneIt offers free transportation from various hotels around the Denali area, making it a good choice for those without a car.

Nenana

TIME FROM DENALI NATIONAL PARK & PRESERVE: **1 HR**

Small-town charm

This small village of a few hundred residents may not be on the map as a major visitor destination, but this rail-belt community is a great place to stop and stretch your legs during the trip to or from Denali National Park & Preserve. Located about an hour from both Fairbanks and Denali, Nenana sits along the south bank of its namesake river, upon traditional Lower Tanana Athabascan lands. The town was settled as a camp for workers during construction of the Alaska Railroad, and is also the spot where then-president Harding drove the final spike to mark its completion in 1923. Since then, it's remained a place for weary travelers to take a break while exploring a bit of small-town life.

Start at the **Historic Alaska Railroad Depot** *(free)*, with a small souvenir shop (craft items, postcards, artwork) tucked in the former depot. Find local history in the back rooms: weathered articles on dog sledding, a model of the 1930s SS *Nenana* river steamboat, and a blasted-open safe that looks like it's been

Historic Alaska Railroad Depot

robbed (actually, someone just lost the keys). Be sure to look at the vintage machinery in the beautifully restored depot office.

Across the street, take a peak in the **Wildlife Museum** *(free)*, which has an astonishing collection of taxidermy – ptarmigans, Dall sheep, bearskins and even a bison. There's also a massive moose named Lightning that you can ride (climb up into the saddle for a photo op – $20). The shop has game jerky (venison, elk, antelope), smoked cheeses and artwork of Alaskan wildlife.

Nearby, **AK Rustic Company** *(akrustic.com)* stocks beautifully made handicrafts, including aurora photographs, hand-turned birch bowls and jewelry featuring cured fish-skin pieces by the Salty Sisters. You'll also find clothing, hats and other Alaskan essentials, along with a snack counter that's quite popular for its creative root beer floats.

From here, take a stroll along A Street, Nenana's main strip, which is dotted with mural-lined buildings, a grocery store, several statue-dotted parks and another shop, the **3 Rivers Trading Post** *(3riverstradingpost.com)*. Next to it, **These Girls Got Nuts** is a whimsically decorated snack wagon for munching on cinnamon sugar pecans, coconut vanilla cashews and other creative combinations.

Reach Nenana via the George Parks Hwy, or see it from the Alaska Railroad's north–south route, traveling south from Fairbanks or north from Denali.

THE NENANA ICE CLASSIC

Nenana's most famous attribute has to do with a wintery game of chance. Each year, as soon as ice covers the entire river surface, a wooden tripod attached to a wire and timer is set up for all to see, and people from all over the world buy chances to guess the exact date and time the ice will 'go out' in the spring. Once the tripod moves 100ft downstream, it trips the wire and stops the clock. With over $200,000 up for grabs, it's been a popular and fun way to say farewell to winter's snow and cold since railroad workers thought it up in 1917.

EATING & DRINKING BEYOND DENALI: OUR PICKS

Monderosa Bar & Grill: Some 5 miles north of Nenana, this old-school dive serves up one of Alaska's best hamburgers. *noon-8pm* $

49th State Brewing: An indoor-outdoor brewery and pub in Healy that packs in the crowds with great food, quality beers and live music. *11am-midnight* $$

The Black Bear: Serves the region's best coffee, plus hearty breakfast fare and creative dinner options (brisket bowls, jackfruit tacos, coconut curry). *7am-9pm* $$

Prospector's: Outstanding brick-oven pizzas plus dozens of craft brews on tap at this atmospheric spot covered with old photos and animal pelts. *11am-midnight* $$

Fairbanks

GOLD-RUSH HISTORY | ALASKA NATIVE CULTURE | NORTHERN LIGHTS

GETTING AROUND

Like Anchorage (p142), Fairbanks is easy to navigate if you have a vehicle, especially since many attractions are on the outskirts of town. The public bus system (MACS) provides decent service around town – but only on weekdays – for $1.50 per ride, or you can buy a day pass for $3. Additionally, tour companies will usually provide transportation to and from most hotels. Ask when you're making a booking. Fairbanks has a few car-rental options, most of which are at Fairbanks International Airport. Some larger hotels provide a shuttle to the airport, railroad depot, and major shopping and dining outlets. Inquire at booking.

A spread-out settlement (more town than city), Fairbanks at first glance seems like a land of strip malls and parking lots. But its compact downtown and scenic riverside are rewarding places to explore, and it boasts some lovely green spaces as well as a botanical garden that are ideal for walking and bird-watching. You'll also find an impressive university collection of art and craftwork showcasing Alaska's diverse Indigenous peoples, the finest vintage car museum in the state, and a park full of timber buildings from Fairbanks' early days as a gold-mining center.

The town is home to some truly fascinating characters – sled-dog breeders, crusading environmentalists, oil workers, college students, military personnel, bush pilots and other intrepid souls who are undeterred by living in a place of such extreme temperature swings: summertime highs can easily reach above 90°F, while wintertime lows plunge to –40°F or colder (including the all-time low of –66°F).

A Showcase of the Alaskan Interior
Exhibitions, films and information

An ingenious mix of museum, info point and cultural center, the **Morris Thompson Cultural & Visitors Center** *(morristhompsoncenter.org; free)* makes a great first stop when exploring Fairbanks. The beautifully designed building is packed with insightful multimedia exhibitions related to Alaska's history and the rich traditions of the Athabascan people. You may feel as if you're entering another realm (the mystical Interior) as you wander through recreations of a salmon smokehouse, a hunting camp (complete with curious grizzly bear), a pocket of snow and a winter cabin. There are finely crafted artifacts (a chief's basket made of

Morris Thompson Cultural & Visitors Center

king salmon skins, masks, beautifully beaded mittens), and videos that delve into Alaska Native languages.

Various films show throughout the day in the theater, exploring topics related to Indigenous traditions of the northern people, the aurora borealis, the canine rangers of Denali, Fairbanks' boomtown days and the construction and impact of building the Alaska pipeline. On Fridays (at 11am), the center hosts a native elder for conversation and a demonstration on traditional practices, crafts and ways of life.

The expansive space is also home to the Fairbanks Visitor Bureau and Alaska Public Lands Information Center. It's an excellent place to plan further travels in the region, especially in more remote areas, with maps and advice available from rangers for all Alaska public lands.

Outside, you can wander the grounds, see mosaics on the ground inspired by Athabaskan artwork, and peak inside a historic cabin from the early 1900s. The simple two-room abode with its wood-burning stove and eye-catching wallpaper gives a glimpse of living conditions during the early gold-rush days.

☑ TOP TIP

Attend and cheer on the athletes of the World Eskimo Native Olympics (WEIO), held each July. This multiday event features tests of skill and strength, plus a fantastic artisan market, and pageants for adults and children representing their tribal affiliations with fur, hides and beading authentic to the Interior.

EATING IN FAIRBANKS: CASUAL FARE

Tanana Valley Farmers Market: Bakery items, crepes, charcuterie, coffee and Thai food amid a veggie- and craft-filled market. *11am-4pm Wed & 9am-4pm Sat May-Sep* $

The Crepery: Extremely popular downtown spot with a small courtyard and a delicious variety of sweet and savory crepes. *7am-6pm Tue-Fri, 9am-6pm Sat, 11am-5pm Sun* $

Big Daddy's: Feast on slow-smoked ribs, juicy brisket, bowls of baked beans and creamy mac 'n' cheese at one of Alaska's best barbecue spots. *11am-9pm Mon-Sat* $$

Thai House: A local favorite with all the hits, from crispy tofu appetizers to flavor-packed drunken noodles. *11am-3pm & 4.30-9pm Mon-Sat* $$

FAIRBANKS

☆ Running Reindeer Ranch (4.5mi)
 Black Spruce Dog Sledding (10mi)

University of Alaska Museum of the North

Pioneer Park

★ HIGHLIGHTS
1. University of Alaska Museum of the North

● SIGHTS
2. Alaska Centennial Center for the Arts
3. Antler Arch
4. Bear Gallery
5. Creamer's Field Migratory Waterfowl Refuge
6. ET Barnette plaque
7. footbridge
8. Fountainhead Museum
9. Georgeson Botanical Garden
10. Golden Heart Plaza
11. Growden Memorial Ballpark
12. Harding Car
13. Large Animal Research Station
14. Lend Lease Monument
15. Morris Thompson Cultural & Visitors Center
16. Pioneer Museum
17. Pioneer Park
18. Presbyterian church
19. SS Nenana
20. Unknown First Family
21. Walter Harper and his dog Snowball
22. Wickersham House Museum
23. Yukon Quest Headquarters

● ACTIVITIES
24. Alaska Fishing and Rafting Adventures
25. Canoe Alaska
26. Riverboat Discovery
27. Wedgewood Wildlife Sanctuary

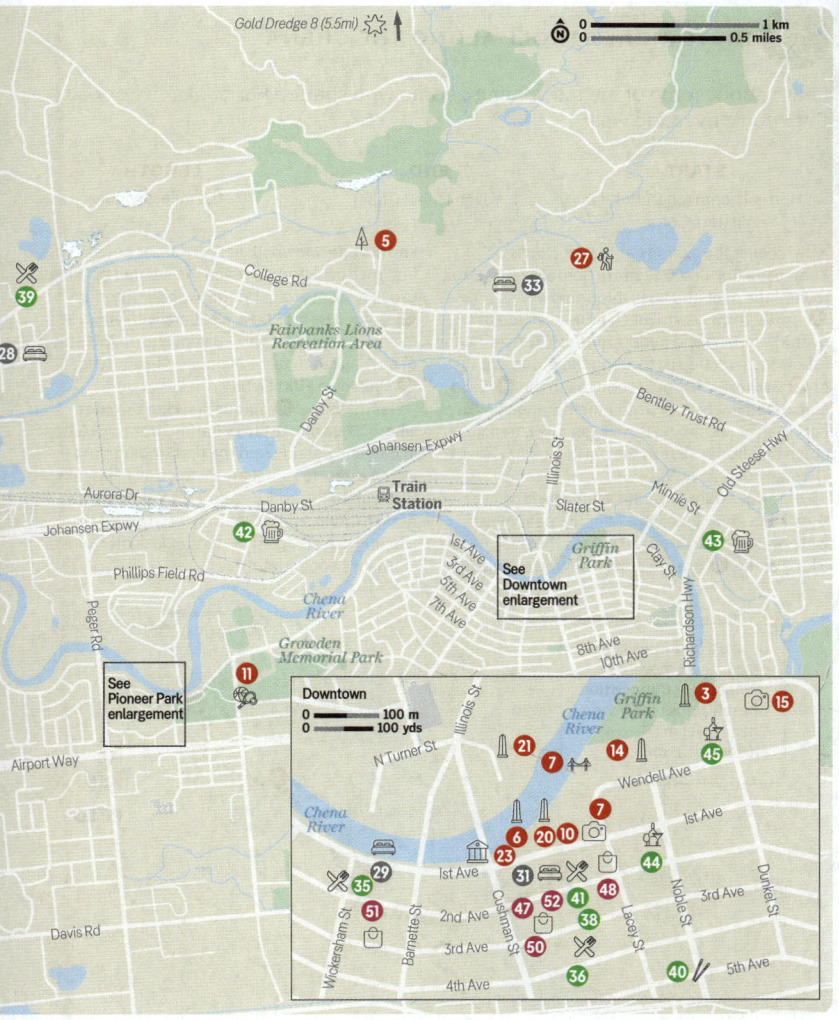

● SLEEPING	**35** Big Daddy's
28 Billie's Backpackers Hostel	**36** Jazz Bistro on 4th
29 Bridgewater Hotel	**37** Pump House
30 Pike's Waterfront Lodge	**38** Soba
31 Springhill Suites	**39** Tanana Valley Farmers Market
32 Sven's Basecamp Hostel	**40** Thai House
33 Wedgewood Resort	**41** The Crepery
● EATING	**● DRINKING & NIGHTLIFE**
34 Alaska Salmon Bake	**42** HooDoo
43 Latitude 65	**50** Lichen
44 Lavelle's Taphouse	**51** Solstice Books
45 Midnite Mine	**52** Two Street Gallery
● ENTERTAINMENT	**● TRANSPORT**
46 Palace Theatre	**53** Tanana Valley Railroad replica train
● SHOPPING	
47 Arctic Travelers Gift Shop	
48 Big Ray's	
49 Great Alaskan Bowl Company	

HISTORICAL STROLL ALONG THE CHENA

Learn about some of the fascinating people who shaped Fairbanks' history on this scenic riverside walk.

START	END	LENGTH
Morris Thompson Cultural & Visitors Center	Yukon Quest Cabin	0.5 miles; 1 hour

After seeing the exhibits at the 1 **Morris Thompson Cultural & Visitors Center** (p316), stroll toward the river and pass through the 2 **Antler Arch** – a striking landmark made of over 100 moose and caribou antlers. Turn left and follow the riverside path along the green expanse of 3 **Griffin Park**. You'll soon reach the 4 **Lend Lease Monument**, which commemorates Alaska's importance in keeping Russia (and by extension much of Europe) alive in the battle against Nazi Germany during WWII.

Off to your right, take the 5 **footbridge over the Chena River** for a view over the peaceful waterway. On the opposite side of the river, have a look at the 6 **bronze statue of Walter Harper and his dog Snowball**. In 1913 Harper became the first man in history to reach the summit of Denali. Cross back over the bridge, wander through 7 **Golden Heart Plaza**, a square with views of a clock tower, winter wildflowers and an 18ft statue of an Alaskan family – Malcolm Alexander's 8 **Unknown First Family**.

Nearby is the 9 **plaque marking the spot where ET Barnette disembarked** from a riverboat in 1901 and established the first trading post – which a year later became known as Fairbanks. Stroll up to the sod-covered 10 **Yukon Quest Alaska Cabin**, where you can learn about the exciting dogsledding races that kick off from Fairbanks each winter.

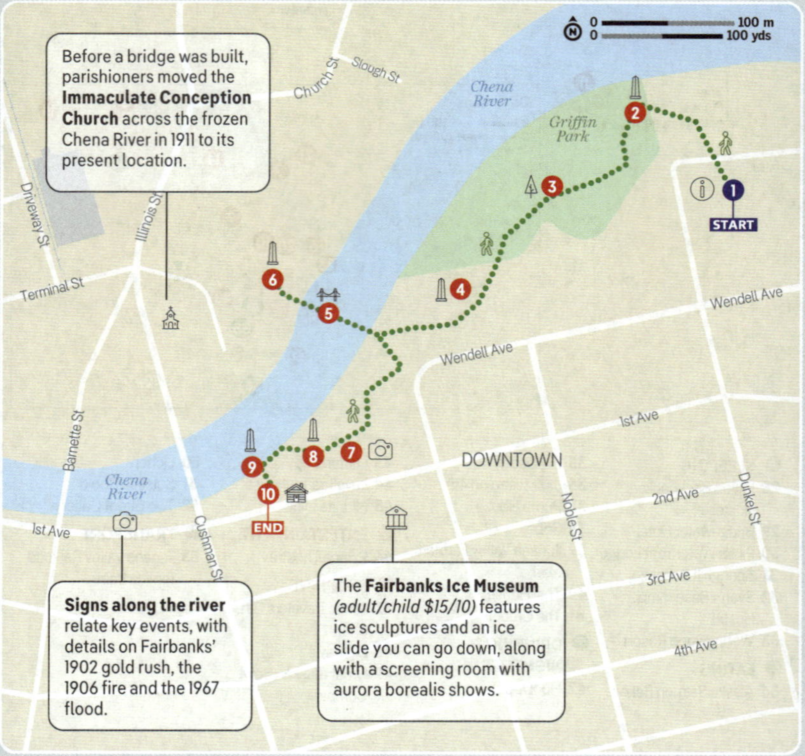
0 100 m
0 100 yds
Before a bridge was built, parishioners moved the **Immaculate Conception Church** across the frozen Chena River in 1911 to its present location.
Church St
Slough St
Chena River
Griffin Park
START
END
Driveway St
Illinois St
Terminal St
Wendell Ave
Wendell Ave
1st Ave
Barnette St
DOWNTOWN
Chena River
2nd Ave
Noble St
Dunkel St
1st Ave
Cushman St
3rd Ave
4th Ave
Signs along the river relate key events, with details on Fairbanks' 1902 gold rush, the 1906 fire and the 1967 flood.
The **Fairbanks Ice Museum** *(adult/child $15/10)* features ice sculptures and an ice slide you can go down, along with a screening room with aurora borealis shows.

Step into the 1900s at Pioneer Park
Historical buildings, food and activities

Run by the Fairbanks North Star Borough, **Pioneer Park** *(pioneerpark.us; free)* is a charming look into the region's unique history. With 44 acres of parkland, museums and historical buildings, there's much to explore. Have a wander inside the **SS Nenana**, a hulking stern-wheeler launched in 1933 that once plied the Yukon River. Today, it's full of vintage photos and exquisitely detailed miniature dioramas of villages and settlements from decades past. Nearby, you can wander through the **Harding Car** – a 1905 railcar that carried President Warren Harding and his entourage during his 1923 visit to Alaska to drive home the final spike marking the completion of the Alaska Railroad.

Many buildings were moved here from other parts, and you can stroll the wooden sidewalks past a 1904 **Presbyterian church** (services still held on Sundays) and numerous log cabins, many of which now host craft shops, casual restaurants and museums. Stop by the **Wickersham House Museum**, Fairbanks' oldest home (built in 1904), to learn about the adventurous judge and congressional delegate who helped develop the territory. Around the corner, the large **Pioneer Museum** has old photos and knickknacks (dogsleds, boat wheels, taxidermy, road signs) that shed light on key events in Fairbanks – like the devastating flood of 1967.

There's plenty of artwork for sale – check out the latest exhibit at the **Bear Gallery** *(fairbanksarts.org)* on the 3rd floor of the **Alaska Centennial Center for the Arts**, built to resemble a southeast Alaska tribal hall.

Kids will want to hop aboard the **Tanana Valley Railroad replica train** *(adult/child $3/2)* for a loop around the park, and nosh on ice cream at the food stands (there's also souvlaki, tacos and pizza). For something more substantial, have a meal at the Alaska Salmon Bake (p322).

A Gold Rush–Era Comedy
Mischievous musical theater

In the evening, it's worth returning to Pioneer Park for the Golden Heart Redux, a one-hour comedy that explores frontier-era Fairbanks and the town's sometimes sordid past through whimsical song and dance numbers. The show happens nightly at the intimate **Palace Theatre** *(akvisit.com; adult/child $35/16)*. Buy tickets online.

Paddle the Chena
Leisurely day on the river

One of the best ways to experience the Chena is to get out on the water. Located on the edge of Pioneer Park, **Canoe Alaska** *(canoealaska.com)* rents canoes, kayaks (single or double) and stand-up paddleboards for a float down the scenic, serpentine waterway. It's an easygoing paddle with the current, and you'll disembark at the Pump House, a

BEST EVENTS IN FAIRBANKS

Golden Days: Staged in the third week of July; commemorates the city's golden past with a parade, rubber-ducky races, bar crawl (in old-time apparel) and street fair.

Midnight Sun Festival: Celebrate the June solstice with live performances throughout the day, along with food and craft vendors.

World Eskimo-Indian Olympics: This four-day mid-July event features athletic competitions, as well as dancing and cultural performances.

Festival of Native Arts: Come in February for a weekend celebrating the rich heritage of Alaska's Interior Native People through song, dance, art and crafts.

Tanana Valley State Fair: From late July to early August, you can join the fun at the fair, amid fiddling, giant cabbages, amusing rides and big concerts.

TOP STORES IN FAIRBANKS

Solstice Books: An indie bookshop with a well-curated selection of new and used titles (including plenty of Alaska fare), plus author readings.

Lichen: Quality apparel and gift ideas for the home: stylish graphic T-shirts with subtle Alaska themes, deer-hide earrings and scented soy wax candles.

Two Street Gallery: In a small downtown shopping complex, browse unique works – paintings, prints, photos, ceramics and more.

Arctic Travelers Gift Shop: This family-owned shop stocks a wide variety of souvenirs: artwork, mugs, jewelry, clothing and knives (like eco ivory ulus).

Big Ray's: One-stop shop for fishing rods, winter jackets, sleeping bags and hiking boots.

Great Alaskan Bowl Company: Peruse finely crafted wooden bowls and Alaska-made souvenirs.

5.5-mile journey from your starting point, which takes two to three hours on average *(single/double kayak $60/80)*. Afterwards, they'll give you a ride to your starting point. For a longer outing, with a greater chance to see moose and other wildlife, paddle the Scenic Lower Chena route *(single/double kayak $100/130)*. Canoe Alaska will shuttle you to the starting point upriver near the Nordale Rd in the North Pole; from there, it'll take you four to six hours to make the 17-mile journey back to Pioneer Park, where you'll finish. You'll need to reserve this one at least 24 hours in advance.

Fairbanks' Finest Museum

Indigenous artifacts and cutting-edge installations

As the largest city in the Interior and northern regions of Alaska, Fairbanks is also home to the first official University of Alaska campus, providing professional, technical and science-based learning for students from all over the world, including those interested in climate change and Arctic research. Make your first stop the **University of Alaska Museum of the North** *(uaf.edu/museum; adult/child $22/16)*, a glimmering white architectural jewel set high on a hill overlooking the Tanana Valley. Here, Alaska's natural and cultural history comes to life with outstanding, interactive

EATING IN FAIRBANKS: OUR PICKS

Alaska Salmon Bake: In Pioneer Park, this casual indoor–outdoor eatery serves grilled wild Alaska salmon and all the fixings. There's also crab, halibut and prime rib. *5-9pm* $$

Pump House: Historic gold rush–era furnishings, outdoor dining and great food make this a popular spot along the Chena River. *4-10pm daily, plus 10am-2pm Sun* $$$

Soba: An atmospheric Moldovan restaurant serving hearty *pelmeni* (dumplings), *mamaliga* (polenta with stewed pork) and other delicacies. *11am-8pm Sun-Thu, 11am-10pm Fri & Sat* $$

Jazz Bistro on 4th: Reserve ahead for this intimate spot with beautifully prepared Cuban and Latin American dishes and live jazz. *6-11pm Mon-Sat* $$$

University of Alaska Museum of the North

exhibits. Start off on the main level exploring the Gallery of Alaska, which covers Indigenous heritage by region and features beautifully crafted clothing, masks, basketry and carvings, along with wildlife (taxidermy) like musk oxen, polar bears and rare birds. Short films show Yup'ik dancing, whale hunting and key events from the past – like the horrific Aleut evacuation during WWII.

On the upper level, you can wander amid some of the museum's artistic treasures like the tiny ivory carving known as the Okvik Madonna, an exquisite work from Punuk Island created around 2000 years ago. There are also landscape paintings of Denali and thought-provoking contemporary works like the Great Alaska Outhouse Experience that visitors are encouraged to enter and sit within. The 2nd floor is also home to the awe-inspiring 'Place Where You Go to Listen,' a soundscape emanating from Earth's magnetic forces, including the aurora borealis.

Stroll Among the Peonies
Botanical blooms and events

You'll earn serious bragging rights – and see some spectacular blooms – by visiting the **Georgeson Botanical Garden**

BASEBALL AT MIDNIGHT

The lights above the field at **Growden Memorial Ballpark** haven't worked in more than 20 years, but no one really cares. Illumination has never been needed for games during Fairbanks' seemingly endless summer nights, particularly on June 20 or 21 when the Alaska Goldpanners host their historic summer solstice game. What started as a challenge between two local bars back in 1906 has morphed into one of the state's best loved baseball games, with teams made up of summer collegiate players. The game starts at 10pm and lasts until just past 1am. The best part of the night happens around midnight when the game is briefly halted, and fans and players alike join in a rousing rendition of the 'Alaska Flag Song'.

DRINKING IN FAIRBANKS: OUR PICKS

HooDoo: Sip German-style gose, Brut IPA and other creative brews in the taproom or by the fire pits in the spacious biergarten. *3-8pm Tue & Wed, from 11am Thu-Sun*

Lavelle's Taphouse: Buzzing space in the heart of downtown with around three dozen beers on tap. *3-11pm Mon-Fri, 11am-midnight Sat, 8.30am-10pm Sun*

Latitude 65: Near downtown, this spacious brewery has an array of well-balanced beers and ciders, plus a food truck with excellent barbecue. *noon-9pm Mon-Sat, until 8pm Sun*

Midnite Mine: One of Fairbanks' best-loved downtown dives, with a pool table, a rock and country soundtrack, and outdoor seating. *10am-2am Mon-Sat, from 1pm Sun*

EQUINOX MARATHON

Known as one of the toughest trail runs in Alaska, the Equinox Marathon has taken place since 1963 by intrepid Nordic ski coaches at the University of Alaska Fairbanks as a way to inspire athletes to get moving on their fall dryland training. The 26.2-mile race is now an autumnal equinox cornerstone of runner life in the Interior, with hundreds participating in the full, half or hiker categories, testing their mettle against steep altitude changes as the course winds up and around Ester Dome and back up and down again before finishing at the UAF campus. Don't want to race? Hike along the beautiful Equinox Marathon trail system and cheer on these hardy souls who have raced in rain, sun and snow over the event's 60-year history.

Sandhill cranes, Creamer's Field Migratory Waterfowl Refuge

(uaf.edu/afes/places/gbg; suggested donation $8), the northernmost botanical gardens in North America. Stretching across 8 acres, the gardens are famous for their enormous and varied peonies, which bloom in June and July. There are also loads of wildflowers, a food garden, and the Babula Children's Garden: kids will enjoy getting lost in the hedge maze or splashing about in the water garden and flume. Keep an eye out for butterflies, native songbirds and migratory birds.

As part of the University of Alaska, the gardens are also used in research. It's a pleasant stroll from the nearby Museum of the North.

If you're around on a Thursday, don't miss Music in the Garden, a free, family-friendly event featuring live jazz, blues, folk and world-music bands. Two different groups play (at 6pm and 7.30pm) from late May to mid-August.

Close Encounters with Musk Ox and Reindeer

Tour the LARS

If you can't make a trip to the Arctic for a little wildlife observation, consider visiting a research station at the university where you can see musk oxen, reindeer and even wood bison. The **Large Animal Research Station** *(LARS; uaf.edu/lars; tour adult/child $20/15)* is a 134-acre facility on the University of Alaska Fairbanks campus dedicated to the study of ungulate (hooved) animals and their adaptations to northern environments. Viewing areas outside the fenced pastures allow a free look at the herds any time, but for deeper insight into these creatures, book a spot on the public tour. These happen at 10am, noon and 2pm from Tuesday to Sunday. Purchase tickets in advance (they sell out) from the LARS Gift Shop, which opens at 9.30am.

Admire Alaskan Autos
Early-20th-century beauties
In a state with so few highways, the **Fountainhead Museum** *(fountainheadmuseum.com; adult/child $20/10)* is a surprisingly comprehensive collection of over 80 working antique vehicles, highlighting the evolution of the automobile from the late 19th century, as well as motor-vehicle history in Alaska. There are plenty of rarities, including 10 automobiles that are the only ones of their kind. Check curiosities, like the fully electric Columbia Mark XIX Surry from 1903 or the 1905 Sheldon, the very first car manufactured in Alaska. Mannequins wearing striking clothing from the 1860s through the 1930s help set the mood, and show that cutting-edge designs weren't limited to vehicles. In 2026, the museum merged with the Pioneer Air Museum, adding more than 50 vintage airplanes to the Fountainhead collection in a sprawling 90,000-sq-ft space 1 mile west of Pioneer Park.

Spot Migratory Birds in a Wildlife Sanctuary
Birds and walking paths
Creamer's Field Migratory Waterfowl Refuge *(friendsofcreamersfield.org; free)* is a former dairy transformed into a 2200-acre refuge. Walking paths, ranging in length from a quarter-mile (Chickadee Loop Trail) to 2 miles (Boreal Forest Trail) wind through meadows, wetlands and woodlands, with interpretive signage in each. The Farmhouse Visitor Center has a few displays on the birds and the dairy's history, and you can also borrow binoculars if you don't have a pair.

Come in late summer to see the avian stars of Creamer's Field: the sandhill cranes. Standing 3ft tall, with a wingspan of over 6ft, these are among the largest migratory birds to pass through Alaska. The annual Tanana Valley Sandhill Crane Festival, held over a week in mid-August, celebrates these leggy birds' return with nature walks, guided wildlife-watching, photography workshops and more.

Other activities happen throughout the year: winter track walks (February), spring migration celebration (April) and holiday craft nights (December), plus naturalist-led wildlife-watching walks three times a week in the summer. During the winter, staff groom trails for excellent Nordic skiing or walking.

Walk or Run the Trails of Wedgewood
Forest and lake views
For walkers and hikers, the **Wedgewood Wildlife Sanctuary** *(free)* offers accessible trails (from half a mile to 1.4 miles) that meander through 75 acres of spruce forests and along Wander Lake, where beaver families are often seen splashing around and hauling birch branches to build dams. Color-coded, well-marked rails are dotted with benches, a couple of overlooks and interpretive signs to add context to the natural environment. You can even connect by trail

OFFBEAT ADVENTURES FROM FAIRBANKS

Go Dogsledding:
Take a husky-powered adventure in summer (by wheeled cart) or winter (sled) with **Black Spruce Dog Sledding**.

Pan for Gold:
On a two-hour tour at **Gold Dredge 8**, you'll learn about the history of mining, ride a replica railroad and try your hand at gold panning.

Cross the Arctic Circle:
Make the 200-mile journey north to the Arctic Circle by plane or van, including the reputable **Northern Alaska Tour Company**.

Walk with Reindeer:
At **Running Reindeer Ranch**, you can go for a walk with reindeer through the boreal forest.

Go Fishing:
Alaska Fishing and Rafting Adventures leads scenic trips along the Chena River to fish for trophy Arctic grayling and other species.

A SECRET SCENIC DRIVE

KattiJo Deeter, professional dog musher, Iditarod finisher and kennel owner at Black Spruce Dog Sledding @*blacksprucedogsledding*

One of the best-kept secrets in the Fairbanks area is the drive east of town on the Steese Hwy that takes you over Cleary Summit, and then Twelvemile Summit and Eagle Summit. Keep going and you'll eventually reach the towns of Central and Circle, a Native community with a bar, restaurant and rooms for the night. Circle is around 150 miles from Fairbanks, but the drive is spectacular because you get above the tree line and you get into a lot of fire-burned areas as well. You'll see mountaintops and snowy peaks, which just seem to go on forever.

Beaver

to the Creamer's Field Migratory Waterfowl Refuge, so you can easily up the mileage if you wish. There's ample (free) parking in the adjoining Wedgewood Resort.

Ride the Riverboat Discovery
Steamboat excursion on the Chena

One of Fairbanks' most memorable journeys is the ride aboard the **Riverboat Discovery** *(riverboatdiscovery.com; adult/child $95/55)*. The three-hour tour navigates the Chena River on a historic stern-wheeler, stopping at a replica Athabascan village as well as the riverfront home and kennels of the late Susan Butcher, four-time winner of the Iditarod sled-dog race. You'll also see a bush pilot take off and land next to the boat, and the pilot will share the vital role these planes played in accessing remote parts of Alaska. The boat leaves from Steamboat Landing, a craft-filled store and replica trading post on the west side of town.

DRIVE THE DALTON HIGHWAY

Fairbanks is the best place to rent a vehicle and procure essential supplies for a journey along one of Alaska's most famous roads (p383 has complete details). Stop in the **Alaska Public Lands Information Center** (p41) for road conditions.

Beyond Fairbanks

Experience the Interior's wild beauty at Chena Hot Springs or the Delta Junction area. You'll also find Santa and reindeer in the North Pole.

The settlements within a 100-mile drive of Fairbanks offer a glimpse of what it's like to live, work and play in rural Alaska without needing to venture too far beyond the city. Many families commute to Fairbanks for school, medical appointments and even jobs, preferring to live a remote lifestyle with access to a larger city within an hour's drive.

You'll quickly find yourself in the wilderness as soon as you leave the city limits. This is the place for memorable experiences you won't find in other parts of Alaska. You can visit the land of Santa in the North Pole, explore a historic roadhouse complex in Big Delta and soak in steaming hot springs in Chena, which also makes an ideal spot for watching the northern lights.

Places
North Pole p327
Chena Hot Springs p328
Big Delta p328
Delta Junction p329

North Pole
TIME FROM FAIRBANKS: **20 MINS**

Visit Santa's realm
For legions of children around the world, the North Pole is a mystical, magical place where snow falls year-round and tiny elves work day and night for the man in red – Santa Claus. And in North Pole, Alaska, you can imagine you're actually there. Aside from street names like Kris Kringle Dr and Mistletoe Ln, North Pole has a number of activities centered around the Christmas holiday. Check out the **Santa Claus House** *(santaclaushouse.com; free)* the cornerstone business for all things Santa. You can pay Santa a visit, purchase holiday-themed gifts and decorations, and peer in the windows of his old-fashioned workshop (elves not included).

Feed reindeer
A short stroll from the Santa Claus House, you can pay a visit to the **Antler Academy** *(santaclaushouse.com/reindeer.asp; tour adult/child $8/6)*, where a group of reindeer live. On a short tour, the reindeer handlers will take you into each of the two pens and tell you all about the herd (there are usually eight reindeer here), while you feed the reindeer from small cups full of pellets. Tours happen every half-hour from 11am to 6.30pm.

GETTING AROUND

If you don't have a vehicle, the MACS bus system does a decent job of moving people around Fairbanks and the North Pole area on weekdays – there's no weekend service. A one-way ticket costs $1.50 *(day pass $3)*. If you don't have a car and want to visit the area's prime attraction, Chena Hot Springs Resort offers transportation *(one-way $90)*, which you can book on the resort's website *(chenahotsprings.com/chena-shuttle)*.

GET A LETTER FROM SANTA

It's been a Christmas tradition since 1952, with millions of recipients around the globe receiving a letter from Santa. Real letters printed on Santa's iconic stationery – and postmarked of course from the North Pole – can be ordered from the Santa Claus House *(santaclaus house.com/ santalettercombo. asp)*. There are many options, including a classic letter along with a deed to 1-sq-in of Santa's kingdom ('a toehold in the North Pole'). Kids aren't the only ones who can get in on the action. You can also order letters for newly married couples, pets, recent graduates and not-so-good adults. Kids can and do write back at the North Pole address. The best letters get displayed on the letter walls toward the front of the store.

Chena Hot Springs
TIME FROM FAIRBANKS: 1¼ HRS

Myriad activities and steaming pools

One of Fairbanks' best-known getaways is the **Chena Hot Springs Resort** *(chenahotsprings.com)*, which is open all year long. There's much to do here, with hiking trails and an activity desk where you can rent bikes or canoes, take an ATV tour, go dog-sledding or hop in the saddle for a horseback ride. There's also an ice museum and a geothermal greenhouse.

Whether you get active or not, you won't want to miss a soak in the steaming **mineral pools** *(adult/child $20/17)*. Visitors have been drawn to these relaxing waters ever since two gold miners stumbled across the springs in 1905. The indoor pool and hot tubs are for all ages. The outdoor pool (known as the hot springs lake) boasts fine views of forested slopes, and it is for adults only (age 18 and up). The pool complex stays open from 7am to 11:45pm. Towels are available for rent *($5)*.

Extend your stay by booking a cabin, yurt or traditional hotel room; you can also pitch a tent in the campground (p341).

Between late August and early April, when night skies darken, aurora viewers head to Chena Hot Springs for its wide open spaces and absence of artificial lighting to view the glorious northern lights.

Big Delta
TIME FROM FAIRBANKS: 1½ HRS

Explore a historic roadhouse property

The **Big Delta State Historical Park** *(self-pay admission $5)* contains an array of beautifully preserved buildings from the early 1900s spread across a 10-acre property – a former roadhouse and homestead – abutting the riverside. You could spend an hour or two on a self-guided walk, peeking inside the wooden cabins and learning about the past through the exhibitions and displays within them. A short stroll from the parking lot, Rika's Roadhouse is named after Rika Wallen, a hardworking Swedish woman who ran the roadhouse from 1917 until the mid-1940s. She kept it open year-round, grew vegetables and fruit, and raised livestock, which allowed her to serve fresh farm-sourced meals to travelers passing through. Inside the roadhouse, old photos, vintage furnishings and a pot-bellied stove give a glimpse of living conditions at the time. Rika's grave is also on the property.

Other buildings of interest include an old telegraph station used by the US army during WWII, a sod-roofed cabin full of furs and old mining equipment, a Swedish-style barn (Rika's) of old sleighs and riding tack, the remnants of Rika's garden, and a weather-beaten 30ft boat once used on

Chena Hot Springs

the local waterway. Nearby, ferry scales and old photos attest to the rustic method of crossing the river before the bridge was built.

Delta Junction
TIME FROM FAIRBANKS: 1¾ HRS

Insight into early-20th-century travel

Near the intersection of the Alaska–Canada Hwy (aka the Alcan) with the Richardson Hwy, you'll find a quaint vestige from the early 20th century. The **Sullivan Roadhouse** *(free)* is another classic log structure that was built in 1906 to serve travelers along the Valdez–Fairbanks Trail. In 1997 the cabin was moved, log by log, from Fort Greely to its present location and now serves as a museum with a collection of exhibits dedicated to travel in Alaska in the early 1900s – the roadhouse era. The multi-room cabin gives lots of insight into road travel in those days – don't miss the Yukon barrel stove (an improvised heater made from a 100-gallon fuel barrel) that served as a drying spot (for wet wintery clothes worn by travelers), room heater and hot plate for warming irons and tea kettles.

Next door, you can grab a bite at the old-school **Buffalo Center Drive-In** *(facebook.com/buffalocenterdrivein)*, a takeaway spot with picnic tables where you can enjoy the best burgers for miles around.

BIRTH OF THE ALASKAN ROADHOUSE

When the gold rushes of the early 1900s brought thousands of eager prospectors to Alaska, the Valdez–Fairbanks Trail became the primary route to claims in the Interior. Hacked into the rocky surfaces of the Chugach mountain range, the trail was first meant for horses and pack mules, but later evolved into a winter road, and then one for automobiles when motorized transport became popular.

To meet a demand for accommodations and food along the way, roadhouses cropped up at regular intervals along the trail (now the Richardson Hwy). Known for plentiful meals and warm places to spend the night, roadhouses were a hub of communication and commerce, and served as the seat of a town's structure, as can be seen at Big Delta.

Tok & the Taylor Highway

REMOTE WILDERNESS | SCENIC DRIVES | GOLD PANNING

GETTING AROUND

Tok is a trade and service center for those making the long trek to or from destinations around the Interior, especially via the Alaska–Canada Hwy, known as the Alcan. Tok is a true highway town, so the most obvious form of transportation here is the automobile. That said, 40-Mile Air *(40-mileair.com)* does offer a charter service between Tok, Delta Junction (p329) and Fairbanks (p316).

You'll need a sturdy vehicle to drive the Taylor Hwy toward Chicken or Eagle. Most rental agencies prohibit driving this road. Instead, rent a 4WD or truck from a specialty outfitter like Alaska 4X4 Rentals *(alaska4x4rentals.com)* or Go North *(gonorth-alaska.com)*.

Near the intersection of three important highways, Tok (rhymes with 'soak') began as a camp for construction crews working on the Alaska–Canada Hwy in 1942. The road was built shortly after the US entered WWII to ensure an overland route for supplies and personnel to reach bases in Fairbanks and Anchorage. Tok is part of the ancestral lands of the Upper Tanana Athabascans, and tribal influence is felt across the community.

Some 12 miles east of Tok lies the Taylor Hwy, a mostly unpaved mountain road that winds its way into a far northeastern corner of Alaska known locally as 'Fortymile.' Driving the challenging wilderness road is an adventure in its own right, though it's also worth stopping in the tiny towns of Chicken and Eagle. Both have deep roots in Alaska's early gold mining, and still draw summertime gold miners and those seeking to get away from civilization. The history and personalities are worth the effort to get there.

Fishing or Floating in Tok
Cast a line or pick up a paddle

Tok is blessed with an abundance of lakes and rivers, so anglers will find plenty of places to fish for rainbow trout, burbot, grayling and pike. Check in with **Tok Visitors Center** (also the Public Lands Information Center) for tips and current conditions.

Try **Four-Mile Lake** (off Taylor Hwy, Mile 4.1), **Hidden Lake** (Alaska Hwy Mile 1240) and **Jan Lake** (Alaska Hwy Mile 1354) for flat-water fishing, and **Tok River Overflow** (Glenn Hwy/Tok Cutoff Mile 104.5) or **Little Tok River** (Glenn/Tok Cutoff Mile 98.2) for some excellent fly-fishing for rainbows. Make sure to have an Alaska fishing license on your person, bear spray, insect repellent, and clothing suited for the conditions.

Many people like to combine fishing with paddling on the lakes around Tok, and rental outlets for canoes, kayaks and

TOK & THE TAYLOR HIGHWAY

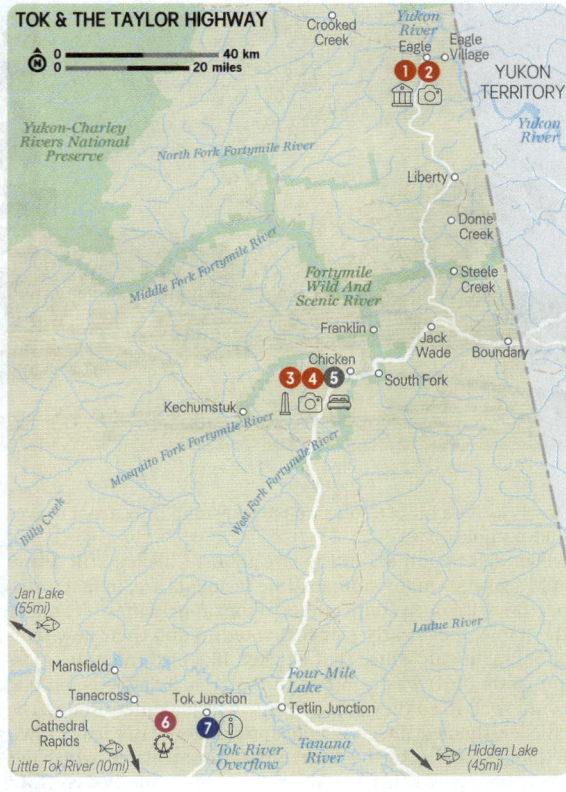

- **SIGHTS**
- 1 Eagle Courthouse
- 2 Fort Egbert
- 3 giant chicken sculpture
- 4 Pedro Gold Dredge
- **SLEEPING**
- 5 Chicken Gold Camp & Outpost
- **ENTERTAINMENT**
- 6 Mukluk Land
- **INFORMATION**
- 7 Tok Visitors Center

rafts may be found in both Fairbanks and Anchorage with **Alaska Outdoor Gear Rentals** (p302).

Oddball Alaskan Landmark
Surreal theme park

For a unique Tok experience, stop by **Mukluk Land** *(mukluk land.com; 1-5pm Tue-Sun)*, billed as 'Alaska's most unique museum.' Established in the 1980s to give road-weary travelers (and parents of bored kids) a place to stretch their legs and learn about Interior Alaska, Mukluk Land has vintage games like Skeeball, a bouncy castle, antique machines used during the building of the Alaska Hwy, a gold-panning exhibit and a big playground full of head-scratchers like 'Santa's Rocket Ship.'

Exploring Chicken
Gold-mining lore

Load up on supplies (fuel, snacks, water and cash) in Tok, then hit the road. From Tetlin Junction (12 miles east of Tok), turn left onto the Taylor Hwy. From here, it's another 65 miles to Chicken along a mostly paved road, but take things

☑ TOP TIP

Looking to see the towering mountains from above? Try Tok Air Service *(tokairservice.com)* for a flightseeing or hiking adventure and experience this remote piece of Alaska in a different way.

THE ALCAN HIGHWAY

One of the great engineering feats of the 20th century, the Alcan, short for 'Alaska–Canada Hwy,' stretches 1387 miles from Dawson Creek in British Columbia to Delta Junction in Alaska. The highway was famously punched through the wilderness in a mere eight months in 1942, as part of a WWII effort to protect Alaska from expansionist Japan. Over 10,000 soldiers, including 4000 Black troops from the Deep South, labored in harsh conditions – swarms of summer mosquitoes, bitter winter cold, swamps and mountains of mud. It remains the only year-round overland route that links Alaska to the Lower 48. Drivers planning a trip should check out **The Milepost** *(themilepost.com)*, the quintessential print (or digital) reference to have along the way.

slowly as it's a bit of a roller coaster of small hills, frost heaves and potholes.

Founded by miners in the late 1800s, Chicken still draws gold seekers – many summertime residents are, in fact, prospectors with deep connections to the off-grid lifestyle. As for the name, those early pioneers voted to dub their new tent-city 'Ptarmigan,' since that chicken-like bird (now the Alaskan state bird) was rampant in the area. Trouble is, no-one could spell it, so they opted for its near lookalike. Today, the chicken-themed kitsch is widespread. You can't leave town without stopping by the **giant chicken sculpture**, which lies near the town's other important landmark, the **Pedro Gold Dredge**. Operating from 1938 to 1967, this massive dredge – now a national historic site – mined over 50,000oz of gold over the years. You can wander around the old machinery, which functions as an outdoor museum of sorts.

The main nexus of town is the **Chicken Gold Camp & Outpost** *(chickengold.com)*, which has an RV park, campground, cabins, cafe and gift shop, along with various activities for visitors. You can try your hand at gold panning *(per day $25)*, for which you'll probably need to rent shovels, buckets and other equipment *(from $17)*, and get a lift to the site on Myers Fork Creek 2 miles away *($14 return)*. With a bit of hard work (and luck), you might find small gold nuggets and/or fine specimens of opal, amethyst, jasper and petrified wood.

Party at Chickenstock

The town's big music fest

Plan your visit for the second weekend in June when hundreds come to the tiny town for **Chickenstock** *(chickenstock musicfest.com)*, an annual celebration of music, dancing and Alaska-style fun. Held at the Chicken Gold Camp & Outpost

Chicken Gold Camp & Outpost

over two days, this wild clucking time features music genres of all types, and dressing up is encouraged. This event sells out quickly every year, as do campsites and rooms across the town.

Tracing the Past in Eagle
Settlement on the edge of wilderness

It's just over 92 miles from Chicken to Eagle where the Taylor Hwy comes to an abrupt end. The going is much rougher on this stretch, as the 'highway' is mostly unpaved and quite narrow in places (not recommended for RVs), with steep, sharp curves and no shoulders. Be prepared: there's no cell service – and some overlanders recommend having two spare, full-sized tires and/or a tire plug repair kit to avoid getting stranded. As you snake up through the mountains past dramatic vistas, you'll need to slow way down on those hairpin curves – watch out for rocks (and rockslides), massive potholes and long stretches of washboards. You'll need 3.5 hours or more to complete the journey.

After so much driving through wilderness, reaching the town of Eagle feels like a surprise. One of the better-preserved towns from the gold-rush era, Eagle sits along the mighty Yukon River, once a major port for steamships ferrying people and supplies to the far northern reaches of the territories. Today you can spend a few hours exploring the town and its quiet streets, many of which are part of the Eagle Historic District. Don't miss the **Eagle Courthouse** or the three buildings of **Fort Egbert**, a restored military post from the late 1800s and early 1900s.

THE NORTHERN LIGHTS

One of the most compelling reasons to visit Interior Alaska during the winter is a chance to gaze into the heavens at the aurora borealis, or northern lights. Visible when solar storms send highly charged proton and electron particles toward Earth's gaseous atmosphere for a glorious collision of green, red and occasionally violet, the northern lights are creations of ancient lore and present-day scientific wonder.

A possibility between September and April, the aurora is a spectacle that often, but not always, appears in the northern sky, and the further north you get, the brighter the show. In Fairbanks, the winter tourism boom has much to do with aurora tours taking visitors to the outskirts of town and further afield.

Wrangell-St Elias National Park & Preserve

GLACIERS | HIKING | MINING HISTORY

Stretching across some 13 million acres, America's largest national park is a land of towering peaks, braided rivers and myriad glaciers – over 3000 at last count. The stats are incredible: Wrangell-St Elias is larger than Switzerland, with taller mountains, but far more difficult to access. Only two roads lead into this remote preserve: both are rugged routes that quickly immerse you in the wilderness. Near the road's end, the tiny town of McCarthy is the only settlement in the park, and it hums with activity in the summer as visitors arrive for glacier hikes, white-water rafting, scenic flights and trekking. In the winter, the town goes into hibernation.

A short distance from McCarthy, Kennicott (also spelled Kennecott) preserves the history of a once bustling mining town, with its 19th-century structures now serving as an open-air museum maintained by the national park. Kennicott is also the starting point for walks on Root Glacier and challenging hikes to mountain overlooks.

Wander an Old Mining Town
Architecture and exhibits

Surprising for the well-preserved architecture in a remote location, the former industrial town of Kennecott Mines is an extraordinary example of 20th-century industry and technology. After arriving from McCarthy, get your bearings at the National Park–run **Kennecott Visitor Center**. You can pick up maps, get info on trails and catch free ranger talks hosted several times a day.

Next, hit the dusty lane through town. You may feel as though you've slipped back to the 1900s as you wander past the old schoolhouse, recreation hall and train depot. Various buildings

GETTING AROUND

If you're not driving the McCarthy Rd (p338), you can take a **Wrangell Mountain Air** flight from Chitina *(one-way $215)* or book the **Kennicott Shuttle** *(one-way/return $109/169)* from Glenallen. For drivers, the road ends at the Kennicott River. Pay for parking in one of the lots *(per day $12)*, cross the pedestrian bridge, and walk (0.75 miles) or take the free shuttle to McCarthy. From there, **Copper Town Shuttles** run at least hourly between McCarthy and Kennicott *(one-day/multiday pass $15/20)*. You can also walk the 4-mile route (take the forested Wagon Rd Trail parallel to the road), but it's not very scenic.

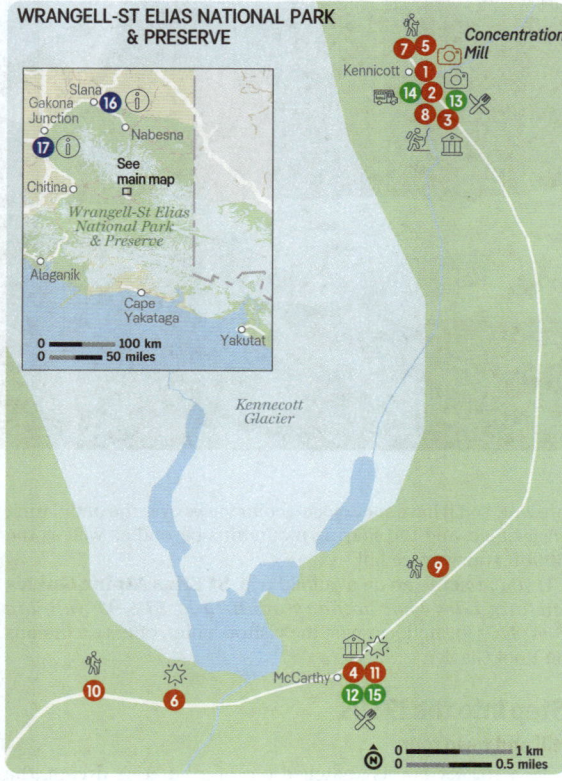

WRANGELL-ST ELIAS NATIONAL PARK & PRESERVE

⭐ HIGHLIGHTS
1 Concentration Mill

● SIGHTS
2 Kennecott General Store
3 Kennecott Visitor Center
4 McCarthy-Kennicott Historical Museum

● ACTIVITIES
5 Bonanza Mine Trail
6 McCarthy River Tours
7 Root Glacier Trail
8 St Elias Alpine Guides
9 Toe of the Kennicott Glacier Trail
10 West Glacier Trail
11 Wrangell Mountain Air

● EATING
12 Golden Saloon
13 Kennicott Glacier Lodge
14 Meatza Wagon
15 Potato (The)

● INFORMATION
16 Slana Ranger Station
17 Wrangell-St Elias Visitor Center

are open to the public and packed with curios from the past. Don't miss the Historic Post Office, with old photos showing what life was like for workers and their family members. There are also several films you can watch, covering the inner workings of the mill and the vast natural wonders of the national park. Next door, you can peer at the shelves of display items at the **Kennecott General Store**. Take a peek at the inventory list, describing the goods for sale, with their original price (highly elevated given the distance to ship these items) and their cost in today's dollars – a case of lemons for $12.60 in 1917 would cost over $215 today.

Walk Across a Glacier
Views from the ice

Wrangell-St Elias National Park is home to an astonishing 3121 glaciers. Among the easiest to reach is Root Glacier, accessible by hiking 2 miles from the mill-town site along the well-marked **Root Glacier Trail**. From there, you can strap on crampons and tighten your grip on your hiking poles (both recommended) and step out upon the creaking ice surface. As you go, avoid walking on the edge of the glacier, where rotting ice can be

☑ TOP TIP
The national park has several info points, including the excellent **Wrangell-St Elias Visitor Center** off the Richardson Hwy, which has exhibits, nature films and short trails. The **Slana Ranger Station** is gateway to the little-visited northern section, accessed via the Nabesna Rd, which is dotted with hiking trails and primitive camping spots.

BEST ADVENTURES IN THE NATIONAL PARK

McCarthy River Tours: Offers everything from easygoing four-hour excursions on the Kennicott River to seven-day white-water adventures through the Chugach Mountains.

Wrangell Mountain Air: Fly past soaring mountain peaks on a spectacular scenic flight. Can also drop you into remote corners of the national park for a backpacking adventure.

St Elias Alpine Guides: Apart from glacier excursions, this outfitter offers alpine hikes, ice climbing, rafting and fly-in paddling trips.

Bonanza Mine Trail: It's a challenging but rewarding 9-mile round-trip hike from Kennicott up past abandoned mines to staggering views on clear days.

West Glacier Trail: An easygoing 2-mile out-and-back trail through forest and out to the edge of the Kennicott Glacier.

present. You'll have some spectacular views over the undulating river of ice, and the soaring mountains beyond as well as the 6000ft stairway ice fall.

If you prefer to go on a guided trip, **St Elias Alpine Guides** *(steliasguides.com; half-day adult/child $115/95, full-day $160/140)*, located just past the visitor center, offers excursions on Root Glacier.

Step into the 1930s

Mill and town tour

Like a rickety fantasy hatched out of a lunatic's dream, the **Concentration Mill** is a soaring 14-story building that once processed the copper mined out of the surrounding mountains. You can only enter via two-hour tours led by **St Elias Alpine Guides**, but this is highly recommended for a chance to peak into a truly surreal tableau of 20th-century mining equipment. The tour through the building is preceded by a historically minded walk through town, where your guide will point out key buildings of interest and describe the life of the workers, bosses and families during the heyday of mining operations. You'll then ascend to the top of the Concentration Mill, don your hard hat and work your way through the building past chutes, gears and massive machinery, while getting an idea of the harsh reality of working here.

Meet the Locals in McCarthy

Fascinating frontier town

Once the red-light district and drinking strip for bored miners bivouacked at the 'dry' mining town of Kennecott, McCarthy today is one of Alaska's most colorful little frontier towns. A muddy assortment of unnamed streets are dotted with a hodgepodge of eateries, guesthouses, dwellings and a single

Root Glacier Trail (p335)

convenience store. It's home to a handful of year-round local residents and dozens of seasonal workers from around the globe all drawn to the beauty of the awe-inspiring wilderness surrounding the town. You can get a dose of local history at the **McCarthy-Kennicott Historical Museum** *(mccarthy kennicotthistoricalmuseum.com; free)*. Set in the old railroad depot, the small collection contains historical photographs, mining artifacts and a model of McCarthy in its heyday.

Hike to the Toe of the Glacier

Easy trail from McCarthy

One of the best short hikes you can do in the region is to walk out to the terminal point or **'toe' of the Kennicott Glacier Trail**. To get there from McCarthy, follow the wagon road, which runs parallel to the main road, toward Kennicott. After three-quarters of a mile, take the forked path off to the left. You'll pass through forest and soon reach an open expanse that leads down to mounds of glacial silt and melt pools, sometimes dotted with small icebergs. You can explore to your heart's content here; just be bear-aware, and be mindful not to step on any of the vegetation – the dandelion-like dryas plants are particularly delicate. It's a level, easy path, around 3 miles round trip from McCarthy.

LIFE IN REMOTE ALASKA

Brandon Roos, horseback riding guide, shares insight into living in the remote Interior. @bdangerroos

McCarthy is a small town and tightly woven community. People look out for one another and enjoy meeting new people. There's just one bar in McCarthy, but it's always a lively gathering spot – even on Monday night. There are 30 or so year-round residents, who stock up before winter. Once the heavy snows arrive, the only way out is by snow machine – or you can take your chances on the road. You have to be resourceful to live out here. A friend described how a serpentine belt on his truck broke down, but he managed to craft an alternate part out of dog leashes lashed together.

 EATING & DRINKING IN MCCARTHY-KENNECOTT: OUR PICKS

Meatza Wagon: The Kennecott food truck has delicious fish tacos and a signature meatball sub sandwich, with tables overlooking the glacier. *11am-5pm Tue-Thu, 11am-7pm Fri-Sun* $$

Kennicott Glacier Lodge: Casual lunches or set-price multicourse dinners (reservations required) in the welcoming dining room or out on the balcony. *7am-8pm* $$$

Potato (The): McCarthy's best-loved restaurant is a buzzing spot for burritos, bangers and mash, lentil and spinach falafel, and their famous rosemary garlic fries. *8am-9pm Tue-Sun* $$

Golden Saloon: A buzzing McCarthy nightspot with a meaty menu (barbecue, burgers), craft beer and a weekly lineup of open-mic, trivia and live music. *noon-midnight* $$

DRIVE TOUR

Motor the McCarthy Road

Today's McCarthy Rd is yesterday's railbed of the Copper River and Northwestern Railway. This 60-mile road from Chitina to McCarthy offers spectacular views of the Chugach Mountains and the rushing Copper River. The road is rough but passable for most vehicles. However, traditional rental agencies prohibit travel on this road, so consider renting from a specialty outfit like Alaska 4X4 Rentals *(alaska4x4rentals.com)* or Go North *(gonorth-alaska.com).* Allow three hours.

❶ Chitina
Small town Chitina, on Copper River's banks, is a former stage-line terminus for workers living at Kennecott Mine or McCarthy. The train passage ended in 1938, but the line wasn't transformed into a road until 1971. Road conditions are better than in the past, but be wary of potholes, washouts and tire-shredding railroad ties that occasionally resurface. There are no services from Chitina to McCarthy, so food, water and a spare tire (with tools) are essential.

The Drive: See the confluence of the mighty Chitina and Copper rivers as you cross Copper River bridge and pavement becomes gravel. At Mile 1.6 turn into the parking area.

❷ Copper River
Fishing for sockeye and chinook salmon in Copper River is popular and families from the Ahtna tribe have spinning wheels in the silty water to capture their allotment

Kuskulana Bridge

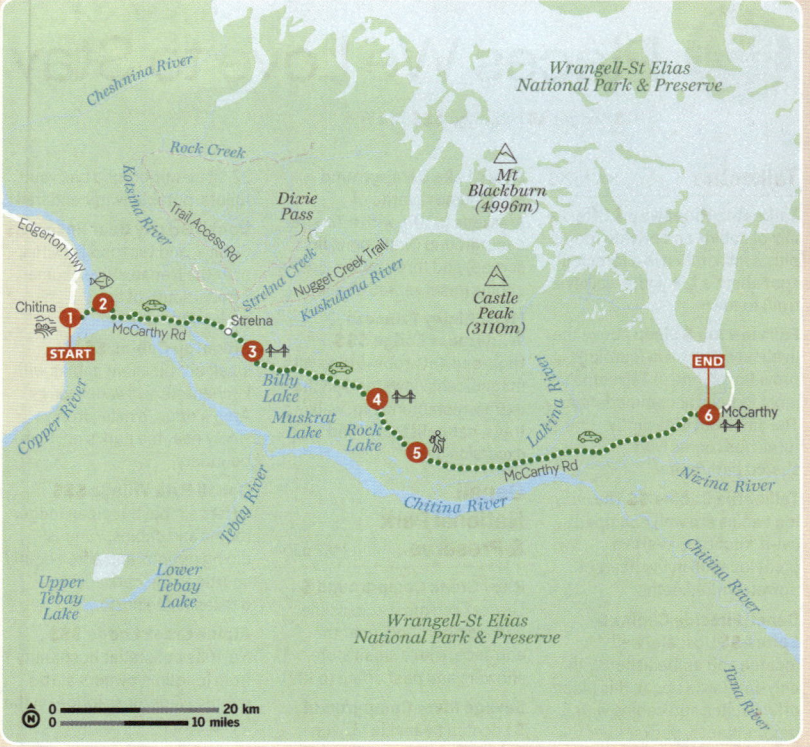

of subsistence fish. On clear days, you can see snowcapped Mt Drum (12,010ft) to the north.

The Drive: Slow down for the dramatic views around Mile 5. Near Mile 15, the road enters a low valley between ridges of gravel (lateral moraines) made by a receding glacier.

3 Kuskulana Bridge

At Mile 17.2, the one-lane Kuskulana Bridge towers above the roadway as a testament to the engineering prowess of 1910. Pull off after crossing the bridge and walk the trail underneath for a better view.

The Drive: Around Mile 20, relatively shallow permafrost means abundant muskeg and swampy lowland. Keep an eye out for browsing moose.

4 Gilahina Trestle

At Mile 29, you'll reach an impressive relic from 1911. The railway once traveled over this wooden trestle, which stretches 890ft long and 90ft high. A short walking trail takes you closer.

The Drive: Keep watch while driving past the hills to your next stop at Mile 34.8. This is a good place to spot Dall sheep.

5 Crystalline Hills

Pull off for a chance to look for wildlife and stretch your legs. The Crystalline Hills trailhead starts a 2.5-mile loop amid lush forests and striking views of the mountain-backed Chitina River valley.

The Drive: At Mile 44.5 you'll cross Lakina River, which is partially fed by melting glacier, before passing Long Lake a mile later.

6 McCarthy Bridge

Around Mile 60, McCarthy Rd ends at the Kennicott River, where a vehicle-free bridge leads you by foot to a free-spirited community (p336). Make the short walk into McCarthy for a meal, live music and local personalities.

Places We Love to Stay

$ Budget $$ Midrange $$$ Top End

Talkeetna
MAP p293

Talkeetna Hideaway $ Offers a mix of cabins and private rooms plus a full kitchen in a forested spot about a 12-minute walk (via trail) to town.

Fairview Inn $ Sleep above the liveliest bar in town (earplugs provided) in one of Talkeetna's most famous accommodations. The small but pleasantly furnished rooms have shared bathrooms.

Talkeetna Cabins $$ The cozy log cabins are well equipped (wi-fi, kitchens, TVs) in a great location in the heart of downtown Talkeetna.

Denali Fireside Cabins & Suites $$ Upscale, well located and embellished with only-in-Alaska decor, this place offers suites and cabins with gas fireplaces, decks and kitchenettes.

Talkeetna Roadhouse $$ The real Alaskan deal, this 1917 roadhouse has an old-time setting with small private rooms, a bunkroom, and several rustic cabins out back.

Talkeetna Alaskan Lodge $$$ Perched on a bluff overlooking town, this enormous high-end lodge has shuttle service, lovely rooms, a restaurant with panoramic views, and top service.

Denali State Park
MAP p301

K'esugi Ken Campground $ Tent and RV sites and two public-use cabins, all bookable online. Great views, especially from walk-in tent sites 1 and 2.

Byers Lake Campground $ Longtime favorite of Alaskans (p301), with a 73-site campground (first come, first served) and three public-use cabins (reserve well ahead).

Mt McKinley Princess Wilderness Lodge $$$ High-end 460-room lodge with magnificent views, and all the extras: restaurant, bar, walking trails, naturalist talks and excursion desk.

Denali National Park & Preserve
MAP p304

Riley Creek Campground $ Largest and most accessible park campground, near the entrance, with a small store, showers and post office (p309).

Savage River Campground $ Located near Mile 13, with excellent access to hiking at Savage River or Mountain Vista areas (p309).

Teklanika River Campground $ Get a taste of remote wilderness at this campground near Mile 29. You need a permit and three-night stay to use your own vehicle. Otherwise use a camp bus.

Camp Denali $$$ A legendary destination near the end of the Park Rd, with 19 attractive timber cabins, and gear for you to go fishing, canoeing or cycling.

Beyond Denali

Brushkana Creek Campground $ Near Mile 105 of the rugged Denali Hwy, this 22-site campground has vault toilets, potable water and trails.

Denali Grizzly Bear Resort $$ Cabins, and tent and RV sites, near the Nenana River, some 8 miles south of the park entrance.

Ridgetop Cabins $$ Six small but pleasant cabins with kitchenette and valley views. Atop a ridge, 6 miles from Healy near the park's northern boundary.

Denali Park Village $$$ Offers simple but clean lodge rooms and cabins, various dining options and a free hourly shuttle to the park entrance 8 miles to the north.

Alpine Creek Lodge $$$ No-frills but stellar hospitality from longtime owners at this remote wilderness lodge on the Denali Hwy.

Fairbanks
MAP p318

Billie's Backpackers Hostel $ A landmark since 1991, with kindhearted hosts, a mix of shared and private rooms, and a homey atmosphere.

Sven's Basecamp Hostel $ Meet adventurous travelers from around the globe at this welcoming spot with cabins, tented bunkrooms, campsites and delightful treehouses.

Bridgewater Hotel $$ The best affordable option in downtown has tidy rooms (with mini fridge, microwave, coffee maker) and free airport or train station transportation.

Pike's Waterfront Lodge $$$
Boasts an enviable river-facing location, with classic rooms (brass lamps, dark wood, satiny bedspreads) and log cabins, plus a billiards table, library and steam room.

Springhill Suites $$$ A northerly branch of the Marriott empire has Zen-like modern rooms and a small indoor pool in a great downtown location.

Wedgewood Resort $$$ A great option for families: each of the suites has a living room, full kitchen and balcony, and walking trails (p325) are nearby.

Beyond Fairbanks

Granite Tors Campground $ One of several campgrounds on the Chena Hot Springs Rd, this one has roomy sites with river access and hiking along a 15-mile loop trail.

Hotel North Pole $$ Boasts 70 modern, well-equipped rooms (microwaves, coffee maker, wi-fi), plus a Santa Suite, with a fitness room, free breakfast and fresh cookies baked daily.

Chena Hot Springs Resort $$ Huge complex with lodge rooms, cabins, yurts, campground and RV park. Loads of activities apart from the famous springs (p328).

Borealis Basecamp $$$ Amid boreal forest some 28 miles north of Fairbanks, stay in igloo-shaped pods with clear ceilings for prime stargazing in the winter.

Tok & the Taylor Highway MAP p331

Young's Motel $$ A Tok institution with good service, reliable wi-fi and Fast Eddy's restaurant. Standard rooms or cabin-style lodgings.

Chicken Gold Camp & Outpost $$ Stay in a cabin (rustic or modernized), pitch a tent or park your RV. Free wi-fi for guests. There's also gold panning and a cafe and restaurant (p332).

Falcon Inn B&B $$ Eagle's best lodging option has a log-cabin lodge with a deck overlooking the river, and a private apartment and river house nearby.

McCarthy-Kennecott MAP p335

Base Camp Kennicott $ Pitch a tent or park your RV at this riverside spot at the end of the McCarthy Rd. Also has tent lodging (BYO sleeping bag).

Ma Johnson's Hotel $$$ Former boarding house with charming, uniquely furnished rooms and antique-filled sitting room full of historical knickknacks.

Kennicott River Lodge & Hostel $$$ Offers a mix of lodge rooms (with shared bathrooms) and dry cabins (no water), in a striking location at the end of the McCarthy Rd.

Kennicott Glacier Lodge $$$ The walls heave with history in this atmospheric lodge with small rooms (some with private bathrooms) and grand views right from the porch.

Pike's Waterfront Lodge

Above: Grizzly bears, Brooks Falls (p358); Right: Salmon fisher, Kodiak (p346)

Researched by
Mara Vorhees

Kodiak & Katmai

BROWN BEARS AND WILDERNESS

Especially famous for wildlife-watching and sportfishing, Kodiak Island and Katmai on the peninsula also show off a surprising history and rich Indigenous culture.

Kodiak Island and Katmai National Park are among Alaska's most storied destinations – wild and pristine, rife with animal life and isolated from much human disruption. Straddling the Shelikof Strait, south of Homer, this region is home to tree-covered mountain peaks, old-growth forests and seemingly endless miles of rugged, untrammeled shoreline. Most intriguing of all, the biggest brown bears on Earth roam this vast swath of wilderness. Watching them gather in numbers to feed at salmon-filled streams is one of the great highlights of a visit to Alaska. Beyond the bears, there is plenty of adventure here – hiking, kayaking and fishing – plus one of Alaska's most welcoming small towns to retreat to at day's end.

Originally called Koniag, the Kodiak Archipelago is the ancestral homeland of the Sugpiaq (or Alutiiq) people. Russian explorers arrived in 1784, establishing their first American settlement here (but not before slaughtering and enslaving thousands of Alaska Native residents). The Russians later used the island as a base to explore the mainland and set up other fur-trading centers. After the transfer to US control, Baptist missionaries arrived to convert and 'civilize' the populace, followed by fisherfolk and naval personnel. Today, the archipelago is a hodgepodge of these peoples and cultures who have met and mingled over the centuries – or not. The wilderness islands are dotted with Alutiiq villages and Russian-speaking outposts, which have persisted thanks to their isolation.

THE MAIN AREAS

KODIAK
Historic town near pristine wilderness. **p346**

KATMAI NATIONAL PARK & PRESERVE
Legendary place for observing brown bears. **p358**

KODIAK & KATMAI | THE GUIDE

Find Your Way

To reach Kodiak Island, there are daily flights from Anchorage and the ferry from Homer. Remote Katmai National Park & Preserve sits on the Alaska Peninsula and is accessible by floatplane.

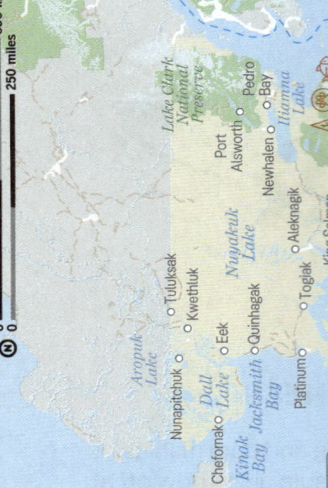

Kodiak, p346
Visit museums full of cultural artifacts, then head out of town to explore rugged shorelines, WWII ruins and bear-stalked streams.

Katmai National Park & Preserve, p358
Stroll from the floatplane to the viewing platform where open-mouth brown bears catch salmon leaping through the river.

CAR
Kodiak Island is mostly wilderness, but some 140 miles of road connect the main town (also called Kodiak) with various points around the northeast side of the island. Hire a car in Kodiak to explore.

FLOATPLANE
Floatplane is the primary transportation for Katmai National Park (from King Salmon, Kodiak or Anchorage). Floatplanes also take passengers into Kodiak National Wildlife Refuge and to remote lodges and other islands in the archipelago.

Holy Resurrection Cathedral (p347), Kodiak

Plan Your Time

Kodiak Island is worth several days of exploration. Most people come to Katmai National Park for a pricey one-day visit, but with advance planning it's possible to spend more time.

If You Only Have One Day

- Hop on a floatplane to **Frazer Lake** (p355) in Kodiak National Wildlife Refuge or to **Katmai National Park & Preserve** (p358) and spend the day marveling at massive brown bears fishing and feasting in preparation for winter. Tour operators in Kodiak will know which location has the most bears, depending on the timing.

Four Days or More

- Consider staying a few days at a **wilderness lodge** (p356) for bear viewing, fly fishing and kayaking – though it's pricey. Or dedicate one day to bear watching, then spend your remaining time exploring Kodiak Island, including its excellent **museums** (p347), **WWII history** (p351), remote **beaches** (p353) and **hiking trails** (p350). Look out for bears all around!

Seasonal Highlights

SPRING
Wildflowers and animal sightings during the migration of birds and gray whales (often in April and May).

SUMMER
July to September are prime time for bear viewing at both Kodiak and Katmai.

FALL
Summer crowds disperse and the bears leave Brooks Falls. Vote for your favorite fat bear during **Fat Bear Week** (p361).

WINTER
Ample snowfall is a magical backdrop to skiing and snowshoeing, though most tours and lodgings close from October to April.

Kodiak

HISTORIC TOWN | PRISTINE WILDERNESS | CULTURAL HISTORY

GETTING AROUND

Most people fly into Kodiak from Anchorage on one of Alaska Airlines' three daily flights. The airport is about 7 miles south of town on Chiniak Rd. The Alaska Marine Highway System ferry from Homer (10 or 14 hours) runs four times a week, docking downtown beside the Kodiak Visitor Center.

There is no shuttle service into town, but taxis such as **Eben Taxi** *(907-942-2626)* charge about $25 into town. Once there, you can get around on foot, but you'll want to rent a car (p353) to explore the island. A bicycle is also a good option; rent one from **58 Degrees North**.

Kodiak is one of outback Alaska's most pleasant towns: big enough to have a few good restaurants and a local microbrewery, but small enough to be walkable and more than a little folksy. The locals are a congenial bunch who passionately love their island and are eager to share its delights. Glimpses of onion domes through the standard strip-mall architecture hint at an erstwhile Russian heritage, while crowds of trawlers in the harbor testify to Kodiak's modern mantle as one of Alaska's largest fishing ports. In fact, there are more than 650 working boats, including the state's largest trawl, longline and crab vessels. The fleet and the 12 shore-based processors include the *Star of Kodiak,* a WWII vessel converted into a fish plant downtown.

Despite its hardworking reputation, there's plenty for outsiders to do in Kodiak, including two excellent museums and a state park, rich with WWII history. It's also a fine base for adventures elsewhere on the island.

Wild Kodiak

Brush up on bears and whales

A great introduction to the island's wildlife is the **Kodiak National Wildlife Refuge Visitor Center** *(fws.gov/refuge/kodiak)*, with informative, kid-friendly displays on the island's diverse ecosystems. The 12-minute film touches on the many wonders of the refuge. The star of the film and exhibit is the Kodiak brown bear, the refuge's most famous resident, with insights into its life cycle, diet and ongoing threats.

Hoping to spot a big bruin? Depending on the food supply, they are sometimes seen at **Buskin River State Recreation Site** near the airport, further south at **Bell's Flats**, or – less romantically – at the **Kodiak Island landfill**. Get tips from rangers here on your best bet for sightings.

Alutiiq Museum

Kodiak's Many Cultures
Alutiiq and Russian roots

The original inhabitants of the Kodiak archipelago were the Alutiiq, also called the Sugpiaq. In recent decades, the Alutiiq have experienced a cultural revival, with renewed interest in the Sugpiaq language, traditional arts and subsistence living. Reopened in 2025 after renovation and expansion, the excellent **Alutiiq Museum** *(alutiiqmuseum.org; adult/child $10/free)* traces the history of the community and culture over several centuries. Exhibits showcase both historic artifacts and contemporary works, demonstrating the diverse and dynamic Alutiiq community that persists in Kodiak today.

Downtown Kodiak also has many visible reminders of its Russian roots – not least the oldest surviving Russian structure in Alaska. The **Kodiak History Museum** *(kodiakhistorymuseum.org; adult/child $10/free)* occupies Erskine House, built in 1808 as a storehouse for precious sea-otter pelts. The building itself is something of a time capsule, with 200-year-old moss still visible between its spruce-log chinking. Inside, exhibits cover all periods of Kodiak's history. Items of interest include a rare triple-hatch Alutiiq canoe covered in sea-lion skin and artifacts from Pavlovsk (the town's original name). Exhibits also detail the interesting history of Erskine House itself.

Also nearby are several photogenic Russian Orthodox churches, easily recognized by their distinctive onion domes. Established in 1794, **Holy Resurrection Cathedral** serves the oldest Russian Orthodox parish in the New World (though the current building dates to 1945). Inside, a carved wooden reliquary contains the remains of St Herman, an 18th-century missionary who established a school for Alaska Native students.

ALUTIIQS IN KODIAK

Dehrich Isuwik Chya is an Alutiiq and the Language & Living Culture Manager at the Alutiiq Museum. *@alutiiqmuseum.*

The Alutiiq/Sugpiaq people have lived on Kodiak Island for at least 7800 years. Where did they come from? Alutiiq legend says that Kodiak was once close to the Alaska Peninsula, separated only by a small stream. A sea otter swam through the stream, driving Kodiak and the mainland apart. Then, the first people paddled from the Alaska Peninsula to Kodiak searching for a chief's missing daughter. They found a land filled with resources and convinced their families to move there. The rest is history!

Learn more about the Alutiiq people at the Alutiiq Museum. Taikina! – You should come!

☑ TOP TIP

The **Kodiak Island Visitor Center** has loads of helpful info about the island. Staff will happily advise on some of their favorite hikes, upcoming local events and transportation tips.

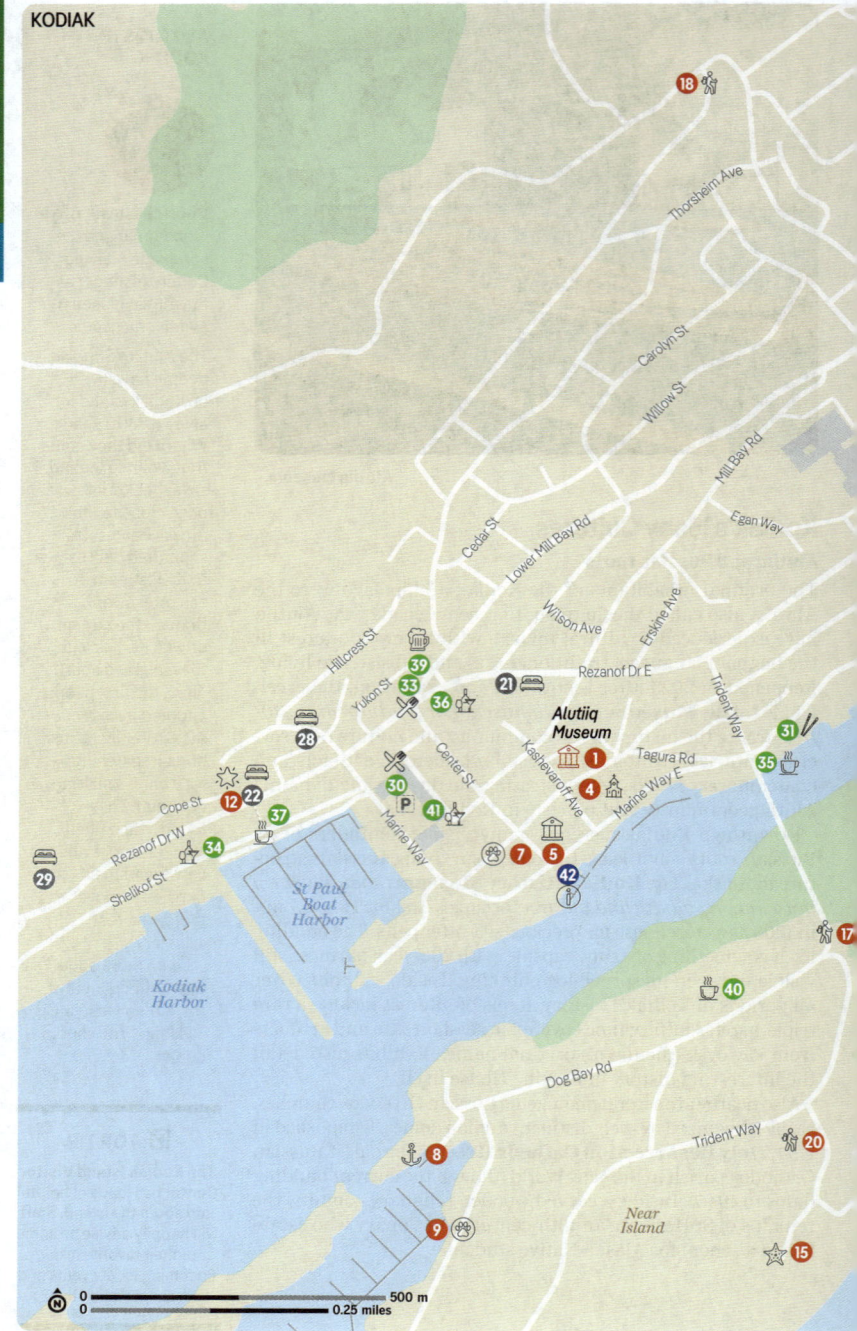

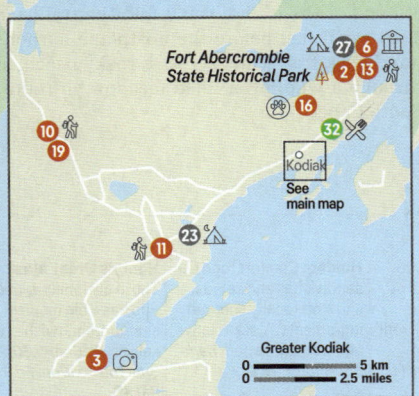

KODIAK & KATMAI KODIAK

★ HIGHLIGHTS
1. Alutiiq Museum
2. Fort Abercrombie State Historical Park

● SIGHTS
3. Bell's Flats
4. Holy Resurrection Cathedral
5. Kodiak History Museum
6. Kodiak Military History Museum
7. Kodiak National Wildlife Refuge Visitor Center
8. St Herman Harbor

● ACTIVITIES
9. Adventures in Kodiak
10. Anton Larsen Pass Loop & Peak
11. Barometer Mountain Trail
12. Fish n Chip Charters
13. Gertrude Lake
14. Kayak Kodiak
15. Kodiak Fisheries Research Center
16. Kodiak Island landfill
17. North End Trailhead
18. Pillar Mountain Trailhead
19. Pyramid Mountain Trailhead
20. South End Trailhead

● SLEEPING
21. A Downtown BnB
22. Best Western Kodiak Inn
23. Buskin River State Recreation Site
24. Channel View Vacation Rentals
25. Cliff House
26. Cranky Crow Guest House
27. Fort Abercrombie State Historical Park Campground
28. Kodiak Compass Suites
29. Ocean Bay Bed & Breakfast

● EATING
30. Henry's Great Alaskan
31. Kodiak Hana
32. Mel's Crazy Cakes & Robert's Super Secret Sauces
33. Nuniaq

● DRINKING & NIGHTLIFE
34. B & B Bar
35. Bean & Bloom Coffeehouse
36. Double Shovel Cider
37. Harborside Coffee & Goods
38. Island Espresso
39. Kodiak Island Brewing Co
40. Near Island Coffee
41. Village Bar

● INFORMATION
42. Kodiak Island Visitor Center

● TRANSPORT
see 14 58 Degrees North

Fort Abercrombie State Historical Park

HARBOR LIFE

Life in Kodiak revolves around the ocean. In the center of town, **St Paul Boat Harbor** is a hive of activity from early morning until evening. Along the waterfront, a series of colorful illustrated panels celebrates the community's connection to the sea, highlighting the fish, the fishing, the seafood industry and more.

Speaking of seafood, this is also the location of the **Kodiak Crab Festival** every year at the end of May. The five-day extravaganza includes fun runs, art shows, live music, guided history and nature walks, kids' activities and lots of street food. Special thematic events include the fish toss (as silly as it sounds) and a fishers' memorial service.

Hiking Trails & Marine Life

Exploring Near Island

Just across from downtown Kodiak, Near Island is a small, mostly uninhabited island – home to a working harbor and a fisheries research center, but not much else. A network of walking trails and wild beaches makes it ideal for exploration.

The short Channelside Trail (sharp right off the Alimaq Bridge) leads to **St Herman Harbor**, Kodiak's larger harbor and a hub of sea life. Harbor seals and sea lions haul out on the docks, while bald eagles are often spotted perched overhead.

A turnout on the left side of the bridge provides access to the **North End Trail**, a 1.2-mile loop through forest lined with salmonberry bushes. A stairway leads down to the shoreline, where you can search the tide pools for starfish, sea anemones and other marine life. At low tide, you can also cross to the neighboring island, Twin Islet, for more exploration.

At the south end of the island, you'll find the trailhead for the **South End Trail** just before the floatplane harbor. The 1.5-mile out-and-back trail leads across a rocky beach, along a cliff and through a wildflower-filled meadow en route to a lookout on South Cape.

EATING IN KODIAK: OUR PICKS

Mel's Crazy Cakes & Robert's Super Secret Sauces: Besides fancy cakes and salsas, they also serve a mean biscuits-and-gravy breakfast. *7-10am Thu-Sat* **$**

Kodiak Hana: Tuck into Kodiak's best seafood at this elegant Japanese restaurant with waterfront deck seating. *11.30am-9pm Sun-Thu, to 10pm Fri & Sat* **$$**

Nuniaq: Comfort food like sandwiches and salads, show off locally sourced ingredients. Alaska Native and woman-owned. *11am-3pm Mon-Fri* **$$**

Henry's Great Alaskan: The lively family-friendly pub has a big menu of fried seafood, sandwiches and salads. *11.30am-9.30pm Sun-Thu, to 10pm Fri & Sat* **$$**

Afterward, head up the road for a visit to the **Kodiak Fisheries Research Center**. Opened in 1998 with funds from the *Exxon Valdez* oil-spill settlement, the center has a few interesting exhibits about local marine life, including a 19ft Cuvier's beaked whale skeleton suspended from the ceiling. Downstairs there is a small aquarium and kid-friendly touch tanks, but opening hours are limited (Tuesday afternoons only, at the time of research).

WWII Memorial
History and scenery at Fort Abercrombie

Fort Abercrombie State Historical Park *(dnr.alaska.gov/parks; parking $5)* is a 221-acre expanse of peaceful forest trails, trout-filled lakes, sandy beaches and surprising historical artifacts. One of four fortified installations on the island, Fort Abercrombie was built by the US Army during WWII as a part of its coastal defense system. During the Aleutian Campaign, the forts played an important role in protecting the island's naval base.

Paths lead up to bunkers, mounted artillery and other remnants from WWII, with information panels giving historical insight to the place. The small but impressive **Kodiak Military History Museum** *(adult/child $5/free; noon-4pm Fri-Mon)* is actually housed inside a former ammunition magazine. This volunteer-run, interactive site lets you try on uniforms and helmets, tap away at working typewriters, listen to shortwave radios and clamber aboard the regulation army jeep.

History aside, the trail network at Fort Abercrombie is delightful. Stroll around **Gertrude Lake** or enjoy the open views in the wildflower-filled meadows. Take in the breezes from atop the sea cliffs, then make your way down to the water's edge, where you can wander among the tidal pools in search of sea creatures.

Fort Abercrombie is located about 4.5 miles northeast of Kodiak town. It's a doable bike ride, mostly following the bike trail that runs alongside E Rezanof Dr. Otherwise, you can get there by taxi for $20.

Kodiak Mountaintops
Reaching hard-earned summits

The Kodiak area has dozens of hiking trails, though many are not well maintained or marked. Windfall and overgrowth can make routes hard to follow, so a detailed map or navigation app is recommended.

The 1270ft **Pillar Mountain** summit overlooks Kodiak, with its sentinel wind turbines on top. More a bumpy dirt road than a

WARTIME KODIAK

In June 1942, Japanese forces bombed the US naval base at Dutch Harbor, then invaded and occupied two outer Aleutian islands, Attu and Kiska. Kodiak became the primary staging area for the Aleutian campaign, with its naval base and joint operations center for three military branches. Fort Greely and three subposts (including Fort Abercrombie) defended the base with fixed artillery batteries, radio and radar stations, observation towers, and ammunition bunkers. Up to 10,000 infantry troops were stationed on the island. The threat of a Japanese attack on Kodiak was very real but never materialized. In May 1943, the US regained Attu after a devastating but decisive battle, and the Japanese abandoned Kiska soon after.

DRINKING IN KODIAK: CRAFT CREATIONS AND LOCAL VIBES

Kodiak Island Brewing Co: Bring your own food to nosh as you sample the microbrews, including the signature Liquid Sunshine. *noon-7pm*

Double Shovel Cider: Brews naturally gluten-free ciders with real ingredients, from pineapple to Arctic Rose. Craft cocktails also on the menu. *noon-9pm*

B&B Bar: It's got a rough reputation, but this 1889 classic is the oldest bar in the state (with the original liquor license on the wall to prove it). *noon-5am*

Village Bar: Friendly local spot where the waitress knows everyone by name. After-hours menu (after 10pm) will take care of your late-night munchies. *1pm-2am*

BEST KODIAK EXCURSIONS

Kayak Kodiak: Scenic and highly informative kayak tours led by a NOAA marine biologist.

Fish n Chip Charters: With over 30 years of experience, Captain Dave offers memorable boat trips fishing for king salmon, Pacific halibut, ling cod and more.

Kodiak Survival School: A Navy SEAL veteran offers wilderness survival courses and one-of-a-kind tours, including multiday adventures in the backcountry.

Kodiak Connections: Ani leads a wide variety of thematic walking tours around town, focusing on food, drink, history and culture.

Adventures in Kodiak: Captain Lee specializes in marine-wildlife tours. Take a ride in the *Trophy II* in search of whales, sea lions, puffins and bears.

Pillar Mountain

trail, this is a quick and easy way to get a glimpse of the island's velvety greenness and enjoy a bird's-eye view of the town. Drive north up Thorsheim Ave and turn left on Maple Ave, which runs into Pillar Mountain Rd to where the turbines slice through the fog. It's 2 miles one-way, with miles of trails along the ridge.

The 2-mile climb up **Pyramid Mountain** (2400ft) ascends a steep, exposed shoulder of alpine tundra, rewarding hikers with pleasant views of the valley and Anton Larsen Bay. Keep an eye out for bears, upland birds and wildflowers. There are two different trails, both of which start on Anton Larsen Bay Rd. Avoid the brush-choked easternmost trail. Instead, continue west to the **Anton Larsen Pass** traihead (about 11 miles northwest of town).

On the same road, you'll find the trailhead for **Anton Larsen Pass Loop & Peak**, a scenic alpine ridge walk. The majority of the 5-mile-loop route follows a green U-shaped valley lined with wildflowers and excellent views.

At a peak elevation of 2500ft, **Barometer Mountain Trail** is a tough grunt that requires serious grit and plenty of scrambling. The path bends through trees at the start, then branches uphill through high bushes, before following a steep open ridge. Views from the summit are staggering. The 4-mile out-and-back trail starts just past the airport runway on Chiniak Rd.

DRINKING IN KODIAK: CAFFEINE FIX

Harborside Coffee & Goods: Strong coffee and decadent cinnamon rolls start your day off right. *6am-6pm*

Bean & Bloom Coffeehouse: 'Bean' is for coffee, and 'bloom' is for plants for sale. But the best part is its delightful waterside setting. *7am-4pm Wed-Mon*

Near Island Coffee: This little drive-through is a perfect place to refuel before or after exploring Near Island. (Don't worry, you can walk through too.) *6am-4pm*

Island Espresso: Serves pizza, ice cream and (of course) espresso – a bit of an identity crisis, but they win for the earliest opening hours. *5.30am-6.30pm*

Beyond Kodiak Town

Kodiak Island (and the entire archipelago) is an outdoor wonderland – prime for wildlife-watching, remote beach swims and scenic hikes.

Kodiak Island acts as a kind of ecological halfway house between the forested Alaskan Panhandle and the treeless Aleutian Islands. The velvety green mountains and towering sea cliffs make a dramatic backdrop for spotting wildlife, fly fishing, and exploring along empty roads and hiking trails.

Kodiak played an important role in WWII when the island became a staging area for the North Pacific operations. You'll see elements of this history not only at Fort Abercrombie, but at weathered pillboxes all along the coast.

And of course, wherever you go, be on the lookout for the island's namesake bear, the mighty creature who has earned his place in legend and lore.

Places

Pasagshak Road p353
Kodiak National Wildlife Refuge p355
Kodiak Archipelago p356

Pasagshak Road

TIME FROM KODIAK: 1½ HRS

Beach-hopping and history-hunting

Drive south on Chiniak Hwy, passing tidal flats and stunning shorelines on your way. About 30 miles south of town, turn right on Pasagshak Rd and continue south for another 16.5 miles through beautiful scenery. Around Mile 9, the road passes **Pasagshak River State Recreation Site**, a picturesque setting where the river meets the bay of the same name. This tidal river reverses direction with the tides four times a day, creating interesting challenges for local fishers.

Just past the 11-Mile market, an unsigned pullout leads to **Surfers Beach**, the longest stretch of sand on the island. It's a magnificent spot for beachcombing, sunbathing and, yes, surfing (for the brave).

Continuing along Pasagshak Rd, you'll drive through the Kodiak Rocket Launch complex, where access remains open apart from the occasional launch. Somewhere after Mile 16, the road ends at **Fossil Beach**. This remote shoreline is flanked by cliffs, all studded by varied concretions (where sand and silt has been cemented in minerals). Look carefully and you'll see ancient shells and animals and other protuberances from the past. Fossil Beach is best at low tide, when you can make your way around the eastern flank to spot more fossils entombed in the sandstone.

GETTING AROUND

To explore Kodiak Island, rent a vehicle from **Kodiak Car Rentals** or **Do North**. Some areas may require 4WD, but it's not essential for the destinations or experiences covered here. Floatplanes (p357) also fly travelers into the wildlife refuge, to remote lodges and other islands in the archipelago.

TERMINATION POINT LOOP HIKE

The much-loved 5-mile loop to Termination Point traverses lush forest and stunning coastline, with a rewarding clifftop climax.

START	END	LENGTH
White Sands Beach	White Sands Beach	5 miles; 2½ hours

You'll find the ❶ **Termination Point Trailhead** at the end of Monashka Bay Rd, near the parking lot for White Sands Beach. Follow signs for the ❷ **interior trail**, which winds northeast through forest. The fern- and moss-laden path passes bogs and tall Sitka spruce, reaching a ❸ **beaver pond** at Mile 1.6. Skirt the pond's north side and stay left to continue north.

You're nearly there as you reach Mile 2.2, where a small ❹ **wooden sign** points to Termination Point. On this headland jutting into the sea, you'll continue through the windblown grasses and wildflowers. The trail culminates at the stunning ❺ **Termination Point overlook**, high above the lapping waves. In summer, the peninsula blooms with mountain iris and cow parsnip.

Retrace your steps to the forest, then follow the ❻ **coastal trail**, which mostly hugs the shoreline. Around Mile 3.3, you'll reach a scenic ❼ **cove beach**. The path winds back into the forest and emerges a mile later at a longer stretch of ❽ **rocky beach**. It's a photogenic scene, with an old driftwood shelter and thick ropes strung through the trees. The going gets steeper from here (both ascending and descending), though it's only 0.7 miles until you end back at ❾ **White Sands Beach**.

This is also the Monashka Mountain trailhead, marked on the main sign in the parking lot. Don't worry, you're in the right place!

For a scenic extension, follow the signs to take a short detour to **Pelenga Bay**.

Never mind the unlabeled forks, as they all hook back to the main trail.

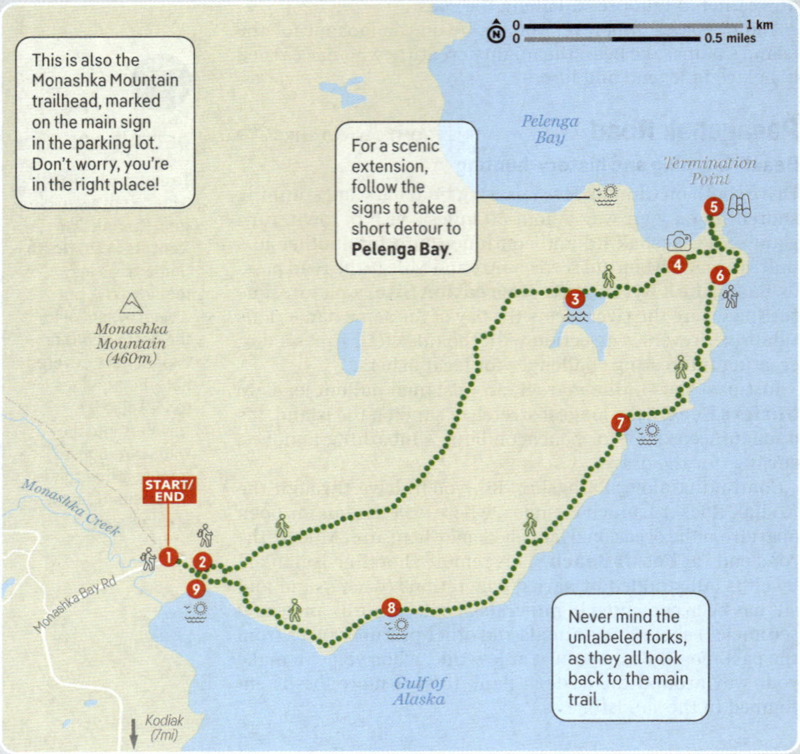

High atop this eastern cliff, there are vestiges of Kodiak's role in WWII. Follow narrow cattle trails up the hillside, across flower-filled meadows and out to the clifftops. A series of bunkers and the crumbling remains of a searchlight station are perched on **Narrow Cape**, unmarked and unmaintained. Several of these bunkers contain some impressive works of street art, while others are flooded or dangerously close to the cliff edge. Keep an eye out for wildlife, including the herd of scraggly bison that roams the area.

Kodiak National Wildlife Refuge

TIME FROM KODIAK: **50 MINS**

Bear viewing at Frazer Lake

To observe the magnificent Kodiak bear in its natural habitat, tour operators and charter floatplanes take bear spotters on half-day tours into the wildlife refuge to **Frazer Lake**.

In the 1950s, scientists from the Alaska Department of Fish & Game introduced sockeye salmon into this previously barren lake. When the salmon returned to spawn, however, they were unable to ascend the 10m waterfall on the Dog Salmon River. So the scientists built a fish ladder that allows the fish to bypass the falls. A weir now guides the fish to the entrance of the pass. Thanks to this successful intervention, Frazer Lake is now the second-largest salmon run on Kodiak Island, providing sustenance for both human and ursine residents.

For wildlife-watchers, Frazer Lake is the most accessible and surefire place to observe Kodiak bears in the wild, with as many as 10 bears fishing here at peak times (late May through August). Some photographers complain that the 200ft fish ladder spoils perfect wildlife photos. On the contrary, the construction is actually a poignant reminder of the interconnectedness of nature: the bears are here for the salmon, and the salmon rely on the fish ladder – without it, there wouldn't be any wildlife photos at all.

Multiday bear-tracking adventures

For a more immersive bear-viewing experience, book a multiday stay at the **Kodiak Brown Bear Center** *(kodiakbearcenter.com; 3-night, 4-day package from $5600)*, a luxurious lodge overlooking Karluk Lake. The lodge is owned and operated by Koniag, the Native corporation of the Alutiiq people. Packages include room and board, as well as twice-daily outings for bear observation.

A more rustic option is **Kodiak Treks** *(kodiaktreks.com; per person per night from $450)*, a remote lodge on an island in Uyak Bay. Noted bear biologist Harry Dodge leads guests from the lodge, by boat and boot, to various viewing spots, with at least one night camping in the wilderness. Packages including fishing and kayaking at the lodge, in addition to adequate room and board, and excellent bear guiding.

THE BIGGEST BEAR

At 2812 sq miles, the Kodiak National Wildlife Refuge covers the southern two-thirds of Kodiak Island, as well as several smaller islands in the Kodiak Archipelago. The wildlife refuge is the chief stronghold of the Kodiak brown bear. An estimated 3500 bears reside in the refuge and the surrounding area – the highest density of brown bears in Alaska. After some 12,000 of years of isolation on the islands, Kodiak bears, aka *Ursus maximus middendorffi*, are a distinct subspecies of brown bears that are found elsewhere in North America. Thanks to the island's bountiful rivers and forests, they are the largest of the brown bears, with males reaching 5ft tall (on all fours) and 1500lb.

BEAR COUNTRY

Kodiak National Wildlife Refuge is one of several sites that are set up for observation of brown bears, as they feast on spawning salmon. See p45 to explore your options.

MASSACRE AT REFUGE ROCK

Grigory Shelikov and his crew of Russian explorers first landed on Kodiak Island in 1784, establishing their first settlement at Old Harbor on the southeast side, across from Sitkalidak Island. The Alutiiq people did not trust the Russians' intentions. After initial resistance, they fled to a hidden 'refuge rock,' or Awa'uq, on the far side of Sitkalidak Island. When the Russians discovered the whereabouts of the Alutiiq, they launched a brutal attack – firing cannons, obliterating the temporary settlement, killing hundreds and enslaving the survivors. It was arguably the worst massacre in North American colonial history, marking the beginning of the subjugation of the Alutiiq people.

Also on Uyak Bay, **Spirit of Alaska Wilderness Adventures** *(spiritofalaska.com; per person for 3 days from $2800)* is a former salmon cannery and bunkhouse, repurposed into a modern, hydro-powered wilderness lodge. Wildlife-watching is superb (both on-site and off-site trips), as is kayaking and hiking. Prices include lodging, transportation and activities, but guests are in charge of their own meals.

Kodiak Archipelago

TIME FROM KODIAK: **10-30 MINS**

Russian roots in Ouzinkie

The year-round population is only 200 souls at the tiny village of Ouzinkie, located about 10 miles north of Kodiak, on the west end of Spruce Island. Most residents are of Russian-Aleut ancestry. The heart of the village is the **Nativity of Our Lord Russian Orthodox Church**, which dates to the 1890s. At the eastern end of the island, Monk's Lagoon is the site of **Sts Sergius & Herman of Valaam Chapel**, built in 1898 on the site of St Herman's grave. Charter planes make the short journey to Spruce Island, but Monk's Lagoon is accessible only by boat.

 EATING & DRINKING ON KODIAK ISLAND: OUR PICKS

Java Flats: Serves heavenly baked goods, sandwiches and salads, not to mention the java. Located 10 miles from town. *6am-6pm Wed-Sun* **$**

Rendezvous: The classic roadside bar and grill fires up tasty halibut burgers and hosts a good lineup of live music. *11am-11pm* **$$**

Olds River Inn: Book a table for beautifully prepared seafood, craft beer and molten-lava chocolate cake. *4-8pm Thu-Sun* **$$$**

Kodiak bears

Adventure on Afognak Island

Afognak Island lies about 25 air miles north of Kodiak Island in the archipelago. Along the north and east side of the island, some 125,000 acres are protected in pristine **Afognak Island State Park**. Amid old-growth forests and picturesque bays, self-sustaining adventurers can get their fill of kayaking, hiking, fishing and wildlife-watching. Unique species here are endangered marbled murrelets and Kodiak brown bears, as well as Roosevelt elks, found on only two other islands in Alaska. The park has three beautifully set public-use cabins: reserve through Reserve America and charter a plane through any air service.

Shack up on Shuyak Island

The northernmost island in the Kodiak Archipelago, remote and undeveloped Shuyak is 54 air miles north of Kodiak. **Shuyak Island State Park** occupies almost all the island's 47,000 acres, with virgin Sitka spruce forest and rugged shorelines dotted with secluded beaches. Otters, sea lions and Dall porpoises inhabit offshore waters, while black-tailed deer and a modest population of Kodiak brown bears roam the interior. The state park has developed a small network of trails on the western side of the island, especially around the **Big Bay ranger station** and the four public-use cabins. The cabins are on Big Bay, Neketa Bay and Carry Inlet. Reserve through Reserve America and charter a plane through any air service.

TOURS & FLIGHTS

Most operators visit Frazer Lake or Katmai National Park, depending on weather and bear-viewing conditions. Unless otherwise noted, the floatplanes dock on a small pond off Mill Bay Rd, 1 mile north of town.

Sea Hawk Air: Operates a six-passenger floatplane on 5½-hour tours, with three hours on the ground. Departs from St Herman Harbor on Near Island.

Kingfisher Aviation: Runs four-hour flightseeing excursions with one to two hours on the ground.

Kodiak Island Expeditions: This husband–wife team (a former park ranger and a pilot) offers both half- and full-day bear excursions.

Vertigo Air Taxi: Trips range from one-hour flightseeing to four-hour bear excursions, in addition to air taxi services.

Andrew Airways: Kodiak's largest bear-viewing operator offers scenic flights and bear-spotting tours in their signature orange-and-yellow floatplanes. Departs from St Herman Harbor on Near Island.

Katmai National Park & Preserve

BROWN BEARS | SPORTFISHING | DRAMATIC SCENERY

GETTING AROUND

Most visitors to Katmai fly with Alaska Airlines from Anchorage to King Salmon, where several air taxis and one boat operator travel to Brooks Camp. Several operators also run day trips directly from Anchorage, Homer, Kodiak, Dillingham and other nearby towns.

Inside the park, visitors fan out over Katmai's 6400 sq miles by chartered floatplanes, backcountry hiking or multiday paddling trips.

It's not easy to reach Katmai National Park & Preserve – and it's certainly not cheap – but sportfishers and wildlife enthusiasts agree it's worth the time and money. This wild and wonderful place is renowned for epic sportfishing, unusual volcanic landscapes and beloved, salmon-trapping brown bears. Unconnected to Alaska's main road network, this vast wilderness is a once-in-a-lifetime destination that demands careful planning and quite a lot of cash.

Visitors arrive by plane or boat at Brooks Camp, 35 miles east of King Salmon, where they can get spine-tinglingly close to 1000lb brown bears pawing giant salmon from the river. Around camp, there are also opportunities for fishing and hiking. Those lucky enough to land a reservation at the lodge or campground can also take a trip to the Valley of Ten Thousand Smokes to see the startling aftermath of the 1912 Novarupta volcanic eruption.

Bear-Watching at Brooks Camp
Spy on salmon-feasting behemoths

Every year, hundreds of brown bears emerge from hibernation and make their way to **Brooks Falls**, a small but important waterfall in Katmai National Park. Around the same time, salmon begin their journey up Brooks River to spawn in Brooks Lake. At this crossroads, salmon can be seen leaping into the jaws of waiting bears. Brown bear concentrations peak in July, when dozens are fishing at or near the falls.

Upon arrival at **Brooks Camp** *(nps.gov/katm/planyourvisit/brooks-camp.htm)*, visitors must attend a mandatory bear safety talk given by a park ranger. Despite Katmai's dense bear population (up to two bears per sq mile) only two serious human–bear incidents have been recorded in 100 years – a testament to fine park management.

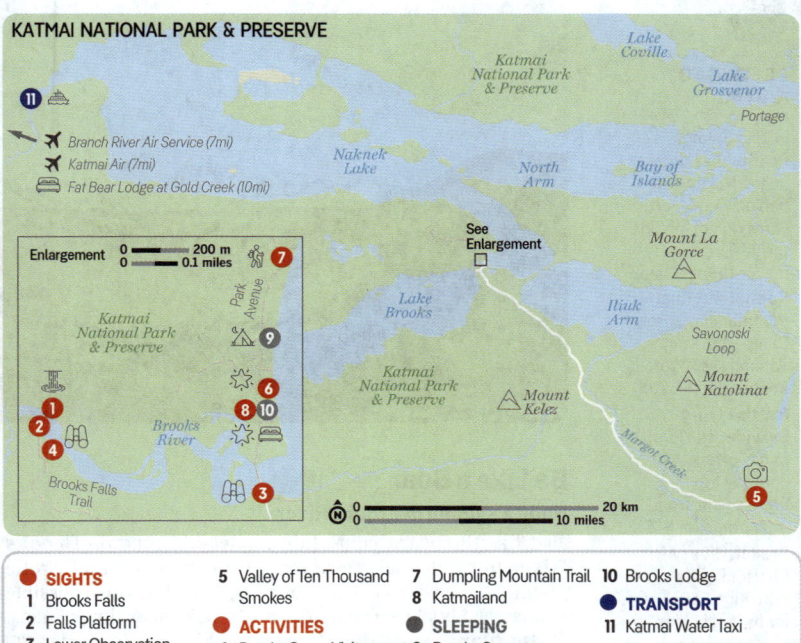

KATMAI NATIONAL PARK & PRESERVE

SIGHTS
1. Brooks Falls
2. Falls Platform
3. Lower Observation Platform
4. Riffles Platform
5. Valley of Ten Thousand Smokes

ACTIVITIES
6. Brooks Camp Visitors Center
7. Dumpling Mountain Trail
8. Katmailand

SLEEPING
9. Brooks Camp Campground
10. Brooks Lodge

TRANSPORT
11. Katmai Water Taxi

The camp has three bear-viewing areas. From the lodge, a dirt road leads to a floating bridge over the river to the **lower observation platform**. From here you can see the bears feeding in the mouth of the river or swimming in the bay.

A half-mile farther from camp, a marked trail leads to Brooks Falls and two more viewing platforms. The first is **Riffles Platform**, which sits above some shallows that occasionally draw sows trying to keep their cubs away from aggressive males at the falls.

The double-decker observation **platform** at the falls is the prime viewing spot, where you can photograph salmon making spectacular leaps or hungry bears waiting at the top of the cascade. At the peak of the salmon run, there might be more than a dozen bears here. The platform holds 40 people, and during early to mid-July it will be crammed with photographers, forcing rangers to rotate people on and off.

Brooks Camps' bear season is relatively short, but chartered floatplanes and guides also operate trips to other bear-viewing areas from June to October.

☑ TOP TIP

Before you arrive, you can check out the lay of the land (and the behemoths that roam it) on the Brooks Falls bear cams. Find the 24-hour live stream on the national park website or *explore.org*.

PARADISE FOR BEARS

There are a handful of other famous places in Alaska to view bears in the wild. See **Bears, Bears, Bears** (p45) to choose the best option for you.

GETTING TO KATMAI

In King Salmon, float-planes dock on the Naknek River behind the airport. Fares do not include the $30 park entry fee for Brooks Camp.

Katmai Air: Charter a floatplane to Brooks Camp from King Salmon ($430) or Anchorage ($1370).

Rust's Flying Service: The Rust family offers a one-day trip to Brooks Falls from Anchorage for $1345.

Branch River Air: Charter flights from King Salmon for fly-out fishing, flight-seeing and bear-viewing, including Brooks Camp.

Katmai Water Taxi: The boat runs five times daily between the King Salmon boat launch and Brooks Camp. The $225 fare includes airport or lodging transfers.

Adventuresmith Explorations: The 'Grizzly Ship' is a small-vessel, three-day cruise along the Katmai coast, bookended by sightseeing days in Kodiak.

Be Like a Bear

Hook a salmon in Brooks River

Just like the bears, come July, anglers descend on **Brooks River** to catch sockeye salmon, rainbow trout and Arctic grayling. The river is fly-fishing only, though it's also possible to charter a boat to troll in nearby Brooks and Naknek Lakes. **Katmailand** (*katmailand.com; fly fishing per day from $85*) offers guided trips for both types of fishing, weather permitting. Lodges in King Salmon (p363) also take their guests fishing on the Alagnak and Naknek Rivers.

Fishing populations in Katmai are carefully managed by the Alaska Department of Fish & Game. Sportfishing licenses are required for nonresidents aged 16 and older (and most residents, too). Because both humans and brown bears are often drawn to the same catch, it's important to follow safe bear-country practices, including maintaining a distance of at least 50yd from any bear. Anglers should stop fishing and move away (cutting the line, if necessary) well before a bear gets within this distance.

All fishing is catch and release, except in the section of river downstream from the bridge, where anglers may keep one fish per day.

Backcountry Hikes

Explore Katmai on foot

Katmai has few formal hiking trails, aside from the short trails within the Brooks Camp. The only developed and maintained trail from camp is a half-day trek to the top of **Dumpling Mountain** (2440ft). The trail leaves the ranger station and heads north past the campground, climbing 1.5 miles to a scenic overlook. It then continues another 2.5 miles to the mountain's summit, where there are superb views of the surrounding lakes.

Valley of Ten Thousand Smokes

Experienced backpackers can explore the backcountry by following river bars, lakeshores, gravel ridges and other natural routes. One option is to take the tour bus out to the **Valley of Ten Thousand Smokes** *(one-way $65)*, and hike the 23 miles back (or vice versa). The dirt road cuts through dense boreal forest and requires several stream crossings.

If you're backpacking, you'll need to camp at least 1.5 miles outside the Brooks Camp Developed Area. The national park recommends campers set up an electric fence around their tent as a bear deterrent.

Katmai Waterways

Paddle the Savonoski Loop

The Savonoski Loop is an 80-mile paddling route through the wilds of Katmai National Park. Depending on the route, experienced paddlers can spend five to 10 days navigating the waterways of Katmai. From Brooks Camp, the route heads northwest to the Bay of Islands in Naknek Lake. A portage connects to windy Grosvenor Lake. For the return trip, the Grosvenor River connects to the Savonoski River and Back to Brooks Camp. Fure's Cabin is a public-use cabin at Bay of Islands, but camping is required at other locations in the park. **Arctic Wild** *(arcticwild.com)* offers an eight-day guided canoe and camping trip along this route. The **Fat Bear Lodge at Gold Creek** *(alaskasgoldcreeklodge.com)* also organizes half-day or full-day kayaking tours in this area for its guests.

Otherworldly Views at the Valley of Ten Thousand Smokes

Marvel at volcanic landscapes

The only road in Katmai is 23 miles long. It's a scenic traverse of the park that leads from the lodge, past wildlife-inhabited

FAT BEAR WEEK

Katmai brown bears spend their summers consuming as much salmon as possible, building up their stores of fat, so they can survive up to six months of hibernation without food or water. Bears lose up to one-third of their body weight during winter hibernation.

During one week in October, aka **Fat Bear Week** *(fatbearweek. org)*, Katmai park rangers create an online tournament bracket, where the bear-loving public can vote for the fattest bear. Aside from introducing the contenders and allowing daily vote casting, the website also has live events highlighting the bears and their ecosystem. Vote early and vote often: only one big teddy earns the title of Fat Bear!

Brown bear fishing for salmon, Brooks River (p360)

THE DAY THE SKY TURNED BLACK

Petr Kayagvak was the first to witness the 1912 Novarupta eruption: 'The Katmai mountain blew up with lots of fire... and fire came down the trail with lots of smoke,' as he later described. He rushed back to his village of Savonoski as the sky grew pitch black. The villagers gathered water in containers and turned boats upside down lest they be filled with ash. After three days of darkness, they saw the devastation: fish, birds and porpoises were floating on the pumice-covered bay. Dead salmon dotted the lake, and streams were buried beneath ash. The Novarupta eruption forever changed their lives. The Alutiiq fled the devastation and created a new community some 230 miles away, which survives to this day (now known as Perryville).

meadows and river valleys, and ends at the **Valley of Ten Thousand Smokes**. The first stop is the Robert F Griggs Visitor Center for sweeping views of the valley and displays on the area's natural history and photographs from the past.

The surreal landscape is the result of the 1912 Novarupta volcanic eruption, the largest of the 20th century. Over three days, pumice and ash rained down and countless smoke vents jetted hot steam skyward. After the magma stopped flowing, some 40 sq miles of forested wilderness had been transformed into a landscape of smoking valleys, blackened mountains, and small holes and cracks, fuming with steam and gas.

Katmailand *(katmailand.com; per person $105)* runs a daily seven-hour tour to the volcanic valley from Brooks Lodge. A ranger gives talks and answers questions during the trip, and there's plenty of opportunity for photo stops. Upon arrival at the visitor center, you can take in the views across nearly 12 miles of barren, moonlike valley, with snowcapped peaks beyond. After a lunch break, the ranger leads an optional hike down to the valley floor where you can get an up-close look at the volcanic landscape. The hike is not particularly long (3.4 miles round trip), but it's uphill on the way back (about a 1000ft elevation gain). Book well in advance for this popular tour.

Places We Love to Stay

$ Budget $$ Midrange $$$ Top End

Kodiak Town
MAP p348

Fort Abercrombie State Historical Park Campground $ Nine wooded sites (including four walk-in sites) in a delightfully mossy forest overlooking a scenic inlet.

Buskin River State Recreation Site $ Located near the airport, the 15-site rustic campground has a self-guided nature trail and good salmon fishing. Bears like to fish here, too.

Cranky Crow Guest House $ A comfortable, affordable option in a residential area north of town, offering both ensuite and shared-bathroom options, plus a shared kitchen and cozy common areas.

Ocean Bay B&B $ Two apartments have private entrances, full kitchens, living area, and expansive ocean and mountain views.

Cliff House $$ Adorned with murals, three sweet rooms overlook the channel, while friendly hosts offer a wealth of local insight.

Channel View Vacation Rentals $$ Owned by a fifth-generation islander, the B&B is lovingly decorated with historic photos, fossils and original creations. The channel view is also lovely. Three-night minimum.

A Downtown BnB $$ Also called 'Room with a Car,' these well-equipped studio apartments include the use of a Fiat 500. Three-night minimum.

Kodiak Compass Suites $$ Kodiak's newest hotel is this handsome all-suite option, located right downtown with mountain and channel views.

Best Western Kodiak $$ The large centrally located motel has modern rooms, a good restaurant and airport-shuttle service.

Kodiak Island

Pasagshak River State Recreation Site (p353) $ Six first-come, first-served tent sites on the peaceful banks of the Pasagshak River.

Smiling Bear $$ In a scenic setting near Monashka Bay, this pet-friendly B&B makes guests feel at home in two comfy suites.

Olds River Inn (p356) $$ Near Kalsin Pond, the beloved restaurant and brewery offers two modern cabins with kitchens and outdoor decks, and easy access to good fishing.

Kodiak Brown Bear Center (p355) $$$ The remote fly-in lodge on Karluk Lake offers multiday packages for bear-viewing and fishing.

Spirit of Alaska Wilderness Adventures (p356) $$$ Fly in to this former salmon cannery overlooking Uyak Bay, for wide-ranging wilderness adventures.

Kodiak Island Resort $$$ Fronting Larsen Bay, this renowned fly-in fishing lodge has appealing all-wood cabins, outstanding cooking and superb service.

Katmai National Park & Preserve
MAP p359

Brooks Camp Campground $ Reservations for this coveted national park campground fill quickly when they open in the first week of January.

Brooks Lodge $$$ The lodge at Brooks Camp has 16 rustic rooms and cabins with twin bunkbeds and ensuites. Reservations by lottery: apply in December for the year after next.

King Salmon

Antlers Inn $$$ This friendly place has simply furnished rooms and suites near the airport in King Salmon.

King Salmon Lodge $$$ Fly fishing and bear-watching are on offer at this relatively affordable fishing lodge, located about 3 miles west of town.

Crystal Creek Lodge $$$ This gorgeously crafted wooden fishing lodge sits on the Naknek River, about 7 miles south of King Salmon.

Fat Bear Lodge at Gold Creek (p361) $$$ About 5 miles west of town, this fishing and wildlife lodge gets top marks for rustic but luxurious lodgings and fantastic food.

Researched by
Melody Burdette

Nome & the Arctic

INUPIAT TRADITIONS, TUNDRA AND ROAD TRIPS

The land of endless summer days and aurora-filled winter nights is an unforgettable place to experience Inupiat culture and rugged tundra wilderness.

Welcome to Alaska's far north, where the land stretches wide to the Arctic Ocean and human history runs deep. This is the ancestral homeland of the Inupiat, who have thrived for thousands of years in one of the planet's harshest climates.

Winter can lock the coast in ice for months, snow may fall in midsummer, and wind rips across the unbroken tundra. Though decidedly modern, life here still follows an ancestral rhythm of hunting, fishing and gathering. Harvests are shared, celebrations are communal, and traditions are carried forward in everyday life.

Nome anchors the Seward Peninsula, known for its gold-rush past and as the legendary finish line of the Iditarod (p369). Beyond town, three gravel roads cut through hundreds of miles of tundra, rivers and mountains, leading to Alaska Native villages, hot springs and landscapes that feel limitless. Utqiaġvik, at Alaska's northernmost tip, looks out over the Arctic Ocean, where bowhead whaling and 24-hour daylight (and darkness) shape life at the top of the world.

Some visitors on tight schedules tick off the Arctic with a day trip from Fairbanks – but to really understand this region, you'll want to linger, explore, and let its scale work on you. The distances here are immense, and the solitude is profound. More than a destination, the Arctic is a reminder of both human resilience and the wilderness itself.

THE MAIN AREAS

NOME
Gold-rush history and tundra exploring. **p368**

UTQIAĠVIK
Inupiat culture, top of the US.
p379

DALTON HIGHWAY
Sprawling and remote Arctic road trip. **p383**

For places to stay in Nome & the Arctic, see p387

Left: Fall landscape at Salmon Lake (p374); Above: Dalton Highway (p383)

Find Your Way

Nome lies on the Seward Peninsula and juts into the Bering Sea. Far north, Utqiaġvik is the biggest 'city' in Arctic Alaska. East of there is the 414-mile Dalton Highway, which reaches the Arctic Ocean.

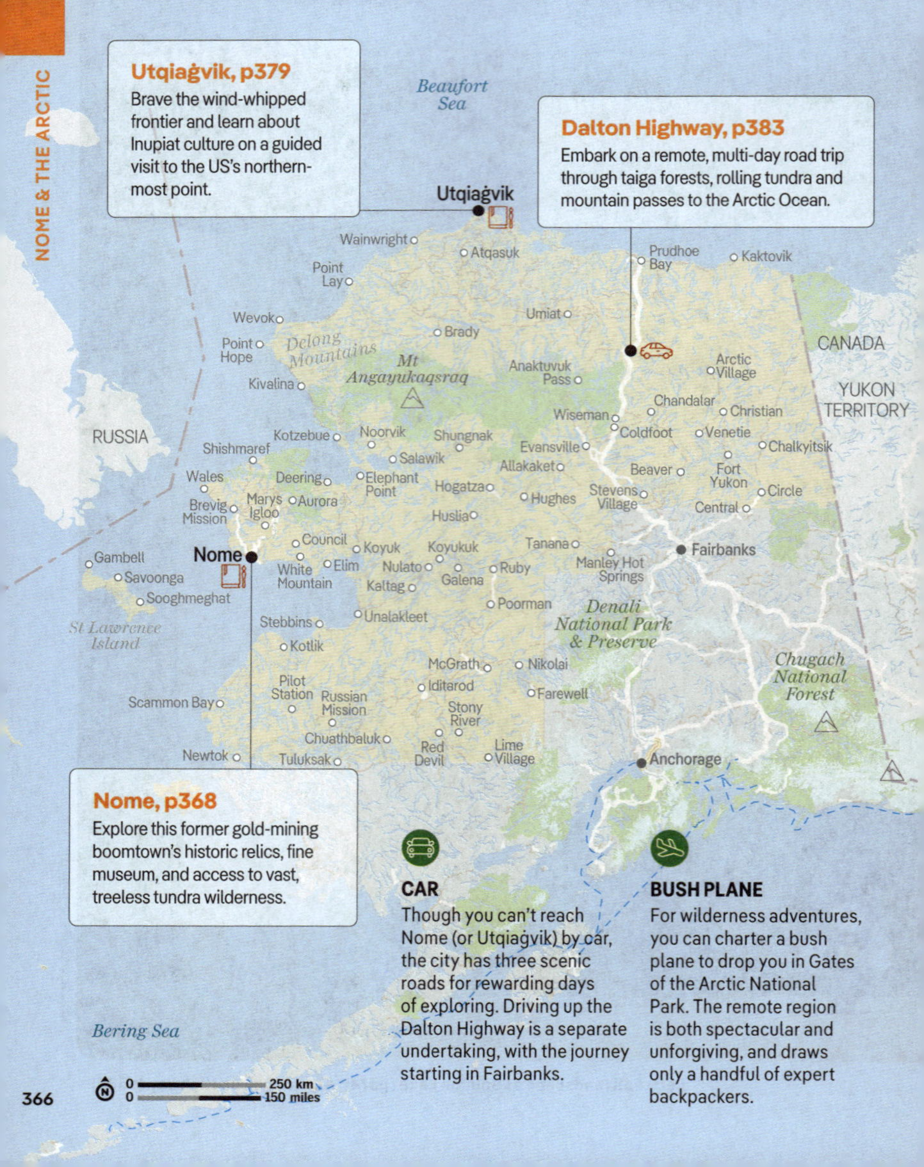

Utqiaġvik, p379
Brave the wind-whipped frontier and learn about Inupiat culture on a guided visit to the US's northernmost point.

Dalton Highway, p383
Embark on a remote, multi-day road trip through taiga forests, rolling tundra and mountain passes to the Arctic Ocean.

Nome, p368
Explore this former gold-mining boomtown's historic relics, fine museum, and access to vast, treeless tundra wilderness.

CAR
Though you can't reach Nome (or Utqiaġvik) by car, the city has three scenic roads for rewarding days of exploring. Driving up the Dalton Highway is a separate undertaking, with the journey starting in Fairbanks.

BUSH PLANE
For wilderness adventures, you can charter a bush plane to drop you in Gates of the Arctic National Park. The remote region is both spectacular and unforgiving, and draws only a handful of expert backpackers.

St Joseph Church (p369), Nome

Plan Your Time

Nome's sprawling highways make for three rewarding days of exploring. Most people spend just one night in Utqiaġvik. Allow four days for a Dalton Highway road trip.

Pressed for Time

● If you only have a day to explore the Arctic, fly into **Utqiaġvik** (p379) and take a guided tour to the US's northernmost point. The chances of spotting beluga whales, polar bears, common eiders and other Arctic wildlife is high. Afterwards, explore the **Inupiat Heritage Center** (p379), the best place to connect with traditions still thriving here today.

Three Days to Explore

● Base yourself in **Nome** (p368), and start with the impressive **Carrie M. McLain Memorial Museum** (p370). Afterwards, road trip to **Council** (p372) where driftwood beaches, abandoned railcars and misty ridgelines mark the way. Over the next two days, explore Nome's other highways for sweeping tundra, hot springs, mountain views, and rusted-out mining relics.

Seasonal Highlights

SPRING
Spring arrives with shore-fast ice typically breaking up around May. This is peak **birding** season, with over 100 unique species migrating near Nome.

SUMMER
Longer, warmer days are ideal for **road trips** and **hikes**. In June, Utqiaġvik celebrates the whale harvest with the **Nalukataq Festival** (p380).

AUTUMN
From autumn to spring, the **northern lights** dance across the sky. Nome closes out summer with quirky fun at the September Bathtub Race.

WINTER
Subzero temps don't stop the crowds here – thousands pack Nome's streets to cheer mushers across the finish line of the **Iditarod.**

Nome

GOLD MINING LORE | BIRDING | ROAD TRIPS

✓ TOP TIP

Make the **Nome Visitor Center** your first stop in town: the extremely helpful staff will load you up with brochures, advice and coffee. You can also use the wi-fi. Just up the street, the **Bering Land Bridge Visitor Center** doles out information on adventures to the remote fly-in park.

Nome clings to the edge of the Bering Strait and inhabits one of the wildest and most westerly parts of mainland America. It's a frontier town weathered by salt, wind and long seasons of ice.

Gold put Nome here. In 1898, three prospectors immortalized as the 'Three Lucky Swedes' struck it rich in a creek outside of town – and the population rocketed from zero to nearly 20,000 within two years. The boom burned hot and fast, and though fires and storms erased most of the historic buildings, echoes of the gold rush remain: rusting dredges marooned in rivers, locomotives sinking into tundra, and hobbyists panning sand on the beach.

Today, Nome's energy returns in bursts. Every March, mushers thunder down Front St to finish the Iditarod. Summer brings birders and open access to three remote gravel roads that lead deep into the tundra toward hot springs, hikes, and villages at the edge of the continent.

Hidden Stories of Downtown Nome
A stroll through culture and time

Start your exploration of Nome at the center of it all: **Anvil City Square**. This full-block park is the gathering place for local events throughout the year, hosting everything from Fourth of July festivities to the Midnight Sun Festival's quirky

---

 GETTING AROUND

The town is flat, compact, and easy to cover on foot – though you'll want good waterproof shoes for the mostly unpaved lanes. Beyond the main drags, renting a car is the best way to explore (but brace for sticker shock – gas and rental prices are high). The airport is 1.4 miles outside town; you can walk or take a local cab for a flat $8 per person (cash only). Some hotels offer free shuttles worth reserving ahead, as cell service can be spotty. Check your coverage before you go.

NOME

SIGHTS
1 Anvil City Square
2 Burled Arch
3 Carrie M. McLain Memorial Museum
4 Richard Foster Building
5 St Joseph Church

ACTIVITIES
6 Iditarod Trail Sled Dog Race

SLEEPING
7 Aurora Inn
8 Noxapaga Suites

EATING
9 Airport Pizza
10 Milano's Pizzeria
11 Pingo Bakery
12 Polar Café
13 Trinh's Floral and Coffee

DRINKING & NIGHTLIFE
14 Board of Trade Saloon
15 Breakers Bar
16 Polar Bar

INFORMATION
17 Bering Land Bridge Visitor Center
18 Nome Visitor Center

IDITAROD REVELRY

Nome's biggest celebration revolves around snow, dogs and sledding. In early March, the Iditarod Trail Sled Dog Race officially kicks off near Anchorage, with around 40 mushers and their canine athletes heading off on the 1100-mile race. Roughly 10 days later, the first racers make their way down Front St in downtown Nome, crossing the finish line under the **Burled Arch**. Every hotel, spare room and couch fills with out-of-towners and a carnival spirit fills the streets. Expect craft fairs, dog sled rides, kennel tours, live music and dance parties. Plan well in advance.

bathtub race. Most famously, it's where mushers cross under the Burled Arch at the end of the **Iditarod Trail Sled Dog Race**. As you stroll the park, you'll spot the (alleged) world's largest gold pan standing upright and 20ft wide, and statues honoring the Three Lucky Swedes who first struck gold here, as well as the Inupiat boys who assisted them.

The north end of the park is anchored by one of Nome's oldest buildings: **St Joseph Church** (affectionately nicknamed 'Old St Joe's Hall'). The church and its tall spire were originally located on Front St as a beacon for seafarers, and

EATING IN NOME: OUR PICKS

Milano's Pizzeria: Charming, cozy spot with a menu ranging from wood-fired pizza to sushi and flavorful bulgogi bibimbap. *11am-10pm Mon-Sun* **$$**

Pingo Bakery: Nome's best breakfast and lunch spot serves up delicious meals with a menu that changes daily, based on whatever is fresh. *hours vary* **$$**

Airport Pizza: Neither in the airport, nor exclusively pizza, this place nevertheless has tasty pizzas, burgers and Asian fare. *11am-10pm Mon-Sun* **$$**

Polar Cafe: A classic greasy spoon with big windows facing the ocean, serving breakfast and lunch options. *7am-3pm Mon-Sun* **$$**

CANINE SOLDIERS

Leon Boardway, a writer, photographer and historian, shares a little-known story from Nome's past.

During WWI, when France was under attack from the Germans, the French couldn't cross snow-covered mountain passes to resupply little villages. So in Nome, these old-time mushers rounded up over 100 sled dogs and shipped them to France in a top-secret operation. Code name: Hairy Alaska. The dogs were amazing. They took 90 tons of supplies over the mountains and transported wounded soldiers on the way back. After the war, the dogs were awarded the French War Cross, the country's highest honor. It was the first time it was ever given to animals.

---

built in 1901 during the gold mining boom. By the 1920s, the city's population had plummeted from 20,000 to fewer than 900, and the Jesuits abandoned the structure. It was used for storage by a mining company until 1996, when the city purchased it and moved it to its current home. It only opens for rare community events, though, so you'll likely have to admire it from the outside.

It all comes together a few blocks north at the **Carrie M. McLain Memorial Museum** *(nomealaska.org/memorial-museum; free)*. Beautifully curated and more impressive than you'd expect for a fly-in town of around 3650 people, the museum profiles the history of Nome and Western Alaska, starting with Indigenous crafts and subsistence. Wooden snow goggles, combs for collecting berries, and a reproduction *umiak* (driftwood-and-walrus-skin boat) sit for you to admire. Further along, you can pull a dredge lever to watch a video about Nome's gold miners, or open a door into a saloon to hear the raucous sounds of Nome's boom days circa late 1890s. Don't miss the photos of legendary law enforcement officer and gunslinger Wyatt Earp, who spent time in Nome. There are also exhibits (and short films you can watch) that rotate through more recent topics about the area.

The museum is housed in the standout **Richard Foster Building**, which houses two other important points of interest in Nome: The Katirvik Cultural Center, an important gathering ground for local elders, and the Kegoayah Kozga Public Library. The latter has a robust collection of titles about Alaska Native culture, and you can grab wi-fi there or use a computer to get online.

Back by the waterfront, be sure to stop by the Nome Visitors Center. This one-room treasure trove overflows with photos, artifacts, and even a taxidermied musk ox. Poke around the display cases, and engage the eager staff to hear stories about Nome's colorful past and present.

Strolling a Golden Beachfront
Riches past and present

Golden sand beaches mean something a little different in Nome. Instead of palm-fringed shorelines, 'golden sand' takes on a literal meaning with sparkling, hidden wealth buried along and just off shore.

One mile east of downtown lies the epicenter of Nome's famed gold rush. The beach is still open to recreational mining, and

---

 DRINKING IN NOME: CAFES AND BARS

Trinh's Floral and Coffee: Cozy with a wide array of specialty coffees, pastries, and breakfast options. Try the tasty breakfast burrito! *hours vary.*

Board of Trade: Nome's oldest drinking den, with pool tables, old photos, and good music. *10am-2am Mon-Thur, to 3am Fri & Sat, closed Sun*

Polar Bar: A classic dive bar on Front St, which also has a handy liquor store attached. *9am-10pm, Mon-Sun*

Breakers Bar: Join the bearded, hat-wearing crowd at this aging spot on Nome's main drag. *2pm-2am Mon-Sun*

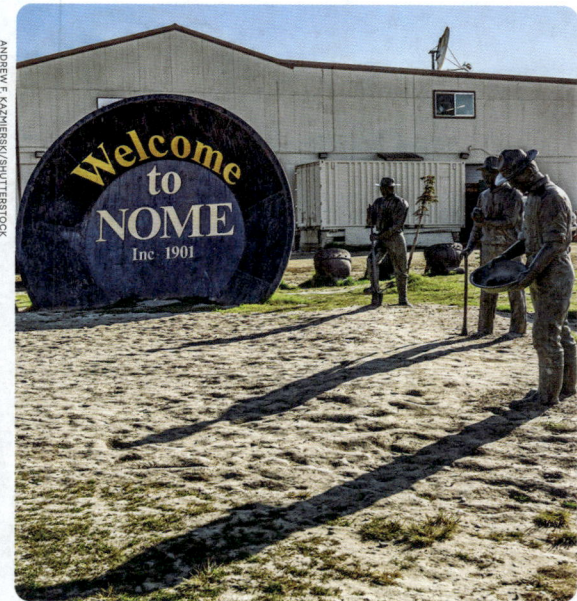

'World's largest gold pan' and statues of the Three Lucky Swedes (p369)

all summer long you can watch miners set up work camps along the shore. Some will pan or open a sluice box right on the sand, while the more serious prospectors mount dredging rigs onto small pontoon boats and anchor offshore. From these Rube Goldberg machine-like contraptions, they will spend up to four hours underwater in wetsuits pumped with hot air from the engine, essentially vacuuming the ocean floor.

Miners are generally friendly, and occasionally you can coax one into showing you their gold dust or nuggets. If you catch the fever, practically every gift shop and hardware store in town sells black plastic gold pans. As you're panning, think about the visitor who, while simply beachcombing in 1984, found a 3.5in nugget at the eastern end of the seawall that weighed 1.29oz – and remember that gold's now worth around $2000 per ounce.

Across from the beach just past East N Street, sits a **Mine Machinery Graveyard**. About a half-mile farther out of town, you can take even more impressive photos at **Swanberg's Gold Dredge**, abandoned since the 1950s. A boardwalk with interpretative signs leads you out for a close-up look. In the evening, herds of musk ox can sometimes be seen grazing in the nearby fields.

DIY HIKING

If you're well prepared and the weather holds, the backcountry surrounding Nome can be hiking heaven. Though there are no marked trails in the region, the area's three highways offer rare access into the tundra and mountains. The lack of trees and sprawling topography makes route-finding fairly simple: just pick a point and go for it. For more direction, the Nome Visitors Center is a great stop for advice on popular destinations and current trail conditions (as well as how to get there).

MIDNIGHT SUN FESTIVAL

The Iditarod isn't Nome's only big event. Plan a trip around the Midnight Sun Festival if you prefer warm(er) weather. Held on the weekend closest to the summer solstice, it offers many chances to take part. You can run a 5K on the beach, brave the Polar Bear Swim (dip your whole body to receive a certificate), or cheer on locals as they push off on homemade watercraft for the 5-mile Nome River Raft Race. There's also a parade, where out-of-towners are often invited to join the judges' panel, plus a reenactment of a gold-rush-era robbery.

Beyond Nome

The real reason to come to Nome is to explore the region's mountain valleys, rolling tundra and wild coastlines.

Places

Council p372
Salmon Lake p374
Pilgrim Hot Springs p374
Teller p376
Anvil Mountain p378

Radiating east, north and northwest from Nome are its finest features: three gravel roads, each offering passage into a land of sweeping tundra, crystal-clear rivers and rugged mountains. Along the way, you'll find some of the best chances in Alaska to see waterfowl, caribou, bears and musk ox. There are also some surreal sights, including rusting train carcasses and tiny villages snuggled at the edge of the world.

But be prepared: there's no gas and few other services along Nome's highways. Instead, you'll encounter route-shrouding dust, rocks and narrow elevated sections of road that can easily dump you into a marsh. The roads can shred the toughest tires, and going slow is key. Take twice as long as you would on pavement.

GETTING AROUND

Unless taking an organized tour, a car is essential for exploring this part of Alaska. Hire vehicles from the Aurora Inn or, if you're a guest, Dredge No. 7 Inn. Some Airbnbs also rent cars. Expect sticker shock: prices start at $200 per day and fuel costs $7 per gallon.

Tell a local contact where you're going and when you'll be back. There's no cell service once you leave town.

Council

TIME FROM NOME: 3HR

Beaches, wetlands and ghostly ruins

On sunny days, the miles of beach outside Nome beckon – and the 73-mile drive to the village of Council offers the most landscape diversity out of all Nome's road trips. For the first 30 miles, the road hugs the glimmering Bering Sea coastline, passing a motley but photogenic array of shacks, cabins, tipis and Quonset huts used by Nome residents as summer cottages and fishing or hunting camps. Alaska Natives have hunted and fished here for millennia, and the many depressions dotting the landscape are the sites of former camps.

At Mile 22 sits the Safety Roadhouse, the last stop on the famous Iditarod Trail Sled Dog Race (p369) before the finish in Nome. Every inch of this watering hole's interior contains something to keep your eyes entertained: dollar bills line the walls and ceiling, and a finishing banner from the 1986 race hangs proudly in the back room.

Just beyond, a gravel turnoff on the left leads to a boardwalk with interpretive signs overlooking Safety Sound – and what used to be the eastern edge of the Bearing Land Bridge. Continue another 10 miles along the wide stretch of coastline. It's worth pulling over: the beachcombing here is unrivaled, and a quick ocean dip (if you're brave) is tempting on sunny days.

'Last Train to Nowhere'

LAST TRAIN TO NOWHERE

In all of northern Alaska, it's certainly among the most-photographed landmarks: a set of steam locomotives, utterly out of place and time, moldering on the Arctic tundra. Dubbed the 'Last Train to Nowhere,' the three engines first ran the elevated lines of New York City in the 1880s, until Manhattan switched from steam to electric trains. In 1903, the upstart Council City & Solomon River Railroad purchased the locomotives and transported them north, hoping to profit by linking inland mines to the coast. By 1907, the operation went belly-up, and six years later, a powerful storm destroyed the Solomon River bridge, stranding the 'Last Train's' engines on the tundra forever.

At Mile 32 lies **Bonanza Crossing**, where a river ferry once linked Nome to the town of Solomon. Established in 1900 and once home to a population of 1000 (and seven saloons), the town was destroyed by a 1913 storm and further devastated by the 1918 flu epidemic. Just past the bridge lies a truly wild sight: the iconic steam engines of the **Last Train To Nowhere** half-sunk into the tundra, still pointed expectantly towards the hills they were meant to chug into.

From here, the road turns away from the shore and climbs into the hills. At Mile 40, **Lees Dredge** sits abandoned on the Solomon River. In 1912 almost 40 dredges worked the Seward Peninsula, and while many can be seen from the road, this one is the most picturesque if you're up for a little bushwhacking. The road continues to Stookum Pass at Mile 53, offering sweeping tundra views. There's a parking area at the top so you can pull off and admire the sights, or hike on the nearby ridge. On clear days, the coast is visible to the south, and the White Mountains to the east.

As you descend from the pass towards Council, you'll notice something unique pop up: trees. They're not a sight you come by often in the tundra, so admire the spruce and birch as you wind your way north. Several river banks are easily accessible from the road to dip your feet in on a nice day.

The road ends at Mile 73 at the village of Council – or, rather, the road ends at the banks of the Niukluk River, and Council is on the other side. Most homes here serve as weekend getaways for Nome residents, with no year-round residents. Locals drive across the river, but tourists with rental cars should stay put. There are no services or shops in Council, but the Niukluk is an excellent place to fish for grayling.

NOME GOLD RUSH

In 1898, Nome became the epicenter of the first true Alaskan gold rush in 1898. Three Swedish prospectors, blown off course in a small boat, discovered gold deposits in a river near Cape Nome. The nascent city, which hadn't even existed two years previously, briefly exploded into Alaska's largest, with over 20,000 hardy souls squeezed into makeshift wooden buildings or saggy canvas tents on the beach. Nome attracted an abnormally high number of unsavory characters. Holdups, gambling, sex work, fist fights, drunkenness and robbery became endemic. The frenzy didn't last long, though – by 1910, the town quickly reinvented itself as a small but stable settlement on the edge of the Bering Sea.

Salmon Lake

TIME FROM NOME: 1½HR

Big adventures on the Kougarok Road

Also known as the Nome-Taylor road, a day trip out on the 84-mile Kougarok road quickly immerses you in the mountainous, remote splendor of the tundra and offers stops for history, a hot-spring dip, and free-form exploration.

As soon as you leave Nome, all signs of town fall away. Rolling green hills rise toward the jagged 'sawtooths' of the Kigluaik Mountains, and the Nome River keeps you company for the first 20 miles as you wind inland. In July, wildflowers cover the tundra in a shock of color that is truly breathtaking.

A series of bridge crossings mark your progress into the wild. At Mile 13, the Nome River Bridge is a favorite local fishing spot for grayling and Dolly Varden trout. Further on, the Grand Central River Bridge frames a striking view back into the valley, and the Crater Creek crossing reveals water braiding its way into the mountains beyond. Each stop is worth pulling over to take in the vistas and maybe spot sockeye salmon wiggling in the current.

Just before Mile 40, **Salmon Lake** comes into view, backed by low mountains and edged with sandy shoreline. This sparkling body of water invites exploration and bird-watching (keep an eye out for the rare bluethroat), or even a lakeside lunch break. The Bureau of Land Management (BLM) maintains a free campground here with picnic tables and a pit toilet (rustic but spectacular) and a perfect place to linger.

Pilgrim Hot Springs

TIME FROM NOME: 2½HR

Head for a soak and historical stroll

It's well worth taking a detour to **Pilgrim Hot Springs** if traveling in a reliable 4WD vehicle. The turnoff (on your left) for the 7-mile spur road appears just before Mile 54 and takes

Landscape near Kougarok road

you on a true Alaskan side quest: climbing to a beautiful alpine ridge, crossing shallow streams (especially after heavy rains), and ending at a small parking area.

The Alaska Native-owned operation is rustic and truly beautiful. There are primitive trails for exploring, elevated cedar hot tubs overlooking the Kigluaik Mountains for soaking, and a hot pool surrounded by a small deck with chairs. Beyond the springs, a cluster of aging buildings from the early settlement stands among the trees. During the gold rush, this was the site of a roadhouse and saloon, and later an orphanage for children who lost their parents to the 1918 influenza epidemic. If you'd like to linger, campsites and cabins are available. Entry is $10, payable at the igloo gatehouse.

Back on the Kougarok Road, Mile 60 crosses the Pilgrim River where you'll see rare groves of cottonwood, willow, and alder, with Arctic terns flitting past. Beaver dams are often found here, and moose (cows and calves) sometimes feed along the shoreline. If you're here in July and August, sockeye and Chinook salmon can be seen swimming under the bridge en route to Salmon Lake to spawn.

The road continues uphill from the bridge, offering sweeping views of lakes and river valleys. Near Mile 68, you'll cross another bridge, this one spanning the Kuzitrin River. Built in 1917, this metal bridge once spanned the Chena River in downtown Fairbanks before being dismantled and barged north in the 1950s.

At Mile 84, the road ends at the wooden Kougarok Bridge, one of the best areas to spot herds of musk ox and fish for grayling, Dolly Varden, and salmon. Beyond this point, the road turns into an ATV track that trails back into the tundra. Take a moment before you begin the slow journey back to Nome to imagine ancient peoples traveling through here

SERPENTINE HOT SPRINGS' HEALING LEGACY

Tucked deep within Bering Land Bridge National Preserve, Serpentine Hot Springs has been a gathering place for centuries. Long before miners built the quirky stone 'bathhouse' that still shelters soakers today, Inupiat families came here to seek healing in the mineral waters and spiritual power among the granite tors. Oral histories tell of shamans performing ceremonies amid the rock spires, and many locals still consider the springs sacred. A boggy 20-mile trail leads in from the end of Kougarok Road, though most visitors arrive by small plane. Whether you come to soak or simply walk the tundra among ancient stones, Serpentine is one of the Seward Peninsula's most evocative sites.

ST LAWRENCE ISLAND: BETWEEN TWO WORLDS

Just 36 miles from Russia, St Lawrence Island sits closer to Siberia than to mainland Alaska. For thousands of years, its Yupik residents have lived across this strait, and today Gambell and Savoonga remain strongholds of traditional culture. Ivory carving – often from legally harvested walrus tusks – sustains many families, with intricate masks and figures that reflect centuries of artistry. During the Cold War, the island also served as a strategic listening post, monitoring Soviet activity across the water. Few visitors make it here – travel is expensive and must be arranged with local guides – but St Lawrence offers one of the clearest windows into a culture and landscape that bridges two continents.

on foot – you're just 55 miles from the eastern boundary of the Bearing Land Bridge National Preserve.

Teller

TIME FROM NOME: 2½HR

Tundra vistas and village life

If you're pressed for time, locals may tell you to skip a day trip out to the village of Teller – but this 73-mile journey through the sweeping Arctic tundra to the coast (ending just 55 miles away from Russia) is well worth the drive. There are ample chances to spot musk oxen along the way, and a portion of the reindeer herd is communally owned by families near Teller. The birding is fabulous, too.

Leaving Nome, the drive takes you past Anvil Mountain and then within view of the Bering Sea. On clear days, you might glimpse **Sledge Island** (originally named Ayak Island), an uninhabited island just 5 miles offshore. Around Mile 14, keep an eye out for rough-legged hawks, gyrfalcons and other raptors that nest in the rocky outcroppings to your right.

Hiking opportunities are numerous – though here as elsewhere, you won't find officially marked trails. Just pick a point and go for it. Near Mile 21, you will see a turnoff on the right where you can pull off and head along a ridgeline with sweeping views of the countryside.

Nearing Mile 26, you'll drive the bridge over the Sinuk River, the largest crossing on this route. It's worth pulling over to take in views of the mountain-backed gravel bars and rippling water, which are often full of salmon on their return upriver in late summer.

At Mile 40, a rough dirt road, owned by the King Island Native Corporation, leads to summer fishing camps at **Wooley Lagoon**. Islanders request visitors not to approach the lagoon, but you can drive a portion of the road or stop at the hillside

Caribou near Teller

just off the main Nome-Teller road to collect fresh spring water flowing there (believed to have healing properties).

Around Mile 54, an abandoned wooden dredge sits pretty on Gold Run Creek, though reaching it requires a bit of bushwhacking through serious willow thickets. While here, look for songbirds and shorebirds. You might even spot the rare bristle-thighed curlew in the low scrub. Less than a mile further along, you'll pass a small-scale working mining operation that was once known as Sullivan City. It's private property, though, so keep moving.

For the next 15 miles, there's no sign of human habitation until you make the awe-inspiring descent into the town of Teller. The coastline sweeps away dramatically, revealing this wind-hardened subsistence community of about 240 residents, which overlooks the slate-gray waters of the Bering Sea. The feeling of remoteness is immense. A drive through town reveals salmon curing in seaside huts, lone fishers heading offshore and kids playing basketball on a court that looks impossibly small amid the vast tundra in the distance. Beyond town, a tapering gravel spit near the mouth of Grantley Harbor teems with ATVs and boats. Roald Amundsen, one of the greatest figures in polar exploration, landed here after his legendary 70-hour airship flight over the North Pole on May 14, 1926. In 1985, Teller again made the headlines when Libby Riddles, then a Teller resident, became the first woman to win the Iditarod.

Today, with rising sea levels and melting permafrost, Teller remains on the front lines of climate change – though this resilient community has no plans to relocate, unlike other remote Alaskan villages.

TRADITION VERSUS MODERNITY

Throughout the 20th century, advances in transportation, communication and social services reshaped remote Northern Alaska. Bush planes made the region more accessible, and towns like Nome and Utqiaġvik grew into commercial hubs serving the smaller villages in their orbit. Political and legal battles brought more schools and better healthcare, while the 1971 Alaska Native Claims Settlement Act turned villages into corporations and residents into shareholders.

Today, residents engage in a fine balancing act – coping with the challenges of the 21st century while preserving the values, practices and links to the land that have been passed down through generations and sustained for millennia.

NOME'S AVIATION FIRSTS

Nome has always punched above its weight in the sky. In 1926, Roald Amundsen's airship *Norge* drifted into Nome after the Arctic's first flight across the region, a moment that stunned locals who raced to the beach to watch it land. During WWII, Nome was a key transfer point for the Lend-Lease program, as American pilots ferried aircraft to Soviet allies across the Bering Strait – from P-39 fighters to transport planes. Today, bush pilots keep Nome connected, flying groceries, mail, and medevac patients across the roadless Seward Peninsula. Whether blimps, bombers, or Beavers on floats, aviation here has always been more a matter of necessity than novelty – and remains a lifeline for the region.

White Alice Communications System, Anvil Mountain

Anvil Mountain

TIME FROM NOME: **20MIN**

Panoramic views, Cold War relics

The climb up 1062ft **Anvil Mountain** is the closest hike to Nome – and the only one that can be reasonably pulled off without a car. It's about two miles from town and a half-mile to the summit through wonderful summer wildflower patches. If you're not up for the hike, you can cheat a bit (well, a lot) by taking the road to the top – go slowly on this rough, pockmarked road.

At the summit, you'll find the giant parabolic antennas of the **White Alice Communications System**. Dubbed 'Nomehenge' by locals, these four massive structures were installed in the 1950s as part of a Cold War-era network spanning western Alaska and used for some 20 years. They were phased out in the 1970s with the advent of satellite communications.

On clear days, you'll have fine views of Nome, with the shimmering Bering Sea just beyond. In other directions, you'll see a seemingly endless expanse of rolling hills and tundra valleys. While summer is the best time for hiking, autumn brings a flash of color to the tundra, and nights offer spectacular views of the northern lights (clouds and solar activity permitting).

To start, follow Bering St out of town until it becomes the Nome-Teller Hwy. About 2.5 miles in, turn right on the Dexter Bypass and look for an obvious dirt road climbing the hillside on your left about half a mile in. From the bottom to the top and back is about 3 miles round trip, with just over 1000ft of elevation gain. Keep an eye out for musk oxen – they're commonly spotted in the area.

Utqiaġvik

HERITAGE | POLAR BEARS | AMERICA'S NORTHERNMOST POINT

Utqiaġvik sits at the very edge of the map, 330 miles north of the Arctic Circle, where endless tundra meets the ice-choked Arctic Ocean. For two months in summer, the sun never sets, and for two months in winter, it never rises. Life here is lived between extremes, and somehow, it's full of vitality. The Inupiat have thrived in this landscape for millennia, and seasonal subsistence whaling still anchors community life.

That thread of tradition runs right alongside modern life, funded in part by North Slope petroleum. You'll find sturdy schools, a borough headquarters, and a heritage center that tells the community's story in its own voice. Wander through town and you might pass under whale bones arching over the beach, see traditional umiaks pulled up on racks, or hear ATVs rattling down gravel streets. Utqiaġvik isn't just the far north – it's living proof of resilience, adaptation, and pride at the top of the world.

Inupiat Art & Culture
Learning about Indigenous traditions

The main draw in town is the **Inupiat Heritage Center**, a beautifully curated modern museum that doubles as a community gathering place. Inside are several well-curated galleries, a gift shop, and a bright studio space in the back where local craftspeople hone baleen sculptures and jewelry – and are more than happy to talk about their art.

Exhibits highlight not only the immense challenges of life in the Arctic but also the creativity and resilience that have carried Inupiat culture forward. What you see here isn't just history on display, it's living memory. The galleries lead past poster-sized portraits of local elders and beneath a 35ft replica of a bowhead whale. Look closer to spot miniature hunting scenes carved out of ivory, headdresses trimmed with loon and raven feathers, and masks of striking variety. Along a back corridor, a display of Arctic birds serves as a handy primer

GETTING AROUND

The only way here is by air, on daily (and pricey) flights from Anchorage, with smaller hops to North Slope villages available. Utqiaġvik is walkable when the weather allows, but strong winds make flat-fare taxis a welcome option (cash only). Rental cars are available near the airport. Download offline maps before you arrive, as cell coverage is patchy, and carry bear spray if venturing outside town – polar bear encounters are rare but possible.

- **SIGHTS**
1 71 North Tours
2 Iñupiat Heritage Center
3 Utqiaġvik
4 Utqiaġvik Presbyterian Church
5 Whalebone arch

- **ACTIVITIES**
6 Tundra Tours

- **SLEEPING**
7 King Eider Inn
8 Latitude 71 BnB
9 Top of the World Hotel

- **EATING**
10 Mario's Pizza
see 9 Niġġivikput Restaurant
11 Osaka
12 Sam & Lee's Restaurant

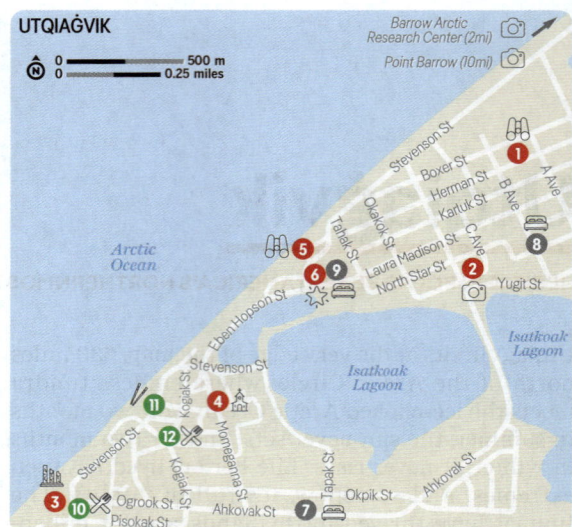

UTQIAĠVIK'S BIGGEST EVENT

The **Nalukataq Festival** is held in late June, after the spring whaling season ends. Depending on how successful the hunt has been, celebrations can last anywhere from a few days to more than a week. It's a rare cultural experience and one of the best reasons to visit Utqiaġvik. The main event is the blanket toss, in which locals use a sealskin tarp to toss people into the air – much like bouncing on a trampoline. The object of each jumper is to reach the biggest heights, which replicates ancient efforts to spot game in the distance.

for spotting the region's specialties – keep an eye out later for the spectacled eider, red-throated loon or crested auklet.

A climate-controlled gallery to the right of the entrance immerses you in traditional whaling and hunting culture and will leave your jaw dropped. Among other things, the displays in this room detail the painstaking work of building traditional *umiak* boats, including the ancient practice of spinning waterproof thread from caribou sinew to stitch the bearded seal-skin hulls. Each whaling crew has its own flag (a few are hung proudly here), and a camp mock-up shows how hunters live out on the ice during the whaling season. At the end of the exhibit, don't miss the chance to try on an Inupiat parka, quite possibly the warmest piece of clothing you'll ever wear.

If you're lucky enough to catch artists working in the back studio, stop for a chat. Their stories – of navigating shifting ice, witnessing climate change firsthand, and keeping traditions alive – are as memorable as the exhibits themselves.

Roaming the Lanes of Utqiaġvik

Architecture, views and monuments

You won't find many big-ticket attractions in Utqiaġvik, but a free-form wander through town is a worthwhile education. The streets are a living gallery of modern Arctic life layered with deep tradition: modern homes sit beside weathered Quonset huts, and shiny snowmachines sit parked next to racks of handmade sleds and traditional *umiaks* built to travel across sea ice.

One of the best views in town is through the **whalebone arch** behind the Top of the World Hotel. Through it, you'll see a horizon that, even in midsummer, sometimes still holds floating ice. A short walk away, the blue and white-painted **Utqiaġvik Presbyterian Church** (active since 1899) offers services in both Inupiat and English, and a signpost out front points north: just 1250 miles to the pole (yes, that one). Across the street at the Arctic Slope Regional Corporation, ask to peek at the lobby display cases: three mastodon tusks recovered from the tundra rest on a block, and delicate baskets woven from baleen sit on display, a vestige of an art form not frequently practiced today. Keep heading north and you'll reach the corners of Apayauk and Ogrook streets, where low earthen mounds mark **Ukpiaġvik,** a historic Inupiat settlement over 2000 years old that faces the ocean.

Daily life here is built to coexist with permafrost. As you wander, notice that most houses perch on pilings or are surrounded by antenna-like thermosiphons to keep their foundations from thawing the earth. Beneath your feet, water and waste run through an intricate system of heated 'utilidors,' wooden tunnels ingeniously built with lumber shipped up after Mt St Helens erupted in 1980.

Along the waterfront, the constant battle with erosion and climate change is impossible to ignore. Shipping containers sunk into the beach act as storm barriers, sprawling clusters of sandbags brace the shoreline, and a new seawall made of boulders barged from Nome is underway. If your timing's right, swing by the **Barrow Arctic Research Center** just outside town to get a glimpse of the climate science happening right on the frontlines.

Where the Land Runs Out

Tour to the northernmost point in the US

Point Barrow, a narrow spit of land jutting into the frigid Arctic Ocean, is the northernmost extremity of the US. Located just 12 miles north of Utqiaġvik, it would seem an easy jaunt to get there – but the 'road' is really just a remote stretch of deep sand and gravel. It also traverses Alaska Native lands, so you'll need to join an authorized tour to make the trip. Several tour operators go partway, but only **71 North** will take you all the way out to the point.

This small Inupiat-owned outfitter runs an immersive 2-hour tour in a big-tired vehicle built to glide through the shifting terrain. The journey passes several unique sights: a blue-and-gold football field stands out against the terrain where the local high school team, the Whalers, play games at the edge of the world. Past that, a metal runway and abandoned military buildings mark where the Navy operated until 1980.

From here, the sand deepens and the spit narrows. You glide past clusters of wind-bitten fishing camps leaning against the elements, whimsical 'palm trees' with stalks made of driftwood and fronds made of baleen, and bowhead whale bones of all sizes from past harvests. Birders and nature lovers should keep an eye out: eiders and phalaropes skim the lagoons, while murres, black guillemots, and sandpipers wheel overhead. Offshore, you might glimpse spotted seals hauled out on the

☑ TOP TIP

Apart from ticking off the town's handful of key sights, you can also stroll the gravel roads and gray-sand beaches to view *umiaks* (traditional boats), giant bowhead whale jawbones, fish-drying racks and the jumbled Arctic pack ice that, even in July, spans the horizon.

BEST TOURS IN UTQIAĠVIK

71 North Tours: This is the only tour that takes you to Point Barrow – the northernmost point of North America. Along the way, learn about Inupiat culture and, with luck, see some wildlife.

Tundra Tours: Top of the World Hotel runs half-day summer tours that include a tundra walk, a drive to the end of the road system, and a narrated tour around the Inupiat Heritage Center.

Wilderness Birding Adventures: Small-group birding tours to the Arctic region, including a three-day Utqiaġvik trip in October to spot the elusive, pink Ross's gull. Also runs a spring migration tour in June.

ANCESTRAL TRADITIONS

Vernon Amaulik Edwardsen, captain of the Amaulik whaling crew and founder of 71 North Tours, talks about sacred, deep-rooted traditions in Utqiaġvik.

'The reason why we're up here is to pursue a subsistence lifestyle, which is part of our culture. Subsistence, for those that don't know, is living off the land. We want to continue to maintain these traditions that have been passed on from generation to generation. It's not for everybody, but it's what we love to do. Whaling requires year-round preparation, and we still use traditional skin boats when we hunt. The meat harvested from the bowhead will be shared with the entire community. We make sure no one goes hungry here.'

Whalebone arch (p380), Utqiaġvik

ice, and if you're really lucky, polar bears often patrol the shoreline, though the best chance of sightings is in the spring.

At the point itself, the feeling of remoteness is absolute: as is the silence when the wind dies down. To the north, the Arctic Ocean; to the south, the entirety of the North American continent. Standing at Point Barrow is as humbling as it gets: a moment suspended between two oceans and the edge of the world.

 EATING IN UTQIAĠVIK: OUR PICKS

Osaka: Cozy Japanese-run spot serving teriyaki platters, bento boxes and sushi rolls, alongside burgers and breakfast fare. *9am-10pm Mon-Sun* **$$$**

Niġġivikput Restaurant: Great place to linger over hearty breakfasts, fish and chips, sandwiches and salads. *7am-8pm Mon-Sat, 8am-8pm Sun* **$$**

Sam & Lee's Restaurant: Local favorite with a cheery interior and a wide menu of delicious Chinese-American fusion dishes. *9am-1.30am Mon-Sun* **$$**

Mario's Pizza: Pizzas, sub sandwiches and Philly cheesesteaks with a view of the Arctic Ocean. *11am-10pm Mon-Thur, to 11pm Fri & Sat, 4pm-10pm Sun* **$$**

Dalton Highway

SPRAWLING TUNDRA | ARCTIC CIRCLE | REMOTE VILLAGES

Two hours north of Fairbanks, the smooth pavement runs out and a modest sign announces the start of one of North America's most legendary drives: the Dalton Highway. Known locally as the Haul Road, this 440-mile route runs all the way to Deadhorse at Prudhoe Bay, shadowing the Trans-Alaska Pipeline through boreal forest, mountain passes, endless tundra, and ends at the edge of the Arctic Ocean.

It's a road built for industry to supply Alaska's northern oil fields, but it's also a famous, rugged corridor into some of the most remote and wild country you can reach by vehicle. The Dalton doesn't coddle. Chipseal gives way to long gravel stretches studded with potholes, dust flies behind every passing truck, and services are few and far between. But if you come prepared, the payoff is a front-row seat to landscapes that seem to shift in geological time.

Driving Across the Arctic
Mountains, tundra and history

The grand adventure north kicks off long before Mile 0. In fact, the Dalton Highway begins some 85 miles north of Fairbanks, so plan on an extra two hours of driving before you even reach the start line. Snap your obligatory photo at the 'Welcome to the James Dalton Highway' sign, then brace yourself. The pavement quickly gives way to gravel, dust and blind curves, and a final sign delivers the challenge ahead: speed limit 50 mph – for the next 414 miles.

Dalton's first few miles roll gently, with the silvery line of the pipeline often in view, until the road tilts down toward the broad sweep of the Yukon River. At Mile 56, the wood-decked Yukon River Bridge creaks under your tires. It's a genuine feat of engineering at over half a mile long, and one of only four bridges that span this impressive river. On the north side, the Bureau of Land Management-run **Yukon Crossing Visitor Contact Station** is worth a pause for maps, road updates, and a quick lesson in Arctic ecology. Across the way, **Yukon**

GETTING AROUND

Most major rental car companies do not allow travel on the Dalton Highway, so you'll have to go with a specialty service like Alaska Auto Rental in Fairbanks, which equips vehicles with spare tires and a CB radio. Fill up on fuel at every stop and watch out for potholes: hitting one at a moderately high speed can easily blow a tire.

If you don't want to drive, Dalton Highway Express runs 10-seat passenger vans twice a week from June through August, stopping at key places along the way. One-way fare from Fairbanks to Deadhorse is $435.

DALTON HIGHWAY

● HIGHLIGHTS
1 Arctic Interagency Visitor Center

● SIGHTS
2 Arctic Circle Sign
3 Atigun Pass
4 Finger Mountain
5 Gates of the Arctic National Park and Preserve
6 Gobbler's Knob
7 Prospect Creek
8 Wiseman

● ACTIVITIES
9 Arctic National Wildlife Refuge
10 Northern Alaska Tour Company

● SLEEPING
11 Arctic Getaway Bed and Breakfast
12 Boreal Lodge
13 Coldfoot Camp
14 Deadhorse Camp
15 Galbraith Lake Campground
16 Yukon River Camp

● EATING
17 Aurora Hotel
18 Trucker's Cafe

● INFORMATION
19 Yukon Crossing Visitor Contact Station

☑ TOP TIP

Drive with extreme caution. There's no cell reception on the Dalton Highway, and it can be a long wait until help arrives if things go sideways.

River Camp offers hot food, gas, and a quick reality check: this is one of your last guaranteed fuel stops until Coldfoot.

Beyond the Yukon, the road begins to climb. Spruce forest thins into open, rocky hills where wind scours the ridges. At the gnarled 40-ft **Finger Mountain**, a short interpretive trail loops just beyond the granite outcrop that has been used for generations as a landmark when navigating the high country. Keep your eyes peeled for hawks riding thermals overhead, and wildflowers tucked into the lee of boulders here.

At Mile 115, you pass the imaginary line of the **Arctic Circle** (stop for a photo at the sign) and soon after, **Gobbler's Knob** offers your first big look at the Brooks Range with its blue-gray teeth on the horizon. The Trans-Alaska Pipeline snakes alongside you towards Pump Station 5, its looping arcs engineered to withstand permafrost's freeze-thaw cycles. You'll then pass **Prospect Creek**, which experienced America's lowest-recorded temperature in 1971: -80° F.

Coldfoot (p387) appears like a mirage at Mile 175 after hours of empty road: a mining settlement turned traveler's stop where you can fill your tank, grab a hot meal at the **Trucker's Cafe,** and swap stories with folks hauling to Prudhoe Bay. Across the road, the **Arctic Interagency Visitor Center** is a bona fide trove of information on local geology, wildlife, and public lands, with rangers happy to help you make the most of your time this far north. If you need a rest, Marion Creek Campground lies just 30 minutes up the road in a pocket of spruce trees, with a short trail leading out of the campsite to a waterfall nearby.

Sitting on a spur road 14 miles north of Coldfoot is **Wiseman**, a historic gold-mining village turned year-round home to a handful of hardy residents. Tidy log cabins line the quiet lanes, and you can book a walking tour with local guide Jack Reakoff through **Northern Alaska Tour Company** to hear him spin stories about Arctic life, exploration, and subsistence traditions of the area. Just outside town, the pipeline ducks underground, and the road begins a beautiful, steady climb as you skirt the edge of the Arctic National Wildlife Refuge. The staggering, western limestone face of Skukapak Mountain (4459ft) looms ahead at Mile 194 as you wind your way past the Chandalar Shelf toward **Atigun Pass**. Dall sheep are often visible on the mountain slopes here, so keep your eyes peeled.

Atigun Pass marks the Continental Divide and is Alaska's highest year-round pass at 4,739ft. Crossing it feels like stepping into another world – south of the pass, the valleys are hemmed in by spruce; north of it, the trees vanish and are replaced by an open sweep of tundra that rolls to the horizon. In midsummer, the pass is a riot of wildflowers; by August, the reds and golds of autumn creep in. Limestone cliffs alongside the road catch light in pale stripes, and braided rivers wind through gravel beds below.

From here, the Dalton skirts the edge of the Arctic National Wildlife Refuge. At **Galbraith Lake Campground**, a handful of stunning sites sit between two great wildernesses: to the east, the Refuge's folded mountains; to the west, the crags of Gates of the Arctic National Park (p386). In June and July, the sun swings in a lazy circle overhead, never dipping below the horizon.

North of Galbraith, the Brooks Range gives way to the rolling Arctic Coastal Plain, a low, waterlogged expanse where permafrost lies just beneath the surface and ponds pock the tundra. The road here is straighter, the sky somehow bigger, and you'll share it all with caribou herds and long-haul trucks bound for the oil fields.

The Dalton Highway ends in Deadhorse, a remote industrial outpost at the edge of the Arctic and the gateway to the Prudhoe Bay oil fields. There's no real 'town' here – just a scatter of rigs, machinery, and modular housing for workers who keep the North Slope running. Travelers can't continue further without a guide, so refuel at the Aurora Hotel (p387) café before joining an Arctic Ocean Shuttle tour (book ahead through Deadhorse Camp (p387)). If conditions allow (and you're brave), a quick plunge into the frigid Arctic is the ultimate badge of honor for reaching the northernmost drivable point in the US. You'll have to save a toast for the long road back south, however: Deadhorse is a dry town.

THE ALASKA PIPELINE

Love it or loathe it, if you're driving Alaska's Dalton Highway, the Trans-Alaska Pipeline will be your traveling companion. The steely tube, 4ft wide and 800 miles long, parallels the highways from Prudhoe Bay on the Arctic Ocean down to Valdez, Alaska's northernmost ice-free port. En route, it spans 500-odd waterways and three mountain ranges, transporting about 500,000 barrels of crude oil per day to tankers waiting in Prince William Sound. Especially good views can be had on the Dalton Highway at the Yukon River crossing, and at the spur road to Wiseman. Just north of Fairbanks, you can walk right up to the pipeline and stand under it.

VENTURE INTO THE ARCTIC NATIONAL WILDLIFE REFUGE

Straddling the eastern Brooks Range, the **Arctic National Wildlife Refuge** is a vast wilderness home to grizzlies, musk ox, Dall sheep and the second-largest caribou herd in North America. More than 20 rivers cut through the region, many ideal for multiday paddles, along with the four highest peaks in the Brooks Range. For adventurers, photographers and lovers of truly wild places, it's an appealing destination. With no facilities or trails, most visitors fly in by bush plane. However, there is one place where it can be accessed by car; just north of Atigun Pass on the Dalton Highway, where the road and the refuge briefly touch.

Gates of the Arctic National Park & Preserve

Gates of the Arctic National Park and Preserve

Fly-in adventures, untouched backcountry

Remote and pristine, **Gates of the Arctic National Park & Preserve** spans 27,000 sq miles of wilderness. Unless you're an experienced backcountry traveler, it's best explored by air – Northern Alaska Tour Company runs flightseeing trips from Fairbanks with sweeping views and no need for extra gear. For those ready to immerse, Alaska Alpine Adventures leads backpacking and rafting expeditions with transport, food, and expertise included. Be aware, creature comforts end at Fairbanks: there are no visitor services, shops, or restaurants in the park. Respect the wild – animals here rarely encounter people, and travelers are guests in one of the Earth's last truly untamed landscapes.

Places We Love to Stay

$ Budget $$ Midrange $$$ Top End

Nome MAP p369

Aurora Inn $$$ Nome's most hotel-like accommodations with comfortably furnished rooms, some with views of the sea.

Dredge No 7 Inn $$$ Welcoming inn with attractive, well-equipped rooms located 1.5 miles north of the center.

Noxapaga Suites $$$ Rents out polished modern apartments that come with kitchens, laundry and high-speed internet.

Outside Nome

AkAu Gold Resort $$$ Seven miles north of town, a great base for adventures, and gold panning on-site.

Salmon Lake Campground $ Scenic lakeside spots with picnic tables and barbecue pits on the Kougarok Rd, and camping here is free.

Pilgrim Hot Springs $ Enjoy the lovely views off the Kougarok Rd, with simple cabins and steaming hot springs.

Utqiaġvik MAP p380

Top of the World Hotel $$$ North America's northernmost hotel is surprisingly plush, with boutique-style rooms and a good restaurant.

King Eider Inn $$ The cozy rooms have wood-post beds, and there's an inviting fireplace in the lobby.

Latitude 71 BnB $$$ B&B with a homelike vibe, and the rooms and common areas are full of Alaska artwork.

Dalton Highway MAP p384

Coldfoot Camp $$$ Small, rustic rooms with private bathrooms set in trailers, or pitch a tent for free.

Boreal Lodge $$ Welcoming place in Wiseman with wood-paneled rooms and cabins surrounded by forest.

Arctic Getaway Bed and Breakfast $$$ These inviting off-the-grid log cabins near Wiseman make great bases for exploring the region.

Deadhorse MAP p384

Brooks Camp $$$ The huge, institutional-like complex has simple rooms with private bathrooms. Food is included.

Aurora Hotel $$$ Overlooking Colleen Lake, the 432-room hotel has snug rooms and ample amenities.

Deadhorse Camp $$$ Basic, clean rooms with shared bathrooms. It also runs a shuttle to the Arctic Ocean.

Northern lights over Wiseman (p385)

Richardson Hwy (p195)
DCRANE/SHUTTERSTOCK

TOOLKIT

The chapters in this section cover the most important topics you'll need to know about in Alaska. They're full of nuts-and-bolts information and valuable insights to help you understand and navigate Alaska and get the most out of your trip.

Arriving
p390

Getting Around
p391

Money
p392

Accommodations
p393

Family Travel
p394

Health & Safe Travel
p395

Food, Drink & Nightlife
p396

Responsible Travel
p398

LGBTIQ+ Travelers
p400

Accessible Travel
p401

Nuts & Bolts
p403

Arriving

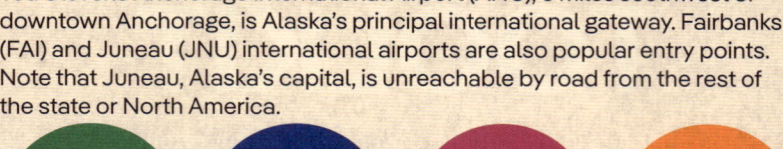

Ted Stevens Anchorage International Airport (ANC), 5 miles southwest of downtown Anchorage, is Alaska's principal international gateway. Fairbanks (FAI) and Juneau (JNU) international airports are also popular entry points. Note that Juneau, Alaska's capital, is unreachable by road from the rest of the state or North America.

Visas

Australians, New Zealanders and Europeans, among others, can enter visa-free for 90-days. However, an ESTA travel authorization is needed *($21; esta.cbp.dhs.gov)*. Those who do need visas may need a multiple-entry if taking a cruise.

SIM Cards

Most travelers opt for prepaid eSIMs from companies such as **Airalo** *(airalo.com)*, **Holifly** *(esim.holafly.com)* and **Simtex** *(simtex.io)*, but you can get physical SIMs at GCI, ATT, Verizon and Fred Meyer locations around Anchorage.

Wi-Fi

Complimentary wi-fi is available in both ANC terminals powered by the Cisco Web-Authentication Network. Connect to 'ANC Free WIFI', accept the terms and conditions, and browse away.

ATMs

You'll find ATMs near the baggage carousels in the arrivals terminal. The fee is $3 – on par with ATMs in town, so no reason not to pull out here.

Transport from the Airport

	Anchorage	Juneau	Fairbanks
BUS	25min $2	35min $2	45min $1.50
UBER/LYFT	15min $25	15min $40	15min $25

MULTIPLE RE-ENTRY VISAS

Due to its geographic position sharing a land border with Canada's Yukon Territory and British Columbia as opposed to the contiguous United States, citizens of the 155 countries that are not part of the Visa Waiver Program may need a multiple re-entry visa (B-2 Visitor's Visa) if coming from the Lower 48 by cruise ship (and by road, obviously). Since most cruise ships aren't American-flagged vessels, an 1886 law requires a stop in a foreign port before returning to the US – hence a usual stop in Canada. Check ahead for your cruise-ship routing.

Getting Around

A vehicle greatly enhances travel in most populated parts of Alaska, but far-flung communities unreachable by road are numerous – ferries and charter flights are your new best friends. The train travel is epic, too.

TRAVEL COSTS

Car rental
$175–350/day

Fuel
From $4 per gallon

Denali Star train from Anchorage to Fairbanks
Adult/child $221/111

Flight from Juneau to Anchorage
From $229

Car Hire

To rent a vehicle in Alaska, you must have a valid driver's license, be at least 21 years of age and possess a major credit card (or be prepared to pay a large cash deposit). An International Driving Permit (IDP) is not required, but is certainly recommended to avoid potential confusion/issues.

Plane

Alaska Airlines *(alaskaair.com)* is the main airline, servicing over a dozen destinations in Alaska. With 75% of the state inaccessible by road, small, single-engine planes called 'bush planes' (including floatplanes and beachlanders) are the backbone of intrastate transport. Fares vary by plane type, size, passenger numbers and flying time, but are quite pricey.

TIP

Airport car hire hits your wallet with an extra airport tax (11.11% in Anchorage, for example). Rent in town if possible.

MIND THE MOOSE!

Moose-vehicle collisions are a serious problem – some 500 accidents are reported annually and the Alaska Department of Fish & Game estimates hundreds more go unreported. You do not want to collide with an 800–1600lb moose, so headlights on (day or night) and always scan the road ahead. Slow down, give them space and don't get lost in the landscape as you drive.

Ferry

Alaska Marine Highway *(dot.alaska.gov/amhs)* ferries call at 35 ports. Nine regular vessels serve four main regions: Southeast (Ketchikan up to Skagway), the cross-gulf route (Juneau to Whittier), Southcentral Alaska (Prince William Sound, Kenai Peninsula and Kodiak) and the Southwest (Alaska Peninsula and Aleutian Islands).

Train

The **Alaska Railroad** *(alaskarailroad.com)* runs a year-round service between Fairbanks and Anchorage, plus summer services (late May to mid-September) from Anchorage to Whittier and from Anchorage to Seward. The historic **White Pass & Yukon Railroad** *(wpyr.com)* offers scenic and hiker services from Skagway to Carcross in the Yukon.

Road Conditions

Only 20% of Alaska is accessible by road but what asphalt there is leads to spectacular scenery. Driving is generally easy – low grades, few sharp bends – but rental companies may prohibit driving the Dalton Hwy, the Taylor Hwy, the road to McCarthy and the Denali Hwy. **Alaska 511** *(511.alaska.gov)* offers real-time road condition info.

DRIVING ESSENTIALS

Drive on the right

Speed limit is 20mph in business districts, 55mph on secondary roads and 65mph on motorways

.08
Blood alcohol limit is 0.08g/100 mL

Money

CURRENCY: US DOLLAR ($)

ATMs & Credit Cards

In Alaska ATMs are everywhere: banks, gas stations, supermarkets, airports and even some visitor centers. Alaskan merchants are willing to accept just about all major credit cards. Visa and Mastercard are the most widely accepted cards, but American Express and Discovery are also widely used.

Tipping

While not mandatory, tipping in restaurants is socially obligatory. Not doing so could cause an uncomfortable situation.
Restaurants 15–20% is customary.
Tour guides 10–20% of the tour cost; up to 30% for above and beyond acts.
Taxis/Uber Around 10–15%.

Taxes

Alaska is one of five states that doesn't charge state sales tax, though local sales taxes are applied in some boroughs and municipalities (up to 5% in Juneau, for example). Short-term room-rental taxes are sometimes applied, such as Anchorage's 12% room tax.

Digital Payments

Tapping your phone with mobile payment services such as Apple Pay and Google Pay is common in bigger cities. Mobile payment apps such as Venmo, Cash App and Zelle are also firmly embedded.

HOW MUCH FOR...

city bus fare
$2

Anchorage museum entry
$25–30

four-hour kayak tour from Ketchikan
$149

seven-day Denali National Park pass
$15

HOW TO... Save Money on Cruising

A popular way to see large swaths of Alaska's incredible nature and scenery is from the water. But luxury cruise ships cost a pretty penny. One pleasurable workaround is to take advantage of Alaska's maritime public-transport system, the **Alaska Marine Highway** (dot.alaska.gov/amhs). While certainly not luxurious, AMH's ferry boats cost a fraction of a cruise, offer the chance to see wildlife from the decks, and even have good, inexpensive food served onboard.

LOCAL TIP

Spotty internet is too often the norm in rural Alaska, so many rural businesses are cash-only. Others have high credit card minimum purchases. Keep cash in various bill sizes handy.

THE ALASKA COST

There's no sugar-coating it: Alaska is pricey. Labor and materials cost a premium, to say nothing of transport costs from the Lower 48 and from Anchorage to Alaskan settlements reachable only by plane. Expect to pay $250 to $600 (or more) per night for a standard, two-queen room in the heart of any city during high season (May to September; double in more rural areas and full-service lodges). Those $18 fish and chips back home? They're $36 here. One pleasant exception? Espresso! Prices are often on par with most of the Lower 48 (insert shrug emoji here).

Accommodations

Camping

Camping is extremely popular in Alaska and those toting tents will be spoiled for choice. From rustic, primitive sites to posh glamping outposts, campgrounds occupy some of the nation's most stunning scenery. Book out reservable campsites and public-use cabins as early as possible – up to seven months in advance for Alaska State Parks and six months out for US Forest Service (USFS) locations.

Wilderness Lodges

Remote wilderness lodges offer some of Alaska's most lavish accommodations in some of its least accessible places. For prices from $500 to $1200 a night, these all-inclusive, off-the-grid hideaways are often reachable only by boat or air taxi, and leave guests nearly on their own amid some of the state's most spectacular scenery. Guided hikes, fishing and bear viewing, among other activities, fill the days.

Hotels, Motels & B&Bs

Hotels and motels are often the most expensive lodgings you can book and tend to be monopolized in summer by tour groups and cruise ships. B&Bs can be an acceptable compromise between sleeping on the ground and sleeping in high-priced lodges. Some B&Bs are a bargain, and most are cheaper than major hotels, but expect $150 to $250 per night for a double room.

Public-Use Cabins

Alaska's public-use cabins offer rustic getaways (no running water, usually no mattresses, outhouses) near the road system, inside national parks or in more far-flung locales. Hundreds of public-use cabins are managed around the state by various agencies, including USFS, and range in price from $35 to $90 per night, reservable up to 180 days in advance.

HOW MUCH FOR A NIGHT IN A...

remote cabin
$75

fishing lodge
$300–600

midrange Anchorage hotel
$300

Hostels

America's most expensive state offers limited options for budget travel, but Alaska is home to 20 or so hostels, including in Juneau, Anchorage and Fairbanks. These budget facilities offer bunk rooms with kitchen facilities and other common areas for nightly fees ranging from $30 to $65. Find listings on **Alaska Hostel Association** *(alaskahostelassociation.org)*.

BEDS VS CRUISE SHIPS

Alaska is a secluded destination, and things get even more isolated upon arrival, with many of the state's most spectacular locales inaccessible by road. A finite number of beds are available, and cruise lines often block rooms a year in advance (cruising brings in nearly two million passengers annually). It's smart to make reservations at least six months ahead of travel to avoid disappointment between June and August. The shoulder season of May and September is a bit less urgent, but two to three months out is recommended.

Family Travel

The great outdoors is as appealing to kids as it is to older travelers. While kid-centric museums, amusement parks and other typical family-oriented entertainment aren't very plentiful here, the entire state is a spectacular backdrop to wide-ranging adventure, wildlife-watching and memorable journeys, whether boating past calving glaciers in a national park or flying in a small plane over the highest peaks in North America.

Facilities
Diaper-changing stations are common in airports, shopping-mall bathrooms and some restaurants, but the latter can be a mixed bag – a portable changing mat can't hurt. Most hotels can provide cribs or cots for little ones if you reserve ahead.

Dining Out
In typical American fashion, families are well catered to when dining out: kids menus are ubiquitous (and the fish sticks are of much higher quality!). High chairs and booster seats are readily available upon request, and folks in general are tolerant of child dining antics. You can beat the crowds and often find other families dining by arriving around 5pm or so.

Getting Around
Children two and older require a full-fare ticket on Alaska Airlines. Children between two and 11 years old are offered discounted fares (save 50%) on Alaska Railroad as well as Park Connection Motorcoach. RV rentals are especially popular with families.

BEST SPOTS FOR KIDS

Talkeetna
Take a jet-boating adventure, rent a bike for scenic rides, and snack at food trucks around town (p292).

Denali National Park & Preserve
Offers hikes for all levels, evening campground programs and junior ranger activities (p303).

Fairbanks
Antique cars, canoe trips and migratory birds, plus day trips to hot springs and the North Pole (p316; reindeers and Santa included).

Glacier Bay National Park
Spot whales, puffins, mountain goats (and with luck, bears) while boating past glaciers and floating icebergs (p109).

BE A JUNIOR RANGER
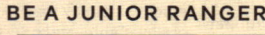

Kids can earn a very cool badge through the Junior Ranger Program, available at various national parks, including Denali, Glacier Bay and Wrangell-St Elias. To earn the badge, kids complete an activity book with questions and games, and for some parks complete an activity (such as a hike, while making observations along the way). The program is aimed at five- to 12-year-olds. Some parks have a range of activities for younger and older kids, with plenty of insight into wildlife. Adults can enjoy it too, and everyone is likely to gain a deeper understanding of the surrounding environment.

Health & Safe Travel

HYGIENE & HEALTHCARE

There is a high level of hygiene found in Alaska, so most common infectious diseases will not be a significant concern for travelers. Healthcare is widely available in the main population centers as is rapid evacuation to major hospitals. However, healthcare costs in Alaska, as throughout the USA, are extremely high. Travel health insurance is essential for foreign visitors.

Tidal Mudflats

Extreme tidal variation around Anchorage, Cook Inlet and Turnagain Arm exposes mudflats, which erroneously appear explorable. They're not. The mudflats are estuaries of quicksand-like mud and can trap someone in a vice-like grip in seconds. It's a deadly proposition combined with one of the world's fastest moving tides. People have died. Never walk on the mudflats.

Winter Driving

Driving long distances during Alaska's long winters is a time-consuming and hazardous process. Tire chains are not used in the state, except on delivery trucks or semi-trucks in extreme conditions, so if you are not comfortable driving in snow and ice, consider renting a 4WD vehicle or using other transportation options.

BUGGING OUT

Alaska is a buggy place. Mosquitoes, black flies, no-see-ums and deer flies wreak havoc between May and September. DEET-based repellents are recommended.

WILDLIFE ROAD SIGNS

Caribou crossing

Moose crash alert

Bear crossing

Sunburn

Due to Alaska's long summer days, sunburn is a primary concern for anyone trekking or paddling. Fairbanks and other places in the Interior can get quite hot (above 90 °F) in the summer, so don't forget the sun protection. Apply sunscreen with a high SPF to exposed skin, even on cloudy days, and wear a hat and sunglasses.

BEAR SPRAY

Bear spray is an essential accessory for Alaskans. If you plan any walks in the wilderness, it's best to have a can at the ready (in a holster at your side, not stuffed in your backpack). One canister costs $30 to $50, and cannot be flown, so plan to buy it from an outdoor store after you arrive.

Food, Drink & Nightlife

When to Eat

Breakfast (7am to 10am, later on weekends) Tuck into classic diner fare or head to a cafe for breakfast burritos and lattes.

Lunch (noon to 2pm) Enjoy fish and chips off a food truck or burgers from an old-fashioned roadhouse.

Dinner (5pm to 8pm) Prime time for tucking into fresh-off-the-boat seafood and grilled steaks. Many places close early.

Where to Eat & Drink

Restaurants You'll encounter Pacific Rim cuisines, fresh game and local produce; pretension and white-tablecloth attitude are foreign concepts.

Bars Many bars double as restaurants, serving big portions of protein to soak up the booze on those long Alaskan nights.

Cafes Main-street cafes are the mainstay of small-town Alaska, serving breakfast, lunch and dinner. There's often halibut and salmon on the dinner menu.

Roadhouses In the Alaskan hinterlands, roadhouses are lodging, food and drinking spots all rolled into one.

MENU DECODER

Crab cake Crabmeat bound with breadcrumbs and eggs, then fried.

Seafood chowder Creamy potato-based soup with clams, salmon and/or other seafood.

Fish and chips Fried fish (cod or pricier rockfish or halibut) served with French fries.

Bowls Base of rice, creatively topped with veggies, seafood, pork belly, tofu or other ingredients.

Breakfast burritos Scrambled eggs with bacon or sausage, wrapped in a tortilla and served with salsa.

Box lunch Sandwich, chips and possibly fruit cup and dessert, ready to take on the day's outing.

Black cod (aka sablefish) Typically served marinated in miso, with rice and vegetables.

Fireweed Wildflower used to flavor ice cream and other desserts.

Jerky Salt-dried meat, often made from wild game.

Reindeer chili Hearty meat stew spiced with ground chilies and beans.

HOW TO... Eat Alaskan King Crab

Alaska's famed king crabs are among the biggest crab species in the world. And tackling them at the dinner table requires a bit more work than your average meatloaf. Upon arrival, take the legs and pull backwards on the hinge to separate the larger cartilage. Use a Crabinator or similar flatware crab-cracker utensil to tear away the shell and expose the succulent meat. There's also meat in the shoulder, which can be torn away by hand. To get at that claw meat, break it off at the hinges and crack the shell (a normal crab cracker usually suffices). To eat it, tear off bits of that tender, distinctly sweet crabmeat and dip it in drawn butter (or not). Bear in mind: the Bristol Bay red-king-crab harvest is sometimes cancelled due to depleted female populations. When it's closed, king crab on menus is likely unsustainably caught in Russia.

HOW MUCH FOR...

a latte
$6

a pint of craft beer
$8

a gourmet burger
$18

a fusion bowl
$18–25

a king-crab eggs Benedict
$28

an AK halibut & chips
$36

an alder-grilled salmon
$35–50

a fine-dining meal for two
$250

HOW TO... Prepare Salmon in the Wild

You'll want to clean your salmon within two hours of catching it, using a designated cleaning station. Using a sharp fillet knife, scale the fish (start at the tail and run the knife down the skin toward the head repeatedly until both sides of the fish are scaled). Rinse off residual scales and any slime that appears during this process. Gut the fish by cutting down the center of the belly from the anus (vent) to the head forward of the pectoral fins and use your hands to remove the internal organs, including any roe/milt and remaining entrails if necessary. Remove the fillets on the first side by placing the knife behind the front pectoral fin and cutting down until you hit the backbone; then run the knife along the backbone horizontally down to the tail, cutting through the ribs. Repeat the process on the second side. Once the fillets are out, remove the ribs by slowly running the knife down the edge of the fillet, being careful to stay as parallel to the fillet as possible to minimize meat loss. Small pin bones will remain – remove them with tweezers beforehand or as you eat. Clean the fillets with water and cook them to your liking, depending on your circumstances (over a campfire or on an alderwood grill can't be beat). Season them minimally – a bit of salt and pepper, and maybe a squeeze of lemon. Divine!

Reduce, Reuse, Recycle

The discarded fish remains can be cut up and thrown back into the river, which not only keeps bears at bay, but provides a source of nutrients for other fish in the river.

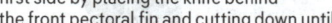

FOOD OF THE GODS

Alaska is home to one of the world's last bastions of wild Pacific salmon and intact salmon-producing ecosystems. The state is home to five varieties of wild salmon (Chinook salmon, sockeye salmon, chum salmon, pink salmon and coho salmon), as well as rainbow trout and cutthroat trout. In Alaska, you don't even need to ask if the salmon on the menu is farmed or wild – salmon farming is illegal (though fish hatcheries – facilities that enhance fisheries using existing wild stocks – are common).

What that means for visitors is that Alaska salmon will be the most divine expression of this internationally celebrated seafood that is likely to ever cross your plate. Chinook, also known as king salmon, is the most coveted of the bunch, but any variety of salmon here is going to be a memorable meal. You'll find salmon served as burgers, grilled or smoked with alderwood (which imparts a cedar-type flavor), as a spread for your morning bagel, baked in parchment, poached in wine and cooked over a campfire, among other methods. Even the discarded parts of the salmon (a king's neck or belly fins, for example) are life-changing, but you'll need to befriend a commercial fisher for that experience.

Salmon's peak season is May through September (conveniently paralleling tourist season). King salmon runs first, followed by sockeye, pink, chum and coho, the latter still spawning through the end of October. If it's on the menu – order it! Is it possible to tire of salmon in Alaska? Not likely!

Responsible Travel

Climate Change & Travel

It's impossible to ignore the impact we have when traveling; Lonely Planet urges all travelers to engage with their travel carbon footprint, which will mainly come from air travel. While there often isn't an alternative, travelers can look to minimise the number of flights they take, opt for newer aircrafts and use cleaner ground transport, such as trains. One proposed solution — purchasing carbon offsets — unfortunately does not cancel out the impact of individual flights. While most destinations will depend on air travel for the foreseeable future, for now, pursuing ground-based travel where possible is the best course of action.

The **UN carbon footprint calculator** shows how flying impacts a household's emissions

The **ICAO's Carbon Emissions Calculator** allows visitors to analyse the CO2 generated by point-to-point journeys

Buy Local

Shopping at locally owned businesses is easy in Alaska, where Alaskans pride themselves on shunning nationwide big-box stores, chain restaurants etc in favor of local choices. Buzzwords include Made in Alaska, Grown in Alaska and Silver Hand Program.

Support Local Artists

Alaskans are a creative and crafty bunch. You'll find plenty of places to purchase unique works (paintings, ceramics, jewelry, clothing) made in Alaska in art-minded towns like Homer (p272) and Talkeetna (p296).

Travel to the End of the Road

Learn about life in the Arctic on a **71 North** (p381) tour run by Iñupiat guides in Utqiaġvik. You'll get insight into traditional subsistence lifestyles and with luck see wildlife (whales, seals, perhaps even a polar bear).

Green Adventures

Consider taking a low-impact tour rather than a motorboat or a helicopter excursion. Kayaking and canoeing are more immersive, with fewer crowds and plenty of opportunities to experience Alaska's wild beauty.

TRAVEL GREEN

Long distances have conditioned Alaskans to love motorized transit but there is a definite push to use non-motorized ways to explore. In Anchorage, you can rent a bike and use over 120 miles of paved bike trails/multi-use trails.

EXPERIENCE CORDOVA'S REGENERATIVE TOURISM MODEL

Rooted in Indigenous values of stewardship, Cordova's regenerative tourism model makes it easy for visitors to leave this destination better than they found it through tours that support environmental restoration and cultural revitalization, and grow regenerative industries *(cordovachamber.com/regenerative-tourism)*.

Choose Sustainable Seafood

Wild-caught Pacific cod, Pacific salmon and Pacific sablefish (black cod) from Alaska waters are some of the most sustainable fish you can eat; king crab out of season likely comes from Russia and is harvested unsustainably.

Consider Small Ship Cruises

While all travel causes certain environmental and cultural impacts, by their very size, cruise ships leave a heavy wake. Organizations like **Friends of the Earth** *(foe.org/cruise-report-card)* give out grades for the environmental impact of various cruise ships.

Drink Local Craft Beer

Alaska ranks an impressive fourth place in the USA for breweries per capita – nearly 60 suds makers produce excellent craft beer, some using Alaska's superior, glacially fed water to do so. No need to drink 'imported' macro beers here.

Seek out Alaska Native Initiatives

Alaska Native initiatives, such as Anchorage's **Oomingmak Musk Ox Producers Co-op** *(qiviut.com)* and **Sealaska Heritage** *(sealaskaheritage.org)* in Juneau are excellent ways to support local Indigenous communities.

Fish Sustainably

Alaska boasts year-round saltwater fishing (except for halibut, lingcod, rockfish, Tanner crab and resident king-crab fisheries). Pay attention to frequently updated fishing regulations on openings and bag limits – these are designed to protect species from overfishing.

Market-Minded Shopping

You can assemble a first-rate picnic at one of Alaska's many farmers markets *(alaskafarmersmarkets.org)*, like Homer's (p274).

Sleep Outdoors

Lower your carbon footprint by camping. If you lack gear, you can rent some (p302).

Renewable Energy

Mainly due to exorbitant electricity costs (which are twice the national average), remote Alaska communities have embraced renewable energy. Kodiak is a renewable energy pioneer – since 2014, nearly 100% of the city's electricity comes from renewable energy.

RESOURCES

adventuregreenalaska.org
Certified sustainable Alaskan businesses.

dnr.alaska.gov/parks
Volunteering opportunities and internships in Alaska's state parks.

ankn.uaf.edu
Alaska Native Knowledge Network.

LGBTIQ+ Travelers

Alaska is a conservative state and, while Alaskans affect a live-and-let-live attitude, they don't always exhibit these values with regards to LGBTIQ+ visitors. As a result, the gay community in Alaska tends to be less open than in major US cities. If in doubt, same-sex couples may want to err on the side of discretion, especially outside Anchorage and Juneau.

Close-Knit Community in the Capital

Alaska's most progressive city is a tiny pocket of liberalism in a conservative state. Although Juneau no longer has any dedicated LGBTIQ+ bars, you'll find a vibrant and supportive community here, with regular meetups and events throughout the year. Check Southeast Alaska LGBTQ+ Alliance *(akseagla.org)* for gatherings, which range from yoga classes and group hikes to potlucks and crafting nights at a local brewery. They also hosted their first (of hopefully many) Pride Parade in 2025. Juneau Drag *(facebook.com/juneaudrag)* stages drag shows once or twice a month at different venues (including the Alaskan Bar).

FUN TIMES IN FAIRBANKS

Fairbanks Queer Collective *(fbxqc.com)* is a grassroots organization with a focus on youth mentorship, community education and legal advocacy. They also host events throughout the year, including cookouts, clothing swaps, singalongs, gender euphoria parties and volunteer days. Check their Facebook or Instagram page for the latest happenings.

Same-Sex Marriage

In 1998 Alaska passed a constitutional amendment banning same-sex marriages. In 2015, when same-sex marriage was legalized in the USA (including Alaska), public opinion polls began swinging toward greater acceptance. Nevertheless, bills introduced to codify same-sex marriage in state statutes and overturn the state constitutional ban have failed. In summary, it's legal, but not supported by the conservative majority.

KEEPING THE LAST FRONTIER FABULOUS

Mad Myrna's *(madmyrnas.com)*, located in downtown Anchorage, is a fixture among Alaska's LGBTIQ+ residents and visitors. Regular cabaret and drag shows and DJ nights make the bar a hangout for all. Mad Myrna's bustles during Pride Month each June and welcomes all humans to enjoy the events.

Anchorage PrideFest

Anchorage's weeklong PrideFest, held annually at Delaney Park every June, is Alaska's biggest LGBTIQ+ event. The event has been a fixture in Alaska's scene since 1977, when participants wore bags over their heads to avoid potentially being fired.

RESOURCES

Identity Inc *(identityalaska.org)* Anchorage-based nonprofit community center and LGBTQIA2S+ resource hub.
Southeast Alaska LGBTQ+ Alliance *(akseagla.org)* Offers links and travel lists geared to gay visitors out of Juneau.
Alaskans Together for Equality *(alaskanstogether.org)* Statewide organization devoted to education and advocacy for Alaska's lesbian, gay, bisexual and transgender communities.
Interior Alaska Center For Non-Violent Living *(iacnvl.org)* Offers a hotline and a variety of resources for Interior Alaska's LGBTIQ+ community.

Accessible Travel

Given its rugged landscapes, Alaska isn't at the top of anyone's accessible travel list, but there is no shortage of tour and transport operators who have upgraded their framework for passengers with mobility issues, cruise ships, scenic flights and ADA facilities in Alaska State Parks among them.

Cruising Alaska's Waterways

All Alaska Marine Highway vessels are accessible to persons with disabilities – each ship is outfitted with elevator access and all cabin vessels include at least one wheelchair-accessible cabin.

Airport

Complimentary wheelchair/assistance service for reduced-mobility passengers is available at Anchorage's Ted Stevens Anchorage International Airport. The Alaska Airlines Fly for All (App Store/Google Play) app is designed for travelers with disabilities.

Accommodation

Large city hotels and most chain hotels should have a room or two retrofitted for guests with disabilities. In the wild, you'll find some wilderness guiding companies equipped for handling clients with wheelchairs on rafting and kayaking expeditions.

ALASKA PUBLIC LANDS INFORMATION CENTERS

The state's four **Alaska Public Lands Information Centers** (APLIC; nps.gov/anch/planyourvisit/hours.htm) in Anchorage, Fairbanks, Ketchikan and Tok can provide information, maps and campground guides to state and federal parks with wheelchair-accessible attractions.

ANCHORAGE PARATRANSIT

AnchorRIDES (facebook.com/anchorrides; 907-343-6543) offers ADA paratransit service for individuals experiencing disabilities that prevent them from using Anchorage's public-transit system. Visitors are also eligible for service, but you'll need to fill out a Visitors Application Form online (muni.org).

Senior Travel

Alaska is a popular destination for older travelers, many of whom arrive by cruise ship. It hits all the right notes: great outdoors, solid infrastructure and excellent medical care.

Challenges

Some activities will be difficult to experience for travelers with mobility issues. Flightseeing, glacier trekking, and some fishing and bear-viewing adventures often require participants to step up, down and over significant obstacles.

RESOURCES

Access Alaska (accessalaska.org) Includes statewide tourist information on accessible services and sites.

Challenge Alaska (challengealaska.org) A nonprofit organization dedicated to providing recreation opportunities for those with disabilities.

Alaska Department of Natural Resources (dnr.alaska.gov/parks/asp/access.htm) A comprehensive list of ADA facilities in Alaska State Parks including trails, campgrounds, viewpoints and historic sites.

Society for Accessible Travel & Hospitality (sath.org) Lobbies for better facilities and publishes *Open World* online magazine.

Solo & Female Travel

Alaska has long attracted solo adventurers. However, police are few and far between compared to the Lower 48, and violent crime rates are high. Solo/female travelers should employ all the usual tactics and avoid venturing too far off the beaten path.

Independence Day (Fourth of July) parade, Skagway (p122)

Nuts & Bolts

OPENING HOURS

Banks 9am–4pm/5pm Monday to Friday; 9am–1pm Saturday (main branches)

Bars and clubs City bars and clubs until 2am or later (brewery taprooms stop serving at 9pm)

Post offices 9am–5pm Monday to Friday; noon–3pm Saturday

Restaurants and cafes Cafes/coffee shops from 7am or earlier; some restaurants open only for lunch (noon–3pm) or dinner (5–10pm, later in cities)

Shops 10am–8pm/6pm (larger/smaller stores) Monday to Friday; 9am–5pm Saturday; 10am–5pm Sunday (larger stores)

Smoking or Vaping

Prohibited in retail stores, bars, restaurants and recreational/cultural facilities.

Internet Access

Spotty rural cell service means even small towns often have free internet access at libraries.

Tap Water

Tap water in Alaska is safe, but you should purify surface water from lakes and streams.

GOOD TO KNOW

Time zone
Alaska Time (GMT/UTC minus nine hours)

Country code
+1

Emergency number
911

Population
742,000

Electricity
120V

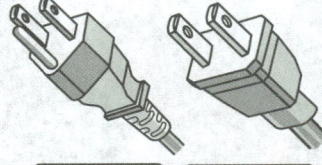

Type B
120V/60Hz

Type A
120V/60Hz

PUBLIC HOLIDAYS

Alaska's notable deviation from the standard USA holiday calendar is Alaska Day, which commemorates the formal transfer of present-day Alaska territories to the United States from the Russian Empire.

New Year's Day January 1

Martin Luther King Day Third Monday in January

Presidents' Day Third Monday in February

Seward's Day Last Monday in March

Easter Sunday Late March or early April

Memorial Day Last Monday in May

Independence Day (Fourth of July) July 4

Labor Day First Monday in September

Columbus Day Second Monday in October

Alaska Day October 18

Veterans' Day November 11

Thanksgiving Day Fourth Thursday in November

Christmas Day December 25

STORYBOOK

THE ALASKA
STORYBOOK

Our writers delve deep into different aspects of Alaskan life.

A History of Alaska in 15 Places

The story of America's largest, most sparsely populated state.

Regis St Louis

p406

Meet the Alaskans

In Alaska, Native communities, long-timers, and newcomers are stitched together by resilience, humor, and generosity.

Melody Burdette

p410

Russian Imperialism & Tlingit Resistance

How a feisty Alaska Native clan shaped America's geopolitical landscape.

Mara Vorhees

p412

Alaska by Air

Aviation built Alaska's identity – connecting remote towns, carrying supplies, and shaping a culture defined by flight.

Melody Burdette

p414

Horned puffin at Resurrection Bay, Kenai Peninsula (p217)

A HISTORY OF ALASKA IN
15 PLACES

The flow of history over the vast landmass today known as Alaska has one common thread: the resources. From its earliest inhabitants to its modern dwellers, it's the rich bounty of Alaska's minerals, wildlife, timber and physical space that both sustains and drives the story of America's largest, most sparsely populated state. By Regis St Louis.

JUST HOW AND when humans first came to the land the Aleuts called Alyeska (or Alaxsxaq) – 'the Great Land' – is something of a mystery, with many of the ancestors of the Alaska Native tribes we know today likely trekking across an ice-age-era land bridge 15,000 to 30,000 years ago. They sustained themselves through fishing, hunting and foraging: lifestyles that continue today despite the attempts by later arrivals to destroy their culture. And like so many people who followed over the centuries, those first tribes came in pursuit of the land's natural resources, including migrating wildlife they used for food and clothing.

Alaska's modern history closely follows that original trajectory, with an ebb and flow of people and groups drawn to this place to leverage the bounty under, on and over the land, sometimes by violent or careless means. From the first Europeans seeking travel corridors and fur pelts, to the stampeders on the hunt for gold, to the modern American oil fields or visitors who come today to experience the state's wild beauty, the story of Alaska has been written in the way its inhabitants interact with the disparate spaces they call home.

1. University of Alaska Museum of the North
THE FIRST ALASKANS
The ancestors of today's diverse Native Alaska population left behind a remarkable collection of artifacts. Among the oldest are 14,000-year-old microblades made of chert unearthed at Swan Point in the interior. Beautifully crafted carvings – like the tiny 2000-year-old Okvik Madonna - allude to an artistry still practiced today. There are also expertly made objects essential to survival in the harsh elements: waterproof parkas made of the intestines of walruses; bags fashioned out of fish skins; and extremely light kayaks fashioned from driftwood and animal hide. The objects here, which span the centuries, provide an excellent bridge between past and present.

For more on the the University of Alaska Museum of the North, see p322.

2. Holy Resurrection Cathedral
THE RUSSIANS ARRIVE
While many view Russia's legacy in Alaska as quaint orthodox churches, the truth of Russia's occupation is far more complicated. After first mapping Kodiak Island in 1769, Russian explorers and fur traders opened an outpost on the island in 1784 and massacred many Alutiiq people. Two years later, forced assimilation schooling began for Native children. Not all of the era's Russian occupiers were bad, however. The missionary and future St Herman arrived in 1794 and ultimately became a protector, shielding the Alutiiq from the other Russians. His remains are inside the Holy

Resurrection Cathedral, which he founded upon his arrival.

For more on the Holy Resurrection Cathedral, see p347.

3. Castle Hill
THE US BUYS ALASKA

Short on cash after the Crimean War and facing a decimated population of sea otters whose lucrative pelts they'd been chasing, Russia offered to sell its Alaskan holdings to the United States. With the American Civil War behind them, President Andrew Jackson and his Secretary of State William Seward locked on 'manifest destiny' and struck a purchase deal with Russia in March 1867: $7.2 million, or about 2¢ per acre. Seven months later and thousands of miles away from Washington, DC, on Castle Hill in Sitka, the transfer was made complete as the Russian flag was lowered and the American flag raised.

For more on Castle Hill, see p87.

4. Klondike Gold Rush National Historical Park
PROSPECTORS STREAM NORTH

Everything changed in 1896 on a remote corner of southeast Alaska. A few lucky prospectors discovered gold in Canada's Klondike region, and the rush was on. Miners landed on the shores of the soon-bustling boomtown of Skagway to prep for their 500-mile trip over the mountain passes. An estimated 1000 hopeful men passed through the town daily. Lawlessness became rampant, and the infamous con man 'Soapy' Smith ruled the town through his gang of ruffians. His reign ended in a dramatic lawman shootout on Juneau Wharf, and today many historic buildings preserve the memory of that extraordinary era.

For more on Klondike Gold Rush National Historical Park, see p123.

5. Denali National Park & Preserve
OLD LAND, NEW PARK

The Athabascan people used what is now Denali National Park and Preserve in Alaska as hunting grounds. But gold was found near Kantishna in 1905 and the big-game hunters followed the stampede. Stunned by the destruction, noted hunter and naturalist Charles Sheldon mounted a campaign to protect the region. From this, Mt McKinley National Park was born in 1917. In 1980, the park was enlarged by 4 million acres and renamed Denali National Park and Preserve.

For more on Denali National Park and Preserve, see p303.

6. Historic Alaska Railroad Depot
BUILDING A TRAIN LINE

Interest in gold and other mineral deposits sparked interest in building a railroad to reach deep into Alaska's interior. Various companies had constructed small sections of railway from Seward northward in the early 1900s, but in 1914 the federal government got involved. So began a nearly decade-long project, involving more than 4500 laborers, to link Seward with Fairbanks via Anchorage. In 1923 President Warren Harding traveled to Nenana to drive the final ceremonial stake where two rail sections met, becoming the first president to visit the then-territory. But it came at a cost for him. Harding died in Seattle just one week after leaving Alaska.

For more on the Historic Alaska Railroad Depot, see p314.

Holy Resurrection Cathedral (p347)

7. Seward Community Library & Museum
DREAMING UP A NEW FLAG
The seaside town of Seward is where one young artist dreamed up a design much loved today by everyone in Alaska. In 1927 the American Legion sponsored a contest for teenagers, with a $1000 scholarship and a gold watch to whoever could produce the best flag design for the territory. Benny Benson, aged 14, a Unangax̂ Alaska Native student living in a Seward orphanage, drew his inspiration from the heavens: seven gold stars representing the Great Bear (Big Dipper) along with the north star on a field of midnight blue. After Benny's win, the flag flew for the first time on top of his orphanage.

For more on Seward Community Library & Museum, see p245.

8. Palmer Museum of History & Art
NEW DEAL IN AN ALASKAN VALLEY
The Great Depression and dust bowl devastated the livelihoods of American farmers in the Lower 48 states, which led President Franklin D Roosevelt to crank out solutions in his 'New Deal.' Among them: resettling bedraggled farmers to so-called colonies for a fresh start – including Alaska's Matanuska Valley. About 200 families made the long trip from Minnesota in 1935, founding the Matanuska Colony in what became Palmer. The tough landscape and lack of suitable farming tools presented serious challenges to the newly arrived Minnesotan families. By 1940 over half had fled, but those that remained shaped Palmer into what it is today.

For more on the Palmer Museum of History & Art, see p166.

9. Alaska State Museum
WAR COMES TO ALASKA
In June 1942, Japan invaded the Aleutian Archipelago and occupied the islands of Attu in Kiska. The occupation of US soil by a foreign invader provided the justification for the US military to forcibly relocate over 800 Alaska Native Unangax̂ to the southeast, where they lived under horrifying conditions until the end of the war (85 of them died from diseases exacerbated by malnutrition and poor sanitation). White residents on some islands, such as Unalaksa, were permitted to stay at their homes. You can learn more about this little discussed period of Alaska's past by exploring the exhibits of Alaska's best history collection, located in Juneau.

For more on the Alaska State Museum, see p96.

10. Downtown Nome
AN EPIC SLED DOG RACE
In 1948, Joe Redington Sr arrived in Alaska and settled a homestead only a few hundred feet from the historic Iditarod Trail, an old dogsled mail route from Seward to Nome. Redington was fascinated by the Iditarod Trail and the famous 'serum run' that saved the town of Nome from diphtheria in 1925, when mushers used the trail to relay medical supplies across Alaska. Worried that snowmobiles might replace sled dogs, Redington proposed an Anchorage–Nome race along the historic trail, and then staged the first 1049-mile Iditarod in 1973. Alaska's 'Last Great Race,' the world's longest sled-dog event, was born.

For more on Downtown Nome and the Iditarod, see p368.

11. Alaska Aviation Museum
BUSH PLANES ACROSS ALASKA
Over 80% of Alaskan communities are not connected to a road or highway system, with only one mile of road for every 40 square miles of land. Many parts of the state simply couldn't be reached without a plane. Versatile aircraft like the 1955 Piper 'Super Cub' played an instrumental role in accessing rural regions, whether landing on water, snow, tundra or rocky riverbanks. At the Alaska Aviation Museum in Anchorage, you can view historic airplanes, and learn about famous pilots like Don Sheldon (1921–1975), who took visitors on scenic flights into Denali and pioneered the technique of glacier landings.

For more on the Alaska Aviation Museum, see p158.

12. The Trans-Alaska Pipeline
THE OIL BOOM
In 1968, petroleum geologists discovered massive amounts of oil in Prudhoe Bay on the edge of the Arctic Ocean. But how to transport it from the far north slope? Enter the Trans-Alaska Pipeline System, constructed between 1973 and 1977, and

The Trans-Alaska Pipeline (p385)

stretching 800 miles from Prudhoe Bay to Valdez to move billions of barrels of oil across the state. Like gold before it, oil forever changed Alaska's economy, forcing officials to settle the long-delayed land claims with Alaska Natives and creating an ebb and flow of oil earnings that today make up a large portion of the state's operating budget and funding shortfalls.

For more on the Trans-Alaska Pipeline, see p385.

13. Kenai Fjords National Park
PROTECTING ALASKAN WILDERNESS

In 1980, with a flourish of Jimmy Carter's presidential pen, the Alaska National Interest Lands Conservation Act doubled the amount of land under control of the NPS, with an additional 100 million acres added to the state's portfolio of protected land. As a direct consequence, and against the wishes of many in the pro-development and pro-mining lobbies, seven new national parks appeared on maps of Alaska: Kenai Fjords, Glacier Bay, Wrangell-St Elias, Katmai, Gates of the Arctic, Lake Clark and Kobuk Valley. It wasn't only national parks that were added – national wildlife refuges, wilderness areas, the Iditarod National Historic Trail and conservation areas were also announced.

For more on Kenai Fjords National Park, see p248.

14. Valdez Museum
ALASKA'S WORST ENVIRONMENTAL DISASTER

Where oil drilling happens, environmental impacts follow. But few are so disastrous as the 1989 oil spill that decimated the coastline and wildlife in Cordova and across the Prince William Sound. On March 24, 1989, the tanker Exxon Valdez ran aground near Valdez, ultimately spilling 11 million gallons of oil into the sound. The impact was nearly immediate, as the black slick spread across 1300 miles of shoreline in and around Cordova, ultimately killing hundreds of thousands of animals and billions of fish eggs. The cleanup continues even today, and some species may never recover.

For more on the Valdez Museum, see p193.

15. Sealaska Heritage Institute
RESILIENCE OF ALASKA'S NATIVE PEOPLE

Unveiled in 2015, the headquarters of the Sealaska Heritage Institute in Juneau symbolizes the remarkable renaissance of Alaska Native culture in the southeast. The Tlingit, Tsimshian and Haida have occupied these lands for countless generations, but faced grave threats from Russians and later American settlers, with the loss of lands, cultural oppression and forced assimilation. Today, interest in Native culture is at an all-time high, and this new eye-catching, sustainably designed building is one of the most celebrated landmarks in the state capital. Both the interior and the exterior serve as a giant canvas for top artists, with exquisite carvings and an iconic clan house within.

For more on the Sealaska Heritage Institute, see p98.

MEET THE ALASKANS

Alaska is a land of deep roots and restless hearts: Native communities, long-timers, and newcomers stitched together by resilience, humor, and generosity. Melody Burdette introduces her people.

ASK AN ALASKAN where they're from, and you'll usually get two answers: the town they live in now and the story of how they ended up there. Some families can trace their roots back thousands of years – Alaska is still home to more than 228 federally recognized tribes, each with its own languages, traditions, and governance. And then there are people (like me) who arrived more recently, drawn by the siren song of the state's mountains, wilderness, and wide-open possibility. Everywhere you turn, you meet folks who came for a season and never left. Alaska is stitched together from all of these stories – less a melting pot and more a quilt, pieced from independence, resilience, and community in equal measure.

Life here moves with the rhythm of the seasons. Summer is a riot of 24-hour sunlight and restless activity: nets straining with salmon, berry buckets filled to the brim, kids sticky-fingered from eating as they pick. Bush planes buzz overhead, skimming remote gravel bars that double as airstrips, connecting even the most far-flung cabins to the outside world. By fall, the tundra blazes crimson and gold, a last burst of fire before the cold sets in, and hunters stock their freezers for the long winter ahead. Then comes the darkness, months when surviving winter becomes a badge of honor. It means gallows humor, thawing frozen pipes with hairdryers, and the warmth of gathering with community. We keep each other close with solstice bonfires, dinner parties, craft nights, and the simple ritual of neighbors checking in on neighbors. By spring, snowmachines give way to ATVs, and the rivers crack open with a roar, carrying the promise of another cycle.

Work in Alaska is as varied as the seasons themselves. Oil still pays a large share of the state's bills, but many Alaskans piece together livelihoods from government jobs, healthcare, tourism, aviation, guiding, fishing or small businesses. The entrepreneurial streak here is less about ambition than necessity, a survival strategy passed down through generations. And the politics reflect that same spirit of independence. Outsiders often label Alaska conservative, but the truth is far more nuanced: roughly 60% of voters have no party affiliation at all. Simply put, Alaskans don't like being put in a box – or told what to do.

Even in 2025, being 'from Alaska' carries an aura beyond state lines – rugged, adventurous, self-reliant. But what lingers most is the big-heartedness. Strangers stop when your car won't start at 30 below. Neighbors drop off moose stew when the power cuts. The grit is legendary, but it's generosity that keeps communities stitched together. Stay long enough, and you may find yourself stitched into that quilt too, carrying forward the humor, resilience, and contradictions that make Alaska unlike anywhere else.

> **Who & How Many?**
>
> Alaska is home to just over 730,000 people, with nearly half living in the Anchorage and Matanuska-Susitna Valley region. Around 15% of the population identifies as Alaska Native – one of the highest proportions of any US state.

DRAWN BY ADVENTURE

Like many Alaskans, I'm a transplant from out of state. I was born in Georgia, then bounced around big coastal cities before moving into a van to explore the hidden corners of the American West during the pandemic. I floated up to Alaska early in that journey and spent a summer nearly exhausting the road system with friends. The more I saw, the harder it was for me to imagine living anywhere else. Two years later, I made the move for good and haven't looked back.

Some days, I truly can't believe my fortune to live in a place where seeing glaciers on your daily commute or spying Denali rising in the distance is commonplace – and yet, it is. But living here is more than outdoor sights: it's a commitment to learning in the broader sense – to steward the land, to explore it, and connect with the history of a place that evolves every day.

Pictured above: Sketch of Sitka (p87) in 1868

RUSSIAN IMPERIALISM & TLINGIT RESISTANCE

How a feisty Alaska Native clan shaped America's geopolitical landscape. By Mara Vorhees.

IN THE LATE 18th century, Russian explorers and traders sailed across the Bering Sea, settling first on Kodiak Island and later on Baranof Island, claiming Alaska's vast territory for the Tsar and Empire. But if not for the resistance of the Tlingit, the North American continent would look very different today.

First Encounters

Under the ruthless leadership of Grigory Shelikhov – the self-proclaimed 'Russian Columbus' – the Russian Empire established its first American settlement in 1784 on Kodiak Island (see p347). Here, Russian colonizers massacred and enslaved the Alutiiq (p356), gaining control of the surrounding archipelago.

Shelikhov's more diplomatic successor, Alexander Baranov, set his sights on the Alaskan mainland at Yakutat, with limited success. Finally, in 1799, he made landfall on Baranof Island, near present-day Sitka, where he negotiated with local Tlingit clans. He promised trade and protection in exchange for permission to build a fort at Gájaa Héen, 7 miles north of the Tlingit village at Noow Tlein (p87). Here, they founded Fort St Michael, a rough-hewn settlement of Russian and Creole hunters and Alutiiq and Aleut conscripts.

Battle at Fort St Michael

For several years, the Russians maintained a tense but mostly peaceful coexistence with their Tlingit hosts. However, the uncultured hunters and workers were inconsiderate and cocky – and sometimes cruel – in their interactions with the Alaska Natives. Their large hunting parties ravaged sea otter colonies and raided Tlingit food stores. They raped women and disrespected clan elders. Finally, the Tlingits could no longer tolerate the Russian presence.

In 1802, a coalition of Tlingit clans launched a surprise attack on the Russian interlopers. Led by the warrior K'alyáan (pronounced *Kat-li-AN*), the Kiks.ádi clan raided and plundered Fort St Michael, while other clans ambushed Russian hunting parties at sea. They destroyed the settlement, taking some 250 lives, burning the fort and driving the Russians off the island. It was a huge victory for the Tlingit, but a Kiks.ádi shaman predicted that the Russians would return.

Battle at Indian River

Incensed by the Tlingit betrayal, Baranov prepared for revenge, assembling a flotilla of armed ships and canoes, further strengthened by the arrival of the Russian naval ship *Neva*. The Kiks.ádi, meanwhile, built a defensive fortification at Indian River, known as Shis'g'i Noow (p92). Constructed from spruce saplings, the fort was designed to repel cannon fire, and its strategic location near the tidal flats prevented Russian ships from approaching too closely.

In 1804, Baranov led a force of 800 Russian, Aleut and Alutiiq hunters against the Tlingit at Indian River. Again led by K'alyáan, the clans fought off the ground attack and wounded Baranov, while the fort withstood cannon fire from afar. After this show of Tlingit strength, the Russians revised their tactics. Hundreds of kayaks tied to the *Neva* pulled the warship closer to shore, allowing it to bombard the fort at closer range. The Russians had also managed to destroy the Tlingit gunpowder supply before the battle, and K'alyáan knew they could not withstand the assault for long.

Survival March

Much to the Russians' surprise, the Kiks.ádi did not surrender. Instead, they chose to retreat, abandoning Shis'g'i Noow under the cover of darkness and embarking overland on a 'Survival March.' Hundreds of men, women and children ventured across the island, traveling through dense forest and over precipitous peaks. They finally arrived on the eastern shore, where they were able to signal for help to their relatives in Angoon. The Kiks.ádi had survived.

Economic Warfare

Just as importantly, the Kiks.ádi had not surrendered. They did not win the battle, but they redefined the war. Insisting that Sitka was still their territory, they set up an economic blockade, stationing their warriors around Peril Strait and blocking trading parties from exchanging with the Russians. The Tlingit were unified in this latest act of resistance. No clans were willing to defy the trade embargo. British and US merchants were also happy to exclude their Russian rivals. And without any trading partners, the Russians were stymied.

In the summer of 1805, Baranov invited the Kiks.ádi back to Sitka. K'alyáan was unwilling to accept the Russian claim to Tlingit territory. But the two leaders reached a compromise: the Russians were allowed to stay and occupy Sitka (which they renamed New Archangel), and the Tlingit were allowed to return from exile without fear of reprisal and rebuild a village nearby. Baranov and K'alyáan agreed, 'From now on, we will be brothers.'

An Uneasy Truce

And so the Kiks.ádi returned to their homeland and rebuilt alongside the Russian settlement of New Archangel. Resentment and distrust permeated both communities, but the uneasy truce endured. However, the Tlingit at large were still wary. Various clans launched attacks on Russian outposts in Yakutat and Nuchek Island. Rumors swirled that warriors from other villages were organizing and amassing in case of Russian attempts at expansion. New Archangel was an unconvincing Russian enclave surrounded by an unwelcoming Tlingit Nation.

Russian America continued for the next 60 years. They did establish smaller settlements in other parts of Alaska, and missionaries had some success in converting Alaska Natives to Russian Orthodoxy. The Russian population increased, mainly due to intermarriage. But the Russian Empire was never able to establish a significant stronghold and eventually decided to sell the Alaskan territory, giving up its presence in North America.

STORYBOOK

ALASKA BY AIR

Aviation built Alaska's identity – connecting remote towns, carrying supplies, and shaping a culture defined by flight. By Melody Burdette.

IN ALASKA, AVIATION isn't a luxury – it's a lifeline. With over 80% of communities unreachable by road, bush planes serve as school buses, mail carriers, grocery trucks, and ambulances, connecting people and supplies across vast wilderness. The hum of a small propeller plane overhead isn't unusual, it's daily life.

A History Written in the Sky

Alaska's love affair with flight began in the early 20th century. In the 1920s and '30s, dog teams still hauled supplies across the wilderness, but aviation quickly proved faster, more efficient, and in the long run, cheaper. Early bush pilots built legendary reputations by flying in all seasons, often without reliable maps or instruments, landing wherever they could: gravel bars, frozen rivers, even tundra patches. They delivered medicine to villages, hauled gold, and stitched the state together.

Names like Russ Merrill, Bob Reeve, and Noel Wien still echo through Alaskan aviation history. Wien, founder of Wien Air Alaska, is often called the father of Alaskan aviation for proving that small aircraft could reliably connect towns spread across the Interior and Arctic. Bob Marshall, a forester and writer, explored Alaska by air as

Pictured clockwise from top left: Lake Hood Seaplane Base (p157); Flightseeing tour, Denali National Park & Preserve (p303); Ted Stevens Anchorage International Airport (p390); Flightseeing, Kenai Fjords National Park (p248)

much as on foot, journaling how the wilderness looked from above. More recent figures, like Roman Dial, an adventurer known for pairing packrafts, bikes, and airplanes, carry the tradition of inventive, risk-taking travel forward.

The Bush Pilot Spirit

If the frontier had a face in Alaska, it would look like a bush pilot. Flying low over rivers, mountains, and endless tundra, they embody daring and necessity. Their planes are as specialized as pickup trucks: Super Cubs and Beavers on bushwheels for gravel bars, Otters and Cessnas on floats for remote lakes, ski-equipped planes for glacier landings. Many date back decades but are endlessly repaired and modified.

Each May, bush flying takes center stage at the Valdez Fly-In & Short Takeoff and Landing (STOL) Competition. Pilots from Alaska and beyond test their skills, coaxing planes into the air in as little as 19 feet or stopping in less than 40. It draws thousands, but more importantly, it celebrates a shared culture of skill, storytelling, and survival that still defines Alaskan aviation.

Cargo, Tourism, and Global Connections

Not all of Alaska's aviation happens in tiny cockpits. The state is also a global freight hub. Anchorage's Ted Stevens International Airport ranks among the busiest cargo airports in the world and serves as a refueling stop for trans-Pacific flights between Asia and North America. FedEx and UPS both maintain major hubs here, and giant cargo planes share the skies with bush pilots threading valleys a few hundred miles away.

Tourism, too, leans heavily on air travel. Visitors board floatplanes in Anchorage or Juneau to reach remote lodges, bear-viewing sites, and fishing camps. Flightseeing tours skim across Denali's granite ridges or land on glaciers that would take days to reach by foot. For many travelers, the highlight of a trip to Alaska is that single unforgettable moment when a small plane banks low over an alpine valley or touches down on a turquoise lake.

The Challenges of Flying in the North

Flying in Alaska is not for the faint of heart. The same landscapes that make it spectacular also make it treacherous. Pilots face sudden fog, high winds funneled through mountain passes, and snow squalls that appear without warning. Dead-end canyons can trap the unprepared, and the lack of remote weather stations means much of Alaska still relies on 'pilot reports' radioed in from the air.

Even the ground poses problems. Many airports sit on permafrost-frozen tundra that is thawing at alarming rates due to climate change. As it melts, runways buckle, crack, and sink, creating dangerous landing conditions. Bethel Airport, one of the state's busiest regional hubs, required a $10 million reconstruction in 2019 to fix thaw damage. Engineers experiment with solutions like pile foundations or imported gravel, but projections suggest Alaska may face billions in runway repair costs by mid-century. In a state where aviation is essential, it's a looming crisis.

Everyday Life in the Air

Even with the challenges, Alaska has more pilots per capita than anywhere else in the USA – about six times the national average – and over 9,000 registered aircraft serving more than 750 landing areas. Lake Hood, next to Anchorage's main airport, is the busiest seaplane base in the world. On summer afternoons, its waters churn with pontoons lifting off toward the Susitna Valley or dropping anglers into hidden trout streams.

For rural residents, flying is as normal as driving. Kids board planes for school sports, elders fly to regional hospitals for care, and groceries and mail arrive weekly on small Cessnas. Tickets can be pricey, but without them, communities would just be cut off.

Why It Matters

Aviation in Alaska isn't just infrastructure – it's identity. It's the roar of an engine over the Brooks Range, the lifeline of a medevac in a snowstorm, the thrill of a glacier landing, and the daily rhythm of mail drops in villages far from any road. It's history and necessity, grit and romance.

For travelers, understanding aviation here means understanding Alaska itself. To see the state from above, whether from the seat of a floatplane skimming into a turquoise lake or the window of a 737, is to glimpse how Alaskans have always seen their home: vast, untamed, and held together by flight.

INDEX

A

accessible travel 401
accommodations 393, *see also individual regions*
activities 18, 30-1, 50-1, 52-3, 367, **52-3**, *see also individual activities*
agate 266
air travel 390, 391, *see also flightseeing*
aviation history 408, 414-15
Lake Hood Seaplane Base 157-8
milk run 80
Nome 378
Alaska Day Festival 90
Alaska Native culture 16-17, 74, 412-13, *see also* Haida culture, Tlingit culture, Tsimshian culture
Aak'w Village 102
Anchorage 146, 148, 154-5
Haines 120
Juneau 98
Kenai 263-4
Ketchikan 66-8, 70
Kodiak 347
Sitka 90-1
Alaska Railroad 38-9, 156-7
Alaska State Fair 167
Alexander Archipelago, the 56-135, **58-9**
accommodations 134-5
activities 60-1
climate 60-1
festivals & events 60-1
itineraries 60-1
navigation 58
travel seasons 60-1

Map Pages **000**

travel within the Alexander Archipelago 58
weather 60-1
Alyeska Resort 174-5
Anan Creek Bear Watch 78
Anchor Point 277
Anchorage 24-5, 28-9, 137-81, 142-58, **138-9, 144-5, 147**
accommodations 181
activities 140-1
climate 140-1
drinking & nightlife 143, 149-51, 154, 156
entertainment 143
festivals & events 140-1, 157
food 143, 149, 151, 155, 156
itineraries 140-1
navigation 138-9
shopping 151, 155
tours 146, 149-50, 152-3, 157-8, **153**
travel seasons 140-1
travel within Anchorage 138, 142
weather 140-1
Anchorage Museum 148
animals 8-9, 40-3, 52-3, *see also individual species*, wildlife refuges & sanctuaries
Anvil Mountain 378
aquariums
Alaska SeaLife Center 247-8
Sealaska Heritage Institute 98, 409
Sitka Sound Science Center 91
archaeological sites & ruins
Douglas Island 103
Dyea 132-3
Landmark Gap Trail North 313
Last Train to Nowhere 373
Petroglyph Beach State Historic Site 79
architecture
Cordova 203
Utqiaġvik 380-1

Wrangell-St Elias National Park & Preserve 334-5
Arctic, the 364-87, **366**
accommodations 387
activities 367
climate 367
festivals & events 367
itineraries 367
navigation 366
travel seasons 367
travel within the Arctic 366
weather 367
area codes 403
art galleries, *see* galleries & art museums
arts & cultural centers
Cordova Center 202
Inupiat Heritage Center 379-80
Jilkaat Kwaan Cultural Heritage Visitor Center 119
Juneau Arts and Culture Center 96
K'esugi Ken Interpretive Center 302
Morris Thompson Cultural & Visitors Center 316-17
arts festivals, *see also* cultural events
Alaska World Arts Festival 31
Festival of Native Arts 321
Talkeetna Art Festival 296
ATMs 390, 392
aurora borealis 41, 333

B

B&Bs 393
backpacking 51, *see also* hiking
Denali National Park & Preserve 308
Lake Clark National Park & Preserve 278
Ptarmigan Lake 257

baseball 323
beaches
Discovery Beach 265-6
Fossil Beach 353, 355
Nikiski Beach 266
Nome 370-1
Outside Beach 279
Petroglyph Beach State Historic Site 79
Surfers Beach 353
White Sands Beach 354
bear spray 395
bears 42, 44-5
Admiralty Island National Monument 107-8
Anan Creek 78
Cooper Landing 238
Denali National Park & Preserve 309-10
Glacier Bay National Park & Preserve
Katmai National Park & Preserve 358-9, 361
Kodiak 346, 355-6
Lake Clark National Park & Preserve 278
Sitka 91
beer 48
Anchorage 143, 149-51
Cordova 202
Girdwood 176-7
Palmer 165, 167
Skagway 131
Talkeetna 297-8
berries 71, 279
bicycle travel, *see* cycling, mountain biking
Big Delta 328-9
birdwatching 51, *see also* eagles
Fairbanks 325
Kenai 264
Prince William Sound 210
Sitka 93
Tern Lake 244
Turnagain Arm 162
Whittier 210
Blackstone Bay 213-14
boat tours, *see* boat travel, cruises

boat travel 34-7, 51, 391, see also cruises
  Chena River 326
  Cordova 198, 200
  Homer 281
  Glacier Bay National Park & Preserve 112-13
  Kodiak 350-1, 352
  Sitka 91, 93-4
  Talkeetna 294, 296
  Valdez 191-2
books 33
bore tide 226
breweries, see beer
Bridal Veil Falls 195
bridges
  Kuskulana Bridge 339
  McCarthy Bridge 339
  Million Dollar Bridge 207
  Veilbreaker Skybridges 174-5
bus tours 306, 307-8
business hours 403

cabins 393
  Caribou Creek Cabin 243
  David St Lawrence/Harry Robb Cabin 295
  East Creek Cabin 243
  Fred's Creek Cabin 93
  Homesteader's Cabin 261
  Kenai Peninsula 280
  Manitoba Cabin 230
  Ole Dahl Cabin 295
  Raven's Roost Cabin 85
  Resurrection Pass Trail 243
  Shelikof Cabin 93
camping 43, 393
  Denali National Park & Preserve 305
  Haines 121
  Kenai Fjords National Park 253
  Summit Lake 231
  Turnagain Arm 162
  unmarked campgrounds 228
canoeing, see kayaking & canoeing
Cantwell 314
canyons 194
Captain Cook State Recreation Area 265-6
caribou, see reindeer
car travel 12-13, 391, see also road trips
  road closures 307
  road safety 227
  winter driving 395
cathedrals, see churches & cathedrals

caves 75
cell phones 390
cemeteries
  Dena'ina Athabascan Eklutna Cemetery 161
  Slide Cemetery 133
chapels
  St Nicholas Chapel 261
  Sts Sergius & Herman of Valaam Chapel 356
Chena Hot Springs 328
Chicken 331-2
children, travel with 51, 394, see also family travel
Chilkoot Trail 126-8, 133, **127**
Chitina 338-9
churches & cathedrals, see also chapels
  Church of St Nicholas 283
  Holy Assumption of the Virgin Mary Russian Orthodox Church 261
  Holy Resurrection Cathedral 347, 406-7
  Nativity of Our Lord Russian Orthodox Church 356
  St Joseph Church 369-70
  St Michael's Cathedral 90
  St Nicholas Orthodox Church 277, 279
  St Nicholas Russian Orthodox Church 98
  Transfiguration of Our Lord 282
  United Protestant Presbyterian Church 166
  Utqiaġvik Presbyterian Church 380-1
clamming 282
climate 30-1, see also individual regions
climate change 156, 398-9
clothes 32
  cruise travel essentials 35
  gear rental 302
coffee 154
  Anchorage 156
  Homer 273
  Kodiak 352
  Palmer 165
  Seward 248
  Skagway 129
Cooper Landing 232-8, **233**
  accommodations 284
  drinking 234
  food 234
  shopping 237
  tours 234-5, **235**
  travel within Cooper Landing 232

Cordova 198-204, **199**
  accommodations 215
  drinking 200, 203
  festivals & events 203
  food 200, 201
  shopping 203
  tours 204
  travel within Cordova 198
costs 41, 392
Council 372-3
courses 202
crab 46-7, 396
credit cards 392
cruises 34-7, 392, 393
  Cordova 198, 200
  Juneau 105-6
  Kenai Fjords National Park 248, 250
  Misty Fjords National Monument 72-3
  Prince William Sound 188-90
  Turnagain Arm 179
  Valdez 188, 190-1
  Whittier 210, 212
  cultural centers, see arts & cultural centers
cultural events
  Cordova Iceworm Festival 31
  Girdwood Forest Fair 177
  Great Alaskan Lumberjack Show 70-71
  Little Norway Festival 31
  Nalukataq Festival 380
  World Eskimo Native Olympics 31
culture 410-11
currency 392
cycling 50, 398
  Anchorage 152-3
  Dyea 132-3
  Haines 121
  Juneau 106
  Primrose 255-6
  Prince of Wales Island 74-5
  Seldovia 279-80
  Skagway 132
  Wrangell 79-80
cycling tours 152-3, **153**

Dall sheep 43
Dalton Highway 29, 383-6, 387, **384**
dangers, see safety
Deadhorse 387
Delta Junction 29, 329
Denali, see Denali National Park & Preserve
Denali Highway 313

Denali National Park & Preserve 25, 41, 303-15, 407, **288-9**, **304**
  accommodations 340
  activities 290-1
  climate 290-1
  festivals & events 290-1
  navigation 288-9
  planning 305
  tours 305, 306-8, 313, **313**
  travel within Denali National Park & Preserve 289, 303
  weather 290-1
Denali State Park 300-2, **301**
disabilities, travelers with 401
dogs 370, see also Iditarod Trail Sled Dog Race
  Black Spruce Dog Sledding 325
  DogGoneIt 314
  Husky Homestead 312
  Ididaride 251
  Sled Dog Kennels 305
drinking 396-7, see also individual regions, beer, coffee
driving, see car travel
driving tours, see road trips
Dyea 132-3

Eagle 333
Eagle River 159, 161
eagles
  Alaska Raptor Center 91
  American Bald Eagle Foundation 119
  Chilkat Bald Eagle Preserve 119
earthquakes 257
Eklutna Lake 161
electricity 403
emergencies 403
environmental issues 156, 398-9
etiquette 32
events, see festivals & events
Exxon Valdez 191

Fairbanks 25, 29, 316-26, **318-19**
  accommodations 340-1
  drinking 323
  entertainment 321
  festivals & events 321, 323, 324

Fairbanks *continued*
  food 317, 321, 322
  shopping 322
  tours 321-2, 325, 326
  travel within Fairbanks 316
  walking tours 320, **320**
fairs
  Fairbanks 321
  Haines 120
  Palmer 167
family travel 51, 394
  Santa Claus House 327
farms 167-8
female travelers 401
ferry travel, *see* boat travel, cruises
festivals & events 30-1, *see also individual regions*, arts & cultural events, fairs, music festivals, sporting events
films 33
fishing 14, 51, 236, 238
  Anchorage 146
  Cooper Landing 232-3, 235, 236
  Cordova 204
  Fairbanks 325
  Homer 276
  Katmai National Park & Preserve 360
  Kenai Peninsula 262, 263
  Ketchikan 68-9
  Seward 251-2
  Summit Lake 231
  Talkeetna 299
  Tok 330-1
flag of Alaska 98
flightseeing 18, 414-15
  Denali National Park & Preserve 297-8
  Juneau 106
  Kenai Peninsula 241
  Kodiak 357
  Misty Fjords National Monument 73
  Tok 331
  Wrangell-St Elias National Park 336
food 46-9, 396-7, *see also individual locations*, berries, crab, salmon

food festivals
  Ketchikan Blueberry Arts Festival 71
  Kodiak Crab Festival 47
  Taste of Homer 274
food tours
  Juneau 106
  Talkeetna 299
forests & rainforests
  Chugach National Forest 179
  Lowell Point State Recreation Site 256
  Tongass National Forest 69
forts
  Fort Kenay 261
  Fort McGilvary 256
  Fort William Seward 119-20
Fourth of July 254, 296

galleries & art museums, *see also* museums
  Alaska Native Art Gallery 296-7
  Aurora Dora 297
  Bunnell Street Arts Center 272-3
  Dancing Leaf Gallery 297
  Homer Council on the Arts 273
  Norman Lowell Gallery of Alaska 277
gardens, *see* parks & gardens
Gates of the Arctic National Park & Preserve 41, 386
gay travelers, *see* LGBTIQ+ travelers
geocaching 229, 231
Girdwood 24-5, 172-5, 181, **173**
Glacier Bay Day Boat 112-13
Glacier Bay National Park & Preserve 23, 41, 109-14, 135, **110**
glaciers
  Beloit Glacier 214
  Blackstone Glacier 213-14
  Columbia Glacier 190
  Exit Glacier 252-3
  Grand Pacific Glacier 113
  Grewingk Glacier 280-1
  Kennicott Glacier 337
  Knik Glacier 169, 171
  Lamplugh Glacier 113
  Laughton Glacier 132
  Lawrence Glacier 214
  LeConte Glacier 84
  Margerie Glacier 113
  Matanuska Glacier 160, 197
  Meares Glacier 190-1
  Mendenhall Glacier 100-1

  Reid Glacier 113
  Root Glacier 335-6
  science 250
  Sheridan Glacier 205
  Spencer Glacier 178, 180
  Tebenkof Glacier 213
  Worthington Glacier 196-7
gold panning
  Crow Creek Gold Mine 177
  Gold Dredge 8 325
  Kenai Lake 236-7
  Nome 374
  Resurrection Pass Trail 227
golf 79
Gustavus 111

Haida culture 67-8, 98
Haines 115-21, **116-17**
  accommodations 135
  drinking 119, 120
  entertainment 120
  festivals & events 120
  food 118, 120
  shopping 115, 118
  tours 118, 120-1
  travel within Haines 115
health 395
Healy 311-12
helicopter tours
  Juneau 105
  Spencer Glacier 180
heli-skiing 193-4
Hickory 312
highlights 6-7, 8-19
hiking 11, 50-1, 52-3, *see also* walking, walking tours
  Anchorage 146, 149
  Chilkoot Trail 126-8, 133
  Cooper Landing 235-6
  Denali National Park & Preserve 305, 306-7, 308-9
  Denali State Park 300-1
  Eagle River 159, 161
  Glacier Bay National Park & Preserve 111
  Haines Junction 121
  Harding Icefield 253-4
  Homer 274-5
  Hope 226-7, 228
  Juneau 102-3, 104-5, 106
  Kachemak Bay State Park 280-2
  Katmai National Park & Preserve 360-1
  Kenai Mountains 230
  Ketchikan 69-70
  Kodiak 351-2
  Lowell Point State Recreation Site 256-7
  Matanuska-Susitna 170
  Mendenhall Glacier 101

  Nome 371
  Palmer 167
  Petersburg 85-6
  Primrose 255-6
  Prince of Wales Island 74-5
  Ptarmigan Lake 257
  Resurrection Pass Trail 242-3
  Seldovia 279, 280
  Sheridan Glacier 206-7
  Sitka 94
  Skagway 131-2
  Skilak Wildlife Recreation Area 240
  Termination Point 354
  Turnagain Arm 179
  Valdez 191-2
  Whittier 210, 212
  Wrangell 79-80
  Wrangell-St Elias National Park 336
historical parks
  Big Delta State Historical Park 328
  Fort Abercrombie State Historical Park 351
  Independence Mine State Historical Park 170
  Klondike Gold Rush National Historical Park 123, 129, 407
  Sitka National Historical Park 92
  Totem Bight State Historical Park 67
historic buildings & sites 15
  Alaska State Capitol 98
  Castle Hill 407
  Concentration Mill 336
  Creek Street 62-3
  Governor's Mansion of Alaska 97-8
  Hope Social Hall 225
  K'Beq' Cultural Heritage Interpretive Site 237-8
  Matanuska-Susitna Borough Building 166
  Petroglyph Beach State Historic Site 79
  Pioneer Park 321
  Richard Foster Building 370
  Russian Bishop's House 90
  Wickersham State Historic Site 98
historic railways, *see* scenic railways
history 15, 406-9
  American presidents 298
  aviation 408, 414-15
  Awa'uq 356
  gold rush 123, 129, 374, 407

homesteading 111, 260, 262
John, Moosemeat 244
Russian imperialism 406-7, 412-13
Tlingit culture 84-5
train travel 407
Tsimshian community 70
Wada, Jujiro 249
WWII 119-20, 211, 256-7, 351
Homer 27, 267-76, **268-9**
  accommodations 285
  drinking 270, 273, 275
  festivals & events 274
  food 270, 272, 274
  shopping 270, 272-3, 274
  tours 275
  travel within Homer 267
  walking tours 270, **270**
Hope 27, 222-8, **223**
  accommodations 284
  food 224, 225
  tours 224, 225, **225**
  travel within Hope 222
Horsetail Falls 195
hostels 393
hotels 393
hot springs
  Chena Hot Springs 328
  Goddard Hot Springs 93
  Pilgrim Hot Springs 374-6
  Serpentine Hot Springs 375

ice skating 264
Iditarod Trail Sled Dog Race 31, 369, 372-3
  Hickory 312
  Iditarod Trail Headquarters 171
  Iditarod Trail Mile Marker Zero 249
insects 395
Interior Alaska 286-341, **288-9**
  accommodations 340-1
  activities 290-1
  climate 290-1
  festivals & events 290-1
  itineraries 290-1
  navigation 288-9
  travel seasons 290-1
  travel within Interior Alaska 289
  weather 290-1
internet access 390, 403
internet resources 399
Inupiat culture 379-80
islands
  Admiralty Island National Monument 107-8
  Afognak Island 357
  Douglas Island 103

Kodiak 27, 343-63, 346-52, **344, 348-9**
Kodiak Archipelago 356-7
Kruzof Island 93
Kupreanof Island 86
Shuyak Island 357
Sledge Island 376
Spruce Island 356
St Lawrence Island 376
itineraries 22-9, **23, 25, 27, 29**, see also individual locations

Juneau 22-3, 96-108, **58-9, 97, 99**
  accommodations 134-5
  activities 60-1
  climate 60-1
  drinking & nightlife 103, 107, 108
  festivals & events 60-1
  food 102, 103, 104, 105, 106
  itineraries 60-1
  navigation 58-9
  shopping 107
  tours 105-6, 107-8
  travel seasons 60-1
  travel within Juneau 58, 96
  weather 60-1

K

Kachemak Bay State Park 280-2
Katmai National Park & Preserve 42, 358-63, **344, 359**
  accommodations 363
  activities 345
  climate 345
  festivals & events 345
  itineraries 345
  navigation 344
  travel seasons 345
  travel within the Katmai National Park & Preserve 344, 358
  weather 345
kayaking & canoeing 10, 51, 52-3
  Blackstone Bay 213-14
  Captain Cook State Recreation Area 265-6
  Cooper Landing 235
  Fairbanks 321-2
  Glacier Bay National Park & Preserve 111, 114
  Haines 118
  Hope 224
  Katmai National Park & Preserve 361

Kenai Fjords National Park 250-1
Ketchikan 71
Kodiak 352
Lake Clark National Park & Preserve 278
Moose Pass 239, 241
Petersburg 83-4
Prince of Wales Island 74-5
Sitka 91, 93
Spencer Glacier 180
Tok 330-1
Kenai 258-64, **259**
  accommodations 285
  festivals & events 260
  travel within Kenai 258
  walking tours 261, **261**
Kenai Fjords National Park 24-5, 42, 245-54, 409, **246**
  tours 248, 250-1
  travel within the Kenai Fjords National Park 245
Kenai Mountains - Turnagain Arm National Heritage Area 229-31
Kenai Peninsula 217-85, **218-9**
  accommodations 284-5
  activities 220-1
  climate 220-1
  festivals & events 220-1
  itineraries 220-1
  navigation 218-19
  tours 240, 242-3, 251, **240, 243**
  travel seasons 220-1
  travel within the Kenai Peninsula 218
  weather 220-1
Kennecott 334-5
Ketchikan 22-3, 62-71, **64-5**
  accommodations 134
  drinking 63, 68, 71
  festivals & events 70-1
  food 66, 67, 68, 69
  shopping 63
  travel within Ketchikan 62
King Salmon 363
Knik 171
Knik Glacier 169, 171
Kodiak 27, 346-52, **344, 348-9**
  accommodations 363
  activities 345
  climate 345
  drinking 351, 352
  festivals & events 345
  food 350
  itineraries 345
  navigation 344
  tours 352
  travel seasons 345

travel within Kodiak 344, 346
walking tours 354, **354**
weather 345
Kodiak Archipelago 356-7
Kodiak bears, see bears
Kodiak National Wildlife Refuge 355-6
Kupreanof Island 86

Lake Clark National Park & Preserve 42, 278
lakes & lagoons
  Blueberry Lake 196-7
  Byers Lake 301
  Chilkoot Lake 115, 118
  Eklutna Lake 161
  Frazer Lake 355
  Gertrude Lake 351
  Grewingk Glacier Lake 280-1
  Juneau Lake 243
  Kenai Lake 236-7
  Lake Hood 157-8
  Lost Lake 255-6
  Ptarmigan Lake 257
  Robe Lake 190
  Salmon Lake 374
  Summit Lake 231
  Tern Lake 244
  Triple Lakes 308
  Westchester Lagoon 152
  Wooley Lagoon 376-7
languages 33
LGBTIQ+ travelers 400
libraries
  Hope Community Library 225
  Seward Community Library & Museum 245, 247
literature 33
live music
  Anchorage 154
  Girdwood 177
  Homer 275
  Seward 253
  Skagway 129
lodges, see wilderness lodges
lookouts, see viewpoints
Lowell Point State Recreation Site 256-7

markets
  Anchorage 143
  Haines 115
  Homer 274
  Soldotna 260

419

Matanuska Glacier 160
McCarthy 28-9, 336-9
medical services 395
memorials, monuments & statues
  Copper River Hwy 207
  Denali State Park 301
  Fairbanks 320
  Homer 270
  Kodiak 351
  Petersburg 83
Mendenhall Glacier 100-1
Midnight Sun Festival 31, 371
military sites
  Haines 119-20
  Kodiak 351
  Lowell Point State Recreation Site 256-7
  Whittier 211
mines
  Chicken 331-2
  Denali Highway 313
  Girdwood 177
  Hope 226-7
  Juneau 103-4
  Kenai Lake 236-7
  Kennecott 334-5
Misty Fjords National Monument 72-3
mobile phones 390
money 392
moose 43, 391
Moose Pass 239, 241
mosquitoes 266, 395
motels 393
mountain biking 18
  Eklutna Lake 161
  Girdwood 176
  Primrose 255-6
  Sitka 95
mountains
  Anvil Mountain 378
  Cecil Rhode Mountain 234-5
  Chugach Mountains 200
  Devils Thumb 86
  Dumpling Mountain 360-1
  Finger Mountain 384
  Mt Alyeska 174-5
  Mt Fairweather 113
  Mt Ripinsky 121
  Mt Roberts 102-3

Pillar Mountain 351-2
Pyramid Mountain 352
mudflats 395
museums, see also galleries & art museums
  Alaska Aviation Museum 158, 408
  Alaska State Museum 96-8, 408
  Alutiiq Museum 347
  Anchorage Museum 148
  Carrie M. McLain Memorial Museum 370
  Clausen Memorial Museum 83
  Colony House Museum 166
  Cooper Landing Historical Society Museum 238
  Cordova Historical Museum 202
  Fountainhead Museum 325
  Haines Sheldon Museum 118
  Hammer Museum 118
  Historic Alaska Railroad Depot 314-15, 407
  Hope & Sunrise Historical Society Museum 224, 225, 226
  Juneau-Douglas City Museum 98
  Knik Museum and Mushers Hall of Fame 171
  Kodiak History Museum 347
  Kodiak Military History Museum 351
  Last Chance Mining Museum 104
  Matanuska Valley Agricultural Showcase 167
  Maxine & Jesse Whitney Museum 192
  McCarthy-Kennicott Historical Museum 337
  Mukluk Land 331
  Oscar Anderson House 143
  Palmer Museum of History & Art 166, 408
  Pioneer Museum 321
  Pratt Museum 267, 271
  Prince William Sound Museum 210
  Seward Community Library & Museum 245, 247, 408
  Sheldon Jackson Museum 90-1
  Sitka Historical Museum 90
  Skagway Museum 129

Soldotna Homestead Museum 260, 262
Southeast Alaska Discovery Center 66
Strawberry Point History Museum 111
Talkeetna Historical Society Museum 292, 294
Tongass Historical Museum 66
University of Alaska Museum of the North 322-3, 406
Valdez Museum 193
Wickersham House Museum 321
Wildlife Museum 315
Wrangell Museum 77, 79
music 33, see also live music
music festivals
  Chickenstock 332-3
  Girdwood Forest Fair 31

national parks & preserves 40-3, 52-3
  Denali National Park & Preserve 303-10, **304**
  Gates of the Arctic National Park & Preserve 386
  Glacier Bay National Park & Preserve 109-114, **110**
  Katmai National Park & Preserve 358-62, **359**
  Kenai Fjords National Park 248, 250-4, **246**
  Lake Clark National Park & Preserve 278
  Wrangell-St Elias National Park & Preserve 334-339, **335**
nature tours
  Haines 301-2
  Denali National Park & Preserve 307-8
  Denali State Park 300-2
Nenana 314-15
nightlife 396-7, see also individual locations
Nikolaevsk 283
Ninilchik 282-3
Nome 368-71, 408, **366**, **369**
  accommodations 387
  climate 367
  festivals & events 367
  itineraries 367
  navigation 366
  travels seasons 367
  travel within Nome 366, 368
  weather 367

northern lights 41, 333
North Pole 327
notable buildings, see historic buildings & sites

Old Valdez 195
opening hours 403
outdoor activities, see activities

P

Palmer 26-7, 163-8, 181, **164**
parks & gardens, see also historical parks, national parks & preserves, state parks, state recreation sites
  Bojet Wikan Fisherman's Memorial Park 83
  Georgeson Botanical Garden 323-4
  Griffin Park 320
  Lu Young Park 210
  Potlatch Park 67
Pasagshak Road 353, 355
people 19, 403, 410-11
permits 41
Petersburg 81-6, 134, **82**
Pilgrim Hot Springs 374-6
planning 32-3
population 403, 410-11
Primrose 255-6
Prince of Wales Island 73-5, 134
Prince William Sound 182-215, **184-5**
  accommodations 215
  activities 186-7
  climate 186-7
  festivals & events 186-7
  itineraries 186-7
  navigation 184-5
  tours 196-7, 206-7, **197**, **207**
  travel seasons 186-7
  travel within Prince William Sound 184
  weather 186-7
Ptarmigan Lake 257
public holidays 403

rafting 10, 50, see also kayaking & canoeing
  Haines 121
  Healy 311-12
  Hope 222, 224
  Kenai River 234-5
  Keystone Canyon 194

Spencer Glacier 180
Wrangell-St Elias National Park 336
rail trips, *see* scenic railways, train travel
rainforests, *see* forests & rainforests
reindeer 43
  Antler Academy 327
  Reindeer Farm 168
  Running Reindeer Ranch 325
research centers, *see* science & research centers
responsible travel 398-9
rivers
  Brooks River 360
  Chena River 320-2
  Copper River 204, 338-9
  Kasilof River 262
  Kenai River 232-5
  Little Susitna River 170
  Russian River 232-3
  Savage River 306-7
road trips 12-13, *see also* cycling tours
  Dalton Highway 383-5
  Fairbanks 326
  Turnagain Arm 162, 179, **162, 179**
  Kenai Mountains - Turnagain Arm Heritage Area 230, **230**
  McCarthy Road 338-9, **339**
  Prince William Sound 196, 206-7, **197, 207**
  Skilak Wildlife Recreation Area 240, **240**
  Talkeetna Mountains 170, **170**
  Turnagain Arm 162, 179, **162, 179**
roadhouses 329
roads
  Alcan Highway 332
  Dalton Highway 383-6
  Kougarok Road 374
  Taylor Highway 330-3
running
  Equinox Marathon 324
  Kenai River Marathon 260
  Mt Marathon Race 247
  Palmer 171
Russian culture
  Eklutna 161
  Kodiak 347, 356
  Nikolaevsk 283
  Ninilchik 282-3
  Sitka 87, 90

safety 395
  bear safety 44-5, 94, 310
  road safety 227
salmon 46-7, 49, 397
  Cordova 204
  Kenai 262
  salmon species 234
Salmon Lake 374
saloons
  Mascot Saloon 129
  Red Onion Saloon 130
scenic railways
  Aurora Winter Train 39
  Coastal Classic 39, 157
  Denali Star 38-9, 157
  Glacier Discovery 39, 157, 178, 180
  Hurricane Turn Flagstop 39, 299
  Spencer Glacier Whistle Stop 178, 180
  White Pass & Yukon Route (WPYR) Railway 130-1
science & research centers
  Barrow Arctic Research Center 381-382
  Kodiak Fisheries Research Center 351
  Murie Science & Learning Center 309-310
  Prince William Sound Science Center 203
seafood, *see* salmon, crab
Seldovia 277, 279-80
Seward 24-5, 245-54, **246**
  accommodations 284
  drinking 248, 253
  festivals & events 254
  food 247, 248
  travel within Seward 245
  walking tour 249, **249**
Sheridan Glacier 205
signs 395
SIM cards 390
Sitka 23, 87-95, **88-9**
  accommodations 134
  drinking 91, 95
  food 91, 93, 94
  shopping 95
  tours 93-4
  travel within Sitka 87
  Sitka National Historical Park 92
Skagway 23, 122-33, **124-5**
  accommodations 135
  drinking 129, 132
  entertainment 129
  food 123, 129, 131
  nightlife 129
  tours 130, 132
  travel within Skagway 122

skiing & snowboarding 51, 52-3
  Alyeska Resort 174-5
  Cordova 202-3
  Kenai Peninsula 220
  Slikok Multi-Use Trails 264
  Tsaltseshi Ski Trails 264
  Valdez 193-4
smoking 403
snowboarding, *see* skiing & snowboarding
Soldotna 258-64, **259**
  accommodations 285
  festivals & events 260
  shopping 260
  travel within Soldotna 258
solo travel 401
spas 175
Spencer Glacier 178, 180
sporting events
  Nenana Ice Classic 315
  Oosik Classic Ski Race 296
  World Eskimo-Indian Olympics 321
state parks
  Afognak Island State Park 357
  Chugach State Park 161
  Denali State Park 300-2
  Kachemak Bay State Park 280-2
  Shuyak Island State Park 357
state recreation sites
  Blueberry Lake State Recreation Site 196-7
  Buskin River State Recreation Site 346
  Chilkoot Lake State Recreation Site 115, 118
  Lowell Point State Recreation Site 256-7
  Pasagshak River State Recreation Site 353, 355
statues, *see* memorials, monuments & statues
summer solstice 157, 241, 321
Summit Lake 231
sunburn 395
sustainable travel 398-9
  food 48
  sustainable cruising 36-7

Talkeetna 25, 292-9, **293**
  accommodations 340
  drinking 297
  festivals & events 296
  food 294, 295, 296, 299
  shopping 297-8
  tours 294, 296, 299
  travel within Talkeetna 292
  walking tours 295, **295**

tap water 403
taxes 392
Taylor Highway 330-3, 341, **331**
Teller 376-7
Tern Lake 244
theatres
  Palace Theatre 321
  Perseverace Theatre 103
time 403
tipping 392
Tlingit culture 67-8, 412-13
  Glacier Bay National Park & Preserve 110
  Haines 119
  Juneau 98
  Petersburg 84-5
  Saxman Village 67
  Wrangell 76-7, 79
Tok 28-9, 330-3, 341, **331**
totem poles 66, 67
  Juneau 98
  Prince of Wales Island 73-74
  Sitka 87
  Sitka National Historical Park 92
  Totem Bight State Historical Park 67
  Wrangell 77
trail running 248
train travel 38-9, 391, *see also* scenic railways
  Last Train To Nowhere 373
trams
  Alyeska Aerial Tram 175, 176
  Goldbelt Tram 102
Trans-Alaska Pipeline 193, 408-9
travel from Alaska 390
travel seasons 30-1
travel to Alaska 390
travel within Alaska 391
trekking, *see* hiking
Tsimshian culture 70, 98
tunnels 208
Turnagain Arm 162, 179, 197, 226

Utqiaġvik 379-82, 387, **380**

Valdez 26-7, 188-94, **189**
  accommodations 215
  drinking 192
  food 190, 193
  tours 188, 190-1
  travel within Valdez 188
Valdez Museum 409
vaping 403

vegetarian & vegan
  travelers 48
viewpoints
  Downtown Anchorage
    Viewpoint 153
  Mendenhall Glacier
    viewpoint 101
visas 390
volcanoes
  Mt Augustine 276
  Mt Edgecumbe 93
  Valley of Ten Thousand
    Smokes 361-362

walking 50-1, 52-3
  Captain Cook State
    Recreation Area 266
  Denali National Park &
    Preserve 310
  Haines 120-1
  Ketchikan 69-70
  Wrangell-St Elias National Park & Preserve
    335-6
walking tours
  Homer 270, **270**
  Hope 225, **225**
  Kenai 261, **261**
  Palmer 166, **166**
  Resurrection Pass 242-3,
    243
  Talkeetna 294, 295, **295**
  Whittier 211, **211**
Wasilla 171
waterfalls
  Bridal Veil Falls 195
  Brooks Falls 358-9
  Horsetail Falls 195
  Juneau Creek Falls 242-3
  Russian River Falls 235-6
  Seward Highway
    Falls 230
water 403
weather 30-1, *see also*
  individual regions
whales
  Glacier Bay National Park
    & Preserve 112-4
  Juneau 105-6
  Kenai Fjords National
    Park 248, 250, 252

Kodiak 346
Petersburg 83-4
Turnagain Arm 162
whaling 382
  Nalukataq Festival 380
Whittier 26-7, 208-12,
  215, **209**
  travel within Whittier 208
  walking tours 211, **211**
Wi-Fi 390
wilderness lodges 393
wildlife 8-9, 40-3, 52-3, *see
  also individual species*
wildlife refuges &
  sanctuaries 40-3
  Alaska Maritime National
    Wildlife Refuge 271-2
  Alaska Raptor Center 91
  Alaska Wildlife Conservation Center 179
  Anan Wildlife Observatory 78
  Arctic National Wildlife
    Refuge 386
  Creamer's Field Migratory
    Waterfowl Refuge 325
  Fortress of the Bear 91

Kenai National Wildlife
  Refuge Headquarters &
  Visitor Center 263
Kodiak National Wildlife
  Refuge 346, 355-6
Large Animal Research
  Station 324
Saint Lazaria 93
Skilak Wildlife Recreation
  Area 240
Stan Price State Wildlife
  Sanctuary 107-8
Wedgewood Wildlife
  Sanctuary 325-6
wolves 43
women travelers 401
Wrangell 22-3, 76-80,
  134, **77**
Wrangell-St Elias National
  Park & Preserve 42, 334-9,
  341, **335**
  tours 338-9, **339**
  travel within Wrangell-St
    Elias National Park &
    Preserve 334

NOTES

Take a water taxi to Kachemak Bay State Park (p280) and follow the Glacier Lake Trail through forest to a waterway full of sparkling icebergs.

See the world's largest collection of totems at Totem Bight State Historical Park (p67) in Ketchikan.

All rights reserved. No part of this publication may be copied, stored in a retrieval system, or transmitted in any form by any means, electronic, mechanical, recording or otherwise, except brief extracts for the purpose of review, and no part of this publication may be sold or hired, without the written permission of the publisher. Lonely Planet and the Lonely Planet logo are trademarks of Lonely Planet and are registered in the US Patent and Trademark Office and in other countries. Lonely Planet does not allow its name or logo to be appropriated by commercial establishments, such as retailers, restaurants or hotels. Please let us know of any misuses: lonelyplanet.com/legal/intellectual-property.

Mapping data sources:
© Lonely Planet
© OpenStreetMap http://openstreetmap.org/copyright

THIS BOOK

The 15th edition of Lonely Planet's Alaska guidebook was written and researched by Regis St Louis, Mara Vorhees, Kevin Raub and Melody Burdette. The previous edition was written by Erin Kirkland and Amy Bushatz. This guidebook was produced by the following:

Destination Editors Melinda Anderson, Melissa Yeager

Production Editor Ailbhe MacMahon

Image Editor Virginia Moreno

Cartographer Dorothy Davidson

Coordinating Editor Andrew Bain

Assisting Editors Sally Davies, Paul Harding, Natalie Howard, Helen Koehne, Jennifer McCann, Jenna Myers, Maja Vatrić

Cover Researcher Daisy Korpics

Thanks Alison Killilea, Kellie Langdon, Darren O'Connell, Saralinda Turner

Paper in this book is certified against the Forest Stewardship Council™ standards. FSC™ promotes environmentally responsible, socially beneficial and economically viable management of the world's forests.

Published by Lonely Planet Global Limited
CRN 554153
15th edition – May 2026
ISBN 9781837584147
© Lonely Planet 2026 Photographs © as indicated 2026
10 9 8 7 6 5 4 3 2 1
Printed in China

Contents

Plan Your Trip

The Journey Begins Here	4
Our Picks	6
Perfect Days	18
When to Go	20
Get Prepared	22
Getting There	24
Getting Around	26
How to Speak French	29
Dining Out	30
Bar Open	34
Showtime	36
Shop	38

The Guide

Neighborhoods at a Glance	42
Old Montréal	44
Downtown	60
Quartier Latin, the Village & HoMa	78
Plateau Mont-Royal	90
Mile End, Little Italy & Outremont	110
Lachine Canal, Little Burgundy & the Southwest	122
Parc Jean-Drapeau	140
Side Trips from Montréal	148
Québec City	162
Day Trips from Québec City	186
Where to Stay	196

Gondola cable car, Mont-Tremblant (p153)

Toolkit

Money	204
Family Travel	205
Food, Drink & Nightlife	206
LGBTIQ+ Travelers	208
Health & Safe Travel	209
Responsible Travel	210
Accessible Travel	212
Nuts & Bolts	213
Language	214

Storybook

A History of Québec in 15 Places	218
Meet the Québécois	222
Au Revoir to Bonjour-Hi	224
A World of Arts in Québec Province	227
Index	230

Land Acknowledgement

Lonely Planet respectfully acknowledges that Canada is the traditional territory of more than 630 First Nations communities as well as Inuit and Métis communities. We offer gratitude to the Indigenous Peoples for their care for, and teachings about, this land.

Blvd St-Laurent (p117)

MONTRÉAL & QUÉBEC CITY
THE JOURNEY BEGINS HERE

Montréal has a split personality. It's a mélange of French and English where people might switch languages mid-conversation. It's the sacred 'City of a Hundred Steeples,' blessed with grand basilicas, and also 'Sin City,' where boozehounds raged during Prohibition. Old Montréal seems like a quaint European village, while Downtown's glassy skyscrapers are the paragon of North American modernity. It's Victorian mansions and brutalist Métro stops; 19th-century industrial factories and green alleys overgrown with gardens. It's Québécois pride and immigrant ingenuity – like a plate of poutine topped with kimchi. It's snow-packed winters and sweltering summers – climatic swings that redraw the landscape every season. With so much variety, choosing sides can be tempting, like pledging fidelity to your favorite Montréal bagel bakery. I abstain from the binary discourse and embrace the in-between. You don't have to pick sides; you get to have it all. And that includes nearby Québec City – a sprinkling of old-world Europe in North America.

John Garry
@garryjohnfrancis

John is a writer, teacher, urban biker, back-alley wanderer, avid museum-goer and long-time theater nerd who's contributed to a dozen Lonely Planet guides. He wrote Plan Your Trip; Old Montréal; Downtown; Quartier Latin, the Village & HoMa; Plateau Mont-Royal; Mile End, Little Italy & Outremont; Parc Jean-Drapeau; Toolkit; A History of Québec in 15 Places; and Au Revoir to Bonjour-Hi.

My favorite experience is strolling up Blvd St-Laurent (p117) – past murals, vintage shops and multicultural restaurants that give Montréal its artsy, international edge.

WHO GOES WHERE

Our writers and experts choose the places which, for them, define Montréal & Québec City.

The aspect of the **Lachine Rapids** (pictured; p134) that really stands out is the sound: from the shores of Verdun the frothing waters make a noise like static. This section of the St Lawrence River feels so formidable that it's no wonder early settlers avoided it. The river's mesmerizing to watch, but after just one look you'll see why digging the Lachine Canal was urgently needed.

Robert Isenberg
@youareheredocs

Robert is a writer, filmmaker and avid cyclist based in Rhode Island. He wrote Lachine Canal, Little Burgundy & the Southwest.

The hill above **Terrasse Pierre-Dugua-de-mons** (pictured; p173) has a postcard-perfect view of Old Québec and the St Lawrence River. In summer it's a great place to enjoy a picnic of local terroir and a bottle of Québec wine. Autumn is breathtaking, and rolling down the hill is fun in winter. It's a peaceful escape in the heart of the old city.

Pamela MacNaughtan
@urbanguidequebec

Pamela is a travel and food writer, road trip addict and croissant snob based in Québec City. She wrote Québec City and Meet the Québécois.

While growing up in Ottawa and living in Montréal, I loved taking off to **the Laurentians** (pictured; p152) for a day or spending a weekend snowboarding at Mont-Tremblant. Seeing snow blanket the evergreens while cruising down from above the clouds is among my most cherished memories. And the best part of any ski day? Warming up in the lodge with an ooey-gooey poutine.

Joel Balsam
@joelbalsam

Joel Balsam is a Canadian freelance journalist and writer of more than a dozen Lonely Planet guidebooks. He wrote about rural Québec for this guide.

GORGEOUS GREEN SPACES

Tree-trimmed parks stretch across Québec's cities, bucolic farms spread over the countryside and Montréal's namesake mountain rises above the skyline like a monument. Green spaces throughout the province aren't merely playgrounds – they reflect what the Québécois prize: natural beauty, local terroir and wide-open fields fit for a festival-crammed calendar. With nearly 2000 parks between them, Montréal and Québec City agree: getting outside is essential. Join locals in their public backyards, where scenes from everyday life unfold.

Urban Greenways

Montréal has around 450 **ruelles vertes** (p102) – green-ified public alleys where communities come together for everything from block parties to barbecues.

Beach, Please

When summer heats up, locals cool off at St Lawrence River beaches like Montréal's **Plage de Verdun** (p132) and Québec City's **Station de la Plage** (p176).

Park with a Past

Québec City's **Plaines d'Abraham** (p165) looks like a peaceful picnic ground, but in 1759 it's where Britain seized Québec from France, reshaping the province's future.

Skyline view from Belvédère Kondiaronk (p105)

PLAN YOUR TRIP OUR PICKS

BEST GREEN SPACE EXPERIENCES

Climb to Parc du Mont-Royal's ❶ **Belvédère Kondiaronk** (p105) for a breathtaking panorama of skyscrapers and the St Lawrence River.

Sail across the St Lawrence to ❷ **Parc Jean-Drapeau** (p140) for cityscape views, summer dance parties and Expo 67 relics.

Cycle the ❸ **Lachine Canal** (p136), a 19th-century industrial waterway transformed into a string of public parks and pretty paths.

Feel the power of Québec's tallest waterfall while crossing a suspension bridge at ❹ **Parc de la Chute-Montmorency** (p186).

Zoom around ❺ **Île d'Orléans** (p190) to pastoral vineyards, organic farms and flower gardens overlooking the St Lawrence.

WINTER WONDERLAND

When the weather outside is frosty, the Québécois bundle up to embrace the glittering snowscape. The outdoor adventures are endless: frozen ponds become ice-skating rinks, public parks turn into snowshoeing courses, and celebrations throughout Montréal and Québec City rejoice in the chilly season's charm. Things get cozier indoors: sugar-shack feasts inspire maple-drizzled indulgences and Scandi-style sauna culture picks up steam around the province. Then there are mountains outside the city – powdered perfection for skiers.

Snow Season

Winter stretches from December to March, but snow might fall anytime from November through April. January and February are coldest – and best for skiing and ice skating.

Underground City

Don't care for the cold? Explore Montréal via the **Réseau de la Ville Souterraine** (RÉSO; p76) – a vast underground network of tunnels connecting Downtown Montréal destinations.

Maple Syrup Feast

By late February, maple sap starts flowing from trees and sugar-shack season gets underway – the best time to feast on hearty Québécois fare.

Sommet Saint-Sauveur, the Laurentian Mountains (p152)

BEST WINTER EXPERIENCES

Race snow bunnies down 42 trails at ❶ **Sommet Saint-Sauveur** (p154), one of many ski resorts climbing the Laurentian Mountains.

Soak in saunas, steam rooms and hot tubs aboard ❷ **Bota Bota** (p59), a floating spa moored in the icy St Lawrence.

Lace up ice skates or don cross-country skis to glide around snow-dusted trails throughout ❸ **Parc Jean-Drapeau** (p145).

Follow Bonhomme – the jolly snowman mascot of ❹ **Carnaval de Québec** (p175) – by participating in three weeks of ice-tastic festivities in Québec City.

Grab a toboggan and zoom down the ❺ **Glissade de la Terrasse** (p175), reaching speeds of up to 70km/h.

AWESOME ART

Québec is a canvas decorated with over 3500 public artworks, 200-plus galleries and dozens of museums. Montréal serves as its cultural capital, home to Canada's largest fine-arts complex and splattered with street art turning drab buildings into eye-catching showstoppers. Québec City keeps pace with outdoor frescoes and exhibitions praising local talent. With its residents surrounded by such visual splendor, it's no wonder Québec also excels in music, theater and dance. Art is in the provincial DNA.

Art for All

Praise Québec's government for all the outdoor sculptures: a 1961 policy mandates that 1% of construction costs for publicly funded buildings be set aside for art.

Mural Town

Montréal is 'Mural City' thanks to two annual graffiti fetes, **MURAL Festival** (p21) and **Under Pressure** *(underpressure.ca)*, decorating avenues with new artwork every year.

Digital Dynamism

Montréal is morphing into a technological arts hub, best appreciated during September's **MAPP_MTL festival** *(@mapp_mtl)*, when city buildings become backdrops for dazzling digital projections.

FROM LEFT: ANNE RICHARD/SHUTTERSTOCK, MILAN SUERE. ARTISTS: SEBASTIAN AYLA AND ARYZ, SANTINOVICHPHOTO.COM/SHUTTERSTOCK

Musée des Beaux-Arts de Montréal (p68)

BEST ART EXPERIENCES

Spend several hours exploring the trove of classical masterpieces and contemporary installations inside ❶ **Musée des Beaux-Arts de Montréal** (p68).

Pop into ❷ **Mile End's art galleries** (p115), including a mural-covered stairwell and the city's first Indigenous artist–run showroom.

Get inspired by the contemporary art center ❸ **PHI** (p57), bringing multisensory magic to Old Montréal.

See summertime street performers, alfresco installations and a can't-look-away 'bad art' exhibit at ❹ **EXMURO** (p181).

Admire First Nations and Inuit art while honoring Québec's Indigenous history at ❺ **Musée de la Civilisation** (p177).

Basilique Notre-Dame (p48)

AMAZING ARCHITECTURE

Québec's cityscapes span four centuries of urban evolution. The historic cores of Montréal and Québec City exude an old-world ambience, their cobblestone streets lined with Victorian facades and elaborate cathedrals. Industrial landmarks along the St Lawrence capture 19th-century ambition, while Montréal's Expo 67 remnants and glassy towers reflect 20th-century optimism. Every block tells a tale.

City Bones

One of the most common building materials in Old Montréal and Québec City is greystone, locally quarried limestone used extensively in the 18th and 19th centuries.

Mountain Tops

Montréal's distinctive skyscape is influenced by its crowning mountain. Under a 1992 law, no city building may exceed the height of Mont Royal.

BEST ARCHITECTURE EXPERIENCES

Sit back as the psychedelic AURA Experience light show spotlights the ornate Gothic Revival interior of ❶ **Basilique Notre-Dame** (p48).

Hop between 19th-century mansions decorating the ❷ **Golden Square Mile** (p77), once the stomping ground of Canada's industrial ruling class.

Book a tour of architect Moshe Safdie's modular masterpiece ❸ **Habitat 67** (p126), his brutalist contribution to the futuristic Expo 67 fair.

Walk the imposing ❹ **fortification walls** (p166) hugging the city to see Old Québec from a colonial soldier's point of view.

Twirl around ❺ **Place-Royale** (p169) to eye centuries-old stone homes with mansard roofs rising from cobblestone streets.

SENSATIONAL STREETS

These boulevards were made for walking. From the fairy-tale charm of Québec City's oldest roads to the serenity of Montréal's green alleys, joining the pedestrian parade is the best way to uncover both cities' souls. These aren't just streets – they're arteries pulsing at the cultural heart of Québec, peppered with gems waiting to be found.

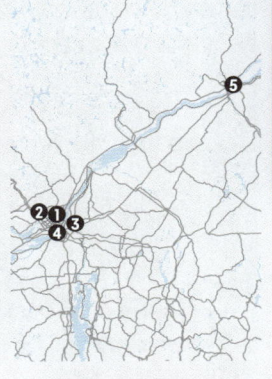

BEST STREETSIDE EXPERIENCES

Experience the multicultural cacophony of ❶ **Blvd St-Laurent** (p95), where over a century's worth of immigrants built new lives in Québec.

Drop by art outlets, clothing boutiques, vintage stores, literary dens and one sensational *fromagerie* along ❷ **Ave Mont-Royal** (p97).

Shop along Rue Ste-Catherine's Downtown stretch by day, then hop between ❸ **LGBTIQ+ bars** (p83) along its Village strip at night.

Take your pick on ❹ **Rue Notre-Dame** (p127) as it shoots between Little Burgundy and Griffintown: perhaps brasseries, comic books, art or antiques.

Skip along ❺ **Rue du Petit-Champlain** (p169), the oldest commercial street in Canada, packed with artisan shops and restaurants.

Bipedal Party

Every summer nearly a dozen Montréal streets close to car traffic, turning over 9km into pedestrian promenades where restaurants and bars spill onto sidewalk terraces.

Count Your Steps

Staircases linking Québec City's lower and upper sections can be steep – particularly the Escalier Casse-Cou ('Breakneck Steps') – a 59-stair climb dating back to the 17th century.

Winter Walking

Don't fret over the fluffy stuff: Montréal spends roughly $200 million on snow removal annually, clearing over 10,000km of sidewalks and streets for pedestrians and drivers.

FROM LEFT: J-PHILIPPE MENARD/SHUTTERSTOCK, ANDRIY BLOKHIN/SHUTTERSTOCK

Marché Jean-Talon (p118)

FANTASTIC FOOD

Get to know Québec through its belly. The province blends French finesse and global influences with a budding locavore movement prizing regional farm fare. Montréal is its gastronomic powerhouse, with 5000 restaurants, 40 microbreweries and dozens of foodie festivals throughout the year. It's all hearty as poutine and sweet as maple syrup – prepare to indulge.

Veggie Valhalla

Montréal is a pioneer of urban agriculture. More than 50 farms on rooftops and balconies grow produce sold to restaurants and markets across the city.

Maple Empire

Québec produces roughly 70% of the world's **maple syrup supply** (p207), fortified with backup reserves to ensure the world never runs out.

BEST CULINARY EXPERIENCES

Flit between food stands at ❶ **Marché Jean-Talon** (p118) and ❶ **Marché Atwater** (p127), where shoppers hunt for farm-grown treats.

Make a reservation at ❷ **Vin Mon Lapin** (p117), a French-Italian bistro with a menu featuring seasonal produce and natural wines.

Choose from over 30 styles of poutine at ❸ **La Banquise** (p93), the legendary 24/7 mess-plate palace going strong since 1968.

Taste the difference between bagels at ❹ **Fairmount and St-Viateur** (p113) so you can argue with locals about who does it better.

Get the full maple-drenched sugar-shack experience with traditional Québécois classics at ❺ **La Bûche** (p167).

WITH KIDS

Put down the iPads: Québec overflows with entertaining activities. Depending on the season, you can climb ropes courses, go ice skating or shriek on amusement park rides until fireworks explode. Interactive museums disguise learning as fun, and the province's prized dishes are perfect for picky eaters. Thank goodness – after all this excitement, everyone will be starving.

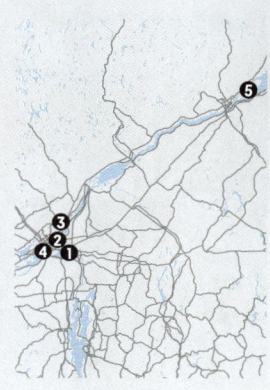

Eat Québécois Classics

Cultivate young palates in Montréal with St-Viateur's bagels and Chez Claudette's cheesy poutine – then try not to giggle while eating 'nun's farts' at **Marché Jean-Talon** (p118).

Take Public Transit

In Montréal, kids 11 and under ride free on buses and the Métro. In Québec City, kids aged six to 12 ride city buses for nix.

Museums for Young Minds

Spend a day flitting between four kid-friendly **Espace Pour la Vie museums** (p84) surrounding Parc Olympique. Discount passes keep prices affordable for families.

BEST EXPERIENCES WITH KIDS

Ride the observation wheel, jump around the pirate park and then catch a science-themed IMAX movie around the ❶ **Old Port** (p52).

Dive into history at ❷ **Pointe-à-Callière** (p47), where kids can join a simulated archaeological dig above 17th-century foundations.

Waddle with penguins and wave at river otters while wandering through five ecosystems under one roof at the ❸ **Biodôme** (p85).

Rent snow tubes to race down the hill above ❹ **Lac aux Castors** (p105) or don skates to zip around the neighboring ice rink.

Fill up on chocolate – cocoa, truffles and summertime ice cream – at the ❺ **Chocolaterie de l'Île d'Orléans** (p192).

Place des Festivals (p64)

FOR FREE

No need to break the bank: Montréal and Québec City offer riches without a price tag, like listening to music at public festivals, tracing murals along city walls and roaming tranquil park trails open to all. Even Montréal's top museums offer occasional free admittance, ensuring savvy travelers rarely need to open their wallets.

Public Performances

Catch open-air shows at Montréal's **Place des Festivals** (p64) or save big at Québec City's **Festival d'Été** (p165) by attending its selection of no-cost concerts.

Free Museum Nights

Montréal museums including **MBAM** (p68), **Musée McCord Stewart** (p70) and the **Centre Canadien d'Architecture** (p131) offer free access on select evenings during the week.

Discount Card

Pinching pennies? Save up to 35% on museums, tours and restaurants with Passeport MTL, valid for three to five top attractions. Purchase online at *mtl.org*.

BEST FREE EXPERIENCES

Watch documentaries and thumb through interactive exhibits in the free-to-visit lobby of ❶ **MEM** (p66), Montréal's immersive social history museum.

Reach the top of ❷ **Oratoire St-Joseph** (p139), a basilica founded by Brother André Bessette, his heart preserved in an on-site reliquary.

Stroll along Blvd St-Laurent and surrounding alleys in the Plateau, where colorful ❸ **street art** (p96) delights on nearly every corner.

Eye fossils, mummies and mammoth tusks at the ❹ **Musée Redpath** (p71), an eccentric natural history collection spread across three floors.

Take a self-guided tour through the sprawling ❺ **Assemblée national du Québec** (p168) to admire its Second Empire architecture.

UNDER THE RADAR

After checking off the must-see museums and colonial-era streets, find the offbeat side of Québec, hidden behind unassuming facades, located in neighborhoods beyond the range of most tourists or waiting outside city limits. These are the spots where you'll rub shoulders with locals – the best places to learn what it means to be Québécois.

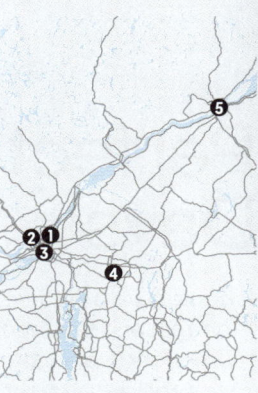

BEST UNDER-THE-RADAR EXPERIENCES

Go on a food crawl through up-and-coming neighborhood ❶ **Hochelaga-Maisonneuve** (p87), sampling baked goods, chocolates, cheeses and craft beer.

Pedal to ❷ **Île de la Visitation** (p121), a tree-lined island connected to industrial ruins along Rivière des Prairies – Montréal's *other* river.

Hunt for slick hats, tailored jeans and must-read paperbacks from ❸ **Downtown stores** (p72) supplying a century of Québec shoppers with grade-A goods.

Drive to the Eastern Townships, where two dozen wineries along ❹ **La Route des Vins** (p161) showcase the local terroir.

Tour the ❺ **Morrin Centre** (p185), Québec's only dedicated English library, with a graffiti-etched crypt recalling its 19th-century prison days.

Cycle to New Sights

Over 12,000km of bicycle paths snake across the province, including the 5000km-plus **Route Verte** (p146) and **hidden rail trails** (p159) linking Montréal to Québec City.

Take a Tour

Licensed guides in Montréal and Québec City keep current on what's cool. Take a tour with Montréal's **Spade & Palacio** (p93) for expert recommendations.

Neighborhoods Worth Knowing

In Montréal, skip along Rue de Castelnau in Villeray (p93) and Rue St-Hubert in La Petite-Patrie (p115), teeming with inventive restaurants, unique boutiques and cafes.

FROM LEFT: MARC BRUXELLE/SHUTTERSTOCK, ANDRY BLOKHIN/SHUTTERSTOCK

Perfect Days

It could take a lifetime to uncover Montréal and Québec City's many wonders. Tighten your focus and get straight to the best spots – blending art, food, history, shopping and must-do outdoor adventures.

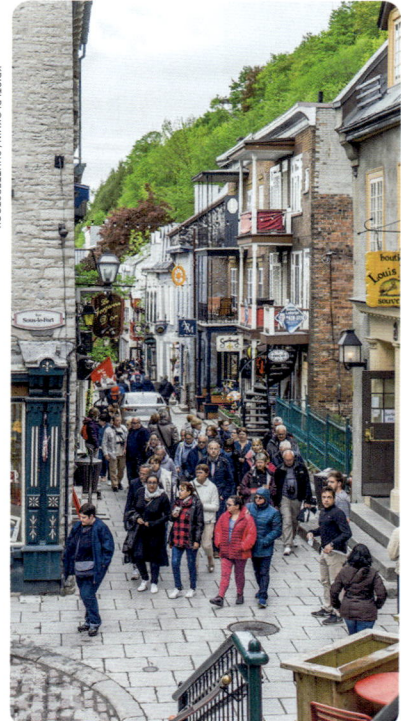

Rue du Petit-Champlain (p170)

DAY 1

Old Montréal

☼ Grab yourself a hearty breakfast at **Olive et Gourmando** (p49) before digesting 5000 years of local history at **Pointe-à-Callière** (p47) – an archaeological museum on top of the city's original foundations. From here, explore shops along cobblestoned **Rue St-Paul** (p50) en route to the sailors' church, **Chapelle Notre-Dame-de-Bon-Secours** (p49).

Lunch: Pop into **Stash Café** (p54) for Polish pierogi or keep it light with a snack from **Le Petit Dep** (p55) on Rue St-Paul.

Old Montréal

☼ Stroll past 18th-century manor **Château Ramezay** (p47) toward Place d'Armes, dominated by the dazzling **Basilique Notre-Dame** (p48). After ogling the Gothic interior, search for stylish souvenirs at Marché Saint Laurent and Montréal-themed prints at poster gallery **L'Affichiste** (p54). Refuel with coffee from **Crew Collective & Café** (p47), housed in a 1920s bank with soaring 15m ceiling.

Dinner: Take a flavor tour through **Chinatown** (p75) or fill up on Japanese at **Fleur et Cadeaux** (p66).

Old Montréal

☾ Beeline to the Old Port: in summer, watch **Cirque du Soleil** (p53) performers catapult through the air; in winter, try an evening soak at **Bota Bota** (p59). Finish with some cocktails at local speakeasies – perhaps whiskey at **Coldroom** (p59) then late-night dancing at petite **Sans Soleil** (p72).

DAY 2

Downtown & Plateau Mont-Royal

☀ Energized by coffee from **Café SAT** (p75), drop by **MEM** (p66) to learn about Montréalers through collections of firsthand accounts. Spend the rest of the morning experiencing the city's multicultural melting pot along Blvd St-Laurent: scope out **vintage stores** (p94), admire **street murals** (p96) and savor a *pastel de nata* (custard tart) around **Little Portugal** (p95).

Lunch: Go classic: either **Schwartz's** (p93) smoked meat or a bagel sandwich from the Ave Mont-Royal location of **St-Viateur** (p113).

Downtown & Plateau Mont-Royal

☀ Trek through Parc du Mont-Royal for panoramic views from **Belvédère Kondiaronk** (p105), then wind down the Grand Staircase to reach Downtown. Get acquainted with Québec and Canadian art at **MBAM** (p68), spread across six floors, before hiking past heritage mansions around the **Golden Square Mile** (p77).

Dinner: Take the Métro to La Petite-Patrie for upscale Thai at **Pichai** (p118) or down pizza and wine at **Marci** (p117).

Little Italy & the Village

☾ Choose between craft brews at **Mellön** (p121) or natural wine from **Mamie** (p119) before deciding how to button the night: indie-band jamming at **Casa del Popolo** (p119), soft jazz at **Dièse Onze** (p102) or all-night EDM at Village club **Stereo** (p86).

DAY 3

Québec City

☀ Catch an early train to Québec City, then grab buttery croissants and espresso at **La Maison Smith** (p164). Engine revved, march to the 18th-century **stone fortifications** (p166) and join a 90-minute tour to explore corners inaccessible without a guide. In summer, roll through **Rue du Trésor** (p170), an open-air art gallery, en route to turreted **Château Frontenac** (p168), the city's architectural eye candy. For St Lawrence River views, skip along nearby **Terrasse Dufferin** (p173), and if it's winter, shriek down its **Au 1884** (p164) toboggan ramp.

Lunch: Belly up to **Le Chic Shack** (p165) for gourmet poutine and made-to-order milkshakes.

Québec City

☀ Wander the cobbled **Rue du Petit-Champlain** (p169), dipping into artisan shops like **Fucklamode** (p164) for clothing and coffee. End the afternoon at **Musée de la Civilisation** (p177), where exhibitions on Indigenous communities reframe Québec's founding stories.

Dinner: Tuck into Québécois comfort food at **La Bûche** (p167), a modern twist on maple-smothered sugar-shack staples.

Québec City

☾ With more energy, see what's playing at the **Grand Théâtre de Québec** (p183) – perhaps stand-up or live music – then unwind at **L'Oncle Antoine** (p169), sipping maple whiskey in an 18th-century stone vault.

WHEN TO GO

Québec's appeal shifts with each season. Winter's icescape transforms with spring's petals and sunny summer's dog days cool as autumn arrives.

Québec experiences all four seasons to their extremes. Snow appears around November or December and blankets the landscape until April, embraced by throngs of ice skaters and skiers who take to frozen ponds and frosty parks. Spring arrives in fits and starts, sweetened by maple syrup and bursting into a floral frenzy by May, when cherry and crabapple trees bloom. Summer is outdoor-festival season, when Montréal's popular thoroughfares become pedestrian promenades, BIXI bikes zip along cycling trails, and crowds catch rays on river banks and outdoor terraces. Autumn becomes an arboreal art show, best appreciated in parks with leafy landscapes and at farmers markets, filled with the fruits of fall's harvest.

Budget Travel

As the temperatures drop below freezing, so do hotel prices, making early January and late February a fantastic time for bargains. Expect to pay top dollar throughout summer and during popular festivals like Carnaval de Québec.

I LIVE HERE

SNOW CYCLISTS

Diego Salamone, co-owner and CEO of Fitz Montréal bike tours, promotes year-round cycling.
@fitzmontrealtours

Cycling in winter is getting more popular every year now that the city is snowplowing the bike lanes. You'll see people out there when it's -20°C, which might sound crazy, but it's the best way to get around, and it beats parking a car in deep snow. If you cycle in the cold, wear an extra layer on your hands and legs – and ensure you have the proper snow tires.

Igloofest (p53)

MORE TREES, PLEASE

Summers in Montréal and Québec City can be heavenly – and hot. Asphalt-slapped streets cause urban heat island effect, trapping heat and roasting neighborhoods. To cool things down, Montréal plans to plant 500,000 trees by 2030, creating natural air-conditioning for a warming world.

Weather Through the Year in Montréal

JANUARY	FEBRUARY	MARCH	 APRIL	MAY	JUNE
Avg. daytime max: **-4°C**	Avg. daytime max: **-4°C**	Avg. daytime max: **3°C**	Avg. daytime max: **11°C**	Avg. daytime max: **19°C**	Avg. daytime max: **24°C**
Days of precipitation: **17**	Days of precipitation: **15**	Days of precipitation: **15**	Days of precipitation: **14**	Days of precipitation: **13**	Days of precipitation: **12**

LET IT SNOW

Warming temperatures throughout southern Québec have meant less snow than a century ago, but there's still no shortage of frosted flakes. Québec City sees over 300cm of annual snowfall, while Montréal receives around 215cm. In 2025 Montréal set a four-day snowfall record: 75cm of fluffy stuff.

Big & Brassy Events

Carnaval de Québec (p175) The world's largest winter carnival transforms Québec City into a frosted fun zone with two weeks of sleigh rides, night parades, maple taffy and 'snow baths' – inspiring *bonhomie* during winter's darkest days. ❄ **February**

Festival international de Jazz de Montréal (p64) Two million jazz-lovers gather to hear legends and newcomers improvise riffs and trills at hundreds of concerts held across the city. ☀ **June and July**

Fierté Montréal (p83) Montréal rolls out the rainbow carpet for the francophone world's biggest LGBTIQ+ gathering, an 11-day fête packed with dance parties, film screenings and performances, climaxing in a celebratory parade. ☀ **August**

Osheaga (p145) Powerhouse performers take to stages around Parc Jean-Drapeau for a three-day music fest featuring everyone from emerging artists to established stars, be it Doechii or Olivia Rodrigo. ☀ **August**

A MAN FOR ALL SEASONS

Montréal tour guide **Thom Seivewright** celebrates his city's cusp seasons.
@montrealexpert

I love when one season shifts into another – those few days when it's not quite summer and not quite fall but something in between. Those are the moments that remind me I'm living somewhere that has four seasons – and how every four months the city completely changes. It's kind of like nature's show, connecting me with nature, which isn't easy to do while living in a city.

Maple sap

MAPLE SYRUP SEASON

Spring is 'sugaring off' season – when farmers tap trees to collect sap for maple syrup. Sap flow depends on freeze-thaw cycles, with warm days and cold nights jumpstarting secretion. The season runs from late February to late April, or whenever buds appear on trees.

Wacky & Wonderful Festivals

Just for Laughs (p64) Visitors leave with sore bellies after two weeks of nonstop jokes, flung at crowds by stand-up greats like past performers Ali Wong, Hasan Minhaj, Jerry Seinfeld and Margaret Cho. ☀ **July**

Nuit Blanche Montréalers stay up way past their bedtime on the first Saturday in March as the city becomes a giant pop-up art space, the creative juices flowing 'til dawn. ❄ **March**

Igloofest (p53) EDM-heads don their favorite retro snowsuits and keep warm by step touching under the moon as DJs spin tunes by Montréal's Old Port. ❄ **January and February**

MURAL Festival Blvd St-Laurent transforms into an open-air art gallery as renowned street artists paint murals on buildings throughout Plateau Mont-Royal, accompanied by block parties featuring digital installations and live performances. ☀ **June**

JULY	**AUGUST**	**SEPTEMBER**	**OCTOBER**	**NOVEMBER**	**DECEMBER**
Avg. daytime max: **26°C**	Avg. daytime max: **25°C**	Avg. daytime max: **21°C**	Avg. daytime max: **13°C**	Avg. daytime max: **6°C**	Avg. daytime max: **-1°C**
Days of precipitation: **13**	Days of precipitation: **10**	Days of precipitation: **13**	Days of precipitation: **12**	Days of precipitation: **15**	Days of precipitation: **17**

Belvédère Kondiaronk (p105), Parc du Mont-Royal (p104)

GET PREPARED FOR MONTRÉAL & QUÉBEC CITY

Clothes

Smart casual Though practicality dictates much Québec fashion, trendy Montréal still dresses up, favoring street-smart attire and baggy silhouettes over suit-and-tie formality.

Winter Follow the three-layer rule: a moisture-wicking base (including leggings or tights), a main layer (perhaps a sweater and pants), plus an insulating jacket. Consider bringing an outer shell to protect against wind and snow.

Accessories In winter, wear warm gloves, heavy socks and a hat to cover the ears.

Boots From December through mid-April, icy streets require warm, water-resistant boots with good grip.

Summer Shorts, tees and dresses all work, but bring an extra layer for cool evenings.

Sneakers In summer, leave the high heels at home: your feet will thank you after slogging along cobblestone streets and gravel park trails.

Manners

Speak French Fluency isn't necessary, but as it's the province's official language, a little French goes a long way. It's a sign of respect to use local salutations.

Follow pedestrian rules Urbanites use sidewalks for commuting, not dawdling: traffic sticks to the right. Need to pause? Step aside.

Kiss, kiss The two-cheek kiss – '*la bise*' – is a convivial Québec greeting, not a French-kissing precursor.

READ

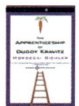

The Apprenticeship of Duddy Kravitz (Mordecai Richler; 1959) A working-class Jewish Montréaler stops at nothing to get rich quick.

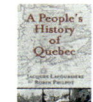

A People's History of Québec (Jacques Lacoursière; 1995) Over 450 years of activity along the St Lawrence River told in 200 pages.

Our Lady of Mile End (Sarah Gilbert; 2023) Short stories of displacement and gentrification in Montréal's hippest 'hood.

The Fat Woman Next Door Is Pregnant (Michel Tremblay; 1978) The lives of seven women converge in comedy and tragedy around Montréal's Plateau.

Words

5 à 7 *'Cinq-a-sept'* (five to seven) refers to the 5pm-to-7pm happy hours, when friends like to gather after work to unwind over food and drinks.

Autoroute Another word for a highway or freeway.

Bonjour-hi Shopkeepers use this bilingual greeting to decipher if someone prefers communicating in English or French. It's a contentious phrase, sparking political debates over the use of English in the French-speaking province (p224).

Casse-croûte 'Snack shack' similar to a diner or deli; serves up traditional Québécois fast food such as hotdogs, hamburgers and poutine (p32).

Dépanneur 'Dep' for short; a convenience store selling beer, wine, lotto tickets and household staples. They often stay open late, and some offer specialty items, artisanal crafts, coffee and lunch fare (p66).

Guichet ATM.

Terrasse Translates to 'terrace' – but it's much more than a patio. English- and French-speaking Québécois use this term to refer to the alfresco social space connected to a bar, cafe or restaurant where people gather to soak up the sun, most often spring through autumn but occasionally year-round.

Sacres Québécois curse words adopted from common Catholic terms like 'chalice,' 'tabernacle,' and 'baptism' (p121).

SAQ 'The Société des alcools du Québec' is the province's chain of state-owned liquor stores – and the easiest place to find hard liquor and wine. SAQs also sell beer, though *dépanneurs* and grocery stores usually carry a wider selection.

 **WATCH**

C.R.A.Z.Y. (pictured; Jean-Marc Vallée; 2005) Being gay isn't easy for a young Québécois in a Catholic francophone family during the 1960s.

I Confess (Hitchcock; 1953) The 'Master of Suspense' filmed this tale of murder and religious morality in Québec City.

Les Orders (Michel Brault; 1974) Québec's 1970 October Crisis comes to life in this docudrama about state-sanctioned incarceration of innocent civilians.

Barkskins (David Slade et al; 2020) New France's colonists, indentured servants and Indigenous inhabitants fight for their lives in this historical TV drama.

Solo (Sophie Dupuis; 2023) A talented drag queen navigates new love and old trauma while performing at a Montréal cabaret.

 LISTEN

Songs of Leonard Cohen (Leonard Cohen; 1967) The debut album of Montréal's beloved musical bard showcases his poetic flair for melancholy.

Funeral (Arcade Fire; 2004) Montréal's indie rock darlings hit the big time with the release of their debut album.

Visions (Grimes; 2012) Claire Boucher (known as Grimes) wrote this breakthrough synth-pop album while cloistered inside her Mile End apartment.

This Is Montreal (CBC; ongoing) Podcast host Ainslie MacLellan digs into Montréal culture with salacious stories and colorful characters.

Bus, Québec City (p162)

GETTING THERE

Most visitors arrive in Québec via one of two airports – Aéroport International Montréal-Trudeau (YUL) or Québec City's Aéroport international Jean-Lesage de Québec (YQB). Depending on your route, a bus, train or personal car may be the more sensible travel option.

Taxis

Taxis receive passengers from signposted pickup posts at Montréal and Québec City airports. Fixed rates from the airport to the city center apply for both cities. YUL to Downtown Montréal costs $49.45 (5am to 11pm) and $56.70 (11pm to 5am). Taxis from Québec City's YQB to Old Québec cost $41.40 during the day and $47.60 at night.

Wi-fi

Wi-fi is free and easy to access in Québec airports. In Montréal, choose the YUL wi-fi network; in Québec City, choose the YQB Gratuit-Free network.

SIM Cards

At Montréal's YUL, retailers ChatR, Rogers and Fido sell SIM cards on the public arrivals level between doors 27 and 28. Québec City's YQB sells SIM cards near the arrival gates.

Bus Passes

Purchase fares for the YUL shuttle to Downtown Montréal with exact change on the bus or at one of the vending machines near door 28 in the international arrivals area. The standard $11 fare works as a 24-hour transit pass to ride the bus and Métro throughout Montréal. At Québec City's YQB, purchase bus tickets for the Réseau de transport de la Capitale (RTC) at the vending machine by the check-in counters in the terminal building.

FROM THE AIRPORT TO THE CITY CENTER

From Aéroport International Montréal-Trudeau (YUL)

| Bus: Rte 747 | 45min, $11 |
| Taxi | 25min, day/night $49.45/56.70 |

From Québec City's Aéroport international Jean-Lesage de Québec (YQB)

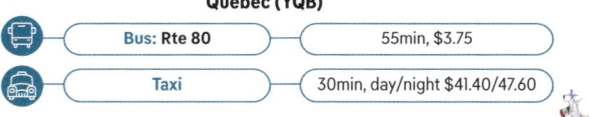

| Bus: Rte 80 | 55min, $3.75 |
| Taxi | 30min, day/night $41.40/47.60 |

TIP

By 2027 Montréal's REM (Réseau Express Métropolitain) train is expected to link YUL to Downtown Montréal's Gare Centrale on a 25-minute ride. Keep a lookout.

OTHER POINTS OF ENTRY

Train & Bus

Canada's VIA Rail *(viarail.ca)* connects Downtown Montréal's Gare Central to over 400 stations throughout the nation – including Québec City's French château-inspired Gare de Palais, a 3½-hour ride away. Montréal links to NYC on a 10-hour trip along Amtrak's Adirondack line *(amtrak.com)*. Most long-distance buses arrive in Montréal at Gare d'Autocars de Montréal.

Boat

Thousands of cruise-ship passengers disembark along Montréal's Old Port and Québec City's Port de Québec – both a short jog to their respective cities' historic cores. Croisières AML *(croisieresaml.com)* sails from Montréal to Québec City on a day-long cruise followed by an evening bus ride back to Montréal.

Car

Montréal is a 75km drive from the US. New York border town Champlain (along I-87) connects to Québec's Saint-Bernard-de-Lacolle (along Autoroute 15), 45 minutes south of Montréal. Driving from Montréal to Québec City can be a breezy 2 ¾-hour straight shot along Autoroute 20 or a leisurely trip along the Chemin du Roy – Québec's oldest thoroughfare.

Jean-Drapeau Métro station

GETTING AROUND

Québec's public transportation showcases the dynamism of its cities. Cycling lanes roll through bustling neighborhoods, ferries cruise along the St Lawrence and Montréal's Métro snakes beneath its streets. Most revealing is the pedestrian choreography of sidewalks, where everyone joins the dance.

Métro

Montréal's underground Métro system races over one million daily riders to 68 stations spread across four color-coded lines covering 69km of track. It's fast, efficient and easy to navigate – and though service is less comprehensive than the bus, it's often preferable, particularly while traveling around the city's traffic-clogged downtown core. Trains operate daily from 5:30am to 1am and until 1:30am on Saturday.

Initially constructed in the 1960s and expanded over the decades, these transit temples are an ode to modernist design. Each brutalist concrete entryway is the work of a different architect, leading to tunnels embellished with over 100 public artworks, including mosaics, sculptures and stained-glass panels.

TIP
Google Maps might be Québec's most popular navigation app, but Citymapper is more comprehensive, with detailed trip planning for all modes of transportation, including subway, bus, ferry, Montréal's BIXI bikes and Québec City's àVélo.

By 2027 the long-awaited Réseau Express Métropolitain (REM) – an above-ground electric light rail system – is expected to be fully operational, providing a Métro alternative with 26 stations connecting Downtown to the airport and suburbs.

Walking

Québec's primary cities are tailor-made for pedestrians, their historic districts chockablock with architecture that inspires slow strolling. Just don't get too caught up in the details. Sidewalks are like mini highways: traffic keeps right, stopping short causes collisions, and if you want to pause for a picture, step out of the way.

Winters can be brutal, but proper attire makes it easy to navigate snowscapes, and in Montréal it's possible to hop around Downtown without stepping outside. The Underground City (Réseau de la Ville Souterraine; p76) links hundreds of shops, restaurants and museums through a network of subterranean tunnels connected to the Métro. Montréal is also blessed with beautiful back alleys known as *ruelles vertes* (green alleyways; p102), a labyrinth of community-run laneways providing tranquil alternatives to bustling boulevards.

Bus

Montréal's STM bus system boasts over 200 routes that make around 8500 stops around the island, but service can be slow and unpredictable, especially around rush hour. It's ideal for reaching places disconnected from the Métro and preferable for travelers with mobility impairments. Montréalers often use a mix of bus and Métro to travel between destinations. The RTC bus system is Québec City's primary public transport option, connecting downtown to the suburbs.

> **TIP**
> Speeding to Montréal's airport? Opt for a taxi over an Uber. Cab drivers can use a dedicated taxi lane, bypassing highway traffic jams and getting you to the airport faster than other cars.

Taxis & Rideshares

It's generally easy to flag down taxis in Québec's biggest cities, but if you prefer to order a car via smartphone, Uber is always an option. Montréal's **Téo Taxi** (*teo.taxi*) operates a lot like Uber, except its fleet of vehicles

---

 PUBLIC TRANSPORT ESSENTIALS

Transit Fare

Fares for Montréal's integrated bus-and-Métro system (STM) cost the same for both modes. They're available for purchase at Métro station kiosks. For the bus, pay with exact change or a prepurchased ticket. Children 11 and under ride for free. Québec City's buses also require exact change.

Bus & Métro Discounts

For extended stays in Montréal and Québec City, consider purchasing an OPUS card ($6) – a reusable smart card that passengers top up; it has discounted rates for bus and Métro fares. The cards are rechargeable: in Montréal, download the **Chrono app** (*artm.quebec/en/chronomobile-application*), choose a fare type, then tap your card to your smartphone to refill it. Québec City uses the **RTC Nomade paiement app** (*rtcquebec.ca*). Cards are available for purchase at Montréal's Métro kiosks and Québec City's RTC info centers.

Montréal's discount pass options include unlimited evening ($6.25, 6pm to 5am), 24 hours ($11), three days ($21.25), 10 rides ($33.25) and one week ($31). Weeklong passes start Monday and end Sunday – suboptimal for midweek purchases.

Québec City's pass options are one day ($10), unlimited weekend ($17.50), five consecutive days ($33.25) and bundles of 20 rides ($63).

Maps

For Montréal transit maps, including bus and Métro routes, visit *stm.info*. For Québec City's bus routes, visit *rtcquebec.ca*.

Bikeshare Fares

If you're only planning to hop on a Montréal BIXI bike several times while visiting, opt for single rides ($1.50 to unlock, 20¢ per minute on a manual bike or 35¢ per minute with an electric boost – plus a $100 security deposit). Serious cyclists can save big by purchasing a monthly membership ($23, 18¢ per minute for rides longer than 45 minutes). Download the BIXI app to pay and unlock bikes with ease.

Québec City's electric àVélo offers single rides ($1 to unlock, 33¢ per minute), 24-hour multi-trip passes ($19, 33¢ per minute for rides longer than 45 minutes), plus month passes for long-term stays.

Hailing a Cab

Several cab companies operate in Montréal and Québec City, so there's no set vehicle design or color. Instead, look for the 'Taxi' sign on their roof for identification. A lit-up sign means the car is available for hire.

is 100% electric. Québec City's **Taxi Coop** *(taxiscoop-quebec.com)* is similar, though you can pay drivers in cash. Prefer to drive yourself? Use **Communauto** *(communauto. com)*, a carshare program where you can sit behind the wheel for round-trip journeys. It's available in both cities.

Bicycle

Montréal is one of North America's best cities for cycling, with over 1000km of interconnected bike paths and nearly 200km of traffic-separated lanes called the REV (Réseau Express Vélo). Flying through town by pedal power is fantastic for seeing the sights quickly. It's also easy, thanks to BIXI – Montréal's year-round bike-share program, with over 900 stations throughout the city.

Québec City's cycling infrastructure grows more robust every year, with plans to build a 150km network of bike lanes by 2035 – though current offerings are best for leisure cruises along the St Lawrence. Bikeshare program àVélo offers electrically assisted bikes at 165 stations between May 1 and November 15.

Ferry

Sail on the St Lawrence in summer to switch up your perspective. In Montréal, a shuttle chugs between the Old Port, Parc Jean-Drapeau and beyond. In Québec City, a scenic boat ride leads across the river to Lévis.

TRAVEL COSTS

Montréal's Métro
$3.75

Québec City's bus
$3.75

10-minute bike-share MTL/QC
$3.50/4.30

ACCESSIBILITY

In Montréal, buses are the best public-transit bet for travelers with reduced mobility. Most of the STM fleet can lower their floors to sidewalk level and extend ramps for wheelchair users. Call 514 STM-INFO (786-4636) to ensure your departure point is accessible. Only 30 of Montréal's Métro stations have elevators. Plan trips using the **STM route planner** *(stm.info)* and click the 'wheelchair accessible' option.

Québec City's most convenient bus routes offer ramp-equipped vehicles, and it's possible to request wheelchair-accessible rideshare services through Uber WAV and **Taxi Lévis** *(taxilevis.ca)*. Avoid steep steps linking Old Québec's Haute-Ville and Basse-Ville by riding the **funicular** between the fortifications and Rue du Petit-Champlain.

Street signs near Hôtel de Ville (p56)

HOW TO... Speak French

French is Québec's official language, and around 90% of Québécois identify as fluent French speakers. You'll see it on road signs, menus and billboards – and though over half the population can converse in English, it's best to come prepared by understanding a little *français*.

Practice Makes Parfait

Download an app Addictive **DuoLingo** (free with add-ons) gamifies language learning – but it's better as a supplement, not an endgame, because it doesn't teach practical conversation skills. If you're serious about speaking French, use **Pimsleur** (starting at $19.95). In each 30-minute lesson, users listen to conversations, repeat phrases and answer questions. It focuses on real-life interactions you'll likely encounter in public spaces. To wrap your ear around the Québécois accent, there's **Mauril** (free), which uses content from CBC and Radio-Canada's audiovisual libraries to immerse learners in French accents heard across the country. Need in-the-moment assistance? Use **Google Translate** to decode tricky menu items and signs in split seconds – along with this book's language guide (p214).

Read and watch Visual learners will appreciate Pierre Corbeil's *Canadian French: A Québécois Phrasebook*, with its collection of useful expressions and linguistic explanations. If you're proficient in French, scan the script of Québec playwright Michel Tremblay's *Les Belles-sœurs* (1968), which employs *joual*, a working-class Montréal dialect, in its dialogue.
Prefer films? Binge-watch your way to fluency with Québécois movies (p23), subtitles on.

Québécois Versus European French

Québécois French hits European ears the way a Scottish brogue hits Americans: intelligible, but occasionally confusing. While the written word doesn't cause consternation, accents can be a different story. Listen for contractions, where words get shortened or merged – like '*je suis*' ('I am'), which sounds more like '*chui*.' Expect to hear relaxed vowel sounds: the 'i' in France often sounds like 'ee,' but in Québec it sounds like 'ih.' Letters 't' and 'd' sound like 'ts' and 'dz', and the letter 'l' is often dropped from the ends of words, turning '*il*' ('he') into 'y.'

LANGUAGE EVOLUTION

French landed on the St Lawrence's shores with European colonizers in the mid-16th century – and as settlements grew, educated laborers from places including Normandy, Brittany and Paris began blending their dialects into a unified sound. After France ceded Québec to Britain in the 18th century, Canada's French speakers found themselves adrift in a vast ocean of English. Cut off from France, the language evolved on its own, incorporating English words for new commercial and technical objects (a car is not a French *voiture* but an English-sounding *char*), creating colorful idioms and curses (p121) and forging a dialect that's distinctly Québécois.

Tourtière

DINING OUT

French proclivities, international palates and a craving for locally grown grub: Québec cuisine comes *tout garni* – 'all dressed' – with everything on it.

Québec fuses global influence and local terroir, forming a tapestry of tastes that acts as an edible timeline. French flavors forged the foundation, with each *boulangerie* (bakery) and wine bar a nod to early colonists. A dash of British style was folded in next, saluting the Union Jack with meat pies and beer. Over the past century, immigrants have introduced port city Montréal to far-off cuisines, adding flavors from China, Eastern Europe, Italy, Portugal and the Middle East.

Chefs sift through this multicultural pantry to craft dishes akin to their cosmopolitan cities, especially in foodie haven Montréal. When sourcing ingredients, however, top restaurants look to Québec's backyard, favoring fresh, seasonal products over imported fare. As a result, kitchens become epicurious laboratories, injecting foreign cuisines with indigenous twists.

Experimentation might reap extravagant results, but Québec's food scene is decidedly relaxed. It's the kind of place where poutine is served at fine-dining restaurants and where sometimes the best dish only costs a couple of toonies.

Farmers Feast

Québec is a locavore's Elysium, with over 28,000 farms producing ingredients essential to regional cuisine. The province produces over 70% of the global maple syrup supply, 25% of the world's cranberries and more cheese than any other Canadian province. Throughout summer, nature's candy takes the form of strawberries in June, blueberries in July and sweet corn around Au-

Best Québec Dishes

BAGEL
Chewy dough torus boiled in honey-sweetened water and oven baked.

PÂTÉ CHINOIS
Québécois shepherd's pie: ground-beef casserole.

PETS DE SŒUR
'Nun's farts' – cinnamon pie dough rolled in brown sugar.

POUDING CHÔMEUR
'Poor man's' bread pudding with maple syrup and cream.

gust. Apples ripen by autumn, hanging like precious rubies across 50 sq km of orchards.

Pork is the province's prized meat. It's ground into sausages, stuffed into pies and reduced to *creton* – a pâté-style paste, best when spread on toast. Foie gras is another popular yet controversial ingredient, made from the fattened livers of ducks and geese. Production involves force-feeding animals via feeding tubes in amounts they wouldn't voluntarily eat. Animal-welfare groups argue the process is cruel; production is banned in several countries worldwide.

While most farms sprawl across rural landscapes, Montréal is making a name for itself as a capital of urban agriculture. Over 50 farms operate within city bounds, supplying restaurants and markets with fresh fare year-round.

Magnificent Markets & Food Tours

The easiest way to experience Québec's home-grown bounty is at a *marché* (market), where farmers pile earth-grown goodies sky-high. Of Montréal's 15 public food markets, **Marché Jean-Talon** (p118) is the largest, with more than 300 stands in summer's peak season, tempting shoppers with stone fruit, wild salmon, cured ham, funky cheese, foraged mushrooms, sugar pies, local honey and homemade ice cream. **Marché Atwater** (p127) comes in second, housed in a brick art-deco beauty steps from the Lachine Canal – ideal for a post-market picnic. In Québec City, **Le Grand Marché** (p168) rules the roost, attracting epicurious crowds with 100-plus vendors and plenty of prepared foods.

If market trips don't satisfy the hunger for agritourism, drive to Québec's farm-laced countryside. **Île d'Orléans** (p190), near Québec City, is the 'Garden of Québec' – a pastoral island where you'll find fruit stands, cheese-making tours and an artisanal chocolate maker among its six charming towns. It's also a fantastic place to sample *vin de glace* – sweet 'ice wine' made from frozen grapes. The signposted, 226km **Chemin du Terroir** (*Path of the Terroir; laurentides.com*) leads to farms and restaurants in the Laurentian Mountains north of Montréal.

Québécois Classics

Traditional Québécois cuisine is heavy and hearty, a reflection of impoverished colonists who worked the land's frosty frontier

Food trucks, Old Port (p52)

FOODIE FESTIVALS

Semaine de la Poutine (p94) Restaurants throughout Montréal craft gourmet versions of Québec's signature mess plate. **February**

Cabane Panache (*promenadewellington. com*) Verdun's Rue Wellington celebrates 'sugaring off' season with all things maple syrup. **March**

Les Premiers Vendredis (p85) On the first Friday of the month, food trucks take over Montréal's Old Port and Parc Olympique. **June to August**

ItalFest (p117) Montréal's Little Italy sizzles with flavors from the homeland. **August**

Québec Table Gourmande (*quebectable gourmande.com*) Dozens of Québec City restaurants serve affordable prix-fixe menus for two weeks. **November**

MTLàTable (*mtlatable.mtl.org*) Restaurants offer reduced-price *table d'hôte* menus spotlighting Montréal's culinary excellence.

POUTINE	**SMOKED MEAT**	**TARTE AU SUCRE**	**TOURTIÈRE**
French fries and cheese curds in gravy.	Succulent brisket that's dry-cured, smoked and steamed.	Decadent pie with brown sugar and maple syrup.	Deep-dish, double-crusted meat pie – best with ketchup or syrup.

Gibeau Orange Julep

Taste the difference between Montréal bagels on a Mile End food crawl (p113).

CASSE-CROÛTE CULTURE

The French term *casse-croûte* translates to 'snack' in English – a simple definition that fails to capture its Québécois meaning. A *casse-croûte* can also be a food joint, often a seasonal roadside shack in rural regions or a late-night corner spot in Montréal. It's the greasy-spoon sister of a canteen, the cousin of a diner and the mother of a modern fast-food counter, serving Québec specialties and US-inspired classics. Menus might advertise poutines, burgers, *steamés* (hotdogs), pogos (corn dogs) and *guédille au homards* (lobster rolls). They proliferated post-WWII, fueled by booming car culture and hungry road-trippers looking for a pick-me-up. While countryside stands close during winter, Montréal spots like **Gibeau Orange Julep** (*orangejulep.ca*) – a three-story, fruit-shaped roadside attraction – keep their summertime nostalgia alive year-round.

and required filling, affordable fare. A classic dinner might center on game meat like moose, deer, rabbit, wild turkey or perhaps a pork-stuffed pie called a *tourtière*.

The menu at a typical *cabane à sucre* (sugar shack) feast, held every spring during maple syrup season, encapsulates the range of this full-belly food. Glazed ham, pea soup, pork rinds, omelettes and *fèves au lard* (baked beans) usually grace the table, all generously drizzled with maple syrup.

At the top of the Québécois food chain sits poutine (p94), a messy plate of French fries traditionally topped with gravy and super-squeaky cheese curds. Invented in rural Québec around the 1950s, the starchy snack started appearing across Canada a few decades later. But don't call it Canadian: as self-described 'poutinologist' Nicolas Fabien-Ouellet argued in an academic paper from 2016, poutine isn't a national dish – it's a Québécois creation with unpretentious, underdog origins indicative of the province's working-class roots.

Despite vociferous insistence on poutine's Québec-ness, the greasy comfort food has been reimagined with international zest. Melted with Portuguese-style São Jorge cheese at Montréal's **Ma Poule Mouillée** (p93) or seasoned with Indian curry sauce at Quebec City's **Le Chic Shack** (p165), poutine's culinary evolution mirrors Québec's transformation into a global melting pot.

International Influences

Québec's culinary roots link directly to France, with its most common styles of restaurants emulating Parisian culture. You'll find wine-loving *buvettes*

FOOD & CULTURE WEBSITES

TOURISME MONTRÉAL
mtl.org

OFFICIAL TOURISM WEBSITE
https://www.mtl.org/en/what-to-do/food. The city's official tourism website has guides on the food scene.

THE MAIN
themain.com. Montréal round-ups related to art, design, food and drink – plus interviews with locals and bite-sized history lessons.

DESTINATION QUÉBEC CITÉ
quebec-cite.com

(small cafes with food and drink), share-plate bistros (casual, intimate eateries) and busy brasseries (larger establishments with substantial mains and beer). Just don't expect all-out Parisian cuisine, particularly in Montréal. Restaurants like **L'Express** (p97) might deliver Left Bank bistro excellence and the croissants at **Le Toledo** (p94) would get Le Cordon Bleu's top grade – but they're a small part of the city's international smorgasbord, influenced by over a century of immigration.

Eastern European Jews introduced bagels, sparking one of Montréal's most heated disputes: are the dough babies better at Fairmount or St-Viateur? Jewish arrivals also started the city's infatuation with smoked-meat sandwiches (p93), stacked on rye bread and smothered in yellow mustard. The Portuguese gave Montréal spicy piripiri chicken (p95). Italians made Québécois picky about pasta (p117). You can find Venezuelan empanadas, Singaporean street food, Caribbean jerk chicken, South Indian dosas (p118) and more here. At varied food market **Le Central** (p65) it's possible for visitors to eat their way around the world without leaving the building.

Thanks to progressive immigration policies, Montréal's culinary map will continue morphing, a fact embraced by fine dining institutions, famous for global flavors and fusions. Still, when it comes to ingredients, the gourmet gurus agree: nothing beats the local stuff.

Prepare for the Meal

Menus throughout the province are often in French – with bilingual exceptions, particularly in Montréal. If a restaurant doesn't provide English options, don't be shy asking your server for help – they're likely used to it. Still, it's helpful to know a few key phrases. In French, *entrée* means 'appetizer,' *le plat principal* means 'main course,' and an *amuse-bouche* is a bite-sized hors d'œuvre. A *table d'hôte* is a fixed-price meal, which usually includes three or four courses. *Apportez votre vin* means 'bring your own wine' – which is fairly common, with roughly 1600 restaurants across Québec sporting BYOW permits.

Reservations are required at popular high-end restaurants in Montréal and Québec City. Book tables at least one week in advance – or possibly a month ahead if you're planning trips to top-rated Montréal restaurants like **Alma** (p117) and Michelin-rated fine diners.

Smoked-meat sandwich

Bar 1608, Château Frontenac (p168)

BAR OPEN

Cozy wine bars, hidden speakeasies, industrial breweries and EDM clubs: Québec's biggest cities have it all. Clink glasses and say 'santé.'

Montréal has been Québec's party capital for over a century. It kept the taps flowing throughout Prohibition and continues to embrace rowdy after-hours antics. Québec City is buttoned up by contrast, with a scene leaning toward intimate beer halls and cocktail bars.

Nights out often start with a post-work *cinq-à-sept* (5pm to 7pm), where groups gather to quaff cocktails, wine or beer. From here, you might stop by a *buvette* to share a bottle of Beaujolais or drop by a brewpub pouring suds made on-site. If you like crafty cocktails, Montréal is a mixology draw where swanky clubs combine high-quality ingredients and top-shelf liquors. There's also a low-ABV and nonalcoholic movement bubbling, with bars like **Bisou Bisou** (p58) proving you don't need booze to have a blast.

Montréalers love to shake it, and electronic dance music (EDM) is often the unifying soundtrack. Locals step-touch everywhere from audiophile oasis **Stereo** (p86) to basement listening bar **Sans Soleil** (p72), along with outside summer festivals and winter shindigs.

Wondrous Wine

When French explorer Jacques Cartier sailed the St Lawrence in the 1500s, he spotted vines on present-day **Île d'Orléans** (p190) and dubbed it 'Île de Bacchus,' after the Roman god of wine. Though it took another 400-plus years for Québec's wine-centric grapes to grow, the province is

---

Best Québec Drinks

BEC
Maple syrup–infused sodas made in Québec.

BIÈRE D'ÉPINETTE
'Spruce beer'; a fermented, low-ABV Indigenous creation.

CARIBOU
Red wine, grain spirits and spices, often mixed with maple syrup.

MAPLE LIQUEUR
Maple syrup blended with whiskey.

slowly gaining recognition as a Canadian *vin*-topia. Over 150 wineries produce more than three million bottles annually, best known for sweet ice wine and cold-hardy hybrids. The Eastern Townships kicked off production in the 1980s and now act as Québec's grape-trellis king. Find your favorite fermented juice on the region's **Route des Vins** (p160), cruising past 20-plus vineyards outside Montréal.

In Montréal proper, natural wine (without artificial additives) is all the rage, served everywhere from fine-dining establishment **Toqué!** (p57), with an impressive 6000 bottles in its cellar, to unpretentious plonk purveyor **Vinvinvin** (p119). Though the occasional local vintner shows up on menus, urban oenophiles tend to favor French and Italian imports.

Craft Brew Revolution

Québec beer is more than **Molsons** – the famous Montréal beer company founded by an English immigrant in 1786. Microbreweries made a splash in the 1980s, starting with Montréal's **Le Cheval Blanc** (p83) as the global craft boom took off. The province now has over 300 microbrewers producing boozy Belgian ales, funky sours, refreshing lagers and floral IPAs. Restaurants rep local makers on their menus (look out for **Brasserie Dieu du Ciel** (p121) and **Brasserie Harricana** – though the best way to sample suds is by visiting a bricks-and-mortar brewery.

Both Montréal and Québec City have 30-odd hop halls each: cozy taverns like MTL's **Réservoir** (p100), industrial warehouses (see **Mellön** (p121)), and spots with seasonal terraces (try QC's **La Barberie** p183). Many serve lunch and dinner, best enjoyed with a flight to sample multiple pours.

Speakeasy City

Unmarked doors, bars within bars and lounges hidden underground: Montréal is saturated with pseudo-speakeasies – a play on Prohibition-era drinking dens running illicit operations. While there's nothing illegal about these contemporary copycats, their elusive entryways add allure. Some come off as kitsch, but others serve as sexy hideaways helmed by master mixologists. Try bespoke cocktails at **Cloakroom** (p71), swill whiskey at **Coldroom** (p59) and sip sake over candlelight at **Big in Japan** (p102).

Cash tips

NEED TO KNOW

Drinking age 18

Opening hours Bars 5pm to 3am, big clubs typically Thursday to Saturday, Montréal parties from 10pm (picking up steam around midnight).

Tipping Tip 15% of the bill at cocktail clubs, between $1 and $2 per drink at a bar.

Tickets Lining up outside a club isn't fun in freezing temperatures; visit websites to purchase tickets in advance.

Events In Montréal, check Resident Advisor *(ra.co)* to search for pop-up parties and purchase tickets.

Dress code Bars and clubs tend to be relaxed; most clubs have coat-check services ($1–5) so you don't have to dance in a parka.

QUEBECANO
Americano (espresso with hot water) renamed by cheeky baristas.

VIN DE GLACE
'Ice wine'; made from grapes that freeze on the vine before they're harvested.

CIDRE DE GLACE
Ice wine's apple-based cousin.

ZAMALEK
Montréal-based maker of nonalcoholic hibiscus karkade – a cold Egyptian tea.

Place des Arts (p63)

SHOWTIME

Montréal is Canada's unofficial arts capital. Québec City adds francophone flair to North American stages. Get ready for an encore.

Québec is a creative hotbed, its list of performance superlatives stretching on longer than a Celine Dion power ballad. The only challenge? Where to focus the spotlight.

In addition to pop diva Dion, the province is responsible for producing a symphony of genre-spanning music celebs. There are singer-songwriters Leonard Cohen and Rufus Wainwright, jazz pianists Oscar Peterson and Diana Krall, indie darlings Arcade Fire and Patrick Watson – and Québec City's hip-hop trio Loco Locass, famous for rapping enthusiastically in French. They co-star on the cultural stage with Montréal playwright Michel Tremblay and filmmakers Denis Villeneuve and Denys Arcand – Arcand's *Les Invasions Barbares* (2003) is the only Canadian movie to win an Oscar for Best Foreign Language Film. They're joined by dance companies, circus artists and stage actors, all bolstered by an arts-based infrastructure supporting the talented trove.

Montréal's Place des Arts is Canada's largest cultural complex – and Québec City's Grand Théâtre hosts hundreds of shows every year, alongside tiny cabarets, arthouse cinemas, intimate concert halls and a bevy of annual festivals.

Live Music

Montréal's live music venues form an eclectic soundtrack. You might catch rising rock stars at grungy **Casa del Popolo** (p119) or tap your toes to trumpets at basement jazz den **Dièse Onze** (p102). Big-time pop artists perform at the **Centre Bell** (p65) stadium and old-school punk bands jam at **Foufounes Électriques** (p63). The classics echo around **Place des Arts** (p63), home of the city's symphony orchestra and North America's largest francophone opera house.

Québec City provides Montréal's string players stiff competition thanks to **Orchestre symphonique de Québec** (OSQ), Canada's oldest symphony orchestra, which shares the **Grand Théâtre de Québec** (p183) with the terrific **Opéra de Québec**.

Theater & Cabaret

Montréal is Québec's scene-stealing drama queen. Theaters showcase everything from avant-garde plays (go to **Usine C** (p89)) to splashy American musicals (try **Espace St-Denis** (p89)). English-speaking stand-up comics cut their teeth at the **Comedy Nest** *(comedynest.com)* with the hopes of headlining July's **Just for Laughs festival** (p64). There's also a cabaret culture showcasing burlesque beauties (visit the **Wiggle Room** (p86)) and drag artists (see **Cabaret Mado's** (p86) lip sync assassins).

Québec City holds its own: local thespians perform at the intimate **Théâtre Périscope** (p183) and multimedia company Ex Machina reimagines classic stories with new technologies at **Le Diamant** (p183). If French isn't your forte, check if the production is in English. Don't expect subtitles.

Circus

Unlike text-based dramas, circus transcends language – no subtitles are needed while you watch acrobats fly. This universality makes it a natural art form for bilingual Montréal, birthplace of international Big Top juggernaut **Cirque du Soleil** (p53). Since the company's 1984 launch, Montréal has become an epicenter for *nouveau cirque*, which shirks Ringling Brothers razzmatazz for story-driven, emotionally rich performances. See it year-round at circus venue **TOHU** (p119) or catch it on sidewalks and public squares during July's **Montréal Complètement Cirque** *(montrealcompletementcirque.com)*.

LONELY PLANET'S TOP...

Fabulous Festivals

Festival d'Été de Québec Over 150 performances turn downtown Québec City into a nonstop 11-day concert in July.

Francos Brush up on your French before June, when this francophone music fest takes over Montréal.

Festival Bach *(festivalbachmontreal.com)* Sounds of baroque bigwig Johann Sebastian come 'Bach' to Montréal's concert halls every November.

Underground & EDM

Piknic Électronik Dancers groove in Parc Jean-Drapeau on summer Sundays as the sun dips behind the city.

ÎleSoniq It's all about beats per minute at this two-day EDM dance-a-thon in August.

Suoni Per Il Popolo *(suoniperilpopolo.org)* This June music festival in Mile End marches to the beat of avant-garde drummers.

Festival d'Été de Québec (p165)

ENTERTAINMENT BY NEIGHBORHOOD	
Old Montréal	In summer Cirque du Soleil entertains the masses along the Old Port. In winter, Igloofest turns the riverfront into an icy rave.
Downtown	Home to Place des Arts, Centre Bell and a grand public space dedicated to Montréal's festivals, this is where most magic happens.
Quartier Latin, the Village & HoMa	Cabarets, clubs and concert venues host stand-up comics, rock bands and drag queens.
Plateau Mont-Royal	Burlesque dancers, jazz musicians and indie up-and-comers perform in upstairs lounges and basement dives.
Lachine Canal, Little Burgundy & the Southwest	Alternative tunes and lesser-known musicians play at Théâtre Beanfield.
Parc Jean-Drapeau	Crowds sail across the St Lawrence for summertime festivals.
Québec City	Top concert venues like Grand Théâtre de Québec are a quick cab ride from the Old Town.

Rue St-Paul (p50)

SHOP

Style is synonymous with Montréalers, known for being sartorially savvy and invested in art. Québec City delights with old-world elegance.

Québec fashion has come a long way since its 17th-century beaver-pelt days. Montréal is now North America's third-largest clothing manufacturer (behind New York and Los Angeles), with formidable home-grown designers championed by local shoppers.

Some of the province's glossiest department stores come with a Québec pedigree – like Holt Renfrew Ogilvy, a luxury retailer formed by the merger of two humble stores that started selling fabrics and furs in the 19th century. Its Downtown Montréal destination now carries brands like Chanel. Then there's La Maison Simons of Québec City, a 19th-century dry-goods shop that transformed into a national department store chain. Footwear empire Aldo started in Montréal, along with high-end streetwear company SSENSE and sophisticated femme designer Nadya Toto. They're complemented by emerging designers and small boutiques crafting styles sold solely in Québec.

Beyond fashion, both cities brim with distinctive knickknacks thanks to a collection of art galleries, gift shops, bookstores and antiques emporiums stocked with Canadian creations.

Made in Montréal

Downtown Montréal carries big-name international brands, but it's local designers operating out of tiny neighborhood storefronts who contribute to the city's stylish aesthetics. In the Plateau, **Le Cartel** (p97) collaborates with Montréal creatives to craft streetwear matching the neighborhood's edgy art scene. While shopping the racks of Mile End's **atelier b** (p114), you can see teams of sewers making T-shirts on-site. Montréal highlights native fashion brands every August during the **M.A.D. Festival** (madfestival.ca), an arts-and-fashion event with a pop-up market for local makers.

Sustainable Style

Bid fast fashion *adieu*. These days, Montréal trendsetters are all about *friperies* – which translates to 'thrift stores'

– and Blvd St-Laurent acts as their upcycle runway. Between Downtown's **Eva B** (p73) and Mile End's **Annex Vintage** (p114) there's an abundance of dynamite shops selling retro statement pieces and secondhand duds. The highest concentration is around Rue Maguire in Mile End, and more shops decorate **Ave Mont-Royal** and **Rue St-Denis** (p94). These stores aren't all about faded band tees and Levis, either. You might find tailored Americana-inspired jackets at **Palmo Goods** or Jazz Age ball gowns at **Les Folles Alliees**. Some shops invite lingering, like **Café Camas**, a thrift store and coffee shop. Prices attract both budget shoppers and big spenders.

In Québec City's Old Town, it's all about historic decor. Rue St-Paul is the town's 'Antiques Row,' lined with shops like **Antiquités Bolduc** (p182), a cabinet of 19th- and 20th-century curios.

Local Art

Nearly half of Québec's working artists reside in Montréal, evident in its abundance of artisan markets and galleries. The most affordable pieces are prints sold by mom-and-pop shops around the Plateau, Mile End and Little Italy.

In Québec City, **Rue du Trésor** (p170) is the best place to hunt for local art. Between mid-May and mid-October, creatives hang their work along the street, turning it into a beautiful bazaar.

> **LONELY PLANET'S TOP ART SHOPS…**
>
> **Where to Buy Art in Montréal**
>
> **L'Affichiste** Flip through vintage posters and contemporary prints fit for a Wes Anderson film.
>
> **L'Original** Montréal street artists fill this gallery with splurge-worthy statement pieces and small paintings.
>
> **Affiche en Tête** Find an affordable print by a local artist and get it framed in-house.
>
> **Gift Shops in MTL & QC**
>
> **Artpop** Come here for quirky tees, bags and city-inspired art.
>
> **Boutique de Noël** (p170) Christmas comes 365 days a year inside this holly-jolly shop hocking Québec-themed ornaments.
>
> **Le Petit Dep** Sip hot cocoa while choosing artisanal treats for the closet and kitchen inside this charming chain.
>
>
>
> **Le Petit Dep (p55)**

SHOPPING BY NEIGHBORHOOD

Old Montréal	Souvenirs, high-end art and apparel fill store windows along Rue St-Paul.
Downtown	Go beyond the big-name brands hugging Rue Ste-Catherine: this neighborhood is home to a smattering of historic clothing outlets.
Quartier Latin, the Village & HoMa	Peruse antique stores and bookshops hocking queer lit (p83) and Lonely Planet guides (p88).
Plateau Mont-Royal	Vintage stores, bookshops and art outlets abound along St-Laurent, Mont-Royal, St-Denis and Duluth – all shopping sensations.
Mile End, Little Italy & Outremont	Head up Blvd St-Laurent in Mile End and Little Italy for designer boutiques, trendy thrift stores and artsy gift shops.
Québec City	Old Québec's Quartier Petit Champlain is the oldest commercial district in North America, abuzz with boutiques lining its namesake cobblestone street. More shops flank Rue St-Jean outside Old Québec's ramparts.

MONTRÉAL & QUÉBEC CITY

THE GUIDE

Chapters in this section are organized by neighborhood. Neighborhoods are delineated by a specific local character or identity, where you'll find unique experiences, local insights, insider tips and expert recommendations.

Old Montréal
p44

Downtown
p60

**Quartier Latin,
the Village & HoMa**
p78

Plateau Mont-Royal
p90

Mile End, Little Italy & Outremont
p110

**Lachine Canal, Little Burgundy &
the Southwest**
p122

Parc Jean-Drapeau
p140

Side Trips from Montréal
p148

Québec City
p162

Day Trips from Québec City
p186

Where to Stay
p196

Basilique Notre-Dame (p48)
KALIM SALIBA/SHUTTERSTOCK

NEIGHBORHOODS AT A GLANCE

Find the places that tick all your boxes.

Downtown (p60)

LIVE PERFORMANCES, REGAL ARCHITECTURE AND ART

Magnificent museums, gilded age mansions and renowned performing arts venues pepper streets stacked with skyscrapers and shopping malls.

Lachine Canal, Little Burgundy & the Southwest (p122)

MONTRÉAL'S TENACIOUS SUBURBS

Cycle along the Lachine Canal's riverside parks to reach industrial-era neighborhoods reinvented as hotbeds for creatives and foodies.

Mile End, Little Italy & Outremont (p110)

ARTY AESTHETICS AND INTERNATIONAL TASTES

New-wave restaurants and old-school eateries mix with wine bars, breweries, creative clothing stores and Montréal's largest food market.

Plateau Mont-Royal (p90)

STYLISH STREETS LEAD TO PRETTY PARKS

Crafty boutiques, cocktail bars and cafes line blocks enlivened by murals, all crowned by a peaceful mountain oasis.

Old Montréal (p44)

THE CITY'S HISTORIC CENTER

History unfurls along atmospheric plazas lined with soaring cathedrals and greystone facades neighboring the action-packed Old Port.

Quartier Latin, the Village & HoMa (p78)

FROM AFTER-HOURS SCENES TO OLYMPIC DREAMS

Montréal's east side packs in brasseries along Rue St-Denis, rainbow flags on Rue Ste-Catherine and a series of natural science museums.

Parc Jean-Drapeau (p140)

ALFRESCO FESTIVALS AND FRESH AIR

Tree-lined footpaths wind through two connected St Lawrence River islands brimming with outdoor adventures for all seasons.

Researched by John Garry

OLD MONTRÉAL

THE CITY'S HISTORIC CENTER

Montréal's story starts here – amid crooked alleyways and the lively plazas of the city's oldest streets, all tumbling toward the St Lawrence River.

Founded as the devout Catholic colony Ville-Marie in 1642, Vieux-Montréal (Old Montréal) quickly became an important fur-trading outpost for New France along the St Lawrence River before ceding to British control in the 1760s. While its greystone facades whisper of saintly 18th-century nuns, greedy 19th-century bankers and steely 20th-century industrialization, its abundance of shops, restaurants and recreational spaces tell another tale – of a trendsetting city that's just getting started. Spin around Place d'Armes for wow-worthy architecture, traipse shop-lined Rue St-Paul, and then hop on a boat at the revitalized Old Port to appreciate the waterway that made it all happen. Nearly 400 years since its founding, Old Montréal continues to reinvent itself.

TOP TIP

Need a break from cement? Between spring and autumn, hop on an Old Port ferry or a BIXI bike and head to Parc Jean-Drapeau (p140).

Place d'Armes (p56)

See page 197 for places to stay in Old Montréal.

☆ Highlights

▼ ❶ Pointe-à-Callière
Stand atop the foundations of Ville-Marie to learn about Montréal's legacy, stretching back 5000 years. **p47**

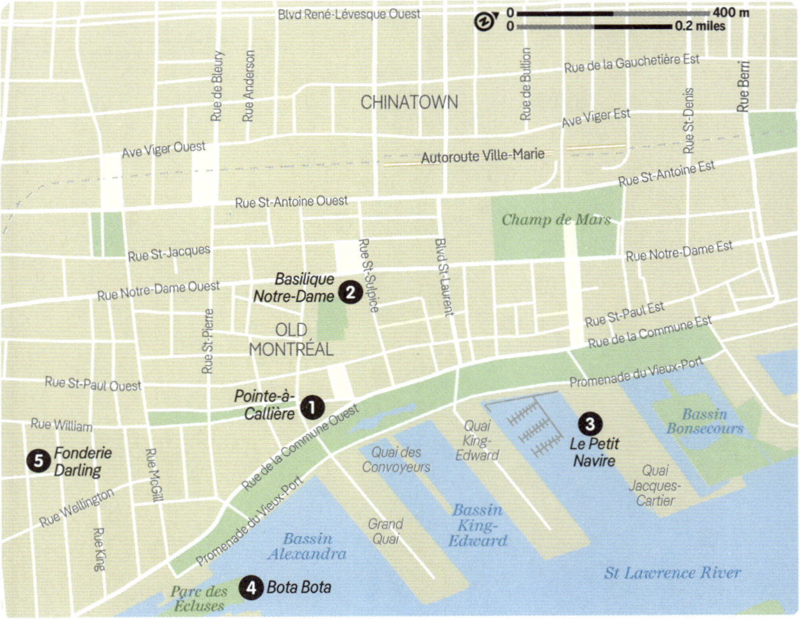

❷ Basilique Notre-Dame
Take in the Gothic Revival exterior of this glorious church before witnessing the captivating light show inside. **p48**

❸ Le Petit Navire
Rock with river waves on an ecofriendly tour of the St Lawrence River, wine glass in hand. **p57**

❹ Bota Bota
Beat winter's doldrums by soaking in Jacuzzis and saunas on this ferry boat-turned-spa bobbing in the Old Port. **p59**

❺ Fonderie Darling
Join Montréal's creative crowd for gallery shows and outdoor performances at this repurposed metal foundry. **p57**

Getting Around

Métro
Take the orange line to Square-Victoria (west), Place-d'Armes (central) or Champ-de-Mars (east) and walk south from Downtown into Old Montréal.

Bus
Bus 14 runs along Rue Notre-Dame in Old Montréal between Rue Berri and Blvd St-Laurent. Bus 55 stops along Blvd St-Laurent. Bus 50 runs along Rue de la Commune by the Old Port.

Walk & Bicycle
Most major sights line walkable Rues St-Paul and Notre-Dame. Cobblestone streets make cycling a bit bumpy. Riding along the Old Port offers access to the Lachine Canal and beyond.

OLD MONTRÉAL SOUTH

★ HIGHLIGHTS
1. Basilique Notre-Dame
2. Pointe-à-Callière

● SIGHTS
3. Caserne Centrale de Pompiers Building
4. Fonderie Darling
5. Grand Quai
6. PHI
7. Sacred Fire Productions

● ACTIVITIES
8. Bota Bota
9. Port of Montréal Tower

● SLEEPING
10. Épik
11. Hôtel Gault
12. Hôtel Nelligan
13. Hôtel Uville
14. Le Petit Hôtel
15. LHotel
16. Place d'Armes

● EATING
17. Barroco
18. Brit & Chips
19. Ciccio's
20. Dandy
21. Dispensa
22. Le Beau Marché
23. Le Cartet
see 10 Le Petit Dep
see 4 Le Serpent
24. L'Orignal
25. LOV
26. Mandy's
see 10 Máti
27. Monarque
28. Olive et Gourmando
29. Restaurant Mélisse
30. Stash Café
31. Titanic
32. Toqué!
33. Wolf & Workman

● DRINKING & NIGHTLIFE
34. Buvette Pastek
35. Clandestino
36. Crew Collective & Café
37. Les Sœurs Grises
38. Nhâu Bar
39. Structure
40. Tommy Café

● SHOPPING
41. Espace Pepin
42. L'Affichiste
see 10 Librairie Maktaba
43. L'Original
44. Marché Saint Laurent
45. Rooney

Dig into Montréal History

MAP P46

Awesome archaeology at Pointe-à-Callière

This is where Montréal was born – above remnants of Fort Ville-Marie, the city's first French settlement, and on grounds occupied by people for thousands of years. The fascinating, informative **Pointe-à-Callière** *(pacmusee.qc.ca; $29)* archaeology museum and National Historic Site invites visitors to explore an underground labyrinth connecting six pavilions covering roughly 5000 years of local history. It's a fantastic first stop in the city, providing context for the making of Montréal. Budget a couple of hours.

Begin with **Crossroads Montréal**, an exhibit exploring the region's Indigenous underpinnings and growth as a commerce hub. It's located in the foundational remains of the 19th-century Royal Insurance Company building, which overlays the city's first Catholic cemetery. Next, stroll through the city's first collector sewer to see **Where Montréal Began** – on the actual site where Paul de Chomedey de Maisonneuve and Jeanne Mance founded **Ville-Marie** (p49) in 1642. Continue with **Building Montréal**, featuring an informative mini-film chronicling the spread of human activity on the island since the arrival of hunter-gatherers.

Several interactive exhibits appeal to kids, including **Come Aboard!**, focusing on the lives of pirates and privateers, and **Archaeo Adventure**, an archaeological dig simulation. Temporary exhibits cover more Montréal heritage and history.

Take a break at **Bistro L'Arrivage**, the main pavilion's 2nd-floor restaurant, with pretty river views. Continue to the 3rd-floor belvedere for an Old Port panorama.

For more history, skip a couple of blocks west to Pointe-à-Callière's free-to-visit **Caserne Centrale de Pompiers** building on Place d'Youville. The Flemish-style firehouse from 1904 tells many tales from Montréal's inflammatory parliamentary past.

If Walls Could Talk

MAP P51

Old Montréal's historic homes

Skip through 500 years of Montréal history inside **Château Ramezay** *(chateauramezay.qc.ca; adult/child $14.50/6)*, a three-story manor built in 1705. The French-style home came with a hefty cost for former Montréal governor Claude de

CONFUSING CARDINAL DIRECTIONS

No, Google Maps isn't gaslighting you: in Montréal, what's called 'north' is really northwest, 'south' is often east – and you can blame 17th-century colonists for any internal-compass incertitude. When the French laid out their settlement's street grid, they treated the St Lawrence River as its guiding star. Streets running parallel to the river were labeled 'west' and 'east', and anything perpendicular became 'north' and 'south.' They weren't entirely wrong. The St Lawrence technically flows west to east from Lake Ontario to the Atlantic Ocean, but it swerves northward around Montréal, making the original French design slightly off-kilter. The result? A city built around geocentric river logic instead of cardinal directions – and, as some like to say, 'the only city where the sun sets in the north.'

This is a reliable Montréal chain.

EATING IN OLD MONTRÉAL: BEST CAFES

MAP P46 & P51

| **Crew Collective & Café:** Order coffee just to drool over the immaculately preserved interior of the former Royal Bank of Canada, built in the 1920s. *8am-4pm* | **Structure:** Descend into this micro-roaster's subterranean cafe with a hexagonal coffee counter and shelves lined with beans. *7am-4pm Mon-Fri, from 8am Sat & Sun* | **Chez Mère Grand:** French owner Roman Beiso presides over this cozy cafe and kitchen serving sandwiches, pastries and espresso drinks. *hours vary* | **Tommy Café:** Sun streams through high-arched windows into this tri-level corner cafe with regal crown moulding, foaming cappuccinos, toasts and bowls. *8am-6pm* |

TOP EXPERIENCE

Basilique Notre-Dame

This is Montréal's grande dame of Catholic churches, open since 1829 and raised to the rank of minor basilica in 1982. Its Gothic Revival twin towers soar 69m high, its midnight-blue ceiling glitters with 24-karat gold stars, and its stained-glass windows (imported from Limoges) depict the city's history. No wonder Céline Dion got hitched here in 1994 – Basilique Notre-Dame is a showstopper.

SHAWN.CCF/SHUTTERSTOCK

Amazing Interior

Inside the main hall, look for the 7000-pipe **Casavant Frères organ** and the swirling staircase leading to the **Pulpit of Truth**, with prophets Ezekiel and Jeremiah crouched at its base. It's hard to believe this hand-carved forest of ornate wooden pillars was constructed without a single nail.

Venture beyond the main hall to admire the 20-ton bronze altarpiece in the **Notre-Dame-du-Sacré-Coeur Chapel**.

Catholic Convert

Dig Notre-Dame's design? So did its New York–based architect, Irish Protestant James O'Donnell. He converted to Catholicism before dying in 1930, ensuring his final resting place could be the church crypt.

The Aura Experience

For a psychedelic encounter with the divine, plan a trip around the Moment Factory's **Aura Experience**, a 25-minute cinematically soundtracked light show highlighting the basilica's elegant architecture in three distinct acts. It's an ecclesiastical rock concert. Arrive 15 to 30 minutes before showtime to wander around the illuminated stations – and don't miss the trippy portrait of Marguerite Bourgeoys glowing on the altar's left-hand side. For the perfect seat, aim for three or four pillars back from the pulpit to take it all in.

TOP TIPS

- Panels inside the church provide backstories on the art. Download the pamphlet on *basiliquenotredame.ca* for even more insight.

- Planning on the Aura Experience? Skip the daytime sightseeing.

- For more regal architecture, step inside the Bank of Montréal across Place d'Armes.

PRACTICALITIES

- basiliquenotredame.ca
- daytime sightseeing/ Aura Experience $16/37
- hours vary

Ramezay, who went into debt financing its steeply pitched roof and stately fieldstone walls – a bold design, considering his neighbors primarily lived in wooden houses at the time.

These days the home is a small museum recounting local history from Indigenous settlement through the 20th century, with 30,000 objects in its permanent collection. Costumed guides offer tours, included with entry (daily in summer; weekends in winter). Their New France–style garb might come off as cheesy theatricality, but the knowledgeable staff impart valuable insight.

Even if you don't go inside, plan to visit the manor's formal French garden, planted with vegetables, medicinal herbs and ornamental flowers. It's free to visit and open from spring through autumn.

Historic home buffs should also plan a visit to **Lieu Historique de Sir George-Étienne Cartier** *(parkscanada.gc.ca/cartier; adult/child $4.50/free)*. The National Historic Site, open to the public on select days from mid-June to mid-December, consists of two houses owned by Cartier (1814–73), a politician who lobbied to unite Canada and was posthumously dubbed Father of the Confederation. Exhibitions in the first home explore Cartier's life and career; the second is a meticulous restoration of his Victorian abode, dripping in 1860s design. It's lovely around December, with decor befitting a 19th-century bourgeois Christmas.

Honor Montréal's Sailors & Saints MAP P51
Explore the charming Chapelle Notre-Dame-de-Bon-Secours

The enchanting **Chapelle Notre-Dame-de-Bon-Secours** *(margueritebourgeoys.org; free)* and its connected **museum** *(adult/child $14/5)* are chock-full of charm. First, there's the architecture – a resplendent French Regime construction from 1771, built after a fire destroyed the original 17th-century building. Artist François-Édouard Meloche added the current tromp l'œil motif between 1886 and 1889, each mural depicting a scene from the Virgin Mary's life.

Then there's the nautical mystique. Gaze toward the vaulted ceiling to see model-boat votives floating above eye level. In the late 18th century, Bon-Secours – overlooking Montréal's port – became a place of pilgrimage for people who survived the arduous Atlantic crossing. Sailors gifted the church votives as gratitude for their successful voyage, and

Arrive before opening to avoid wait times.

FROM MISSION TO METROPOLIS

Montréal wasn't initially built for commerce; it was built for religious conversion. In 1642 a band of French Catholic colonizers, backed by the Société Notre-Dame de Montréal, landed on the banks of the St Lawrence with the intention of 'saving' the Indigenous population by converting them to Catholicism. Paul de Chomedey, Sieur de Maisonneuve, a 30-year-old nobleman-turned-governor, led the missionaries alongside Jeanne Mance, a determined 35-year-old nurse. They dubbed their new settlement Ville-Marie (City of Mary) – honoring the Holy Virgin – and set to work, clinging to their faith despite disease, starvation and Iroquois attacks. By 1650 the settlement's raison d'être had flipped from Holy Father fervor to fur trading, and in 1705 'Ville-Marie' became 'Montréal', though the city remained a Catholic stronghold for centuries.

🍽 EATING IN OLD MONTRÉAL: BRUNCH — MAP P46

Dandy: Comfy banquettes buzz with hungry hordes helping themselves to ricotta pancakes, yolky breakfast bowls and boozy brunch cocktails. *10am-4pm* $$	**Olive et Gourmando:** Enjoy heaping sandwiches, salads and all-day breakfast plates at this homey hang steps from the Old Port. Expect summer crowds. *8am-6pm* $$	**Restaurant Mélisse:** White walls, green vines and floor-to-ceiling windows adorn this Mediterranean-inspired restaurant with a popular weekend brunch. *hours vary* $$	**Le Cartet:** Grab gourmet snacks to go or stay for solid brunch-lunch fare like sizzling egg skillets and veggie bowls. *7:30am-4pm Mon-Fri, 9am-3:30pm Sat & Sun* $$

PIONEERING WOMEN

What do Celine Dion, Madonna, Hilary Clinton and approximately two-thirds of all French Canadians have in common? They're descendants of the Filles du Roi (Daughters of the King), a group of roughly 800 marriageable women sent to settlements in New France (including Montréal) between 1663 and 1673 to fix a population problem: there weren't enough gals. Intendant of the colony Jean Talon and France's Louis XIV came up with the idea: pay for the women's passage from France, provide them with a dowry, give them the freedom to choose their husband, and then offer bonuses for bearing 10-plus children. These brave pioneers, who swapped uncertain fates in Europe for the harsh realities of an unknown place, contributed to a major population boom – and quite literally birthed a new nation.

in the 19th century a statue of the Virgin Mary as 'Star of the Sea' was added atop the chapel's river-facing belvedere. Leonard Cohen fans will recognize her as 'our Lady of the Harbor,' featured in his lilting song 'Suzanne'.

This church stands today thanks to Marguerite Bourgeoys (1620–1700) – New France's first teacher and Canada's first female saint. Bourgeoys championed education for girls of all backgrounds (including the Filles du Roi) and defied convention by developing one of the Catholic Church's first uncloistered nun communities. She launched the chapel's initial construction in 1655. QR codes throughout the church provide deeper context. Bring headphones to listen.

The attached museum tells Bourgeoys' story, descends into the chapel's crypt to see artifacts spanning thousands of years of local history, and then climbs to the bell tower for Old Port views.

Skip down Montréal's Oldest Street

MAPS P46 & P51

Shopping on Rue St-Paul

Walk along Rue St-Paul – first paved with cobblestone in the 1670s – and you might forget you're in North America. With the sing-song sounds of *'Bonjour'* pouring out of the doors of 19th-century buildings, this is as close as you'll get to a historic French village without crossing the Atlantic. This strip of Rue St-Paul covers roughly 1.2km. Budget a couple of hours for leisurely shopping.

Start by admiring the metal dome crowning **Marché Bonsecours** (marchebonsecours.qc.ca), a sprawling neoclassical structure from the 1840s. The building has been everything from a farmers market to a concert venue – and it even served briefly as Montréal's city hall (1852–78). These days it houses tourist-targeted shops and cafes, though the architecture eclipses the indoor offerings.

Continue west through **Place Jacques-Cartier** and you'll find more souvenirs, art galleries and coffee shops. Search **L'Empreinte Coopérative** (lempreintecoop.com) for Québec-made crafts, then admire canvases created by local street artists at **L'Original** (loriginal.org) – all grade-A graffiti glam with accessible price points.

Rue St-Paul is also a veritable restaurant row with international appeal. You'll find Polish pierogies, French wine, Greek, Italian, Indian and more. The choicest spots congregate west of Blvd St-Laurent.

European style dissipates around Rue McGill, where Cité Multimedia – a collection of industrial warehouses and glassy tech offices – firmly plants Montréal in urban North America's modern aesthetics.

GALLERIES & GRAFFITI

Modern art fans should head to the gallery spaces around **Mile End** (p115) or tour Plateau Mont-Royal to see some of North America's best **street art** (p96).

OLD MONTRÉAL NORTH

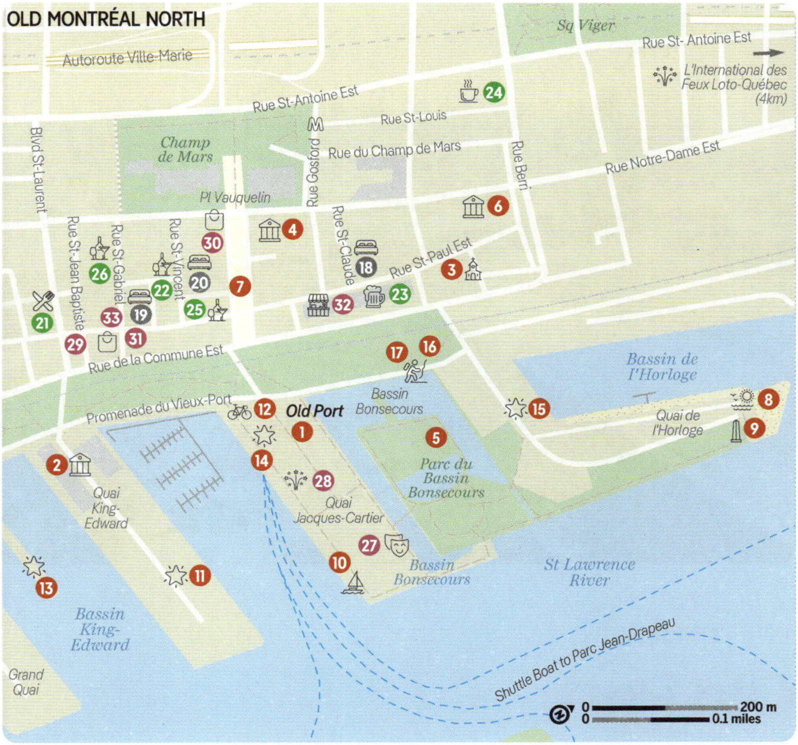

🟠 HIGHLIGHTS
1. Old Port

🔴 SIGHTS
2. Centre des Sciences de Montréal
3. Chapelle Notre-Dame-de-Bon-Secours
4. Château Ramezay
5. La Grande Roue de Montréal
6. Lieu Historique de Sir George-Étienne Cartier
7. Place Jacques-Cartier
8. Plage de l'Horloge
9. Tour de l'Horloge
10. Wet Set MTL

🔴 ACTIVITIES
11. Croisères AML
12. ÉcoRécréo
13. Montréal Bungee
14. Petit Navire
15. Saute-Moutons
16. Tyrolienne MTL Zipline
17. Voiles en Voiles

⚫ SLEEPING
18. Auberge Alternative
19. Auberge du Vieux-Port
20. Hôtel William Gray

🟢 EATING
21. Modavie

🟢 DRINKING & NIGHTLIFE
22. Bisou Bisou
23. BrewSkey
24. Chez Mère Grand
25. Coldroom
26. Velvet

🔴 ENTERTAINMENT
27. Cirque du Soleil
28. Igloofest

🔴 SHOPPING
29. Galerie Images Boréales
30. Galerie Le Chariot
31. L'Empreinte Coopérative
32. Marché Bonsecours
33. Wachiya

 EATING IN OLD QUÉBEC: LUNCH

Plant eaters can order tofu.

MAP P46

Titanic: Sink into this sub-floor dining room among Old Montréal's worker bees for sandwich-style plates with Mexican and Italian influences. 10:30am-4:30pm Mon-Fri $

Ciccio's: Wash down paninis, antipasti and salads with well-pulled espresso shots from this cheery 1950s-style sandwich counter. 9am-8pm $

Brit & Chips: Imagine the St Lawrence is the Thames as you nosh on fish and chips. (Keep it Québécois: sub fries for poutine.) 11am-9pm Sun-Thu, to 10pm Fri & Sat $$

LOV: Enjoy plant-based takes on North American classics (burgers, bowls and pastas) and biodynamic wines at this West Coast–style veggie Valhalla. hours vary $$

TOP EXPERIENCE
Old Port

Montréal's historic center for maritime trade, the Vieux-Port (Old Port) is now a recreational fun zone stretching along a 2km promenade paralleling the St Lawrence River. Explore its four major *quais* (quays; concrete platforms reaching into the river) for a host of family-oriented adventures and seasonal festivals – or to hop on a boat tour and sail away from the crowds.

DON'T MISS
- Plage de l'Horloge
- La Grande Roue
- Cirque du Soleil
- Igloofest
- Centre des Science de Montréal
- Port of Montréal Tower

Quai de l'Horloge

The Old Port's easternmost quay is a summertime sensation thanks to **Plage de l'Horloge** (Clock Tower Beach), an urban sand patch open June to September that's dotted with sea-blue umbrellas, lounge chairs and misting stations (swimming isn't allowed). Grab a drink from the on-site bistro (serving slushies, wine and water) and enjoy views of the St Lawrence flowing beneath Pont Jacques-Cartier. Admission is free outside ticketed events, such as evening DJ sets for 18-and-over

PRACTICALITIES
- oldportofmontreal.com ● prices and hours vary by activity
- many experiences close in winter

crowds. It's a fantastic spot to watch fireworks erupt over the river during **l'International des Feux Loto-Québec** (p145). The scene is anchored by the cream-white, 45m-high beaux-arts **Tour de l'Horloge**, constructed in 1922 to honor sailors lost in WWI.

Parc du Bassin Bonsecours

Walkways from the Promenade du Vieux-Port and Quai de l'Horloge lead to this tiny park, dominated by **La Grande Roue de Montréal** (lagranderouedemontreal.com; adult/child $27.50/15). This is Canada's tallest observation wheel, with 42 roomy gondolas that whisk riders 60m into the air for 360-degree views. With temperature-controlled cabins, leather seats and a smooth ride, it's the Cadillac of Ferris wheels, open year-round. Expect long summer lines; beat the ticket queue by purchasing online in advance.

Quai Jacques-Cartier

Most people stop by this quay between spring and summer to see acrobats fly under the Big Top with **Cirque du Soleil** (cirquedusoleil.com; from $83), one of the city's most famous exports. These gravity-defying shows rarely disappoint – don't pass up a chance to see a home-turf performance.

Come mid-January, crowds return for alfresco fête **Igloofest** (igloofest.ca), a four-week outdoor electronic music festival where people bundle up in vintage ski suits to dance under the stars. Grooving to a lineup of renowned DJs is the best way to heat up Montréal's coldest months.

Quai King Edward

Enjoy a riverside excursion at the **Centre des Science de Montréal** (centredessciencesdemontreal.com; adult/child $28/18.50). Hands-on exhibits appeal to budding scientists, tech tots and anyone young at heart. There's also an immersive IMAX movie theater playing science-themed films on a seven-story screen with a 32,000-Watt sound system. Accessibility is a cornerstone of the museum, making this a fantastic option for folks with limited mobility or developmental disabilities.

Grand Quai

The **Grand Quai** is like the Old Port's greatest hits on one 305m-long dock. Step inside the Port Center to explore *All Aboard*, a free, interactive, kid-friendly exhibit on Montréal's role in the global supply chain. Catch rays on the 2nd-story green roof, with 24,000 flowering plants blooming around the terrace. The **Port of Montréal Tower** (port-montreal.com; adult/child $15/10) is a 65m-high observatory with hands-on displays, panoramic views and a glassed-in cage where visitors can see straight down to the docks below. It's open June to September and one week around Christmas and Spring Break.

Expect summertime swarms: the Grand Quai welcomes over 60,000 cruise-ship passengers from May through October.

TOP TIPS

● If there's time for just one viewpoint, choose La Grande Roue.

● For food, try seasonal spots along the Promenade du Vieux-Port, around La Grande Roue and on Quai Jacques-Cartier. Most offerings tend toward overpriced mediocrity. Walk into Old Montréal's winding streets for tastier fare.

● Rent quadricycles and paddle boats from **ÉcoRécréo** (ecorecreo.ca; from $29) at its Quai Jacques-Cartier window. They're perfect for zipping along the promenade or paddling around Bassin Bonsecours.

● Head to Quai Jacques-Cartier for river tours (try Petit Navire) and to ride the river shuttle to Parc Jean-Drapeau (navettesfluviales.com; p140).

ALL-AGES THRILLS

From March to December, you can fling yourself from Canada's highest bungee jump, a 64m platform located at **Montréal Bungee** (montrealbungee.com; from $179) on Quai des Convoyeurs. The child-friendly **Tyrolienne MTL Zipline** (mtlzipline.com; adult/child $20/17) is a 25m-high, 365m-long thrill ride that soars over Bassin Bonsecours (May to September). Kids go bananas for ropes courses around pirate-themed adventure park **Voiles en Voiles** (voilesenvoiles.com; from $29), open April to October.

OLD MONTRÉAL

MORE SHOPS WORTH A GANDER

L'Affichiste: Karen Etingin's poster gallery sells designs by local artists along with stacks of vintage belle époque and mid-century modern ads. *laffichiste.com*

Librarie Maktaba: Moroccan ottomans invite lounging inside this Middle Eastern–themed literary den with a thoughtful selection of English-language reads. *maktaba.online*

Marché Saint Laurent: Forget chintzy souvenirs. Grab your MTL swag (prints, totes, artisanal MAPSle syrup) from this boutique-cafe off Place d'Armes. *marchesaintlaurent.com*

Rooney: On-trend streetwear, shoes and accessories – including hard-to-find international brands – make this a magnet for fashion hounds. *rooneyshop.com*

Espace Pepin: You can have it all: flowing dresses and smart polos in the corner store, then clean-lined home goods and a cafe down the street. *thepepinshop.com*

JON BILOUS/ALAMY

Admire Indigenous Art
Gallery-hopping and shopping

MAPS P46 & P51

Celebrate art of the First Nations (Indigenous groups recognized by the Canadian government) by spending time at the neighborhood's best free galleries dedicated to homegrown creators.

Start at **Sacred Fire Productions** (*productionsfeuxsacres.ca*) – a nonprofit gallery space run by passionate entrepreneur Nadine St-Louis, who is of Mi'kmaq, Acadian and Scottish descent. Shows rotate every three months to highlight different Indigenous makers. A small shop sells prints, jewelry, books and more artisanal items.

At two-floor **Galerie Images Boréales** (*imagesboreales.com*) you can peruse work by Inuit artists from all over Nun-

---

 EATING ON RUE ST-PAUL: OUR PICKS MAPS P46 & P51

Stash Café: Sit in a church pew and fill up on traditional Polish comfort food such as pierogies at Stash, going strong since the 1970s. *hours vary* **$$**

Wolf & Workman: Dining on elevated pub grub in this 1830s stone building recalls when Britain ruled Montréal. *11:30am-1am Mon-Fri, from 10am Sat & Sun* **$$**

Máti: Dig in beneath seafoam-shaped light fixtures at this earth-toned Greek spot with shareable plates and cocktails mixed with Mediterranean liquors. *hours vary* **$$$**

Modavie: Live bands jazz up daily dinner and weekend brunch at this French bistro with old-world charm. *11:30am-11pm Mon-Fri, from 10:30am Sat & Sun* **$$$**

Le Petit Dep

avut (Canada's Arctic north). Upstairs is packed with stone, ivory and fossilized bone sculptures of revered animals including owls, eagles, bears and wolves. Head downstairs for a selection of Indigenous-made ornaments and clothes.

Wachiya *(wachiya.com)* sells work by the Eeyou Istchee's Cree community – northern Québec's largest traditional territory of the Cree people. Step inside the Rue St-Paul shop to find fur-lined mittens, hand-stitched bags and leather shoes adorned with geometric motifs.

End with the impressive sculpture collection at **Galerie Le Chariot** *(galerielechariot.ca)*. Open since 1980, this Inuit art gallery displays 2000 pieces in its permanent showroom, along with furs, jewelry and more Indigenous-made souvenirs.

MONTRÉAL'S ORIGINAL INHABITANTS

Indigenous groups were present in Montréal at least 5000 years ago, according to archaeological evidence. By the time Jacques Cartier showed up in 1535, the St Lawrence Iroquois were well established on the island and its surrounds, living in villages and cultivating the land. The Europeans' arrival brought disease, displacement and centuries of violence that decimated the Montréal's First Nations inhabitants' numbers, but they didn't disappear. Over 35,000 Indigenous-identifying people reside in Greater Montréal today. They make up Québec's largest Indigenous population, and include members of Mohawk communities Kahnawà:ke and Kanehsata:ke. Honor them at the annual August **International First Peoples' Festival** *(presenceautochtone .ca)*, a 10-day celebration of Indigenous culture.

 DRINKING IN OLD MONTRÉAL: BEST MARKET-CAFES — MAP P46

Le Petit Dep: Step behind the mint-green facade of this upscale *dépanneur* (convenience store) chain for artisanal treats. *8am-8pm Sun-Thu, to 10pm Fri, to 6pm Sat*

Dispensa: Premade pastas and olive oils, maybe, but most folks cram into this market around midday for stacked subs and Italian sweets. *7:30am-5pm Mon-Fri*

Le Beau Marché: Parisian owner Charles presides over this grocery-cafe with a petite baked specialty: eggy *canelés*. *7:30am-7:30pm Mon-Fri, from 8:30am Sat & Sun*

Mandy's: This solid Montréal chain sells grab-and-go wine cans and doubles as a cafe with grain bowls and seasonal salads. *11am-9pm Mon-Fri, to 8pm Sat & Sun*

INVESTIGATE MONTRÉAL'S OLDEST GRUDGES

Old Montréal's streets may seem serene today, but its monuments tell tales of centuries-old grievances. Time to eavesdrop.

START	END	LENGTH
Place Jacques-Cartier	Place d'Youville	1.5km; one hour

Start at ❶ **Place Jacques-Cartier** (p50) and gaze uphill to see a stone-etched showdown. British Admiral Horatio Nelson, who died defeating the French, looks from ❷ **Nelson's Column** (1809) toward a monument honoring French naval officer Jean Vauquelin (1927), who fought British forces. Together they embody centuries of Anglo-Franco feuding. ❸ **Hôtel de Ville** (City Hall) rises east, where French president Charles de Gaulle ended a 1967 balcony speech with '*Vive le Québec libre!*' ('Long live free Québec!') – a rallying cry for Québec separatists who desired independence from Canada.

Next, stand at the center of ❹ **Place d'Armes**. To the west, two skyscrapers vie for attention: the eight-story New York Life Building (1889), Montréal's first skyscraper, and the 23-story Aldred Building, which stole the city's 'tallest tower' title in 1931. Look east toward two snooty statues: *The English Pug and the French Poodle* (2013). An English pug owner judges the French Catholic Basilique Notre-Dame (p48); his French counterpart glares at the British-influenced Bank of Montréal. From here, follow Rue St-Jacques, dubbed Canada's Wall St, to see a modern war waged at ❺ **Crew Collective & Café** (p47): the fight for seats in Montréal's most beautiful coffee shop.

End at ❻ **Place d'Youville**, where 39 First Nations communities agreed to peace with New France in 1701. Peace unraveled with the British conquest of 1760. The fight for Indigenous rights continues.

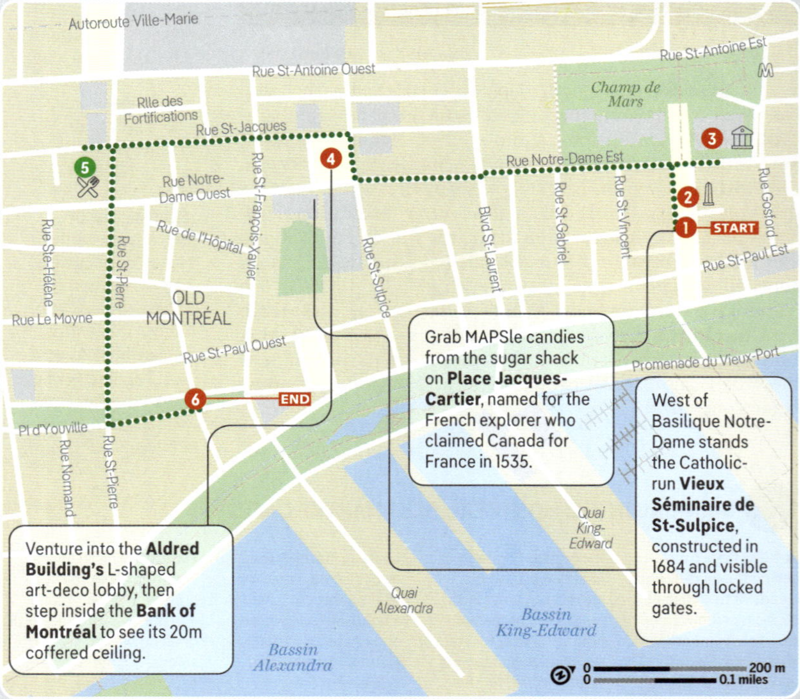

Grab MAPSle candies from the sugar shack on **Place Jacques-Cartier**, named for the French explorer who claimed Canada for France in 1535.

West of Basilique Notre-Dame stands the Catholic-run **Vieux Séminaire de St-Sulpice**, constructed in 1684 and visible through locked gates.

Venture into the **Aldred Building's** L-shaped art-deco lobby, then step inside the **Bank of Montréal** to see its 20m coffered ceiling.

Get Artsy Fartsy

MAP P46

Contemporary exhibits at PHI and Fonderie Darling

Leave the landscape paintings behind. Head west of Blvd St-Laurent to trade Rue St-Paul's conventional galleries for experimental art.

First up is **PHI** *(phi.ca)*. Formerly Centre Phi and Foundation Phi, it celebrates the intersection of art, design and technology in three Old Montréal buildings with galleries, live performance spaces and a cinema. Many exhibits lean immersive – no surprise, given founder Phoebe Greenberg's theater background. Admission to the 451 and 465 Rue St-Jeanne spaces is free. For film screenings at 407 Rue St-Pierre, see what's playing and reserve tickets in advance (suggested $20 donation). The organization plans to unify its spaces under one roof by 2028; check the site for updates.

Head further west for **Fonderie Darling** *(fonderiedarling.org; $8)*, a cavernous two-room gallery in what was a 19th-century metal foundry. Scope the calendar for openings, when you can peek inside the upstairs studios of the 12 artists in residence. On summer Thursdays, performance artists take over the stone patio near the entrance from 5pm to 10pm, June to August. Scan the schedule to see who's on; admission is free. Cap off your art crawl with a meal at **Le Serpent** *(5:45-10:30pm Wed-Sat)*, an upscale industrial space serving Italian bistro bites that's linked to Fonderie Darling's main gallery.

Sail the St Lawrence

MAPS P46 & P51

Le Petit Navire's ecofriendly tour

Get acquainted with Montréal's *fleuve* (river that flows into the sea) on a seasonal boat tour departing from the Old Port. You can be drenched to the skin on a jet-boat trip to the Lachine Rapids with **Saute-Moutons** *(jetboatingmontreal.com)*, take it slow while dining on a 750-passenger ship with **Croisères AML** *(croisieresaml.com)* or speed off to a St Lawrence island on a jet-ski tour with **Wet Set MTL** *(wetsetmtl.com)*.

If you'd rather experience the water sans noisy motor or cruise-style crowds, opt for a ride with **Petit Navire** *(lepetitnavire.ca)*. From mid-May to mid-October, the company's carbon-neutral fleet – all Japanese lifeboats repurposed as quiet electric vessels that rock gently with the river's

MONTRÉAL'S TOP TOURS

Montréal tour guides are experts – literally. In order to legally lead tours on public property, guides must be licensed by the city. This includes completing 240 hours of rigorous coursework at the Institut de tourisme et d'hôtellerie du Québec (ITHQ) and renewing their license annually. Québec City is the only other Canadian city with the same guidelines. If you're looking for 'non-touristy tours' rooted in local charm, try **Spade & Palacio** *(spadeandpalacio.com)*. Its **Montréal Mural Art** tour dives deep into graffiti and **Beyond the Market** takes visitors to Little Italy's hidden culinary gems. **Fitz Montréal** *(fitzmontreal.com)* specializes in bike tours, pedaling everywhere from Old Montréal to the Plateau. You can also rent its sturdy bikes (starting at $45) to explore solo.

All these restaurants require reservations.

 EATING IN OLD MONTRÉAL: WORTH A SPLURGE ——— MAP P46

| **Toqué!:** Go for the seven-course tasting menu at this fine-dining star, sourcing ingredients from artisan farmers since 1993. *11:30am-1:45pm & 5:30-9:30pm Tue-Sat* **$$$** | **Monarque:** Dine à la carte in the brasserie or try the Salle à Manger's tasting menu at this boisterous, wine-walled restaurant on Montréal's former Wall St. *hours vary* **$$$** | **Barroco:** Restaurant romance, from soft jazz to oysters to knockout European-style dishes. *6-10:30pm Sun-Thu, 5:30-11pm Fri & Sat* **$$$** | **L'Orignal:** Winter's antidote? Gorging on classic Québécois dishes (venison, wild boar, rabbit) in a cozy dining room. *5-10pm Wed & Thu, to 11pm Fri & Sat* **$$$** |

HIGHWAY H₂O

The St Lawrence River is Montréal's lifeline, a 1200km highway from Lake Ontario to the Atlantic, linking Europe to North America's interior. It's how the city's major players arrived: the Iroquois, Jacques Cartier, Paul de Chomedey de Maisonneuve and the waves of immigrants who followed.

The river sparked battles, powered a 19th-century industrial boom and still fuels commerce today: 39 million tons of goods move through Montréal annually, making it Canada's second-busiest port. It's a migratory superhighway too, attracting 400 bird species and over 80 land and aquatic mammals, including the endangered St Lawrence beluga – one of these white whales stunned Montréal with a rare visit in 2012. The river is also a source of sustenance: when you drink from the tap, you're tasting the St Lawrence (filtered, thankfully).

Bota Bota

waves – takes groups of 20 to 30 people on intimate sailing adventures to Montréal's coastal treasures. Most popular is the 45-minute **Old Port of Montréal Tour** *(adult/child $30/14)*, which departs from **Quai Jacques-Cartier** (p53) to the Lachine Canal, takes in close-ups of **Silo No 5** and **Habitat 67** (p126), and then loops back along the Old Port. Guests can order drinks (beer, wine and water; plastic sales are offset by donations) while the captain provides a historical deep dive. It's a breezy, ecofriendly way to spend an hour connecting with the river that started it all.

One of Montréal's best bars for mocktails.

🍸 DRINKING IN OLD MONTRÉAL: APERITIFS, BEER AND WINE — MAPS P46 & P51

| **Buvette Pastek:** Swirl Old World and Québec vinos around stemmed glasses inside this oenophile outlet with light bites and monthly wine tastings. *hours vary* | **Les Sœurs Grises:** Raise a glass to Montréal's 18th-century Gray Nuns (Les Sœurs Grises) inside this laidback, bi-level, blonde-wood beer joint. *hours vary* | **BrewSkey:** Get high on hops while watching brewers in the beer lab below Marché Bonsecours or sit on the seasonal terrace. *hours vary* | **Bisou Bisou:** It's always summer at this low-level bar with Mediterranean island vibes pouring expertly low-ABV apéritif cocktails. *4pm-midnight Tue-Sun* |

Soak, Steam & Sweat

MAP P46

Relax at Bota Bota

Melt above the mighty St Lawrence at **Bota Bota** *(botabota.ca; packages from $75)*, the floating Finnish spa steaming along the Old Port piers at Rue McGill.

Water is in the DNA of this four-floor pleasure palace. Originally built as a ferry back in the 1950s, it was revamped in 2010 with saunas, steam rooms, heated pools and cold plunges. It's also kitted out with terraces, hammocks and meditation rooms, where visitors can unwind while feasting their eyes on impressive views of the city skyline and Silo No 5.

The basic Water Circuit package includes access to the spa's top two floors and an outdoor garden. Massages, facials and food cost extra (and they're not necessary to reap Bota Bota's bodily benefits). Reservations for the Water Circuit are highly recommended on Saturdays, though some walk-ins are accepted outside of peak times.

Bota Bota is open year-round, though it's particularly magical in winter, when visitors soak in alfresco hot tubs, dispelling winter's chill above the frozen St Lawrence. Bring a bathing suit, a pair of sandals and a water bottle. Bota Bota provides towels and bathrobes.

MONTRÉAL'S SOCIAL HISTORY

Explore more history at **MEM** (p66), a museum with hundreds of first-person Montréaler interviews, and **Musée McCord Stewart** (p70), with a fantastic permanent exhibition on Indigenous life in Canada.

LAST SILO

Look west along the Old Port toward Pointe du Moulin, and you'll see **Silo No 5**, a monument to Montréal's industrial past. Constructed in four stages between 1906 and 1958, the 500m-long, 66.4m-high behemoth shot into the sky as Montréal became the world's largest grain port. When Silo No 5 shuttered in 1994, the result of Montréal's grain-trade decline, it was the only remnant of the port's era as a global grain hub. It's reviled as a waterfront blight, revered as an architectural icon and the subject of long-awaited redevelopment plans by the Canada Lands Company.

Brown libations are the specialty here.

 DRINKING IN OLD MONTRÉAL: SPEAKEASY-STYLE COCKTAIL BARS MAPS P46 & P51

Coldroom: Enter this underground lounge by ringing the doorbell reading 'Patience' – which you may need while waiting for a seat. *5pm-1am Sun-Thu, from 3pm Fri & Sat*

Clandestino: Mezcal and tequila splash into glasses around this red-hued, leaf-fringed basement bar with plush retro couches. *Muy caliente. 8pm-1am Mon-Wed, to 2am Thu-Sat*

Nhâu Bar: Sink into a velvet booth to sip cocktails from seashells in this sleek Vietnamese-themed den below restaurant Hà. *5pm-1am Tue & Wed, to 3am Thu-Sat*

Velvet: Walk through a candlelit passageway to a subfloor, stone-walled EDM dance club in the underbelly of a 1754 inn. *10pm-2am Thu, to 3am Fri & Sat*

Researched by John Garry

DOWNTOWN

LIVE PERFORMANCES, REGAL ARCHITECTURE AND ART

Museums, mansions and malls stand next to Montréal's most lauded performing arts venues, towering above a vast subterranean city.

Downtown (Centre-Ville in French) slopes from Old Montréal to leafy Mont Royal with office-crammed skyscrapers, wide boulevards and department stores. Most people come here for shows and festivals around Place des Arts or to see some of the city's best museums. The Quartier des Spectacles sits east, where vestiges of Montréal's 20th-century Sin City days linger between cultural centers abutting Chinatown's hand-pulled-noodle parlors. The Golden Square Mile, Canada's most exclusive 19th-century neighborhood, rises northwest – now the territory of McGill University students, who skip between its remaining mansions on Mont Royal's southern slopes. Rue Ste-Catherine cuts east–west through it all, a bustling artery teeming with pedestrians and lined with shops.

TOP TIP

For a bird's-eye view of Downtown's skyscrapers, take the steep 1.4km ascent to Parc du Mont-Royal's Belvédère Kondiaronk (p105) from the top of Rue Peel near McGill University.

Chinatown (p75)

See page 197 for places to stay Downtown.

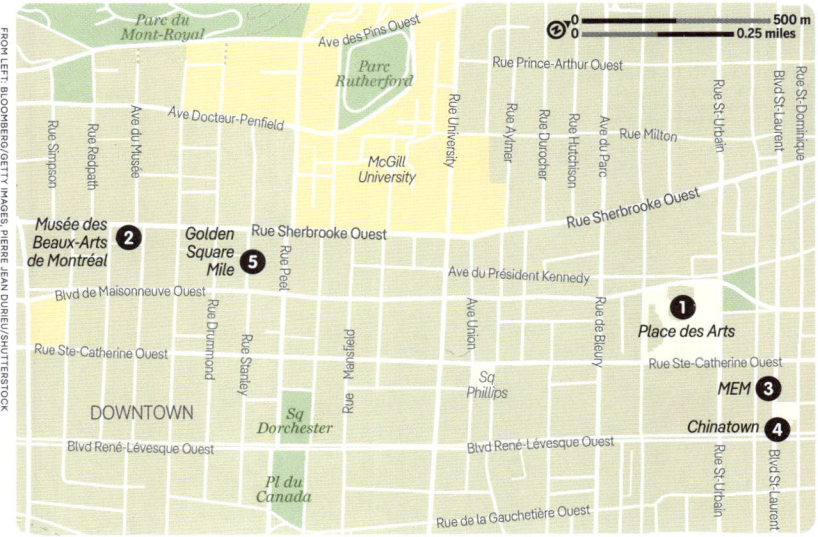

⭐ Highlights

◀ ❶ Place des Arts
Snag tickets to an opera, symphony, ballet or play at Canada's largest performing arts complex. **p63**

❷ Musée des Beaux-Arts de Montréal
Wander through centuries of art spread across MBAM's five pavilions, each an architectural triumph. **p68**

❸ MEM
Hear stories from Montréalers in mini-documentaries throughout this accessible social history museum. **p66**

❹ Chinatown
Chow down on hand-pulled noodles, delicious dumplings, chewy bao buns and traditional dragon's beard candies. **p75**

❺ Golden Square Mile
Pass baronial mansions on a walking tour through a neighborhood colonized by Canada's railroad-era elite. **p77**

🚶 Getting Around

Métro
The green line runs east–west through Downtown's center, with stops at St-Laurent (near MEM), Place-des-Arts, McGill (near Musée McCord Stewart) and Guy-Concordia (near MBAM). The orange line follows the southern edge.

Bus
Bus 150 runs east–west along Blvd René-Lévesque. Bus 1 runs along Blvd de Maisonneuve, stopping at Place-des-Arts. Bus 24 goes east–west along Rue Sherbrooke.

Walk
Beat winter snow and summer rain by walking through the Underground City (p76), a network of tunnels linking Métro stations and sites throughout the neighborhood.

🟠 HIGHLIGHTS
1. MEM
2. Place des Arts

🟤 SIGHTS
3. Esplanade Tranquille

⚫ SLEEPING
4. Auberge du Plateau
5. Hotel 10
6. Hotel Manoir Sherbrooke
7. Hotel Monville

🟢 EATING
8. Bloom Sushi
9. Cadet
10. Café Parvis
11. Dragon Beard Candy
12. Fleur et Cadeaux
13. Hoang Oanh
14. Kamùy
15. Le Central
16. Montréal Pool Room
17. Noodle Factory
18. Pâtisserie Bao Bao Dim Sum
19. Pâtisserie Coco
20. Qing Hua Dumplings
21. Restaurant Chinatown Kim Fung

🟢 DRINKING & NIGHTLIFE
22. Bar Pamplemousse
see 39 Café SAT
23. Café Tranquille
24. Club Pelicano
25. La Finca
26. Mintar
27. Osmo x Murasan
28. Poincaré
29. Sans Soleil

🔴 ENTERTAINMENT
30. Agora de la Danse
31. Art Souterraine
32. Club Soda
33. Duceppe
see 35 Festival international de Jazz de Montréal
34. Foufounes Électriques
see 35 Francos
see 35 Grand Marché de Noël de Montréal
see 35 International Frst Peoples' Festival
35. Jazz Fest
36. Le Balcon
see 2 Les Grands Ballets Canadiens de Montréal
see 35 Montreal en Lumiere
37. Mtelus
see 2 Opéra de Montréal
see 38 Orchestre Métropolitain
38. Orchestre Symphonique de Montréal
39. SAT

🔴 SHOPPING
40. Eva B
41. Eva D
42. Henri Henri
43. Indiana Jeans
44. Pantalons Supérieur
45. Word

Applaud Great Performers

MAP P62

See shows at Place des Arts

Place des Arts *(placedesarts.com)*, Canada's largest performing arts complex, spreads across six performance halls at the heart of Quartier des Spectacles. With roughly 900 shows and events attended by a million spectators annually, there's a little something for everyone.

For the classically inclined, try **Opéra de Montréal** *(operademontreal.com)*, North America's biggest francophone opera house, presenting everything from traditional scores to contemporary pieces sung by a mix of Canadian and international vocalists. Performances take place in the acoustically astounding Salle Wilfrid-Pelletier. Spectators aged 18 to 34 receive a 30% discount on single tickets.

This hall is also where point-perfect ballerinas twirl for the **Grands Ballets de Canadiens** *(grandsballets.com)*, Québec's first professional ballet company. Of the company's six annual shows, *The Nutcracker* is a perennial favorite, delighting holiday audiences with Montréal-born choreographer Fernand Nault's take on Tchaikovsky's score since 1964. The 18-to-34 crowd receives a 40% discount.

Venezuelan conductor Rafael Payare oversees the **Orchestre Symphonique de Montréal** *(osm.ca)*, playing over 100 concerts per year in the Maison Symphonique space and beyond. Expect approachable programming such as Disney's *Fantasia* along with works by Mozart, Mahler, Rachmaninoff and more. Folks aged 35 and under pay $40 for single tickets.

The offerings continue with the **Orchestre Métropolitain** *(orchestremetropolitain.com; from $31)*, which also plays inside Maison Symphonique and democratizes classical music by bringing shows to communities throughout Montréal.

Programming at the 1500-seat **Théâtre Maisonneuve** features contemporary dance, comedy and theater. The 421-seat **Cinquième Salle** hosts intimate, avant-garde performances and multimedia events; the 128-seat **Salle Claude-Léveillée** offers a cozy setting for smaller shows. Check the Place des Arts website for schedules.

Even if you don't see a performance, it's worth touring the compound. A pretty pedestrian plaza connects the theaters from outside, and a tunnel with public art links Place des Arts to the **Underground City** (p76).

Sit on the terrace in summer!

MORE LIVE ACTS DOWNTOWN

MTELUS: It's been a skating rink, a cinema, a porn house, a nightclub, and now a 2000-plus-seat concert hall with musical acts and DJ sets as eclectic as its history. *mtelus.com*

Foufounes Électriques: Divey, three-floor 'Electric Buttocks' started playing punk power chords in 1983 and has kept its commitment to alt tunes. *foufounes electriques.com*

Club Soda: Crowds pop into this midsize Quartier des Spectacles concert hall for indie jams, hip-hop, country, punk parties, comedy shows and drag. *clubsoda.ca*

Agora de la Danse: Montréal's leader in contemporary dance showcases modern and experimental movement by homegrown and international troupes. *agoradanse.com*

Duceppe: Founded in 1973 by Montréal actor-director Jean Duceppe, this French-language theater company celebrates Québec playwrights. *duceppe.com*

DRINKING DOWNTOWN: CAFES

MAPS P62 & P67

Café Tranquille: Overlook the crowds in Esplanade Tranquillé from this 2nd-story cafe with generous seating and two terraces. *10am-10:30pm*

Côte Café: Teeny-weeny Côte grinds beans from local roaster Zab, best enjoyed on its streetside patio a few blocks west of MBAM. *6am-6pm*

La Finca: UQAM's kids love this airy cafe with light brunch fare and a tiny market of artisanal wine, beer, coffee beans and quirky cards. *8am-4pm*

Osmo x Murasan: Enjoy java and Japanese-influenced drinks beneath the disco ball in this space-age bunker spinning electro tunes. *8am-6pm Mon-Fri, from 10am Sat & Sun*

MORE DOWNTOWN FESTIVALS

Drawing two million spectators annually, the **Jazz Fest** is the city's best-attended festival, but it's just one of many events buzzing about **Place des Festival**.

Montréal en Lumière: This event brightens Montréal's darkest months with food, an outdoor skating rink, live performances, and illuminated art. It happily coincides with Nuit Blanche (*nuitblanchemtl.com*), a one-night-only arts festival that doesn't quit 'til dawn. February to March; *montrealenlumiere.com*

Francos: Hosts around 150 French-language music concerts over nine days in summer. June; *francosmontreal.com*

Just for Laughs: Brings stand-up comedians to town for the world's biggest yuck-yuck fest. July; *montreal.hahaha.com*

Grand Marché de Noël de Montréal: Transforms the plaza into a Christmas market with around 60 artisan booths. November to January; *noelmontreal.ca*

Festival international de Jazz de Montréal

Jam to Live Jazz
Festivals and concerts

MAPS P62 & P67

In the 1920s jazz music jumped the US border and migrated to Montréal. Its rebellious rhythms poured from the city's clubs like champagne, seeping into Montréal's sonic landscape. Though its popularity waned in the 1960s and '70s, the 1980 launch of the **Festival international de Jazz de Montréal** (*montrealjazzfest.com*) sparked a revival. It's now the world's largest jazz fest, with around 3000 musicians giving 500 performances across 10 days between late June and early July. Around 350 of those concerts are alfresco jam sessions outside Place des Arts – all free for the public.

It's tucked inside Maison Alcan (p77).

 EATING DOWNTOWN: CAFES WITH BREAKFAST & LUNCH — MAPS P62 & P67

Caffettiera: Get a proper Italian espresso in this peppy color-blocked cafe and aperitivo bar with Italian pastries and focaccia sandwiches. *7:30am-6pm* $

Mintar: Head upstairs to watch staff prep smoothie bowls, salads, coffees and flat top-grilled sammies in the open kitchen below. *hours vary* $

Améa Café: Order Mediterranean-style lunch or grab a pastry before finding a nook in the surrounding atrium. *8am-4pm Mon-Fri, from 9am Sat, 10am-3pm Sun* $$

Cafe Aunja: 'There' (*aunja* in Farsi) delivers a slice of Iran with rose-flavored teas, tisanes and sandwiches. *9am-7:30pm Mon-Fri, 10am-7pm Sat, to 6pm Sun* $

There's also plenty of quality jazz to enjoy outside of June's jamboree. **Upstairs Jazz Bar & Grill** *(upstairsjazz.com)* hosts everyone from local legend Jim Doxas to McGill University's finest students in its cozy club (which is downstairs, ironically). Check the schedule and reserve seats online to ensure admittance. There are usually one to three sets per night; lesser-known acts are often *gratis*. Come hungry – there's a full dinner menu (burgers, steak, nachos).

On Wednesdays there's more jazz at **Le Balcon** *(lebalcon.ca; from $20)*, a multigenre cabaret space in the St James United Church on Rue Ste-Catherine. Splurge on front-row seats to enjoy a three-course preshow dinner or sit in the mezzanine to sip cocktails while swaying to tunes.

Go Coocoo for the Canadiens

MAP P67

Tour Centre Bell's hockey arena

Montréal's love of hockey runs deeper than Québec's maple syrup reserves, so it's no surprise the highest-capacity arena in the National Hockey League (NHL) sits smack-dab in the city's center. The **Centre Bell** *(centrebell.ca)* seats over 21,000 hockey heads, who gather in Hab gear from October to April to cheer on the Canadiens. ('Hab,' the Canadiens' nickname, is short for 'Habitants' in French, which translates to 'settlers' – referencing the province's early French inhabitants.) If you want to see the home team play live, score tickets online *(nhl.com/canadiens)* and show up early – doors open 90 minutes before scheduled matches, and you can grab drinks and food within the arena.

If a game isn't on the cards, opt for an hour-long Centre Bell **walking tour** *(centrebell.ca/en/guided-tours; adult/child $22/13)* to get a close-up of the place where the Canadiens fight for puck supremacy. Guides lead groups to the press box (where reporters watch games), alumni lounge (where former Canadiens hang pre- and post-match) and the news conference room where coach Martin St Louis meets the press. If it's a non-game day, you'll also get to peek inside the locker room, following in the footsteps of players like Nick Suzuki.

HOCKEY'S HUMBLE BEGINNINGS

There's plenty of debate over the location of hockey's ancient origins – but when it comes to the modern game, Montréal is its undisputed epicenter. According to the International Ice Hockey Federation, students at McGill University played the first officially organized indoor match in 1875. The game's popularity snowballed from there, with seasonal tournaments and a championship prize called the Stanley Cup – the oldest trophy in North American sports – introduced in 1893 and awarded to a Montréal squad. By 1917 the city had given birth to the National Hockey League (NHL), today's premier league for puck pros. The NHL's oldest continually operating team? The Montréal Canadiens, founded in 1909. The most decorated? Also the Canadiens, owners of 24 Stanley Cups – though their last win in 1993 feels like ancient history.

Try Indian street food at Le Super Qualité.

EATING DOWNTOWN: NO-FUSS FOOD MARKETS

MAPS P62 & P67

Marché Artisans: Crepes, pizzas, charcuterie, cheese, ice cream and souvenirs: get it all around this 750-sq-meter market connected to the Fairmont hotel. *8am-6pm* **$$**

Le Cathcart: An enormous skylight lets sun into this upmarket Underground City food court, packed with Downtown's white-collar crowd at lunchtime. *hours vary* **$$**

Time Out Market: Counters representing popular Montréal restaurants serve Thai, Japanese, Indian and more on the Centre Eaton's 2nd floor. *hours vary* **$$**

Le Central: Search for international cuisine inside this industrial Quartier des Spectacles center with long communal tables. *hours vary* **$$**

See a Divine Circus

MAPS P62 & P67

Acrobats at Le Monastère

Montréal is North America's center for circus arts, best known as the birthplace of **Cirque du Soleil** (p53). The internationally renowned troupe might only stop in town for a couple of months annually, but there are still plenty of chances to catch other exciting circus companies (unrelated to Cirque) at performance halls year-round.

For death-defying acts, see what's on at nonprofit **Le Monastère** *(le-monastere.ca; from $37.50)*, which transforms a 19th-century neo-Gothic church into a non-religious circus cabaret. It's set up like theater-in-the-round, with performers on a central stage ascending heavens-high on everything from silks and straps to trapeze and stacked chairs. The cabaret's comedic relief usually performs in French, but don't worry: there's no language barrier when it comes to physical comedy and juggling.

Arrive 20 to 30 minutes before curtain to enjoy the full experience. Grab a bag of popcorn, order an adult beverage and get ready to watch talented acrobats soar among the rafters.

MORE JAZZ MUSIC
Head to the Plateau for a sound bath in bass strings and brass by heading down to **Dièse Onze** (p102), a basement jazz spot on Rue St-Denis.

Meet All Kinds of Montréalers

MAP P62

Visit MEM: Centre des Mémoires Montréalaises

What makes Montréal tick? **MEM** *(memmtl.ca; adult/child $15.50/free)* provides answers through interactive exhibits and mini documentaries that span centuries of history. No fluff here – permanent exhibit *Montréal* digs deep, featuring around 100 firsthand accounts from a diversity of locals. You might hear from *dépanneur* owner Imad Abdalla, spin around town with disability activist Maude Massicotte, celebrate a Stanley Cup win for the Canadiens and learn a few Franglish phrases. The rotating exhibits use an equally thoughtful, human-first approach to Montréal storytelling.

If you're short on time or pinching pennies, the free-to-visit lobby is still worth exploring. After trailing past MEM's historic sign exhibit, bop to the 2nd floor, packed with hands-on MAPS, fast facts and a 13-minute movie about the evolution of Blvd St-Laurent, where MEM is located. Don't miss the gift shop – it doubles as a cafe and a *dépanneur*. Best of all, this

continues on p70

THE CONVENIENT DÉPANNEUR

A *dépanneur* is more than a convenience store – it's a Montréal institution. Derived from the French verb 'to help out', 'deps' (the local abbreviation) are neighborhood lifelines for groceries, cleaning supplies, snacks, the occasional deli treat and three beloved vices – beer, cigarettes and lotto tickets. They first appeared in 1970, capitalizing on a legal loophole: small merchants with no more than two employees could stay open on nights and weekends, continuing to sell goods when other stores closed. Over 1000 deps dot the city today, each with a personality reflecting the metropolitan mosaic.

Head downstairs post-dinner to speakeasy San Soleil (p72).

 EATING DOWNTOWN: DYNAMIC UPSCALE DINNERS — MAPS P62 & P67

Kamùy: Sail to the West Indies in this glass-walled restaurant with a terrace for reinvented Caribbean classics such as jerk chicken. *5-10:30pm Wed-Sun* **$$**

Nora Gray: Try velvety pasta ribbons and sharing plates in this Italian-style joint with bitters-forward cocktails and exceptional service. *5-10pm Tue-Thu, to 10:30pm Fri & Sat* **$$$**

Cadet: Seedy St-Laurent gets sophisticated at this industrial, softly lit preshow spot on Blvd St-Laurent with tapas-style veggie plates and fish. *5-11pm* **$$$**

Fleur et Cadeaux: Sake pours from tinted bottles and diners sit at a rectangular bar as staff meticulously prepare bite-sized Japanese dishes. *5-10:30pm* **$$$**

★ HIGHLIGHTS
1 Musée des Beaux-Arts de Montréal
2 Musée McCord Stewart

● SIGHTS
3 Cathédrale Marie-Reine-du-Monde
4 Centre Bell
5 Dominion Square Building
6 La Guilde
7 Musée Redpath
8 Place Ville Marie
9 Square Dorchester
10 Sun Life Building

● ACTIVITIES, COURSES & TOURS
11 Atrium Le 1000

● SLEEPING
12 Ambrose House & Cafe
13 Auberge Les Bons Matins
14 Auberge Saintlo Montréal
15 Fairmont the Queen Elizabeth
16 Hôtel Le Germain
17 Le Mount Stephen
18 Ritz-Carlton
19 Sofitel Montréal Golden Mile

● EATING
20 Cafe Aunja
21 Le Cathcart
22 Le Taj
23 Marché Artisans
24 Mono
25 Time Out Market

● DRINKING & NIGHTLIFE
26 Améa Café
27 Bar Dominion
28 Bar George
29 Caffettiera
30 Cloakroom
31 Côte Café
32 Grumpys Bar
33 Upstairs Jazz Bar & Grill

● ENTERTAINMENT
34 Le Monastère

● SHOPPING
35 Boutique Tozzi
36 Divine Chocolatier
37 Holt Renfrew Ogilvy
38 La Maison Simons

TOP EXPERIENCE

Musée des Beaux-Arts de Montréal

Founded in 1860, the Musée des Beaux-Arts de Montréal (MBAM), also called the Montreal Museum of Fine Arts (MMFA), is an encyclopedic bastion of creativity with roughly 47,000 works spread around five pavilions covering 53,000 sq meters. You'll find Egyptian mummies, Renaissance portraits, decorative furniture, multimedia installations, a masterful collection of modern Montréaler paintings and more. Budget a few hours.

DON'T MISS

The Arts of One World

ᐅᒪᒪᖅᑐᖅ uummaqutik

Storm Brewing over Hochelaga

Mathieu David Gagnon electronic instrumentals

Embrace

Portrait of the Lawyer Hugo Simons

Napoleon in Ceremonial Robes

Global Connections

Most journeys begin on Level 4 of the **Jean-Noël Desmarais Pavilion**, home of permanent exhibit **The Arts of One World**. Its 10 galleries showcase over 1200 objects covering every continent and spanning the 4th millennium BCE to today – and despite its vastness, the assemblage is easy to digest. Each room is a mindful meditation on cultural connectivity across space and time. Ancient African masks stare at works by contemporary African artists; Ming Dynasty porcelain appears next to Chinese decor owned by Canada's 19th-century elite. Don't miss Nadia Myre's moving *Oceanus Procellarum* (2019) west of the elevator bank. Her wallpaper art comments

PRACTICALITIES

- mbam.qc.ca ● adult/under 25 $30/free ● 10am-5pm Tue & Thu-Sun, to 9pm Wed

on European colonization in America, with references linking ancient Byzantine weaving to Hochelaga, Montréal's 16th-century Iroquoian village.

Early to Modern International Art

Get a crash course in art history by exploring the four-floor **Michael & Renata Hornstein Pavilion for Peace**, with around 500 artworks covering everything from the Middle Ages (Level 4) to the present day (Level 1). Start with Level 1's Impressionists (Matisse, Monet, Renoir) and works by Picasso. Search for his sexual *Embrace*, painted when he was 90. For local history, spend time with German painter Otto Dix's *Portrait of the Lawyer Hugo Simons* (1925). Simons, the sitter, brought the portrait from Dusseldorf to Montréal, where he settled after escaping Nazi Germany.

Level 2 goes from baroque to the Age of Enlightenment, with a room dedicated to the Napoleonic era. Stare into the steely eyes of Emperor Bonaparte in François-Pascal-Simon Gérard's portrait *Napoleon in Ceremonial Robes* – which the subject supposedly loved. Before leaving, snap a *Self Portrait* in the frosted two-way mirror by Yannick Pouliot (2016) – an opportunity to create a contemporary rococo masterpiece.

Québec & Canadian Art

The **Claire & Marc Bourgie Pavilion** celebrates local heritage over six levels spanning the 18th century to the 1980s. Start on Level 4, showcasing Indigenous ingenuity, then make your way down to see Canadian art transform over 400 years.

Carve out time to see the work of Canadian modernists on Level 1, including a section dedicated to Marc-Aurèle Fortin, whose whimsical paintings of Montréal and the Québec countryside recall works by Van Gogh. Gaze into his soot-colored *Storm Brewing over Hochelaga* (1940), depicting a bucolic section of pre-industrial Montréal framed by a neon sky.

On Level S1, pull out headphones to contemplate Montréal-born Jean-Paul Riopelle's kaleidoscopic abstract mosaics from the 1950s. QR codes connected to three enormous canvases link to electronic instrumentals, designed by Mathieu David Gagnon in 2023 and inspired by Riopelle's work.

Inuit Art & Design

Peruse drawings, photographs, paintings and sculptures at ᐅᒻᒪᖅᑐᖅ **uummaqutik: essence of life** – a celebration of Indigenous creativity inside the **Michael & Renata Hornstein Pavilion**. Scan the QR code at the entrance to follow the digital audio guide, designed for people with visual impairments and offered in three languages – Inuktitut, French and English. Audio clips feature commentary from First Nations artists and asinnajaq, the exhibit's Inuit curator. Design lovers should head to the neighboring **Liliane & David M Stewart Pavilion** (under construction at research time) to admire seven centuries of decorative art.

TOP TIPS

- Visitors over 26 pay $15 from 5pm to 9pm Wednesday.

- Families enter for free from 10am to 1pm Saturday.

- Adults over 65 enter for free from 10am to 1pm Tuesday.

- Hungry? Try **Beaux Arts Bistro** on Level 2 of the Jean-Noël Desmarais Pavilion, or hold out for an Italian sandwich at nearby lunch counter **Mono**.

- Check the schedule for guided tours, free with admission and offered in English or French.

- Drop off your coat at the entrance: underground passages connect all pavilions.

- There's tons to see. Start with the pavilion that piques your interest most.

ARCHITECTURE TIME WARP

MBAM's five pavilions showcase over a century of architectural transformation. On Rue Sherbrooke's south side, there's Habitat 67 designer Moshe Safdie's modernist entrance (1991), which is connected to a glassy addition designed by two Montréal firms (2016). On Sherbrooke's northwestern corner, a beaux-arts beauty (1912) links to a brutalist heavyweight (1976). On the northeastern corner, a geometric white-marble block (2011) is juxtaposed with a Romanesque Revival church (1894).

MONTRÉAL'S PAST, PRESENT & FUTURE

Join tour guide **Thom Seivewright** *(@montrealexpert)* for one of his signature 'quickie tours' Downtown.

Let's go to the **Place Ville Marie** esplanade. There's a vista down McGill College Ave leading your eye to Mont Royal, the city's namesake – and in my opinion, its heart and soul. Castles line the foot of the mountain, all beautiful buildings from the 18th and 19th centuries. Look for the giant ring by local artist and landscape architect Claude Cormier, who passed away in 2023. He left his signature around Montréal and this was his last big piece of public art. Cormier intended the ring to be a portal through which you can see the city's past, present and future.

Musée McCord Stewart

continued from p66

museum is accessible for people with limited mobility, ensuring this museum about everyone welcomes everyone, too.

Where Histories Intersect

MAP P67

Explore the Musée McCord Stewart

Sift through centuries of Canada's social history at this mid-size **museum** *(musee-mccord-stewart.ca; adult/child $20/free)* near McGill University. The collection consists of over 1.5 million artifacts – one of North America's largest historical collections – with fashion, photography, paintings, prints, decorative arts and more all on display. Budget an hour or two, and buy tickets online to save money.

 EATING DOWNTOWN: OUR PICKS

MAPS P62 & P67

Cafe Parvis: Kick back in this two-floor parlor with 1970s pizzazz for pizza, sandwiches, coffee and wine. *hours vary* **$$**

Le Taj: Expect Indian authenticity in each bite, perfected since 1985. The clay wall panels were created for Expo 67. *5-10:30pm Sun-Thu, to 11pm Fri & Sat* **$$**

Montréal Pool Room: Billiards? *Non.* Steamed hot dogs (called *steamés*)? *Oui.* Order yours all-dressed, with onion, cabbage and mustard. *10:30am-4am* **$**

Bloom Sushi: Each piece of plant-based sushi is a flavor explosion, as delicate and exciting as a cherry blossom bursting. *hours vary* **$$**

The museum's assemblage spreads across three floors. **Indigenous Voices Today**, the permanent 1st-floor exhibit, ruminates on centuries of Indigenous life in Canada, with artifacts and testimonies from First Nations people reflecting on cultural knowledge, colonial trauma and resilience. Spend time at the exhibit entrance with Cree artist Kent Monkman's massive three-panel painting, inspired by the museum's collection.

Rotating exhibits on the top two floors examine local history, with past exhibits covering topics such as Montréal's 19th-century costume balls and the transformation of Little Burgundy's Black community.

Exhibits aside, stop by to hang out. The gift shop sells Montréal-themed swag by local makers. On-site **Cafe Notman** – named for 19th-century Canadian photographer William Notman, whose work decorates the walls – sells filling sandwiches and salads. Then there's the pedestrianized **Museum Alley** – a yellow-pink-blue take on the classic **Ruelle Verte** ('Green Alley,' p102). With seating designed by architecture firm KANVA, it's an inviting place to break from Downtown's bustle.

Nerd out over Natural History

MAP P67

Artifacts at Musée Redpath

There's a touch of Hogwartsian magic to the natural history collection at McGill University's **Musée Redpath** *(mcgill.ca/redpath; by donation)*. It's less 'stodgy museum' and more 'cabinet of curiosities,' with hodgepodge exhibits related to paleontology, zoology and mineralogy scattered across three floors. Find the 2.5-million-year-old *Australopithecus africanus* skull near an ancient Egyptian mummy, seemingly uncoiling behind its glass case (Floor 3). Then, hunt for taxidermied animals with Canadian pedigree before stumbling upon an ancient woolly mammoth hair and a table piled with glittering rocks (Floor 2).

Views from the 3rd-floor wraparound balcony are particularly striking, staring down the toothy grin of a Gorgosaurus from the Late Cretaceous Epoch. The Greek Revival greystone structure, completed in 1882, is equally mesmerizing – and one of the nation's oldest museum buildings. Search the museum's west-side base stones and you might spot 470-million-year-old fossils hidden in the facade – fitting for a house of natural science.

WRITTEN IN STONE

Old Montréal and Downtown's array of greystone buildings don't just define the two's architectural landscapes; they also hold some of the city's oldest secrets. Locally quarried, blue-gray limestone was prized in the 17th and 18th centuries for its ability to withstand fire and cold. It then became a 19th-century status symbol, lending structures like the Redpath Museum their stately appeal. Search their facades to spot some ancient surprises: aquatic fossils embedded over 400 million years ago, back when Montréal lay beneath a vast inland sea. The city's history isn't only written in stone, either. Scan the bricks of 19th-century buildings, like those on Rue Milton, and you might see tiny paw prints – remnants of a time when bricks dried outside (instead of being kiln-fired) and Montréal's kittens got curious.

Come for classic cocktails and seafood-forward dishes.

 DRINKING DOWNTOWN: BARS WITH OLD-SCHOOL STYLE — MAP P67

Cloakroom: A men's tailoring store guards this slender speakeasy where bartenders craft made-to-measure cocktails. How fitting. *4pm-1am Sun-Thu, to 3am Fri & Sat*

Bar George: Sir George Stephen's Victorian mansion-turned-men's club now houses a wood-paneled restaurant and bar, ideal for sipping smoky scotches. *hours vary*

Bar Dominion: If this storied wood-and-tile tavern's taps could talk, they'd sing of the original 1927 hotel restaurant and a century of revelry. *4pm-1am*

Grumpys Bar: Reading works by Montréal's Mordecai Richler? Toast the late author at the dimly lit dive he supposedly loved. *5pm-1am Sun & Mon, 3pm-3am Tue-Sat*

Follow Indigenous Footsteps

MAP P67

Rue Peel's art-and-history trail

A centuries-old secret lies beneath cement-smacked Rue Peel: this was once the site of a thriving Iroquoian village. Between 2016 and 2019, archaeologists unearthed over 2000 artifacts, including pottery shards and ceramic pipes, all remnants of the Indigenous community that lived here from approximately 1350 to 1460.

In 2023 the city of Montréal and the nearby Mohawk community, Kahnawà:ke, paired up to create an interpretive walking trail along the historic street. It features 11 stations, each with two spherical bronze sculptures created by Mohawk artist MC Snow and Montréal artist Kyra Revenko. Together, they form a pair of seats, representing a desire for dialogue between Indigenous and non-Indigenous communities. The trail might not be on Montréal's most scenic thoroughfare, but it offers a thought-provoking way to recontextualize the city – through the eyes of its first inhabitants.

Download the **Portrait Sonore app** *(portraitsonore.ca)* and follow the *Our Ways* podcast as you stroll the street. Each stop features information about the art, along with ancestral stories from First Nations descendants and historians.

The walk starts at Rue Smith (near the **Lachine Canal**, p122) and ends at Ave des Pins (near **Parc du Mont-Royal**). Each stop takes roughly five to 10 minutes. Venture out on a sunny day with headphones and a fully charged phone. Budget an hour or two.

Upon finishing, walk 10 minutes to **La Guilde** *(laguilde. com)* – a nonprofit founded in 1906 to promote Inuit and First Nations art. The gallery and exhibition space showcases historical and contemporary works, drawing a direct line from Rue Peel's original inhabitants to today.

A FLAG FOR ALL MONTRÉALERS

When Jacques Viger, Montréal's first mayor, designed the city's coat of arms in 1833, he incorporated symbols from ethnic groups living side by side, in an effort to unite divided parties. There was an English rose, a Scottish thistle, an Irish shamrock and a beaver for the fur-trading French – all joined by a crimson saltire. When the city raised its first flag in 1939, it modified Viger's design to include a French fleur-de-lys instead of the beaver and a red cross representing the city's Christian founders. Still, something was missing: recognition of the land's original inhabitants. That 'something' was added in 2017 – a white pine tree, the Great Tree of Peace, which grows its needles in clusters of five and symbolizes the five-nation Haudenosaunee Confederacy (or Iroquois), finally acknowledged.

Hats, Pants & Paperbacks

MAP P62

Downtown's enduring stores

Forget the fast fashion on Rue Ste-Catherine. Downtown is home to some of Montréal's most storied shops, each a time-tested jewel box that invites slow shopping. Set aside an afternoon to browse their wares.

Come here post-dinner at Fleur et Cadeaux (p66).

DRINKING DOWNTOWN: BEER & COCKTAILS

MAP P62

Club Pelicano: Splash into craft cocktails inside this art-deco, pool-themed bar where DJs spin tunes; upstairs is Peruvian seafood restaurant Tiradito. *hours vary*

Poincaré: At this 2nd-floor Chinatown lair beers are artisanal, fries are fermented and the seasonal rooftop pulses at night. *4pm-1am Sun-Wed, to 2am Thu-Sat*

Bar Pamplemousse: Order 5oz pours to sample some of the 20-odd beers on tap at this tavern with Mediterranean bites. *4:30pm-1am Sun-Thu, to 2am Fri & Sat*

Sans Soleil: Tables by the DJ booth vanish around 10pm as dancers take over this Japanese-influenced listening room. *6:30pm-1am Mon-Wed, to 2:30am Thu-Sun*

Henri Henri

Begin at **Henri Henri** *(henrihenri.ca)*, a leather-scented hat supplier selling all styles of chapeaux since 1932. The hockey term 'hat trick' – when a player scores three goals in a game – originated here thanks to a deal the owners made with the NHL Canadiens: a free hat for their wins. Local legends such as Jean Béliveau (memorialized on a wall near the entrance) regularly came in to collect their caps.

While you're less likely to spot a Hab (nickname for the Canadiens) in store today, you'll be joined by hardcore hat aficionados who come here for everything from fedoras to homburgs, Baileys and Borsalinos. Master hat-maker Sylvain Labbé, who spent nearly two decades designing headpieces for Cirque du Soleil acrobats, also crafts bespoke fits for all head sizes.

A few blocks west is **Pantalons Supérieur** (Superior Pants), a family-owned clothing shop established in 1924. Fourth-generation denim dynamo Mitch Stroll helps customers find the perfect fit, offering on-site alterations on one of two sewing machines humming away in the jean-jammed outlet.

You could get lost thumbing through racks in thrift store **Eva B** *(boutiqueevab.com)*, established in 1987 and stuffed to the hilt with all sorts of treasures: Hawaiian shirts, Cabbage Patch dolls, Rollerblades and prom dresses primed for a second chance to dance. There's also a small on-site cafe

CANADIAN BRANDS & HISTORIC COMPANIES

Indiana Jeans: In 1991 this boutique transformed a corner of Blvd St-Laurent into the Wild West with boots, jeans, buckles and bags. *indiana-jeans.com*

Divine Chocolatier: Sugar fiends started flocking to this shop owned by Belgian chocolatier Richard Zwierzynski in 1976. *divinechocolatier.com*

Holt Renfrew Ogilvy: Canadian heavyweights Ogilvy (founded in 1866) and Holt Renfrew (1837) joined forces, now hocking Gucci, Chanel, Dior and more from this six-floor department store with a 2nd-floor restaurant. *holtrenfrew.com*

La Maison Simons: Originally a Québec City dry-goods shop founded in 1840, this fashion retailer now sells stylish duds at department stores nationwide. *simons.ca*

Boutique Tozzi: Stylists guide shoppers to high-end labels sourced everywhere from Canada to Copenhagen in three Crescent St stores: two for masc fits and one for femme attire. *boutiquetozzi.com*

WHEN MONTRÉAL BURNED RED

In the 1920s, Montréal was a town of vice where you could find burlesque, betting houses – and, most importantly, booze. The city never enacted Prohibition laws, so alcohol flowed freely, drawing crowds of tap-happy tipplers from the neighboring US. Mobsters ruled the roost, meaning prostitution ran rampant, and around Rue Ste-Catherine, covering today's Quartier des Spectacles and the Quartier Latin, was dubbed the Red Light District. Burlesque icon Lili St Cyr, who splashed onto the scene in the 1940s, wrote that every night in Montréal was akin to New Year's Eve in NYC. By the 1950s, officials had started scrubbing Montréal's streets and, by the early 2000s, little remained of this area's promiscuous past – save for Café Cleopatre, a storied strip joint where the red lights still flicker.

Eva B (p73)

– and a sister store, **Eva D**, selling higher-end femme attire one block south.

If you're more into paperbacks than apparel, finish at the **Word** *(thewordbookstore.ca)*, a living-room-sized bookstore selling all sorts of literature you didn't know you needed: Balzac collectibles, *Harry Potter* in Latin and plenty of titles in both French and English. Founders Adrian King-Edwards and Lucille Friesen started pushing books on McGill University's students in 1975. Their shop, housed in a 19th-century brick building, devoid of computers and perfumed with the earthy aroma of yellowed pages, feels virtually unchanged – part of the charm.

SENSATIONAL CIRCUSES

For more flying acrobats, check out **Cirque du Soleil** (p53) under the Old Port's Big Top in summer and see what's playing on the north side of town at performance center **TOHU** (p119).

Dance Under the Dome MAP P62

Immersive experiences at Société des Arts Technologiques

It's all about the visuals at nonprofit **SAT** *(sat.qc.ca)*, a 44,000-sq-ft creative incubator where art, technology and music collide. Most people come here to get lost in the **Satosphere**, a convex concert hall with an 18m-diameter dome and

157 loudspeakers delivering immersive, 360-degree audiovisual experiences. It's soundtracked by DJs spinning genre-spanning sets, with a heavy focus on EDM (check the schedule to see what's on and purchase tickets in advance). The Satosphere also showcases short films and digital art exhibits. Third-floor restaurant **Pavillon** serves natural wines and small plates.

Not up for a full-on dance party? Get a jolt of energy at the connected **Café SAT** *(8am-5pm Mon-Thu, to 10pm Fri)*, serving its fruit-forward house brew (made in collaboration with Montréal roaster Jungle) alongside a small food menu. Show up on Fridays from 5pm to 10pm, when the cafe turns into an electronic listening room with DJs spinning tunes for crowds sipping microbrews. While grooving to the beat, clock the coffee counter: a wood-cut mashrabiya (oriel window) tells SAT's history in binary code.

Fill up on Asian Cuisine

MAP P62

Food tour through Chinatown

Montréal's **Chinatown** is tiny, spanning roughly one square block, but its options for Asian cuisine seem endless. Look for the red-and-gold *paifang* gates marking the area's four corners to find steamy dim sum, hand-pulled candies and delectable dumplings. Come hungry and spend an afternoon grazing.

Enter the microneighborhood through its northern gate on Blvds St-Laurent and René-Lévesque to bite into Vietnamese tradition at **Hoang Oanh** *(10am-6pm)*. You could fill up on its signature *banh mi* (a baguette sandwich stuffed with your choice of meat or tofu and smothered in mayonnaise) or grab a handheld *banh bao* (an eggy, garlic-seasoned pork bun).

Head next to **Qing Hua Dumplings** *(11am-9:30pm Sun-Thu, to 10pm Fri & Sat)* – a sit-down dumpling den with more than 30 types of its namesake flavor bomb. Each order comes with 15 – get a pack to share, dunking them in vinegar, soy sauce or hot chili oil.

For Chinese baked goods with Parisian panache, hop across the street to **Pâtisserie Coco** *(9am-8pm Sun-Thu, to 9pm Fri & Sat)* and pick up a tray to collect your treats – perhaps custard buns, black-sesame brioche loaves or packets of chewy mochi to save for later.

Continue the sweets tour at **Dragon Beard Candy** *(12:30-4:30pm Mon-Thu, to 7pm Sat & Sun)* – a bite-size counter making teeny confections dating back to China's Han Dynasty. Watch as the Candy Master repeatedly pulls sugar dough, creating thousands of strands – a 'dragon's beard' – used to wrap a peanut-sesame-chocolate-coconut filling. Each made-to-go box comes stuffed with eight pieces, which never seems like enough.

For more tempting desserts, pop into **Pâtisserie Bao Bao Dim Sum** *(10am-6pm)* for warm, chewy treats packed with flavors like lotus root and red-bean paste.

Still hungry? Stop at the **Noodle Factory** *(noon-9pm Wed-Sun)*, a cash-only dive where chef Lin Kwong Cheung whacks

CHINATOWN'S RESILIENCE

In 1902 French-language newspaper *La Presse* first used the term 'Quartier Chinois' to reference Chinatown, though at that point the city's Chinese population was already a key part of Québec's multiethnic makeup. The first major wave of Chinese immigrants arrived in the late 19th century, following completion of the transcontinental railroad in British Columbia. Young men beelined for Montréal, building tight-knit social networks with the hopes of finding work and escaping the racism they encountered out west. By 1911, roughly 1300 Chinese people lived in the city – and by 1915 nearly 50 Chinese-operated businesses filled the surrounding streets. Real estate developments have slashed the neighborhood's size by roughly two-thirds since the 1960s, but resilient residents and shopkeepers hang on. In 2022 Québec granted Chinatown heritage status, protecting its historic core from being transformed into condos.

MONTRÉAL'S UNDERGROUND METROPOLIS

You'd never know it while strutting the city sidewalks, but hidden underground is a vast 33km network of tunnels. These tunnels connect the Métro with 2000-plus shops, restaurants, apartment buildings, hotels, museums and much more. This is the Underground City, officially called RÉSO (Réseau de la Ville Souterraine). It first appears like a run-of-the-mill shopping mall – a disappointment to those imagining a magical metropolis – but it's a remarkable feat of engineering, dating back to 1964 and dotted with public art, including a piece of the Berlin Wall. Roughly 500,000 Montréalers pass through it daily (it's a welcome reprieve from weather extremes). RÉSO is also the site of **Art Souterraine** *(artsouterrain.com)*, a three-week spring festival transforming 6km of passageways into a labyrinthine art gallery. Visit *montreal undergroundcity.com* for a handy map.

and kneads hand-pulled noodles into delicate strips. Order Shanghai (thick noodles) or house-style (thin) – and if you like heat, don't skimp on the sweet house-made hot sauce.

If you've got room for more, finish at **Restaurant Chinatown Kim Fung** *(8am-3pm & 5-10pm)*, hidden up an escalator in the rear of shopping mall Place du Quartier. Come here for Cantonese dim sum and Sichuan platters, which servers roll out on trolleys to entice their tables.

Spin Around Square Dorchester   MAP P67

Beautiful buildings and 19th-century ghosts

Stand atop one of the Venetian-inspired bridges on this pretty **square's** northern corner for an architectural eyeful. To the north is the **Dominion Square Building** (1930; titled after the park's former name) – a Lombard Romanesque Revival heavyweight with an Alabama Rockwood limestone facade. To the east, the hulking beaux-arts **Sun Life Building** (1914–33) rises 122m into the sky – it was the largest edifice in the British Empire upon completion. Look for the 13 statues perched on top of **Cathédrale Marie-Reine-du-Monde** *(1870–94; mariereinedumonde.org)* – diagonally across from the park's southeastern corner – one of the city's four basilicas. Modeled after St Peter's Basilica in Rome, the baroque beauty forms the shape of a cross, covering 4700 sq meters. Step inside to get a look at the 77m-high dome. Placards on building facades, including Dominion Sq, offer more detailed architectural and historical information, along with a numbered map highlighting intriguing structures nearby.

As for the square, it's peppered with monuments and sprinkled by a green Victorian-inspired fountain (2019). Notice the fountain's 21st-century twist: it's sliced in half, nodding to the square's shrunken footprint, scaled back when parking for the Dominion Square Building cut into the space.

Then there's the history you can't see. Thousands of bodies supposedly rest underground, remnants of Square Dorchester's days as a 19th-century cemetery for cholera victims. Latin crosses in the pavement mark the graveyard's presence, a quiet reminder of the park's darker past.

THE GOLDEN SQUARE MILE'S ELEGANT ARCHITECTURE

Between 1870 and 1900, around 60 business moguls built palatial homes along what's now dubbed the Golden Square Mile. Admire their mansions.

START	END	LENGTH
Holt Renfrew Ogilvy	Roddick Gates	2.5km; 1½ hours

In the 19th century, families on these streets accounted for nearly 80% of Canada's wealth. Today you'll still find moneyed Montréalers at department store ❶ **Holt Renfrew Ogilvy** (p15). Holt Renfrew was the British royal family's official fur supplier in the late 1800s. Next up is ❷ **Mount Stephen** (p71) – once home to Canadian Pacific Railway baron Sir George Stephen, then a gentlemen's club, and now a hotel. More mansions delight along Rue Sherbrooke between Stanley and Drummond.

North is the ❸ **Mount Royal Club**, which splintered from Montréal's St James Club in 1899. The St James was supposedly too liberal. Next door sits the French Second Empire–style ❹ **Maison Louis-Joseph Forget** (1884). Forget was one of the first French Canadians to join Montréal's Scottish-dominated aristocracy. Across the street rises the ❺ **Maison Alcan** complex, blending five historic buildings (1872–1928). Step through the art-deco entrance for a breather in the colorful public atrium.

Continue east past the ❻ **Ritz-Carlton** (1912), dubbed the 'Grande Dame of Sherbrooke St,' and head north up Ave du Musée along ❼ **MBAM** (p68). After climbing steep steps to Ave des Pins, walk east to McGill University past turreted, Queen Anne Revival–style ❽ **Maison Lady Meredith** (1894), then wind downhill past the Greek Revival ❾ **Musée Redpath** (p71) to ❿ **Roddick Gates**, where yesteryear's glamor gives way to modern skyscrapers.

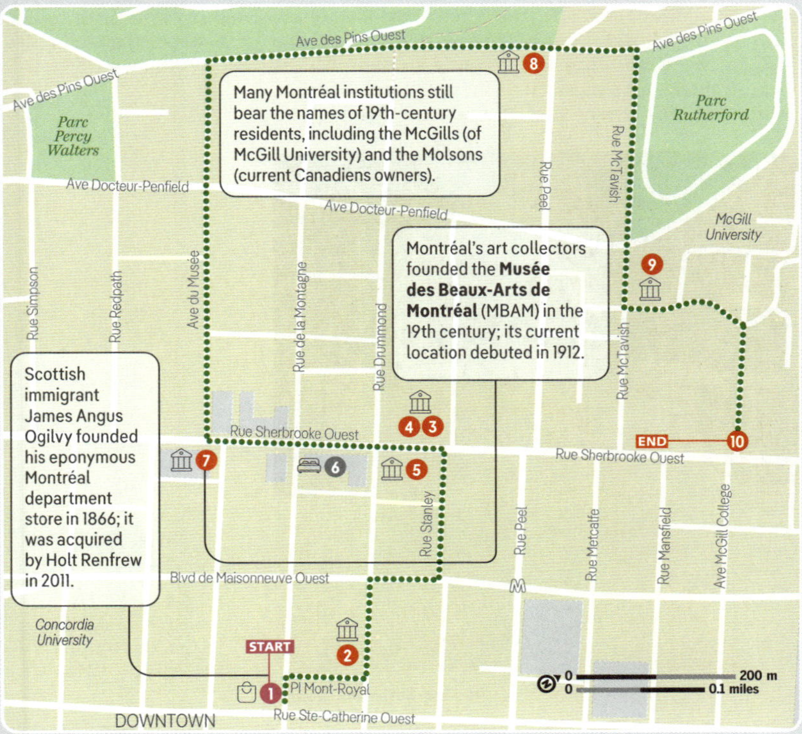

Many Montréal institutions still bear the names of 19th-century residents, including the McGills (of McGill University) and the Molsons (current Canadiens owners).

Montréal's art collectors founded the **Musée des Beaux-Arts de Montréal** (MBAM) in the 19th century; its current location debuted in 1912.

Scottish immigrant James Angus Ogilvy founded his eponymous Montréal department store in 1866; it was acquired by Holt Renfrew in 2011.

Researched by John Garry

QUARTIER LATIN, THE VILLAGE & HOMA

FROM AFTER-HOURS SCENES TO OLYMPIC DREAMS

Beer joints, gay bars and the country's largest natural science complex stretch along Montréal's east side. There's a little something for everyone.

Rue St-Denis is the place to be in the Quartier Latin, where UQAM students rub shoulders with theatergoers and a ragtag mix of street urchins – gritty ghosts from the neighborhood's glory days. The Village (also called the Gay Village) comes alive once night descends, with dance clubs and LGBTIQ+ bars along Rue Ste-Catherine bumping from dinner 'til dawn. Beyond the main drag, a smattering of boutiques and restaurants provide quiet sophistication. Further east there's up-and-coming Hochelaga-Maisonneuve (HoMa). Though the 1976 Olympics put this industrial francophone neighborhood on the map, its renaissance has only recently arrived. Explore the residential area's artisanal revitalization before seeing the natural science museums around Parc Olympique.

TOP TIP

Hop on the Métro at Quartier Latin's Berri-UQAM station and you can get nearly anywhere: HoMa (east), Little Italy (north), Verdun (west) and Parc Jean-Drapeau (south).

Rue Ste-Catherine (p83)

See page 199 for places to stay in Quartier Latin, the Village & HoMa.

Highlights

❶ Biodôme
Wander through five ecosystems to see Atlantic puffins, river otters, yellow anacondas and golden lion tamarins – all under one roof. **p85**

▶ ❷ Insectarium
Observe hundreds of butterflies flitting around a barrier-free greenhouse, where winged wonders occasionally land on outstretched arms. **p85**

❸ Écomusée du Fier Monde
Learn about the Centre-Sud's communities inside an art-deco bathhouse-turned-museum. **p80**

❹ Stereo
Rave until the sun comes up inside this Village club renowned for its impeccable sound system and wide DJ roster. **p86**

❺ Rue Ste-Catherine
Clink glasses with the LGBTIQ+ crew at one of the many bars lining the heart of Montréal's historic gayborhood. **p83**

Getting Around

Métro
Orange, green and yellow lines stop at Berri-UQAM in the Quartier Latin; green continues east to Beaudry and Papineau in the Village, then on to Pie-IX and Viau for Parc Olympique and HoMa.

Bus
In the Village, bus 24 runs east–west along Sherbrooke (to the north); bus 34 runs east–west along St-Catherine (to the south). In the Quartier Latin, bus 30 runs north–south along Rues Berri and St-Denis.

Walk
Follow Rue St-Denis north from the Quartier Latin to Plateau Mont Royal. Rue St-Catherine links Downtown and the Village.

QUARTIER LATIN, THE VILLAGE & HOMA

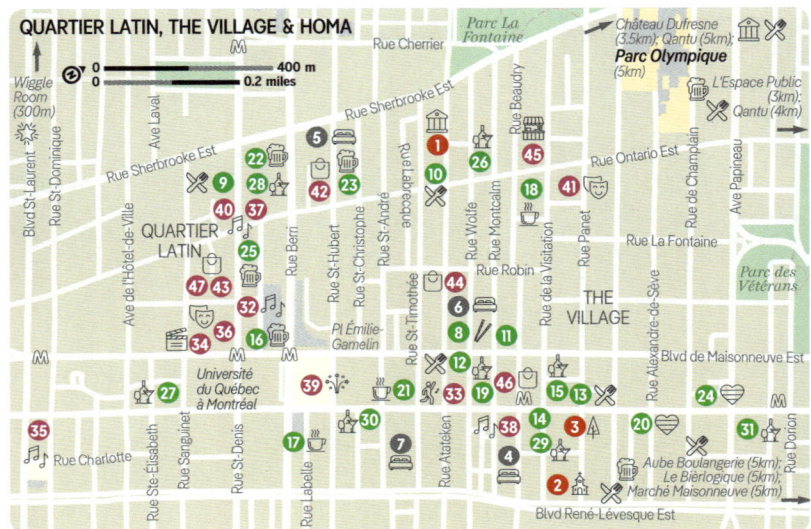

- ● **SIGHTS**
- 1 Écomusée du Fier Monde
- 2 Église St-Pierre-Apôtre
- 3 Parc de l'Espoir

- ● **SLEEPING**
- 4 Bed & Breakfast du Village
- 5 Hôtel Château de l'Argoat
- 6 La Loggia Art & Breakfast
- 7 M Montreal

- ● **EATING**
- 8 Le Blossom
- 9 Le Café Big Trouble
- 10 Le Mousso
- 11 Le Red Tiger
- 12 O'Thym
- 13 Saloon
- 14 Tendresse

- ● **DRINKING & NIGHTLIFE**
- 15 Aigle Noir
- 16 Brasseurs du Monde
- 17 Café Léo
- 18 Café Sfouf
- 19 Club Unity
- 20 Complexe Skye
- 21 La Graine Brûlée
- 22 L'Amère a Boire
- 23 Le Cheval Blanc
- 24 Le Cocktail
- 25 Le Saint-Bock
- 26 Marion Tavern
- see 29 Motel Motel
- 27 Newspeak
- 28 Randolph Pub
- 29 Renard
- 30 Stereo
- 31 Stud

- ● **ENTERTAINMENT**
- 32 Bistro à Jojo
- 33 Cabaret Mado
- 34 Cinémathèque Québécoise
- 35 Club Soda
- 36 Espace St-Denis
- 37 Le 4e Mur
- 38 Le National
- 39 Les Jardins Gamelin
- see 34 Sommets du Cinéma d'Animation
- 40 Turbo Haüs
- 41 Usine C

- ● **SHOPPING**
- 42 Aux Quatre Points Cardinaux
- 43 Camellia Sinensis
- 44 Espace Vintage
- 45 Fromagerie Atwater
- 46 L'Euguélionne
- 47 Pause Friperie
- see 15 Priape

MONTRÉAL'S BEST MARKETS

Marché Maisonneuve feels like a quaint neighborhood market compared to Montréal's largest fresh-produce outposts: **Marché Atwater** (p127) and **Marché Jean-Talon** (p118), two fantastic spots to spend an hour grazing among food stands.

Get to Know the Working Class

Dive in at Écomusée du Fier Monde

Montréal's blue-collar crowd gets its due at this history museum inside an **ex-bathhouse** (ecomusee.qc.ca; adult/child $14/8). Permanent exhibit **All the Livelong Day! The Joys and Sorrows of Life in a Working-Class Neighbourhood** examines the rise, fall and current reinvention of Centre-Sud, a 20th-century neighborhood now split into a patchwork of communities, including the Village.

Visitors loop around the balcony – which overlooks the bathhouse's former pool – to see photos, artifacts and multimedia displays that show the daily life of laboring families who kept Montréal's industrial-era factories afloat. The pool area below hosts temporary art shows. Allow 45 minutes to take it all in.

Between its brick facade and cathedral-worthy ceiling, the building's 1927 art-deco bones are arguably the museum's greatest assets. In 1905 the City of Montréal estimated 75% of working-class homes lacked places to bathe. Public bathhouses like this one – formerly the Bain Généreux – became important community hubs, promoting personal hygiene. With architecture this nice, a rinse must've felt very regal.

Go to the Movies
Canadian films at Cinémathèque Québécoise

Join cinephiles by sinking into seats to see avant-garde films, animated shorts and cult classics at **Cinémathèque Québécoise** (*cinematheque.qc.ca; adult/child $13/11*), founded in 1963 to safeguard Québec's audio-visual heritage. New releases get screened in concert with footage from the institution's impressive archive, which holds 40,000 films and videos and 30,000 television broadcasts. Most movies showcase Québec makers, with plenty of Canadian directors and international titles in the mix.

In addition to screenings, there's a series of free-to-visit art exhibits throughout the year, showcasing new works alongside selections from the vault's exhaustive collection of posters and photographs.

Head to the cafe pre- or post-film to discuss your favorite Québec directors over coffee, beer or wine – most enjoyable (when weather permits) when sitting on the outdoor terrace. If you're visiting in May, check out **Sommets du Cinéma d'Animation** (*sommetsanimation.com*), a five-day animated film festival.

Order the fluffy pancakes or flavorful breakfast burrito.

> ### WHAT'S IN A (STREET) NAME?
>
> For over 200 years a Village street slicing from the St Lawrence River to **Parc La Fontaine** (p103) bore the name of Jeffery Amherst, commander-in-chief of North America's British army (1758–1763), who led the capture of Montréal during the Seven Years' War. When it came to warfare, Amherst didn't stop at guns; he also proposed biological destruction. In 1763, Amherst suggested giving smallpox-infected blankets to the Indigenous communities in an attempt, as he wrote, to 'extirpate this execrable race.' In 2019 Montréal gave him a demotion. The street was renamed Rue Atateken, which is a Kanien'kéha (Mohawk) word roughly translating to 'brotherhood' and denoting equality. As for Amherst, he's not entirely gone. Block-long Rue du Square-Amherst still bears his name, a small but potent reminder of North America's dark colonial past.

EATING IN THE QUARTIER LATIN, THE VILLAGE & HOMA: CAFES

Le Café Big Trouble: This colorfully off-kilter brunch-and-coffee counter on Rue St-Denis recalls the street's hip heydays. *8am-4pm Thu-Sun* **$$**

La Graine Brûlée: If an eight-year-old from 1995 opened a vegetarian coffeehouse, this would be it – vintage video-game den, excessive carnival decor and all. *7am-10pm* **$**

Café Sfouf: Settle into this boho hang with the work-from-anywhere crowd for tartines (toasts) topped with Lebanese flavors. *8am-6pm Tue-Fri, 8:30am-5pm Sat & Sun* **$**

Café Léo: UQAM students study amid art-adorned white walls in this cafe-gallery with coffee from local roaster Zab. *7:30am-6pm Mon-Fri, from 8:30am Sat & Sun* **$**

THE SOUL OF ST-DENIS

The Quartier Latin has been through a lot – and no street tells the story better than Rue St-Denis as it runs from Blvd René-Lévesque to Rue Sherbrooke. Victorian facades recall its 19th-century heyday as an exclusive neighborhood for wealthy francophones. The brutalist buildings of the Université du Québéc à Montréal (UQAM) harken back to its bohemian renaissance in the 1980s and '90s, when college students made this Montréal's cool-kid kingdom. Then there's the recent fast-food chain infiltration – indicators of the street's downward decline. Graffiti decorates facades with flavors of punk days past, and some hip spots linger – such as the **Cinémathèque Québécoise** (p81) and the new (yet nostalgically '90s) **Cafe Big Trouble** (p81). But homelessness is prevalent, and though a slow revival appears underway, a spate of recent media ponders if St-Denis is dead.

L'Amère a Boire

Cheers Beers on Rue St-Denis
A tour for hops heads

Rue St-Denis might not sparkle with the same boisterous energy that made it famous a few decades ago, but one thing remains steadfast: it's a great place to grab a beer. Spend an evening trying the Quartier Latin's best.

Kick off the taste tour with a four-beer flight at **Brasseurs du Monde** *(11am-1am Mon-Fri, from 10am Sat & Sun)*, serving ales made at its St-Hyacinth microbrewery. This two-story spot with solid pub fare takes *'l'art de la bière'* (the art of the beer) seriously.

Next, walk up St-Denis until you see the holy beer mural outside **Le Saint-Bock** *(3pm-3am Sun-Thu, from noon Fri*

Reservations required. All meals start by 6:30pm.

EATING IN THE VILLAGE: OUR PICKS

Le Red Tiger: Sidle up to the canary-yellow bar for Vietnamese street food like deep-fried pancakes and crunchy imperial rolls. *5-10pm Mon-Thu, to 11pm Fri & Sat* **$**

O'Thym: Menus change weekly at this minimalist outpost for epicurious omnivores. Expect game and greens sourced from Québec farms. BYO wine. *5:30-10pm* **$$$**

Tendresse: Come to this zinnia-colored vegan restaurant for the three-course dinner menu (from $31) – an ode to tofu. *5-10pm Mon & Wed-Fri* **$$**

Le Mousso: You'll need a few hours to enjoy chef Antonin Mousseau-Rivard's 12-course menu at this seasonal neo-Nordic star of Montréal's dining scene. *6-10pm Thu-Sat* **$$$**

& Sat). Choose from more than 40 beers on tap – its headiest selections are brewed in-house.

See how the lagers compare at malt-scented **L'Amère a Boire** (*4pm-1am Mon-Wed, 2pm-3am Thu-Sat, 2pm-12:30am Sun*), all brewed on-site and best enjoyed on one of two terraces.

Finish east at **Le Cheval Blanc** (*3pm-3am Tue-Sat, to 1am Sun & Mon*) on Rue Ontario – Montréal's first microbrewery, pouring homemade craft since the 1980s. The digs might seem dingy, but the suds remain stellar and there's occasionally live music. Raise a glass to the bar that started it all.

Follow MTL's LGBTIQ+ Rainbow
Queer history in the Village

When it comes to queer life, Montréal is tops. The city's annual Pride parade – **Fierté Montréal** (*fiertemontreal.com*), held in early August – is the largest LGBTIQ+ gathering in the francophone world. But the road to acceptance wasn't always paved with rainbows. Explore the Village's pink past on this brief walking tour, less than 1km.

Start outside the Catholic **Église St-Pierre-Apôtre** (*diocesemontreal.org*), constructed in 1851, to ponder Christianity's historic influence on queer Montréal. The city's first recorded rumblings of LGBTIQ+ life date back to 1648, when an unnamed military drummer with the French garrison was charged with 'crimes of the worst kind' – a phrase historically used to describe homosexual acts. Initially sentenced to death, he was offered a bargain by Québec's Catholic Bishop: kick the bucket or become New France's executioner. The musician swapped his drumsticks for the axe.

Luckily, this church doesn't share such antiquated ideology. In 1996 St-Pierre-Apôtre inaugurated the **Chapel of Hope** – the world's first chapel dedicated to victims of AIDS. The illness devastated Montréal's LGBTIQ+ community.

Next, head to **Parc de l'Espoir** (Park of Hope) on the corner of Rues Panet and Ste-Catherine, founded in 1991 by ACT UP Montréal as a memorial for those lost to HIV/AIDS in Québec. For years, mourners tied ribbons inscribed with the names of loved ones to trees here. Today, a red ribbon embedded in the ground keeps their spirit alive.

continues on p86

Snap a picture in the mural-covered bathroom.

MONTRÉAL'S STONEWALLS

Montréal didn't have one version of Stonewall, New York City's legendary LGBTIQ+ uprising against police brutality; it had two. The first occurred in 1977, when police stormed Downtown leather bar Truxx and nearby Le Mystique, arresting 146 men on trumped-up morality charges. The following day, more than 2000 protesters flooded city streets. Their voices were heard: by the end of the year Québec had become the first Canadian province to ban discrimination based on sexual orientation. The second event erupted in 1990, when police raided Sex Garage, an LGBTIQ+ loft party, and beat 400 partygoers in the street. The violence led to a 36-hour riot, galvanizing locals to organize and fight for LGBTIQ+ rights. When Montréalers march in August's Pride parade, it's on pathways paved by these brave revolutionaries.

DRINKING ON RUE STE-CATHERINE: BEST LGBTIQ+ BARS

Renard: A 'Fox' with a split personality: weeknights he's a 5 à 7 cocktail-with-dinner gentleman; at weekends he's a dance-'til-dawn diva. *3pm-1am Sun-Wed, to 3am Thu-Sat*

Aigle Noir: Four bars, three floors, and a series of slot machines where you might see leather-clad bears gambling for a lucky night: shoot your shot. *8am-3am*

Stud: It's a veritable zoo at this bi-level 'men's bar', its two dance floors packed with leather bears, pool sharks, furry pups and, occasionally, fresh-faced bucks. *2pm-3am*

Saloon: This queer-centric alternative to dance dens serves dinner until 8pm before doubling down on cocktails. *5pm-midnight Sun-Thu, to 1:30am Fri & Sat*

Stade Olympique

TOP EXPERIENCE

Parc Olympique & Espace Pour la Vie

Four museums, a leaning tower from the 1976 Olympics and glorious green spaces linking them all: no one's getting bored at this cultural oasis, central to 'Space for Life,' the largest natural science complex in Canada. Spend a day or more seeing the exhibits, or simply walk the grounds to appreciate architecture ranging from art-deco delights to space-age spectacles.

DON'T MISS

- Biôdome
- Insectarium
- Jardin Botanique
- Montréal Tower
- Planétarium
- Les Premiers Vendredis
- Stade Olympique

Stade Olympique

Constructed for the 1976 Summer Olympics, the **Stade Olympique** is an impressive monument to Montréal's mid-20th-century architectural ambitions – though its costly construction remains controversial. It's dominated by the 165m-high **Montréal Tower**, which extends over HoMa at a 45-degree angle, making it the tallest inclined tower worldwide. A new glass-cabin funicular will open in fall 2026, whisking riders to an observation deck for a sweeping island panorama.

PRACTICALITIES

- parcolympique.qc.ca
- espacepourlavie.ca
- 1 Espace Pour la Vie museum adult/child $23.75/12.25

On the first weekends of June, July and August, come hungry for **Les Premiers Vendredis** *(lespremiersvendredis.ca)*, Canada's largest food-truck gathering, which packs Parc Olympique's esplanade (outside the stadium) and the **Old Port** (p52) with snack stands dishing up all kinds of cuisine.

Biodôme

From outside, the **Biodôme** looks like an enormous dinosaur egg – fitting for this 'House of Life', constructed as the velodrome (cycling track) for the 1976 Olympics. The space now features five of America's ecosystems under one roof, with 2500 animals representing around 200 species. Wave to capybaras in a **Tropical Rainforest**, see what's lurking underwater around the **Gulf of St Lawrence** and observe otters playing in the **Laurentian Maple Forest**. You can also hop alongside puffins on the **Labrador Coast** and waddle with penguins around the **Sub-Antarctic Islands**. Set aside a couple of hours, visit midweek to avoid crowds and follow the self-guided circuit to ensure you see everything.

Planétarium

This **museum**, shaped like a pair of whirling sci-fi spaceships, hurls visitors light years from Earth inside two high-tech, domed theaters featuring movies about astronomy. Films skew kid-friendly. (Recent flicks traveled to the icy dunes of Mars and explored distant planets throughout the Milky Way.) Ensure you reserve tickets for the correct language: films are offered in English and French on a rotating schedule. Choose one film or a double feature.

Insectarium

See the world from a bug's point of view inside this dynamically designed **museum** housing thousands of living and preserved insects. Budding entomologists enjoy burrowing underground to a suite of interactive exhibits, while adults appreciate the 9m domed cathedral lined with 3000 framed specimens – one row arranged chromatically, another grouped by categories like 'Impressive Legs.' Most magnificent is the **Great Vivarium**, a sawtooth-topped greenhouse where butterflies emerge from chrysalises, even in winter, to flutter freely through the air.

Jardin Botanique

Open since the 1930s, the **Jardin Botanique** has blossomed into the world's third-largest botanic garden, with 10 exhibition greenhouses and 20 outdoor gardens covering 75 hectares. Admire Ming dynasty design around the **Chinese Garden's** Lac de Rêve (Dream Lake), get in touch with Indigenous foliage around the **First Nations Garden** and glide through the **Japanese Garden** with its traditional pavilions, tea room and the largest bonsai 'forest' outside Asia. Visit between May and October, when seasonal petals turn outdoor exhibits into natural art shows.

TOP TIPS

- Reserve timed entry tickets online in advance.

- To see Espace Pour la Vie's five museums, which include Parc Jean-Drapeau's offsite **Biosphère** but not Stade Olympique, save money by purchasing a SOLO Passport *($87; bigger discounts for families)*.

- Download the user-friendly Espace Pour la Vie app for visits to the Biôdome and Insectarium, which trade interpretive museum signs for digital guides.

- Join a guided tour of the Jardin Botanique, free with a museum ticket *(amisjardin.com)*.

- An underground tunnel links the Biôdome and Planétarium.

- For food, grab vegan cafe fare from Espace Végo inside the Planétarium, or try Jardin Botanique's seasonal cafe-terrace.

THE BIG OWE

The Olympic Stadium has two nicknames: the Big O, for 'Olympics,' and the Big Owe, for taxpayers, who saw the concrete structure become an endless cash vacuum. The cost to build it in time for the 1976 Games ballooned from an initial $120 million to $900 million when it finally opened. That number jumped to $1.47 billion by the time the city paid it off three decades later.

continued from p83

Veer west on Rue Ste-Catherine, passing street poles decorated in tubular Pride flags, en route to **Priape** *(priape.com)*. When this gay-centric shop opened in 1974, it marked the gayborhood's gradual move from Downtown to the Village. It's now a three-level emporium specializing in hand-crafted leather fetish gear and adult toys.

Continue on Ste-Catherine to the Beaudry Métro station, outfitted with six rainbow pillars in 1999, and look for *Le Rêve de Ron Farha* (The Dream of Ron Farha), a mural by street artist XRAY. Ron's dream? A march through Montréal to raise HIV/AIDS awareness. His legacy lives on through the Farha Foundation, which has since donated over $10 million to HIV organizations across Québec.

End inside **L'Euguélionne** *(librairieleuguelionne.com)*, a queer feminist bookstore stocked with French and English literature, including a stellar zine selection. Pick up a pamphlet by a contemporary artist to uncover the city's latest LGBTIQ+ stories, hot off the presses.

Clap for Classic Drag

A night at Cabaret Mado

Hairline-high eyebrows, puckered lips and a wardrobe screaming 'clown chic' – that's what to expect when Montréal drag pioneer Mado Lamotte takes the stage at her eponymous Rue Ste-Catherine **cabaret** *(mado.qc.ca; tickets from $34)*. Mado – who goes by Luc Provost offstage – started treading the boards in 1987, long before *RuPaul's Drag Race Canada* sashayed onto TV screens. Don't expect death drops – she saves those tricks for her roster of younger performers. Lamotte, instead, is a cunning bilinguist, serving as impresario at her intimate venue – and following in the high heels of local drag legend Armand Larrivée Monroe, who paved the way by opening the city's first dedicated drag bar in 1972.

This isn't the only drag show in town. Lip-sync assassins slay stages at **Le Cocktail** and **Complexe Sky**. Wigged wonders sometimes strut across the 2nd floor of **Café Cleopatre** (p74). Queens and kings occasionally shake it at the **Wiggle Room** (p103) and **Club Soda** (p63). But Cabaret Mado feels like a blast from the drag past, offering a look at a historic slice of Village culture.

Plan your visit to see long-running *Mado Reçoit*, with a rotating cast of queens ranging from schlocky to exceptional, and purchase tickets in advance to ensure admittance. Unlike many establishments along Rue Ste-Catherine, this isn't a gay bar; crowds tend to be female-forward. Save your bills: though tipping is normal at most drag shows, you're not expected to toss loonies and toonies at this talent.

WHERE TO GO DANCING

Stereo: Melodic house and transcendental techno flood the speakers of this all-hours dance floor, revered by Montréal club kids for its exceptional sound system. *tixr.com/groups/stereo*

Motel Motel: Pass the tiny cocktail lounge up front to reach the cozy dance floor hidden in back, its LED ceiling glowing like a Lite-Brite board on acid. *@motel_motel_*

Turbo Haüs: Up-and-coming bands play to petite crowds in this lower-level bar and music venue known for rocking punk and metal music, along with open-mic nights on Tuesdays. *turbohaus.ca*

Newspeak: Groove freely to the sounds of electronic music in this 300-person, bunker-style dance den, named after Orwell's fictional language in the dystopian *1984*. *newspeakmtl.com*

Club Unity: This club is the definition of 'bi' – two dance floors with two different styles of music and an all-are-welcome rooftop with LGBTIQ+ flavor. *clubunity.com*

Hochelaga-Maisonneuve

Eat Artisanal in HoMa
Small-batch food tour

Hochelaga-Maisonneuve is more than its most recognizable landmark – the Olympic Stadium, rising above the neighborhood like the handle of a giant's saucepan. The working-class francophone area is having a renaissance, and the best way to experience its wealth is with your belly.

Begin at **Aube Boulangerie** *(7am-6pm)*, where you can watch bakers prep croissants, financiers, scones and baby-sized bread loaves as you wait in line to order coffee made with beans by local roaster Jungle.

CLINK MORE PINTS
If you're big on beer, head to Mile End and Little Italy (p110) to taste what's pouring from some of the city's tastiest taps, including Brasserie Harricana and Czech-influenced Mellön (p121).

 EATING IN QUARTIER LATIN, THE VILLAGE & HOMA: BARS WITH FOOD

Marion Tavern: This light, bright corner cocktail bar serves flatbreads and artisanal beers later than most – a fantastic 'last call' in the Village. *4pm-3am* **$$**	**Blossom:** Lounge beneath cherry blossoms and choose from an long list of sakes and makis inside this glass-walled, neo-Japanese joint. *5-10pm Tue-Thu, to 10:30pm Fri & Sat* **$$**	**Le 4E Mur:** It's speakeasy kitsch, complete with Sin City–era burlesque and a hard-to-decipher brick-wall entrance. Visit *le4emur.com* for a clue. *5pm-3am Wed-Sun* **$$**	**Randolph Pub:** Tabletop tournaments rage inside this brewpub with over 1000 board games geared to all tastes. *4pm-1am Sun-Thu, to 2am Fri & Sat* **$**

WHERE TO SHOP IN THE VILLAGE

Aux Quatre Points Cardinaux: Find your way with this encyclopedic assortment of maps, globes, atlases and aerial photographs and commendable collection of Lonely Planet guides. *aqpc.com*

Fromagerie Atwater: Prep a charcuterie board with a superb selection of meats and cheeses. Opt for a local *fromage* such as the Bête-à-Séguin, a camembert from Ísle-aux-Grues on the St Lawrence River. *fromagerieatwater.ca*

Camellia Sinensis: Order an oolong to go, peruse the white canisters of loose leaf or grab a seat to compare your favorites with a tea tasting ($5 per cup). *camellia-sinensis.com*

Pause Friperie: Search for vintage and upcycled attire sold at prices even UQAM's thriftiest college students can afford. *pausefriperie.com*

Espace Vintage: Your grandmother's long-lost storage unit or a well-curated vintage store? Squeeze between Russian dolls and 1950s lampshades to decide for yourself. *@espacevintage419*

Take your joe to go and head to **Marché Maisonneuve** *(marchespublics-mtl.com; 9am-6pm Tue-Sat, to 5pm Sun & Mon)*, Montréal's third-largest public market, where bakers, butchers, fishmongers and cheese connoisseurs sell snacks. After finding something tasty, drop by **Le Bièrlogique** *(lebierologue.com)* to pick out a Québec-made can of beer or bottle of wine. (In Montréal you're legally allowed to drink alcohol in certain designated picnic spots while consuming a meal. Bring your spoils to nearby **Parc Maisonneuve**).

With your picnic polished off, stop by local bean-to-bar chocolatier **Qantu** *(qantuchocolate.com)*, which crafts award-winning chocolates from Peruvian cacao. Staff members offer visitors a chance to taste-test treats before buying – perhaps the plummy Morrópin or honey-kissed Oh La Vache. Chocolate fiends can also organize 1½-hour **factory tours** *($44; 11am Sat)* to explore the production process.

Say '*santé*' to HoMa by finishing up at microbrewery **L'Espace Public** *(tasting room 2287 Ave Letourneux; hours vary Wed-Sun)*, an industrial beer-making factory with communal picnic tables overflowing onto a seasonal terrace. Sours are the specialty: try a five-pour flight to sample what's on tap.

Château Dufresne

Tour an Elegant Estate
Gilded glamor at Château Dufresne

Nothing inspires real-estate envy like visiting this grand beaux-arts **mansion** *(chateaudufresne.com; adult/child $14/7)* facing Parc Olympique. Constructed from 1915 to 1918, the château was modeled after the Petit Trianon in Versailles and decked out with interiors fit for a king: parquet floors, stained-glass windows and coffered ceilings with frescoes by Italian artist Guido Nincheri.

Bourgeois Montréal brothers Oscar and Marius Dufresne commissioned the three-story home, which the family sold in 1948. Oscar lived on one side – it's largely empty today, allowing visitors to focus on architectural elements and mythological frescoes (crane your neck in the living room to see 15 paintings depicting Orpheus and Eurydice). Marius occupied the other, furnished with the latest styles of the Dufresne days. Bring headphones: QR codes throughout the museum offer context on Guido Nincheri's artwork. There's scant information provided otherwise; join a guided tour (3pm, weekends only) for a more thorough experience.

SEE LIVE PERFORMANCES

Espace St-Denis: This block-long complex includes a theater for musicals, a cabaret for stand-up comics and French brasserie Le Molière for pre-performance dining. *espacestdenis.com*

Usine C: Centre-Sud's former jam factory now crams its facility with experimental theater, dance, music and mixed-media performances. Join artists for a post-show drink in the cafe. *usine-c.com*

Les Jardins Gamelin: From May to September, Place Émilie-Gamel transforms into an outdoor recreation center with gardens, games and live shows. *jardinsgamelin.com*

Le National: Opened in 1900 as North America's first francophone theater, this intimate Village institution transitioned to presenting an eclectic lineup including indie bands and French-speaking comics. *latulipe.ca*

Bistro à Jojo: Booze, blues and rock 'n' roll: get it all at this Rue St-Denis venue, jamming to live tunes since 1975. *bistroajojo.com*

Researched by John Garry

PLATEAU MONT-ROYAL
STYLISH STREETS LEAD TO PRETTY PARKS

Creative energy spills from the cafes, bars, bookstores, vintage shops and historic haunts of this bohemian playground, decked out in colorful homes with spiral staircases.

Splashed in street art, brimming with boutiques and bookended by gorgeous green spaces, the Plateau – as it's commonly called – is home to some of the city's most sought-after real estate. Since the 19th century it's evolved from a mix of bourgeois families in greystones and working-class immigrants in multiplexes to a center of Jewish life, an outpost for Portugal and, most recently, a magnet for newcomers from France. Blvd St-Laurent (dubbed the Main) runs north–south through it all, historically dividing English and French speakers. These days it's the hip heart of the neighborhood, along with action-packed Ave Mont-Royal and Rue St-Denis, forming a mosaic of Montréal's artsy, international spirit.

TOP TIP

After exploring the Plateau's main thoroughfares, wander around its quiet, residential side streets to admire candy-colored town houses and leafy *ruelles vertes* (green alleyways; p102).

The Plateau

See page 199 for places to stay in Plateau Mont-Royal.

Highlights

❶ Ave Mont-Royal
Find vintage threads, artist prints, baked goods and enormous street murals along this thoroughfare, perpetually abuzz. **p97**

❷ Belvédère Kondiaronk
Hike to Parc du Mont-Royal's most magnificent overlook for panoramic views of Downtown's skyscrapers and the St Lawrence River. **p105**

❸ Schwartz's
Get your fingers greasy on a smoked-meat sandwich at Montréal's favorite delicatessen, serving brisket since 1928. **p93**

❹ Ave Duluth
Pop into boutiques, restaurants and bars along this cobblestone street in summer, when it becomes a pedestrian pathway. **p97**

❺ L'Original
Admire work by Montréal artists, including muralists whose signature styles you might recognize on the Plateau's streets. **p95**

Getting Around

Métro
Take the orange line to Sherbrooke (south) or Mont-Royal (north) along Rue Berri.

Bus
Bus 55 travels along Blvd St-Laurent, bus 30 runs along Rue St-Denis, bus 80 follows Ave du Parc and bus 11 chugs along Ave Mont-Royal and (until 2027) up Parc du Mont-Royal.

Walk & Bicycle
For walking, Blvd St-Laurent and Rue St-Denis are the neighborhood's most energetic north–south thoroughfares. For cycling, follow the bike lanes along Rue St-Denis and east–west along Rue Rachel.

NORTHEAST OF PLATEAU MONT-ROYAL

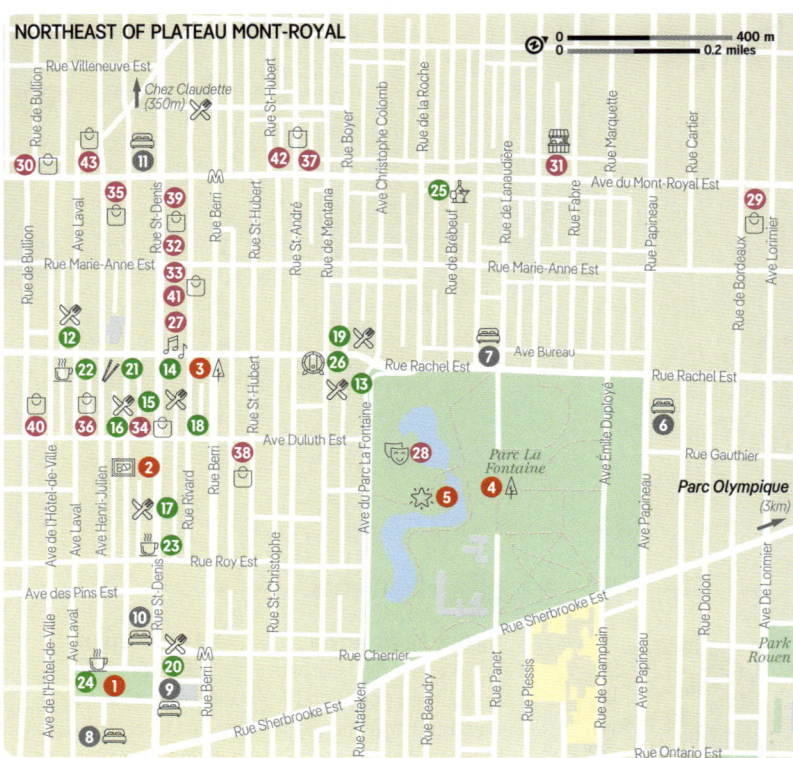

⭐ SIGHTS
1. Carré St-Louis
2. Livart
3. Parc de la Bolduc
4. Parc La Fontaine

⭐ ACTIVITIES, COURSES & TOURS
see **2** Espace Thomas
5. Patin Patin
see **23** Spade & Palacio

⬤ SLEEPING
6. Accueil Chez François
7. Auberge de La Fontaine
8. Gingerbread Manor
9. Hôtel de l'ITHQ
10. Kutuma Hotel & Suites
11. Sonder Le Guerin

⬤ EATING
see **38** Au Pied de Cochon
12. Café Chez Téta
see **38** Khyber Pass
see **30** Kitano Shokudo
see **35** Kouign Amann
13. La Banquise
14. La Binerie
15. La Panzeria
16. La Prunelle
see **11** Le Toledo
17. L'Express
18. L'Gros Luxe
19. Ma Poule Mouillée
20. Momo
see **5** Robin des Bois
21. Yokato Yokabai

⬤ DRINKING & NIGHTLIFE
see **38** Bar Vivar
22. Café Replika
23. Le Club Café
24. Le K
25. Le Rouge-Gorge
26. Projet Pilote

⬤ ENTERTAINMENT
27. Dièse Onze
28. Théâtre de Verdure

⬤ SHOPPING
29. Affiche en Tête
30. Artpop
31. Bleu & Persillé
32. Café Camas
see **2** Café Mimi
33. Club 777
34. De Stiil
35. Hadio
36. La Grande Ourse
37. Le Cartel
38. Les Chocolats de Chloé
see **11** Les Folles Alliees
39. L'Original
40. Magasin Général Lambert Gratton
41. Marché Floh
42. Multimags
43. Palmo Goods

Savor Smoked Meat
MAP P100
Order a sandwich at Schwartz's

Eating smoked meat is a Montréal must and **Schwartz's** *(10am-11pm Sun-Thu, to midnight Fri & Sat)* is the best place to try it. The meat has been made the same way since 1928, when Romanian Jewish immigrant Reuben Schwartz opened this shop. It's cured for 10 days, smoked overnight and sliced by hand to order – and crowds can't get enough. Some diners go for the rib steak and poutine, but the juicy brisket sandwich is best, stacked higher than Mont Royal between two pieces of mustard-slathered rye bread.

Prepare to wait in line for the sit-down experience, or save time by ordering yours to go from the deli next door, where you'll find a counter and some tables in back. You could also prep a DIY feast and take it to **Parc du Mont-Royal** (p104): order smoked meat by the pound, grab a loaf of rye and pick out some fixings – perhaps pickles, peppers and coleslaw. Bring napkins – you'll need them.

Plunge into Poutine
MAPS P92 & P100
A fried food crawl

Plateau Mont-Royal serves some of Montréal's best takes on a culinary trio synonymous with Québec: fries, gravy and cheese curds. Compare poutines across the neighborhood – or pick one *poutinerie* and go all-in.

When it comes to name recognition, **La Banquise** *(24hr)* takes the cake. Expect weekend wait times, a small price to pay for choosing from over 30 curd concoctions perfected since the 1980s. Carnivores: come hungry for the T rex, topped with ground beef, pepperoni, bacon and sausage. Up-all-nighters: venture here for a gravy-doused nightcap.

Across the street, **Ma Poule Mouillée** *(10am-9pm Tue-Sun)* brings poutine to the Azores with tangy São Jorge cheese, chicken and chorizo, all glazed in a special garlicky sauce. Nab a window seat to gloat at the Banquise competitors – or grab yours to go and nosh in **Parc La Fontaine** (p103).

For a classic *casse-croûte* (snack shack) experience, try diner **Patati Patata** *(11am-2am)*, slimmer than a French fry and

> This is a sustainably-minded, zero-waste business.

UNDERRATED MONTRÉAL

Say *au revoir* to the tourist hit list with tips from Danny Pavlopoulos, founder of **Spade & Palacio** (@spadeandpalacio).

Swap **Schwartz's brisket** for **Serrano's chicken**.
 Danny: They cut up Peruvian chicken and smother it in homemade spicy sauce.

Instead of the **Old Port** (p52), see the **Lachine Canal** (p136).
 D: Bike towards Verdun, passing repurposed industrial buildings and Atwater Market.

Instead of **Rue St-Paul** (p50), stroll **Rue de Castelnau**.
 D: It's a pedestrian strip in summer for people-watching and performances.

Instead of **MBAM** (p68), visit **Fonderie Darling** (p57).
 D: You're going to see art with cool locals who are probably in the art scene, too.

Instead of **Basilique Notre-Dame** (p48), try genuflecting at **Cathédrale Marie-Reine-du-Monde** (p76).
 D: It's a replica of St Peter's – the Vatican. What else do you want?

DRINKING IN PLATEAU MONT-ROYAL: BEST CAFES
MAPS P92 & P100

Dispatch Coffee: Baristas serve espresso made with award-winning beans in a concrete space overlooking the Main. 7:30am-6pm Mon-Fri, from 8am Sat & Sun

Le Club Café: Cyclists love this coffee shop with two street-facing terraces, ample seating and bike-repair services. 7:30am-6pm Mon-Fri, from 9am Sat & Sun

Café Replika: Toast photos of anthropomorphised animals before downing espresso and taking a peek at the mural outside. 8am-5pm Mon-Thu, from 9am Sat & Sun

Cass Café: Order the Quebecano (Americano made with Québécois pride), brewed with beans from local roaster Binocle. 8am-5pm Mon-Fri, from 9am Sat & Sun

A MARVELOUS MESS

The year: 1957. The town: Warwick, northeast of Montréal. A customer walks into restaurant Le Lutin Qui Rit and asks owner Fernand Lachance for cheese curds atop his fries. Lachance obliges, muttering it'll be a *'maudite poutine'* – a 'hell of a mess.' The name apparently stuck – and so did the snack. That's one of many poutine origin stories; others argue the name comes from *pouding*, French for pudding. Regardless, poutine spent the next half-century climbing the culinary ladder from rural junk food to upscale restaurant mainstay (**Au Pied de Cochon** (p97) serves theirs with foie gras). It also sizzles as a source of Québec pride, celebrated every February during Montréal's **Semaine de la Poutine** *(lapoutineweek.com)*, when restaurants compete to craft the city's finest 'mess.'

open since 1996. Get the breakfast poutine (eggs, bacon and sausage), crowned with its signature olive.

Then there's cozy **Chez Claudette** *(11am-11pm Tue-Sun, from 4pm Mon)* – a nearby Mile End institution since 1982 that gives all other *poutineries* a run for their gravy. You might leave smelling like a fry cooker, but after trying one of its 40 variations – like the smoked-meat Céline, a nod to Québec's favorite pop diva – you'll start belting the praises of Montréal's best 'mess' plate.

Thrift on Three Streets   MAPS P92 & P100

Upcycled fashion on St-Laurent, Mont-Royal and St-Denis

When it comes to secondhand clothes, the Plateau is first-rate. Dig through some of the city's best thrift shops along the neighborhood's main arteries.

Start your search on Blvd St-Laurent at **Magasin Steal Street** *(@steal.strt)*, where cowboy boots and 1970s pinup mags bookend racks of graphic tees and jeans. Next door, **Kitsch'n Swell** *(boutiquekitschnswell.com)* channels retro-rockabilly vibes with clothing for gals who aspire to Bettie Page silhouettes. Further north is **La Caravane Vintage** *(lacaravanevintage.com)*, where owner Erika Devile has been restoring vintage denim, leather and plaid since 2019.

Move on to Ave Mont-Royal for **Palmo Goods** *(palmogoods.com)* – a small, handpicked selection of quality vintage rooted in collegiate, military and Americana styles with options ranging from affordable to top dollar. One block east, **Hadio** *(@hadio514)* stocks everything from $10 tees to used Converse sneakers in its creaky wooden-floored *friperie* (French for 'thrift store'), always overflowing. For Parisian sophistication, there's **Les Folles Alliees** *(@follesalliees_mtl)*, with a selection of showstopper costumes and shiny accessories fit for an Alphonse Mucha painting. Clock the mirrors, embellished with the Czech artist's art-nouveau style.

On Rue St-Denis, take a breather inside **Cafe Camas** *(@cafe.camas)*, a coffee shop and thrift store with leather couches up front and funky sweaters in back. Continue south for Y2K fashions at **Club 777** *(club777vintage.com)*, then finish big at **Marché Floh** *(marchefloh.com)*, where three crammed floors separate punk-rock attire (basement), masc streetwear (ground floor) and femme flair (upstairs).

Try the apple-stuffed chausson aux pommes.

EATING IN PLATEAU MONT-ROYAL: BAKED GOODS & BREAKFAST   MAPS P92 & P100

Kouign Amann: Scents of butter and caramelized sugar waft around this pastry palace, specializing in its namesake Breton cake. *7am-3pm Wed-Fri, to 4:30pm Sat* $

Le Toledo: French pastries (cakes, eclairs, quiches, croissants) are made with local ingredients by an army of bakers, visible through glass windows. *7am-6pm* $

La Binerie: Sit around the zigzag counter in this old-school, two-floor, buttercream-colored spot for eggs, crepes and Québécois classics. *hours vary* $$

Bagels Etc: Grab a red vinyl booth for classic greasy-spoon specialties, including bagel sandwiches. *7:30am-4pm* $$

Parc du Portugal

Tour Little Portugal
MAP P100

Tiles, tarts and chicken

Over 50,000 people in the greater Montréal area have Portuguese roots – many connected to immigrants who settled in the Plateau throughout the 1950s and '60s. Though their descendants have largely moved elsewhere, a stretch of Blvd St-Laurent from Ave des Pins to Rue Marie-Anne – dubbed Petit Portugal – feels like a European portal, no passport needed.

Start by admiring the azulejo (glazed tile)–adorned entrance of **Parc du Portugal**, with a monument dedicated to the neighborhood's first Portuguese residents. Look south

SHOP, SOAK & SEE DOWN RUE ST-DENIS

L'Original: Local muralists sell canvases, some at affordable prices, inside this two-floor gallery with paint-splashed studios upstairs. *loriginal.org*

Espace Thomas: Beat bad-weather blues with a day pass (from $54) at this church turned fitness center. Relax around the Finnish-style spa, pool and roof deck. *espacethomas.ca*

Livart: Once a presbytery, these holy halls now house contemporary art galleries, artist studios and a colorful shop selling books, paintings and prints. *lelivart.com*

Café Mimi: Stop in this basement delicatessen with Balkan treats and meats to greet owner Lily Mlabenovich, who emigrated to Montréal from the former Yugoslavia in 1981.

Carré St-Louis: Gorgeous greystone row houses with Crayola-crayon paint jobs line this pretty square anchored by Le K, a petite seasonal cafe.

 EATING IN PLATEAU MONT-ROYAL: INTERNATIONAL LUNCH FARE MAPS P92 & P100

La Panzeria: Take a trip to Puglia inside this St-Denis cafe by ordering a deep-fried, cheese-stuffed *panzerotti* (dough pocket). *hours vary* $$

Arepera: Pews line the entrance to this restaurant praising Venezuelan arepas (meat, cheese and veggie-stuffed corn cakes). *11:30am-9pm Tue-Sat, 10am-3pm Sun* $$

Cafe Chez Téta: *Manouche* (Lebanese flatbreads) accompany cardamom coffee and chunky pistachio halva lattes. *9am-7:30pm Wed-Fri, to 5pm Sat & Sun* $

Yokato Yokabai: Warm up with a steaming bowl of pork-based *tonkotsu* ramen accompanied by handmade noodles. *hours vary* $$

SEE MAGNIFICENT MURALS

Montréal is Canada's 'Mural City,' splattered in buckets of kaleidoscopic paint. Explore streets around Blvd St-Laurent – a veritable open-air art gallery.

START	END	LENGTH
Corner Rues St-Dominique and Napoleon	53 Rue Milton	1.6km; one hour

Look up on the corner of Rues St-Dominique and Napoleon to see singer-songwriter **1 Leonard Cohen's two-story eyes** (Kevin Ledo, 2017), watching over the neighborhood where he spent the latter half of his life. En route to Blvd St-Laurent, find the photorealistic portrait of **2 Jackie Robinson** (Fluke, 2017), who played minor league baseball in Montréal before breaking the major league color barrier in 1947.

Next stop is 3860 Blvd St-Laurent, where Montréal artists Axe Lalime and Zek One preserved **3 Karma goID** (2024), the work of local graffiti legend Scaner, who passed in 2017. Notice the gold clover, Montréal's official symbol, on the right. Continue south toward 3725 Blvd St-Laurent to greet the street's gray-haired mascot, **4 a graffiti-loving grandma** (by street-art team TYXNA), then take in **5 Seven Deadly Sins** on the wall of Dirty Dogs (Buff Monster, 2016).

Veer west on Rue Prince Arthur to 3598 Rue St-Famille to see **6 Personal Topography** (Klone Yourself, 2016) – a reflection on the way bodies collect experiences like tree trunk rings – then bop one block south, where the heterochromatic eyes of **7 Sarah McDaniel** (Drew Merrit, 2017) look toward *Cash Grocery* (Matéo, 2016).

Finish at 53 Rue Milton's **8 La liberté vandalisée** (Freedom Vandalized; Escif, 2024), a modern take on Eugène Delacroix's revolutionary-themed painting **La liberté guidant le peuple** (1830) – it's layered with defiant graffiti tags.

> Murals may get added or destroyed around the neighborhood over time. To see the best up-to-date artwork, join a Spade & Palacio tour (p57).

> Visit during early June's **MURAL Festival** *(muralfestival.com)*, when international wall-scrawlers make their mark and Blvd St-Laurent turns into an arty block party.

to Rue Vallières, graced by a mural of Portuguese *fado* singer Amália Rodrigues. (Cue up her soulful *Vou Dar de Beber à Dor* for full effect.) To the north, a building-sized portrait honors Portuguese diplomat Sousa Mendes, who defied government orders by issuing thousands of visas to help Jewish refugees flee Nazi-occupied Europe in the late 1930s.

Continue south to **Les Anges Gourmets** *(7am-4pm Tue-Sat)*, where sugar-sweet *avós* (grandmas) started serving *pastel de nata* (custard tarts) nearly half a century ago. Order six minis in various flavors – they're best when sprinkled with cinnamon.

Switch to savory at **Coco Rico** *(10am-9pm Sun-Wed, to 10pm Thu-Sat)*, founded in 1970 and considered the city's first outpost for Portuguese-style rotisserie chicken, now a Montréal cuisine staple. The unfussy counter serves its birds with *piripiri* (Swahili for 'pepper pepper'), a fiery sauce inspired by Portuguese-African cooking. Get yours on a sandwich and scarf it down counterside.

Prefer fish? Grab a table at **Casa Minhota** *(10am-11pm Tue-Sat, to 10pm Sun)*, where tiled walls and *arroz de marisco* (seafood rice) bring a touch of Lisbon to the Plateau.

Dip Down Duluth

MAPS P92 & P100

A car-free promenade in summer

From mid-May to mid-October, **Ave Duluth** *(avenueduluth.ca)* closes to cars between Blvd St-Laurent and Rue St-Hubert. Join pedestrians on this 750m brick-paved stretch by stopping in boutiques, imbibing on streetside terraces and admiring murals decorating its buildings.

For shopping, flip through lit at English-language bookstore **De Stiil** *(destiil.com)*, each title handpicked by Brittany-born writer-turned-shop owner Aude Le Dubé – then step behind the turquoise facade at **Magasin Général Lambert Gratton** *(@magasingenerallambertgratton)* to find everything from vintage kitchenware and old-school candies to Montréal-inspired print art and top-shelf jams. If you've got kids in tow, stop by **La Grande Ourse** *(boutique lagrandeourse.ca)*, an old-world treasure chest that shirks iPad playtime for nontoxic toys crafted by local makers using materials like wood, wool and cotton. Finish with a sugar fix at **Les Chocolats de Chloé** *(leschocolatsdechloe.com)*,

Sister cafe Ohayo serves delicious brunch-lunch fare.

SHOP LOCAL ON AVE MONT-ROYAL

Artpop: Around 80 creatives fill this small shop with quirky souvenirs such as poutine magnets, CBC-branded socks and postcards of street art. *artpopmontreal.com*

Le Cartel: Savvy streetwear serves as canvases for muralists, photographers and graphic designers at this clothing brand and art collective. *lecartelclothing.com*

Multimags: Flip through hard-to-find design magazines in English and French, pick up the *Montréal Gazette* or pick out a coffee-table Taschen tome. *presse commercecorp.com*

Bleu & Persillé: Find your favorite Québec cheese and pair it with other local products sold on-site, such as Qantu chocolate (p88) and Miel honey test tubes. *bleuetpersille.ca*

Affiche en Tête: Pick out affordable local art, such as Sébastien Beaupré's Montréal-themed photographs and André-Anne Guay's Québec-inspired collages, at this frame-and-prints purveyor. *afficheentete.ca*

EATING PLATEAU MONT-ROYAL: DINNER

MAP P92

L'Express: Serving 'Left Bank bistro' on this side of the Atlantic since 1980, beef tartare, brisk waiters, black-and-white tiles and all. Reservations required. *11:30am-2am* **$$$**

Kitano Shokudo: Fish, Japan imported or Québec caught, stars in *chirashi* bowls at this seasonally-minded restaurant. *11:30am-1:30pm & 5:30-8:30pm Mon, Tue, Thu & Fri* **$$$**

Au Pied de Cochon: Meat in a can. Meat on poutine. Meat in dessert. Foie-gras essence in cocktails. It's fatty, decadent and quintessentially Québécois. *5-11pm Wed-Sun* **$$$**

Momo: Vegan sushi rolls? More like avant-garde flavor bombs with styles ranging from funky cheese to garden fresh, all elevating Japanese tradition. *hours vary* **$$**

CELEBRATED STAIRCASES

Dubai has skyscrapers, Brooklyn has brownstones, and Montréal has twirling outdoor staircases, an architectural element synonymous with the city. Common in neighborhoods like the Plateau, Mile End and Villeray, these features date to the mid-19th century, when a population boom led to strong housing demand. The solution? Multiplexes: residential buildings with units stacked atop one another. City laws required them to be set back from the street, so to maximize interior space while conforming to rules, new constructions got creative and placed upper-unit stairs outside. Considered dangerous eyesores, they were banned in the 1940s, but Montréalers reignited their corkscrew-step romance in the 1970s. They might be harrowing in ice storms and horrible on moving day, but when you look down a street of spiraling iron, it's easy to see why they're beloved.

a primary-colored chocolate truffle shop where each square morsel gets made in-house.

You'll find plenty of BYOW (bring your own wine) restaurants along the strip, where visitors join the boozy summer block party without breaking the bank. After finding artisanal Canadian beer, cider or wine at **Lejeune & Frères** (@lejeuneetfreres), enjoy your adult juice of choice at **Khyber Pass** *(5-11pm)* with Afghan kebabs or at **La Prunelle** *(5:30-10pm Sun-Wed, to 10:30pm Thu-Sat)* with a French-style duck breast.

There's often a free alfresco weekend concert to attend (usually between noon and 8pm), plus several weeklong festivals highlighting local gastronomy gurus such as microbrewers

There's also beer, natural wine and bistro-style food.

 DRINKING IN THE PLATEAU MONT-ROYAL: WINE & BEER — MAPS P92 & P100

Bar Vivar: Score bar seats to watch chefs prep Spanish tapas (tortillas, croquettes) while sipping old-world wines. *11:30am-9pm Wed-Fri, 10am-9pm Sat, to 4pm Sun*

Réservoir: Beers come with bite at this warmly lit, two-floor brewery boasting a summer deck overlooking Duluth. Try the sour candy-flavored Mont Royal. *hours vary*

Projet Pilote: A spiral staircase ascends to 2nd-floor tanks where the magic is made in this soaring-ceiling distillery with occasional live music. *5pm-1am*

Le Rouge-Gorge: Grab a two-top table to sample wines inside this upscale, unstuffy bar guarded by a tiny *rouge-gorge* (robin). *3pm-midnight Sun-Tue, to 1am Wed-Sat*

Ruelle verte **(green alley)**

and cheese-makers. Check the avenue's official website for programming details.

Amble Through Alleys MAP P92

The Plateau's *ruelles vertes*

Back alleys in most urban areas get a bad rap for being ugly gutters – except in Montréal, where hundreds serve as community corridors called *ruelles vertes* (green alleys). The city officially recognizes more than 450 of these linear laneways, providing front-row seats to the backstage lives of Montréalers. You might run into flower-filled gardens, weekend block parties, outdoor dinner hangs or an occasional impromptu concert. Some sport eye-catching murals. Many peek into the back windows of private triplexes. In the Plateau you can walk south to north almost entirely along these peaceful paths, many of which come alive in early summer evenings.

Find your own way (consult the map on *ruellesvertesde montreal.ca*) or take a 900m, 20-minute tour by starting

FOOD, GLORIOUS FOOD
For more foodie fun, take an affordable **international food tour** (p114) through Mile End or book a reservation at lauded Little Italy bistro **Vin Mon Lapin** (p117).

continues on p102

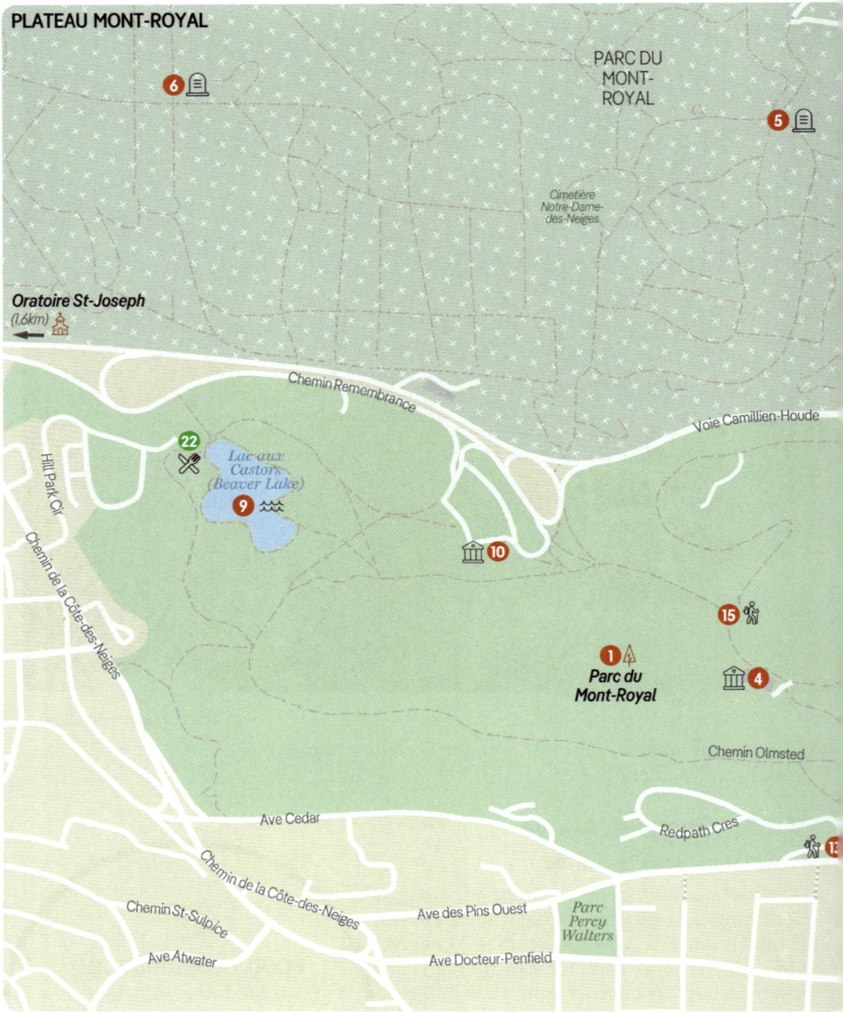

PLATEAU MONT-ROYAL

HIGHLIGHTS
1 Parc du Mont-Royal

SIGHTS
2 Avenue Duluth
3 Belvédère Camillien-Houde
see 4 Belvédère Kondiaronk
4 Chalet du Mont-Royal
5 Cimetière Mont-Royal
6 Cimetière Notre-Dame-des-Neiges
7 Croix du Mont-Royal
8 Georges-Étienne Cartier Monument
9 Lac aux Castors
10 Maison Smith
11 Parc du Portugal
12 Shaar Hashomayim Cemetery

ACTIVITIES, COURSES & TOURS
13 Chemin le Serpentine
14 Chemin Olmsted
15 Summit Loop

EATING
16 Arepera
17 Bagels Etc
18 Casa Minhota

19 Coco Rico	● **DRINKING &**
20 Les Anges Gourmets	**NIGHTLIFE**
21 Patati Patata	**24** Big in Japan
22 Pavillon du Lac	**25** Bootlegger
aux Castors	**26** Cass Café
23 Schwartz's	**27** Dispatch Coffee

28 Majestique
29 North Star Machines
30 Réservoir

● **ENTERTAINMENT**
31 Wiggle Room

● **SHOPPING**
see 34 Kitsch'n Swell
32 La Caravane Vintage
33 Lejeune & Frères
34 Magasin Steal Street

RUELLES VERTES RULE

The green glow-up of most *ruelles vertes* is a recent development. First carved out as routes to pass through farmland, they were reimagined in the 19th century to follow British-style urban design: as lanes for the transportation of coal and ice – and as backdoor entrances for servants. When cars then became ubiquitous in the 1950s, alleys were paved, and over the next few decades they became trash-packed eyesores. Mayor Jean Drapeau planted the first seeds for a *ruelle* renaissance in the 1980s by developing 58 laneways into parks, and though the project wilted in 1988, the idea didn't die. In 1995 Montréal's first *ruelle verte* blossomed in Plateau Mont-Royal. By 1997 Montréal's government had decided to start funding similar green initiatives throughout the city. These eco-quarters now span nearly every borough, turning concrete corridors into pocket-sized Edens.

Parc La Fontaine

continued from p99

west of **Carré St-Louis** (p95), a pretty square lined with stately Victorian greystones. Begin between **Avenue Laval** and **Avenue de l'Hôtel-de-Ville**, where a graffiti-strewn alley zips north to Ave des Pins. Continue to Rue Roy on regular streets, then head east to **Ruelle Gaston-Michaud**, opposite a school basketball court. Follow the alley's vine-covered fences to **Avenue Duluth** (p97), a pedestrian walkway in summer, then jog a few blocks east past restaurant **L'Gros Luxe** to **Ruelle de la Bolduc**. Skip north to end at

See sister Italian restaurant Miracolo's more-is-more decor.

DRINKING IN PLATEAU MONT-ROYAL: COCKTAILS & LIVE MUSIC MAPS P92 & P100

Bootlegger: Absinthe flows, live music blares and there's a daily 5 à 7 at this New Orleans–inspired sipping saloon. *5pm-1am Sun-Thu, to 3am Fri & Sat*

Big in Japan: A bow-tied waiter takes orders behind the labyrinthine bar, swirling like a dragon's tail in this sexy, unmarked speakeasy beside Patati Patata. *5pm-3am*

Dièse Onze: Check the calendar to see who's playing before bopping into this subfloor jazz cellar for blue notes and boulevardiers. *6pm-1am Thu-Tue*

Majestique: The decor (vintage globes, jeroboams, a mascot bunny bead) are as eclectic as the cocktail list and fish-forward tapas menu. Come for the 5 à 7 oyster special. *4pm-3am*

The Plateau's Other Park
MAP P92
Hang out in Parc La Fontaine

Stretching 40 hectares across the Plateau, **Parc La Fontaine** is the city's eastern answer to **Parc du Mont-Royal** (p104). The city converted the grounds, formerly farmland, into green space in the late 19th century and eventually added two waterfall-linked ponds – ideal for summer strolling and winter snowshoeing.

In warm months, folks flock to its green fields, perimeter bike paths and **Théâtre de Verdure** *(montreal.ca/lieux/theatre-de-verdure)*, an outdoor amphitheater with free programming from late June through August. Check the schedule for an eclectic mix of circus, music, dance, film and theater events.

When winter blows in, ice skaters take to the frozen pond and cross-country skiers glide along 5.2km of groomed trails. **Patin Patin** *(patinpatin.ca/en)* offers skate and ski rentals inside the park chalet from mid-January to early March.

The chalet doubles as the restaurant and event space for **Robin des Bois** *(robindesbois.ca)*, where you can drop in for sandwiches, soups, coffee and beer – and possibly catch a live jazz set, drag brunch or dance party, all listed on the website's calendar.

Giggle at the Wiggle Room
MAP P100
Canada's best burlesque

Lili St Cyr – the 1940s striptease starlet dubbed 'Montréal's most famous woman' by Canadian documentarian William Weintraub – would be proud. When it comes to modern burlesque, nothing beats her hometown.

Montréal's **Wiggle Room** *(wiggleroom.ca; tickets from $37)* is Canada's only full-time burlesque cabaret – and one of the few woman-owned burlesque businesses in North America. Frenchy Jones presides over the pasty party with aplomb, bringing a feminist point of view to an art form historically designed for the male gaze. In addition to feather-boa femmes, shows here may include gender-bending boylesque, drag, stand-up and live music. There's a ragtag quality to each performance – from the itty-bitty stage to the tassel-twirling talent, which runs the gamut from basic to brilliant. (If you're looking for pure polish, head elsewhere.)

Shows run Wednesday to Sunday, starting at 8pm. Arrive early to choose your seat – the bar opens at 7pm. Themed shows take place throughout the week – check the schedule to see what's on or try Wednesday night's *Voix de Ville*, a long-running variety show where audience members vote for their favorite acts.

MORE ICE RINKS WITH SKATE RENTALS

Esplanade Tranquille: The city's largest refrigerated rink covers 1500 sq meters in the heart of Downtown's Quartier des Spectacles from mid-November to early April. Video projections illuminate the ice at night.

Parc Jean-Drapeau: Follow the forested ice trail winding through this island park during winter festival Fête des Neiges (p145).

Parc du Mont-Royal: Join the blade brigade on a refrigerated rink beside Lac aux Castors (p105) or sit on a circular bench at its center as crowds glide by.

Atrium Le 1000: Take to the ice year-round at this glass-domed indoor rink, located on the ground floor of 1000 De la Gauchetière, which dominates Downtown's skyline.

Parc Maisonneuve: Ring around the icy outdoor oval in this HoMa park shadowed by the Olympic Stadium's Montréal Tower (p84).

TOP EXPERIENCE

Parc du Mont-Royal

The 'Mountain' – as locals call it – is more like a noble hill, rising 233m above sea level. But a modest label dismisses its dynamism. Inaugurated in 1876 and designed by green-space guru Frederick Law Olmsted (of Central Park fame), Parc du Mont-Royal is a 280-hectare symphony of woodlands, meadows and winding trails, majestic no matter the season.

DON'T MISS

Belvédère Kondiaronk

Chalet du Mont-Royal

Chemin Olmsted

Belvédère Camillien-Houde

Lac aux Castors

Maison Smith

Croix du Mont-Royal

Tam-Tams du Mont-Royal

An Angelic Entrance

Approach the park from Plateau du Mont-Royal to greet the bronze-winged Goddess of Liberty, soaring atop the **Sir Georges-Étienne Cartier Monument**. Cartier (1814–37), a political heavyweight who improved English–French relations in Canada, graces the sculpture's eastern side, holding a document inscribed with a message: *Avant tout, soyons Canadiens* (Above all, be Canadian).

On warm-weather Sundays, stone-faced Cartier vibrates to the beat of **Tam-Tams du Mont-Royal** – a free, informal event where people from all walks of life groove to a cacophonous chorus of tam-tams (bongo-style drums). They're joined by crafty folks selling homemade treats and trinkets,

PRACTICALITIES
- lemontroyal.qc.ca
- 6am–midnight
- free

plus the occasional group of faux sword–swinging LARPers (Live Action Role Players).

Lookout Points

This is Mont Royal's must-see: the sprawling **Chalet du Mont-Royal**, a beaux-arts lodge constructed in 1932, with steps descending to the **Belvédère Kondiaronk** – a half-moon terrace with the park's most spectacular viewpoint. Visitors jockey for railing space on sunny days, looking toward Downtown's skyscrapers, the St Lawrence River and Vermont's distant mountains in the US. Bonus points for spotting the 21-story Leonard Cohen mural towering over Rue Crescent.

The chalet is cavernous, with big bay windows, grand chandeliers and canvases by 13 Canadian artists depicting Montréal's history. Look up: 32 wood-carved, nut-clutching squirrels serve as sentinels, lurking in the rafters. You'll also find a small cafe, gift shop and information kiosk – plus clean bathrooms and seats to rest weary legs.

A Holy Monument

Roughly 190m from the Camillien-Houde lookout stands the **Croix du Mont-Royal** (Mont Royal Cross), a skyline icon. Erected in 1924, the 33m-tall construction – made of 1830 pieces and weighing 26 tons – commemorates the spot where Montréal founder Maisonneuve (p49) carried a wooden cross in 1643. According to legend, when floods threatened the fledgling colony that year, Maisonneuve prayed to the Virgin Mary to save his village, promising her a cross atop the mountain if the town was spared. Mary apparently came through.

Lac aux Castors & Maison Smith

Built in 1938 on a former beaver-dammed marsh, **Lac aux Castors** (Beaver Lake) is now the park's clover-shaped epicenter for year-round recreation.

Stop by the mid-century modern **Pavillon du Lac aux Castors** along the lake's northwestern banks to rent outdoor gear and games for all seasons. From late June to September it's all about rowboats, Mölkky (Finnish bowling) and spikeball sets. Winter sports rule from December to March: lace up ice skates to twirl around a refrigerated rink, snow tube down the lake's southern hillside, or choose between cross-country skis and snowshoes to explore the park's frosted frontier. Nonprofit park-preservation group **Les Amis de la Montagne** *(lemontroyal.qc.ca)* provides rentals. Check the website for pricing.

End your excursion with the après-sport crowd in the pavilion's top-floor **cafe** *(9am-6pm)* for snacks and drinks, served year-round.

TOP TIPS

● The park has multiple entry points, but most people choose between two: the gradual slope near the western edge of Rue Rachel in Plateau Mont-Royal or the steep climb from the northern tip of Rue Peel in Downtown.

● It's legal to imbibe at designated picnic areas in Montréal parks – but alcohol must be accompanied by a meal. To drink legally, bring your picnic to Lac aux Castors, near Maison Smith, or the grassy patch behind Chalet du Mont-Royal – and ensure your meal is more substantial than a bag of chips. These picnic spots double as places to grab food and use the restroom.

ANIMALS ALL AROUND

With 180 bird species and 20 types of mammal, you're sure to spot wildlife while wandering Mont Royal. Seeing squirrels and raccoons is par for the course, as is catching sight of birds like white-breasted nuthatches – which flit among seed-filled feeders around the Summit Loop from November to April, the best time for birding. Les Amis de la Montagne occasionally leads bird-watching walks.

Choose Your Trail

The park's many trails (*chemins* in French) weave in and out of each other with clear, easy-to-follow signage.

To see all the park's major sites, choose **Chemin Olmsted**, snaking from the Cartier monument to the Summit Loop over a moderately inclined 4.4km crescendo. It's a poem in trail form, as Olmsted intended, weaving around the mountain and passing Beaver Lake until arriving at its exclamation point – Belvédère Kondiaronk. The dirt-and-gravel trail is meticulously maintained, even with winter snow and spring mud, making it a magnificent option for cyclists, joggers and hikers all year. It's also possible to reach Kondiaronk via a shorter, steeper climb along the footpath south of Cartier's statue – look for the Quartier Général gate off Ave Duluth.

Once at Belvédère Kondiaronk, continue onto the 2.2km **Summit Loop**, lined with bird feeders popular with black-capped chickadees. Detours lead to Mont Royal's cross and Belvédère Camillien-Houde.

When entering the park from Downtown, amble up **Chemin le Serpentine** on Ave des Pins – which connects with the sweat-inducing Grand Staircase, a 1.4km athletic alternative to reach Belvédère Kondiaronk, jogging up steps from the top of Rue Peel.

SCULPTING MONT ROYAL

Despite legend, Mont Royal isn't a volcano. The dome formed 125 million years ago when magma bubbled beneath the surface but never broke free. Time sculpted what's seen today, with wind and rain its primary tools – along with glaciers, which turned the mountain into an island archipelago when they melted roughly 13,000 years ago. Mont Royal's rocky bones – a mix of gabbro (volcanic rock) and fossil-laced limestone – hold the memories of its turbulent past.

Chemin Olmsted

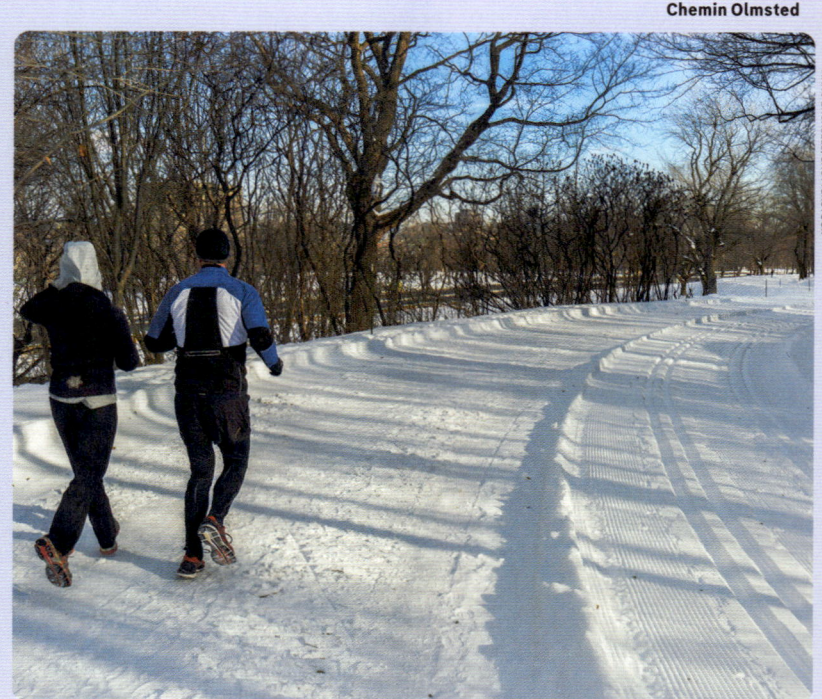

Be a Pinball Wizard

MAP P100

Hit flippers at North Star Machines

In 2015 it was technically illegal to serve alcohol and play pinball in the same Montréal establishment. When **North Star Machines** *(5pm-1am Sun, Mon, Wed & Thu, to 3am Fri & Sat)* opened that year, it did both.

The rule dates back to 1955, when Mayor Jean Drapeau started cleaning up the city's red-light reputation (p74). Pinball, associated with gambling and juvenile delinquency, had to go – so he signed a bylaw making it illegal to play the game in public spaces. Drapeau relaxed the ruling in 1977, but under one condition: pinball and pints must remain separate.

Enter the team behind North Star Machines (named after Montréal's now-defunct North Star Coin Machine Company), which lobbied for two years to change Drapeau's draconian rule.

In 2017 the pinball palace won – a boost for anyone who likes downing beers while slamming flippers (the levers used to control pinballs). These days you'll find powerhouses plugging away along the 2nd-floor barcade's 13 vintage arcade games, each decorated with themes like cinema classics (*Pulp Fiction*), big-name bands (The Beatles) and throwback video games (*Flash Gordon*). Look closely and you'll notice each machine has an addition Drapeau would've dreaded: a pint-sized cup holder.

After ordering a drink and posing for pictures in the old-school photo booth, grab some game tokens under the neon 'Currency Exchange' sign and start fiddling those flippers like an old-fashioned delinquent.

> **MORE CULTURE ON THE MAIN**
>
> Little Portugal isn't the only international clan to call Blvd St-Laurent home. Head south along the street to taste the flavors of **Chinatown** (p75), or head north for espresso-loving **Little Italy** (p117).

Explore Mountain Mausoleums

MAP P100

Cemeteries bordering Parc du Mont-Royal

Mont Royal became prime real estate for the dearly departed centuries ago. Indigenous people buried their dead here before Europeans arrived, and by the mid-19th century Montréal had relocated its burials to the holy hill once city cemeteries reached capacity. Over a million permanent residents now occupy the necropolis north of Parc du Mont-Royal, spread among a series of serene cemeteries. Pay your respects.

Roughly 900,000 souls rest north of the park's **Lac aux Castors** (p105) inside **Cimetière Notre-Dame-des-Neiges** *(cimetierenotredamedesneiges.ca; free)*, the largest cemetery in Canada. Established in 1854 as a Catholic burial ground and inspired by Paris's Père-Lachaise, the 139-hectare site is possibly the city's finest, with about 20 Montréal mayors, including Jean Drapeau, choosing it as their final resting place. Visit the website for a guide to notable sites like the **Pietà Mausoleum**, with its full-scale marble replica

---

SENSATIONAL SNOWBLOWERS

Montréal is North America's snowiest city, receiving around 191cm of it annually. Despite the pummeling by powder, roads remain surprisingly clean – but that wasn't always the case. Before the 20th century, clearing snow was a physically taxing endeavor done with horse-drawn plows and manual shovels. Smaller streets and rural roads would close during winter's harshest wallops, isolating communities and making travel nearly impossible. Things started changing in 1925, when local farmer Arthur Sicard invented the Sicard snowplow and snowblower. His contraption – modeled after a wheat thrasher – mounted on a truck, scooped up snow, then blasted it more than 25m away. Montréal bought its first snowblower in 1928, beginning its snow-removal revolution.

MONTRÉAL'S SECULAR SAINT

Legendary singer-songwriter Leonard Cohen (1934–2016) towers over the city he called home with a **nine-story mural** overlooking the Plateau (p96) and another **21-story mural** visible from Mont Royal (p105). The tributes feel apt – his music unites Montréal's many faces. Born into an affluent Jewish family from Westmount, Cohen spent his life living between two Montréals. He went to synagogue in the Catholic shadow of **Oratoire St-Joseph**, penned English poetry in a French-speaking city and left his wealthy enclave to perform in seedy downtown cafes. These dualities defined his work, riding a line between sacred (like 'Suzanne'), erotic ('Chelsea Hotel #2'), devotional and rebellious (listen to the biblical 'Story of Isaac'). Montréal may still squabble over language and religion, but Leonard Cohen is one thing most people can get behind.

of Michaelangelo's famous sculpture in Rome. Wandering the grounds sans guide is equally rewarding, as the patchwork of forests and gardens is shaded by a canopy of nearly 13,500 trees.

East of here – and north of Parc du Mont-Royal's **Maison Smith** (p105) – lies **Cimetière Mont-Royal** *(mountroyal cem.com; free)*, founded in 1852. Its terraced grounds slope over 67 hectares covered in century-old trees and granite headstones serenaded by over 100 species of bird. Some 200,000 people lie buried beneath it all, including Montréal author Mordecai Richler, brewery mogul John Molson and Anna Leonowens – the travel writer and social activist immortalized as governess Anna in musical *The King and I*. Follow the green line in the cemetery's main road, which connects the south entrance to the northern Outremont gate, where you can pick up self-guided tour MAPS inside the cemetery office.

The **Shaar Hashomayim Cemetery** *(shaarhashomayim .org/cemetery; free)*, established by Montréal's Ashkenazi Jewish community in 1863, sits just east of Cimetière Mont-Royal. Enter on Rue Foret to find folk star Leonard Cohen's grave, then cue up his haunting 'Hallelujah' – a musical poem about faith, love and loss.

TOP EXPERIENCE

Oratoire St-Joseph

Canada's tallest church – and the only Montréal building rising above Mont Royal – soars nearly 130m into the heavens alongside the city's landmark mountain. This Catholic basilica is the world's largest shrine honoring Jesus' earthly father and a major site for pilgrims, some of whom crawl up the church's 300 steps on their knees. Don't worry – you can opt to ride the escalator instead.

Brotherly Beginnings

This granite temple's story starts in 1904, when Alfred Bessette – Brother André (1845–1937) – established a 4.5m-by-5.5m wooden chapel across from Collège Notre-Dame. Brother André was said to have miraculous healing powers, and as word spread, the chapel quickly became overwhelmed by visitors. Construction on the current Italian Renaissance–inspired basilica began in 1924 but was halted after the 1929 stock market crash. It was finally completed in 1966.

Like the basilica, the brother's legacy took time to mature: he was beatified in 1983, canonized in 2010 and named the Patron Saint of Family Caregivers in Canada in 2016.

Seeing the Basilica

St Joseph's Oratory spreads across eight floors, linked by elevators, escalators and staircases. If you're short on time, zip to Level 4's prayer-hushed **Votive Chapel**, warmed by hundreds of candles leading to Brother André's black-granite tomb. After paying your respects, ride a series of escalators to Level 8 and admire the basilica interior's stark art-deco design.

There's also a Level 3 cafeteria, a Level 5 terrace with northwestern Montréal views and a Level 6 exhibit offering more information on Brother André – along with his heart, preserved as a reliquary.

TOP TIPS

● Arrive via the blue line's Côte-des-Neiges Métro station, linking to Outremont and Little Italy (p117).

● Pair your visit with a walk through the Cimetière Notre-Dame-des-Neiges, 10 minutes away on foot.

● Unless you're planning to pray, visit outside the basilica's **Mass times** *(11am & 12:30pm Sun).*

PRACTICALITIES

● saint-joseph.org/en
● 6:30am-9pm
● free

Researched by John Garry

MILE END, LITTLE ITALY & OUTREMONT

ARTY AESTHETICS AND INTERNATIONAL TASTES

Beloved bagel bakeries, upscale bistros, laid-back wine bars, independent boutiques and Montréal's largest market: arrive with an empty belly and a shopping bag.

Immigrants and artists spent the past century transforming these neighborhoods into destinations for foodies and fashionistas. Mile End, an industrial 20th-century manufacturing district and Jewish hub, was once a 'mile' from the city's northern border. Today it's the cusp of Montréal cool, its streets lined with trendy restaurants, indie stores and murals. Little Italy, on the western side of the Petite-Patrie borough, started waving red, white and green flags in the early 1900s, and the neighborhood's culinary makeup is now a mélange of European, Latin American, Asian and Middle Eastern influences. Outremont moves from mansions lining Parc du Mont-Royal, home to wealthy francophones, to brick multiplexes belonging to stylish Montréalers to a Hasidic stronghold.

TOP TIP

Residential Outremont puts a pep in its step along Ave Bernard and Ave Van Horne (between Aves McEachran and Park), both sprinkled with restaurants and shops.

Cafe, Mile End

See page 199 for places to stay in Mile End, Little Italy & Outremont.

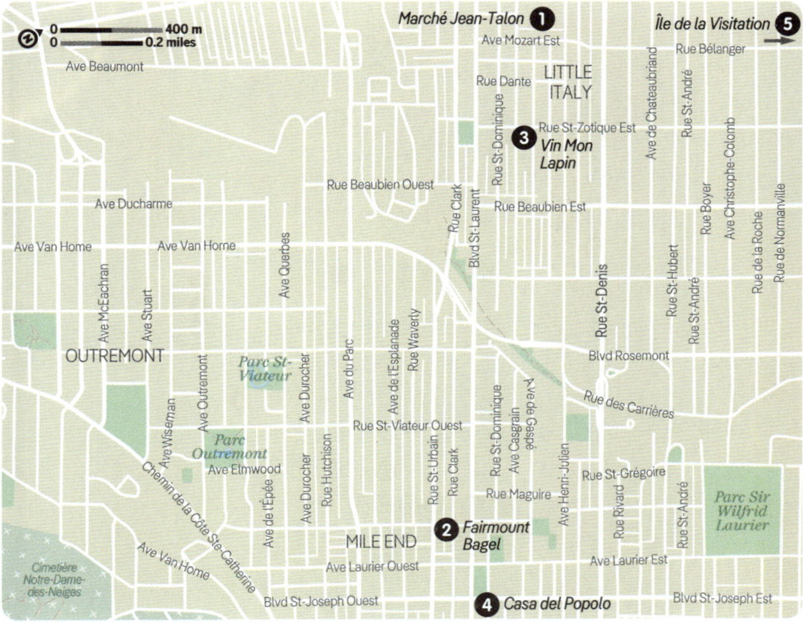

Highlights

❶ Marché Jean-Talon

Cruise Montréal's most dynamic food market for its cornucopia of Québec-produced veggies, meats, cheeses and sweets. **p118**

❷ Fairmount Bagel

Try a fresh-baked dough halo from what many see as the city's first bagel bakery – then see how St-Viateur Bagel compares. **p113**

❸ Vin Mon Lapin

Reserve a table at this intimate restaurant reimagining a French bistro with Montréal flair in the heart of Little Italy. **p117**

❹ Casa del Popolo

Groove to the tunes of Montréal's up-and-coming indie musicians before they hit the big time. **p119**

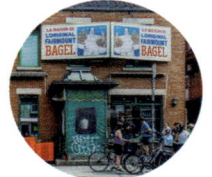

❺ Île de la Visitation

Cycle to factory ruins along an island laced with walking trails in the Rivière des Prairies. **p121**

Getting Around

Métro

Take the orange line to Laurier for Mile End. Ride the orange or blue lines to Jean-Talon for Little Italy. Outremont has its own station on the blue line.

Bus

Bus 55 runs north–south along Blvd St-Laurent through Mile End and Little Italy; bus 46 zigzags through Mile End and Outremont; bus 80 runs along Ave du Parc, linking Outremont to Downtown and beyond.

Walking

Blvd St-Laurent is the main artery connecting Mile End and Little Italy. For more dining and shopping, stroll east on Ave Fairmount and Rue St-Viateur.

FROM LEFT: CATHERINE ZIBO/SHUTTERSTOCK, ELI UNGER/SHUTTERSTOCK

Join the Bagel Debate

MAP P112

Fairmount versus St-Viateur

Forget hockey fights and political battles – Montréal's most enduring rivalry is soft and slightly sweet. Who makes the city's best fire-baked dough ring: Fairmount Bagel or St-Viateur Bagel? Try the baked bounty from both of these Mile End institutions and decide for yourself. (And whatever you do, don't even consider espousing the virtues of New York–style bagels here.) The Montréal bagel is notably lighter, sweeter and thinner than its American cousin. The rings are also boiled in a honey-and-water solution before baking in a wood-fired oven.

Begin at **Fairmount Bagel** *(24hr)* – Montréal's first bagel bakery, opened by Jewish Ukrainian immigrant Isadore Shlafman in 1919 and run by his grandchildren today. Look behind the counter of its current Fairmount Ave address – a tiny Mile End torus temple since 1949 – to see the traditional Montréal bagel-making process in action. Each dough baby gets pulled from a mound, hand-rolled, poached in honey-sweetened water and doused in a specific topping. They're then lined up on a long plank (called a *sheeba*) and baked in a wood-burning brick oven. The result? Crispy exterior, slightly chewy interior – and lines of customers trailing out the door to place orders. Get yours with sesame or poppy seeds – or possibly *tout-garni* ('all dressed', with a bold caraway-forward mix of spices) – along with a tub of cream cheese for dipping. These bagels are best fresh; dig in as soon as you step outside.

St-Viateur Bagel was founded in 1957 by Polish Holocaust survivor Myer Lewkowicz. Its opening ignited the now-famous rivalry, with an array of other bagel bakeries springing up across the city in the years to come. For the original experience, stop by **263 Rue St-Viateur** *(6am-midnight)*, which has a setup similar to Fairmount's. (Look for a sign reading 'La Maison du Bagel'.) If lines are long, skip a few blocks east to **158 St-Viateur** *(6am-10pm)*, or try one of its several other worthy locations heating up gluten goodies.

When the weather permits, take your spoils to nearby **Café Olimpico**, grab a coffee and bite into your bagel on the sizable terrace. St-Viateur also sells bagel sandwiches at **1127 Ave Mont-Royal** *(7am-8pm)* – along with bagel-themed swag such as plushies and sneakers. Order sandwich toppings ranging from savory (try the smoked-salmon 'Traditional') to sweet (go for the ricotta-fig jam 'Joe Bagel'). Wait times for inside dining can be outrageous – order yours to go. Once you're done, the debate begins.

BAGELS ACROSS BORDERS

Raegan Steinberg *(@babiesandpancakes)* – the Montréal-born restaurateur behind brunch icon Arthurs, salad bar Dirty Greens and American bistro Romies – discusses all things bagel.

I've got a controversial take on Montréal bagels: the Montréal bagel does not lend itself well to sandwich-style eating because it's small, and as you bite into it, everything explodes out. For that I prefer – dare I say it – an American-style bagel. But there's still nothing better than a warm Montréal bagel ripped into pieces and dipped into cream cheese or salted butter. I'm a salty-sweet girl, so I also love bagels topped with cheese and jam. You can grab bagels from the iconic places, but there are many delicious neighborhood spots that make them with a fire-burning oven, too.

 DRINKING IN MILE END, LITTLE ITALY & OUTREMONT: CAFES — MAP P112

Pastel Rita: No need to worry about finding coffee and dildos before getting that tattoo: this pastel-pink cafe has everything you need. *8am-6pm Mon-Fri, at 9am Sat & Sun*

Café Alphabet: Sip Greek-style iced cappuccinos, chilled milk frothed on top, while sitting on the quiet terrace where the 'Mile' ends. *7am-7pm Mon-Fri, from 8am Sat & Sun*

Café Bravo: Listen to tunes by local artists repped by Bravo Musique & Talents, located upstairs from this ground-floor cafe and record shop with 1970s aesthetics. *8:30am-6pm*

Café Éclair: Plop on a velvety green stool along the oval coffee counter for a breather while shopping along Blvd St-Laurent. *8am-5pm Mon-Sat, from 9am Sun*

WHERE TO SHOP IN MILE END

Drawn & Quarterly: Jump into a comic strip inside the bookshop of this cult Montréal publisher representing leading North American cartoonists. *drawnandquarterly.com*

Au Papier Japonais: Loraine Pritchard and Stan Phillips started selling handmade, conservation-quality paper imported from Japan in 1993, each piece pretty enough to frame. *aupapierjaponais.com*

atelier b: On-site artisans have been crafting this smart set of sustainable, colorful clothes for adults and kids – many designs gender neutral – since 2011. *atelier-b.ca*

Annex Vintage: Surrounded by vintage shops along Blvd St-Laurent, Annex stands out with its local art, quirky magazines, feminine accessories and Y2K styles. *annexvintage.com*

Boutique Unicorn: Québec and Canadian brands decorate this minimalist shop dedicated to hip threads and shoes.

Wilensky's Light Lunch

Taste the World's Flavors
A Mile End food tour

Hop across the globe on a budget-friendly cuisine crawl covering roughly 500m. For an appetizer, fly to the West Indies with Jamaican patties from **Lloydie's** *(Rue St-Viateur; 11:30am-9pm)* – bringing Caribbean flavors to Québec since the late 1980s. Due east, Israeli-owned **Falafel Yoni** *(11am-9pm)* packs its signature fried chickpea balls into fluffy pitas; eat yours outside beneath the red-and-white awning. Next stop is **Perogi Lili** *(11am-7pm Wed-Sun)* on Ave Fairmount, a counter dishing up sweet and savory homemade

The cauliflower cake, a menu mainstay, is a must.

MILE END, LITTLE ITALY & OUTREMONT: BEST BRUNCHES & BAKED GOODS

Cheskie's: Ex New Yorker Cheskie Lebowitz started selling his challah loaves, babka rolls, poppy-seed *hamantaschen* and more in 2002. *8am-11pm Sun-Thu, 7am-5pm Fri* $

Larrys: Brunch at the U-shaped bar of this hip bistro, where sun streams through St-Laurent windows onto crowds devouring breakfast sandwiches. *9am-10pm Tue-Sun* $$

Bernie Beigne: Glazed doughnuts drip in the window of this old-school sweets salon boxing up apple fritters and cinnamon ties with its funfetti variety. *10am-6pm Wed-Sun* $

Le Butterblume: A yolk-yellow door opens to this bright brunch spot with an attached bakery serving items that rotate biweekly. *11am-3pm Tue-Thu, 10am-4pm Sat & Sun* $$

Ukrainian dumplings (called *varenyky*). In winter, warm up with steamy borsch and a piping cup of nonalcoholic *glühwein* (mulled wine). Continue east on Fairmount to **Drogheria Fine** *(11am-6pm)*, a small window where servers stuff Chinese takeout containers with pillowy Italian gnocchi doused in a sweet Calabrian red sauce. Add cheese or red-pepper flakes for extra flavor, then join the crowds eating streetside with chopsticks. For local Jewish flair, grab a stool inside nearby **Wilensky's Light Lunch** *(10am-4pm Tue-Sat)*, serving the Wilensky Special (bologna, salami and mustard on a roll) since 1932. Cross the street for a return to Italy at coffee shop **Fame** *(9am-6pm)*. The menu's star is the Zabaione – an espresso drink made like the classic Italian dessert, frothy egg yolk on top.

Go Gallery Galavanting

MAP P112

Contemporary art in Mile End

Mile End's transformation from working-class enclave to creative hotbed is most evident around the neighborhood's eastern blocks, where industrial buildings have been repurposed as gallery spaces. Works on display rival collections in Montréal's contemporary art museums – except here, admission is free.

Start at **daphne** *(daphne.art)* – Montréal's first Indigenous-run art center, co-founded by four Anishnaabe and Kanien'kehá:ka creatives to promote work by artists of First Nation, Métis and Inuit descent. Check the website for opening events and artist talks.

Next, head one block east to **5455 and 5445 Ave de Gaspé**, a complex constructed in the 1970s and repurposed as a gallery hub in 2014. Begin at **Centre Clark** *(centreclark.com)*, accessible from the street, an artist-run company filling two exhibition spaces with physical and virtual works. From here, enter the complex's northern 5455 entrance and walk to the gray door labeled **Musée Romeo's**. Get ready to climb: what first appears to be a stairwell is actually an art gallery with 12 street art–style murals decorating 12 floors.

Back on ground level, stroll south through the de Gaspé building to peek into **Elektra** *(elektramontreal.ca)*, where virtual creations blink behind glass walls, and **Atelier Circulaire** *(ateliercirculaire.org)*, dedicated to printmaking – book hour-long guided tours in advance.

FROM GARMENTS TO VIDEO GAMES

Look at the modest edifice of **5505 Blvd St-Laurent** to see a century of Mile End history embedded in brick. Constructed in 1904 for clothes manufacturer Peck & Co, the building became the epicenter of Montréal's booming garment industry and a magnet for Jewish immigrants, who toiled in the neighborhood's factories. By the 1930s, Peck & Co had shuttered, Jewish families had moved west and immigrants from Portugal, Greece and Italy had moved in. The garment industry gasped its last breath in the 1980s and artists filled the void – followed by French gaming titan **Ubisoft Entertainment**, which colonized the Peck building in the 1990s. Like Peck & Co, Ubisoft became a magnet for workers, who reshaped the neighborhood in their image. Some cry gentrification; others see history repeating itself.

DRINKING IN MILE END, LITTLE ITALY & OUTREMONT: CAFES AROUND LA PETITE-PATRIE

MAP P116

Ferlucci: The 1990s are alive inside this teeny coffee shop with addictive amaretto cookies and a Blockbuster-worthy VHS collection. *7am-9pm Mon-Fri, from 8am Sat & Sun*

Zab Café: 'Wake the funk up,' as a sign demands inside this local roaster's Little Italy cafe with hardcore brew sure to give you the 'coffee sweats.' *8am-5pm*

Café Pista: Laptops in back, baristas in front and summer cold brews enjoyed outside in the shadow of a church. *7:30-6pm Mon-Fri, from 8am Sat & Sun*

Café des Habitudes: Lose your shoes before entering this socks-preferred vegan coffee shop with events like open-mic nights and knitting workshops. *hours vary*

MILE END, LITTLE ITALY & OUTREMONT

THE GUIDE

- ● **SIGHTS**
  1. Notre-Dame-de-la-Défense
  2. Rue de Castelnau
- ● **ACTIVITIES**
  3. Les Faiseurs
- ● **EATING**
  4. Alati-Caserta
  5. Café San Gennaro
  6. Caffè Italia
  7. Le Kahéra
  8. Marci
  9. Montréal Plaza
  10. Pichai
  11. Vin Mon Lapin
- ● **DRINKING & NIGHTLIFE**
  12. Brasserie Harricana
  13. Café des Habitudes
  14. Café Pista
  15. Ferlucci
  16. Mamie
  17. Mellön
  18. Polari
  19. Ratafia
  20. Zab Café
- ● **ENTERTAINMENT**
  21. ItalFest
- ● **SHOPPING**
  22. État de Choc
  23. Ex-Voto
  24. Le Palais Bulles
  25. Marché Jean-Talon
  26. Oui Manon
  27. Pony

Between June and September, end at **Champ des Possibilities** (Field of Possibilities; popmontreal.com/about/marche-des-possibles), a park at Ave de Gaspé's northern edge that's home to seasonal events and art displays. No matter the month, stop by to see its defining feature: Ola Volo's 2019 mural, *Walla Volo* – a whimsical interpretation of a Mile End artist, her blonde hair unfurling across five stories.

Give Little Italy a Big Hello

MAP P116

Food, frescoes and festivals

The early-20th-century *nonnas* who originally settled this neighborhood would be pleased. Little Italy, or Petite-Italie (stretching between Blvd St-Laurent and Rue St-Denis from Rue St-Zotique to Rue Jean-Talon), remains Montréal's biggest bastion for Europe's brash boot, serving some of the strongest espressos, yummiest pizza and sweetest cannolis in town. Inhale them all in an hour or two.

Start with espresso shots at **Caffè Italia** *(hours vary)*, pulled from an Italian-made La Spaziale machine. This no-frills counter cafe, established in 1956, retains its 20th-century charm: expect macchiato-loving septuagenarians – the opposite of Mile End's laptop-toting cold-brew connoisseurs.

For those with southern Italian tastes, make a quick trip east to the **Café San Gennaro** *(7:30am-7:30pm Tue-Sat, to 4pm Mon, 8am-6pm Sun)*. This family-owned spot serves thick, square slices of Sicilian pizza and *bombolones* (cream-filled doughnuts), which are stuffed with flavors like pistachio and Nutella.

A few blocks northeast, save room for some sweet ricotta-piped cannolis from **Alati-Caserta** *(closed Mon)*, its crispy pastry shells kissed with a secret ingredient – a dash of red wine. It's been open since 1968 and makes everything from scratch in-house.

Repent for your sweet-eating sins across the street at **Notre-Dame-de-la-Défense** *(Church of the Madonna della Difesa; diocesemontreal.org)*, a Catholic church known for frescoes designed by Italy-born Guido Nincheri – the same artist behind Château Dufresne – who has been nicknamed 'the Michelangelo of Montréal'. Look up at the temple's angelic dome, painted in the 1930s, for a controversial surprise: former Italian dictator Benito Mussolini riding a horse.

Visiting in August? Don't miss **ItalFest** *(italfestmtl.ca)*, a 10-day festival when Little Italy celebrates its cultural heritage along Blvd St-Laurent.

Ask for the house-made hot pepper sauce.

WHAT MAKES THE MAIN

Daniel Bromberg *(@themain)* is a tour guide, writer and co-founder of city-centric magazine *The Main*.

The Main (nickname for Blvd St-Laurent) was nicknamed 'the corridor of immigrants', because – historically speaking – it welcomed people from all over the world as they arrived in Montréal and settled along this street. For a long time it was an invisible dividing line between the Anglo Protestant communities and the French Catholic communities. Nowadays, it's more of a bridge where people come together – and a great place for cultural and culinary exploration. I love stretches that go through the gates of **Chinatown** (p75), **Little Portugal** (p95) and Mile End – but I think there's something extra special about entering Little Italy's archway.

EATING IN MILE END, LITTLE ITALY & OUTREMONT: RESERVATIONS REQUIRED

MAPS P112 & P116

Vin Mon Lapin: At this classic French bistro with a modern Montréal makeover, wines are funky, veggies are fresh and plates are shareable. *5-10:30pm Tue-Sat* **$$$**

Montréal Plaza: Between its innovative, internationally influenced tasting menu and grandiose desserts, this fine diner flabbergasts. *5-11pm Tue-Sat* **$$$**

Marci: Melted candle mounds light up Petite-Patrie's cool crowd, sharing pizzas and wine in this bilevel, cork-ceilinged bar-resto. *5-10:30pm Tue-Sat, to 9:30pm Sun* **$$**

Alma: Travel from Mexico's coast to its mountains with a multicourse tasting menu featuring heirloom corn from Tlaxcala pressed into tortillas. *6-11pm Tue-Sat* **$$$**

WHERE TO SHOP IN LITTLE ITALY

PONY: Don't be fooled by the stuffed toys. Montréal artist Gabrielle Laïla Tittley's clothing shop is an adult *Pee-wee's Playhouse*, huggable phallus plushies included. *ponymtl.com*

État de Choc: It's like the Apple store for international chocolate, each bar laid out with reverence in a minimalist space. *etatdechoc.com*

Ex-Voto: Trendy fits, cutesy home decor and gifts: you're bound to fall in love with something inside this shop dedicated to local brands and sustainable makers. *exvoto.ca*

Oui Manon: Searching for a Montréal-themed mug? Come to this shop with local artist designs, most items printed on-site. *ouimanon.com*

Le Palais Bulles: This bright, bold store bubbles with things like cat clocks, pretzel sculptures and fashionable kids clothes sure to make children the envy of the playground. *lepalaisbulles.ca*

Fill up at Montréal's Biggest Market

MAP P116

Gourmand adventure at Marché Jean-Talon

Marché Jean-Talon *(marchespublics-mtl.com)*, open since 1933, is Little Italy's big belly, packed with pyramids of farm-fresh produce, meats and glazed pastries. In peak summer season, roughly 300 vendors ply their wares beneath four open-air hangars, and in winter the market erects walls to keep shoppers cozy. Come hungry and get ready to graze: this is Montréal's largest food market, with something for all appetites.

For a taste of quintessential Québec, start with raw-milk goat cheese produced by **Fromagerie de la Ferme**, followed by ma-

EATING IN MILE END, LITTLE ITALY & OUTREMONT: INTERNATIONAL FLAVORS

MAP P116

Pichai: Petite-Patrie gourmands pack into this hip restaurant for shareable plates with revelatory takes on Southeast Asian cuisine. *5-10:30pm Wed-Mon* **$$**

Le Super Qualité: Order huge dosas, crispy *puri* (shells with yogurt filling) and more spicy South Indian street-food favorites. *5-9:30pm Sun-Wed, to 10pm Thu-Sat* **$$**

Le Kahéra: Nefertiti's profile adorns this Egyptian street food *dépanneur*. Try the Ful – a slightly spicy pita sandwich. *9am-7pm Mon-Fri, from 10am Sat & Sun* **$**

Damas: Whether opting for tasting menu or meze plates, don't overdo it on the made-to-order pita: you'll want room for more Syrian specialties. *5:30-10:30pm* **$$$**

Marché Jean-Talon

ple syrup–coated salmon at neighboring **Délices de la Mer**. Forgo tropical sorbet at **Havre-aux-Glaces** and keep it Canadian by opting for cranberry. Try cured ham aged for six months in the Eastern Townships at **Les Cochons tout Ronds** and grab a bag of dried mushrooms scented like maple candies (called Candy Caps) at **Les Chapeaux Gourmand**. For dessert? Stop by **La Fournée des Sucreries de l'érables** for nuns farts ('*pets de soeurs*', a Québec specialty) – each bite an angelic sugar bomb, despite the name. You'll also find plenty of souvenirs (spices, candies) and foods ideal for picnic spreads throughout the market. Visit its website for a map.

CONCERTS, CLASSES, ARTS & ACROBATS

TOHU: Methane from a former landfill powers this complex in St-Michel with circus shows, architecture tours and a public park. *tohu.ca*

Casa del Popolo: The 'House of the People' hosts experimental performances and indie bands (including Arcade Fire before they got big) in four intimate halls with nightly performances. *casadelpopolo.com*

Les Faiseurs: Paint handmade ceramics crafted by Montréal artists ($38 to $54) in this Little Italy coffee shop. French speakers can sign up for introductory pottery classes ($75). *lesfaiseurs.ca*

Galerie Noël Guyomarc'h: Thanks to owner Noël's keen eye, each piece of jewelry displayed in this shop-showroom seems fit for a museum. *galerie noelguyomarch.com*

Théâtre Rialto: This 1920s beaux-arts movie theater acts as a performing arts venue promoting up-and-coming local talent. *theatrerialto.ca*

 DRINKING IN MILE END, LITTLE ITALY & OUTREMONT: WINE ———— MAP P116

Vinvinvin: This terrifically tiled wine den sorts sips by categories like 'mineral', 'punk' and '*pas tranquille*' (unruly). *3pm-1am Sun-Thu, to 3am Fri & Sat*

Polari: Romance is in the air at this unpretentious natural wine bar with self-branded condoms and a sign reading 'Stay queer, stay rebel.' *4-11pm*

Mamie: The name means 'Grandmother,' hence the grannycore aesthetic, plus homemade food so good you'll beg for seconds. *noon-1am Thu-Sun, from 4pm Mon & Wed*

Ratafia: Tipplers, teetotalers and sweet tooths love the extensive list of wines, nonalcoholic drinks and desserts. *5-11pm Tue-Thu, to midnight Fri & Sat*

JUMP INTO JEWISH HISTORY

The Plateau and Mile End served as epicenters for Montréal's Jewish community, tens of thousands strong, from 1900 to 1950. Their mark remains.

START	END	LENGTH
Bagg Street Shul	Musée du Montréal Juif	3km; two hours

Begin outside ❶ **Bagg Street Shul**, Québec's oldest surviving synagogue, built as a two-family complex in 1889 and converted into a house of worship in 1921. From here, skip through ❷ **Parc Jeanne-Mance**, once known as Fletcher's Field – a 20th-century gathering place for Jewish families. The **Croix du Mont-Royal** (1924) overlooks – a constant reminder of the city's Catholic dominance.

Head west on Ave Mont-Royal past the mural of Hymie and Freda Sckolnick, who sold meals to Jewish garment workers from luncheonette ❸ **Beauty's**, family run since 1942. Save your appetite for Jewish-French fusion bakery ❹ **Hof Kelsten** and order the croissant *tout-garni* (everything-seasoned croissant) with cream cheese. Munch while moving into Mile End along Ave Laurier, past a ❺ **mural of Montréal author Mordecai Richler**, who wrote vividly about the local Jewish experience in this neighborhood, then stroll north along Ave Esplanada to ❻ **Collége Français**. Peer above the Pavilion Montaigne on Ave Fairmount to spot the grand, ghostly arch of a defunct synagogue, B'Nai Jacob Synagogue (1918), still visible above the new structure.

Jog back toward Blvd St-Laurent, passing Jewish food favorites ❼ **Fairmount Bagel** (p113) and ❽ **Wilensky's Light Lunch** (p115) en route to the ❾ **Musée du Montréal Juif** (*museemontrealjuif.ca*), where rotating exhibitions on Jewish culture and events like Yiddish language classes keep Mile End's heritage alive.

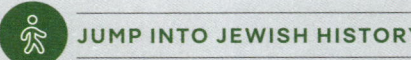

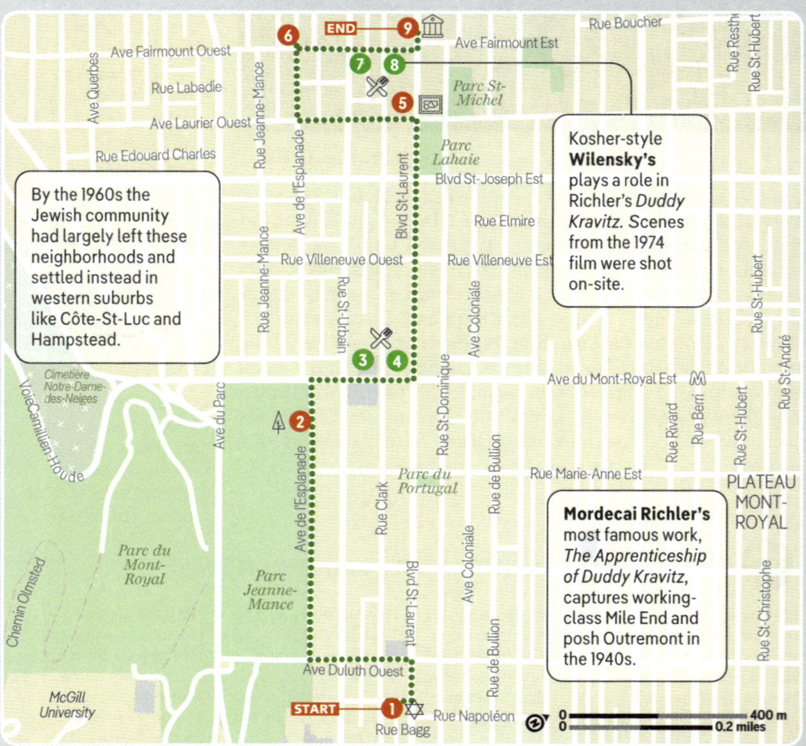

By the 1960s the Jewish community had largely left these neighborhoods and settled instead in western suburbs like Côte-St-Luc and Hampstead.

Kosher-style **Wilensky's** plays a role in Richler's *Duddy Kravitz*. Scenes from the 1974 film were shot on-site.

Mordecai Richler's most famous work, *The Apprenticeship of Duddy Kravitz*, captures working-class Mile End and posh Outremont in the 1940s.

See Montréal's Other River

MAPS P112 & P116

Cycle to Île de la Visitation

When it comes to rivers, Montréal's St Lawrence gets all the love – but cycle to the city's north side and you'll fall for the Rivière des Prairies – or as the Kanien'kehá:ka (Mohawk) aptly named it, the 'River Behind the Island.' Along this urban waterway sits the **Parc-nature de l'Île-de-la-Visitation** – a 34-hectare green space rooted around industrial ruins from the Moulins du Sault-au-Récollet site. Between 1726 and 1960, Montréal manufacturers exploited the hydraulic potential of the Sault-au-Récollet rapids to produce wheat, wool, nails and paper. In 1998 the city transformed the abandoned Moulins building into a people's park where locals trade urban speed for life in the slow lane.

Start by grabbing a bike at Plateau rental and tour company **Fitz Montréal** (*fitzmontreal.com; 10am-5pm/24hr $45/55*), near Parc La Fontaine. The journey north is simple: follow Rue Rachel west to St-Denis, where a protected cycling lane speeds north to Little Italy. If you're feeling famished, stop for coffee at **Zab Café** (p115), located along St-Denis, or take a quick detour to **Marché Jean-Talon** (p118) to grab snacks for later.

From here, continue east on Rue Bélanger, then north on Ave Christopher Colomb until it dead-ends at Blvd Gouin. Follow Blvd Gouin east to the park, past Victorian houses with grassy lawns – a sure sign urban Montréal is miles away.

Upon reaching the park, lock your bike on racks beside **Le Festigoût Cafe** (*10am-5pm Sat & Sun*), selling soup and sandwiches from a stone house with a scenic terrace overlooking the rapids. Tree-trimmed footpaths stretch along Montréal's mainland and Île de la Visitation, the bridge-connected island where turtles sun themselves on the rocks and mallards paddle along the river.

Cycling here covers roughly 11km one way. Budget three hours and enjoy a waterfront picnic. Plan your trip between snow-free spring and autumn.

> ### HOLY LINGUISTICS
>
> Tabernacle. Chalice. Sacrament. Host. In English these words might evoke images of seemingly harmless holy choirs and communion cups, but yell them in Québécois French and you're spewing some of the province's dirtiest profanities. These are *sacres* – Québec's signature swear words, which take aim at one of its defining institutions. While the naughtiest English-language swear words often focus on terms and taboos related to sex and bodily functions, Québec's foulest language stems from its Catholic upbringing. Linguistic historians say this sacred swearing developed in the 19th century as a rebellious pushback against religious control. As Catholic fervor fades, some wonder how long these slurs will survive. For now, however, they're part of local parlance – so think twice before yelling '*Tabarnak!*' in a crowd. It may not go down well.

 DRINKING IN MILE END, LITTLE ITALY & OUTREMONT: BREWERIES & COCKTAIL BARS

MAPS P112 & P116

Brasserie Harricana: Sip suds in the sophisticated dining room of this Mile-Ex brewery, hopped up since 2014. Try the smoky-umami Wild Marchen. *hours vary*

Mellön: Like a good head on your beer? Order a Czech-style *snyt* (two parts beer, three parts foam) or *mliko* (Czech for 'milk', a foam-filled glass). *hours vary*

Brasserie Dieu du Ciel: A fixture of Québec's craft-beer scene since 1998, this heavenly hops star shows no signs of fading. *hours vary*

Bar Henrietta: The din of diners and clinking cocktails bounces off white bricks in this softly lit bar bringing 'Portuguese tavern' to trendy Mile End. *4pm-3am*

Researched by Robert Isenberg

LACHINE CANAL, LITTLE BURGUNDY & THE SOUTHWEST

MONTRÉAL'S TENACIOUS SUBURBS

On the other side of the tracks – and along a legendary canal – Southwest Montréal offers a new wave of entertainment and outdoor diversions.

Southwest Montréal is Downtown's funky sibling, a mishmash of suburbs where waves of immigrants have gained a footing for the past two centuries. Blocks of squat apartment buildings extend in all directions, iconic curved staircases leading to their upper storeys, while vintage storefronts line old commercial strips. Yet a lot has changed as well: where industry once pulsed and canals were once dug, a new generation of young professionals has birthed energetic hot spots. Branch away from the glamour of Old Montréal to find thriving neighborhoods full of global restaurants, buzzing art centers and elaborate cycling networks. Meanwhile, a long chain of riverside parks offers wide-open views of the St Lawrence.

TOP TIP

Meals, museums and nightlife await you at any time of year in Southwest Montreal, but doors fly open and activities abound in the warmer months.

Lachine Canal

See page 196 for places to stay.

Highlights

❶ Lachine Canal
Flanked by parks and paths, this 200-year-old waterway cuts through 14km of Southwest Montréal. **p136**

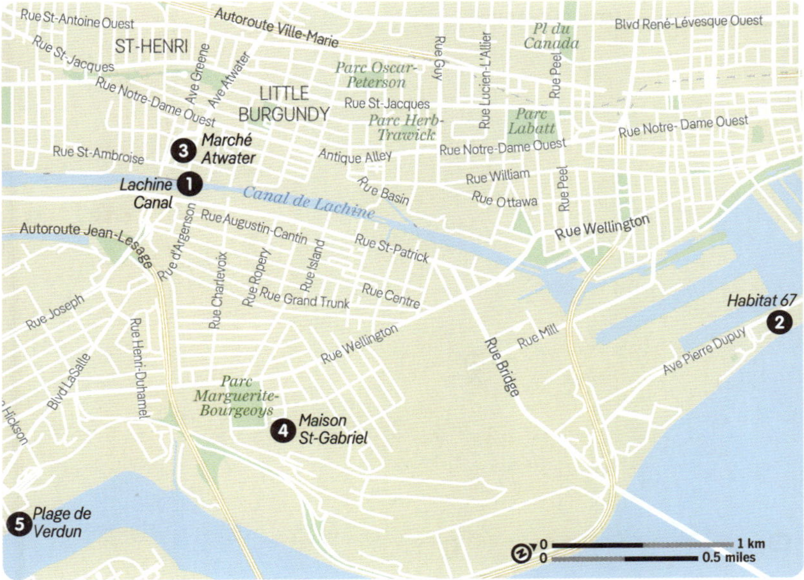

❷ Habitat 67
The brutalist housing development in the Cité du Havre is one of the most striking designs in the world. **p126**

❸ Marché Atwater
Farmers and florists congregate at this art-deco masterpiece to sell their goods at charming stalls. **p127**

❹ Maison St-Gabriel
History comes alive at this storied compound, where costumed interpreters lead you through 17th-century living quarters. **p138**

❺ Plage de Verdun
Convenient and beautifully designed, Verdun beach is a place for swimming and sunbathing in the middle of the city. **p132**

Getting Around

Walking & Biking
Southwest Montréal is easy to get around on foot or by bike. The terrain is mostly flat, with pleasant sidewalks, well-marked bike lanes and lots of city parks.

Taxi
You may want to skip the endless residential blocks between attractions. Rideshare apps are popular, as is the all-electric fleet of Montréal-based Téo Taxi *(teo.taxi/en)*.

Métro
The orange line will take you to Little Burgundy, with stops at Lionel-Groulx and Place-Saint-Henri stations, then Vendôme in Westmount. The green line goes to Verdun and additional points west.

LACHINE CANAL, LITTLE BURGUNDY & THE SOUTHWEST

● SIGHTS
1. Arsenal Art Contemporain
2. Canal de Lachine
3. Centre Canadien d'Architecture
4. Dare-Dare
5. Dorchester-Clarke Park
6. Musée des Ondes Emile Berliner
7. Musée et Centre d'Art de Montréal
8. Théâtre Beanfield
9. Westmount Athletic Grounds

● ACTIVITIES
10. Bruno Vélo

● SLEEPING
11. Gite L'Imprévu

● EATING
12. Bagels Le Trou
13. Brasseur de Montreal
14. Café Gentile
15. El Gordo Montréal
16. Foiegwa
17. Le Tequila Bar
18. Le Vin Papillon
19. Marché Bagels on Greene
20. Memento! Brasserie Artisenal
21. Oorja
22. Satay Brothers

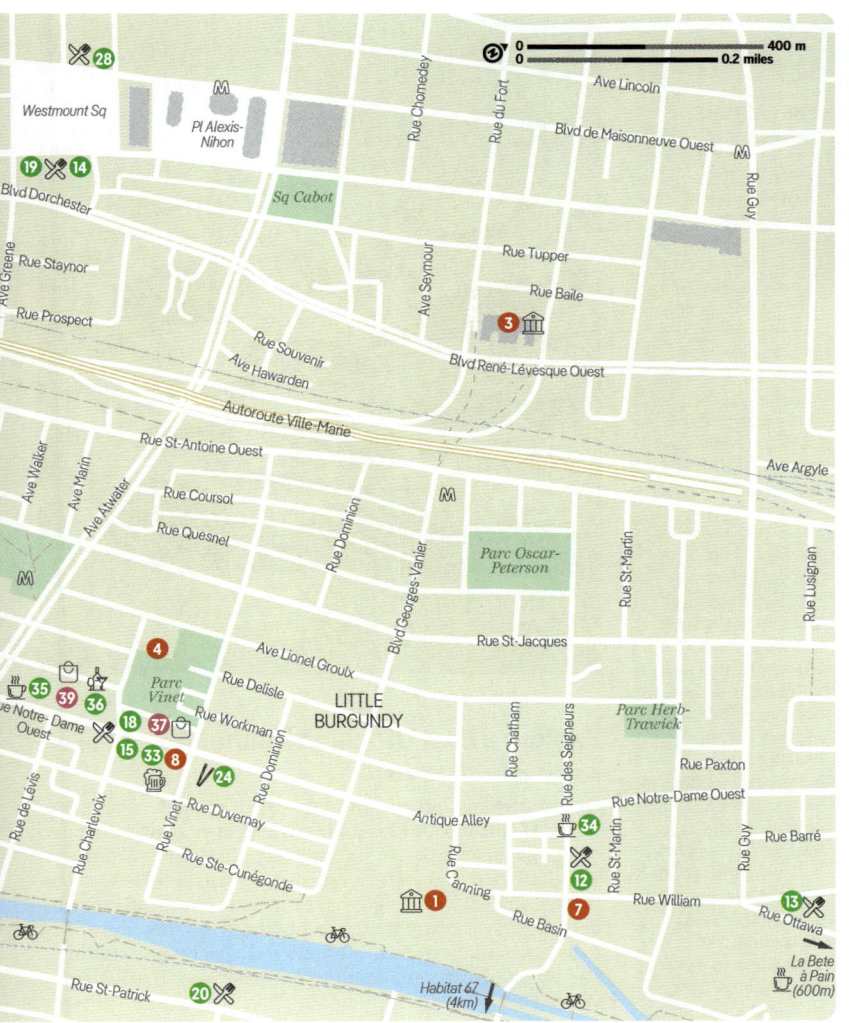

23 Schnitzel & Cie par Bagel St-Henri	28 Taverne Sur Le Square
24 Shushu Thai Bar À Nouille + Riz	29 TRAN Cantine
25 Siboire Notre-Dame	● **DRINKING & NIGHTLIFE**
26 Tacos Frida	30 BarBara
27 Tacos Tin Tan	31 Bistro Bar Notre-Dame
	32 Bon Délire

see 40 Brulerie Aux Quatre Vents
33 Burgundy Lion
34 Café Lali
35 Café Lili & Oli
36 La Drinkerie Ste-Cunégonde

● **SHOPPING**
37 Aesop Petite Bourgogne
38 Crossover Comics
39 Librairie Livresse
40 Marché Atwater
41 Notre-Dame-du-Vintage

THE LACHINE CANAL

Where there's a will, there's a way. Early colonists wanted to bypass the Lachine Rapids way back in the 17th century, but funding and engineering problems stymied every attempt to dig a new canal. The unusual name (French for 'China') refers to that era's dream of a Northwest Passage, which would connect Europe to East Asia. The 14km channel was finally opened in 1825, and its seven locks allowed barges to ease past the St Lawrence without the need for grueling portages. The canal triggered massive industrialization in Southwest Montréal, and immigrants poured into the city over the next century. With the construction of the St Lawrence Seaway, the **Canal de Lachine** was closed to commercial shipping in 1970 and gradually transformed into a linear park.

Habitat 67

Explore a Lost Utopia at Habitat 67 — MAP P124

A masterpiece in concrete

One of the most provocative structures in modern architecture is **Habitat 67**, a LEGO-like arrangement of prefabricated blocks at the edge of the St Lawrence River. Fans admire its imaginative design, which anticipated a hyper-dense urban future. Critics find it ugly and strange, saying it's disconnected in every way from the Montréal skyline. Love it or hate it, Habitat remains a functional apartment building – and an enduring monument to Expo 67, Montréal's historic World Fair.

Israel-born architect Moshe Safdie dreamed up Habitat for his college thesis; the concept combined box-like suburban homes with the stackability of high-rises. Angular concrete was popular at the time, and other Expo 67 pavilions shared

EATING IN LITTLE BURGUNDY: OUTSTANDING BRASSERIES — MAP P124

Foiegwa: Enjoy brunch, seafood and cocktails at this vintage diner with caricatures. *5:30-11pm Mon-Thu, 10am-2pm & 5:30-11pm Fri, 9:30am-3pm & 6-11pm Sat & Sun* **$$$**

Brasseur de Montréal: The setting's raw and industrial, but the service, burgers and craft beers are down-home. *11:30am-11pm Wed-Sat, 10:30am-10pm Sun* **$$**

Memento! Brasserie Artisenal: Amid arty mismatched seating and otherworldly lamps, fill up on craft beers and poutine. *3-11pm Mon-Wed, to 1am Thu, to 3am Fri, noon-11pm Sat* **$$**

Siboire Notre-Dame: Brick walls and bicycle-frame lamps enhance this craft-beer enclave with poké and veggie burgers. *noon-midnight Sun-Wed, to 1am Thu-Sat* **$$**

this brutalist aesthetic, but Habitat is also known for its leafy landscaping and cozy units; in fact, nearly all of its apartments are owned and occupied as condos. In 2023 one apartment garnered attention for its $1.4 million asking price.

Habitat hosts regular 90-minute **tours** *($58)* from May to November, in both French and English. Guides lead visitors through mostly outdoor spaces, revealing the design's subtleties and surprises, as well as the inside of one residence. The property stands on Cité du Havre, an industrialized peninsula that faces Old Montréal. Tours must be reserved in advance; if you're driving, turn off busy Ave Pierre Dupuy and announce yourself at a secure gate. Ironically, this egalitarian utopia was once impossible to reach by public transit; today the 777 bus drops you off at its threshold. Cité du Havre also has its own bike path, which runs the length of the peninsula and connects seamlessly with the Lachine Canal route.

EXPO 67
The Habitat complex wasn't the only permanent structure to result from Expo 67. Learn more about how this massive fair (p144) transformed Montréal's skyline – and the city's reputation for creative vision.

Shop Through the Ages in Marché Atwater

MAP P124

A lively art-deco market

For nearly a century **Marché Atwater** *(marchespublics-mtl.com)* has been the commercial keystone of Southwest Montréal, drawing customers to this long brick building with its 45m-high clock tower. The hangar-sized structure has always served as a food market, and even the advent of modern supermarkets hasn't sullied its importance; if anything, Marché Atwater is more beloved than ever, and residents and tourists alike come here to walk the corridors and browse displays of produce and flowers.

Part of its appeal is the vintage aesthetic: Québec architect Ludger Lemieux designed the Marché in a distinctive art-deco style, with sharp vertical lines and bold rectangular windows. The market opened to the public in 1933 and has operated continuously ever since. It's easy to find at a bend in the eponymous Ave Atwater. Greengrocers occupy the contained outer hall in winter, and their stalls extend into the parking lot in warmer months, along with an outdoor food court. Deeper in, specialty shops sell quality meats, cheeses and jarred goods. For sit-down meals, savor an espresso and pastry from **Brulerie aux Quatre Vents** *(Four Winds Roastery; brulerie4vents.com)*, grab a grilled sandwich at **Boulangerie Première Moisson** *(First Harvest Bakery; premieremoisson.com)* or score some remixed Japanese favorites – such as 'sushi tacos' – at **Sushi Shop** *(gingersushi.com)*.

The Marché is also convenient for urban visitors as it's located at the edge of Little Burgundy, a stone's throw from the Lachine Canal and one block from a scenic pedestrian bridge. There are many parking spaces in adjacent lots and streets, but strolling here on foot or coming by bike and picking out artisanal ingredients feels downright Parisian. You're

COOLEST STOPS ON RUE NOTRE-DAME

Dare-Dare: Founded in 1985, this artist-run cooperative partly operates inside a shipping container. Hosts a wide range of cultural events and regularly changes its church-style sign. *dare-dare.org/en*

Notre-Dame-du-Vintage: This eclectic antiques shop lures customers with curios displayed in the front window and an art-nouveau sign.

Librairie Livresse: This bright little space is everything you want in an indie bookstore. Titles in French and English, plus regular author events.

Crossover Comics: Browse shelves packed with comic books, graphic novels and manga, plus a stockpile of adventure games. *shopcrossovercomics.ca*

Aesop Petite Bourgogne: The bold, minimalist design is reason enough to visit this luxe beauty supply store. *aesop.com/us*

NO CRYSTAL STAIR

Montréal is the birthplace of many significant fiction writers, and a standout is Mairuth Sarsfield, author of the 1997 bestseller *No Crystal Stair*. This powerful novel takes place in Little Burgundy in the 1940s and centers on the Willow family. The story reveals the challenges and adaptations of a single Black mother and her three daughters, who are newcomers in a diverse neighborhood. Sarsfield painstakingly recreates streets and historical landmarks as they appeared in the mid-20th century, giving the prose a photorealistic authority. Taking its name from the Langston Hughes poem 'Mother to Son,' *No Crystal Stair* has become a classic of Canadian literature – and an illuminating take on Montréal's working-class past.

also just a few steps away from Rue Notre Dame and its wealth of attractions.

Sample Southwest Montréal's Art Scene

MAPS P124 & P130

Art for all tastes

Tucked into a cluster of new apartment buildings, **Arsenal Art Contemporain** *(mtl.org; $15)* is a voluminous show space for international artists, and it's little wonder that the sprawling property spent much of the 1800s as a shipyard. The 1st floor is dedicated to a high-ceilinged gallery that presents rotating exhibitions of paintings and sculpture. The 2nd floor is usually reserved for Canadian artists and solo shows, and a vast multipurpose space holds intermittent public events. The gallery is closed Monday and Tuesday.

The building was fully renovated in 2012, and today it contains more than 7400 sq meters of floor space. The private institution was founded by art collectors Pierre and Anne-Marie Trahan, who have since established satellite Arsenal locations in Toronto and New York.

Just two blocks down William St is the **Musée et Centre d'Art de Montréal** *(Montréal Art Center & Museum; montrealartcenter.com; $9.20)*, a dynamic community hub for artists of all media and skill levels. This facility is also housed in a renovated historic building, dating back to 1879, and the rooms are divided into classrooms, rentable studios and a theater for screenings and live performances.

Visitors to the museum are welcome to take a self-guided audio tour in English or French and browse its eclectic collection. The rooms have boldly painted walls and an old-school directoire style – it makes you think of a chateau designed by Wes Anderson. Feeling inspired? Join a live drawing class on Thursdays, or even submit finished works to the Global Art League Competition.

Finally, there's **Espace Verre** *(Glass Space; espaceverre.qc.ca)*, a busy workshop in the very middle of Montréal's port area. Once a fire department, the handsome stone building has been repurposed for glass artisans: thousands of unique pieces are heated and shaped in Espace Verre's studio space, thanks to an arsenal of special ovens, torches and tools. The facility hosts one-hour **tours** *($12)*, demonstrating use of the equipment and the creative process behind glass art. Tours are a little tricky to arrange, as you'll have to make reser-

EATING ON RUE NOTRE DAME: BEST ASIAN

MAP P124

| **Satay Brothers:** Legendary spot serving flavorful Singaporean street food. Its fair prices appeal to a younger crowd. *11am-11pm Thu-Sun, 5-11pm Mon-Wed* **$** | **Oorja:** Come here to sample spicy treats from around the world in a stately, earth-toned dining room. *5-10pm Tue-Sun* **$$** | **TRAN Cantine:** Ordering from the counter is fast and easy, but the *pho* and *bahn mi* are worth sitting down for and savoring. *11:30am-8pm Mon-Sat* **$$** | **Shushu Thai Bar À Nouille + Riz:** Authentic noodles, soups and dumplings in an low-key setting. *11am-2:30pm & 4:30-9:30pm Mon-Wed, 11am-2:30pm & 4:30-10pm Thu & Fri, 3-10pm Sat & Sun* **$$** |

Musée et Centre d'Art de Montréal

vations five working days in advance and at least six people must sign up. Inquire at *info@espaceverre.qc.ca*.

Whether or not you can secure a tour, the building also houses an elegant shop, **Vitrine** *(9am-5pm Mon-Fri)*, where you can browse a boundless variety of glass vessels and sculptures. Espace Verre stands in the middle of a lonely row of warehouses and industrial buildings, but it's not as remote as it feels; the Lachine bike path takes you within a block of the studio; alternatively, you can hop a cab in Little Burgundy and arrive here in under 10 minutes.

SPRINGTIME ON THE LACHINE CANAL

Thomas Yeo is beverage director at the Barroco Group and co-owner at Bon Délire.

My favourite part of the Southwest is the stretch of the Lachine Canal that runs through St-Henri. Montréal is (in)famous for being a winter city, and that means when spring finally comes we really embrace it. The canal in particular blooms to life the moment the snow melts. I love to grab some great cheese and a bottle of wine at the **Atwater market** (p127), then stroll west along the water. You can see the city skyline without being a part of it and check out great local businesses along the way. From beer gardens to boat rentals to bakeries, there's something for everyone. When your wine runs out, pop into my bar, **Bon Délire** (p139), for a cocktail to wrap up a perfect St-Henri day!

🍽 EATING ON RUE NOTRE DAME: BEST LATIN — MAP P124

Le Tequila Bar: Spend a whole night sipping margaritas among trippy murals; also try the tacos and wraps. *5pm-3am Thu-Sat, 5pm-midnight Tue & Wed* $$

Tacos Tin Tan: Named after a Mexican film star, Tin Tan boasts an incredible Mexican-inspired ramen bowl. *11:30am-11pm Thu-Sat, to 10pm Sun-Wed* $

El Gordo Montréal: Follow up a flavor-blasting entrée with a gourmet churro at this hip spot. *5-10pm Mon-Wed, 11:30am-11pm Thu & Fri, 10am-11pm Sat, 10am-10pm Sun* $$

Tacos Frida: Enjoy simple tacos in endless arrangements amid Lucha Libre–themed decor. *11am-10pm Tue-Sat, 11am-9pm Sun* $$

LACHINE CANAL, LITTLE BURGUNDY & THE SOUTHWEST

VERDUN

SIGHTS
1. Auditorium de Verdun
2. Dock 5160 Cultural Centre
3. Plage de Verdun

EATING
4. BENELUX Brasserie Artisanale
5. Chez Boss & Fils
6. Janine Café
7. Les Street Monkeys
8. Restaurant Verdun Beach
9. Rita

DRINKING & NIGHTLIFE
10. Bar Social Verdun
11. Church Street Pub
12. Le Trèfle

Appreciate Design at the Centre Canadien d'Architecture

MAP P124

A building that honors buildings

The **Centre Canadien d'Architecture** *(CCA; $10)* began as a jaw-dropping Second Empire–style mansion in the middle of Montréal, with high windows, decorative turrets and elaborate finials. Originally built in 1876, it later housed the Lords Shaughnessy and has since been known as the Shaughnessy House.

In the 1970s Montréal architect Phyllis Lambert purchased the Shaughnessy House to prevent developers from tearing it down. She then spearheaded the CCA, which incorporated the mansion into a larger complex. Today the two structures are interconnected, and they make up a massive public museum dedicated to architecture.

The museum hosts rotating exhibits on diverse architectural themes, from individual projects to provocative concepts such as climate change and gentrification. Each exhibit uses a wide range of multimedia – like archival photographs, video projections and even extracted building materials – to illustrate architectural movements and ideas. Not surprisingly, the museum itself consists of spacious halls that demonstrate different materials and design techniques. Students and professional architects will appreciate these displays the most, but the museum is open to all; exhibits are easy to digest, and bilingual plaques are written for the general public. The CCA also maintains a world-class library with 12,000 volumes; many are the kind of image-rich coffee-table books that could occupy enthusiasts for hours.

The museum is closed Monday and Tuesday. Admission is free on Thursday, when the CCA is open until 9pm. Free audio guides are available upon request.

See a New Band at the Théâtre Beanfield

MAP P124

A musician's favorite stage

The front of the **Théâtre Beanfield** *(theatrebeanfield.ca)* looks like an old movie house, and a vertical marquee still reads 'Corona,' from the building's early days as a silent-film cinema. First opened in 1912, this auditorium has seen a lot of changes over the past century, including several different owners, waves of renovation and at least one serious fire. Just as Little Burgundy has experienced a renaissance in recent

OTHER THEATERS OF SOUTHWEST MONTREAL

Théâtre Paradoxe: This beautiful church was repurposed in 2014 as a performance venue, mostly for concerts. *en.theatre paradoxe.com*

Théâtre Desjardins: Live bands, French-language stand-up comics and drag shows – they all take place under the Théâtre Desjardins roof. *theatredes jardins.com/en*

Club La Roue: Known as 'The Wheel Club' in English, this rollicking little music venue hosts respected bands, up-and-comers and 'Hillbilly Night' open-mics. *wheelclub ndg.com*

Centre Culturel et Communautaire Henri-Lemieux: This 40-year-old cultural center has a 115-seat theater with music and dance recitals. *ccchl.ca*

Segal Centre for Performing Arts: This massive facility contains one full-sized theater, a studio and a cinema. Rotating programs in English and French. *segalcentre.org/en*

 DRINKING IN VERDUN: BEST PUBS

MAP P130

Le Trèfle: 'The Clover' is a classic neighborhood Irish pub – with a French twist. The menu's full of guilty pleasures. *4pm-3am Mon-Fri, 10am-3am Sat & Sun*

Church Street Pub: The lively main bar and well-used pool table are great in winter; summer means a bustling rooftop terrace. *noon-1am*

BENELUX Brasserie Artisanale: Housed in a vintage bank, this brewpub churns out tasty IPAs and giant pretzels. *noon-3am Fri-Sun, 3pm-3am Mon-Thu*

Bar Social Verdun: Stop by for the outdoor seating, impressive central bar, live music and wide selection of microbrews. *3pm-3am Wed-Sat, to 1am Sun & Tue*

VAGUE À GUY

One of the most magical spots in Montréal is **Vague à Guy**, a consistent rise of water that mimics perfect ocean breakers. Translating literally as 'Guy's Wave,' Vague à Guy is better known in English as 'The Eternal Wave.' River surfing has gained popularity across Canada, and many surfers prefer turning their boards against the current to enjoy a kind of treadmill effect. Part of Vague à Guy's draw is its proximity: the adjacent park is free to visit, and the swells rise right near the shore. The river is still intense, and signs warn about the dangers of putting in your board. Still, Vague à Guy remains popular with both newbies and pros, and warm days can bring crowds.

years, so too has this theater's stage. Today the Théâtre Beanfield is named after a Canadian internet provider and is among the most beloved concert venues in Montréal.

The elegant proscenium has hosted big-name bands including Soul Asylum and Mogwai, but Théâtre Beanfield is also the perfect place for fans to catch tours of lesser-known musicians or just hear fresh sounds. The theater has the rounded interior and decorative ceilings of an opera house and seats 925. While it's most frequented by young audiophiles, the space also hosts stand-up comedians, art exhibitions and private rentals.

You can find a schedule and buy tickets on the theater's website or at *evenko.ca*. To buy advance tickets in person, visit the **Centre Bell** (p65) in Downtown Montréal.

Play in the Sun Around Plage de Verdun MAP P130

A sandy stretch for all

The riverside borough of Verdun has come a long way in recent years, and a slew of trendy pubs and restaurants have helped transform this working-class district of 70,000 residents into a coveted place to live. The only thing that was missing: a place to sunbathe in the warmer months. So the city built itself a crescent of sand, and the **Plage de Verdun** opened to the public in 2019.

The beach is modest, with a maximum capacity of about 400 people, but it's a great place to wade into the river on a scorching day. The waters are shallow and practically still in this part of the river, but many will appreciate the presence of lifeguards in summer. The surrounding **Parc Arthur Thierren** is expertly landscaped, with greenery and accessible walkways; there's a paid parking lot just steps away, and the entrance is about a 10-minute walk from De L'Église Métro station, the main Verdun stop on the green line from Downtown Montréal.

Parc Arthur Thierren is thick with diversions as well, including an outdoor swimming pool, a skate park, a baseball diamond and a dog run. On arrival the first thing you'll see is the massive **Auditorium de Verdun**; this complex contains two ice rinks, one in an historic brick building from 1939 and the other in a glittering glass addition, the Scotty Bowman Arena, opened in 2021. Each hosts a variety of junior-league sporting events. The area can get pretty quiet in winter, but you'll still spot a few runners and cross-country skiers braving the bluffs.

EATING IN VERDUN: HIP SPOTS MAP P130

Janine Café: This paragon of brunch spots has high-backed chairs, an autumnal color palette and gorgeous platters. *9am-3pm* $$

Rita: The only thing that could rival the pizzas at this trendy Italian place is the maple-infused 'Unemployed Pudding.' *5-10pm Mon-Sat* $$

Les Street Monkeys: These elaborate bowls interweave Cambodian cuisine with fusion creativity. *5:30-11pm Thu-Sat, 5:30-10pm Sun, Mon & Wed* $$$

Chez Boss & Fils: Blended East Asian and Mediterranean flavors make for a perfect Verdun date night. *6-11pm Thu-Sat, to 10pm Wed* $$$

THE SOUTHWEST

- **SIGHTS**
- 1 Parc Ignace Bourget
- 2 Parc King George
- 3 Parc Westmount
- 4 Théâtre Paradoxe

- **EATING**
- 5 Entre Deux
- 6 Park Restaurant
- 7 R.E.A.L Bagels
- 8 Ristorante Donato

- **ENTERTAINMENT**
- 9 Cub La Roue

BIKE RENTALS IN SOUTHWEST MONTRÉAL

Bixi (bixi.com): Rideshare company with stations across the city, including in Southwest Montréal. The app is free; monthly membership is $23, then 18 cents per minute for both manual and e-bikes. Scan QR codes with your phone to ride.

Ma Bicyclette (mabicyclette.ca): Located right on the Lachine Canal bike trail; rents out a wide range of models, from hybrids to tandems to electric cargo bikes. Learn popular routes from its staff, then get revved up at the on-site cafe.

Bruno Vélo (brunovelo.com): Bruno Vélo turns urban cycling into an all-year adventure thanks to its fleet of fat-tire bikes and organized group events, including area gravel rides.

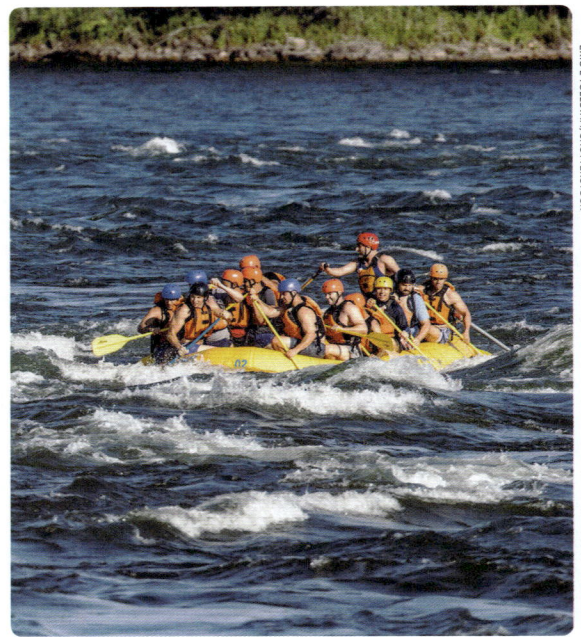

Lachine Rapids

Conquer the Current on the St Lawrence MAP P130
Buoyant fun on the river

The St Lawrence River is a mighty beast, and the segment that flows along Southwest Montréal is among its most dynamic parts. When you stand on Verdun's riverfront parks and gaze at the opposite shore, you're looking across about 7km of fast-moving water. The river bottlenecks around Goat Island, resulting in the Lachine Rapids, a frothing channel that has taunted boaters for centuries. The powerful rush of water over rocks is audible from the shore, and you can easily see why the Lachine Canal was built: to bypass this treacherous waterway.

Nowadays there are lots of ways to embrace these thrilling currents. The rapids are ideal for whitewater rafting, and the river's width and diverse surfaces make for an inclusive environment: rookies can paddle in calmer riffles, while seasoned

ALONG THE ST LAWRENCE WATERFRONT

Maison Nivard-de-St-Dizier: Now a museum and cultural center, this stone cottage has stood here since 1710. Browse artifacts, join an archaeological simulation or catch a concert in the grounds.

Verdun Municipal Greenhouses: The Grand Potager (Big Vegetable Garden) houses active greenhouses and hosts workshops and occasional tours. *grandpotager.ca/en*

Verdun Dancing Terrace: This concrete-floored space is open during the warmer months, hosting popular swing, zumba and yoga classes.

Dock 5160 Cultural Centre: An art gallery, a theater, live concerts and so much more can be found here.

Quenneville Bay Observation Deck: Find serenity on a wooden platform overlooking a scenic St Lawrence inlet.

 EATING IN SOUTHWEST MONTRÉAL: BEST BAGELS MAPS P124 & P133

R.E.A.L Bagels: Watch these freshly baked rings come out of the brick oven and get stacked on a metal trough. *5am-9pm* $

Marché Bagels on Greene: Bagels, plus coffees, torpedo-roll sandwiches and a rainbow of pasta salads. *7am-5pm Mon-Sat, 8am-4pm Sun* $

Bagels Le Trou: Joyful murals and heaping bagel sandwiches make this a favorite morning destination in Griffintown. *7:30am-6pm Mon-Fri, 8am-4pm Sat & Sun* $

Schnitzel & Cie par Bagel St-Henri: Tiny, German-owned bakery in Westmount serving bagels, pastries and massive ham slices. *8:30am-2pm Wed-Sat, 9am-2pm Sun* $

rafters can brave Class IV froth when the water level is high. **Rafting Montréal** *(raftingmontreal.com; adults/teens/kids $61/51/44)* caters to different group sizes and skill levels, providing guides, instruction and all necessary equipment. The popular company is headquartered at the western end of the Canal de l'Aqueduc and operates between May and October. The minimum age is six.

If you're confident with a paddle, go it alone with **Espace Navi** *(espacenavi.ca; 1/2hr $28/42)*, a kayak-rental service with a major branch on the shores of Verdun. You can reserve your own craft, then shove off into the river's current. Espace Navi organizes a wide range of group excursions and tours as well; many of these take place in the colder months, when you'll have to wear layers – chunks of ice will float past your bow. The most dramatic outing takes place during fireworks displays over the water.

All Ears at the Musée des Ondes   MAP P124
Audio through the ages

Don't turn that dial! Everywhere you look in the **Musée des Ondes Emile Berliner** *(Wave Museum, MOEB; moeb.ca; $15)* you'll see vintage radios, restored turntables and vinyl records from across the past century. Founded by a group of hobbyists in 1992 – the so-called Club des Vieilles Lampes (Old Lamp Club) – the museum pays tribute to audio technology from household stereos to radio communication with astronauts. Antique gadgets are displayed on the museum's shelves, and docents are more than happy to explain every button and antenna. The museum is named after Emile Berliner (1851–1929), the German-American innovator who invented the gramophone record.

Part of the museum's cachet is its symbolic setting: the RCA Building. Media giant RCA helped pioneer recorded music in the early 20th century, and the brand's distinctive logo is still stamped on new CDs, tablets and monitors, though the company has long dissolved. In its heyday, then-RCA Victor maintained an important branch in Montréal, where music for vinyl records was recorded and mixed. Fittingly, the MOEB founders secured a space inside the old headquarters, and here it has remained since its first public exhibit in 1994.

The museum is open Wednesday to Friday; advance online reservations are strongly recommended. It's a 10-minute walk from the Place Saint-Henri Métro station on the orange line.

MUSICIANS OF MONTRÉAL

Céline Dion: Vocal superstar Dion grew up in the Montréal suburb of Charlemagne. Her first album hit No 1 in Québec when she was only 12 years old.

Leonard Cohen: Poet-musician Cohen grew up in a Jewish household in Westmount. Covers of his 'Hallelujah' remain a Canadian karaoke favorite.

Arcade Fire: The indie-rock supergroup was founded back in 2001 in Montréal and has wowed critics and fans with its vulnerable power ballads.

Patrick Watson: Both quiet and contemplative, Watson is the quintessential singer-songwriter. He grew up in Hudson, west of Montréal.

Godspeed You! Black Emperor: Founded in Montréal, Godspeed has become famous for its long-building crescendos, epic instrumentals and intense political messaging.

 DRINKING IN SOUTHWEST MONTRÉAL: BEST WINE SPOTS   MAPS P124, P130 & P133

| **BarBara:** Rich entrées and a warm setting make BarBara a Little Burgundy favorite. It has a substantial collection of orange wines. *8am-1am* | **Le Vin Papillon:** Standout dishes include melt-in-your-mouth ham topped with cheese. Staff can help guide you through the well-curated wine list. *5-10:30pm Tue-Sat* | **Entre Deux:** This cozy Westmount eatery can make the simplest dish sophisticated, and the wine list pairs seamlessly. *5-11pm Mon-Sat* | **Restaurant Verdun Beach:** A friendly little bistro with a selective list of wines by the glass, plus beers and cocktails. *5:30-10pm Tue-Thu, to 11pm Fri & Sat* |

CYCLING TOUR: THE LACHINE CANAL

Grab a *bicyclette* and pedal this historic canal trail through the heart of Southwest Montréal.

START	END	LENGTH
CNR Wellington Bridge	Pointe René Lévesque	12.5km; 45 minutes

Start at the ❶ **CNR Wellington Bridge**, a defunct swing bridge that permanently stands on its own island. Head south to ❷ **Hangar 1825**, an industrial building covered in wraparound abstract murals by French artist Ankhone. Keep riding to the ❸ **Atwater Footbridge**, just a block from **Marché Atwater** (p127).

Cross the canal and grab an espresso at ❹ **Café Ma Bicyclette** (cafemabicyclette.ca). Once you arrive at the ❺ **Côte-Saint-Paul Lock** you can admire the engineering from a second footbridge. Back on the north side of the canal, arrive at the ❻ **Gauron-LaFleur Station**; keep an eye out for its two green-painted former drawbridges.

On the south side again, reach the ❼ **Lachine Canal Lock**, which used to admit boats into the channel. To fully appreciate the history of this canal, visit the ❽ **Musée de Lachine**. This 17th-century stone building is being renovated, but sculptures are displayed outside. Explore ❾ **Parc René Lévesque**, a skinny peninsula of trees and picnic tables.

Push down your kickstand at ❿ **Pointe René Lévesque**, a perfect spot for sunsets on the river.

The **St-Gabriel Lock** is one of five historic locks that once eased watercraft through the canal.

In summer, check out the **Fur Trade at Lachine National Historic Site**, a stone building with thoughtful exhibits.

Night riders will spot the **Farine Five Roses Sign**, an iconic neon sign erected in the 1940s.

Experience Jewish History at the Musée de L'Holocauste

MAP P133

A sobering pilgrimage

In the great constellation of the Jewish diaspora, Montréal is a very bright star: immigrants arrived from Great Britain as early as the 18th century, and the city is now home to a robust Jewish community. But as the **Musée de l'Holocauste** *(museeholocauste.ca; adult/student $12/10)* notes in its chilling permanent exhibition, Canada joined the US in rejecting Jewish refugees in the 1930s, condemning untold numbers to Nazi death camps.

Housed in a nondescript office building across from Mackenzie King Park, the museum takes visitors on a self-guided loop through two floors. Using an exhaustive collection of period artifacts, the exhibits methodically chronicle the rise of fascism in Europe and the disintegration of Jewish life. This is Canada's only museum dedicated to the Holocaust, and the photographs, pamphlets and newspaper clippings don't pull any punches. The tour ends with an eternal flame – and the names of communities erased by the genocide.

On the 1st floor, a bright Jewish Public Library has a wide range of popular titles, as well as a selection of antique volumes and sacred texts. The complex also hosts regular events and guest speakers.

The museum is closed Saturday.

Sled, Swim & Throw Discs at Parc Ignace Bourget

MAP P133

Get outside, in countless ways

From the top of the Pente à Neige (Snow Slope) you can see the towers of Downtown Montréal on the horizon, along with snow-blanketed lawns and ranks of trees all around. This impressive hill in the middle of **Parc Ignace Bourget** transforms into a snow-tubing track in winter, with several expertly laid runs. The community initiative is known as **Ma Côte Newman** *(centremgrpigeon.com/macotenewman)*, and anyone can fly down the slopes on inflatable doughnuts (for free) between December and March. Make sure to reserve a session online before heading out.

Of all the parks in Southwest Montréal, Parc Ignace Bourget is the most action-packed. The diamond-shaped property has activities for every season: a playground, baseball field,

JEWISH MONTRÉAL

Waves of Jewish immigrants arrived in Montréal over the past two-plus centuries, and today the city is a major hub in the diaspora, with 82,000 residents tracing their lines back to Sephardic and Ashkenazi ancestors. Southwest Montreal was a popular destination for many first-generation families, and their influence on local neighborhoods is still visible; Montréal has about a dozen synagogues and a slew of kosher restaurants, many scattered around the **Musée de l'Holocauste**. This community may not be obvious to passing tourists, but one contribution stands out: the Montréal bagel. Thinner and crispier than their New York cousins, these bagels are traditionally boiled in honey water, giving them a distinct sweetness.

 EATING IN WESTMOUNT: BEST FINE DINING — MAPS P124 & P133

| **Park Restaurant:** Some of the finest Japanese dishes in Montréal. *11:30am-2:30pm & 5-11pm Fri & Sat, 11:30am-2:30pm & 5:30-10pm Tue-Thu* $$$ | **Taverne Sur Le Square:** Fine-dining classics, plus gourmet burgers and mac and cheese. *5-10:30pm Tue-Sat* $$$ | **Café Gentile:** Serving Sicilian classics since 1959, from racks of lamb to veal scallopini. *8am-3pm Mon, to 10pm Tue-Thu, to 11pm Fri, 9:30am-11pm Sat, 10am-3:30pm Sun* $$$ | **Ristorante Donato:** Inventive Italian fish, pizza and pasta in a suave dining room. *11:30am-2pm & 5-10pm Sun, Tue & Wed, 5-10pm Mon, 5-11pm Sat, 11:30am-2:30pm & 5-11pm Thu & Fri* $$$ |

PARKS OF WESTMOUNT

Parc Westmount: The district's flagship green space dates back to the turn of the century and includes water features, greenhouses and the regal stone Victoria Community Center.

Parc King George: This sloped park has a swimming pool for the summer, a sledding hill for the winter and tennis courts for just about any season.

Westmount City Hall: This small park in the middle of the neighborhood is most notable for its permanent Pavillon de Boulingrin (lawn bowling field), which local players take very seriously.

Westmount Athletic Grounds: The football field, playground and running track here are all free and open to the public.

Dorchester-Clarke Park: Catercornered to the athletic grounds is this picnic-ready urban park.

Maison St-Gabriel

basketball court and swimming pool, plus permanent ping-pong tables made of concrete and a 12-basket disc golf course. The park is open every day and free for public use. The closest Métro station is Angrignon, the last stop on the green line; walk 1km north on Rue Irwin.

Time Travel at Maison St-Gabriel   MAP P130

A vivid colonial recreation

Sleeping in a stone room. Boiling lard into soup. Turning vats of pig blood into sausage. Life wasn't easy in the late 17th century, and it's hard to even imagine what the average French colonist experienced during those early years, but a visit to the **Maison St-Gabriel** *(maisonsaintgabriel.ca; adult/child $15/5)* brings these daily routines to life, thanks to costumed interpreters and multiple floors of period furniture and hand tools.

Maison St-Gabriel is no ordinary farm; it was established by a wealthy Frenchwoman, Marguerite Bourgeoys (1620–1700), who was deeply devoted to the Catholic Church. Bourgeoys took it upon herself to found the Congregation de Notre Dame, a religious colony near Ville-Marie, the village that would become Montréal. Laborers arrived in the form of young colonists, both male migrants from France and the **Filles du Roi**

 DRINKING IN SOUTHWEST MONTRÉAL: BEST CAFES   MAP P124

La Bete à Pain: Espresso drinks, fresh pastries and magnificent cakes are on offer at this Griffintown hub. *7am-7pm Mon-Fri, 8am-6pm Sat & Sun* **$$**

Café Lili & Oli: Stop in for freshly baked muffins and one of the best iced coffees in town. *7am-10pm Mon-Thu, to 8pm Fri, 8am-8pm Sat & Sun* **$$**

Brulerie Aux Quatre Vents: Tucked into Marché Atwater, the 'Four Winds' cafe has served magical espressos since 1997. *8am-6pm Mon-Fri, to 5pm Sat & Sun* **$$**

Café Lali: Painting-infused Lali executes brilliant foam art. *7am-4pm Mon-Fri, 9am-4pm Sat & Sun* **$$**

(King's Daughters; p50), poor teenagers without marriage prospects. The property also served as a school; although the sexes were separated, the women weren't expected to live a fully cloistered life.

As the guides tell it, only one major tragedy befell the colony: in 1693 the house caught fire and partly burned down. Otherwise, life was fairly consistent; workers raised crops and livestock, churned their own butter and spun their own wool. Each floor of the museum contains a treasure trove of artifacts that illustrate the highly manual existence of the house's residents. The river has since been diverted, so it no longer runs past the property, and suburban houses surround the museum on all sides, but the lovingly preserved Maison feels like a time machine.

Reserve tours in English or French on the website. The museum is closed Monday and Tuesday.

Climb the Secret Stairs of Westmount MAP P124
Slopes, steps and sights

A large residential neighborhood west of Downtown Montréal, Westmount is known mostly for its pleasant parks and attractive houses. Rising over these rooftops is Mont Royal, the 764m-high hogback hill that puts the 'mount' in Westmount.

Westmount doesn't have the nightlife or dining scene of its youthful neighbors, but this is a prime spot to simply walk around, thanks to even sidewalks, quiet side streets and increasingly impressive views as you venture upward. As a rule, the houses get grander the higher you go, with an eclectic mix of stately old domiciles and modernist new builds.

The secret, though, is the small network of stairways that abruptly climb the slopes. Wedged between lawns and privacy fences are public concrete steps that provide shortcuts from one avenue to the next. Just east of Westmount Park, one staircase starts on Victoria Ave and rises to Grosvenor Ave, then to Roslyn Ave. Another, mysteriously identified as 'Boom boom chuck Steps' on Google Maps, starts at the intersection of the Boulevard and Renfrew Ave, then ascends in three stages to Summit Cres. There are two shorter staircases as well: one extends between Rue Cedar Crescent and Lansdowne Ave, the other between the dead-end on Aberdeen Ave and Sunnyside Ave.

The logical endpoint for all this hiking is the **Oratoire St-Joseph**, which offers a spectacular view of the southwestern skyline and is worth its own visit. Be sure to bring snacks and water, as you won't find anywhere to resupply up here.

LITTLE BURGUNDY'S BLACK HISTORY

At the intersection of Rues des Seigneurs and St-Jacques, search for Gene Pendon's 88-sq-meter mural of Montréal jazz pianist Oscar Peterson. It's a striking reminder of the Black community that once ruled these streets. In the 1880s railway jobs enticed Black men from the US and Caribbean to settle in the train track–adjacent St-Antoine neighborhood, laying the groundwork for an English-speaking enclave with its own churches, clubs and community centers. By the 1920s it had been dubbed the 'Harlem of the North' – a jazz hot spot where Louis Armstrong played and Peterson honed his craft. In the 1960s Mayor Jean Drapeau's 'urban renewal' plans razed much of the district and displaced residents; the area was then rebranded as Little Burgundy. The name stuck, and the Black community never fully recovered.

 DRINKING IN LITTLE BURGUNDY: FUN PUBS ———— MAP P124

Bon Délire: Roughly translating as 'good crazy,' Bon Délire is a cavernous dive bar with welcoming service and a superlative beer selection. *5pm-3am*

Bistro Bar Notre-Dame: No need to dress up; shoot pool with locals and try one of the video poker games. *11am-3am*

La Drinkerie Ste-Cunégonde: This place is as playful and welcoming as its name. Serves craft beers, cocktails and lobster rolls. *4pm-3am*

Burgundy Lion: Enjoy upmarket pub food and quality beers in a greenhouse-like setting next to Théâtre Beanfield. *11:30am-3am Mon-Fri, 10am-3am Sat, 10am-1am Sun*

Researched by John Garry

PARC JEAN-DRAPEAU

ALFRESCO FESTIVALS AND FRESH AIR

Stroll along the river, dance under summer's sun, ice-skate through winter and explore outdoor artwork: it's a year-round island escape.

Exhale around Parc Jean-Drapeau's 268 hectares, spread across two islands lapped by the St Lawrence River. Île Ste-Hélène, closest to Old Montréal, evolved over centuries from Indigenous land to colonial estate to military outpost to 19th-century public park. The city expanded its boundaries and built Île Notre-Dame for Expo 67 – an ambitious world's fair with futuristic flair – using river-dredged sediment and excavation debris from Montréal's Métro system. Memories of the exposition live on in public art and repurposed pavilions, like the striking Casino de Montréal, while festivals throughout the year plant the park firmly in contemporary times. Budget half a day to explore or plan a trip around a high-octane event.

TOP TIP

For food, there's the Ste-Hélène Bistro-Terrasse near the Métro and Le Montréal in the casino, but you're better off bringing a lunch or snacks.

Parc Jean-Drapeau

See page 196 for places to stay.

☆ Highlights

❶ Biosphère
Admire the webbed steel skeleton of this Expo 67 dome turned into a natural science museum. **p142**

❷ Piknic Électronik
Dance outdoors as the sun sets over the St Lawrence River on summer Sundays. **p143**

❸ Plage Jean-Doré
Kayak the perimeter of an artificial lake, then jump into its waters for a refreshing finish. **p145**

❹ Bike Link
Pedal from Parc Jean-Drapeau to the southern shores hugging Montréal's white-capped river. **p147**

◀ ❺ L'International des Feux Loto-Québec
Take in the fireworks lighting the sky from amusement park La Ronde. **p146**

 Getting Around

Métro
Take the yellow line from Berri-UQAM to Jean-Drapeau, which drops visitors by the Biosphère near the heart of Île Ste-Hélène.

Bus
Bus 777 stops at Jean-Drapeau and the casino. In summer, bus 767 stops at Jean-Drapeau and La Ronde; bus 768 stops at Jean-Drapeau and Plage Jean-Doré.

Ferry & Bicycle
In summer, sail to Île Ste-Hélène via **ferry** (navettesfluviales.com; adult/child $6/free) from the Old Port's Quai Jacques-Cartier. Cyclists can take the Cité du Havre route, passing Habitat 67, or via Pont Jacques-Cartier.

PARC JEAN-DRAPEAU

- **SIGHTS**
  1. Biosphère
  2. Habitat 67
  3. Jardins des Floralies
  4. Plage Jean-Doré
  5. Tour de Lévis

- **ACTIVITIES**
  6. Aquazilla
  7. Bike Link
  8. Circuit Gilles-Villeneuve
  9. Complexe Aquatique
  10. Escalade FQME
  11. Patin Patin

- **EATING**
  12. Ste-Hélène Bistro-Terrasse

- **ENTERTAINMENT**
  13. Fête des Neiges
  14. Grand Prix du Canada
  15. ÎleSoniq
  16. La Ronde
  - see 16 L'International des Feux Loto-Québec
  - see 17 Osheaga Festival Musique et Arts
  17. Piknic Électronik

Appreciate Futuristic Architecture
Bop inside the Biosphère

The **Biosphère** *(espacepourlavie.ca/biosphere; adult/child $23.75/12.25)* is Parc Jean-Drapeau's visual pièce de résistance, rising above the tree line as an architectural emblem of Expo 67. American inventor Buckminster Fuller designed the geodesic dome, originally wrapped in an acrylic skin, as the festival's US pavilion. A 1976 fire destroyed the covering but left the most striking features intact: a webbed skeleton of steel tubes reaching 62m high and 76m across.

Today the dome houses one of Espace Pour la Vie's five science museums (p84), with exhibits related to climate change, biodiversity, sustainable living, ecotechnologies and more. The center also has interactive and multimedia displays, including hand-pumps and water spouts. Programs generally appeal to elementary-school-aged children, with plenty of activities available for curious minds.

For those more interested in architecture, make a beeline for Level 5. Floor-to-ceiling windows offer spectacular tower views and give visitors a chance to inspect the dome's beams and scan Montréal's distant skyline.

The Biosphère is located just a short walk away from the Jean-Drapeau Métro stop. The subway station provides access to the island year-round.

Dance Until Dusk

Outdoor EDM at Piknic Électronik

Summer Sundays are a sonic celebration thanks to **Piknic Électronik** *(piknicelectronik.com; tickets from $24)*, a weekly alfresco EDM fête from May to October. The party began in 2003 and quickly became a hit, with a soundtrack by a roster of internationally acclaimed DJs and attracting club kids, queer crowds, young families and Montréal's original 1990s raver community.

You can spend all day bopping between beats on two dance floors, playing yard games (volleyball, cornhole), kicking back in hammocks and filling up at food trucks serving *casse-croûte* (snack shack) classics such as burgers and poutine. Bring snacks for a proper picnic; alcohol must be purchased on-site.

The party takes place by the Jean-Drapeau Métro overlooking the St Lawrence River. Dancing begins around 5pm; crowds step-touch until dark. Save money and ensure entry by purchasing tickets online at least 24 hours in advance. If you're big on EDM, check out **OfF Piknic** events – a spin-off series of summer concerts grooving on Fridays and Saturdays.

Piknic Électronik's other spin-off endeavors include a free **Petit Piknic** event program, which is geared towards families. It is hosted on several afternoons throughout the summer from noon to 3pm, and features tailored music acts and other family-focused activities and attractions. These include games, hammocks, sports, children's entertainers and mocktails; noise-cancelling headphones are available in limited quantities for children. Standard Piknic Électronik entry is free for children under 12.

EXPO 67'S LEGACY

Without Expo 67 – the 1967 International and Universal Exposition celebrating the centennial anniversary of the Canadian Confederation – there would be no Parc Jean-Drapeau and no Métro connecting it to Montréal. There would be no Biosphère, no Habitat 67 (p126) and no La Ronde (p146). Montréal's psyche might not swirl with the same spirit of optimism – the mindset that made the 1976 Olympics seem possible; the nerve to think every pop-up festival today will come together. Expo 67 wasn't just a world's fair – it was a feat, with over 50 million people touring nearly 100 pavilions representing 62 participating nations spread across two river islands over the course of six months. Mayor Jean Drapeau was instrumental in its success, overseeing the short four-year-plus preparation process – a mission impossible that panned out, now ingrained in Montréal's DNA.

TIME-HOP AROUND EXPO 67 SCULPTURES

Expo 67 can seem like a distant Montréal dream – except on Île Ste-Hélène, where artwork resurrects the World Fair's attitude of optimism.

START	END	LENGTH
Puerta de la amistad	Signe solaire	2.4km; 1½ hours

Arrive via Métro and walk south to the red steel ❶ **Puerta de la amistad** (Friendship Gate) by Mexican artist Sebastiàn. Though created in 1993, it marked the signing of the North American Free Trade Agreement between Canada, Mexico and the US, fostering a friendly cross-cultural exchange similar to Expo 67.

Next, look toward the St Lawrence River for ❷ **Trois disques**, abstract sculptor Alexander Calder's 22m-high steel symphony, its three dancing discs frozen mid-motion since 1967. From here, scan the treetops for 9m-tall ❸ **Phare du Cosmos**, Yves Trudeau's addition to Expo 67's 'Man the Explorer' pavilion – a robotic giant now guarding the park's modern-day adventurers.

To the west, the white granite pillars of ❹ **La Ville imaginaire** rise like ancient ruins – artist João Charters de Almeida's gift to Montréal in 1997 to celebrate the World Fair's 30th anniversary. For another Expo 67 creation, wander up Chemin du Tour de l'Isle to Québec sculptor Robert Roussil's ❺ **Migration**. Its cast-iron shape evokes an animal, with 11 points directed at the earth, sky and some distant destination.

Continue to the ❻ **Biosphère** (p142), the fair's most recognizable remnant, then end with a final flash of futurism at ❼ **Signe solaire**, a bronze oval meant to be glimpsed from a speeding car – a dazzling flash, gone in an instant, just like the famous festival.

> Expo 67 created a global village, with dozens of participating nations promoting innovative technologies with lofty promises of keeping the world peacefully connected.

> The fair's theme was 'Man and His World', and pavilions explored relationships between human culture, science, technology and the environment.

> Montréal demolished most Expo 67 pavilions around the mid-1980s, with few retaining their original form – like the France and Québec Pavilions (now a casino).

Splash Through Summer
Where to swim and paddle

Between late June and early September, beat summer's heat at **Plage Jean-Doré** *(parcjeandrapeau.com; adult/child/family $8.50/4.50/20.50)*, an artificial gold-sand beach overlooking the oblong lake on Île Notre-Dame. The facilities are safe, clean and ideal for kids, who can splash all day in the 15,000-sq-meter swim zone or hop around **Aquazilla** *(aquazilla.com; per hr adult/child/family $22/17/70)*, a floating obstacle course. It's also possible to **rent canoes, kayaks, pedal boats and paddle boards** *(from $17.25)* to row beyond the beach and explore lagoons within **Jardins des Floralies**, overgrown with greenery. Picnic facilities and snack bars serve food and beer back at the beach.

If you prefer a pool, bring a towel to the **Complexe Aquatique** *(parcjeandrapeau.com; adult/child/family $6.50/3/15)* on Île Ste-Hélène. It's dedicated to both recreational lap and free swimming, with a gradual slope and padded bottom ideal for beginners.

Chill Outdoors in Winter
Skate, ski, cycle and climb

Bundle up between late December and March to make the most of island ice-capades. Outdoor enthusiasts can sled down Espace 67's natural slope, cross-country ski through 7km of tree-lined rails or journey through the park on snowshoes and fat bikes. Ice-skating is most popular, thanks to a 500m refrigerated trail connected to a large rink where pros let loose.

Visit on Saturday evenings for **Slide and Groove** *(parcjeandrapeau.com)* events, when DJs turn the scene into a frosty disco as colorful lights bounce off the ice. **Patin Patin** *(patinpatin.ca; rentals from $9)* rents equipment for all activities from an Espace 67 shed near the Métro.

For more adrenaline-pumping playtime, have a go at ascending the **Escalade FQME** ice cascades, which are frozen over a 12m-high rock-climbing wall by La Ronde. Book a session with **La Liberté Nord-Sud** *(labertenordsud.com; $76.50)*, which provides expertise from professional guides and technical equipment.

Cold-weather skeptics, fear not: warming huts are dotted throughout the park to offer reprieve from the elements.

The official Parc Jean-Drapeau website also provides a full schedule of winter activities, with updates on the condition of various facilities. This is updated daily.

CYCLING SOUTHWEST
Montréal's most scenic bike path is arguably along the Lachine Canal, with a route connecting to Parc Jean-Drapeau. Follow the trail southwest to pass Atwater market and visit trendy **Verdun neighborhood** (p132).

MORE EVENTS AROUND THE PARK

Osheaga: Over 100 bands perform at this three-day festival in August, featuring celebrated pop stars and local indie artists. *osheaga.com*

ÎleSoniq: It's all about beats per minute at this two-day August festival where crowds dance to techno, house, EDM and trance. *ilesoniq.com*

L'International des Feux Loto-Québec: From late June through July the world's largest fireworks competition lights up La Ronde's night sky. *laronde.com*

Fête des Neiges: Families celebrate the snowy season with winter sports and performances over four weekends between late January and February – hot cocoa included. *parcjeandrapeau.com*

Grand Prix du Canada: F1 race-car fans pack stands around the Circuit Gilles-Villeneuve for three days devoted to the need for speed. *gpcanada.ca*

Scream on Roller-Coasters
Visit La Ronde on Île Ste-Hélène

Adrenaline junkies go berserk for Québec's largest amusement park **La Ronde** *(sixflags.com/larondeen; from $43)* thanks to more than 40 rides and attractions on offer from mid-May to late October. **Chaos** – a seven-story, 360-degree loop – lives up to its name; **Goliath** catapults riders through space at 110km/h; and **Le Monstre** – the world's highest dual-tracked wooden coaster – has been making Montréalers see stars since the 1980s. Though originally built for Expo 67, La Ronde is now a Six Flags property and feels less like a 20th-century historical relic and more like a standard amusement park, fried-food stands and all. Even so, views from atop the coasters can be spectacular – and nothing beats the evening **firework displays**, which can be seen on Thursdays at 10pm from late June through July.

EXPO ART & ARCHITECTURE

Remnants of Expo 67 line the St Lawrence waterfront: walk around its **public artworks** (p144) decorating Parc Jean-Drapeau, then head to **Habitat 67** (p126), Moshe Safdie's modular concrete masterpiece Tetris-ed along Cité-du-Havre.

La Ronde

Pedal Scenic Pathways
Cycle along the St Lawrence

Over 25km of bike-friendly paths wind through Parc Jean-Drapeau, linking its two islands to mainland Montréal and the St Lawrence's southern shore. Hopping on a BIXI bike can be a fun, fast way to speed through the scenery – just grab a set of wheels near the Jean-Drapeau Métro. Cyclists with a competitive streak should zip to **Circuit Gilles-Villeneuve** – the race track for the **Formula 1 Grand Prix du Canada**, one of the world's most popular motorsport events and Canada's biggest – which opens up to speedy cyclists throughout summer.

If you're big on cycling, consider following the park's 14km **Bike Link**, which forms part of Québec's **Route Verte** (a signposted 5000km cycle route) and the **Trans-Canada Trail** (the world's longest coast-to-coast bike path), as it glides from Parc Jean-Drapeau along the St Lawrence on a breezy, car-free seaway leading to **Ste-Catherine Lock**. BIXI won't cut it for this serene riverside ride; rent wheels from **Fitz Montréal** (*fitzmontreal.com; from $45*) in the Plateau or **Ça Roule Montreal** (*caroulemontreal.com; from $80*) in the Old Port.

FANTASTIC FLORA & FAUNA

Nearly 16,500 trees cover Parc Jean-Drapeau, its leafy canopy stitched with Siberian elms, Pennsylvania ashes, hackberries and 11 species of maple. Train binoculars on their branches to spot over 200 bird species – especially during the spring and autumn migration seasons, when birders search for the colorful breasts of goldfinches and scarlet tanagers. Raccoons lounge among the canopy too, while groundhogs peek out from their burrows, red foxes dart between bushes and a beekeeping team tends to hives of honey-makers around the rose garden near the Biosphère (p142). Climb 157 steps to the top of **Tour de Lévis** – a tower constructed in 1937 and renovated in 2025 – to admire the scene from a hawk's point of view and eye the park's most common fauna: Montréalers.

Researched by Robert Isenberg and Joel Balsam

Side Trips from Montréal

Southwestern Québec is rich in history, gastronomy and adventure – once you know where to look.

Places

Sainte-Anne de Bellevue p148

Kahnawake Mohawk Territory p149

Pointe-des-Cascades p151

Oka p151

The Laurentians p152

Saint-Jean-sur-Richelieu p159

Mont-Saint-Grégoire p160

Brome-Missisquoi p160

☑ TOP TIP

These locations are spread out and more or less require a car to reach and travel around, though there are some bus and shuttle services, depending on your destination.

The lands directly around Montréal are filled with vineyards, opportunities for outdoor recreation and homey small towns. Drive an hour or two in any direction and you'll find endless diversions: the Laurentian Mountains lure skiers and snowboarders, the confluence of the Ottawa and St Lawrence rivers yields beaches and boating, and the fertile Eastern Townships are a world-class destination for wine enthusiasts.

You can make your base in Montréal and foray out for the day, or overnight in a cozy cottage or chalet, but be sure to spend at least a day in the quieter countryside – whether it's about berms or moguls, snowshoes or paddles, southern Québec has a pastime for every season.

Sainte-Anne de Bellevue

TIME FROM MONTRÉAL: 1HR

Morgan Arboretum

On the westernmost tip of the island of Montréal, the **Morgan Arboretum** *(mcgill.ca/morganarboretum; adult/child $8/4.50)* feels like a faraway forest, with its 245 hectares of protected woods and 25km web of unpaved, multi-use trails. The property is maintained by McGill University and open to the general public every day except Christmas and New Year's Day. Skiing and snowshoeing are permitted, but bicycles should be locked up outside the entrance. You may see leashed dogs on the paths, though this option is reserved for paying members. The 40 species of tree feature prominently – it *is* an arboretum – though Morgan is popular with birders as well, owing to the 170 species that migrate through each year.

Montréal Aviation Museum

If the arboretum is a place for quiet reflection, the **Montréal Aviation Museum** *(mam.quebec; adult/child $15/5)* is geared toward engines and militaria. Established in 1998, the museum occupies an unexpected space: the Old Stone Barn, an antique agricultural building on one of McGill's satellite campuses. The Old Stone Barn was built as an educational facility

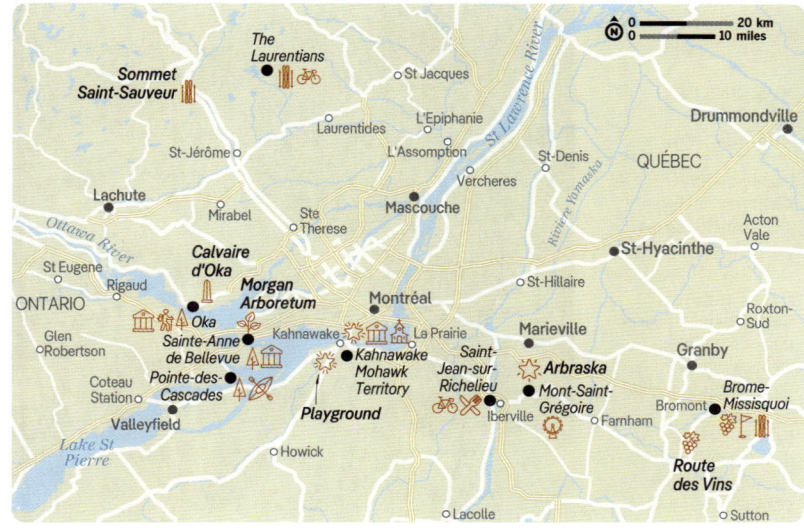

in 1907 at the behest of Sir William McDonald. Today, fans flock to the Blériot XI from 1909 and the Curtiss-Reid 'Rambler' biplane from 1928, among other restored vintage flyers housed inside the de facto flight hangar. Families will also get a thrill out of the on-site flight simulators, along with displays of historic artifacts and a beautifully laid-out art gallery.

Kahnawake Mohawk Territory

TIME FROM MONTRÉAL: **45MIN**

Try your luck at Playground

Across the St Lawrence River from Montréal stands the **Kahnawake Mohawk Territory** *(kahnawaketourism.com)*, a First Nations reservation of about 8000 residents. The main town is clustered on the riverbank directly west of the Honoré Mercier Bridge. One of Kahnawake's biggest tourist draws is **Playground** *(playground.ca)*, a leviathan gambling complex with more than 1000 video machines and 44 card tables. The casino also has four high-end restaurants and a cigar lounge, but there's no hotel on the premises. In a similar vein, the **Mystic Pines Golf & Country Club** *(mysticpinesgolf.com)* next door has a sizable golf course and is open to guests.

Hear a First Nations language

For a richer cultural experience, start your visit at the **Kanien'kehá:ka Onkwawán:na Raotitióhkwa Language and Cultural Center** *(korkahnawake.org; tours $8)*. This facility displays an impressive range of historic artifacts

FIRST NATIONS ROOTS

While the Mohawk and Huron-Wendat are distinct peoples with a complex relationship, their ancestors all spoke versions of the Iroquois language, and Kahnawake has qualities in common with Wendake (p188), the First Nations community just outside of Québec.

MUSEUMS OF SOUTHERN QUÉBEC

Musée du Haut-Richelieu: Tells the history of St-Jean-sur-Richelieu through 15,000 artifacts.

Musée du Fort Saint-Jean: Recounts three centuries of military history in St-Jean-sur-Richelieu and beyond.

Exporail: Musée du Ferroviaire Canadien: Holding a collection of real locomotives and boxcars, the Canadian Railway Museum in Saint-Constant offers interactive exhibits curated by the Canadian Railroad Historical Association.

Musée Lac-Brome: Across seven heritage buildings in Knowlton, this museum explores First Nations and colonial life.

Musée du Chocolat de la Confiserie Bromont: Learn the art of chocolate-making at this confectioner in Bromont.

Powwow dancers, Kahnawake Mohawk Territory (p149)

from daily Mohawk (Kanien'kehà:ka) life, as well as paintings and illustrations of the region's Indigenous people through the ages. A full-scale diorama reveals what a section of a traditional longhouse would have looked like in the centuries before European colonists arrived. The center contains a formidable library on First Nations topics, and a two-year immersion program trains students in the critically endangered Kanien'kehà:ka language. The center is open Monday to Friday; self-guided tours last about an hour.

EATING IN KAHNAWAKE: OUR PICKS

Fire & Ice: Spicy chicken roti and jerk chicken are favorites at this homey Caribbean joint. *11am-7:30pm Thu-Sun* **$$**

Naked Greens: With the motto 'Eat Clean,' health-food grocer Naked Greens makes veggie-rich bowls. The cute space has some seating. *8am-5pm Mon-Fri, 10am-3pm Sat & Sun* **$$**

Robbie's Smokehouse & Burger Bar: Order beef-heavy meals in this cabin-like dining room, right next to the Playground casino. *11:30am-10pm Sun-Thu, 10:30am-11pm Fri & Sat* **$$**

Drunken Dragon: Sushi rolls, sashimi bowls and fusion tacos, plus impressive cocktails and wine list, in Playground's elegant dining room. *5-11pm* **$$$**

Meet a Catholic saint

The lovely **St Francis Xavier Mission** is a stone church that has stood here since 1720. The interior mixes classic Catholic iconography with images of Mohawk people, including the Shrine of St Kateri Tekakwitha. Born into a Kanien'kehà:ka family and nicknamed 'The Lily of the Mohawks,' Tekakwitha (1656–80) was the sole survivor of a smallpox outbreak that left her scarred and visually impaired. She studied with Jesuits, converted to Catholicism and is credited with several posthumous miracles. Tekakwitha was canonized in 2012. Her tomb stands next to the church's altar. The church is open to the public Monday to Thursday and holds Sunday services.

Pointe-des-Cascades

TIME FROM MONTRÉAL: **65MIN**

Get outside at Village des Écluses

In preparation for the Expo 67 world fair, organizers had to consider how to house the thousands of visitors who would flood Montréal. Knowing that some would arrive in campers and tents, they looked to an industrial zone west of the city, right at the mouth of the Soulanges Canal. The new campground proved popular that year, and developers soon added a summer theater and on-site restaurant.

This little settlement would grow to become **Village des Écluses** (Village of the Locks), a kind of all-ages summer camp. The estate maintains many primitive sites, RV hookups and 'prêt-à-camper' canvas military tents, drawing outdoorsy guests from across North America. Live concerts also take place on an alfresco stage throughout the warmer months. The biggest draw is the water: relax on the small beach, lounge by the river on a sprawling wood-floored terrace, or paddle the St Lawrence in a rented kayak *(per hr/day $15/60)*. Village des Écluses also marks the trailhead of the Soulanges Canal Bike Trail, which stretches 24 flat kilometers to the town of Les Coteaux.

Oka

TIME FROM MONTRÉAL: **65MIN**

Make a park pilgrimage

Like many of the old colonies along the St Lawrence, the town of Oka was founded as a religious community, and the **Calvaire d'Oka** remains its most enduring monument. Its four oratories and three chapels date back to the 1740s, when missionaries were actively seeking to proselytize First Nations peoples, and the preserved structures continue to welcome pilgrims seeking spiritual solace. They also make for a photogenic backwoods destination for regular hikers, who follow a 5km out-and-back trail to the well-preserved whitewashed structures. The rugged route is considered moderately challenging due to the hill's 150m prominence. From the top you'll be rewarded with impressive views of the Lac des Deux Montagnes (Lake of Two Mountains).

The **Parc National d'Oka** *(sepaq.com/pq/oka; day pass adult/child $9.85/free)* isn't far from Montréal by car, but the

---

HIGH STEEL

1965 documentary *High Steel* showcased ironworker Harold McComber, who grew up in Kahnawake. The Kanien'kehà:ka had already garnered a reputation for being unafraid of heights and many earned jobs as high-rise builders in New York City. A neighborhood in Brooklyn is still known as Little Caughnawaga (an alternate spelling of Kahnawake).

This storied past is also touched by tragedy: in 1907 a partly built Québec Bridge, which had drawn many workers from Kahnawake, unexpectedly collapsed, and killing 75 laborers, including at least 33 Kanien'kehà:ka men. The Québec Bridge disaster is considered one of the worst construction failures in modern history.

WHY I LOVE SOUTHERN QUÉBEC

Robert Isenberg, Lonely Planet writer

I grew up in small-town Vermont, and Montréal was only a 2½-hour drive from my family's house, making it the closest major city. Our TV antenna picked up French programming. Classmates had French names. I regularly spotted Québec license plates on Main St. Through the years, Montréal and its environs have served as a getaway – a place for excitement and reflection. Québec is very much a foreign country to this New Englander, yet the cultural values and daily rhythms are so familiar. The moment I cross the border, my intermediate language skills come flooding back and I fall into the *joie de vivre* for which French Canada is famous.

forested hills and wetlands feel like a remote wilderness to urbanites seeking an expedient getaway. If you're bringing a tent along, you can set it up in the park's sizable campground, which is located on the forested flatlands next to the Ottawa River. All of these sites are within a short walk of the Plage du Parc (Park Beach), a relaxing stretch of sand with changing facilities, picnic tables and kayaks for rent ($35 per day).

Eat Oka cheese

Outside Oka proper, the Trappist monks at L'Abbaye d'Oka, founded in 1881, have carried their faith into a modern-day hustle, with a guesthouse and shop, **Magasin de L'Abbaye d'Oka** *(abbayeoka.ca)* that specializes in one of Québec's favorite cheeses, along with artisanal wine and other fine foods. But don't fill up there. The monks' shop is just one of many stops on the 226km **Chemin du Terroir** *(laurentides.com/en/themes/what-to-do/tourist-routes/chemin-du-terroir)* food trail in the lower Laurentians. Other taste breaks include wineries, a gin distillery and North America's oldest operating water-driven flour mill.

Breeze through town

The town of Oka stands on the same riverbank as the Parc National d'Oka, to the west of the campground. This community of about 4000 people has several historic buildings in its center, including the **Église de l'Annonciation** (Annunciation Church), a steepled stone beauty just steps from the water. A handful of restaurants are located next door. If you need to cross the river to continue west, you can take a 10-minute **ferry ride** *(car/foot passenger $14/3)* from Oka to the town of Hudson.

The Laurentians

TIME FROM MONTRÉAL: **1–2½ HR**

Get some fresh air

For decades, Montréalers have been driving north to *les* Laurentides (the Laurentians) to kick back and relish Québec's pristine scenery – rolling hills, thousands of freshwater lakes, cuter-than-cute villages and cozy log-cabin chalets in which to warm up and breathe it all in. At the heart of the Laurentian Mountains, one of the world's oldest ranges, is Mont-Tremblant, which encompasses many things: a 932m mountain with eastern Canada's most popular ski resort, a village and the province's oldest provincial park. Millions of visitors come to ski or snowboard its powdered slopes, hike or mountain bike its vast network of trails, canoe its rivers, relax at its spas or soak in the rainbow of colors when leaves change every autumn.

Closer to Montréal, towns such as Oka (p151), St-Sauveur, Val-David (the regional hub), Val-Morin and Ste-Agathe-des-Monts make for reasonable day trips from Montréal, with cute boutiques, fine dining and access to activities such as kayaking, cross-country skiing, rock climbing and cycling.

Calvaire d'Oka (p151)

Ski these slopes

The Laurentians are known for skiing, and **Mont Tremblant Resort** *(tremblant.ca; adult/senior/youth/child/peewee (3-4) $149/128/112/85/26)* has achieved rock-star status among travelers willing to drive well over two hours from the big city. Founded in 1938 and home to Canada's first chairlift, this is eastern Canada's most popular ski resort during the season (late November to mid-April), but being so popular can mean the 932m-high mountain's 100-or-so runs and 14 lifts can get mighty crowded on any winter's day, and lift tickets are pricey. Still, you'll realize skiing at Tremblant is worth it when you disembark from the gondola above the clouds and glide past evergreens sagging in marshmallow-white blankets. And

THE OKA CRISIS

In 1990 developers planned to break ground on a golf course on a property near Oka. First Nations residents objected because the site, known as the Pines, overlapped with ancestral burial grounds. What followed was one of the ugliest episodes in modern Canadian history. The Oka Crisis was a 78-day standoff between First Nations protesters, who built defensive blockades, and Canada's Armed Forces, who laid siege outside. Both parties were armed, and a shootout took place on July 11 – the violence resulted in one death on each side. The Oka Crisis culminated in the arrest of most protesters and bitter feelings on both sides, but the development was ultimately halted.

 EATING IN THE LAURENTIANS: MONT-TREMBLANT

| **Casse-Croûte d'en Haut:** Arguably the best poutine in the Laurentians, along with thick-crust pizza, *steamé* hot dogs, burgers and subs. 11am-7:45pm Tue-Sun **$** | **Cucinotto:** Italian fine grocer and lunch counter serving delicious deli sandwiches, pastries and its show-stopper gnocchi poutine. 9:30am-5pm Tue-Sat **$** | **Le Diable Microbrasserie:** The food you want after a day on the slopes: thick-gravy poutine, burgers, Belgian-style beer. 11:30am-9pm Sun-Thu, to 11pm Fri & Sat **$$** | **Maison de Soma:** Seasonal ingredients from its 2.4-sq-km farm served in a modern dining room by waiters who participate in the harvest. 11am-9pm Thu-Sat, to 4pm Sun **$$$** |

THE WIDE-RANGING LAURENTIANS

Named after the St Lawrence River, the Laurentian Mountains (or 'Laurentides') extend 1400km across Central Québec and Labrador. Another beautiful section for outdoors lovers is **Parc National de la Jacques-Cartier** (p195).

while Tremblant's Alps-style resort town might be on the kitschy side, walking its cobblestone streets past upscale resorts and condos, hot chocolate or poutine in hand, remains magical.

Closer to Montréal, **Sommet Saint-Sauveur** (sommets.com; adult/youth/child $93/61/22) is a sprawling ski resort with eight lifts and 42 trails across nearly 58 hectares of forest and rolling slopes. The highland topography is fairly tame, with a maximum of 213m vertical drop, making this a great place for beginners and families to master some powder. Sauveur has many other conveniences as well: it's cheaper and less crowded than Tremblant and you can comfortably drive up, ski throughout the day and return to Montréal by nightfall.

Cycling, kayaking and climbing

Outside of ski season, bicycles replace skis as the premier way to whizz around these scenic hills. The 11.6km **La Villageoise** loop trail connects Mont Tremblant Resort and **Mont-Tremblant Village**, 4km away along the riverfront. If you're in for some bumps and thumps, Tremblant has a huge network of cleverly crafted mountain-biking trails as well as a free 100m **pump track** in the village. Connecting Laval, north of Montréal, to Mont-Laurier through popular tourist hubs such as Mont-Tremblant and Val-David, the 234km **Le P'tit Train du Nord** (ptittraindunord.com) multi-use path is a great way to experience the Laurentians in one fell swoop. Rent a wide range of bikes, including e-bikes and fat bikes, and get trail maps and advice from **Ski & Bike Lab** (skilabtremblant.com) in Mont-Tremblant Village, or from **Le Randonneur** (tremblant.ca/things-to-do/activities/biking) at the main entrance to the resort.

Or get out on the water. After all, the Laurentians are filled with more than 9000 lakes and rivers. Combine an easy self-guided 7km paddle on La Rivière du Nord with a 4km cycle on Le P'tit Train du Nord with **À l'Abordage** (alabordage.ca; 3hr $55) in Val-David. It also runs 11km kayak or canoe paddles down La Rivière du Diable (Devil's River) from Tremblant. **Kayak & Cabana** (kayak-cabana.com) in Labelle offers another easy way to get on the water, with a package that includes a 12km kayak or canoe down calm La Rivière Rouge and a stay in one of its off-grid cabins.

Another popular outdoor sport in the Laurentians is climbing. **Parc Régional de Val-David-Val-Morin** (parcregional.com) has some of the best climbing routes in Québec. Its granite rocks attract climbers from all over, with hundreds of top-roping routes as well as plenty of bouldering options. **Montagne d'Argent** (montagnedargent.com) near Tremblant is another top climbing spot. If you want to learn or brush up on your skills, climbing schools **Passe-Montagne** (ecole-escalade.com) and **Attitude Montagne** (attitudemontagne.com) can show you the ropes. Courses range from several hours to multiday trips, and ice-climbing courses are available in winter.

MORE SKIING DAY TRIPS

All these ski areas are within an hour's drive of Montréal.

Sommet Olympia: Thanks to its well-respected ski school, six lifts and 200m of vertical drop, this is great for families.

Sommet Gabriel: About a third of the 18 trails on offer here would be considered challenging.

Mont Habitant: Equipped with two lifts, 6km of trails and mostly intermediate-level runs, Habitant is as family-friendly as it gets for skiing. monthabitant.com

Mont Avila: Snow-tubing park and plenty of powder, thanks to three lifts and 14 slopes.

Centre de Ski de Fond Gai-Luron: Explore this beautiful cross-country loop through a pine wonderland on skis, snowshoes or a fat bike. skigailuron.ca

Mont Tremblant Resort (p153)

Get steamy at Strøm Nordic Spa

Straddling the Simon River, **Strøm Spa Nordique** (*stromspa .com/en/strom-saint-sauveur*) is a sizable campus with Jacuzzis, saunas and massage chambers. Of Strøm's five locations, this is perhaps the most scenic. Forest encircles the property, and the scenery is awe-inspiring in any season. Drop in for a facial or a thermal experience, or spend the full day here, capping it off with a health-forward dinner at Nord, the spa's on-site restaurant.

Treetop adventures

The Laurentians' newest attraction can be found 40 vertical meters above the town of Mont-Blanc, nestled between the trees and squirrels. Opened in 2022, **Sentier des Cimes** (*treetop-walks.com/laurentides; adult/senior/youth/child $32/30/20/free*) is a 2.7km round-trip wooden footbridge and 40m wooden tower with a mesh hammock on top for some high-altitude chilling. The views are that much more spectacular when the area turns into a kaleidoscope of colors in the fall. The path is accessible, with ramps leading up having a maximum of 6% gradient, and it's built for the whole family, with signage about local wildlife along the trail. At ground level, visit the free museum next door to learn about

TOP SPAS IN QUÉBEC

Scandinave Spa: Mont-Tremblant spa that cascades down a hillside overlooking the Rivière du Diable, with an abundance of pools, waterfalls and cozy nooks. Also in Old Montréal. *scandinave.com/ mont-tremblant*

Strøm: Well-established Nordic spa in St-Sauveur, as well as in Montréal, Les Cantons de l'Est and Québec City. *stromspa.com*

Bota Bota: It's a Nordic spa, but on a boat (a 1950s ferry) just off the shores of Vieux-Montréal with great city views. *botabota.ca*

Nordik Spa-Nature: The largest spa in North America is in Chelsea, with nine saunas and 10 outdoor pools, including an infinity pool that blissfully overlooks the Gatineau Hills. *chelsea.lenordik.com*

Spa Bolton: Cantons de l'Est spa with 25 years of experience hosting polar baths, swims under waterfalls and massages in isolated yurts. *spabolton.com*

VINCENT JIANG/SHUTTERSTOCK

GETTING TO THE LAURENTIANS

Mont Tremblant Resort (p153) offers free shuttle buses between the resort and parking lots scattered around the expansive urban area. It also operates a coach service between Montréal's Trudeau airport and the resort from December to April.

Autobus Galland *(galland-bus.com)* links Montreal's main bus station to Mont-Laurier, with stops in the main hub towns. If you're cycling, **Autobus Le Petit Train du Nord** *(autobuslepetittraindunord.com; $33-85)* takes cyclists, their bikes and/or luggage to one of 20 accommodations in the Laurentians. It also rents out bikes.

the fascinating pisciculture research carried out on this site that managed to repopulate the Laurentians' waterways with trout. It's also worth sampling edible plants made into familiar foods such as milkweed salsa, chanterelle mushroom caramel and sea buckthorn hot sauce at **Gourmet Sauvage** *(gourmetsauvage.ca)* next door. It also does wild foraging tours. **Café Boréal** *(10am to 5pm)* is also on-site and has more forest finds, including vegan clover and balsam fir ice cream.

For more thrills from the treetops, head over to **Acro-Nature** *(sommets.com/en/what-to-do/aerial-hebertism; adult/child $42/35)*, an elevated obstacle course through the forest canopy at Sommet St-Sauveur. From May to October, adults and families can pick from eight different routes and slide down an

EATING IN THE LAURENTIANS: OUTSIDE MONT-TREMBLANT

Le Solstice: Grab an addictive smash burger on the terrace and a natural wine to take camping. In St-Sauveur. *11:30am-8pm Wed-Sun* **$**

Au Petit Poucet: Taste authentic Québécois cuisine like *oreilles de crisse* (deep-fried pork rinds) in a pioneer-style cabin just outside of Val-David. *6:30am-4pm* **$$**

Normal: Ste-Agathe wine bar with local dishes, gussied up: think pork and duck hot dogs and gourmet club sandwiches. *noon-10pm Thu-Sat, 5-9pm Wed* **$$**

L'Épicurieux: Shareable tasting menu featuring local, seasonal produce in an intimate Val-David riverside setting. *5:30-10pm Thu-Sat* **$$$**

Sentier des Cimes (p155)

astonishing 32 zip lines. Further north, **Tyroparc** *(tyroparc.com; prices vary)* has a network of four zip lines, the longest of which is 900m, a via ferrata and a treetop obstacle course.

Another memorable tree-bound adventure is **Tonga Lumina** *(tongalumina.tremblant.ca; adult/child/baby $30/20/free)* by Moment Factory, an immersive journey through sound and light that shares Polynesian legends with a pro-conservation message from the top of Mont-Tremblant from June to October.

Explore national parks

Inaugurated in 1895, **Parc National du Mont-Tremblant** *(sepaq.com/pq/mot; entry $9)* is Québec's oldest provincial park and a natural playground for humans and animal species alike. Covering a massive territory of 1510 sq km, the park, 20 minutes' drive from the Mont Tremblant Resort, protects wild hills covered in rare vegetation such as silver maple and red oak, along with six rivers and a whopping 400 lakes. Wolves, foxes and coyotes roam here, as do black bears, beavers, white-tailed deer, moose (though they're rare) and 200 species of birds. As of 2023, Parc National du Mont-Tremblant is also an International Dark Sky Park.

The park is divided into three sectors. Closest to Mont Tremblant Resort, **Le Diable** is the most popular area and is best

BIKE RENTALS OUTSIDE MONTRÉAL

Southern Québec is replete with bike shops, but rentals are harder to find. There are three solid locations for trail-ready rides. **Cycle LM** *(cyclelm.com)* in Saint-Jean-sur-Richelieu offers a wide range of models, from fat bikes to e-bikes. In the outdoors hub of Granby, the popular Québec company **Sports aux Puces** has a special **VéloGare** *(Bike Station; sapvelogare.com/en)* that rents everything from mountain bikes to carbon roadsters. Finally, in the far-southern town of Dunham you'll find the **E-Mobilité Café** *(emobilitecafe.com)*, which specializes in e-bikes. Budget about $60 to $90 per day for a rental at each of these places.

THE EASTERN TOWNSHIPS

You really could spend weeks driving the rolling byways of the Eastern Townships (Cantons de l'Est, in French) of Québec. The townships begin with Granby and Bromont, just an hour's drive east of Montréal, and extend about 200km at their widest points. The history of these bucolic towns is nearly as checkered as their geography. British Loyalists escaped the American Revolution and settled here, followed by newcomers from the UK, then French Canadians in search of farmland. The townships lie roughly within the district of Estrie, and the region has gained popularity for its beautiful landscapes, ample outdoor activities and ever-growing gastronomic scene. The townships are big enough to merit their own road trip, but several are within a 70-minute drive of Montréal.

Parc National de la Mauricie

for a day trip. Here you can pick up equipment rentals for the park's many activities and speak to knowledgeable Sépaq staff at the **Lac-Monroe Visitors Centre**. Activities include hopping on a bus north to pick up a canoe, then snaking down the Rivière du Diable on a trip of up to three days; descending the mountain to the river by shuffling along ropes on a via ferrata; and hiking trails that range from 20-minute jaunts to ascents of steep mountains. The eastern **L'Assomption** and northern **La Pimbina** sectors have few maintained trails

EATING IN SAINT-JEAN-SUR-RICHELIEU: OUR PICKS

| **Restaurant L'Imprévu Le Bistro:** Classic fine dining: ornate dishes and a prix-fixe option. *11:30am-9pm Wed, 10:30am-10pm Thu & Fri, 5-10pm Sat* **$$$** | **La Plank:** Right near the river, Le Plank redefines guilty pleasures with 'deluxe fast food.' *11:30am-2pm & 4:30-8pm Sun & Tue-Fri, 11:30am-9pm Sat* **$$** | **Capitaine Pouf:** With its bearded-skipper mascot, Capitaine Pouf fries up fish and chips and pours beers. *11:30am-8pm Sun-Thu, 11am-9pm Fri & Sat* **$$** | **Plan B par Bistro Braque:** Savor ornate French creations in this romantically lit bistro. *5:30-11pm Thu & Sun, to midnight Fri & Sat* **$$$** |

and are geared toward fishing for pike, walleye and speckled trout. There are more than 1000 places to choose from throughout the park, including remote refuges and cabins where you might have a whole lake to yourself.

Sharing the Laurentians mountain chain, **Parc National de la Mauricie** (*pc.gc.ca/eng/pn-np/qc/mauricie*; entry $9) is one of just three Parks Canada–managed parks in Québec. Mauricie covers an area roughly a third of the size of Parc National du Mont-Tremblant and doesn't have mountains as steep, but it's highly organized and useful if you already have a Canadian National Parks Pass. Mauricie offers 110km of hiking trails, 150 lakes and affordable equipment rentals, including convenient oTENTik (a mix between a tent and a cabin) campsites.

Saint-Jean-sur-Richelieu

TIME FROM MONTRÉAL: **40MIN**

Cycle the countryside

Unbeknown to many travelers, the southern tip of Québec Province is crisscrossed with hundreds of kilometers of bike trails. To be fair, the former railroad lines are hard to spot; they're often hidden by crops or trees, and they only sporadically intersect with motorways. For cyclists in the warmer months, this is a perfect formula: straight and level paths, wide-open spaces and just the right distance between one town and the next. Many of the trails are smoothly paved and well painted, so bike tourers can roll through the Québec countryside without a single flat tire or need to change gears. All trails are free to access.

One of the most pastoral routes is **La Montérégiade**, a 48km trail that starts in the mill town of Saint-Jean-Sur-Richelieu and shoots in a straight line to Farnham, then zips over to Granby. The full route should take most cyclists about 2½ hours each way, making for a full day if you're planning a there-and-back journey. Alternatively, parking lots are scattered along the route, so you can ride La Montérégiade in segments. All three towns have hotels, and accommodations in Granby are especially affordable if you decide to stay the night. The trail is open and maintained between May and October.

WHOSE PARK IS IT ANYWAY?

In other Canadian provinces, there are national parks and provincial parks, the difference being that national parks are administered federally by Parks Canada, while provincial parks are administered by the province. Not so in Québec. Here, both federal and provincial parks are called national, with most being managed by Québec's Sépaq and only three being run by Parks Canada.

While at first glance, the decision to name provincially administered parks 'national' appears political – Québec considers itself a distinct nation within Canada, and still has a small, but existing, separatist movement – in actuality Sépaq uses the word to show it's just as committed to environmental protection as national parks in Canada and the US.

 EATING IN GRANBY: OUR PICKS

La Maison Chez Nous: Try French favorites such as snails in puff pastry in a country-chic dining room. *5-11pm Wed-Sat* **$$$**

Maison Boire: Enjoy wood-fired delicacies and all-you-can-eat steak-frites in a space reminiscent of a 19th-century country home. *5-10pm Wed-Sat* **$$$**

Bistro Kapzak: The first Polish bistro in Granby, Kapzak elevates classics such as pierogies and *szaszłyk z kaczki* (duck skewers). *4:30-10pm Tue-Sat* **$$**

C'est Belge: Delicious waffles, eggs Benedict and breakfast sandwiches are on offer at Granby's prime brunch location. *8am-2:30pm* **$$**

MAGIC IN THE MOUNTAINS

Lori Anne Jones, an artist, baker and manager at **Café Boréal** (p156), moved to the Laurentians and couldn't be happier. Here's why she thinks you'll love it too. @kingston_1977

This region is full of magic: sparkling lakes, vast forests and mountains that invite both peace and adventure. Each season transforms the landscape into something breathtaking. The air is crisp, the people are welcoming and time slows down. The Laurentians are more than a destination – they're a place where the soul feels rooted, inspired and fully alive. For outdoor lovers, it's a dream come true – every path leads to wonder and every moment reconnects you with nature.

Mont-Saint-Grégoire

TIME FROM MONTRÉAL: **40 MIN**

Go ape at Arbraska

Many Canadians light up when they hear the name **Arbraska** *(arbraska.com/en/parks/mont-saint-gregoire; child 5-7/8-13/14+ from $39/42/47)*, as the Québec-based adventure company has gradually expanded across the country over the past 20 years, delighting generations of outdoorsy youths. This high-flying playground knots together rope ladders, zip lines and hanging bridges, almost always in a wooded location. Arbraska was founded in Rowdon, Québec, and the province has a half-dozen other sites as well, including one in the town of Mont-Saint-Grégoire, within day-trip distance of Montréal.

Arbraska's specialties, such as trampolines and 'aerial games,' have become increasingly popular among ropes-course-style theme parks. This park also hosts activities at night, using colored lights to paint the nets and cables in a scheme designed to mimic an aurora borealis. It adds a thrilling new dimension to the aerial activities. Arbraska is also known for its Arbre-en-Ciel (Sky Tree) Village, which interweaves traditional park equipment in the surrounding woods. The Arbre-en-Ciel appeals mostly to children aged three to seven.

No matter how scary the heights may seem, Arbraska provides helmets, harnesses and thorough instruction, ensuring the safety of every responsible guest. Reservations must be made in advance; most activities are for ages five and up. The basic package includes a zip line and aerial trek. The Mont-Saint-Grégoire park opens for weekends and holidays all year, and daily from July through August.

Brome-Missisquoi

TIME FROM MONTRÉAL: **1HR**

Gastronomy tour

Oenophiles and anyone with a taste for the giggly grape juice, rejoice: this region ferments about 60% of the wine produced in Québec. Born in the 1980s, Québec's wine industry might be relatively young, but unique microclimates that make parts of the Townships up to 2°C than neighboring regions, as well as creative flair, turn the bottles here into a force to be reckoned with.

From May to October, wineries host tours and tastings, and many continue to welcome guests throughout the winter as well. Taste for yourself on a road trip. There are 25 wineries

---

 EATING IN BROMONT: OUR PICKS

Bistro Le 633: Set in a converted 19th-century farmhouse, this bistro boasts an eclectic tapas menu and excellent sangrias. *10:30am-10pm* **$$$**

Comme Chez Soi Bromont: Dine on braised lamb shanks and walleye fillet by a roaring fireplace. *4-10:30pm Sat-Wed, 11:30am-2:30pm & 4-10:30pm Thu & Fri* **$$$**

Le Roux: Try anything from gourmet pizza to duck confit while enjoying knockout views of nearby mountains. *4-10pm Tue-Sat* **$$$**

Chardo: Foodie heaven, with sophisticated reimaginings of beef carpaccio and frog legs. *11:30am-9pm Wed, Thu & Sun, to 10pm Fri & Sat* **$$$**

Ski Bromont

listed on **La Route des Vins** (*The Wine Trail; laroutedesvins.ca*), accessible along seven driving routes ranging from a 32km day trip to a three-day 120km tour. On the way, don't just taste wine; the Townships are also filled with breweries, gin distillers, cideries – including **Clos Saragnat** (*saragnat.com*), the owner of which invented ice cider – and cheese makers (who also have their own driving itinerary at *createursdesaveurs.com/quoi-faire/fromageries-tetes-fromageres*.

If you prefer to get a workout between stops, La Route des Vins also lists four cycling tours – just be prepared for some serious pedaling as the distances between wineries aren't small. **Vélouroute Gourmande** (*veloroutegourmande.com*) and **Tourism Eastern Townships** (*easterntownships.org/guides-and-maps*) also have cycling itineraries, many of which connect with Québec's 5400km **Route Verte** (*routeverte.com*) trail network.

Get busy in Bromont

Brome-Missisquoi is a sizable district at the western edge of the Eastern Townships. For a warm-weather day trip, hop from one winery to the next, then grab lunch or dinner in **Bromont** (*tourismebromont.com*), Brome-Missisquoi's largest and most active town. In summer you can play a round of golf at the **Parcours du Vieux Village** (*parcoursduvieuxvillage.com*); in winter, **Ski Bromont** (*bromontmontagne.com*) offers a wide range of gentle slopes and the most robust night-skiing infrastructure in North America, with 101 illuminated trails.

BROME-MISSISQUOI WINERIES

Domaine du Ridge: Acclaimed vineyard known for its timber-roofed terrace and wedding-ready grounds. *domaine duridge.com*

Vignoble de l'Orpailleur: Centers on an attractive, modern complex with a highly rated in-house restaurant, the Corkscrew. *orpailleur.ca*

Vignoble du Ruisseau: With its elegant gardens and red covered bridge, Ruisseau makes for a blissful guided tour. *levignobleduruisseau.com*

Vignoble de Grenouille: True to its playful name, the mascot representing this 2-hectare, family-owned vineyard is a little smiling frog. *vignoblelagrenouille.com*

Vignoble Sugar Hill: Certified organic, Sugar Hill boasts a variety of reds, whites and sparkling wines. *vignoble-sugarhill.com*

Researched by Pamela MacNaughtan

QUÉBEC CITY

CENTURIES-OLD CITY WHERE FRENCH CULTURE THRIVES

Over 400 years of history meet a modern European sensibility in Québec City, with French-speaking locals, fascinating museums, gourmet eats, cozy cafes and postcard-worthy vistas.

Skip the trans-Atlantic flight to Europe with a trip to Québec City, where history and culture whisper through almost every crevice. Wandering the narrow cobblestone streets of the Historic District of Old Québec (a UNESCO World Heritage Site since 1985) reveals a blend of French and British influences in everything from architecture to food to language. Cap Diamant, a jagged cliff with strategic views of the St Lawrence River, divides Old Québec into two. The fortified city (Haute-Ville) lies above the cliff, and the oldest neighborhoods, Petit-Champlain and Place-Royale, sit at its base (Basse-Ville). Outside Old Québec, St-Jean-Baptiste, St-Roch and Limoilou are vibrant neighborhoods filled with boutiques, music, art, bars and restaurants.

TOP TIP

Wander beyond the old city walls to dine with locals and explore Québec City's vibrant food scene – the menu prices are more affordable too.

Old Québec

See page 199 for places to stay in Québec City.

FROM LEFT: HONESTTRAVELLER/SHUTTERSTOCK, AUDETPHOTO

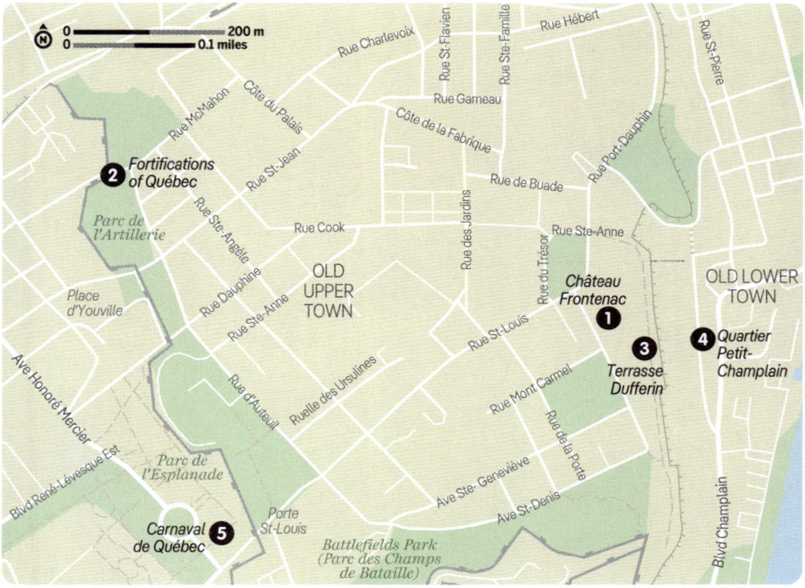

Highlights

❶ Château Frontenac

Perhaps one of the most photographed hotels in the world, and the unofficial mascot of Québec. **p168**

❷ Fortifications of Québec

Admire the stone walls, cannons and murder holes that kept the city safe for centuries. **p166**

❸ Terrasse Dufferin

Visit this boardwalk for sweeping views of the St Lawrence River and Basse-Ville and to listen to local artists. **p173**

❹ Quartier Petit-Champlain

Wander around the historic cobblestone streets of North America's first commercial district. **p169**

❺ Carnaval de Québec

The biggest and oldest winter festival in Canada, where everyone bows down to a giant snowman called Bonhomme (pictured). **p175**

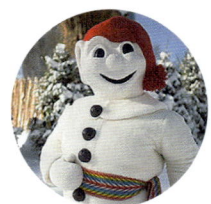

Getting Around

Walking

Most sights are within walking distance, which avoids the frustration of trying to find parking – especially in Old Québec.

Public Transportation

An extensive bus network makes it easy to visit popular sights and local neighborhoods. Download the RTC Nomade app for real-time information and RTC Paiement to buy digital tickets.

Bicycle

Rentals are available year-round. In summer àVelo has hundreds of e-bikes for rent across the city; there are stations in front of Parc Montmorency and near Château Frontenac and Musée de la Civilisation. Download the àVélo app for info.

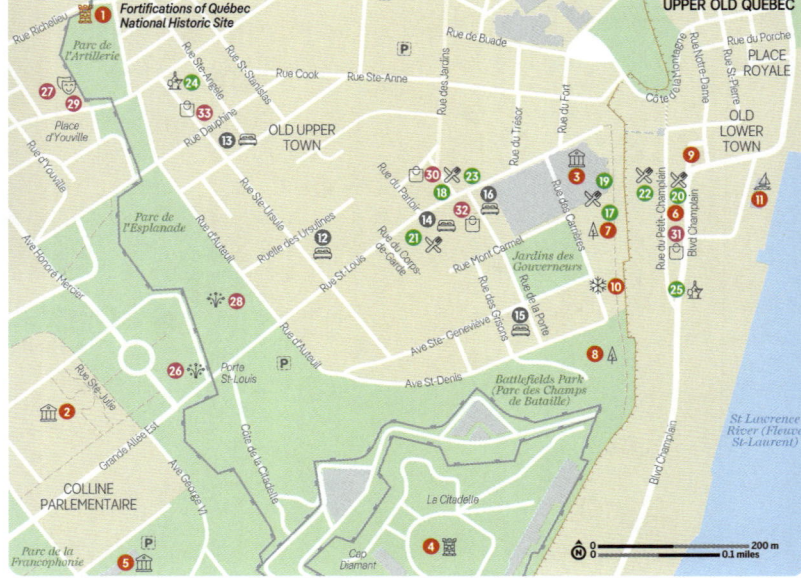

★ HIGHLIGHTS
1 Fortifications of Québec National Historic Site

● SIGHTS
2 Assemblée national du Québec
3 Château Frontenac
4 La Citadelle
5 Musée des Plaines d'Abraham
6 Quartier Petit-Champlain
7 Terrasse Dufferin
8 Terrasse Pierre-Dugua-de-mons
9 Umbrella Alley

● ACTIVITIES
10 Glissade de la Terrasse
11 Lévis Ferry

● SLEEPING
12 Au Petit Hôtel
see 3 Château Frontenac
13 HI Auberge Internationale de Québec
14 Hôtel AtypiQ
15 Hôtel Nomad
16 Maison Kent

● EATING
17 Au 1884
18 Aux Anciens Canadiens
19 Bistro Le Sam
20 Cochon Dingue
21 La Bûche
22 Lapin Sauté
23 Le Continental
see 3 Restaurant Champlain

● DRINKING & NIGHTLIFE
24 Bar Ste-Angèle
25 Terroir

● ENTERTAINMENT
26 Carnaval de Québec
27 Le Diamant
28 Les Fêtes de la Nouvelle-France
29 Théâtre Capitole

● SHOPPING
30 Épicerie Richard
31 Fucklamode
32 Galerie d'Art Inuit Brousseau
33 Marché d'Emma

 DRINKING IN OLD QUÉBEC: BEST COFFEE — MAPS P164 & P178

La Maison Smith: Locally roasted coffee, flaky croissants and nibbles, best enjoyed on the patio in historic Place-Royale. *7am-7pm Sun-Wed, to 8pm Thu-Sat*

Café Apotek: Danish minimalist boulangerie-cafe serving high-quality small-batch coffee and lush desserts in Old Port. *8am-4pm Mon-Fri, 8am-5pm Sat, 9am-5pm Sun*

Fucklamode: Iconic clothing store in Petit-Champlain serving excellent espresso and cappuccino. Don't bother tipping; he doesn't want it. *9:30am-7pm, to 9pm Sat*

Au 1884: Gazebo turned cafe serving locally roasted coffee and light sandwiches. On a hot day, treat yourself to an affogato. *10am-5pm Sun-Thu, to 9pm Fri & Sat*

The Historic Plaines d'Abraham MAPS P164 & P180
Imagine a 20-minute battle that changed Canada

When you're enjoying a picnic under a leafy elm, admiring the Martello Towers or feeling the electric hum of guitars and drums during **Festival d'été de Québec (FEQ)**, it's hard to imagine the **Plaines d'Abraham** as an 18th-century battleground.

The British tried for months to conquer Québec City, bombarding it with incendiary devices and destroying many of its buildings, but they were unable to breach the city's defence and attack on land. All of that changed on September 13, 1759, when a 20-minute battle on the Plaines d'Abraham between British and French forces changed the course of North American history. It was a surprise attack; Marquis de Montcalm and his Indigenous allies thought it was impossible to scale the cliffside to the plains, but General James Wolfe and his troops proved them wrong. When the battle ended, Wolfe and Montcalm were mortally wounded and the French had lost control of Québec City. When the Treaty of Paris was signed in 1763, ending the Seven Years' War, it laid out the boundaries for British North America (including Québec). On July 1, 1867, British North America would become known as Canada.

The **Musée des Plaines d'Abraham** chronicles the Battle of 1759 with period clothing, battle MAPS and immersive videos spread over three floors. Tickets are $17 in summer (July to September) and $13.75 the rest of the year. Other activities include a 45-minute guided bus tour ($4.25) and cross-country skiing in winter.

The Sisters of l'Hôtel-Dieu MAP P178
Soak up hospitality in a historic site of care

At **Monastère des Augustines**, sun-soaked halls with 17th-century wood floors are decorated with religious busts and tapestries that sometimes hide little alcoves of solitude. Visitors walk into a modern three-story glass atrium with floating steel-frame walkways on the 2nd and 3rd floors. On the ground floor a remarkable museum showcases the 320-year history of the cloistered nuns who founded the first permanent hospital in North America, **Hôtel-Dieu de Québec** (1644). A guided tour of the museum's main exhibit, *Augustinian Sisters: Healing Body and Soul*, shines

QUÉBEC CITY'S COLONIAL HISTORY

Jacques Cartier's voyages to the Americas were at the behest of Francis I, who was looking to expand France's territory and establish a western trade route to Asia. In 1535 Cartier landed in Stadacona, an Iroquoian village that was led by Chief Donnaconna. Initial relations between the Europeans and the First Nations people were amiable, but that changed when Cartier took Chief Donnaconna, two of his sons and seven others to France, where all but one died. Met with hostility when he returned to Stadacona in 1541, Cartier fled back to France. In 1608, Henry IV sent explorer Samuel de Champlain to Stadacona to establish a settlement and build up the fur trade. He founded Kebec (Algonquin for 'where the river narrows'), now known as Québec City.

 EATING IN QUÉBEC CITY: BEST POUTINE MAPS P174, P178 & P180

Le Chic Shack: Gourmet poutine with hand-smashed potatoes is the name of the game. Try La Forestière and a boozy milkshake. *8am-9pm* $$	**Snack-Bar St-Jean:** After a night of bar-hopping in St-Jean-Baptiste, dig into a piping-hot order of poutine gyro. *11am-4am Sun-Thu, to 5am Fri & Sat* $	**Chez Gaston:** In St-Roch, this local hot spot makes a mean traditional poutine. *11am-10pm Mon-Wed, to 4am Thu-Sat* $	**Chez Ashton:** Dig into La Galvaude poutine, with fries, chicken, green peas and brown sauce, at this classic local fast-food chain. *11am-8pm Sun-Thu, to 10pm Fri & Sat* $

TOP EXPERIENCE

Fortifications of Québec

At the height of its fur-trading era, the capital of Nouvelle France (Québec City) was under constant threat from the British. Cap Diamant and the surrounding cliffs provided a natural shield, but the northern side of the city was exposed. In an effort to secure the city further, stone fortifications were built between 1690 and 1759, just before the fateful attack by General James Wolfe (p165).

TOP TIPS

- Take the guided walking tour with Parks Canada for access to sites not open to the general public. The guides are fabulous.

- Start at Terrasse Dufferin and end at the Dauphine Redoubt.

- Wear good shoes and bring a water bottle.

PRACTICALITIES

- parks.canada.ca/lhn-nhs/qc/fortifications
- 9:30am-5pm
- all 4 sites $30

Securing Québec City

French General Marquis de Montcalm greatly underestimated the ingenuity of General James Wolfe and his troops, who led an attack on the Plaines d'Abraham after climbing the cliff face – a feat previously thought to be impossible. After Québec was ceded to the British in 1763, they went to work to secure the city, building the fortifications on the western side from the Plaines d'Abraham to Artillery Park, as well as **La Citadelle** (p181), still an active military base.

St-Louis Forts & Châteaux

Hidden below Terrasse Dufferin are the ruins of the St-Louis Forts and Châteaux, home to the French governors first and then the British ones. From this seat of power, river activity was monitored and battles were planned. Interactive displays, artifacts and MAPS offer a glimpse of historical daily life as you wander through the ruins.

Artillery Park & Dauphine Redoubt

From Terrasse Dufferin you can walk along Rue St-Louis to the wall and follow it to Artillery Park, where munitions were made. Continue to the Dauphine Redoubt, where officers and soldiers lived. Each floor of the buildings highlights a different era from French to British.

a light on the sisters' way of life from the time they arrived in 1639 through to 1962, when the hospital became part of Québec's public health system. The transfer effectively ended the sisters' nursing duties and placed their focus entirely on the spiritual comfort and care of the hospital's patients, resulting in a significant decrease in nuns at the monastery. There are hundreds of artifacts to see in the museum, including an apothecary where the nuns made medications, and an impressive collection of medical instruments and paraphernalia.

Take a yoga or meditation class, get a massage or have a wholesome and delicious meal at Vivoir cafe. For a particularly special experience, stay overnight in a traditional nun's cell (they've been modernized to be very comfortable) with a twin bed, a small desk, a pedestal sink and shared bathrooms. En-suite rooms are also available.

Along the St Lawrence
MAPS P178 & P164
See the city from the river

All aboard! From May to October, you can set sail on the St Lawrence River from Québec City on a memorable cruise with **Croisières AML** *(croisieresaml.com/en/our-cruises)*. Soak up scenic views, look for wildlife, enjoy dinner under the stars or watch fireworks set to music (every August).

You can take the AML *Louis Jolliet* on a 90-minute guided sightseeing cruise ($50) with panoramic views of Montmorency Falls and Île d'Orléans with a French and English commentary on Québec City's maritime and colonial history. It's a favourite with daytime explorers.

AML brings the party with its two-hour DJ and cocktail cruise ($50), where the outside decks turn into a vibrating dance floor. In summer it's the hottest club in the city. Also available are weekend brunch cruises and dinner cruises.

Combo bus-and-boat day trips with AML include the **Grosse-Île Irish Memorial National Historic Site**, hiking trails and suspension bridges at Canyon Ste-Anne, and whale-watching in Tadoussac. You can book an AML cruise either online or at its booth, which is located near the boat dock on Quai Chouinard.

Another way to enjoy a fabulous view of **Château Frontenac** (p168) and Old Québec is to take the **Québec–Lévis ferry** *(traversiers.com/en)*, which departs from Gare Fluviale de Québec terminal every 30 to 60 minutes, depending

QUÉBEC CITY FESTIVALS

Carnaval de Québec: Visit Bonhomme's ice palace, watch ice-canoe races and drink Caribou at Canada's oldest winter festival.

Festival d'été de Québec: An 11-day music festival featuring global and local artists on stages across the city.

Les Grand Feux: This themed fireworks festival is the best way to spend August evenings in Old Québec.

Les Fêtes de la Nouvelle-France: A four-day celebration of 17th- and 18th-century Québec, complete with a parade.

Toboggan Festival: Ring in the New Year with outdoor concerts, ice bars and a giant Ferris wheel.

 EATING IN QUÉBEC CITY: QUÉBÉCOIS CUISINE — MAPS P164 & P178

Buffet de l'Antiquaire: Iconic diner in Old Port serving traditional foods since 1976. The breakfast poutine is a great hangover cure. *6am-9pm* $$	**Aux Anciens Canadiens:** Dine on tourtière, wild game, pea soup and other classics in the oldest house in Québec City. *noon-10:30pm* $$$	**La Bûche:** Urban sugar shack serving pâté chinois, a Québécois shepherd's pie, deer tartare and smoked trout. *8am-9:30pm Sun-Wed, to 10pm Thu-Sat* $$	**Chez Boulay:** Modern Québécois with Nordic Québec flavors and local ingredients. *5-9:45pm Mon & Tue, 11:30am-2pm & 5-9:45pm Wed-Fri, 10am-2pm & 5-9:45pm Sat & Sun* $$$

PICNIC LIKE A LOCAL

La Place Boutique Gourmand: The best spot for buying Québec wines and craft beers – and gourmet Bret's chips from France.

Le Grand Marché: Splurge on Québec cheeses, strawberries, charcuterie and fresh baguettes at this large farmers market.

Terrasse Pierre-Dugua-de-mons: Spread a blanket on the grass and enjoy postcard-perfect views.

Plaines d'Abraham: This 1759 battleground is now a public park with big, leafy trees perfect for picnicking in the shade.

Baie de Beauport: Sink your toes into the sand and nibble on Québec terroir at this popular local beach.

on the time of year. The ride takes 15 minutes and fares are under $5.

A Magnificent Castle-Style Hotel   MAP P164
Snap a photo of the Château Frontenac

Towering atop Cap Diamant like a lord surveying his land is the iconic **Château Frontenac**. This luxurious château-style hotel was built in 1893 by the Canadian Pacific Railway to entice elite travelers to explore Canada's rugged beauty and lush offerings. It has since been taken over by Fairmont and then Accor, but the château's continued allure lends credibility to its claim of being the most photographed hotel in the world.

The exterior is imposing, with a tall central tower and fabulous turrets, but the hotel's true charm is revealed when you pass through its revolving doors. The brushed gold and marine blue lobby gives way to a plush, boutique-lined galleria. Throughout, painted ceilings, decorative flourishes, curved grand staircases and crystal-laden chandeliers accentuate the hotel's lavish charm. A walking tour of the hotel reveals a history of royal visits, famous guests and its role in world history, most notably the Québec Conferences of WWII, when William Lyon Mackenzie King, prime minister of Canada, hosted Winston Churchill and Franklin D Roosevelt.

Even if you're not staying here (nightly rates range from $600 to $4500), you can still visit the hotel's public spaces, take the walking tour, dine at **Restaurant Champlain** or **Bistro Le Sam** (p184) or sip cocktails at 1608 Wine Bar.

A French-Influenced Legal System   MAP P164
Tour the Assemblée national

A free 60-minute guided tour of the **Assemblée national du Québec** *(assnat.qc.ca/en/index.html)* offers the chance to learn about Québec's parliamentary history and its civil law system (legal codes and statutes), as distinct from the common law (judicial precedents) found in the rest of Canada. Québec uses the federal common-law system for criminal and constitutional matters. When the Assemblée national is not in session, the tour visits the Salon bleu (National Assembly chamber). Talks detail the 1995 referendum, when the Parti Québécois wanted Québec to secede from Canada, and important political leaders such as René Lévesque and Jean Lesage. Finish with a visit to the grounds to admire

EATING IN OLD QUÉBEC: OUR PICKS   MAP P178

Restaurant Wong: An institution since 1960 serving Chinese fusion and intriguing cocktails such as the 'curry kid'. Reserve. *5:30-9pm Wed-Sun* $$

Chez Temporel: Artists cafe turned French bistro tucked down a quiet street in Haute-Ville. Reservations recommended. *11am-9pm* $$

Le Don: Gourmet plant-based foods that even a carnivore could love. Generous portions. *11am-9pm Mon-Thu, to 10pm Fri, hours vary Sat & Sun* $$

Le Bedeau: Tapas and wine bar where every dish features local ingredients. Try the scallop crudo or asparagus with marscapone. *5:30-10pm Mon-Wed, 11am-10pm Thu-Sun* $$

Château Frontenac

the bronze sculptures. Tours in French and English can be booked online. Bring photo ID.

North America's Oldest Commercial District

MAP P164 & P178

Shop around Petit-Champlain and Place-Royale

Travel back in time to 18th-century Québec, when the narrow cobblestone streets of **Petit-Champlain** and Place-Royale were a thriving commercial district with a large outdoor market and merchant shops in stone houses with

BLACK HISTORY

Join rapper, historian and tour guide **Webster** (@webster_ls) on a tour of Québec City's Black history.

Olivier Le Jeune, the first Black person to live permanently in Canada, arrived as an enslaved person in 1629. There's a plaque in the square of the Seminaire recognizing him as a person of historical importance in Québec and Canada. In a quiet corner I talk about segregation, African American and Afro-Caribbean history and how slavery in those places and here are interconnected and different. In the 20th century Château Frontenac turned down a lot of Black people because it wanted to cater to the Southern states of the US. Hôtel Clarendon was a safe space for Black visitors.

Tours can be booked at qchistoryxtours.ca.

🍺 DRINKING IN OLD QUÉBEC: BEER — MAPS P164 & P178

L'Oncle Antoine: This stone cavern in Place-Royale housed the first woman-owned business in Québec (1754). (Try a shot of maple whiskey too.) *11am-1am*

Bar Ste-Angèle: Meet local characters and enjoy live jazz while sipping a cold beer on Rue Ste-Angèle. *8pm-3am*

Pub d'Orsay: A staple since 1973 with a great beer selection and even better bartenders. *11:30am-10pm Sun-Wed, to 10:30pm Thu, to 11pm Fri & Sat*

Taverne Belley: Look for the pink house in Old Port and settle in for a night of beers and billiards. *noon-3am*

OLD QUÉBEC SHOPPING

Boutique de Noël: It's always Christmas time in this charming boutique near the Notre-Dame basilica. A great spot for Québec-themed ornaments.

Quartier Petit-Champlain: Wander through the oldest shopping district in North America, filled with souvenir shops, artisan boutiques, and local terroir.

Rue du Trésor: Chat to local artists in this iconic open-air gallery space, a local staple since 1960.

Galerie d'art Inuit Brousseau: Intricate Inuit soapstone and basalt carvings by artists from Arctic Canada are on display here.

Old Port: Antique shops and high-end galleries selling Québec art line Rue du Sault-au-Matelot and Réue St-Paul in Old Port.

gabled roofs. Snap a photo of Petit-Champlain from the top of **Escalier Casse-Cou** (1635; Breakneck Steps), the oldest stairs in Québec City, and shop at artisan boutiques on Rue du Petit-Champlain. You won't find popular franchises down here, but you will find gourmet restaurants, lively pubs and Rue Cul-de-sac, best known as **Umbrella Alley**.

The settlement of Kebec started in the spot now occupied by **Église Notre-Dame-de-victoires** (built from 1688 to 1723), which makes an appearance at the end of the movie *Catch Me If You Can* (2002). After the Battle of 1759 against the British, the neighborhood surrounding the church became a busy wharf and warehouse district, with workers living in tenement houses on Rue du Petit-Champlain.

Almost 200 years later a project was launched to restore Basse-Ville in hopes of increasing tourism. In Place-Royale the bones of the gable-roofed stone houses were restored to their original state, and ceramic plaques with merchant names and the buildings' dates of origin were fixed beside doorways. A couple of streets over, on Rue du Petit-Champlain, the houses are complete reconstructions based on historical documents. The blend of French and British architectural styles is representative of the lives lived under both countries' rule.

Layers of History at Notre-Dame-de-Québec

MAP P178

Visit the first Catholic parish north of Mexico

With its holy door, single domed tower, baldachin-capped altar and vibrant stained-glass windows, the **Basilique-Cathédrale Notre-Dame-de-Québec** appeals to secular visitors as well as pilgrims.

French explorer Samuel de Champlain built a church on the site in 1633. After it was razed by fire, the structure was replaced in 1647 with a stone church built by the Jesuits. When François de Laval was appointed head of the Diocese of Québec in 1674, the church was given cathedral status and became the seat of the Roman Catholic Church in North America. Québec City was the continent's first French settlement, and the church was eager to protect the French language and culture. It was then elevated to minor basilica status in 1874 by Pope Pius IX.

The church you'll see today, mostly neoclassical in style, is the work of three generations of Baillairgé master carpenters

EATING IN OLD QUÉBEC: FRENCH RESTAURANTS

MAPS P164 & P178

Bistro 1640: Look for the red roof, sit on the patio and order the tartare or the impressive charcuterie and fromage platter. *8:30am-9pm* **$$**

Lapin Sauté: Charming French restaurant in Petit-Champlain known for rabbit confit and seafood cassoulet. *11:30am-9:30pm* **$$**

L'Entrecôte Saint-Jean: Parisian-inspired bistro serving classics such as steak frites and duck-leg confit. *11:30am-10pm Mon-Sat, 4-10pm Sun* **$$**

Le Continental: Serves a classic French dinner with Caesar salad made tableside, snails in garlic butter and shrimp flambé. *4-10:30pm* **$$$**

A PHOTO-WORTHY TOUR OF OLD QUÉBEC

Discover the architecture, history and charm of Old Québec on this walking tour of historic landmarks, quiet side streets and Instagram-worthy vistas.

START	END	LENGTH
Fontaine de Tourny	Batterie-Royale	4km, 1½–2 hours

From ❶ **Fontaine de Tourny**, follow Rue St-Louis through ❷ **Port St-Louis**, turning right on Côte de la Citadelle. A walking path to the left leads to ❸ **Terrasse Pierre-Dugua-de-mons** (p173), where a staircase leads to Terrasse Dufferin. Grab a chocolate-dipped ice cream at ❹ **Au 1884**.

Continue to ❺ **Rue du Trésor** artists alley and then ❻ **Basilique-Cathédrale Notre-Dame-de-Québec**. From Côte de la Fabrique, turn right on Côte du Palais for a sweet treat at ❼ **Épicerie Québécoise** (p21), then follow Rue Charlevoix past the ❽ **Monastère des Augustines** (p165), a 17th-century monastery turned wellness retreat.

Follow Rue Hamel to Rue des Remparts and take the wooden staircase down to cobblestone ❾ **Côte du Colonel-Dambourgès**. On Rue St-Paul, have coffee and a pastry at ❿ **Les Cafés du Soleil**, then stroll pedestrianized ⓫ **Rue Sault-au-Matelot** with its high-end galleries.

Across Côte de la Montagne is Rue Notre-Dame with its ⓬ **Fresque des Québécois** (p182) mural. Turn right on Rue Sous-le-fort for the famous ⓭ **Breakneck Steps**.

Follow Rue du Petit-Champlain to sample goat cheese at ⓮ **Ferme Audet**, then take the staircase down to Blvd Champlain to find ⓯ **Umbrella Alley** on the left. The junction of ⓰ **Rue Cul-de-sac and Rue Notre-Dame** offers a great photo op of Château Frontenac. Turn right on Rue Sous-le-fort to reach the ⓱ **Batterie-Royale** (p181).

Dating from a church built in 1633, the **Basilique-Cathédrale Notre-Dame-de-Québec** is the oldest church in Canada.

The **Fontaine de Tourny** was a gift from Peter Simons, president of Maison Simons department store, to Québec City on its 400th anniversary.

Terrasse Pierre-Dugua-de-mons offers a postcard-perfect view of Old Québec.

HOLY DOORS

A concept dating back to the 14th century, a Holy Door represents overcoming obstacles and moving towards hope, forgiveness and light. Holy Doors are typically opened every 25 years to mark a special jubilee year, but they're also opened on other notable occasions. After the inauguration of the Holy Door at the Basilique-Cathédrale Notre-Dame-de-Québec in 2013 to mark the 350th anniversary of the founding of the church, the door was opened again in 2015 for the Year of Mercy. Even when it's closed, many visitors derive comfort from placing a hand on the massive bronze door embossed with biblical images. Québec City's Holy Door was last opened in 2024 for the 350th anniversary of the Diocese of Québec and will next be opened in 2049 (unless there's a special dispensation beforehand).

Terrasse Dufferin

(1759–1843). An American arsonist rumoured to be affiliated with the Ku Klux Klan in Canada set fire to the basilica in 1922. The blaze gutted the church, but it was painstakingly reconstructed over seven years, using photographs as reference points. In the funerary chapel you'll find the tomb of St François de Laval, who was beatified in 2014. Visits to the crypt, where four governors of New France and several bishops are buried, are possible from 1:30pm to 3:30pm Friday to Sunday.

EATING IN QUÉBEC CITY: BRUNCH

MAPS P174, P178 & P180

Elli: Drag brunch? Yes, please! Come alone or with friends – hello, bellinis and breakfast tacos. *10:30am Sat & Sun* $$

Café du Monde: Classic French bistro next to the cruise terminal with fancy omelets and eggs Benny. *9am-9:30pm Sat & Sun* $$

Chez Rioux & Pettigrew: No need to fuss over menu options: Sunday brunch is a set menu highlighting local flavors. *9am-1:30pm Sun* $$

Maelstrøm: Popular cafe in St-Roch serving daily brunch, which pairs well with a cold-brew coffee. *9am-3pm* $$

Old Québec Like a Local

MAP P164

See a World Heritage Site without the crowds

A World Heritage Site since 1985, Old Québec is the first place every newcomer visits. The best way to avoid the crush is to wander around before noon, visit museums or relax on a patio in the afternoon, and then hit the streets again around dinnertime. It's easy to spend a full day soaking up the district's ambience, strolling down **Terrasse Dufferin** or laying claim to a patch of grass above **Terrasse Pierre-Dugua-de-mons** to admire the views of Château Frontenac (p168), Old Québec and the St Lawrence River. The main arteries here are Rues St-Jean, St-Louis, du Buade and Côte de famille, each lined with boutiques, restaurants and bars. In summer the pavement water fountain at **Hôtel-de-Ville-de-Québec** is a popular place to cool off, and a large section of Rue St-Jean is blocked off for pedestrians and filled with patios. The true charm of the neighborhood, though, is found in its quiet side streets, where the locals live in houses dating back to the 18th and 19th centuries. There are over 400 years of French and English history here, from the markings of the first farmhouse and the home of the first Black person to live permanently in Canada (p169) to stone walls lined with cannons, religious foundations and artistic corners.

Snow Days

MAP P164

Celebrate life in the frosty season

Spotting a local during winter in Québec City is easy: from toque to heavy boots, they are ready for everything Mother Nature will throw at them. When winter really sets in, it's best to walk in the streets of Old Québec rather than along the sidewalks to avoid ice and snow falling from the buildings' roofs. They're not essential gear, but if you own ice cleats it's worth bringing them to help you stay upright on the city's steep hills. Locals don't cower at home in winter – it's simply too long to stay inside. Instead they give the chilly months a hearty bear hug. Place d'Youville's **outdoor skating rink** is a popular spot, and the Plaines d'Abraham has a great cross-country ski track (rentals available). In late November the **Marché de Noël allemand** (*German Christmas Market; mnaq.ca/en*) opens with outdoor bars, live music, visits from Santa and local artisans in small wooden chalets selling holiday treats. As the Christmas holidays approach, a thick blanket of snow covers the city (most years), a giant

SHOPPING OUTSIDE OLD QUÉBEC

Article 721: On Ave 3e in Limoilou, this small boutique sells Québec-made art prints, skin care, jewelry and clothing.

Coeur de Loup: Local fashion designer Nathalie Jourdain makes clothing to order at her atelier on Rue St-Vallier Est.

Le Knock-Out: Shop for vintage records in this funky shop on Rue St-Joseph Est.

Fanamanga: Indulge in all things Japanese, from manga to cosmetics, sweet treats and snacks.

SAQ: These government-run liquor stores are filled with Québec wines and spirits. Sortilège maple whiskey is a must!

 EATING IN LIMOILOU: OUR PICKS

MAP P174

Franky Johnny: Sandwicherie with a killer Italian option served on fresh focaccia. *11am-3pm Tue-Sun* $	**Soupe et Cie:** Soups from around the world, such as tortilla soup, gazpacho and Korean hot pot. *11am-9pm Mon-Fri, noon-9pm Sat & Sun* $$	**Ô Nicky:** The only all-you-can-eat sushi place in Québec City with a conveyor belt (known as sushi river). Reservations required. *4-9pm Sun, Mon & Wed, to 10pm Thu-Sat* $$	**La Planque:** Slurp fresh oysters followed by duck magret or sweetbreads at this upscale restaurant. *5:30-10pm Tue-Sat* $$$

LIMOILOU & ST-ROCH

● **SIGHTS**
1 Église St-Roch
2 St-Roch

● **EATING**
3 Bati Cantine
4 Chez Gaston
5 Franky Johnny
6 La Planque
7 Ô Nicky
8 Patente et Machin
9 Poulet Frit Wong
10 Smith Café
11 Soupe et Cie

● **DRINKING & NIGHTLIFE**
12 JJacques
13 La Barberie
14 La Korrigane
15 Le Nektar
16 Le Trèfle
17 Maelstrøm
18 Noctem Artisans Brasseurs

● **ENTERTAINMENT**
19 Impérial Bell

● **SHOPPING**
20 Article 721
21 Coeur de Loup
22 Déjà Vu Meubles
23 Fanamanga
24 La Place Boutique Gourmande
25 Le Knock-Out

tree is erected in Place-Royale and twinkling lights convert Old Québec into a living holiday card. On Terrasse Dufferin you can barrel down the **Glissade de la Terrasse**, the oldest tourist attraction in Québec, on a long wooden sled.

If you visit in February, be sure to check out the **Carnaval de Québec**.

Canada's Oldest Winter Carnival MAP P164
Join the February merriment

Over 70 years ago **Carnaval de Québec** (*carnaval.qc.ca*) was created to provide some cheer during the frigid weather in the depths of winter, when the St Lawrence River is heavy with large chunks of ice floe and the crisp air can literally take your breath away. In the early years it was an epic party not suitable for families. Things are different now, much to the chagrin of the older beer-loving generation.

The carnival ambassador is Bonhomme, a 2m-tall snowman with a red knitted toque on his head and a *ceinture fléchée* (French arrow sash, traditionally worn over winter coats in the 18th century to keep the cold out) around his waist. He hangs out in his grand ice palace when he's not busy walking in Old Québec, visiting schools and leading parades. Ice sculptures by artists from around Québec are scattered throughout Old Québec, restaurants build ice bars, and locals carry long, plastic carnaval canes that look like horns to carry alcohol with them as they wander around the city. You can go ice climbing near the marina, party the night away at an outdoor concert, watch the ice-canoe races on the St Lawrence River and drink Caribou, a Québécois winter tipple made with fortified wine and whiskey. A plastic effigy (in the shape of Bonhomme) acts as a passport to all things Carnaval. Buy it online and hang it from your coat zipper.

Just 20 minutes from Old Québec is **Hôtel de Glace**, the only ice hotel in North America. Built anew each January and open until early March, the complex includes hotel rooms, ice bars, a wedding chapel, an ice slide, and ice sculptures and carvings. Every year has a different theme. If you stay at the ice hotel, a warm room next door at Village Vacances Valcartier is included in the rate.

WINTER FESTIVALS & EVENTS

Marché de Noël allemand de Québec: This German Christmas market kicks off at the end of November with artisan kiosks, live music and Santa. *mnaq.ca*

Village Nordik: Held at Québec City's marina from February to March, here you can learn how to ice fish. *villagenordik.com*

Poutine Week: The first week in February is dedicated to Québec's national dish, with local restaurants competing to make the best gourmet poutine. *lapoutineweek.com*

Pee-Wee Hockey Tournament: Hockey fans pack the stands at the Vidétron Centre to watch this 12-day tournament in February. *tournoipee-wee.qc.ca*

Igloofest: An outdoor rave in March with three days of intoxicating music by internationally renowned DJs. *quebec.igloofest.ca*

 DRINKING IN ST-JEAN-BAPTISTE: BEST BARS MAP P180

Le Drague: The only gay bar in Québec City, with multiple dance floors and drag performances. *11am-3am*

Le Projet: A gastropub with ornate vaulted ceilings and 29 microbrews on tap. *3pm-1am Mon-Wed, 11am-3am Thu-Sat, 1am Sun*

Le Sacrilège: In summer the hidden terrace is a perfect place to sip Québec craft beer. *noon-3am*

Bateau de Nuit: Drink with locals in this rustic beer hall with live music and improv nights. *7pm-1am Mon, 8pm-1am Tue & Sun, 8pm-3am Wed-Sat*

A LOCAL'S ST-JEAN-BAPTISTE

Allison Van Rassel (@allisonvanrassel) is a CBC radio host, a journalist and proprietor of deTerroir Café (p182).

Buvette Scott: Wine bar with hip underground vinyl records and a menu showcasing seasonal foods.

Scott's Bodega: Family-friendly spot with tacos made by the owner, homemade sandwiches and local products.

L'Axe du Malt: My favorite spot to get locally brewed beers and ciders. If you want to find something cool and interesting, they'll probably have it.

Couteaux Deva: Dave Fortin is the best knife maker in Québec and one of the best-kept secrets in St-Jean-Baptiste. You can't just show up; you have to plan ahead and make an appointment.

Pâtisserie Chouquette: Classic French pastries that embody savoir faire. Everything is made with seasonal, local ingredients.

Neighborhoods Outside Old Québec   MAP P174
Venture beyond the city walls

Fromageries, *boucheries* (butcher shops), beer and wine shops, and ephemeral patios dot the neighborhoods outside Old Québec, where you'll find that the throngs of tourists are notably absent. In **St-Jean-Baptiste**, a bohemian neighborhood a short walk from the old city walls, the streets are lined with buzzy cafes, micro-restaurants, chocolatiers and steep hills stacked with houses. It's home to young professionals, live music events, poetry readings, jam sessions and the occasional street festival. **St-Roch** is considered the hippest neighborhood in Québec City, with Rue St-Joseph Est running through it like an artery and **Église St-Roch** (the tallest cathedral in the city) standing at its center. It's home to the iconic Imperial Bell, a performing arts theater since 1933, and an eclectic mix of houses squished together like marshmallows.

Across the St Charles River, **Limoilou** is often referred to as an up-and-coming neighborhood, which does it a disservice. Québec hip-hop grew up here in the late 1990s and early 2000s, long before stylish cafes and restaurants appeared on Ave 3e. The neighborhood's signature multistorey brick houses with metalwork staircases winding up the center are reminiscent of Montréal's Plateau. In summer the marina and park along the river offer a welcome reprieve from the heat, street festivals are held and patios take over the sidewalks. **Smith Café** is a go-to for coffee, pizza and coworking.

Two-Wheeled Sightseeing   MAPS P178 & P180
Cycling around Québec City

Navigating Old Québec by car will age you by at least 10 years. In Basse-Ville the streets are pedestrian only after 11am, and Haute-Ville has very little parking and is full of buses, pedestrians and one-way streets. Tuck your vehicle away in a garage, explore Old Québec on foot and then rent an e-bike to branch out into the areas beyond the walls. **Promenade Samuel-de-Champlain** is a popular path with cyclists and runners, stretching from Pont Pierre Laporte to Port de Québec, where it connects with the Corridor du Littoral. The promenade hugs the St Lawrence River, passing public art installations and **Station de la Plage** (Québec City's hottest new beach and pool area). The **Corridor du Littoral**

continues on p179

EATING IN ST-ROCH: OUR PICKS   MAPS P174 & P180

Bati Cantine: Casual dining option serving classic Thai and Cambodian foods like Khmer noodles and Tom Yum soup. *hours vary* $$

Patente et Machin: These kitchen pirates cook impressive meals using domestic stoves. Bring friends and dine family-style. *6-11pm Mon-Sat* $$$

Nina Pizza Napolitaine: Québec City's best Neapolitan pizza spot, with pillowy focaccia, Caesar salad and creamy burrata too. *11am-10pm Sun-Thu, to 11pm Fri & Sat* $$

Poulet Frit Wong: Savor juicy gluten-free fried chicken with a side of creamy Asian-inspired coleslaw. *11am-8pm* $$

TOP EXPERIENCE

Musée de la Civilisation

Perhaps the most significant museum in Québec City, Musée de la Civilisation in Basse-Ville takes an avant garde approach to its exhibitions, challenging mainstream ideas and pushing cultural boundaries. There have been exhibits on poop, the history of beer, French comic *Tintin* and dinosaurs. The true stars of the museum, however, are its permanent installations on Indigenous and Québécois history.

Modernity Meets History

Light pours through large skylights, warming the concrete walkways and illuminating the ruins of a ship on display below. This captivating juxtaposition begins with the building, designed by Israeli-Canadian architect Moshe Safdie (who also designed Habitat 67 in Montréal and the National Gallery of Canada) to incorporate historic buildings and modern additions.

In Other Words, Québec

The largest exhibit, In Other Words, Québec has six themed pavilions spanning 1570 sq meters. The journey begins with the first contact between White colonizers and First Nations people in 1535 and weaves together the histories of the First Nations and the colonizers who claimed Québec as their own, touching on economics, sociology, protesting and belonging.

This Is Our Story

One of the most poignant exhibits on the First Nations and Inuit people, This Is Our Story is a collaboration between 11 Indigenous nations in Québec, who tell their stories and perspectives through art, artefacts and sounds. In this space you'll learn about tumultuous events, and the nations' fears, hopes and dreams.

TOP TIPS

● Buying tickets online is often cheaper and lets you skip the line when you arrive.

● Allow yourself at two to four hours to properly explore the various exhibits.

● On the second Thursday of every month entry is free from 10am to 5pm.

PRACTICALITIES

● mcq.org/en
● 10am-5pm Tue-Sun
● adult/student $26/21

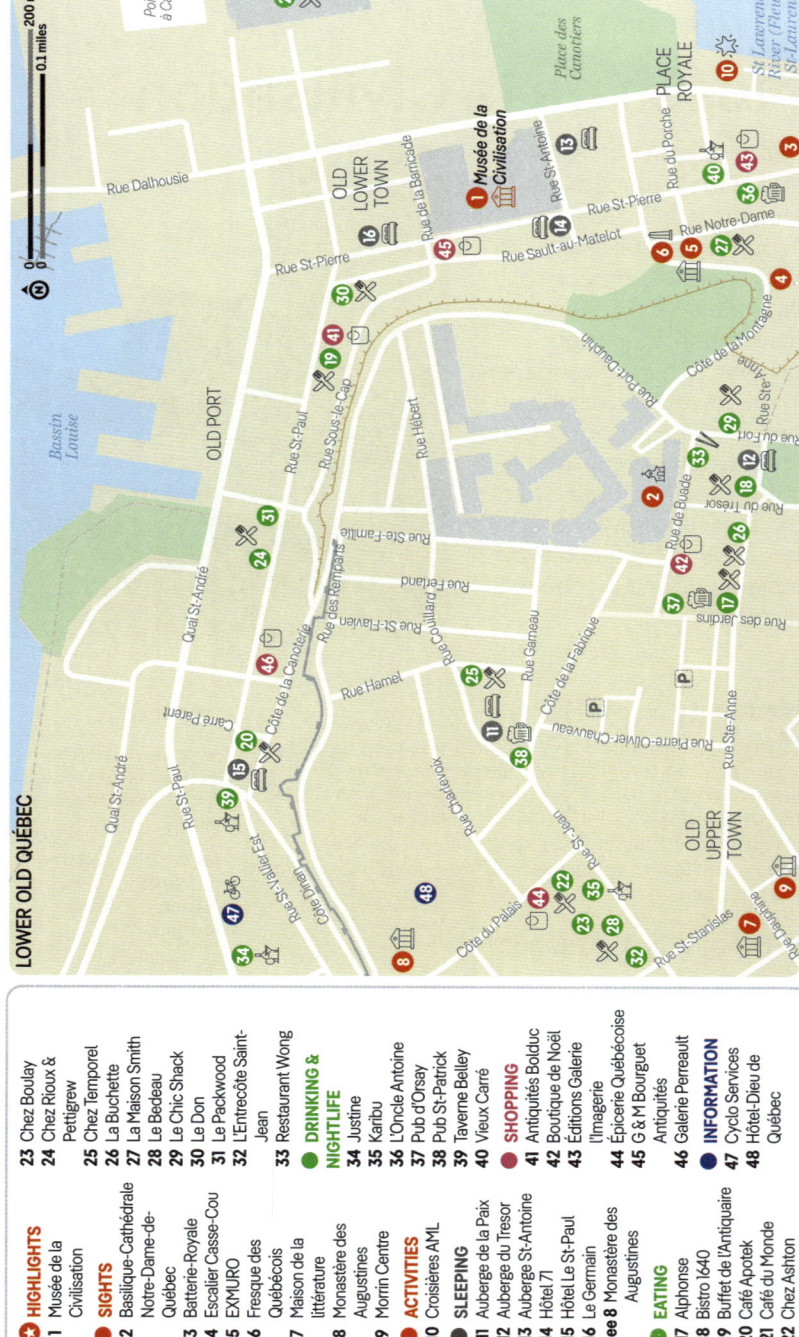

continued from p176

then moves north, passing Domaine de Maizerets, a sprawling park with historic buildings, a pool and a labyrinth. From there it's on to Chute-Montmorency, where you can take a path along the St Charles River to Limoilou or keep pedaling until you reach Wendake.

Ambitious riders may want to tackle the **Route Verte du Québec**, a 5300km trail network that extends into Ontario, New Brunswick and the US. Chat with the folks at **Cyclo Services** about your route, safety equipment needs and which bike rental is best for the journey.

The Birthplace of Poutine   MAP P174 & P178
Experience Québec's culinary icon

Reaching rock star status around the world, the most famous dish to come out of Québec is a delicious accident known as poutine: fries topped with fresh squeaky cheese curds (made by curdling milk, which separates into liquid whey and small pieces of fresh, solid cheese) and smothered with hot brown gravy (called *sauce brune* in Québec). Poutine originated in the 1950s when car travel became popular and *casse-croûtes* (roadside snack shacks) popped up serving burgers, fries, steamies (hot dogs) and bags of fresh cheese curds. The most common claim is that a customer (either in Drummondville or Warwick) was in a rush and asked for his cheese curds to be thrown into his bag of fries and gravy. Soon this *pouding* (Québec slang for 'a messy mixture') became known as poutine, winning the hearts (emotionally and physically) of Québec's working class. In the 1980s poutine started popping up on menus at McDonalds and Burger King, and not long after it spread around the world from London to Laos. It's the perfect meal before, during and after a night of drinking, and every neighborhood in Québec City has at least one poutine spot. **Buffet de l'Antiquaire** (p167) is known for its heart-stopping breakfast poutine, which includes sausage, bacon, ham and hollandaise, and having poutine from **Casse-Croûte Pierrot** delivered directly to the bar is always a solid idea. The first week of February is **Poutine Week** (p175), an excellent time to try a variety of gourmet poutines.

ÉPICERIES

Épicerie Richard: The best option in Old Québec, with fresh produce, wine, bread and canned goods.

Marché d'Emma: Has a wide selection of pantry foods, milk, eggs, craft beer and sometimes fresh produce.

Épicerie Québécoise: Ready-made high-end foods – perfect if you're staying somewhere with a kitchen.

Épicerie Européenne: A gourmet food shop in St-Jean-Baptiste with an amazing selection of cheese, dried meat, wine and fine snacks.

Carotte Joyeuse Épicerie Santé: A natural goods shop with a great produce section, legumes and organic goods.

 DRINKING IN QUÉBEC CITY: WINE BARS & SPEAKEASIES   MAPS P164, P174 & P178

Justine: Look for windows covered with black curtains near the train station – great music, eats and cocktails. *6pm-3am Wed-Sun*

JJacques: Named one of the 50 best bars in Canada, this speakeasy has succulent seafood towers and delicious cocktails. *5pm-1am Sun-Thu, to 3am Fri & Sat*

Karibu: Serves a 100% Québec menu, from wines to umami-packed Asian snack foods. *11:30am-2pm Tue-Fri, 5:30-8:30pm Tue & Wed, 5-9pm Thu-Sat*

Terroir: Relax on the patio with a view of Petit-Champlain while sipping a glass of wine. *11:30am-7pm Thu, to 8pm Fri & Sat, to 6pm Sun*

ST-JEAN-BAPTISTE & AROUND

● SIGHTS
1. Obsérvatoire de la Capitale
2. Plaines d'Abraham
3. St-Jean-Baptiste

● SLEEPING
4. Auberge Jeunesse QBEDS Hostel
5. Château des Tourelles
6. Hôtel Château Laurier
7. Hôtel Krieghoff
8. Le C3 Hôtel

● EATING
9. Buvette Scott
see 7 Café Krieghoff
10. Ciel!
11. Elli
12. Épicerie Européenne
13. Hobbit Bistro
14. Le Billig
15. Nina Pizza Napolitaine
see 15 Pâtisserie Chouquette
see 15 Snack-Bar St-Jean

● DRINKING & NIGHTLIFE
16. Cantook
17. deTerroir Café
18. Le Drague
19. Le Projet
20. Le Sacrilège
21. L'Inox
22. Pub Galway
23. Pub Nelligan's

● ENTERTAINMENT
24. Bateau de Nuit
25. Festival d'été de Québec
26. Grand Théâtre de Québec
27. Théâtre Périscope

● SHOPPING
28. Carotte Joyeuse Épicerie Santé
29. Couteaux Deva
30. L'Axe du Malt
31. SAQ
32. Scott's Bodega

A French-Occupied British Fortress MAP P164
Tour La Citadelle

Sometimes referred to as the Gibraltar of the Americas, **La Citadelle** is the biggest British fortress in North America. After a failed American attack in 1775, the British erected a temporary citadel on the top of Cap Diamant. Inspired by the Fortifications of Vauban in France, La Citadelle's permanent star-shaped stone structure with five bastions was built from 1820 to 1831. Two remnants of the French regime were included, the Cap Diamant Redoubt and the powder magazine; in 1840, armouries, a barracks and a hospital were added. The greatly feared American invasion never happened and the British remained until 1871, when they handed La Citadelle over to the Canadian government.

A guided visit is the only way to visit this active military base, home to Canada's only French-speaking infantry regiment, the Royal 22e, since 1920. The highlight at La Citadelle is its museum, recognized as a Canadian Forces Museum since 1974. The collection is extensive: 15,000 artifacts, 340,000 photographs and over 5000 military documents and books. There are plenty of information panels to read, as well as weapons in cases, flags and displays on the evolution of uniforms. Book tickets online for the one-hour **tour** *(billets.lacitadelle.qc.ca/Online; $22)*. The best time to go is in the morning from Wednesday to Sunday, when tours can be combined with the regiment's musical performance (formerly the changing of the guard).

Creative Québec City MAP P178
Delve into the city's arts scene

Eclectic, fun and sometimes super-weird, Québec City's arts scene is a vibrant part of its appeal. Nonprofit arts foundation **EXMURO** *(exmuro.com/en)* has curated an open-air summer program in Basse-Ville for over 10 years, showcasing the work of artists from Québec and around the world and inviting locals and visitors to interact with Old Québec in new ways. There are quirky street performances and thought-provoking temporary works, such as Ai Weiwei's installation of refugee life jackets that covered the **Batterie-Royale**. Installations move around and change from May to October, but EXMURO's free museum is open year-round and includes a room called the Museum of Bad Art. Consult the website for info on current and upcoming exhibitions.

MAPLE SYRUP, QUÉBEC'S LIQUID GOLD

Québec makes an astonishing 70% of the world's maple syrup. First Nations people used maple sap and bark to cook and cure meat and for medicinal purposes for thousands of years before teaching the colonizers how to get it for themselves, a kind gesture that led to the creation of maple sugar and then, in the early 20th century, maple syrup. This liquid gold contributes $1.1 billion to Canada's GDP, according to the syrup-makers' union. In 2011 and 2012, Richard Vallières convinced a group of thieves to help him rob the maple reserve, replacing nearly 3000 tonnes of syrup with water and sometimes leaving the barrels empty. He's currently serving a 14-year jail sentence and must repay $9 million of the $18 million worth of syrup he stole.

EATING IN QUÉBEC CITY: BREAKFAST MAPS P164 & P180

Le Billig: Known for having some of the best crêpes in Québec City. Popular stop on food tours. *11am-10pm* **$**

Hobbit Bistro: French bistro serving gourmet croque madame, salmon gravlax and boudin sausage. *8am-10pm* **$$**

Cochon Dingue: Tuck into an order of eggs Benny or a full breakfast with eggs, meat of your choice and toast. *8am-9pm Sun-Thu, to 10pm Fri & Sat* **$$**

Café Krieghoff: Neighborhood institution serving affordable hearty meals. Try the breakfast pizza. *8am-2:30pm* **$$**

ANTIQUES & ART BOUTIQUES

G & M Bourguet Antiquités: A lovely father-and-son-run antique shop with Québec antiques, folk art, carved wooden pieces and furniture. *gmbourguet.com*

Antiquités Bolduc: Houses 19th-century curios, housewares, vintage paintings, ceramics and glassware. One of the best antique shops in the city. *lesantiquitesbolduc.com*

Éditions Galerie l'Imagerie: This little shop sells prints, paintings and puzzles with images of Québec by Québec artists. *egiclees.com*

Galerie Perreault: Spectacular gallery showcasing the work of over a dozen North American artists, including Mr Brainwash and Bruno Côté. *galerie-perreault.com*

DéJà Vu Meubles: Shop for vintage furniture, signs, glassware, suitcases and more. A local favourite in St-Roch. *dejavumeubles.com*

Observatoire de la Capitale

A walk through St-Roch's residential streets is the best way to discover many of the city's murals. Great places to start include the Rue de la Salle, the Elvis Snoopy on Rue Kirouac and the overpass pillars on Blvd Charest. The oldest and largest mural is **Fresque des Québécois** (1999) in Place-Royale, depicting important figures in Québec's history.

Visual arts are just the tip of the iceberg, though. Québec City is also home to thriving literary and performing arts communities. Concerts and performances are a window on

DRINKING OUTSIDE OLD QUÉBEC: CAFES — MAPS P174, P178 & P180

Cantook: Choose from more than 15 coffee blends at this popular local cafe. *7:30am-7pm Mon-Fri, 9am-5pm Sat & Sun*

deTerroir Café: Artisanal coffee, cold brew and 'croffles' (croissant waffles served with homemade caramel). *6:30am-4pm Mon-Fri, 8am-5pm Sat & Sun*

Le Nektar: Contemporary cafe in St-Roch with high-quality small-batch coffee. Popular with remote workers. *7am-8pm Mon-Fri, 8am-8pm Sat & Sun*

Le Packwood: Cafe, sandwicherie and quirky boutique near Rue St-Paul's antique shops. *9am-4:30pm*

Québec culture. Even though they're almost always performed in French, they're enjoyable no matter which language you speak.

The City's Best Angle
Take in the views

MAP P180

On the 31st floor of Édifice Marie-Guyart, the 'Horizons Experience' at the **Observatoire de la Capitale** (*observatoire-capitale.com*, $15) sets out to be an exposé of Québec City's history and cultural identity. There are interactive displays and immersion videos, all big and easy to consume in a short time. The Observatoire also offers a 360-degree view of the city, and the smartphone-friendly audio guide is a fun way to learn even more history as you take in the vista. Hold off on buying tickets in advance, and check 'today's view' to see whether you can look forward to clear skies. Timed tickets can be bought online.

Alternatively, soak up panoramic city views at **Ciel!**, the rotating restaurant on the 28th floor of the Hôtel Le Concorde in Montcalm. The brutalist-style building is hard to miss. If you want a table by the window, be sure to make a reservation – and there's still no guarantee.

For a unique prospect on the city, **SkySpa** in Ste-Foy offers a thermal experience (with steam/hot tub and cold plunge) while you soak up sweeping city views.

Irish Québec
Honor the courage of immigrants on Grosse-Île

MAP P178 & P180

Many Irish Québecers can trace their roots back to **Grosse-Île Irish Memorial National Historic Site**, a quarantine island 48km downstream from Québec City. From 1832 to 1937 this island in the St Lawrence processed 4.3 million immigrants, many of whom were Irish. Crosses mark the mass graves of thousands of immigrants who died on the island. Most were Irish people fleeing the potato famine in 1847 who then contracted typhus on the 'coffin ships' traveling across the Atlantic to the Americas. Over 5000 people died here in 1847, leaving behind hundreds of orphans, who retained their Irish names when they were adopted by French-Canadian families. A visit to Grosse-Île chronicles the struggles of those who sought to start a new life in a new country. Book an excursion through **Croisières AML** (*croisieresaml.com/en*).

ARTS AFTER DARK

Le Diamant: Next to Port St-Jean in Old Québec, this venue has a program featuring everything from brash comics to interpretive dance. *lediamant.ca/en*

Impérial Bell: A primo live-music venue that's been a neighborhood staple in St-Roch since 1912. *imperialbell.com*

Grand Théâtre de Québec: The music and comedy performances are good, but watching a movie while the symphony plays the score live is unforgettable. *grandtheatre.qc.ca/programmation*

Théâtre Capitole: With a program ranging from the Thunder from Down Under to Marc Dupré, the Capitole has been an icon since 1903. *theatrecapitole.com/en/shows*

Théâtre Périscope: This unassuming theater in St-Jean-Baptiste is a solid place to experience Québec City's indie arts scene. *theatreperiscope.qc.ca*

 DRINKING IN QUÉBEC CITY: BEST MICROBREWERIES — MAPS P174 & P180

La Korrigane: The owner of this microbrewery crafts her beers using Québécois products. *11:30am-midnight Sun-Thu, to 2am Fri & Sat*

La Barberie: Local hot spot in a quiet corner of St-Roch with great beers. There's another location on Île d'Orléans. *noon-1am*

Noctem Artisans Brasseurs: Things get a little catty here, but don't worry: it's just the beer names (El Gato Lime, Weisskatz, Catnip...). Sit out in summer. *hours vary*

L'Inox: A neighborhood favourite since 1987, L'Inox is a chill place for a drink and to make new friends. *11am-1am*

INDIGENOUS QUÉBEC

Québec's 11 Indigenous nations comprise 10 First Nations; the 11th is Inuit. Together they represent nearly 10% of Canada's total population of Indigenous people, and fit within three geocultural groups: Eastern Woodlands Indigenous Peoples (Algonquin and Iroquois), Subarctic Indigenous Peoples (Cree) and Arctic Indigenous Peoples (Inuit). The nations also include the Kanien'kehá:ka (Mohawk) on Montréal's South Shore; the Huron-Wendat found in Wendake, near Québec City; and also the Algonquian, in the Outaouais and near Abitibi-Témiscamingue, extending into Ontario. The once nomadic Innu reside along the Côte-Nord, and Gaspésie is the ancestral land of the Mi'kmaq people. The Inuit are located in Nunavik. Other groups include the Eeyou (Cree), Atikamekw Nehirowisiwok, Naskapi, Wolastoqiyik (Malecite) and Waban-Aki also (Abenaki).

In 1997 a Celtic cross was erected in Old Québec by John Callery, founder of the Stokestown Park Famine Museum, as a thank you gift to Québec City for welcoming Irish people during the tumultuous 1840s.

Storehouses of Language

MAP P178

Visit the city's French and English libraries

Light pours through the towering triple lancet windows of the **Maison de la littérature**, the epicenter for the preservation of French literature in Québec City. Its shelves are filled with books by French and Québécois authors, and local

 DRINKING IN OLD QUÉBEC: COCKTAIL SPOTS — MAPS P164 & P178

Bistro Le Sam: Channel *The Great Gatsby* while sipping elaborate cocktails and slurping down oysters. Try a Hugo spritz. *11:30am-10pm*

Alphonse: Old pennies cover the bar wall of this bank turned restaurant and cocktail bar. Try a botanist pink. *11:30am-10pm Sun-Wed, to 11pm Thu-Sat*

La Buchette: Sip boozy cocktails under antler chandeliers in a sugar-shack-chic restaurant with a $10 happy hour. Try a Buchette spritz. *8am-10:30pm*

Vieux Carré: Small speakeasy with artisanal cocktails made with Québec products. Try a spicy smash bros. *4pm-1am, Thu-Sun in winter, daily in summer*

Morrin Centre

art exhibitions and literary salons are held here, too. The library that first occupied this space was the Salle de l'Institut (1944–96), run by L'Institut canadien de Québec (L'ICQ), founded in 1848 to strengthen Québec culture and education.

Just across the street is the **Morrin Centre**, an English-language cultural center that's home to the Literary and Historical Society of Québec and a Victorian library with worn wooden floors, big work tables and over 27,000 books. Events include performances by local musicians, afternoon tea time and poetry nights. Purchase a day pass for $5, which helps support the center and its programming.

QUÉBEC CITY TOURS

Free walking tour of Old Québec: A two-hour walking tour winding through the streets and history of Québec. *afreetourof quebec.com*

Evening gourmet food tour: Splurge on an unforgettable food tour through some of Old Québec's best restaurants. *hqst.ca*

St-Roch Broue tour: Drink your way around the microbreweries of Québec City's trendiest neighborhood. *broue-tours.ca*

Bike tour of Old Québec: Take a guided bike tour on a summer evening, complete with a break on the beach. The fat bike tour is a must in winter. *quebecfatbike.com*

Gin and the Québec Garrison Club: A guide in period costume unlocks the history of this 19th-century private club while plying you with local gin. *cicerone.ca*

 DRINKING IN QUÉBEC CITY: BEST IRISH PUBS — MAPS P174, P178 & P180

Le Trèfle: Enjoy a pint of Guinness or Smithwick's and savour beer-soaked Irish mussels at this popular pub. *4pm-1am Tue & Wed, to 3am Thu & Fri, hours vary Sat & Sun*

Pub Nelligan's: Whiskey is the name of the game at this homey Irish pub a short walk from Old Québec's Port St-Jean. *4pm-3am Mon-Fri, 2pm-2am Sat & Sun*

Pub St-Patrick: On a summer day the sprawling patio is perfect for enjoying a cold beer and people-watching in Old Québec. *11am-midnight Sun-Tue, to 1am Wed, 11am-3am Thu-Sat*

Pub Galway: A piece of Galway in Québec City, with 20 beers on tap, Irish whiskeys and Celtic-themed cocktails. *11:30am-3:30am Fri & Sat, hours vary Sun-Thu*

Researched by Robert Isenberg

Day Trips from Québec City

Fire up that engine! The dynamic hills and riverfront around Québec City are full of history and natural wonders.

Places

Chute Montmorency p186
Wendake p188
Île d'Orléans p190
Sainte-Anne-de-Beaupré p192
Parc National de la Jacques-Cartier p195

☑ TOP TIP

Driving is the most common mode of transportation, but many destinations are a reasonable taxi or bike ride from Québec City.

Waterfalls, churches and rolling vineyards: the magic of Québec extends well beyond the city limits. Once you've explored every staircase and alleyway of Old Québec you'll find plenty more enchantments within an hour's drive. This is where some of the first French settlers broke ground to establish the colony of New France. Whether you visit the historic villages just a few kilometers down the St Lawrence River or venture into the forests of the Parc National de la Jacques Cartier, the lands around Québec City are rich in activities and folklore. Meanwhile, the suburb of Wendake is a vivid reminder of just how long First Nations peoples lived in the pre-Columbian forests, building longhouses and cultivating a resilient cultural legacy.

Chute Montmorency

TIME FROM QUÉBEC CITY: **20MIN**

Gaze on the falls

It's hard to convey the sheer magnitude of **Chute Montmorency** *(sepaq.com/destinations/parc-chute-montmorency; adult high/low season $12.60/9.46)*. The cascade of water drops 83m into a nimbus of froth and mist, and vertical walls of sandstone and shale rise on either side, disappearing beneath curtains of forest. Even as you drive past on Rte 138 you can sense the falls' titanic power. The closer you get, the more jaw-dropping Montmorency becomes.

Luckily, the infrastructure around **Parc de la Chute-Montmorency** allows you to get pretty darn close. From the upper parking lot you can walk along a path to an observation platform. On sunny days the lower reaches of the falls are wreathed in rainbows. Further down is a 23m-long suspension bridge, which spans the top of the falls and provides a bird's-eye view of the plummeting water. On the other side, a long staircase zigzags down to the bottom of the falls. The paved trails down here trace a long horseshoe around the

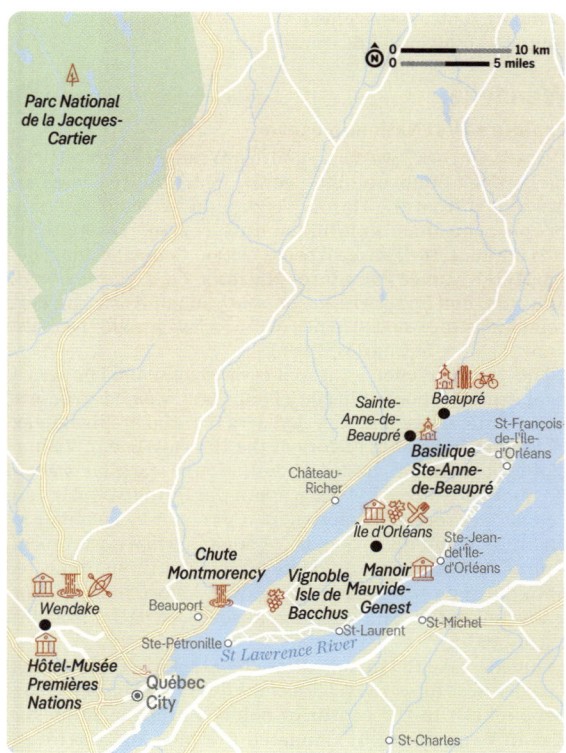

MONTMORENCY'S MONUMENTS

As you explore the Parc de la Chute-Montmorency you'll spy some historic monuments. The main building near the entrance, Manoir Montmorency (p188), is a replica from 1994 of an 18th-century governor's residence. The remains of an old fort from a battle between the British and French, Redoute de Wolfe, stand near the eastern zip-line platform. There is also Wolfe House, which was constructed around 1818 and offers a rare glimpse at the French regime's architecture. These all hint at the plot's long-standing colonial history.

lower waters; as you approach the plunge basin, expect to get soaked in spray.

The park is open daily. If you'd prefer to avoid the long climbs, you can ride the cable car from the upper parking lot to the bottom of the canyon ($14.95 for unlimited same-day trips.)

Zip over the water

For thrill-seekers, the concept is too perfect: you fasten on a helmet, hook yourself to a cable and soar 300m across the Montmorency canyon. The **zip line** *(adult/child $32/24)* is strung between two raised wooden platforms, and everything in between is crashing water and open air, affording you the closest possible view of the falls. Even better, this zip line has two separate cables, allowing you to ride alongside – or even race – a second person. The ride lasts less than a minute, and you only cross once; visitors should still budget about 30 minutes for the full experience, including up to 10 minutes to walk back from the opposite side. Riders must be at least 15 years of age and weigh between 41kg and 99kg. Book tickets through the main Sépaq website.

The upper park is currently undergoing a major revitalization, which includes a full replacement of a via ferrata

MONTMORENCY'S GRAND MANOR

Perched above the thundering falls, the Palladian-style Manoir Montmorency has lived many lives. Built in the 1780s as a summer retreat for Governor Sir Frederick Haldimand, it became a royal love nest from 1791 to 1794, when the British Duke of Kent (future father of Queen Victoria) holed up here with his longtime mistress, Julie de St Laurent. The site later morphed into a timber merchant's home, a hotel and a retirement residence before a fire reduced it to ashes in 1993. What you see today is a faithful 1994 reconstruction housing a gift shop and restaurant overlooking the same dramatic cascade admired by centuries of inhabitants.

climbing route. Management expects to install an improved route by summer 2026.

Wendake

TIME FROM QUÉBEC CITY: **30MIN**

Explore a First Nations museum

Deep in Québec's western suburbs, Wendake is a pretty little borough of about 2000 people. Nearly all residents are descended from the Huron-Wendat, the Iroquois-speaking people who once dominated this region. To spotlight this heritage, the Huron-Wendat Nation Council established the **Hôtel-Musée Premières Nations** *(First Nations Hotel-Museum; hotelpremieresnations.ca)*, an impressive modern complex on the wooded banks of the Akiawenrahk River (also known as the St Charles River.)

The main attraction is the well-curated museum. The permanent exhibit is housed inside a lampshade-shaped structure, where interactive maps, period artifacts and archival images illustrate the long history of the Huron-Wendat. Visitors can choose from a guided or audio tour – each lasts about 90 minutes. Here you'll learn about the Huron-Wendat's ancestral territories, the destruction wrought by colonialism, and the current operations of Wendake's tribal government. One of the most powerful features is a short film, projected onto the main wall, that tells the Wendat origin story. Gorgeous animation and a trilingual script bring the complex legend to life.

Outside, take the main path to the Ekionkiestha' National Longhouse, a full-sized replica of the dwellings Huron-Wendat people built in the centuries before European influence. Gas-lit flames burn in simulated fire pits, and the interior is realistically adorned with skins and drying vegetables. Within a protective timber wall, guides describe the architecture and give an account of daily life in a Huron-Wendat village. To really embrace the experience, you can actually stay the night in the longhouse.

Alternatively, you can book a suite at the Hôtel Premières Nations, which provides luxury accommodations just steps from the museum. Sleep in a well-appointed room, float around the indoor swimming pool and savor traditional flavors at **Restaurant La Traite** *(restaurantlatraite.ca)*, the campus' exquisite on-site restaurant.

A boutique showcasing Indigenous crafts is located just under the museum.

 EATING IN WENDAKE: OUR PICKS

Restaurant La Traite: In a refined setting, La Traite serves masterpieces using locally sourced ingredients. *7am-9pm* **$$$**

Resto Pub Délice: After a good ride on the nearby bike trail, enjoy a hearty breakfast or lunch in this easygoing pub. *7am-10pm* **$$**

Restaurant Le Piolet: The food here's top notch: Le Piolet is both a bistro and a training ground for young cooks. *11:30am-1:30pm Wed-Fri* **$$**

Restaurant Yahwatsira: This easygoing eatery puts a fun, modern spin on traditional Wendat cooking. *11:30am-5pm Mon & Tue, to 7pm Wed-Fri* **$$**

Kabir Kouba Waterfall

THE WENDAKE POW WOW

Each summer, Wendake hosts its **Pow Wow International** *(tour ismewendake.ca)*, a sizable celebration of First Nations heritage. Like many powwows across North America, this event is free and open to the public; visitors can see traditional garments and crafts, and taste a range of foods. The Pow Wow is an important meeting point for members of the Huron-Wendat diaspora, but it also helps educate outsiders about Indigenous roots. Merchants set up tents to showcase their artwork, and dancers perform in a central circle (some performances are ticketed). The festival is typically held at the end of June; the hotel, museum and longhouse get especially busy during this time, so book rooms and tours well ahead.

Embrace the river

The waters of **Kabir Kouba Waterfall** slide gently down a diagonal sedimentary rock face, descending a total of 28m into the narrow canyon. The site is just a five-minute walk from the Hôtel-Musée Premières Nations parking lot and makes for striking photos.

This part of the Akiawenrahk River has a powerful current, and the waters get frothy in the spring, so swimming near the waterfall isn't recommended. A little further downstream, though, you'll find **Canots Légaré** *(Lost Canoes; canotslegare.com)*, a boathouse that rents canoes, kayaks and stand-up paddleboards. This calmer segment is perfect for paddling, and you can follow the same watery routes Huron-Wendat fishers took in generations past.

Walk through legends

What if you entered the forest at night and the land itself told you a story? That's the idea behind **Onhwa' Lumina** *(onhwalumina.ca; adult/child $34/18)*, an immersive educational experience that uses lyrical recorded narration and sophisticated lighting effects to describe the cosmology of the Huron-Wendat. Follow a trail through elaborate sets and cinematic projections – and dress for weather.

JACQUES CARTIER

French explorer Jacques Cartier (1491–1557) was a contemporary of the Spanish conquistadors, but he chose to sail north, into the St Lawrence River. Cartier is believed to be the first European mariner to encounter a number of First Nations peoples, including the Iroquois and Huron-Wendat, and historians generally agree that his interpretation of the Iroquois word *kanata* (village) inspired the name Canada. Like Columbus, Cartier was convinced he could find a direct route to China, and his relentless search for riches has made him an increasingly controversial figure among historians. In many ways the explorer was ahead of his time; he started mapping a region that the French monarchy would not set about colonising until decades after his death, with the bloodier arrival of Samuel de Champlain.

Île d'Orléans

TIME FROM QUÉBEC CITY: **20MIN**

Admire the architecture

As early as the 17th century, French farmers started to till the rich soils of Île d'Orléans, and they built farms and six distinct villages in the Norman style they knew best. Much of this early architecture still stands on the river-island's bucolic hillsides. The best-preserved village is St-Jean-de-l'Île-d'Orléans, which stretches along the southeastern shore and is lined with whitewashed cottages and brightly painted roofs. You'll find a smattering of shops and eateries, as well as a stately stone church and neighboring cemetery. St-Jean's crown jewel is the **Manoir Mauvide-Genest** *(manoir mauvidegenest.com)*, an archetypal French mansion built in 1752. Costumed interpreters guide visitors through the manor house, using period furniture and household items to illustrate upper-class living in New France.

Another standout is the **Seigneurie de l'Île d'Orléans** *(seigneurieiledorleans.com; $22.60)*, a 10-hectare estate near the island's eastern tip. The massive stone house was carefully renovated to serve as a wedding venue, and the grounds have won national attention for their expansive lavender fields and Zen garden. The Seigneurie is open from late June to early September.

St-Jean-de-l'Île-d'Orléans

Wine-tasting on the island

As you drive the northern shore you'll spot several vineyards, the basis for Île d'Orléans' acclaimed wine industry. Grapes already grew here in abundance by the time explorer Jacques Cartier arrived in 1535, and he cheekily named this land mass the Île de Bascuz (Isle of Bacchus), after the Roman god of wine. One of the many wineries is **Vignoble Isle de Bacchus** *(isledebacchus.com)*, which takes its name from Cartier's mythic appellation and comprises 11 hectares of vines. Isle de Bacchus stands on a hillside overlooking the river, and guests can tour the grounds and the many types of wine created there, from dry red to sparkling. Bacchus is conveniently located about 2km east of the main bridge on Rte 368; the rest of Île d'Olreans' wineries are spread out along this main road as well.

Explore Espace Félix Leclerc

Félix Leclerc is considered a Canadian national hero – and that goes double in Québec. Born into a large French-speaking family in 1914, he was a prodigious writer, actor and radio announcer in his formative years, but he earned global acclaim for his songwriting. Leclerc was famous for his playful guitar ballads and soul-searching lyrics. He eventually settled on Île d'Orléans, where he passed away in 1988. **Espace Félix Leclerc** *(felixleclerc.com)* is a music venue converted from

AN ISLAND PILGRIMAGE

Vincent Paris is a master jam-maker and co-owner at **Confiturerie Tigidou** *(tigidou.ca)*.

Just 20 minutes from Québec City, Île d'Orléans offers a journey through 500 years of French-Canadian heritage. Locals call it a *pèlerinage* (pilgrimage) around 72km of rolling farmland, berry fields and centuries-old villages. Known for its legendary strawberries, the island bursts with seasonal bounty from May to October, best enjoyed fresh-picked or transformed into artisan jams.

Locals joke that native islanders are 'sorcerers,' their secrets rooted in tradition and the terroir. Nowhere is this magic clearer than at **La Maison de Thé** *(lamaisondethe.com)*, a tearoom and micro-farm where wild herbs and berries become healing teas and gourmet platters. With garden-to-table offerings and peaceful salons, it's a sanctuary for slowing down and reconnecting with nature.

OTHER WINERIES OF ÎLE D'ORLÉANS

Vignoble Ste-Pétronille: Wine, cider and brandy, plus Neapolitan-style pizza.

Saint-Pierre Le Vignoble: Based on a refurbished barn from the 1930s, Saint-Pierre hosts tastings and community harvests.

Le Vignoble du Mitan: Tour the vineyard, then grab nibbles at the adjacent Gourmet Corner.

Cassis Monna & Filles: Two sisters continue a five-generation winemaking tradition that started in France. Baked goods, a museum and an ice-cream bar.

Domaine Sainte-Famille: Picnics and apple-picking in summer; cross-country skiing in winter; wines, cider and digestifs anytime.

Grange Restaurant-Vignoble: An eclectic global restaurant became a prolific winery in 2016.

a former barn; a museum about Leclerc's life is based in the 2nd floor. Concerts perform on the small stage throughout the summer, and the Espace hosts other cultural events as well. After browsing the modest exhibit, you can spend a warm afternoon walking the 3km trail system that starts just outside.

Float through the maritime museum

The St Lawrence River is among the most important waterways in North America, connecting the Great Lakes to the Atlantic Ocean. Early French settlers imagined it was the first segment of the legendary Northwest Passage. The **Musée Maritime de L'Île d'Orléans** *(museemaritimeio.ca/en)* offers a highly interactive crash course in the river's nautical past. The property is based on a former shipyard, and one of its buildings is a rowboat workshop established in 1837. Stone trenches in the ground mark where vessels were once assembled and dry-docked. The museum has an exhaustive collection of antique tools, and visitors can get an up-close look at the *RF Grant* tugboat, which recently joined the museum's permanent collection.

Savor the Chocolaterie de l'Île d'Orléans

A multifloored emporium of sugary treats, the **Chocolaterie de l'Île d'Orléans** *(chocolaterieorleans.com)* sells everything from boxes of pralines and maple candy to figures shaped like chocolate moose (get it?). In winter, baristas pour mugs of hot chocolate; in the warmer months, many guests lean their bikes against surrounding trees and order ice-cream cones. Regardless of the season, the *chocolaterie* occupies a special place on the island: cross the main road to the Promenade Horatio Walker, which parallels the rocky riverfront, and you'll find a beautiful, unobstructed view of Québec City, standing about 5km upstream.

Sainte-Anne-de-Beaupré

TIME FROM QUÉBEC CITY: **30MIN**

Find sanctuary at the basilica

One of the most moving displays in all of Québec province is the medley of crutches hanging from a pair of stone pillars inside the **Basilique Ste-Anne-de-Beaupré** *(sanctuairesainteanne.org)*. In all colors and sizes, they rise in neat rows toward the vaulted ceiling. According to lore, each crutch

---

EATING IN STE-ANNE-DE-BEAUPRÉ: OUR PICKS

La Grange: Rivaling the pizzas and pasta at this Italian brasserie are the wines and craft beers. *11am-9pm Tue-Thu, to 9:30pm Fri & Sat, to 8pm Sun* **$$**

Radio Café: Eggs Benedict for breakfast or a burger for lunch or dinner – it's all delicious. *7am-9pm Sat & Sun, 8am-9pm Mon-Fri* **$**

Les Trois Becs: Shop at this market for groceries, but stick around for a hearty meal. *9am-5pm Wed-Sun* **$$**

Microbrasserie des Beaux Prés: Great pub grub and outrageously tasty beers. *11:30am-8pm Mon & Tue, to 10pm Wed, to midnight Thu & Fri, to 11pm Sat, to 5pm Sun* **$$**

Basilique Ste-Anne-de-Beaupré

represents a suffering patient who was cured by praying to the church's namesake: St Anne, the patron saint of sailors.

The town of Ste-Anne-de-Beaupré is home to about 3000 residents, so visitors are often shocked to find such a colossal stone church on its outskirts. With its two Gothic steeples and enormous rose window, the basilica would look perfectly at home in medieval France, yet the ambitious structure was completed in 1944, after 18 years of halting construction. Today the church is a magnet for tourists and pilgrims, who admire its ornate carvings and illustrative stained-glass windows. The crutches are easy to spot near the main entrance, though this sacred site is credited with numerous other miracles as well. The basilica is free to enter and welcoming to guests, and you can spend warmer days hanging around the

EATING ON ÎLE D'ORLÉANS: OUR PICKS

Bistro du Hangar: Sidle up to the beautiful wood bar, dig into poké or poutine, then take in a live concert. *11:30am-4pm Sun, to 7pm Mon-Thu, to 8pm Fri & Sat* **$$**

Resto de la Plage: Lobster roll or fish and chips? You'll struggle to decide at this waterfront hangout. *11:30am-8pm Mon-Sat, 9am-8pm Sun* **$$**

Les Ancêtres Auberge & Restaurant: Elegant dishes are served in the handsome, stone-accented dining room of this converted farmhouse. *5-9pm Tue-Sat* **$$$**

Au Poste de Traite: Stay at the inn, then feast on ornate dishes at a romantically lit table. *4-9pm Fri & Sat* **$$$**

CYCLORAMA DE JERUSALEM

Directly across the railroad tracks from the Basilique Ste-Anne-de-Beaupré stands a peculiar structure. With its arabesque arches and onion-dome tower, the **Cyclorama de Jerusalem** *(cycloramadejerusalem.com)* looks like a hexadecagonal Persian palace. Built in 1895, the Cyclorama contains a sprawling, 360-degree painting that measures 110m across. Paul Philippoteaux's landscape depicts the Crucifixion and the skyline of Jerusalem as it likely appeared at the time. Cycloramas were popular in the 19th century, and this is among the largest in the world, but management was forced to close its doors in 2017. The attached gift shop, with a wide range of Christian memorabilia, is open May to October. See the website to arrange a private visit to the Cyclorama from November and April.

Parc National de la Jacques-Cartier

plaza and fountain just outside. Three masses are held each day, and the faithful can receive personal blessings anytime between 10am and 4pm.

Ski Sainte-Anne

Mont-Sainte-Anne *(day pass $47)* is sneaky. Driving through town, you may not notice it right away, but it'll suddenly appear: an 800m hulk looming above Rte 360 with 71 trails cut down its sides. The mountain's proximity to Québec City makes it a perfect winter excursion, and the town of Beaupré transforms from sleepy satellite community into a plucky ski town full of powder-seekers. This side of the Laurentian Mountains doesn't have nearly as many downhill resorts as Montreal, so Mont-Sainte-Anne gets a good amount of traffic. This popularity extends into the night as well, thanks to the resort's 19 illuminated runs. Equipment rentals are available both at the on-site shop and in town.

In summer, mountain bikers can come back to tear up the mountain's single track, with multiple routes for different skill levels.

Pedal from Québec

The moment the mercury hits 5°C, the motorways along the St Lawrence River fill with cyclists. Lycra and drop bars are common sights in Beaupré, in part because the town lies about 35km from Old Québec, making it a great end point for a four-hour ride. A network of rail trails connects the city to the town, and the level pavement is well suited to road bikers who like to go fast. The trails are free to use year-round, though you should expect heavy snow cover between November and April.

Browse paintings at the Galerie d'Art

Just off Rte 360, a narrow driveway leads you into the forest. Here you'll find **Galerie d'Art Mont-Ste-Anne** *(galeriemontsteanne.com/en)*, a secluded stone cottage full of local artwork. The gallery is the brainchild of Italian painter and mosaicist Giovanni Gerometta, who also built the surrounding house by hand in 1976. The sylvan setting feels far from civilization, and outdoor sculptures are scattered across the property. To learn more about Gerometta's extraordinary life, the gallery sells his colorful coffee-table book.

Parc National de la Jacques-Cartier

TIME FROM QUÉBEC CITY: **45MIN**

Hit the trails

In the history of Canadian conservation, **Parc National de la Jacques-Cartier** *(Jacques Cartier River National Park; jacques-cartier.com)* is a heartwarming success story. The public rejected a dam project in this edenic glacial valley, and today the park attracts hundreds of thousands of hikers each year to its 100km of forest trails. These trails vary in terrain and difficulty, and some double as gravel-biking routes. In winter, snowshoers and cross-country skiers flock to Jacques Cartier to explore a snow-covered wonderland. The park is an easy drive from Québec, but there's no need to rush: reserve one of 113 campsites or stay in one of the local chalets or yurts. Daily access to the park is $10.10, payable at the main gate.

Paddle the current

The Jacques Cartier River runs 161km through the Laurentian Mountains. During the warmer months, canoes and kayaks drift down these (mostly) gentle waters. If you're not bringing your own craft, you'll find a **rental center** *(per hr canoe/solo kayak $19.50/17.75, per day life jacket $8.25)* at kilometer 3 on the road that loops through the park. Looking for more action? There's a second rental center at kilometer 10 for whitewater rafting, with multiple circuits and shuttle transportation.

OTHER PARKS AROUND QUÉBEC

Parc des Chutes-de-la-Chaudière: Walk right up to these gorgeous falls just south of Québec. The trail-filled park is free to visit.

Parc des Moulins: Well-trodden paths guide hikers and skiers through the woods – and past a historic stone windmill.

Marais du Nord: Thread your way along 8km of trails in this important wetland. Day entry is $8.

Parc de la Forêt Ancienne du Mont Wright: Scramble over 6.5km of rocky trails in a rare old-growth forest.

Réserve Nationale de Faune du Cap-Tourmente: These marshlands are a birders' paradise thanks to abundant migrations and strategic lookout points.

Where to Stay

Forgo the big-name chains – Montréal welcomes guests with stylish boutique hotels, cozy B&Bs and affordable hostels. Winter is best for budget travel; summer prices come at a premium.

Where to Stay If You Love ...

History, architecture & riverfront fun

Old Montréal (p44) Cobblestone streets, greystone facades and grand old-world architecture lend the city's storied epicenter the air of a European village. Rue St-Paul teems with art galleries, shops and restaurants – and camera-toting tourists.

Live performances, museums & shopping

Downtown (p60) Skyscrapers neighbor heritage mansions and museums, white-collar workers rub shoulders with university students, and shoppers stream down Rue Ste-Catherine. Place des Arts is the gateway to live performances and festivals.

Cool clubs & queer culture

Quartier Latin, the Village & HoMa (p78) Theaters and bars pepper gritty Rue St-Denis, while dance floors and LGBTIQ+ clubs pulse along Rue Ste-Catherine once night descends. Most hotels around here hug quiet, residential side streets.

Artsy boutiques & pretty parks

Plateau Mont-Royal (p90) There's no shortage of sidewalk cafes, hip boutiques and cozy bars around this trendy neighborhood. It's also laced with gorgeous green spaces and bordered by Parc du Mont-Royal, Montréal's beloved 'mountain'.

Food, fashion & boundless creativity

Mile End, Little Italy & Outremont (p110) Stylish Mile End is chockablock with vintage shops and fantastic dining; its influence is most apparent in Little Italy, home to food-topia Marché Jean-Talon, and Outremont's smattering of top-tier restaurants.

Local vibe & hip nightlife

Lachine Canal, Little Burgundy & the Southwest (p122) A quieter alternative to Downtown Montréal. Lots of youthful nightlife, though accommodations are few and far between.

History, art & epicurean pleasures

Québec City (p162) Old Québec has short-term rentals, guesthouses, hostels and hotels. Prices increase during summer, the Christmas break and major festivals.

$$$ Top end $$ Midrange $ Budget

Old Montréal

HOSTEL

Auberge Alternative $
MAP P51

These spick-and-span rooms look toward the silver **Marché Bonsecours dome** with options for shared dorms, women-only spaces and private suites – plus a shared kitchen. There's a sister location on Rue St-Pierre.

RIVERFRONT & ROOFTOPS

Auberge du Vieux-Port $$$
MAP P51

Wake up to St Lawrence River views inside this 1882 Old Port warehouse redesigned as a boutique hotel and end your night on the rooftop, perfect for seeing summer's firework displays.

Hôtel Nelligan $$$
MAP P46

The sumptuous brick-and-wood interior of this hotel, spread across four 19th-century buildings with a lovely rooftop terrace, is visual poetry – fitting for a boutique lodge celebrating Québecois wordsmith Émile Nelligan.

Hôtel William Gray $$$
MAP P51

Comfy rooms, certainly, but you may never leave the common spaces: a three-story glass solarium 'living room', a 4th-floor patio overlooking Place Jacques-Cartier and the rooftop terrace with a river panorama.

MODERN INTERIORS

Hôtel Uville $$
MAP P46

Travel back to the swinging mid-century style of Expo 67 and the 1976 Olympics. Each room is a love letter to the events that put Montréal on the map, vinyl-spinning turntable included.

LHotel $$$
MAP P46

An art gallery's worth of contemporary work decorates the interior of this French Revival building from 1870, formerly a bank, where guests sleep next to everyone from Botero to Warhol.

Place d'Armes $$$
MAP P46

Gaze at the Basilique Notre-Dame, one block away, from the historic bones of four neoclassical buildings cobbled into modern accommodations with electric fireplaces warming winter's coldest days.

INTIMATE BOUTIQUES

Épik $$
MAP P46

Wooden beams and stone walls transport you back to 1723 (the year of construction), while the 10-room boutique's sleek amenities ensure you fall asleep to contemporary comforts.

Hôtel Gault $$$
MAP P46

Built in 1871 for Andrew Gault, the 'Cotton King of Canada,' this former fabric and haberdashery warehouse is now a minimalist lodge where stylish visitors hang their hats in one of 30 spacious rooms.

Le Petit Hotel $$$
MAP P46

Small in size, perhaps, but grand thanks to the Rue St-Paul location's front desk–bistro's buttery baked goods, complimentary bike service and historic brick-walled rooms. There's a second location on Rue Notre-Dame.

Downtown

ON A BUDGET

Auberge Saintlo Montréal $
MAP P67

Grab a dorm room or splurge on a private one and join digital nomads for the free breakfast before clacking away in the coworking space on the western border of Downtown.

Auberge du Plateau $
MAP P62

Rooms inside this 19th-century house turned hostel may be basic, but they're centrally located between the Plateau and Downtown – and there's a rooftop terrace where you can meet fellow travelers in summer.

TOWNHOUSE HOTELS

Ambrose House & Cafe $$
MAP P67

Grab a coffee on the ground floor, then spend your time living like a local in this hotel, merging two 1910 Victorian greystones on a residential street near Mont Royal's entrance.

HOW MUCH FOR A NIGHT IN MONTRÉAL & QUÉBEC CITY

Hostel
$30–150

B&B
$100–250

Midrange hotel
$150–300

High-end boutique
Over $250

Auberge Les Bon Matins $$
MAP P67

Quirky, colorful artwork decorates the brick walls of these spacious rooms with hardwood floors spread out over three stately traditional townhouses at the southern edge of Downtown.

Hotel Manoir Sherbrooke $$
MAP P62

Staying a night in this century-old home at the nexus of Downtown, Quartier Latin and the Plateau feels like sleeping inside a meticulous granny's guesthouse, each room outfitted with vintage flair.

HISTORIC STAYS

Le Mount Stephen $$$
MAP P67

Don't let the 1883 facade of Lord George Stephen's former mansion fool you: aside from the carved-wood bar and restaurant, guests stay in 21st-century accommodations with chromatherapy showers fit for modern royalty.

Ritz-Carlton $$$
MAP P67

Luxury is key at this 130-room bastion for big spenders where Queen Elizabeth II rested her head, Elizabeth Taylor got hitched to Richard Burton, and the Rolling Stones once rented an entire floor.

Fairmont the Queen Elizabeth $$$
MAP P67

In 1969 John Lennon and Yoko Ono staged an infamous 'Bed-In' for peace in Suite 1742. A 2017 update gives new guests good reason to recreate the scene, plush comforters included.

MODERN STYLE

Hotel Monville $$
MAP P62

You may be greeted by robot butler H2M2 (fashioned after *Star Wars'* R2D2) inside this hotel beloved by business travelers for its self-service check-in kiosk and coworking space, between Downtown and Old Montréal.

Hotel 10 $$
MAP P62

Set in an art-nouveau building from 1915, this Blvd St-Laurent designer hotel brings the street's creative energy indoors with pieces by local artists hanging on its walls. Avoid noisy rooms on lower floors.

Hotel Le Germain $$$
MAP P67

The facade's *Dazzle My Heart* mural by Canadian artist Michelle Hoogveld does just that, accompanied by the interior's fashionable loft-style rooms, sophisticated bar and brasserie-inspired restaurant, Le Boulevardier.

Sofitel Montréal Golden Mile $$$
MAP P67

Constructed as an office tower in 1973, this silver high-rise shadowing Rue Sherbrooke's 19th-century mansions and McGill University underwent a 2025 glow-up, adding a dash of Parisian glamour to the Golden Square Mile.

Fairmont the Queen Elizabeth

Quartier Latin, the Village & HoMa

BUDGET-FRIENDLY

M Montreal $
MAP P80

Choose your adventure: shared dorm room with privacy curtains or solo suite with kitchenette, and perhaps dipping into the terrace Jacuzzi or joining a guided stroll through town. Stay for Wednesday's free pasta night.

COMFY B&BS

Hôtel Château de l'Argoat $$
MAP P80

Paintings, photographs and sculptures by established and emerging Québec artists decorate two combined Victorian homes with original woodwork, perched on the border between Quartier Latin and Plateau Mont-Royal.

La Loggia Art & Breakfast $$
MAP P80

This well-maintained residence, built in 1870, outfits its guest rooms with Persian rugs and attractive art. Stay for breakfast, served in the garden when weather permits.

Bed & Breakfast du Village $$
MAP P80

Choose a standard room, budget suite (ideal for families) or private cottage and start your day with a filling breakfast in this quiet oasis steps from the bars on Rue Ste-Catherine.

Plateau Mont-Royal

CONTEMPORARY COMFORT

Hôtel de l'ITHQ $$
MAP P92

Hospitality students provide the service (including breakfast) at this sustainability-focused modern hotel where guests stay in Scandi-style rooms equipped with mini balconies. Hotel profits go toward servers' education.

PARKSIDE B&BS

Auberge de La Fontaine $$
MAP P92

Simple bedrooms in this pretty guesthouse, built in the early 20th century, overlook the northern edge of lovely Parc La Fontaine, close to BIXI stations and a protected bike path.

Accueil Chez François $$
MAP P92

Guests receive a warm *accueil* (welcome) at this tidy five-room inn on Parc La Fontaine's eastern edge, with free parking, a 20% discount at the neighboring cafe and first-come, first-served bike rentals.

COZY DECOR

Gingerbread Manor $$
MAP P92

Hosts Ephraim and Yves turned this three-story manor from 1885 into a cozy B&B with Victorian panache. It's set along a leafy residential street near postcard-perfect Carré St-Louis. Choose a shared or en suite bathroom.

SHORT-TERM RENTALS

In Montréal, short-term rentals such as Airbnb only operate legally between June 10 and September 10, a 2025 law meant to ease housing market demands. A small portion of Rues Ste-Catherine and St-Denis offer short-term rentals year-round.

Kutuma Hotel & Suites $$
MAP P92

With its cheetah-print fabrics, African-themed artwork and Ethiopian restaurant downstairs, staying at this boutique hotel is the closest you'll get to a safari along Rue St-Denis.

APARTHOTEL

Sonder Le Guerin $$
MAP P92

Whether you're working remotely or staying long-term, these modern, fully furnished apartments offer a slice of homestyle comfort close to the Métro.

Mile End, Little Italy & Outremont

BUDGET-FRIENDLY CRASH PAD

Pensione Popolo $
MAP P112

See concerts at legendary music venue Casa del Popolo downstairs, then stumble to your cozy, beatnik abode above. Hotel guests get a 25% discount at the on-site restaurant.

APARTHOTEL

Le Mile-End Hotel $$
MAP P112

Experience life in the local lane in one of these snug, functional one- and two-bedroom apartments with kitchenettes, located in residential Mile End near Parc du Mont-Royal.

Downtown Québec City

BUDGET

Residences Université Laval $
MAP P180

Short-term rentals are available year-round at the Université Laval and come with bedding and towels; bathrooms are shared.

THE GUIDE | WHERE TO STAY

WHERE TO STAY

HI Auberge Internationale de Québec $
MAP P164

A large HI Canada hostel with a full kitchen, a bar, common rooms, dorms and private accommodations. It's in a great location in Old Québec.

Auberge Jeunesse QBEDS Hostel $
MAP P180

This friendly hostel is smack in the middle of Grande-Allée, one of Québec's best streets for nightlife. Rates include a continental breakfast.

Auberge de la Paix $
MAP P178

A quaint no-frills hostel in an 1850s house on Rue du Couillard, the de la Paix has seven dorm rooms and six private rooms.

BOUTIQUE

Au Petit Hôtel $
MAP P164

Tucked away on a quiet street near Monastère des Ursulines, this hotel lives up to its name. Rooms are small and have private bathroom.

Château des Tourelles $
MAP P180

Perched at the end of Rue St-Jean, this three-star hotel has friendly staff. It's a 15-minute walk from Old Québec.

Hôtel AtypiQ $$
MAP P164

A cross between a boutique hotel and a hostel, the AtypiQ has a fully equipped kitchen, a shared dining room, funky murals and space-saving private rooms.

Hôtel Krieghoff $$
MAP P180

This cafe-hotel has modern contemporary rooms with comfortable beds and views of the surrounding neighborhood. Breakfast in the cafe is highly recommended.

Auberge du Tresor $$
MAP P178

At the Tresor, rooms are small but beautiful, with wooden floors and cushy beds. The location, across the street from Château Frontenac, is unbeatable.

ALT Québec $$
MAP P180

Located in Ste-Foy, this family-owned hotel chain focuses on sustainability. The rooms are a good size with very comfortable beds, and the common area has a little corner with gourmet snacks.

Le C3 Hôtel $$
MAP P180

Look for a golden horse cut in half and you're at Le C3, an artsy boutique hotel near the Musée national des beaux-arts. Every room is spacious with artistic flair, crisp white linens and cozy chairs.

Hôtel Classique $$
MAP P180

Located in Ste-Foy near Laurier Mall, this hotel has large rooms (most with a balcony), an indoor pool and a restaurant. Take bus 11 outside the hotel to get to Old Québec.

> **FESTIVAL SEASON**
>
> Book lodging several months in advance when traveling for or around big celebrations, be it Festival international de Jazz de Montréal or Carnival de Québec – and expect to pay a premium.

Hôtel Le St-Paul $$
MAP P178

This recently renovated three-star hotel has rooms with minimal furniture, soft beds and rain showers. It's a less than 10-minute walk from the Gare du Palais train station.

Maison Kent $$
MAP P164

Rooms are huge and come with a kitchenette at this small boutique hotel on Rue St-Louis in Old Québec.

Hôtel 71 $$$
MAP P178

A boutique hotel in a former bank with exposed stone walls, red velvet accents and a large lobby lounge with a fireplace.

Hôtel Nomad $$$
MAP P164

This biosphere-certified hotel near Terrasse Dufferin has beautiful thematic rooms, intriguing art pieces and a houndstooth-clad communal lounge.

HIGHER END

Hôtel Château Laurier $$$
MAP P180

Rooms have been updated recently to compete with the other mid-century modern hotel rooms in the city. The hotel's winding layout can make it easy to get lost.

Le Germain $$$
MAP P178

The owners of this hotel brand are Québécois and have a keen eye for detail. Rooms are soundproof with incredibly comfortable beds and large showers.

Auberge St-Antoine $$$
MAP P178

A hotel-musée that displays artifacts uncovered during its construction. Rooms are spacious, and bathrooms have heated floors.

Château Frontenac (p168), from street below

SOMETHING SPECIAL

Monastère des Augustines $$
MAP P178
Traditional cell rooms come with a single bed, desk, sink and wardrobe – shared bathrooms are across the hall. Regular rooms have double beds and private baths. Silent breakfast is included.

Fairmont Le Château Frontenac $$$
MAP P164
This historic hotel is the city's premium place to stay, with comfortable rooms and small bathrooms. Some of its most unforgettable guest experiences include: panoramas from the hotel's Bar 1608; arrivals by *calèche* (horse-drawn carriage); and remarkable views of the building when it's illuminated at night.

Side-Trips Destinations

THE LAURENTIANS

Hôtel UNIQ $
Sleep in glamping domes in a field surrounded by nature and sing along when fellow travelers inevitably bring a guitar. Mid-May to mid-October only.

Auberge Manitonga Hostel $
Big, sparkling hostel in Mont-Tremblant village, with free coffee and its own bar.

Les Conifères $$
Stay *chez* Catherine at this streamside B&B and cafe in a 19th-century farmhouse. Has a wonderful shared courtyard, kitchen and Jacuzzi.

Fairmont Tremblant $$$
Ski out your door onto Mont-Tremblant Resort. Just completed renovations to dozens of rooms and its facilities.

EASTERN TOWNSHIPS

Auberge Yoga Salamandre $
Retreat to this peaceful lodge in the woods above a stream where volunteers lead daily yoga classes and, if you're lucky, coloring sessions.

Au Saut du Lit $$
Marie-Ève and Maxime's bright yellow and blue New England–style cottage in Magog is a delight.

Au Diable Vert $$
Unique family resort with tree houses, pods, camping and year-round activities, including augmented-reality stargazing.

TOOLKIT

The chapters in this section cover the most important topics you'll need to know about in Montréal and Québec City. They're full of nuts-and-bolts information and valuable insights to help you understand and navigate Montréal and Québec City and get the most out of your trip.

Money
p204

Family Travel
p205

Food, Drink & Nightlife
p206

LGBTIQ+ Travelers
p208

Health & Safe Travel
p209

Responsible Travel
p210

Accessible Travel
p212

Nuts & Bolts
p213

Language
p214

Rue St-Paul (p50)
FARUTXO/SHUTTERSTOCK

Money

CURRENCY: CANADIAN DOLLAR ($)

ATMs
Montréal and Québec City have ATMS in airports, banks and the occasional convenience store, pub and hotel. Expect a fee of $2 to $5.

Discount Cards
Passeport MTL (mtl.org/en/passeport-mtl) offers museum discounts: buy admission for three to five major tourist attractions and save around 35% on ticket prices.

Card Versus Cash
Most businesses accept debit or credit card – it's the most popular way to pay. Many establishments don't accept American Express, aside from higher-end restaurants and hotels. Still, it's wise to keep some hard cash on hand. Though rare, some restaurants, market stands and mom-and-pop shops don't take plastic.

Taxes
There are two types of tax in Québec: the federal goods and services tax (GST), which adds 5% to the selling price, and the Québec sales tax (QST) of 9.975%. Montréal and Québec City also have a 3.5% accommodations tax for hotel and home-share stays.

HOW MUCH FOR A…

Ferry to Parc Jean-Drapeau
$6

24-hour Montréal metro pass
$11

Museum ticket
Free–$30

Place des Arts show
Free–$250

HOW TO… Tip
Tipping is obligatory in restaurants, bars, taxis and hair salons. It's respectful to leave at least 15% of the bill – more for exceptional service. For bellhops and porters it's customary to leave at least $2 per suitcase. At cafes there's usually a tip jar – a dollar or loose change can go a long way. Tour guides appreciate monetary acknowledgement, too; bring cash to tip them 10% to 15%.

NAMING THE COINS
Canadian coins come in 1¢ (penny), 5¢ (nickel), 10¢ (dime), 25¢ (quarter), $1 (loonie, named for the loon on the coin) and $2 (toonie, a portmanteau of 'loonie' and 'two').

TARIFF TUMULT

In 2025 the US started a trade war with Canada, imposing 25% tariffs on Canadian goods and causing the Canadian dollar to tumble against foreign currencies. Canada hit back with a 25% tax on US products including furniture, clothing, and food items ranging from coffee to tomatoes. Québec grocery store Provigo responded by labeling US-grown goods with a 'T,' flagging tariff hikes and nudging shoppers toward local products. At research time the battle showed no signs of ending, so expect price spikes in the years ahead – and opt for Québec-made wares to dodge the tariff commotion.

Family Travel

Budding scientists, fussy foodies, artsy adolescents and tomorrow's ice-hockey pros: Montréal is an action-packed playland for children with all types of tastes. Museums entice families with interactive exhibits at affordable prices, *casse-croûtes* (snack bars) cater to young palates with menu items like cheesy poutine, and outdoor fun is as varied as the seasons. Everyone's going to need a nap.

Get Outside in Every Season

In summer, bounce around **Aquazilla** (p145), floating in Plage Jean-Doré, climb the **Voiles en Voiles** (p53) ropes course along the Old Port or play a round of Finnish bowling on the banks of **Lac aux Castors** (p105). In winter, tube down the gentle slopes of Parc du Mont-Royal, skate through the forest trail in **Parc Jean-Drapeau** (p140) or build a snowman. It's free.

Québec's Kid Cuisine

Québécois comfort food is ideal for fussy foodies. Bite into buttered bagels at **St-Viateur** (p113), one of North America's best bagel bakeries, choose from 30 styles of poutine at **La Banquise** (p93) and order hotdogs from the century-old **Montréal Pool Room** (p70). Prefer sweets? Don't miss the **Cabane à Sucre** at **Place Jacques-Cartier** (p56), a 'sugar shack' where everything's smothered in maple syrup.

MONTRÉAL'S MEMORABLE ACTIVITIES

Biodôme (p85)
Meet animals from five different ecosystems.

Insectarium (p85)
Burrow underground, then watch butterflies flutter between flowers.

Cirque du Soleil (p53)
Cheer on clowns and acrobats under the big top in summer.

Pointe-à-Callière (p47)
Play archaeologist, then learn about pirates that once sailed the St Lawrence.

La Ronde (p146)
Shriek on roller coasters and admire summer's fireworks.

La Grande Roue (p53)
Spin above the Old Port on a temperature-controlled Ferris wheel.

Museum Discounts

Save on **Espace Pour la Vie's** five immersive museums (the **Biodôme, Insectarium, Planétarium, Jardin Botanique** and **Biosphère** pictured) by purchasing a MULTI Passport, which includes entrance for two adults and three children for $149. Passports are valid for 12 months.

SEE QUÉBEC CITY

For kids, Québec City dazzles. Wander through interactive exhibits geared for young minds at the **Musée de la Civilisation** (p177), then join a tour or craft workshop the whole family will love. Get to know the Indigenous Huron-Wendat people on the **Onhwa' Lumina** (p190) forest trek. Make the most of winter by gliding around Place d'Youville's **ice-skating rink** – and pick up speed while tobogganing down the **Glissade de la Terrasse** (p175). For a summertime adrenaline rush, head to the **Chute Montmorency** (p186), a 83m waterfall where adventurers bounce around a playground, zoom on a zip line or brave the via ferrata.

Food, Drink & Nightlife

When to Eat

Breakfast (*déjeuner*; 7am to 11am) Bagels, pastries, crepes, eggs, bacon, sausage and beans.

Lunch (*dîner*; noon to 2pm) Everything from sandwiches and salads to three-course meals.

5 à 7 (*cinq-à-sept*; 5pm to 7pm) Post-work drinks and small plates.

Dinner (*souper*; 5pm to 10pm) Two to three courses: an appetizer (salad or shareable nibbles), a main course (usually meat focused) and possibly dessert.

Where to Eat

Bistro Casual, cozy French-inspired restaurant with moderately priced food and wine.

Brasserie Larger than a bistro, with heartier fare and a focus on beer.

Buvette Wine-centric bar with shareable plates.

Cafe Coffee, pastries and light lunch served through late afternoon.

Cabane à sucre 'Sugar shack' – known for hearty Québécois meals smothered in maple syrup; popular during spring's harvest.

Casse-croûte Greasy-spoon diner, deli or roadside stand serving fast-food snacks.

Marché 'Market' – where local farmers and bakers sell produce, meats, cheeses and sweets.

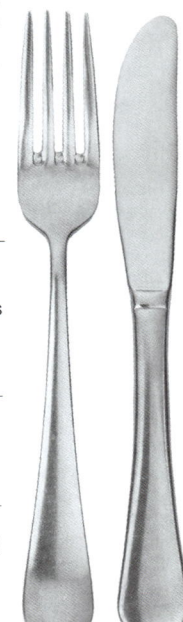

MENU DECODER

Carte Menu.

Amuse bouche Pre-appetizer nibble to 'amuse' the 'mouth.'

Entrée Appetizer.

Plat principal Main course.

Facture Bill.

Table d'hôte A prix-fixe menu with several courses, often offered at fine-dining establishments but occasionally found at midrange restaurants.

Chocolatine Chocolate croissant, called a *pain au chocolat* in France.

Crème glacée The Québécois way to say 'ice cream' – not to be confused with *glace*, which means 'ice cream' in France but simply 'ice' in Québec.

Paté Pasta (noodles), not to be confused with *pâté* (a creamy meat spread).

Apportez votre vin 'Bring your own wine' – indicating a restaurant doesn't serve alcohol but will uncork wine bottles brought by guests.

Vin rouge/blanc/macération Wine that's red/white/skin contact (resulting in orange or rosé).

HOW TO... Enjoy a Night Out

A night in Québec's two principal cities typically starts with a *5 à 7* (*cinq-à-sept*) – a post-work gathering from 5pm on, and perhaps followed by dinner, cocktails, a live performance or dancing 'til dawn. Weeknights last until midnight or 1am, while weekends rage until 3am and beyond, with Montréalers partying later than the rest of the province. For late-night munchies, stop by Montreal's **La Banquise** (p93), open 24/7.

Electronic music is particularly popular in Montréal, where DJs spin beats everywhere from pseudo-speakeasies (try **Sans Soleil**, p72 – line up outside the door) to high-capacity clubs (try **Stereo**, p86 – buy tickets online in advance). Get ready for late nights: these parties usually pick up steam around midnight and can go until morning. Prefer daytime revelry? Attend one of the province's seasonal outdoor events, like **Piknic Électronik** (p143), a Sunday shindig from May to October where Montréalers dance beneath the setting sun.

SERGIY KUZMIN/SHUTTERSTOCK

HOW MUCH FOR A...

Shot of espresso
$3.25

Pint of beer (16oz)
$5–10

Craft cocktail
$12–20

Plain bagel
$1.20

Plate of poutine
$10

Smoked-meat sandwich
$15

Three-course meal at a top-rated restaurant
$60–100

HOW TO...

Savor Maple Syrup

Maple syrup is more than a sugary topping – it's a Québec tradition started by Indigenous communities, picked up by French colonizers and now a cultural cornerstone. Over 5000 maple farms practice the ancient alchemy of transforming sap into sugar during the short 'sugaring off' season between February and March, when sap flows from trees. The province produces around 70% of the world's supply, and this liquid gold contributes $1.1 billion to Canada's economy. Due to the product's dependence on erratic and ever-changing weather, Québec stockpiles the world's only reserve of maple syrup. Three warehouses hold the equivalent of 52 Olympic-size syrup pools, ensuring waffles worldwide never go dry, no matter the success of a harvest.

Québécois take serious pride in all things maple – most evident from March through April, when they head to countryside *cabanes à sucres* (sugar shacks) to celebrate the season's bounty. During these sugar-soaked fests, groups gather inside cabins for traditional meals, often including pea soup, smoked ham, *tourtières*, baked beans, sausage links, pancakes and baby-sized omelets, all smothered in syrup. There's dessert, too, especially maple taffy (*la tire*) – where boiling syrup gets poured onto snow and rolled into lollipops. There's no need to wait for spring to indulge. In Québec, maple syrup gets turned into candies, mixed into sauces, used to glaze meats and dripped into coffee and cocktails.

Can Art

Québec's maple syrup often comes in a can emblazoned with the image of a red, snow-covered cabin with a sugar-maker working in the foreground. The image dates to 1951, when the government held a province-wide call for designs.

QUÉBEC'S LAGER LEGACY

Québec's craft-beer affair might be a 21st-century fling, but the suds romance goes back centuries. New France colonist Brother Ambroise, a Jesuit monk living near Québec City, became the region's first recorded beer-maker in 1646, brewing the heady elixir for his fellow fathers. Jean Talon, Intendant of the colony, entered the beer biz in 1668 by launching Canada's first commercial brewery – which dried up a few years later. New France colonists apparently preferred wine.

Tastes changed after the British conquest, when immigrants from across the pond sought a drink to quench their thirst for home. Enter John Molson, an English-born beer-maker who hopped onto the Montréal scene in 1786 and began building one of Canada's beer behemoths (a distinction now shared with Labatt, operating out of Ontario). The province's craft-beer revolution didn't start for another two centuries, when bars like **Le Cheval Blanc** (p83) popped up in Montréal. Today, over 300 small-batch brewers operate throughout the province, accounting for roughly a quarter of all Canadian microbreweries.

The best way to enjoy the historic juice like a Cicerone (beer sommelier) is by visiting a brewery and tasting what's on tap. Most establishments offer flights or smaller 5oz pours so you can sample several without going overboard. Treat the beer like wine: inspect the color and swirl it in the glass. Sniff for aromas like citrus, flowers, chocolate and honey. Sip – and decide if it's sour, sweet, bitter or maybe umami. If enjoying several pours, start with light beers and move to dark.

LGBTIQ+ Travelers

Pride is citywide in Montréal, home to one of North America's largest LGBTIQ+ neighborhoods. Originally dubbed the 'Gay Village,' it's now inclusively called 'the Village,' with hundreds of queer-friendly businesses like bars, bookstores, clothing shops and drag cabarets– many lining Rue Ste-Catherine and more sprinkled beyond its borders. Québec City's scene is comparatively small but spirited.

Montréal's Never-ending Rainbow

Rue Ste-Catherine might be central to **MTL's LGBTIQ+ nightlife** (p83), but it only represents a piece of the city's pink puzzle. Queer-friendly and queer-owned establishments form an urban archipelago from Verdun to Villeray. Head to the Plateau for drag brunch at **Robin des Bois** (p103) or go bowling at Little Italy's **Notre-Dam-des-Quilles** (@ndq_bar_mtl). In Mile-Ex, eat burgers at lesbian-run **Dépanneur Le Pick Up** (lepickupmtl.com) or down beers at inclusive **Brasserie Harricana** (p121). Visit Villeray to clink wine glasses with queer couples at **Polari** (p119).

POP-UP PARTIES

MTL's party scene goes far beyond Village drinking dens. Homopop's **West End Gays** (@homopop_) is a magnet for dancing to pop and disco, **Queen & Queer** (@queenqueermtl) throws Sapphic soirées under SAT's trippy dome, **Ballroom 4 Community** (@ballroom4community) presents vogue-centric shows, DJ **Reid Bourgeois** (reidbourgeois.com) plays parties for a devout gay crowd and **ElleLui** (@ellelui.mtl) promotes queer, lesbian and trans joy on the dance floor.

Beyond Montréal's Bars

Join **Violet Hour** (@violet_hour_mtl) for LGBTIQ+ readings, check out chickadees with **Queer Birders de Montréal** (facebook.com/groups/queerbirders) and do battle against **Montréal Gaymers** (facebook.com/MTLGaymers). Visit queermtl.tumblr.com for citywide events and read fugues.com for queer Québec news.

PRIDE IN MTL

Fierté Montréal (Montréal Pride; fiertemontreal.com) is the largest LGBTIQ+ event in the French-speaking world, with roughly 750,000 people gathering in August for 11 days of concerts, film presentations, workshops and parties. It all culminates in a free-to-visit parade, thousands of people strong, marching 2.5km along Blvd René-Lévesque.

History Time Hop

Montréal's gayborhood spent the past century migrating from Downtown to the Village. Follow LGBTIQ+ footsteps on a history tour with **Thom Seivewright** (p70), who walks guests through Downtown's rainbow-hued past, then take a self-guided stroll around storied **Village landmarks** (p83).

QUEER IN QC

Most of Québec City's small-but-mighty LGBTIQ+ scene hugs Rue St-Jean within the St-Jean-Baptiste neighborhood. Uber-inclusive **Le Drague** (p175) is the hub for dancing and drag, **Bar St-Matthew's** (@barstmatthews) attracts bear-forward boys and art-packed **Fou-Bar** (foubar.ca) serves queer-friendly mixed crowds. Every Labor Day weekend 50,000 people join forces to celebrate **Fierté de Québec** (Quebec City Pride; fiertedequebec.ca), their colorful flags flying high over Place d'Youville.

Health & Safe Travel

KILLER COLD

Québec's winters are frigid, with temperatures sometimes dropping below -30°C. This puts travelers at increased risk of life-threatening cold-related ailments. Avoid them by wearing warm layers and covering all body surfaces, including the head, neck and fingers, while outside. Watch out for the 'umbles' (stumbles, mumbles, fumbles and grumbles), all symptoms of impending hypothermia. Stay inside during extreme cold snaps.

Health Insurance

Canada might be praised for its taxpayer-funded healthcare system, but unless you're a Canadian citizen, it's not possible to take advantage of the program. If your regular health insurance policy doesn't cover you while abroad, consider purchasing travel insurance to help fund any necessary medical care or prescription drugs while visiting. Paying out of pocket will cost a pretty penny.

Cannabis & Alcohol

Marijuana is legal, but you must be at least 21 years old to purchase and consume the drug. It's illegal to smoke in public places, including parks. All cannabis must be bought at a **Société Québécoise du Cannabis store** *(SQDC; sqdc.ca)*. The legal drinking age in Québec is 18. The primary place to buy alcohol is at an **SAQ outlet** *(saq.com)*.

TAP IS TOPS

It's safe to drink tap water in Montréal and Québec City – the majority of H_2O comes filtered from the St Lawrence River.

ROAD SIGNS

Red 'Arrêt'
Stop.

Green Excepté Dépassement
Drivers should use the far-right lane while driving uphill unless they want to pass on the left.

Yellow jumping deer
Watch out for white-tailed deer in the area.

Yellow moose
Watch out for moose in the area.

Vaccinations & Medications

No need to prove you've been jabbed – Canada doesn't require vaccinations – but ensure you're up to date with routine shots for the measles-mumps-rubella vaccine (MMR), the diphtheria-tetanus-pertussis vaccine and the polio vaccine. If you need over-the-counter medicine, search for big pharmacy chains like **Jean Coutu** *(jeancoutu.com)* and **Pharmaprix** *(pharmaprix.ca)*. Some branches stay open late.

WALK, RIDE & DRIVE

Montréal and Québec City are known for high levels of street safety compared to other North American cities. Pedestrians can generally walk freely through neighborhoods and hop on public transit without fear, though it's smart to keep valuables safely stashed. Drivers, beware: increased car theft around Montréal means it's wise to park in a garage overnight.

Responsible Travel

Climate Change & Travel

It's impossible to ignore the impact we have when traveling; Lonely Planet urges all travelers to engage with their travel carbon footprint, which will mainly come from air travel. While there often isn't an alternative, travelers can look to minimise the number of flights they take, opt for newer aircrafts and use cleaner ground transportation, such as trains. One proposed solution – purchasing carbon offsets – unfortunately does not cancel out the impact of individual flights. While most destinations will depend on air travel for the foreseeable future, for now, pursuing ground-based travel where possible is the best course of action.

The **UN Carbon Offset Calculator** shows how flying impacts a household's emissions.

The **ICAO's carbon emissions calculator** allows visitors to analyse the CO2 generated by point-to-point journeys.

Eat Plant-Based Plates

Reduce greenhouse-gas emissions by going vegan or vegetarian. In Montréal, **Momo** (p97) serves fish-free sushi with inventive flavors, **Tendresse** (p82) dishes out affordable three-course meals and **Vin Mon Lapin** (p117) offers inventive plant-based alternatives to select dishes.

Fill up on Farm Goods

Visit markets supporting local producers and artisans. More than 300 stands fill Montréal's **Marché Jean-Talon** (p118) and over 100 Canadian producers sell tempting treats at Québec City's **Le Grand Marché** (p168).

Make Zero Waste

Champion eateries that reduce, reuse or eliminate waste. Montréal's **Café des Habitudes** (p115) is almost entirely decorated in secondhand furniture and **Cass Café** (p93) uses takeout cups that decompose in soil within 180 days.

No one knows what makes their town tick better than Québec's licensed tour guides. Decode Montréal with help from **Spade & Palacio** (p57), then see QC through the eyes of **Tours Voir Québec** (toursvoirquebec.com).

French is Québec's official language, and using a little *français* in everyday interactions can go a long way. Even a simple greeting shows respect for local culture, making small exchanges friendlier and more meaningful.

Upcycle Your Style

Say *'à bientôt'* to mass-produced fashion – Montréal is all about **repurposed vintage** (p94). Hunt for rehabbed denim at La Caravane Vintage, restored leather at Palmo Goods and gently used tees at Magasin Steal Street.

Take the Train

Hop on VIA Rail to chug between Québec City and Montréal – it's a scenic countryside cruise. Once in Montréal, reduce fuel usage by riding the Métro, which zips between the city's most popular neighborhoods.

Sail Sustainably

Bid *adieu* to gas-powered boat tours. Float along the St Lawrence on an all-electric **Petit Navire cruise** (p57), departing from Montréal's Old Port, or paddle your way to a cleaner planet with **Rafting Montréal** (p135).

Honor Indigenous Culture

The original stewards of America's landscape hold keys to protecting its ecology. You can learn about their Earth-savvy approach to living at the **Musée McCord Stewart** (p70) and August's **International First Peoples' Festival** (p55).

Choose Green Stays

Sleep soundly at a Green Key–certified hotel that's committed to ecofriendly practices. Try **Le Mount Stephen** (p198), a 19th-century mansion modernized for 21st-century tastes, or **Hôtel de l'ITHQ** (p199), run by hospitality students.

Cycle Like a Local

Minimize your carbon footprint by cycling across Québec. There are bike-share programs in Montréal and Québec City, and the **Route Verte** (p179) is a 5000km collection of paved bike paths crisscrossing the province.

It's safe to drink Québec's tap water – carry a reusable water bottle.

Single-use plastic bags are banned in Montréal's shops and restaurants – bring a tote or backpack.

NOT-SO-SWEET FUTURE

Québec's maple syrup farmers are on the front lines of climate change, with extreme weather and invasive insects resulting in sugar-making setbacks. Some scientists predict the syrup's regional sweet spot will shift hundreds of miles north by 2100.

RESOURCES

Offset your carbon footprint in Montréal
https://api.mtl.org/en/carbon-calculator

Download Montréal's BIXI bike app
bixi.com/en/mobile-application

Offset your carbon footprint in Québec City
quebec-cite.com/en/plan-your-trip-quebec-city/carbon-footprint-offset

Accessible Travel

Navigating Québec with physical or cognitive impairments can be challenging. Public transportation isn't fully accessible, plus cobblestone streets and narrow sidewalks make historic centers in Montréal and Québec City tricky for wheelchair users. It's also rewarding: cultural attractions offer plenty of disability-friendly programming. Always call ahead to confirm accessibility standards.

Local Sign Language

Travelers who are deaf should familiarize themselves with a few phrases in Langue des signes québécoise (LSQ), Québec's primary sign language. Visit *aqepa.org/courslsq* to begin.

Airport

Canada's Accessible Transportation for Persons with Disabilities Regulations (ATPDR) mean the nation's airports and airlines must provide accommodations and necessary support for passengers with disabilities. Contact your airline to ensure all accessibility requirements can be met.

Accommodations

Modern hotels, such as Montréal's **Hotel Monville** (p198), incorporate access into their designs, but hotels constructed before the 1990s may lack certain mobility-access features like elevators and ramps. Check with the hotel before booking.

Montréal's Métro

Only about 30 of the city's 68 Métro stations have elevators, making over half the system terrible for travelers with reduced mobility. Visit *stm.info* for a map of accessible stations.

Try a Taxi

Many Montréal bus lines accommodate wheelchair users, but ramps can occasionally be out of order. Call **Taxi Para-Adapté** *(taxiparaadapte.ca)* for faster, smoother service. In Québec City, try **Transport Accessible du Québec** *(taq.qc.ca)*.

PLATES WITHOUT PEEKING

Find out what it's like to dine sans sight at Montréal's **Onoir** *(onoir.com)*, where blind and low-vision waitstaff serve meals in darkened rooms. A percentage of profits goes to local associations supporting the blind community.

SENSORY-FRIENDLY FUN

Autistic travelers and those with sensory sensitivities can enjoy 'peaceful mornings' at **Centre des Sciences de Montréal** and relaxed performances at **TOHU** (p119), and avail of sensory kits provided by **Espace Pour la Vie's museums** (p84).

> **RESOURCES**
>
> **Kéroul** *(keroul.qc.ca)* creates accessible travel itineraries for people with limited mobility in Montréal and Québec City. Visit **Québec for All** *(lequebecpourtous.com)*, a Kéroul-powered database listing over 2000 accessible or partially accessible hotels, restaurants, museums and tourist sites.
>
> Travelers with disabilities can apply for a **CAL card** *(carteloisir.ca/non-resident)*, granting companions free entry to participating cultural sites such as museums.

> Skiing Québec's mountains is a rite of passage, and adaptive programs mean reduced-mobility athletes can join the fun. Daredevils aged eight and up shred slopes at **Owl's Head** *(owlshead.com)*, near Montréal, and **Station Touristique Stoneham** *(ski-stoneham.com)*, near Québec City.

Nuts & Bolts

OPENING HOURS

Hours remain relatively consistent year-round, though businesses involving outdoor tours generally operate seasonally.

Banks 9am to 5pm Monday to Friday, with select Saturday hours

Cafes 8am to 4pm; some close 6pm or later

Restaurants Breakfast 7am to 11am, lunch 11:30am to 2:30pm, dinner 5pm to 10pm, weekend brunch 10:30am to 3pm

Bars, clubs and pubs Bars 5pm to midnight or later; clubs stay open until 3am on weekends; pubs with food service open around lunchtime

Museums 10am to 5pm; most close Monday and a handful stay open late one day a week, typically Wednesday or Thursday

Shops 11am to 6pm

Grocery stores 8am to 10pm

Weights & Measures

Québec mostly uses the metric system, but Canada only transitioned away from the imperial system in the 1970s, so many Canadians still use a mix. Still, distance is measured in kilometers (1.6km equals 1 mile) and speeds are indicated in kilometers per hour (100km/h equals 62mph). Gas is sold in liters (3.75L equals 1 US gallon). Weight is measured in grams and kilograms.

Internet
Wi-fi is widely available. Consult *ville.montreal.qc.ca/cartemtlwifi* (Montréal) or *zapquebec.org* (Québec City) for free service.

Toilets
Public washrooms are scarce. Visit *quebec-cite.com* for a map of QC's downtown toilets.

GOOD TO KNOW

Time zone
Eastern Time (EST/EDT; UTC/GMT minus five hours)

Country calling code
+1

Emergency number
911

Population
9.1 million (all of Québec)

Electricity
Type A 120V/60Hz; Type B 120V/60Hz

Type A 120V/60Hz

Type B 120V/60Hz

PUBLIC HOLIDAYS

Québec observes eight statutory holidays. Select businesses remain open in big cities and tourist areas, but hours are subject to change. Expect packed venues and higher hotel prices. Plan travel around these dates well in advance.

New Year's Day January 1

Good Friday and Easter Monday Late March to mid-April

Victoria Day The penultimate Monday in May (before the 25th)

National Indigenous Peoples Day (non-statutory) June 21

Fête National du Québec (St-Jean-Baptiste Day) June 24

Canada Day July 1

Labour Day First Monday in September

Canadian Thanksgiving Second Monday in October

Remembrance Day (non-statutory) November 11

Christmas Day December 25

Language

Canada is officially a bilingual country with the majority of the population speaking English as their first language. In Québec, however, the dominant language is French. The local tongue is essentially the same as what you'd hear in France, and you'll have no problems if you use standard French phrases.

Basics

Hello. Bonjour. *bon-zhoor*
Goodbye. Au revoir. *o-rer-vwa*
Excuse me. Excusez-moi. *ek-skew-zay-mwa*
Sorry. Pardon. *par-don*
Yes/No. Oui/Non. *wee/non*
Please. S'il vous plait. *seel voo play*
Thank you. Merci. *mair-see*

Directions

Where's...? Où est...? *Oo ay...?*
What's the address? Quelle est l'adresse? *kel ay la-dres*
Can you write down the address, please? Est-ce que vous pourriez écrire l'adresse, s'il vous plaît? *es-ker voo poo-ryay ay-kreer la-dres seel voo play*
Can you show me (on the map)? Pouvez-vous m'indiquer (sur la carte)? *poo-vay-voo mun-dee-kay (sewr la kart)*

Signs

Entrée Entrance
Femmes Women
Fermé Closed
Hommes Men
Ouvert Open
Renseignements Information
Sortie Exit
Toilettes/WC Toilets

Date & Time

What time is it? Y'est quelle heure? *il ay kel er*
It's (eight) o'clock. Il est (huit) heures. *il ay (weet) er*
Morning matin *ma-tun*
Afternoon après-midi *a-pray-mee-dee*
Evening soir *swar*
Night nuit *nwee*
Today aujourd'hui *o-zhoor-dwee*
Yesterday hier *yair*
Tomorrow demain *der-mun*

Emergencies

Help! Au secours! *o skoor*
Leave me alone! Fichez-moi la paix! *fee-shay-mwa la pay*
I'm ill. Je suis malade. *zher swee ma-lad*
I'm lost. Je suis perdu/perdue. *zhe swee-pair-dew (m/f)*
I'm allergic (to...) Je suis allergique (à ...). *zher swee za-lair-zheek (a...)*
Call a doctor. Appelez un médecin. *a-play un mayd-sun*
Call the police. Appelez la police. *a-play la po-lees*
It hurts here. J'ai une douleur ici. *zhay ewn doo-ler ee-see*

Eating & Drinking

What would you recommend? Qu'est-ce que vous conseillez? *kes-ker voo kon-say-yay*
What's in that dish? Quels sont les ingrédients? *kel son lay zun-gray-dyon*
I'm a vegetarian. Je suis végétarien/végétarienne. *zher swee vay-zhay-ta-ryun/vay-zhay-ta-ryen (m/f)*
Cheers! Santé! *son-tay*
Please bring the bill. Apportez-moi l'addition, s'il vous plaît. *a-por-tay-mwa la-dee-syon seel voo play*

NUMBERS

1 **un** *un*
2 **deux** *der*
3 **trois** *trwa*
4 **quatre** *cat*
5 **cinq** *sangk*
6 **six** *sees*
7 **sept** *set*
8 **huit** *weet*
9 **neuf** *nerf*
10 **dix** *dees*

ENGLISH DONATIONS TO QUÉBÉCOIS

Québec French employs a lot of English words; e.g. English terms are generally used for car parts – even the word *char* (pronounced 'shar') for car may be heard.

Québéc-qois?!

There are some key differences between European French and the Québec version (known as 'Québécois' or *joual*). For example, while standard French for 'What time is it?' is *Quelle heure est-il?*, in Québec you're likely to hear *Y'est quelle heure?* instead. Other differences worth remembering are the terms for breakfast, lunch and dinner: rather than *petit déjeuner*, *déjeuner* and *dîner* you're likely to see and hear *déjeuner*, *dîner* and *souper*.

Five Phrases to Learn Before You Go

Do you have any rooms available?
Est-ce que vous avez des chambres libres?
es·ker voo za·vay day shom·brer lee·brer

How much is it per night/person?
Quel est la prix par nuit/personne?
kel ay ler pree par nwee/per·son

I'd like to buy...
Je voudrais acheter...
zher voo·dray ash·tay ...

Do you speak English?
Parlez-vous anglais?
par·lay·voo ong·glay

I'd like to reserve a table for...
Je voudrais réserver une table pour...
zher voo·dray ray·zair·vay ewn ta·bler poor...

SOUND IT OUT

The sounds used in spoken French can almost all be found in English. If you read our pronunciation guides as if they were English, you'll be understood. There are a couple of exceptions: nasal vowels (represented in our guides by o or u followed by an almost inaudible nasal consonant sound m, n or ng), the 'funny' u (ew in our guides) and the deep-in-the-throat r. Syllables in French words are, for the most part, equally stressed. As English speakers tend to stress the first syllable, try adding a light stress on the final syllable of French words to compensate.

As of 2021, nearly 10.7 million Canadians can hold a conversation in French.

The majority of Canada's Francophones (84.1%) live in Québec.

STORYBOOK

STORYBOOK

Our writers delve deep into different aspects of Montréal and Québec City life.

A History of Québec in 15 Places

The story of Québec is embedded in ancient stones and Indigenous settlements, carried along the St Lawrence and found inside magnificent mansions.

John Garry

p218

Meet the Québécois

The Québécois are passionate about their French roots, traditions and culture; they cherish community and family and find pleasure in everyday life.

Pamel MacNaughtan

p222

Au Revoir to Bonjour-Hi

Forget four-letter words. In Montréal, uttering two letters after *'bonjour'* might be the naughtiest thing you can do.

John Garry

p224

A World of Arts in Québec Province

French Canada has fostered some of the most famous artists in the world, and countless more are waiting to be discovered.

Robert Isenberg

p227

A HISTORY OF QUÉBEC IN
15 PLACES

The story of Québec is embedded in ancient stones and Indigenous settlements, carried along the St Lawrence and found inside magnificent mansions. It's told in French, English and Iroquoian, through fur trades and manufacturing, religious zeal and red lights. Explore the streets of Montréal and Québec City to uncover their defining moments. By John Garry

WITHOUT THE ST Lawrence River, there'd be no Québec. The grand waterway linking the Atlantic to the Great Lakes provided a direct path to North America's interior, allowing the French to establish a colonial empire stretching far beyond the river's source. Montréal and Québec City emerged as its trading epicenters, shaped by the goods and people passing through.

When Jacques Cartier first navigated the St Lawrence in 1535, he encountered communities of St Lawrence Iroquoians who already understood the river's value. By the early 1600s those tribes had disappeared – possibly due to warfare with the Haudenosaunee Confederacy (also known as the Five Nations or Iroquois), whose influence grew around present-day Montréal. By the mid-1600s the Huron-Wendat had rooted themselves outside Québec City.

In the coming centuries, these Indigenous groups faced upheaval as European colonizers arrived en masse. The first boats brought fur-seeking Frenchmen and Catholic missionaries, who established Québec City as the capital of New France. The British came next, and by the early 1800s, Montréal had stolen the spotlight as the province's cultural and economic engine. Though Québec joined the Canadian Confederation in 1867, it retained a distinct identity, defined by its French-speaking populace – a linguistic island in an English-speaking sea.

1. Mont Royal
HISTORY'S BEST VANTAGE POINT

When it comes to watching Québec history unfold, there's no better seat in the house than Montréal's crowning mountain. Roughly 125 million years ago, magma surged toward the Earth's surface beneath this site, solidifying into a hard mass of igneous rock. As glaciers carved the softer sedimentary rock around it, this hilltop remained, a steady sentinel through it all: the ancient formation of the Champlain Sea, the arrival of hunter-gatherers over 5000 years ago, the rise of Iroquoian villages through the 1500s and the 1535 entrance of French explorer Jacques Cartier, who climbed its slopes and named it Mont Royal.

For more on Mont Royal, see p104.

2. Place-Royale
WHERE QUÉBEC CITY BEGAN

In 1608, explorer Samuel de Champlain founded France's first permanent settlement in North America along the St Lawrence River. He called it Québec – from the Indigenous Algonquian word 'Kebec,' meaning 'where the river narrows' – now considered the cradle of French Canada. Champlain's bottom line was big business. Furs were wildly lucrative, so he established a fortified trading post at present-day Place-Royale, tapping into Indigenous trade routes to acquire items like beaver pelts. These coveted skins became New France's raison d'être – transforming

North America's landscape and economy while stoking decades of shifting alliances, cultural upheaval and violence for First Nations communities.

For more on Place-Royale, see p169.

3. Pointe-à-Callière
FOUNDATIONS OF RELIGIOUS FERVOR

Modern Montréal's story began here in 1642, where Paul de Chomedey de Maisonneuve and Jeanne Mance laid the foundation for Ville-Marie, the island's first French settlement. Their mission was ambitious: convert the local Indigenous population to Christianity. Within a decade the fragile dream of a Catholic utopia faded as priorities shifted to fur trading, but religion had been embedded in Montréal's DNA. Today a holy cross tops Mont Royal, honoring one Maisonneuve erected in 1643 and watching over 200 churches, four basilicas and a people so saturated in religion they developed *sacres*, a lexicon of profanities that take aim at the church.

For more on the Pointe-à-Callière museum, see p47.

4. Place de la Grande-Paix-de-Montréal
PEACE, PLAGUES AND PERSECUTION

New France's thirst for fur demanded Indigenous partnership, so in 1701, Montréalers decided to broker peace. Around 1300 delegates from nearly 40 First Nations gathered here, now part of Place d'Youville, to sign a treaty ending decades of conflict, invigorating the fur-trading industry and enabling French colonists to pierce North America's heartland. Huron-Wendat leader Kondiaronk, who helped seal the deal, died during negotiations due to an epidemic – possibly smallpox – sweeping the city. Peace didn't last under British rule, and treatment of First Nations communities remained appalling. From the mid-1600s until slavery's abolition in 1834, colonists enslaved over 2000 Indigenous people.

For more on Montréal's Indigenous inhabitants, see p55.

5. Fortifications of Québec National Historic Site
THE BRITISH TAKE OVER

There's no telling what Québec might look or sound like today without the stone-and-wood ramparts circling Québec City's historic core. In 1690, residents started building this 4.6km defensive wall, fearing a British assault. Their fear came to fruition in 1759 during the Seven Years' War, but instead of relying on their fortifications, French troops engaged with the British on the Plains of Abraham – and lost. Britain's victory led to the 1763 Treaty of Paris, which ceded New France to British control. Ironically, the fortifications proved their worth years later when American revolutionaries attacked the city in 1775 – the walls held.

For more on Québec City's wondrous walls, see p166.

6. Lachine Canal
INDUSTRIAL BOAT RACE

Connecting Europe's markets to inland America, the St Lawrence River was a boon for Québec merchants. But there was one major snag: the Lachine Rapids outside Montréal, which prevented passage to the Great Lakes. Built to bypass the barrier, the 14km Lachine Canal supercharged Montréal's industrial boom when it finally opened in 1825. Flour mills, sugar refineries and textile factories crowded its banks until 1959, when construction of the St Lawrence Seaway rendered the canal obsolete. It was closed to boats by 1970 and turned into a drainage ditch, until 21st-century revitalization projects reimagined it as a recreation hub.

For more on the Lachine Canal, see p134.

Pointe-à-Callière (p47)

7. Place d'Youville
EXPLOSIVE POLITICS

Montréal had a five-year fling as Canada's capital (1845–49), sparking political progress and a fiery riot. During this short-but-seismic stint, leaders established a responsible government (led by elected politicians), won offical British recognition of French and enshrined bilingualism in parliament. But tensions between English and French speakers remained, and in 1849, outraged anglophones torched the parliament building. Their grievance? A bill compensating French Canadians for losses during the 1837–38 rebellions – a series of protests against British colonial oppression. The fire gutted the building – now a green patch at Place d'Youville – and the government packed its bags for Toronto.

For more on Place d'Youville, see p56.

8. Le Mount Stephen
MONTRÉAL'S INDUSTRIAL TITANS

When Scottish business mogul George Stephen commissioned an Italian Renaissance mansion on Drummond St in 1880, he joined a who's who of anglophone elites living in palatial homes around Mont Royal's southern base – a district now dubbed the Golden Square Mile. It's estimated that 80% of Canada's wealth lined the pockets of families living here at the turn of the 20th century. Stephen's neighbors, like the Molsons (of the eponymous brewery), laid the groundwork of iconic institutions. Stephen himself helped finance the Canadian Pacific Railway Company, laying steel tracks that linked Canada's provinces – a physical manifestation of the 1867 Canadian Confederation.

For more on the Golden Square Mile, see p77.

9. Boulevard St-Laurent
A GLOBAL GATEWAY

Montréal's oldest northbound thoroughfare became a cultural crossroad after the British came to power in the 18th century, geographically separating the city's English- and French-speaking communities. English Protestants claimed the west, French Catholics took the east, and as waves of immigrants arrived throughout the 19th and 20th centuries, they flooded the dividing line and made it their new home. An international mosaic emerged along Blvd St-Laurent – dubbed 'the Main' – now a walking timeline of Montréal's industrial-era population growth. Chinatown's noodle parlors echo 19th-century migration, along with 20th-century Jewish delis, Portuguese chicken counters and Italian cafes, each a soupçon in Montréal's multicultural melting pot.

For more on Blvd St-Laurent, see p117.

10. Bain Généreux
WORKING-CLASS WOES

When this art-deco bathhouse in Centre-Sud opened in 1927, it solved a dilemma plaguing working-class Montréalers: most homes lacked bathing facilities. The city built Bain Généreux – and many like it – to meet the basic needs of the booming population. By 1941 nearly 100,000 people lived in Centre-Sud, attracted by factories throughout the neighborhood offering low-wage manufacturing jobs. But after WWII, factories shuttered, jobs disappeared and the government razed entire blocks for public projects, displacing residents and reshaping the urban milieu. Montréal's LGBTIQ+ community began settling around Centre-Sud's south side in the 1970s and '80s, lured by cheap rents as police crackdowns pushed them from Downtown.

For more on Bain Généreux, see p80.

11. Place des Arts
SIN CITY'S CURTAIN CALL

As the 1920s roared in, Prohibition laws dried up taps across North America – but not in Montréal. Pleasure seekers hopped the US-Canada border to join the party raging along Rue Ste-Catherine and Blvd St-Laurent, lined with cabarets, brothels and gambling dens where gangsters like Al Capone reportedly held court. When mayor Jean Drapeau took office in the 1950s, he vowed to turn off the red lights, making plans for a grand cultural center to reinvent the neighborhood. In the coming decades, the seedy district was largely swept away and renamed Quartier des Spectacles, anchored by Place des Arts – Canada's largest performing arts complex.

For more on Place des Arts, see p63.

12. Parc Jean-Drapeau
THE GREAT FAIR'S MAYOR

No mayor shaped Montréal more than 'master builder' Jean Drapeau, who ran the city from 1954 to 1957 and again from 1960 to

Hôtel de Ville de Montréal (p56)

1986. His grand plans helped create the Métro, Downtown's skyscraper forest and the underground city beneath it. He also fought to host the 1976 Olympics, which redrew eastern Montréal and plunged the city deep into debt. He's best remembered for Expo 67 – a futuristic world's fair built on what's now his namesake park – which drew over 50 million visitors, boosted Montréal's global stature and forever changed how the city saw itself: as a place where anything was possible

For more on Parc Jean-Drapeau, see p140

13. Hôtel de Ville de Montréal
STRAPLINE

During a 1967 visit to Montréal, French president Charles de Gaulle stood on the balcony of City Hall and declared, 'Vive le Québec libre!' ('Long live free Québec!'). His words echoed nationalist sentiment from the Quiet Revolution – a period of sociopolitical change throughout the 1960s when French-speaking Québécois pushed for greater control over the province's identity and institutions. By invoking their separatist slogan, de Gaulle encouraged the movement's cause. The following year René Lévesque founded the independence-focused Parti Québécois, which won power in 1976 and passed Bill 101, making French the sole official language of Québec. A significant anglophone exodus followed.

For more on the Quiet Revolution and Bill 101, see p224 and p56.

14. Champ des Possibilities
STRAPLINE

Twirling around this community-run, city-sanctioned urban prairie is like spinning through time. On one side, cloistered nuns at the Carmelite Monastery recall Montréal's Catholic beginnings. On another, Canadian Pacific Railroad tracks evoke 19th-century industrialization. Then there's Mile End's 20th-century garment factories, where immigrants toiled until the 1970s and artists made their mark in the 1980s. When French gaming company Ubisoft moved into a former factory in the 1990s, it marked Montréal's rise as a tech hub – it's now a major player in AI and biotechnology. Gentrification followed, but locals fought back. This field stands as proof: the neighborhood isn't giving up.

For more on Champ des Possibilities, see p116.

15. MEM
MODERN MONTRÉAL

A museum spotlighting home-grown voices in mini documentaries, MEM believes that no one knows today's Montréal better than locals. Their stories chart Montréal's evolution into Canada's third-most multicultural city, where today's descendants of European immigrants mix with newcomers from Africa, Latin America, the Middle East and South Asia. They span 19 boroughs, ride 1065km of cycling lanes and fly a city flag redesigned in 2017 to honor Indigenous inhabitants. It's a city under constant construction: between 2021 and 2022, 94% of Downtown's streets were partially obstructed to upgrade infrastructure. Some see chaos; others see growth. Either way, Montréal's story remains a work in progress.

For more on MEM, see p66.

MEET THE QUÉBÉCOIS

The Québécois are passionate about their French roots, traditions and culture; they cherish community and family, and find pleasure in everyday life. PAMELA MACNAUGHTAN introduces her people.

THE STEREOTYPICAL DESCRIPTION of the Québécois is a people with a thick French accent who spurn anything English, consume vast amounts of maple syrup, work when they feel like it and love a good party. There's some truth to this – especially the last part. When you encounter the Québécois outside of Québec, they're often the loudest people in the room, so engrossed in their activities, food, wine and each other that they forget other people are around.

Connecting through shared language, culture and traditions, the Québécois are a fiercely proud people, and the fastest way to their heart is to make an effort to speak French when you're around them. There's no need to be fluent; a couple of words go a long way, and after a few beers with locals, your vocabulary will expand – usually with words not fit for polite company. This small gesture is more than a respect for language preferences; it's an acknowledgement of Québec's distinct culture, society and place within Canada.

The Québécois have lived a slow food, farm-to-table lifestyle for hundreds of years; meals typically include fresh local vegetables; foraged berries, herbs and mushrooms; wild game; and farm-raised meats. Glasses are filled with local beers or wines, and cheese boards are a common way to end a meal. Whether dining alone or gathering with family or friends, meals are a source of pleasure and often last two hours or more. Dining family style is common in restaurants – and the best way to try a variety of dishes.

Art, literature and music are some of the ways the Québécois hold onto their language and traditions. Through these forms of expression they protest against social injustices and biases, expose their souls, celebrate their language and preserve their history. They have a dark humor, and nobody is better at poking fun at the Québécois than the Québécois themselves. The most famous Québécois comedian outside of Québec is Norm MacDonald, who appeared on *Saturday Night Live* from 1993 to 1998. He's not the only famous Québécois, though; there's Québéc's unofficial queen, Céline Dion; one of Hollywood's hottest directors, Denis Villeneuve; and the captain of Québécois hearts, William Shatner.

The Québécois fight vigorously for what they believe in, and while some want their province to separate from the rest of country, the vast majority are proud Canadians. This became abundantly clear during 2025 chatter about Canada becoming the 51st US state: 'Canadian patriotism is on the rise in Québec,' said Émilie Foster, an adjunct professor in politics at Carleton University. 'We prefer to be part of Canada instead of being part of the United States, if we have to choose.'

The French Connection

The population of Québec reached 9.11 million in 2025, with about 80% descended from French colonizers. In the 2021 Census, 74.8% stated French is their mother tongue, 11.2% identified as Québécois, and 50% identified as French or Canadian.

A QUÉBÉCOISE BY CHOICE

I fell in love with the Québécois in 2013, on my first visit to Québec City. During a three-week cross-Canada adventure with VIA Rail, I spent three days here and was captivated by the locals' kindness and the culture's vibrancy. I returned several times that year and eventually based myself in the city for a couple of months in 2014 to be closer to my dad in Ontario, whose dementia was worsening. Moving to Québec City allowed me to trick my mind into thinking I was traveling, while also being only a nine-hour drive from my family. I moved to Québec City full time in 2016, a year after my father's death. In the eight years I've lived here I've become a loud and proud Québécoise with a deep connection to the city and its culture – a connection that has been strengthened by the friendships I've made.

AU REVOIR
TO BONJOUR-HI

Forget four-letter words. In Montréal, uttering two letters after *'bonjour'* might be the naughtiest thing you can do. By John Garry

'BONJOUR-HI!'
This unofficial shopkeeper greeting is ubiquitous in certain corners of Montréal, so common that former Montréaler Bowen Yang lampooned it on a *Saturday Night Live* sketch in 2020. '*Bonjour*-hi,' he sings as a faux Montréal news anchor with a thick Québécois accent – a preamble to five minutes poking fun at French-Canadian Franglish.

It's a seemingly harmless form of 'hello,' usually initiated by a bilingual cashier, who invites customers to pick the lingua franca by responding in their language of choice. It's a one-minute conversation condensed into one second; a linguistic shortcut that tells an entire tale.

But in Québec, the only region in North America where French is the sole official language, two additional letters after *'bonjour'* carry the weight of a 2-ton bomb.

Secret Agent Salutations
Between 2022 and 2023, undercover agents slipped into some 7000 business-

es across the Montréal region, silently waiting to be greeted. Upon receiving a verbal acknowledgment, they attempted a short exchange in French. Afterwards, agents recorded the results, including the business's 'language of greeting' and 'language of service.' The goal? Find out who and where companies didn't use Québec's official tongue. They targeted everyday spots – *dépanneurs*, restaurants, hotels – places frequented by locals and tourists alike.

This wasn't the first time Québec's government spied on stores. Surveillance started in the late 1980s, and the statistics – gathered by watchdog group Office québécois de la langue française (OQLF) – read like a francophone's nightmare. Between 2010 and 2023, French-only greetings dropped from 84% to 72%. Using a French-and-English combo, like '*bonjour-hi*,' rose by over eight percentage points to nearly 12%.

In response to the results, Montréal mayor Valérie Plante condemned the bilingual salute.

'We say "*bonjour*,"' she told English-language newspaper the *Montréal Gazette* in 2024, expressing that Montréalers should feel emboldened to use their mother language - even when speaking to out-of-towners.

A few months later the government released a $2.5-million multimedia campaign to protect French, featuring a commercial with a smiling cabbie and store clerk exclaiming '*Bonjour!*' to the camera. Ride the Métro and you'll see the campaign's signs, picturing three happy friends: '*Montréal se conjugue en français,*' they proclaim. Roughly translated, 'Montréal hangs out in French.'

Dépanneur **(convenience store; p66)**

> **RIDE THE MÉTRO AND YOU'LL SEE THE CAMPAIGN'S SIGNS, PICTURING THREE HAPPY FRIENDS: '*MONTRÉAL SE CONJUGUE EN FRANÇAIS,*' THEY PROCLAIM. ROUGHLY TRANSLATED, 'MONTRÉAL HANGS OUT IN FRENCH.'**

Language of the Oppressor

Language is tethered to Québec's identity. French displaced Indigenous dialects as New France built cities along the St Lawrence in the 1600s. After the British seized power in 1763, many wealthy francophones fled. English became the language of the elite, and though the 1867 Canadian Confederation declared the country bilingual, French became second class.

By the 1960s French-speaking frustrations had reached boiling point. Shut out of economic and political opportunities, francophones began demanding change, sparking the Quiet Revolution. Citizens called for secularism, education reform and greater control over the economy. Catholic influence waned and political action surged. French, long marginalized, was elevated to a dominant force in schools and workplaces. A new motto accompanied the movement: '*maîtres chez nous'* ('masters of our own house').

As the Quiet Revolution roared, Québécois nationalism swelled, pushing back against British suppression of Québec's French identity. Protests became de rigueur, including violent demonstrations led by the separatist group Front de libération du Québec (FLQ). Tensions peaked in October 1970 when the FLQ kidnapped Québec labour minister Pierre Laporte. Laporte's lifeless body was discovered stuffed into the trunk of a car. The assassination shocked the province, shattered the FLQ's public support and marked the beginning of the militant organization's end.

But cries for a free Québec were just beginning. By 1976 the Parti Québécois – led by René Lévesque – had won control of the provincial government, campaigning on a promise to seek Québec's independence and promote the rights of the French language. Though Québec sovereignty never transpired, Lévesque's language reform altered the course of provincial history.

Speak in French, S'il Vous Plaît

In 1977 Lévesque's government passed Bill 101, which declared French the province's only official language and mandated its use in education, work and commerce. It also required all commercial signs to be solely in French. (The law was relaxed in 1993; signs can now include other languages, though less prominently.) The message was clear: learn French or get lost. Over the next two decades an estimated 300,000-plus English speakers got the memo, fleeing for cities like Toronto.

In Montréal, home to Québec's largest anglophone community, businesses occasionally catch Bill 101's heat. In 1996 there was Matzahgate, when the OQLF (the same group that sent spies into stores) attempted to thwart the sale of kosher Jewish Passover products without French labels. In 2013, Pastagate turned the OQLF into a laughing stock after they warned Italian restaurant Buonanotte against using words like 'pasta,' 'antipasti' and 'calamari' on its menu. (In both cases, the OQLF backed down.)

Finally, in 2017, the 'bonjour-hi' backlash came into focus after provincial legislators passed a resolution to make shopkeepers drop the bilingual 'hello.' It never became law, but it did pave the way for Bill 96 in 2022. The new bill requires government employees to speak and write exclusively in French – and gives immigrants a brief six-month grace period to learn the language, necessary to receive public services.

Polyglot Province

Despite the use of 'bonjour-hi,' the OQLF's recent shopkeeper study found that workers still served customers in French 98% of the time. It seems French isn't under assault – it's thriving in a multicultural landscape.

Linguistic purism gets complicated in a city where one-quarter of the population identifies as immigrants. A bilingual greeting isn't always a threat – it's a peace offering in an increasingly global world.

Then again, peace for one community can translate to oppression for another. Saying 'au revoir' to 'bonjour-hi' might celebrate four centuries of Québécois culture, but it still leaves no room for an Indigenous 'hello.'

A WORLD OF ARTS IN QUÉBEC PROVINCE

French Canada has fostered some of the most famous artists in the world, and countless more are waiting to be discovered. By Robert Isenberg.

QUÉBEC PROVINCE IS a pretty great place to live a creative life – just ask any of the 43,000 professional artists who live here. They work in all media: painting, music, sculpture, performance and film, among countless others. The long winters give them time to write, compose, mix colors and edit photographs, and more than 200 performance halls and theaters host dance recitals, plays and improv comedy. Come summer, Montréal and Québec City explode with street festivals, outdoor concerts and public art displays.

There's no single explanation for Québec's robust artistic expression, though part of it may well be that the French diaspora is renowned for its creative spirit – art galleries look as apt in Montcalm and Old Montréal as they do in Paris and the French Riviera. Artistic endeavour among the diaspora dates back to at least the 18th century, with notable pioneers including landscape painter Joseph Légaré, opera singer Emma Albani and novelist Philippe Aubert de Gaspé.

The Canadian government also has a strong reputation for promoting its artists through active programming and financial support from the Canada Council for the Arts. Montréal and Québec City shine a bright light on their cultural institutions, too: Montréal's Quartier des Spectacles is home to more than 30 performance venues, with a total of 38,000 seats. Québec City's Grand Théâtre and Théâtre Capitole are two resplendent structures in a skyline with no shortage of grandeur. Both cities are rich in bookstores, ateliers, concert venues and recording studios. Without even stepping through a door, you can browse Montréal's 1000-plus works of public art, including hundreds of building-sized murals. Québec province has invested heavily in its talent, and the fruits of their labor are everywhere.

Success Stories

Québec province has incubated a remarkable number of breakout stars. Perhaps the most impressive Cinderella story began with a group of street performers in the riverside town of Baie-Saint-Paul, northeast of Québec City. After busking in the street for tourists, this ragtag band of jugglers and fire-throwers joined together to form Club des Talons Hauts (The High-Heeled Club) and developed more cohesive shows at the town's holiday fair. In 1984, under the leadership of accordionist Guy Laliberté and entrepreneur Gilles Ste-Croix, these 20 ambitious clowns and acrobats rebranded themselves under a new name: Cirque du Soleil.

STORYBOOK

Today, Cirque du Soleil is a global phenomenon with more than a dozen established shows and 1200 resident artists. Touring companies travel all over the world, and its permanent theater in Las Vegas holds performances every day of the week. More than 400 million people have seen at least one Cirque du Soleil show, making it one of the most successful circuses of all time. Yet Cirque is headquartered, and remains firmly rooted, in Montréal.

It's not alone. Non-Canadians are often surprised to learn how many household names started out in Québec. Decades before blockbusters like *Bladerunner 2049* and *Dune* hit cinemas, their director, Denis Villeneuve, grew up near the small city of Trois-Rivières and studied film in Montréal. Villeneuve first directed experimental French-language films before catching the attention of Hollywood. Meanwhile, both Céline Dion and Leonard Cohen grew up in Québec province before they became superstar vocalists. Actor William Shatner was raised here and started out performing at the Montréal Repertory Theatre, where he once understudied for fellow Montrealer Christopher Plummer. Meanwhile, before he voiced the lead character in *How to Train Your Dragon*, Jay Baruchel grew up in the Notre Dame de Grâce neighborhood in Montréal, and *Saturday Night Live* comedian Norm MacDonald spent most of his youth in Québec City.

A healthy arts scene shouldn't just be measured by its celebrities, but it's notable that all these stars got their start in Québec province. The arts scenes in Montréal and Québec City – and many places in between – are more active than ever, and it's exciting to imagine who will next emerge onto the international stage.

Connecting with Local Arts Scenes

One of the best ways for visitors to connect with the local scene is through the performing arts. Montréal is a major stop for touring bands and Broadway shows, and they're a great reason to spend a weekend in town. If you don't want to pay a fortune for tickets, Montréal has a good number of smaller theaters and comedy clubs as well, and you can find a jazz band or singer-songwriter performing even on the quietest winter night.

If you're seeking something frugal and spontaneous, Montréal and Québec City have more than their fair share of museums and art galleries, which draw the works of diverse studio artists from around the world. Many of these are top-tier institutions such as the **Musée des Beaux-Arts de Montréal** and the **Musée National des beaux-arts du Québec** – a visit to either is like a survey course in art history. You'll also find lots of private exhibitions and more avant-garde galleries, such as **Fonderie Darling** and **Arsenal Art Contemporain** in Montréal. Most interactive of all is the **Rue du Trésor** (p170) in Québec City, a narrow gauntlet of stalls selling original artwork.

Some basic French enriches many of these experiences, and verbal arts such as poetry readings and stand-up comedy will be hard to enjoy without a strong grasp of the language. But music and fine arts are pretty universal, and most museums have bilingual plaques and brochures.

For travelers spending more time in either city, there's no better place to learn or practice a creative skill. Life drawing classes and semi-formal writing groups get together every week in Montréal, and many organizers are eager for drop-ins. Public-facing institutions like the Musée et Centre d'Art de Montréal are designed to get newcomers involved, through tours of the museum, film screenings or regular holiday markets. Long after you've returned home, you'll likely be looped into open calls for art competitions and film festivals based in Québec; if your own painting or short film is accepted, you'll have a ready-made excuse to return to this arts-loving part of the world.

> THE ARTS SCENES IN MONTRÉAL AND QUÉBEC CITY - AND MANY PLACES IN BETWEEN - ARE MORE ACTIVE THAN EVER, AND IT'S EXCITING TO IMAGINE WHO WILL NEXT EMERGE ONTO THE INTERNATIONAL STAGE

Cirque du Soleil (p53)
THE CANADIAN PRESS/ALAMY

INDEX

ᐅᒪᓯᑦ uummaqutik: essence of life 69

A

Abenaki people 184
accessible travel 212
accommodations 196-201, *see also individual locations*
activities 20-1, *see also* canoeing, climbing, cycling, golfing, ice skating, kayaking, nature & natural history, paddleboarding, sledding & tobogganing, skiing, swimming, winter activities, ziplining
air travel 25
airports 25
Algonquin people 184
ampitheaters, *see* theaters & ampitheaters
animals, *see* wildlife
antiques 182
Arbraska (Mont-Saint-Grégoire) 160
arcades 107
architecture 12
  Arsenal Art Contemporain 128
  Biosphère 142
  Centre Canadien d'Architecture 131
  Château Dufresne 89
  Habitat 67 126-7
  history 151
  Manoir Montmorency (Chute Montmorency) 188

Silo No 5 59
staircases 98
tours 77
area codes 213
art 10-11, 227-9, *see also* murals
  shopping 39, 182
  tours 57, 128
art galleries, *see* museums & galleries
Assemblée national du Québec 168-9
Atelier Circulaire 115
ATMs 204
Auditorium de Verdun 132
Ave Duluth 97

B

B&Bs 197
bagels 113, 134
ballets 63
bars 34-5, *see also* drinking & nightlife
Basilique Cathédrale Notre-Dame-de-Québec 170
Basilique Notre-Dame 48
Basilique Ste-Anne-de-Beaupré (Sainte-Anne-de-Beaupré) 192-3
bathrooms 213
beaches
  Plage de l'Horloge 52
  Plage de Verdun 132
  Plage Jean-Doré 145
  Station de la Plage 176
beer 34-5, 82-3, 169, 183, 207, *see also* breweries & microbreweries
Belvédère Kondiaronk 19, 105
bicycle travel, *see* cycling
Biodôme 85
Biosphère 142
boat tours
  Croisières AML 57, 167
  Québec-Lévis ferry 167-8
  Saute-Moutons 57
boat travel 25, 28
books 23
bookshops 86, 97, 114

Bota Bota 59
Breakneck Steps 170
breweries & microbreweries 35, 121
  L'Espace Public 88
  Clos Saragnat (Brome-Missisquoi) 161
Brome-Missisquoi 160-1
Bromont (Brome-Missisquoi) 161
budgets 204, *see also* free experiences
  accommodations 20, 196-200,
  travel 27-8, 204
burlesque 37, 74
  Wiggle Room 103
business hours 35, 213
bus travel
  to/from Montréal & Québec City 24, 25
  within Montréal & Québec City 27

C

cabaret 36-7, 66, 86, 103, 208
Calvaire d'Oka (Oka) 151
candy 75
canoeing, *see also* kayaking, paddleboarding
  Laurentians, the 154, 158
  Parc National de la Jacques-Cartier 195
car travel 25
Carnaval de Québec 175
Cartier, Jacques 55, 58, 165, 190-1
cash 204
casse-croûte 32
cathedrals, churches & monasteries
  Basilique Notre-Dame 48
  Basilique Ste-Anne-de-Beaupré (Sainte-Anne-de-Beaupré) 192
  Basilique-Cathédrale Notre-Dame-de-Québec 170

Cathédrale Marie-Reine-du-Monde 76
Chapelle Notre-Dame-de-Bon-Secours 18, 49
Église de l'Annonciation (Oka) 152
Église Notre-Dame-des-victoires 170
Église St-Pierre-Apôtre 83
Église St-Roch 176
Monastère des Augustines 165
Notre-Dame-de-la-Défense 117
Oratoire St-Joseph 109
Centre Bell 65
Centre Canadien d'Architecture 131
Centre Clark 115
Chalet du Mont-Royal 105
Champ des Possibilities 116, 221
Château Dufresne 89
Château Frontenac 19, 168
Château Ramezay 18, 47, 49
children, travel with 15, 205
Chinatown 75-6
chocolatiers & confectioners
  Divine Chocolatier 73
  Chocolaterie de l'Île d'Orléans (l'Île d'Orléans) 192
  Dragon Beard Candy 75
  État de Choc 118
  Les Chocolats de Chloé 97-8
  Musée du Chocolat de la Confiserie Bromont 150
  Pâtisserie Coco 75
  Qantu 88
churches, *see* cathedrals, churches & monasteries
Cimetière Mont-Royal 108
Cimetière Notre-Dame-des-Neiges 107
Cinémathèque Québécoise 81

circuses 37
Cirque du Soleil 18, 53, 66
Le Monastère 66
Montréal Complètement Cirque 37
TOHU 119
Claire & Marc Bourgie Pavilion 69
climate 20-1
climbing
Laurentians, the 154
ice climbing 175
rock climbing 145
clubs 34-5, 206, 213, see also drinking & nightlife
Cohen, Leonard 23, 96, 108, 135, 229
confectioners, see chocolatiers & confectioners
Corridor du Littoral 176-9
costs 204, see also budget
accommodations 196
travel 28, 204
Cree people 184
art 55, 71
credit cards 204
Croix du Mont-Royal 105
cruises, see boat tours
culture 222-3, 227-9
currency 204
cycling 27-8, see also fat & winter biking
Brome-Missisquoi 161
Dunham 157
Granby 157
Île de la Visitation 121
Lachine Canal, Little Burgundy & the Southwest 133
Laurentians, the 154, 156
Old Montréal 45
Parc-nature de l'Île-de-la-Visitation 121
Parc Jean-Drapeau 141, 145, 147
Parc du Mont-Royal 106
Plateau Mont-Royal 91
Promenade Samuel-de-Champlain 176
Québec City 163, 176, 179
Saint-Jean-Sur-Richelieu 157, 159
Sainte-Anne-de-Beaupré 194-5
cycling tours
Bike Tour of Old Québec 185
Fitz Montréal 57
Lachine Canal 136, **136**
wine trails 161

dangers 209
day trips, see side trips
de Champlain, Samuel 170
dépanneurs 23, 66
disabilities, travelers with 212
discounts 204
Dominion Square Building 76
Downtown 60-77, **61**, **62**, **67**
accommodations 197-8
drinking 63, 64, 71, 72
entertainment 63
festivals 64
food 64, 65, 66, 70
highlights 61
shopping 65, 72-4
transportation 61
drag 86, 103, 131, 172, 175, see also LGBTIQ+ sites & venues
drinking & nightlife 34, 35, 206-7, 213
speakeasies 35
tours 185
driving 25

Eastern Townships 158
Écomusée du Fier Monde 80-1
EDM 37
Igloofest 175
ÎleSoniq 145
Piknic Électronik 143
electricity 213
emergencies 213
épiceries 179
Escalier Casse-Cou 170
Espace Verre 128-9
exhibits & exhibitions
All the Livelong Day! The Joys & Sorrows of Life in a Working-Class Neighbourhood 80
Aura Experience 48
Building Montréal 47
Crossroads Montréal 47
Indigenous Voices Today 71
Onhwa' Lumina (Wendake) 189
The Arts of One World 68
This Is Our Story 177
Where Montréal Began 47
EXMURO 181
events, see festivals & events

Fairmount Bagel 113
family travel 15, 205
fat & winter biking 20, 147, 154, 157, 185
ferries, see boat travel
Festival d'été de Québec 37, 165, 167
Festival international de Jazz de Montréal 64
festivals & events 21, 37
Art Souterraine 76
Carnaval de Québec 167, 175
Festival Bach 37
Festival d'Été de Québec 37, 165, 167
Festival international de Jazz de Montréal 64
Fête des Neiges 145
Fierté Montréal 83
food 31
Francos 37, 64
Grand Marché de Noël de Montréal 64
Grand Prix du Canada 145
Igloofest 175
ÎleSoniq 37, 145
ItalFest 117
Jazz Fest 64
Just for Laughs 64
Les Fêtes de la Nouvelle-France 167
Les Grand Feux 167
Les Premiers Vendredis 85
L'International des Feux Loto-Québec 145
Marché de Noël allemand de Québec 175
Montréal en Lumière 64
OfF Piknic 143
Osheaga 145
Parc Jean-Drapeau 145
Pee-Wee Hockey Tournament 175
Petit Piknic 143
Piknic Électronik 37, 143
Pow Wow International 189
Québec City 167
seasons 200
Suoni Per Il Popolo 37
Sommets du Cinéma d'Animation 81
Tam-Tams du Mont-Royal 104
Toboggan Festival 167
Village Nordik 175
winter 175
Fierté Montréal 83

films 23
Sommets du Cinéma d'Animation 81
First Nations & Indigenous Peoples, see also Abenaki people, Alonquin people, Cree people, Inuit people, Iroquois people, Mohawk people
art 54, 71-2, 55
festivals 55, 189
history 55-6, 184, 189
languages 149-50
food 14, 30-2, 206-7, see also bagels, poutine, websites 32
food tours 31
Beyond the Market 57
Brome-Missisquoi 160-1
Chemin du Terroir (the Laurentians) 31, 152
Dragon Beard Candy 75
Evening Gourmet Food Tour 185
Gourmet Sauvage 156
HoMa 87-8
Mile End 114-15
Qantu 88
Fortifications of Québec 19, 166, 219
Franglish, see language
free experiences 16, 185
French, see language
Fresque des Québécois 182

galleries, see museums & galleries
gardens, see parks & gardens
gay travelers, see LGBTIQ+ travelers
Glissade de la Terrasse 175
Golden Square Mile 19
golfing
Mystic Pines Golf & Country Club (Kahnawake Mohawk Territory) 149
Parcours du Vieux Village (Brome-Missisquoi) 161
Grand Quai 53
Grand Théâtre de Québec 19, 183
Grands Ballets de Canadiens 63
green spaces, see parks & gardens
Grosse-Île Irish Memorial National Historic Site 167, 183-4
Gulf of St Lawrence 85

H

Habitat 67 126-7
health 209
Henri Henri 73
highlights 6-17
hiking, see walking tours, walking trails
historic sites
  Fortifications of Québec National Historic Site 19, 166, 219
  Grosse-Île Irish Memorial National Historic Site 167, 183-4
  Lieu Historique de Sir George-Étienne Cartier 49
  Plaines d'Abraham 165
history
  architecture 71, 151, 187
  Bain Généreux 220
  Black 139, 169
  Boulevard St-Laurent 220
  burlesque 74
  Catholicism 49, 83, 109, 172
  Champ des Possibilités 221
  Chinatown 75
  colonial 138-9, 165, 187-8
  commercial district 169-70
  Expo 67 143-4
  Filles du Roi 50, 138-9
  immigrants 117
  Irish people 183-4
  Jewish 113, 120, 137
  Lachine Canal 126, 219
  Le Mount Stephen 220
  LGBTIQ+ 83, 86
  literature 128, 184-5
  MEM 221
  Mile End 115
  military 166, 181
  Montréal 72, 74
  Mont Royal 218
  national parks 159
  Oka 153
  Olympic Stadium 85
  Parc du Mont-Royal 106
  Parc Jean-Drapeau 220-1
  parliamentary 168-9
  Place de la Grande-Paix-de-Montréal 219
  Place des Arts 220
  Place d'Youville 220
  Place Royale 218
  Pointe-à-Callière 219
  Québec City 165-6
  St Lawrence River 58
  St-Denis 82
  tours 56
  Wendake 189
  working classes 80-1
hockey 65, 175
HoMa, see Quartier Latin, the Village & HoMa
hostels 197
Hôtel de Glace 175
Hôtel-de-Ville-de-Québec 173

I

ice skating
  Atrium Le 1000 103
  Auditorium de Verdun 132
  Esplanade Transquille 103
  Parc du Mont-Royal 105
  Parc Jean-Drapeau 145
  Parc Maisonneuve 103
  Place d'Youville 173
  Plateau Mont-Royal 103
ice-canoes
  Carnaval de Québec 167, 175
Île de la Visitation 121
Île d'Orléans 190-2
  food 193
Indigenous peoples, see First Nations & Indigenous peoples
Insectarium 85
insurance, health 209
internet access 24, 213
Inuit people 184
  art 54-5, 69, 72, 115, 170, 177
Iroquois people 184
ItalFest 117
itineraries 18-19

J

Jardin Botanique 85
Jardins des Floralies 145
Jean-Noël Desmarais Pavilion 68

K

Kahnawake Mohawk Territory 149-150
  food 150
kayaking, see also canoeing, paddleboarding
  Lachine Rapids 134-5
  Laurentians, the 152, 154
  Oka 152
  Parc Jean-Drapeau 145
  Parc National de la Jacques-Cartier 195
  Pointe-des-Cascades 151

L

La Banquise 93
La Citadelle 181
La Grande Roue de Montréal 53
La Ronde 146
Lac aux Castors 105
Lachine Canal, Little Burgundy & the Southwest 122-39, **124-5, 130, 133, 136**
  drinking & nightlife 129, 131, 135, 138-9
  food 126, 128-9, 132, 134, 137
  highlights 123
  transportation 123
Lachine Rapids 134-5
Laurentians, the 152-9
  transportation 156
language 29, 214-15, 224-6
Le Chariot 55
Leclerc, Félix 191-2
LGBTIQ+ travelers 208
  festivals 83
  tours 83, 86
LGBTIQ+ sites & venues
  Café Cleopatre 86
  Chapel of Hope 83
  Club Soda 86
  Complexe Sky 86
  Le Cocktail 86
  Le Drague 175
  L'Euguélionne 86
  Parc de l'Espoir 83
  Priape 86
  Wiggle Room 86
  Lieu Historique de Sir George-Étienne Cartier 49
Liliane & David M Stewart Pavilion 69
Limoilou 176
Little Burgundy, see Lachine Canal, Little Burgundy & the Southwest
Little Italy, see Mile End, Little Italy & Outremont
Little Portugal 19, 95-6
live entertainment, see performing arts
lookouts, see viewpoints & lookouts

M

Magasin Steal Street 94
Maison de la littérature 184-5
Maison St-Gabriel 138-9
Maison Smith 105
Malecite 184
Manoir Mauvide-Genest (Île d'Orléans) 190
maple syrup 207
Marché Atwater 127-8
Marché Bonsecours 50
Marché Jean-Talon 118-19
Marché Maisonneuve 88
marchés (markets) 206
  Le Grand Marché 168
  Marché Atwater 127-8
  Marché Bagels on Greene 134
  Marché Bonsecours 50
  Marché d'Emma 179
  Marché de Noël allemand de Québec 173, 175
  Marché Floh 94
  Marché Jean-Talon 118-19
  Marché Maisonneuve 88
mausoleums 108
MBAM 68
MEM 66
menus 33, 206
Métro travel 26-8
Michael & Renata Hornstein Pavilion for Peace 69
Mile End, Little Italy & Outremont 110-21, **111, 112, 116, 120**
  accommodations 199
  drinking & nightlife 113, 115, 119, 121
  entertainment 119
  food 114, 117, 118
  shopping 114, 118
Mohawk people 184
  history 81, 149-51
Monastère des Augustines 165, 167

monasteries, *see* cathedrals, churches & monasteries
money 204
Montreal Museum of Fine Arts, *see* Musée des Beaux-Arts de Montréal
Montréal Tower 84
Mont-Saint-Grégoire 160
monuments & statues
Croix du Mont-Royal 105
Nelson's Column 56
Silo No 5 59
Sir Georges-Étienne Cartier Monument 104
Tour de l'Horloge 53
Morgan Arboretum (Sainte-Anne de Bellevue) 148
Morrin Centre 185
mountains
Laurentians, the 152-9
Mont-Sainte-Anne (Sainte-Anne-de-Beaupré) 194
murals
Fresque des Québécois 182
graffiti-loving grandma 96
Jackie Robinson 96
Karma goID 96
La liberté guidant le peuple 96
La liberté vandalisée 96
Leonard Cohen (Mont Royal) 108
Leonard Cohen (Plateau) 108
Leonard Cohen's eyes 96
Personal Topography 96
Sarah McDaniel 96
Seven Deadly Sins 96
tours 96
Musée de la Civilisation 177
Musée de l'Holocauste 137
Musée des Beaux-Arts de Montréal 68-9
Musée des Ondes Emile Berline 135
Musée et Centre d'Art de Montréal 128
Musée McCord Stewart 70-1
Musée National des beaux-arts du Québec 229
Musée Redpath 71
Museum Alley 71

museums & galleries, *see also* exhibits & exhibitions
5455 & 5445 Ave de Gaspé 115
Arsenal Art Contemporain 128
Atelier Circulaire 115
Biosphère (museum) 143
Centre des Science de Montréal 53
daphne 115
Écomusée du Fier Monde 80-1
Elektra 115
Espace Verre 128
EXMURO 181
Exporail: Musée du Ferroviaire Canadien (Saint-Constant) 150
Fonderie Darling 57
Galerie d'Art Mont-Ste-Anne 195
Galerie Images Boréales 54
Galerie Le Chariot 55
Hôtel-Musée Premières Nations (Wendake) 188
Maison St-Gabriel 138-9
MEM 66
Monastère des Augustines (museum) 165
Montréal Aviation Museum (Sainte-Anne de Bellevue) 148-9
Musée de la Civilisation 177
Musée de l'Holocauste 137
Musée des Beaux-Arts de Montréal 68-9
Musée des Ondes Emile Berline 135
Musée des Plaines d'Abraham 165
Musée du Chocolat de la Confiserie Bromont (Bromont) 150
Musée du Fort Saint-Jean (St-Jean-sur-Richelieu) 150
Musée du Haut-Richelieu (St-Jean-sur-Richelieu) 150
Musée et Centre d'Art de Montréal 128
Musée Lac-Brome (Knowlton) 150
Musée Maritime de Île d'Orléans (Île d'Orléans) 192

Musée McCord Stewart 70
Musée Romeo's 115
PHI 57
Planétarium 85
Sacred Fire Productions 54
Société des Arts Technologiques 75
music 23, 36-7, *see also* EDM
history 135
jazz 64-5

national parks & reserves
Parc National de la Jacques-Cartier 195
Parc National de la Mauricie (the Laurentians) 159
Parc National d'Oka (Oka) 151-2
Parc National du Mont-Tremblant (the Laurentians) 157-8
Réserve Nationale de Faune du Cap-Tourmente 195
nature & natural history 71
Biodome 85
Biosphère 142
Great Vivarium 85
Insectarium 85
Jardin Botanique 85
Morgan Arboretum (Sainte-Anne de Bellevue) 148
Parc du Mont-Royal 105
Parc Jean-Drapeau 147
Sentier des Cimes (the Laurentians) 155
Tonga Lumina (the Laurentians) 157
neighborhoods 42-3, **42-3**
Nelson's Column 56
nightlife, *see* drinking & nightlife
North Star Machines 107
Notre-Dame-de-la-Défense 117

observatories
Observatoire de la Capitale 183
Port of Montréal Tower 53
obstacle courses
Acro-Nature 156
Aquazilla 145

Tyroparc 157
Oka 151-2
Old Montréal 44-59, **45, 46, 51**
accommodations 197
drinking & nightlife 47, 55, 58, 59
food 47, 49, 51, 54, 57
highlights 45
shopping 50, 54
transportation 45
walking tour 56, **56**
Old Port 52-3
Olympic Stadium 84
opening hours 35, 213
Opéra de Montréal 63
operas 36, 63
Oratoire St-Joseph 109
Orchestre Symphonique de Montréal 63
outdoor activities, *see* climbing, cycling, golfing, ice skating, kayaking, nature & natural history, skiing, sledding & tobogganing, swimming, water sports, winter activities
Outremont, *see* Mile End, Little Italy & Outremont

paddleboarding, *see also* canoeing, kayaking
Canots Légaré (Wendake) 189
Parc Jean-Drapeau 145
Parc du Mont-Royal 104-6
Parc du Portugal 95-7
Parc Ignace Bourget 137-8
Parc Jean-Drapeau 140-7, **141, 142**
highlights 141
transportation 141
Parc La Fontaine 103
Parc National de la Jacques-Cartier 195
Parc National de la Mauricie (the Laurentians) 159
Parc National d'Oka (Oka) 151-2
Parc National du Mont-Tremblant (the Laurentians) 157-8
Parc Olympique & Espace Pour la Vie 84-5
parks & gardens 6-7, *see also* Parc Jean Drapeau, national parks & reserves
Chinese Garden 85

parks & gardens *continued*
  Dorchester-Clarke Park 138
  First Nations Garden 85
  Japanese Garden 85
  Jardin Botanique 85
  Marais du Nord 195
  Parc Arthur Thierren 132
  Parc de la Forêt Ancienne du Mont Wright 195
  Parc de l'Espoir 83
  Parc des Chutes-de-la-Chaudière 195
  Parc des Moulins 195
  Parc du Mont-Royal 104-6
  Parc Ignace Bourget 137-8
  Parc King George 138
  Parc La Fontaine 103
  Parc-nature de l'Île-de-la-Visitation 121
  Parc Westmount 138
  Westmount Athletic Grounds 138
  Westmount City Hall 138
Pavillon du Lac aux Castors 105
pedal boats
  ÉcoRécréo 53
  Plage Jean-Doré 145
penguins 85
people 213, 222-3, *see also* First Nations & Indigenous peoples
performing arts 36-7, 227-9, *see also* theaters
  Agora de la Danse 63
  Bistro à Jojo 89
  Casa del Popolo 119
  Cinémathèque Québécoise 81
  Cinquième Salle 63
  Club Soda 63
  Duceppe 63
  Espace Félix Leclerc (Île d'Orléans) 191-2
  Espace St-Denis 89
  Foufounes Électriques 63
  Grands Ballets de Canadiens 63
  Le Balcon 65
  Le Diamant 183
  Le Monastère 66
  Le National 89
  Les Jardins Gamelin 89
  MTELUS 63
  Opéra de Montréal 63
  Orchestre Métropolitain 63
  Orchestre Symphonique de Montréal 63
  Place des Arts 63
  Salle Claude-Léveillée 63
  Satosphere 74
  TOHU 119
  Usine C 89
Petit-Champlain 169-70
picnics 168
Pietà Mausoleum 107
Piknic Électronik 143
Place d'Armes 56
Place des Arts 63
Place d'Youville 56
Place Jacques-Cartier 50
Plage de l'Horloge 52
Plage de Verdun 132
Plage Jean-Doré 145
Plaines d'Abraham 165
Planétarium 85
plants, *see* natural history
planning, *see also* budget
  clothes 22
  etiquette 22
  language 23, 29
  Montréal & Québec City basics 22-3
Plateau Mont-Royal 90-109, **91**, **92**, **96**, **100-1**
  accommodations 199
  drinking & nightlife 93, 98, 102
  food 94, 95, 97
  highlights 91
  transportation 91
Playground (Kahnawake Mohawk Territory) 149
podcasts 23
Pointe-à-Callière 18, 47
Pointe-des-Cascades 151
politics 186-7, 220
Port of Montréal Tower 53
poutine 32, 93-4, 165
  history 94, 179
  Poutine Week 175
public holidays 213
public transportation 24-7

Quartier Latin, the Village & HoMa 78-89, **79**, **80**
  accommodations 199
  drinking & nightlife 83, 86
  entertainment 89
  food 81, 82, 87
  highlights 79
Québec City 162-85, **163**, **164**, **171**, **174**, **178**, **180**
  accommodations 199-200
  drinking & nightlife 164, 169, 175, 179, 182, 183, 184, 185
  entertainment 183
  food 165, 167, 168, 170, 172, 173, 176, 181
  highlights 163
  tours 185
  transportation 163
  shopping 169, 170, 173
Québec-Lévis ferry 167-8

raves 175
Redpath Museum, *see* Musée Redpath
Réseau de la Ville Souterraine 76
RÉSO 76
responsible travel 210-11
ridesharing 27
rock climbing 145, *see also* climbing
Rue du Petit-Champlain 19
Rue St-Paul 18, 50
ruelles vertes 99, 102

S

safety 209
Sainte-Anne-de-Beaupré 192-4
  food 192
Sainte-Anne de Bellevue 148
Saint-Jean-sur-Richelieu 159
SAT 74
Schwartz's 93
Seigneurie de Île d'Orléans (Île d'Orléans) 190
Shaar Hashomayim Cemetery 108
shopping 38-9, *see also* bookshops, marchés (markets), thrift & vintage stores
side trips 148-61, 186-95, **149**, **187**
  accommodations 201
Silo No 5 59
SIM cards 24
Sir Georges-Étienne Cartier Monument 104
Six Flags 146
skiing
  Centre de Ski de Fond Gai-Luron 154
  Parc du Mont-Royal 105
  Parc Jean-Drapeau 145
  Mont Avila 154
  Mont Habitant 154
  Mont Tremblant Resort (the Laurentians) 153
  Ski Bromont (Brome-Missisquoi) 161
  Sommet Gabriel 154
  Sommet Olympia 154
sledding & tobogganing
  Au 1884 19
  Glissade de la Terrasse 175
  Toboggan Festival 167
snowshoeing
  Centre de Ski de Fond Gai-Luron (the Laurentians) 154
  Parc du Mont-Royal 105
  Parc Jean-Drapeau 145
  Parc La Fontaine 103
  Sainte-Anne de Bellevue 148
Société des Arts Technologiques 75
Southwest, the, *see* Lachine Canal, Little Burgundy & the Southwest
spas
  Bota Bota 59, 155
  Nordik Spa-Nature 155
  Scandinave Spa 155
  SkySpa 183
  Spa Bolton 155
  Strøm Spa Nordique (the Laurentians) 155
sports 65
Square Dorchester 76
St Francis Xavier Mission (Kahnawake Mohawk Territory) 151
St Lawrence river 134-5
St-Jean-Baptiste 176
Station de la Plage 176
statues, *see* monuments & statues
street experiences 13
St-Roch 176
St-Viateur Bagel 113
Sun Life Building 76
sustainability 210-11
swimming
  Complexe Aquatique 145
  Parc Ignace Bourget 137-8
  Parc King George 138

Plage Jean-Doré 145
Plade de Verdun 132
Spa Bolton 155
Restaurant La Traite (Wendake) 188
Canots Légaré (Wendake) 189

taxes 204
taxis 24-5, 27
Terrasse Dufferin 19, 173
Terrasse Pierre-Dugua-de-mons 173
theaters & ampitheaters
  Centre Culturel et Communautaire Henri-Lemieux 131
  Club La Roue 131
  Segal Centre for Performing Arts 131
  Théâtre Beanfield 131-2
  Théâtre Desjardins 131
  Théâtre de Verdure 103
  Théâtre Maisonneuve 63
  Théâtre Paradoxe 131
  Théâtre Rialto 119
thrift & vintage stores 19
  Annex Vintage 114
  Club 777 94
  Eva B 73
  Eva D 74
  Hadio 94
  La Caravane Vintage 94
  Les Folles Alliees 94
  Magasin Steal Street 94
  Marché Floh 94
  Palmo Goods 94
time zones 213
tipping 35, 204
tobogganing, see winter sports
toilets 213
tours, see also drinking & nightlife, cycling tours, food tours, walking tours
  architecture 77
  art 57, 128
  Atelier Circulaire 115

Château Dufresne 89
Croisères AML 57, 167
drinking 185
Fitz Montréal 57, 121
guides 70, 169
history 56, 181
jet-ski 57
La Citadelle 181
LGBTIQ+ 83, 86
Montréal Mural Art 57
Québec City 185
Saute-Moutons 57
Spade & Palacio 57
Wet Set MTL 57
train travel 25
travel to/from Montréal & Québec City 24-5
traveling with kids 15, 205
travel seasons 20-1
travel within Montréal & Québec City 26-8

Ubisoft Entertainment 115
Umbrella Alley 170
Underground City 63, 76
under-the-radar experiences 17

vaccinations 209
Vague à Guy 132
vegan or vegetarian travelers 210
video games 107, 115, 149
viewpoints & lookouts
  Belvédère Kondiaronk 19, 105
  La Grande Roue de Montréal 53
  Port of Montréal Tower 53
  Secret Stairs of Westmount 139
  Sentier des Cimes 56
  Terrasse Pierre-Dugua-de-mons 173

Tour de Lévis 147
Village, the, see Quartier Latin, the Village & HoMa
vintage stores, see thrift & vintage stores
Village des Écluses (Pointe-des-Cascades) 151

walking 13, 26-7
walking tours 56, 65, 77, 120, 144, 171, 185, **56, 65, 77, 120, 144, 171, 185**
  Free Walking Tour of Old Québec 185
walking trails
  Calvaire d'Oka (Oka) 151
  Chemin le Serpentine 106
  Chemin Olmsted 106
  Chute Montmorency 186-7
  Espace Félix Leclerc 191-2
  Laurentians, the 152-9
  Onhwa' Lumi (Wendake) 189
  Rue Peel 72
  Summit Loop (Parc du Mont-Royal) 106
water 209
water sports, see canoeing, kayaking, paddleboarding, pedal boats, swimming
waterfalls
  Chute Montmorency 186
  Kabir Kouba Waterfall 189
weather 20-1
wi-fi 24, 213
Wiggle Room 103
wildlife 85, 105, 147, 209
wineries 30-2, 34-5
  Brome-Missisquoi 161
  Cassis Monna & Filles (Île d'Orléans) 192

Domaine du Ridge (Brome-Missisquoi) 161
Domaine Sainte-Famille (Île d'Orléans) 192
Grange Restaurant-Vignoble (Île d'Orléans) 192
La Route des Vins (Brome-Missisquoi) 161
Le Vignoble du Mitan (Île d'Orléans) 192
Saint-Pierre Le Vignoble (Île d'Orléans) 192
Tourism Eastern Townships (Brome-Missisquoi) 161
Vélouroute Gourmande (Brome-Missisquoi) 161
Vignoble de Grenouille (Brome-Missisquoi) 161
Vignoble de l'Orpailleur (Brome-Missisquoi) 161
Vignoble du Ruisseau (Brome-Missisquoi) 161
Vignoble Isle de Bacchus (Île d'Orléans) 191
Vignoble Ste-Pétronille (Île d'Orléans) 192
Vignoble Sugar Hill (Brome-Missisquoi) 161
whitewater rafting, see also canoeing, kayaking
  Lachine Rapids 134-5
  Parc National de la Jacques-Cartier 195
winter activities 8-9, see also ice skating, skiing, sledding & tobogganing
  Escalade FQME 145
  La Liberté Nord-Sud 145
  Patin Patin 103, 145
  Slide & Groove 145
  Québec City 173, 175

ziplining 187, 157

NOTES

NOTES

NOTES

NOTES

La Grande Roue (p53) is Canada's tallest observation wheel, with 42 roomy gondolas that whisk riders 60m into the air for 360-degree views.

Visit Bonhomme's ice palace, watch ice-canoe races and drink Caribou at Canada's oldest winter festival, Carnaval de Québec (p175).

All rights reserved. No part of this publication may be copied, stored in a retrieval system, or transmitted in any form by any means, electronic, mechanical, recording or otherwise, except brief extracts for the purpose of review, and no part of this publication may be sold or hired, without the written permission of the publisher. Lonely Planet and the Lonely Planet logo are trademarks of Lonely Planet and are registered in the US Patent and Trademark Office and in other countries. Lonely Planet does not allow its name or logo to be appropriated by commercial establishments, such as retailers, restaurants or hotels. Please let us know of any misuses: lonelyplanet.com/legal/intellectual-property.

Mapping data sources:
© Lonely Planet
© OpenStreetMap http://openstreetmap.org/copyright

FROM LEFT: JON BILOUS/SHUTTERSTOCK, MARC DUFRESNE/GETTY IMAGES

THIS BOOK

The 7th edition of Lonely Planet's Montréal and Québec City guidebook. It was written and researched by John Garry, Joel Balsam, Robert Isenberg and Pamela MacNaughtan.

This guidebook was produced by the following:

Destination Editor
Caroline Trefler

Coordinating Editor
Sarah Bailey

Production Editor
Ursula O'Sullivan-Dale

Image Editor
Compton Sheldon

Cartographer
Hunor Csutoros

Assisting Editors
Imogen Bannister, Lucy Jones,

Helen Koehne, Charlotte Orr

Cover Researchers
Giada de Agostinis, Gwen Cotter

Thanks Alison Killilea, Kellie Langdon, Saralinda Turner

Paper in this book is certified against the Forest Stewardship Council™ standards. FSC™ promotes environmentally responsible, socially beneficial and economically viable management of the world's forests.

Published by Lonely Planet Global Limited
CRN 554153
7th edition - May 2026
ISBN 978 1 83758 418 5
© Lonely Planet 2026
10 9 8 7 6 5 4 3 2 1
Printed in China